D1518466

An Encyclopedia of
American Women at War

An Encyclopedia of
American Women at War

From the Home Front to the Battlefields

Volume 2:
M–Z

Lisa Tendrich Frank, Editor

 ABC-CLIO

Santa Barbara, California • Denver, Colorado • Oxford, England

Library of Congress Cataloging-in-Publication Data

   An encyclopedia of American women at war : from the home front to the battlefields / Lisa Tendrich Frank, editor.
     p. cm.
   Includes bibliographical references and index.
   ISBN 978–1–59884–443–6 (hbk. : alk. paper) — ISBN 978–1–59884–444–3 (ebook) 1. United States—Armed Forces—Women—Biography—Encyclopedias. 2. Women and war—United States—Encyclopedias. 3. Women and the military—United States—Encyclopedias. I. Frank, Lisa Tendrich.

UB418.W65E53   2013
355.0092′520973—dc23   2012018244

ISBN: 978–1–59884–443–6
EISBN: 978–1–59884–444–3

17 16 15 14 13   1 2 3 4 5

This book is also available on the World Wide Web as an eBook.
Visit www.abc-clio.com for details.

ABC-CLIO, LLC
130 Cremona Drive, P.O. Box 1911
Santa Barbara, California 93116-1911

This book is printed on acid-free paper ∞

Manufactured in the United States of America

For Shayna

Contents

List of Entries

M

MAASS, CLARA LOUISE (1876–1901)

Clara Louise Maass was one of the first American women to serve as an Army contract nurse. She is celebrated for her role in a series of yellow fever experiments that proved how the disease is transmitted.

She was born on June 28, 1876, in East Orange, New Jersey. As the eldest of nine children in a working-class German American family, it was important for her to contribute to the family financially. She began wage work at age 15, after three years of high school. She first found employment at the Newark Orphan Asylum, then won admission to the second class of nurses at the Newark German Hospital. She earned half of her previous salary in the program but gained valuable training that included medical lectures and practical experience. Newark German Hospital hired Maass when she graduated in 1895. She nursed typhoid cases and other communicable diseases evident in contemporary cities.

In 1898, the same year that she became a head nurse at Newark German Hospital, Maass applied to be a contract nurse for the U.S. Army. Hundreds of women joined men in the fervor to volunteer following the United States' declaration of war against Spain. The military had an acute need for nurses during the conflict: disease killed over five times as many American soldiers as did combat in the war. Perhaps most feared was yellow fever with its 85 percent mortality rate. The disease was long prevalent in Cuba, where most of the war was fought. Yellow fever was especially dangerous during the summer months—exactly when American troops would be there.

Between October 1, 1898, and February 5, 1899, Maass nursed soldiers in Army field hospitals in Jacksonville, Florida; Savannah, Georgia; and Santiago, Cuba. She returned to Newark German Hospital after her honorable discharge, but the Army called her again on

November 20. This time she was sent even farther from home, to the Field Reserve Hospital in Manila, the Philippines, where she served until May 1900.

Some five months later, Maj. William C. Gorgas, chief sanitary officer of Cuba, summoned Maass to work as a civilian for the Yellow Fever Commission at Las Animas Hospital in Havana, Cuba. After the Spanish-American War, the United States had established military occupation of Cuba rather than granting the island the political independence it had sought from Spain. The United States initiated many programs in Cuba, including a collaborative project between U.S. Army and Cuban medical experts. The study aimed to settle whether infected objects and persons spread yellow fever, as prevailing theory claimed, or whether (like malaria) an insect host carried the disease. Gorgas hoped to explore the possibility of a vaccine to immunize against yellow fever as well. Maass had experience treating yellow fever (along with smallpox, typhoid, and dysentery) from the war against Spain and her time in the Philippines, but she had never contracted the disease.

The commission was undeniably engaged in dangerous work. Dr. Jesse Lazear had been incubating infected mosquitoes when he died of yellow fever. However, Maass volunteered for experiments regarding the transmission of the disease. When she was subjected to the bite of a *Stegomyia fasciata* mosquito (later renamed *Aedes aegypti*) in June 1901, Maass became the only nurse and the only American woman to participate. Along with a desire to help eradicate yellow fever, she stood to earn $100 compensation, a significant contribution

to her household. Maass also believed that by surviving the disease she would develop immunity, which would help produce a vaccine and enhance her individual career as a nurse.

Maass contracted yellow fever, but only a mild case. Because she was regarded as not fully immunized, she was infected again on August 14. Virulent symptoms ensued, including pain, fever, and gastric hemorrhage. Two other participants also contracted fatal cases. Her sister Sophia arrived in Cuba shortly before Clara died on August 24, 1901. The experiments then ended. The knowledge gained regarding yellow fever's transmission led to a change in public health policy: instead of disinfection and fumigation, a program was launched to eradicate the *Aedes aegypti*.

Maass was subsequently memorialized as someone who gave her life for the advancement of science. Cuba issued a postage stamp in August 1951 marking the 50th anniversary of Maass's death. The hospital where she had worked was renamed the Clara Maass Memorial Hospital in her honor the following June. In 1976, she became the first individual nurse depicted on a U.S. commemorative postage stamp.

Laura R. Prieto

See also: Nursing; Spanish-American War (1898).

References and Further Reading

Cunningham, John T. *Clara Maass: A Nurse, a Hospital, a Spirit.* Belleville, NJ: Rae Publishing, 1986.

Fickeissen, Janet L. "Clara Louise Maass." In *American Nursing: A Biographical Dictionary*, edited by Vern L. Bullough, Olga Maranjian Church, and Alice Stein. New York: Garland Publishers, 1988.

Schuyler, Constance B. 1997. "Clara Louise Maass." In *Past and Promise: Lives of New Jersey Women*, edited by Joan Burstyn, 166–67. Syracuse, NY: Syracuse University Press.

MAMMY KATE

(N.D.–N.D.)

Mammy Kate was the name of a Negro slave owned by Stephen Heard, a prominent landholder and politician from Georgia. After Heard was taken prisoner by British forces, she smuggled him out of the fort to safety.

The date of her birth is unknown, but it is believed that Kate was born in Africa. She claimed to have been the daughter of an African king. Kate served as a house slave on Heard's plantation, in present-day Elbert County, Georgia. She was married to Daddy Jack, Heard's gardener.

During the early part of the Revolutionary War, Heard's wife, Jane, and their adopted daughter were captured by Loyalists, who forced them out into a bitter snow storm where they died from exposure. Heard took the loss hard, as did Kate. On February 14, 1779, Heard took part in the battle of Kettle Creek, Georgia, where he was wounded and captured by the British. He was taken to Augusta, where he was imprisoned pending execution as a traitor.

Kate received word of her master's plight and at once made plans to rescue him. She and her husband traveled the 50 miles from the Heard plantation to Augusta, where Kate procured a large woven clothesbasket. She then went to the fort and offered her services as a laundress to the British officers. By all accounts, Kate did an excellent job of cleaning and pressing the officers' clothing, and she soon had an abundance of clients. She seems to have had a special talent for pressing the numerous ruffles that adorned a British officer's shirt. Once she had sufficiently acquired the good will of the British officers, she asked to be permitted to do Heard's laundry as well. The British commander refused her request, stating that Heard was to be hanged and had no need of clean clothes. Kate persisted, however. She argued that the condemned man might as well hang clean and presentable as dirty and degraded, and eventually the British officer gave in and allowed her to visit Heard and do his laundry twice a week.

Kate had become so well known to the soldiers in the British garrison that they did not bother to search her basket during her numerous trips to and from the fort. She was able to take advantage of this trust to sneak food in to Heard so he could keep up his strength during his confinement. When Kate learned Heard's execution was to take place shortly, she decided the moment had come to put into action a plan she had been considering for some time. One evening, just about dark, Kate arrived at the fort to collect her laundry. She made her rounds, as usual, throughout the post before stopping at Heard's cell to collect his things. By all accounts, Kate was an impressively large woman, standing more than 6 feet tall and having a muscular, broad frame. Heard, on the other hand, was a small, diminutive man. When Kate and Heard were alone, she instructed her master to climb into the clothesbasket and keep still. She then covered him with some articles of clothing, hefted the basket to the top of her head as was her custom, and walked out of the fort, with no challenge from any of the guards.

Once outside the gates, she leisurely made her way to a place where she had previously concealed two horses. Kate and Heard mounted the horses and started for Heard's plantation and safety. Along the way, Heard expressed his gratitude for Kate's actions and informed her that he was setting her free as a reward for her loyalty. Kate responded that Heard might set her free, but she was never going to set him free. It was her desire to stay with him as long as she lived.

Good as his word, Heard granted Kate her freedom. He also gave her a small four-roomed house and a parcel of land. After the war, Heard became the governor of Georgia and a prosperous and influential man in the state. Kate had meant what she said about never leaving her master. Until her death, she continued to go to the manor house to care for Heard and his children. On her deathbed, she willed her nine children to the Heard family, one to each of the governor's children.

The date of Kate's death is unknown. She was buried in the Heard Family Cemetery, in Elberton, Georgia, between her husband and Heard.

Robert P. Broadwater

See also: African American Women; American Revolution (1775–1783).

References and Further Reading

Broadwater, Robert P. *Liberty Belles: Women of the American Revolution.* Bellwood, PA: Dixie Dreams Press, 2004.

Cannon, Jill. *Heroines of the American Revolution.* Santa Barbara, CA: Bellerophon Books, 1995.

Hughes, Langston. *Famous American Negroes.* New York: Dodd, Mead & Company, 1954.

MARINER, ROSEMARY BRYANT (1953–)

The first Navy woman to fly a tactical jet, Rosemary Bryant Mariner was also the first to command a squadron of Navy aircraft.

As a child, Mariner dreamed of being a pilot, even after the death of her father, an Air Force pilot, in a plane crash when she was three years old. At age eight, Mariner and her two sisters moved to San Diego, California, with their mother, a former Navy nurse. There she spent many hours watching the planes take off from nearby Miramar Naval Air Station. Mariner earned money for flying lessons by cleaning houses and washing planes at Gillespie and Lindbergh Fields, earning her pilot's license at age 17.

Mariner attended college at Purdue University, where she was the first woman to graduate from the aviation program. In 1973, at age 19, she graduated with a degree in aviation technology. It was the same year that the Navy admitted women to flight school, and Mariner joined the first group of women flight trainees at the Naval Aviation Training Command in Pensacola, Florida. Six of the women went on to win their wings, including Mariner, who graduated in June 1974. They were the first women pilots in any of the armed services since the Women Air Force Service Pilots (WASP) of World War II.

Mariner was selected for jet pilot training in 1975, qualifying in the A-4L, A-4E, and the A-7E, all jet attack aircraft. She accumulated more than 3,500 flying hours in 15 types of aircraft during her Navy career.

Mariner was qualified as a surface warfare officer and in the early 1980s spent almost three years as ship's company aboard USS *Lexington* (AVT-16), during which she stood thousands of hours of engineering and deck watches in order to qualify for her "water wings" (i.e., ship driver). At that time the *Lexington* had 120 enlisted women and 15 female officers in a crew of around 1,700. As a lieutenant commander, Mariner was also a division officer who spent many hours overseeing young enlisted men and women aboard ship.

On July 12, 1990, Mariner accomplished another milestone when she became the first woman to assume command of a naval aviation squadron, Tactical Electronic Warfare Squadron 34, based at the Naval Air Station in Point Mugu, California. Mariner was selected for O-6 command (major aviation shore) and slated to go to Meridian Naval Air Station, but she decided to retire instead. With an extensive background in joint warfare, she served as Chairman of the Joint Chiefs of Staff (CJCS) professor of military strategy at the National War College during her last two years of active duty.

Mariner explained her rise through the ranks of the Navy when she said, "When I hit a wall, I am going to get under it, over it, or around it. Put a wall in front of me and my reaction is to knock it down." Mariner also likes to acknowledge that several combat-experienced male officers and figures like Chief of Naval Operations Elmo Zumwalt, who supported the entry of women into military aviation, mentored her. Mariner notes, "I think it is very important to give men credit, because the military can be a very hostile place for women and we must acknowledge the good guys who risk their careers by supporting women. 'Politically Correct' for most of my career meant 'No Women.'"

Mariner has spoken out on many issues involving women in the military. In her position as president of the Women Military Aviators (WMA) in 1991, she helped fight to repeal the 1948 law banning women from flying aircraft engaged in combat missions. She has been vocal on other issues as well, including the role of women in the armed forces. In a *Washington Post* article (May 11, 1997), she discussed integrated gender training in the armed forces, writing, "Internally, the military must resolve the outstanding issues of gender integration. Externally, we dare not squander our success by pandering to a few vocal critics pushing an anti-woman social agenda at the expense of national security. No amount of nostalgia over manly warriors protecting fair maidens erases the fact that this country cannot go to war without women on the front lines."

Mariner has published widely, especially in support of gender integration based on her own years of experience "in the trenches." Her article "A Soldier Is a Soldier" (*Joint Force Quarterly*, Fall/Winter 1994) was based on an award-winning paper for the National War College and discusses the basic principles for successful gender integration. She is working on a book tentatively entitled *No Excuses: Ending the Gender Wars in the Military.*

Vicki L. Friedl

See also: Cold War (ca. 1947–1991); Women Air Force Service Pilots (WASP).

References and Further Reading

Ebbert, Jean, and Marie-Beth Hall. *Crossed Currents: Navy Women in a Century of Change.* Washington, D.C.: Batsford Brassey, 1999.

Holm, Jeanne. *Women in the Military: An Unfinished Revolution.* New York: Ballantine Books, 1992.

Mariner, Rosemary, "The Military Needs Women." *Washington Post,* May 11, 1997, 7C.

MARTIN, GRACE WARING (N.D.–N.D.), AND MARTIN, RACHEL CLAY (N.D.–N.D.)

American patriots Grace Waring Martin and Rachel Clay Martin were the wives of American Revolutionary War soldiers who disguised themselves in their husbands' clothes, took up arms, and successfully intercepted a dispatch from British soldiers that they handed over to the American side.

Grace and Rachel endured the war at the home of their mother-in-law, Elizabeth Marshall Martin. The Martin house was located west of Charleston, South Carolina, along the border with the Cherokee nation. Their husbands were the eldest of the seven Martin sons, who had all volunteered for service in the Continental Army.

In the absence of men, the women were subject to the abuses of Loyalists, who on one occasion cut open and scattered the feather beds of the house. The women had also provided a safe haven for an injured Continental soldier, hiding him from Loyalists who were searching for him. The fighting soon came close to home for the Martin women, first with the siege of the port of Augusta and afterward the fort at nearby Cambridge, also known as Fort Ninety-Six. Grace's husband, William, was killed during the siege of Augusta, and a British officer passing to Fort Ninety-Six, still under British possession, rode out to the Martin house to deliver the news in hopes that it would devastate the women.

The Martins received word one evening that a courier, guarded by two British officers, would be passing through the area with an important dispatch. Rachel and Grace determined that they would intercept the message and hand it over to Gen. Nathanael Greene. The women disguised themselves in their husbands' clothing, took weapons, and positioned themselves in the bushes at a point along the road where they knew the British party would pass. The women surprised the British and held them at gunpoint, gained their immediate surrender and the handover of the dispatch, and then released them. They sent the dispatch directly to Greene by another messenger.

Later that night the same three British men sought lodging for the night at the Martin home. The women, their disguises never revealed, offered their hospitality. They listened to the men's story of being taken prisoner by two rebel boys and looked at their paroles. The men departed the next day, not knowing that these were the very women who had held them at gunpoint the night before.

Kristen L. Rouse

See also: American Revolution (1775–1783); Espionage.

Reference and Further Reading

Ellet, Elizabeth F. *The Women of the American Revolution*, 3rd ed. New York: Baker and Scribner, 1849.

MAY, GERALDINE PRATT (1895–1997)

Col. Geraldine May was a member of the Women's Army Auxiliary Corps (WAAC, later Women's Army Corps or WAC) during World War II. After the war, she transferred to the new Women in the Air Force (WAF) component, part of the U.S. Air Force. As a WAF officer, May was the first woman promoted to the rank of colonel in the Air Force. May also served as the first WAF director. In this position, she helped establish women's roles in the newest U.S. military branch.

Pratt was born in Albany, New York, on April 21, 1895, and lived in several locations during her childhood. As a high school student, she studied at schools in both Tacoma, Washington, and Bryn Mawr, Pennsylvania. Following her high school graduation, Pratt went on to study at the University of California, Berkeley. Her first job was with the California immigration and housing commission. Prior to joining the military, she held a variety of social work jobs and also served as an executive with the Camp Fire Girls organization. She left the workforce when she married Albert E. May in 1928 and moved to Tulsa, Oklahoma, with her husband. By the time World War II began, however, May's husband had passed away.

When the WAAC began in 1942, May was already 47 years old—two years above the legal age limit for WAAC members. Despite this age difference, the WAAC accepted May to join the first officer candidate class. After completing her training, May was assigned to the Army Air Forces as WAC staff director of the Air Transport Command (ATC) beginning in March 1943. The ATC included 6,000 enlisted women and officers, and May's job included overseeing all of these women. In this capacity, May traveled to U.S. air bases worldwide to provide oversight and advisement regarding women in the Army, their assignments, and policies related to them.

After the war ended, May transferred to the General Staff of the War Department before becoming WAC staff director of the Army ground forces. As Congress debated the Women's Armed Services Integration Act, May moved to Army headquarters in January 1948 to help with the military's planning efforts for after the war. By this time, May had attained the rank of major.

On June 12, 1948, President Truman signed the Women's Armed Services Integration Act into law. Four days later, May transferred to the newly created Air Force to become the director of the WAF. With this appointment, May received a promotion to colonel, becoming the first Air Force woman to attain that honor. At that time, only the director of each women's service component could hold that rank. May held the status as the sole colonel in the WAF until her retirement. She was 55 at the time of her assignment as director of WAF.

From 1948 to 1951, May helped the Air Force establish the WAF service component for women. This job encompassed recruiting, policy making, and long-term planning on how to utilize servicewomen as both regular and reserve members of the new Air Force. As director of WAF, May tried to integrate women into the Air Force as much as possible. However, as director of WAF, May could not control Air Force policy regarding women's utilization and assignment. The director position was an advisory role, and male Air Force leaders could accept or ignore her recommendations as they preferred.

During her three years as director of WAF, May ensured that the Air Force established its own training system for WAFs rather than combining with women in other services as had been previously proposed. She also advocated for utilizing WAFs as broadly as possible and contended with general indifference over the WAF program from many male leaders.

Despite this general indifference, the main problem during May's tenure as director of WAF occurred when Air Force chief of staff Gen. Hoyt Vandenberg commissioned aviatrix Jacqueline Cochran to examine the WAF program and provide input on its status and effectiveness. Cochran had headed the civilian Women Air Force Service Pilots (WASP) program during World War II but was not part of the postwar WAF system. In her 1950 report, Cochran criticized the WAF for lack of attention to such things as femininity, gave specific recommendations for recruiting and retention, suggested stricter physical and mental standards, and also advised that the Air Force reorganize the director's office. Although an Air Force headquarters committee ultimately disagreed with most of Cochran's findings and recommendations, Vandenberg and other leaders paid attention to the report. Many within the WAF believed this incident led to the end of May's military career.

In 1951, May resigned as director of WAF, citing personal reasons. She retired at that time and later held various government posts. May died in 1997 at the age of 102 and is buried in Arlington Cemetery.

Tanya L. Roth

See also: Cochran, Jacqueline (1910–1980); Defense Advisory Committee on Women in the Services (DACOWITS); Women Air Force Service Pilots (WASP); Women in the Air Force (WAF); Women's Armed Services Integration Act of 1948 (Public Law 80-625); Women's Army Auxiliary Corps (WAAC); Women's Army Corps (WAC); World War II (1941–1945).

References and Further Reading

Holm, Jeanne. *Women in the Military: An Unending Revolution*, rev. ed. Novato, CA: Presidio Press, 1993.

Holm, Jeanne. *In Defense of a Nation: Servicewomen in World War II*. St. Petersburg, FL: Vandamere Press, 1998.

Witt, Linda, Judith Bellafaire, Britta Granrud, and Mary Jo Binker. *"A Defense Weapon Known to Be of Value": Servicewomen of the Korean War Era*. Hanover, NH: University Press of New England, 2005.

McAFEE (HORTON), MILDRED HELEN (1900–1994)

An academic administrator of several colleges and the director of the Women Accepted for Volunteer Emergency Service (WAVES) from 1942 until 1945, Mildred McAfee was the first female commissioned officer in the U.S. Navy.

Born in Parkville, Missouri, on May 12, 1900, McAfee graduated Phi Beta Kappa from Vassar College in 1920. She earned her master's degree in sociology from the University of Chicago in 1928. McAfee became a professor of sociology and economics at Tusculum College in Tennessee in 1923. In 1926, McAfee became dean of women at Centre College and then became dean of women at Oberlin College in 1934. In 1936, McAfee became president of Wellesley College. In all of these capacities, McAfee earned great praise from her students and constantly pursued greater rights for women in education.

In 1942, McAfee was invited by an advisory council to serve as the first director of the U.S. Navy's tentative women's naval reserve, the WAVES. This program was designed in response to increasing labor shortages in the Navy. Women would fill positions formerly occupied by men to allow the

Lt. Cmdr. Mildred H. McAfee, director of the WAVES, and First Lady Eleanor Roosevelt inspect one of the rooms in the WAVES barracks at the Naval Training School for Women's Reserve in the Bronx, New York, on August 26, 1943. (AP/Wide World Photos)

men to serve at sea. McAfee accepted the position only after being granted a leave of absence from her post as president of Wellesley. The WAVES were then officially founded on July 30, 1942, with the signing of Public Law 689. This law inserted the wording for the creation of a women's naval reserve into the Naval Reserve Act of 1938. Significantly, this legislation differed from other contemporary women's reserve groups, such as that creating the Women's Army Auxiliary Corps (WAAC), in that it granted women full status as members of the U.S. Navy, although this was understood to be only on an emergency basis. Thus, when McAfee was granted the title of lieutenant commander on August 3, 1942, she became the first female commissioned officer in the U.S. Navy.

McAfee served as the director of the WAVES for the next four years and continually worked to strengthen both the WAVES program and the status of women within the military. Most of the highly educated women who formed the initial officer staff of the WAVES were personally requested by McAfee and accepted because of their relationship with her. McAfee was highly influential in the passing of Public Law 183 on November 8, 1943. This law granted enlisted women allowances for dependents similar to those of enlisted men. This law also promoted the head of the WAVES to the rank of captain, which was then bestowed upon McAfee, making her the first female captain in the U.S. Navy.

It was also under McAfee's tenure that the WAVES became the first program to allow black women to serve in the military, in 1944. While McAfee served as director, the WAVES grew to enlist over 80,000 women, including more than 8,000 officers. McAfee not only instituted basic training programs for these women but also pushed for them to receive specialized training. With this training, WAVES filled between 50 to 70 percent of positions in air training stations, rocket testing sites, and a variety of positions within the naval communications network in 1945. For her service, McAfee was the first woman to be awarded the Navy Distinguished Service Medal, on November 7, 1945. Also, owing at least in part to her leadership, the WAVES program was so successful that the Navy did not cancel it after the end of World War II, claiming that the roles performed by the WAVES were simply too valuable to give up. This choice is generally considered to have paved the way toward the full acceptance of women into the Navy and subsequently all other branches of the American military.

McAfee stepped down from her position as director of the WAVES in February of 1946, returning to her position as president of Wellesley College. McAfee married Douglas Horton, future dean of Harvard Divinity School, the same year. McAfee continued to actively support the role of women in the military, writing a series of sociological papers on the subject as well as on the rights of women more generally. McAfee stepped down as president of Wellesley in 1949. She still continued to serve on a variety of distinguished committees and boards, however, including as president of the American Association of Colleges and as vice president of the National Council of Churches.

McAfee died on September 2, 1994, in a nursing home in Berlin, New Hampshire.

Victoria Wheeler

See also: African American Women; Hancock, Joy Bright (1898–1986); Women Accepted for Volunteer Emergency Service (WAVES); Women's Army Auxiliary Corps (WAAC); Women's Army Corps (WAC); World War II (1941–1945).

References and Further Reading

Ebbert, Jean, and Mary-Beth Hall. *Crossed Currents: Navy Women from World War I to Tailhook.* Washington, D.C.: Brassey's, 1993.

Horton, Mildred McAfee et al. *The Reminiscences of the WAVES.* Annapolis, MD: U.S. Naval Institute, 1971–1979.

"Mildred McAfee Horton Dies; First Head of WAVES Was 94." *New York Times*, September 4, 1994.

McCLELLAND, HELEN GRACE (1887–1984)

A recruit of the American Army Nurse Corps (ANC) during World War I, Helen Grace McClelland served on the French front lines as a reserve nurse. She was assigned to British Casualty Clearing Station number 61, British area, near the convent of Saint Sixte in Belgium. For her extraordinary courage under German station bombings in 1917, during which she saved the life of her tent-mate, nurse Beatrice Mary MacDonald, she received the American Distinguished Service Cross, the United States' second highest combat award, and the British Royal Red Cross, a decoration awarded to Army nurses for exceptional services. She was one of the three women to receive the Distinguished Service Cross during World War I.

McClelland was born on July 25, 1887, in Austinburg, Ashtabula County, Ohio. She was the daughter of Raymond G. McClelland, a pastor at Fredericktown village, and Harriet (Hattie) Cooper McClelland. She was the third child of a large family, with two older sisters and two younger brothers, all born in Ohio: Mary J. McClelland, Florence McClelland, Raymond M. McClelland, and Stewart W. McClelland. When Helen was 13, the McClellands moved to Fredericktown, Knox County, Ohio.

In 1912, she graduated from the Pennsylvania Hospital School of Nursing. She joined the ANC in 1917. Attached to the American Expeditionary Forces (AEF), the U.S. armed forces sent to Europe in World War I, as a member of the Pennsylvania Hospital team, she was sent to Base Hospital number 10 at Le Treport, France, for a support mission between France and Belgium. McClelland was to work with the five British and two American surgical teams on detached duty at the French front, British area. The two American surgical teams chosen for this assignment were recruits from the Pennsylvania and the Presbyterian units.

On July 21, 1917, the ambulances carrying the chosen personnel left Base Hospital number 10 at six in the morning, stopping first at Abbeville in the County of Picardy, France; then at Hesden in the Pas-de-Calais County, France, where they spent the night; then at Proven in Belgium, before finally reaching their stations. McClelland was assigned as a reserve nurse to British Casualty Clearing Station number 61, near Saint Sixte's Convent in Belgium, with Captain Mitchell and Captain Packard. She shared her tent with Beatrice MacDonald from the New York Presbyterian Hospital.

On the night of August 17, the sound of German airplanes woke McClelland and MacDonald. McClelland reported that both of them reached for their tin hats. McClelland covered her head with the hat, trying to protect herself as she could and rolling into a ball. Then German planes began attacking the camp by dropping bombs. Pieces of shrapnel reached their tent and wounded MacDonald in the eye and on the side of her face. McClelland stopped MacDonald's hemorrhage and by doing so saved her life. On October 6, almost 11 weeks after her assignment to Casualty Clearing Station number 61, McClelland's mission was over. On May 25, 1919, she left the ANC. On June 27, 1919, the secretary of war presented her with the American Distinguished Service Cross. She also received the British Royal Red Cross, First Class.

In 1926, McClelland returned to her nursing career at Pennsylvania Hospital before becoming assistant to the school's head, Margaret A. Dunlop. In 1933, she succeeded Dunlop as director of the Pennsylvania Hospital's Nursing Department, running the school for 23 years until 1956, when she retired. During her tenure, McClelland brought major changes to the nursing department by enforcing shorter work days, designing teaching curriculums, and securing national accreditation for the school's nursing program. In 1978, at age 91, she was inducted into the Ohio Women's Hall of Fame, which provides public recognition of the contributions of Ohio women.

In December 20, 1984, at age 97, she died at Fredericktown, Knox County, Ohio, and was buried at the Wayne Baptist Cemetery.

Florence Dupré

See also: American Red Cross; Army Nurse Corps (ANC); Ayres, Clara Edith Work (1880–1917); Nursing; War of 1812 (1812–1815); World War I (1914–1918).

References and Further Reading

American Expeditionary Forces Base Hospital No. 10. *History of the Pennsylvania Hospital Unit: The Great War.* New York: P.B. Hoeber, 1921.

Bellafaire, Judith. *Women in the United States Military.* New York: Routledge, 2011.

Dock, Lavinia L., Sarah Elizabeth Pickett, and Clara Dutton Noyes. *History of American Red Cross Nursing.* New York: Macmillan Company, 1922.

Schneider, Dorothy, and Schneider, Carl J. *Into the Breach: American Women Overseas in World War I.* New York: Viking Press, 1991.

McGEE, ANITA NEWCOMB (1864–1940)

Physician, anthropologist, and the head of female Army nurses during the Spanish-American War, Anita Newcomb McGee played a prominent role in the development of the U.S. Army Nurse Corps (ANC).

Anita Newcomb was born in Washington, D.C., on November 4,

1864, to Simon and Mary Caroline Hassler Newcomb. Her father was an eminent mathematician and astronomer at the U.S. Naval Observatory, and her mother was a granddaughter of Ferdinand Rudolph Hassler, the first superintendent of the U.S. Coast and Geodetic Survey. Anita received early education at private schools in Washington, D.C. She then traveled to Europe, where she took courses at Newnham College, Cambridge University, in England and at the University of Geneva in Switzerland. After returning to the United States, she married William John McGee, the chief geologist of the Atlantic coastal plain division at the U.S. Geological Survey, in February 1888.

While conducting anthropological research into religious colonies such as the Oneida community and Koreshanity with her husband, Anita entered the medical school of Columbian University (now George Washington University) and earned a degree in medicine in 1892. After graduation, she continued her postgraduate study in gynecology at Johns Hopkins University and also started medical practice in Washington, D.C. McGee became a prominent figure in academic and social circles in Washington, D.C., acting as the recording secretary of the Women's Anthropological Society and the vice president of the Daughters of the American Revolution (DAR).

In 1898, when war broke out between the United States and Spain over Cuba's independence, McGee established the DAR Hospital Corps in April for the recruitment and selection of female nurses for military service. Authorized by George M. Sternberg, the surgeon general of the Army, and under McGee's direction, the DAR Hospital Corps acted as an official examining board for female army nurses. As such, the DAR Hospital Corps sorted out applications for army nurses from across the nation and judged the eligibility of each applicant. In the screening process, McGee laid down strict eligibility criteria for the official appointment as an army nurse, which required applicants to be graduates of established training schools for nurses and to be between 30 and 50 years of age. In addition, applicants had to present an endorsement of their moral character and nursing ability from the superintendents of their respective schools, preferably with a recommendation from members of the DAR local chapters. McGee thus attempted to exclude untrained amateurs from the eligible list of nurses, although the large demand for army nurses in the wartime emergency gradually undermined her standards and allowed intrusion of voluntary agencies in the army nursing field.

On August 29, 1898, McGee was appointed as the acting assistant surgeon general of the Army. As a result, the DAR Hospital Corps was disbanded, and thenceforth female army nurses came under the supervision of McGee's new office in the Army. Beginning with the first call for female nurses from the surgeon general on May 7, 1898, and ending in July 1899, McGee had sent out 1,563 female nurses to the Army hospitals. Female nurses worked at overseas hospitals in Cuba, Puerto Rico, Hawaii, and the Philippine Islands, as well as in homeland general hospitals. In addition, some of these nurses also joined the campaign in China during the Boxer Rebellion in 1900 and 1901.

On February 2, 1901, the Army Reorganization Act passed Congress.

McGee drafted section 19 of the act, which provided for the creation of the U.S. ANC as a regular military organization under the female superintendent. After the enactment, McGee resigned her governmental post and instead established the Society of the Spanish American War Nurses to claim veterans' benefits for female army nurses. In April 1904, McGee traveled to Japan with a small group of women nurses to help the Japanese army nursing service during the Russo-Japanese War. McGee worked with female nurses of the Red Cross Society of Japan at the Reserve Hospital in Hiroshima. Her nursing team left Japan in October, but McGee went back to Japan next month as an attaché to the American Legation in Tokyo and visited the battlefields in the northeastern region of China as an observer in 1905. Following her return to the United States, McGee continued her anthropological research while lecturing on scientific and social issues.

On October 5, 1940, McGee died in Washington, D.C., after suffering a cerebral hemorrhage. She was buried with full military honors in Arlington National Cemetery.

Yoshiya Makita

See also: American Red Cross; Army Nurse Corps (ANC); Curtis, Namahyoke Sockum (1861–1935); Hasson, Esther Voorhees (1867–1942); Heavren, Rose (1870–1968); Kinney, Dita Hopkins (1855–1921); Nursing; Spanish-American War (1898).

References and Further Reading

Cirillo, Vincent J. *Bullets and Bacilli: The Spanish-American War and Military Medicine*. New Brunswick, NJ: Rutgers University Press, 1999.

Moldow, Gloria. *Women Doctors in Gilded-Age Washington: Race, Gender, and Professionalization*. Urbana: University of Illinois Press, 1987.

Sarnecky, Mary T. *A History of the U.S. Army Nurse Corps*. Philadelphia: University of Pennsylvania Press, 1999.

McGRATH, KATHLEEN (1952–2002)

Pioneering naval officer Kathleen McGrath became the first woman to command a U.S. warship when she captained USS *Jarrett* in 2000.

Service to the U.S. armed forces was part of McGrath's life from a young age. The eldest of six children, she was born in Columbus, Ohio, in 1952 on an Air Force base. Her father, Vietnam veteran James McGrath, had flown B-52 combat missions during the war. McGrath grew up on Air Force bases all over the country including in Texas, New Mexico, and Guam. After graduating high school in Guam, McGrath went to California State–Sacramento, gaining her degree in environmental science in 1975. She began her career at the U.S. Forestry Service, and when she grew bored of the work there, her father encouraged her to look into opportunities with the Air Force.

When McGrath showed up to the recruitment office in Merced, California, the Air Force recruiter was out to lunch, so she was wandered into the Navy office. Drawn in by the travel and adventure the Navy offered, she joined in 1980. After attending officers' school in Newport, Rhode Island, McGrath was given a job at a Navy personnel office in Yokosuka, Japan. She soon grew frustrated that she was stuck in an office instead of using her training to navigate and drive ships. After a ride on a Navy support vessel where she got to steer the ship, do a man-overboard drill, and stand watch, she became even more convinced of her desire for a more hands-on job.

McGrath went after greater responsibilities and attempted to enroll in the Surface Warfare Officers School. However, at this time the Navy was still hesitant about women's roles in the service and allowed only 17 women each year into the Surface Warfare Officers School. All the spots had already been filled, but McGrath did not let up until she was given a spot. During her time at school, McGrath was trained on many support vessels. She later became successful, working on many different ships between 1983 and 1993. Her talent was noticed, and in 1993 she was given an 18-month opportunity as commander of a salvage ship, *Recovery*. After that, McGrath gained her master's degree in education at Stanford University but still wanted her military career to progress further. Her dream was to command a warship.

In 1993, in part as a result of the difficulty of recruiting enough men, Congress finally revoked the prohibition against women serving on warships. McGrath worked very hard to prove herself as a leader, serving two years in Washington, D.C., at the Navy's personnel bureau. She then moved to San Diego to prepare a destroyer squadron for war.

A huge turning point for women's advancement within the Navy occurred in December 1998 when five women were appointed as commanders of ships. Four of the women, Michelle Howard, Maureen Farren, Ann O'Connor, and Grace Mehl, were assigned to transport ships that were not expected to enter combat zones. However the fifth appointment, the leadership of the warship USS *Jarrett*, was given to McGrath. This made McGrath the first woman to command a U.S. Navy warship. USS *Jarrett* was a missile frigate and, at 453 feet, was one of the smallest ships in the Navy. Yet it was equipped with massive weaponry, including anti-aircraft devices, air and water missiles, torpedoes, and two SH-60 Seahawk helicopters for combat and rescue.

In 2000, McGrath and her crew of 262, including four women, set sail. Their main task was to search the Persian Gulf looking for ships breaking a UN ban by smuggling oil shipments from Iraq. The USS *Jarrett* also led the search for survivors of Alaska Airlines Flight 261, which had crashed nearby. Throughout her appointment as captain, McGrath worked tirelessly, often from 6:00 a.m. until after midnight. Her hard work was noticed, and over her career McGrath was awarded four Meritorious Service Medals, three Navy Commendation Medals, the Legion of Merit, and a Navy Achievement Medal.

After her six-month deployment was up, McGrath transferred to the Joint Advanced Warfighting Unit in Alexandria, Virginia. This allowed her to be closer to her husband, retired Navy officer Greg Brandon, and their two adopted children, Nicholas and Clare. The children were aged 2 and 3 during McGrath's time aboard USS *Jarrett*, but she felt it was important to take the groundbreaking opportunity setting the way for future female Navy leaders.

McGrath died of lung cancer in 2002 at age 50. She is buried in Arlington National Cemetery.

Megan Findling

See also: Cold War (ca. 1947–1991); Vietnam War (1965–1973).

References and Further Reading

"Capt. Kathleen McGrath, 50, Pioneering Warship Commander." *New York Times*, October 1, 2002, B8.

Kimmel, Elizabeth Cody. *Ladies First: 40 Daring American Women Who Were Second to None*. Des Moines, IA: National Geographic Books, 2006.

Thompson, Mark. "Aye, Aye, Ma'am." *TIME*, March 2000, 30–34.

McGUIRE, COLLEEN L. (N.D.–N.D.)

As the first female provost marshal general of the Army and commander of the Criminal Investigation Department (CID), Colleen L. McGuire became the first woman to serve as the head of the Army law enforcement. This honor occurred after nearly three decades of dedicated and honored service in several departments in the military.

McGuire graduated from the University of Montana in 1979, where she joined the Military Police Corps. Her first post was in Germany, where she served the 709th Military Police as a platoon leader, company executive officer, and then as battalion logistics officer. A decade later, she became a staff officer in the Office of the Chief of Public Affairs at the Pentagon. She also served in Somalia as public affairs staff officer in late 1993 and early 1994 and as the battalion operations officer, Law Enforcement Battalion, at Fort Belvoir. In 1998, she commanded the 705th Military Police Battalion at Fort Leavenworth. In 2002, after attending battalion command and senior service college, she went back to Fort Leavenworth as brigade commander at the U.S. Disciplinary Barracks. She was the first woman to hold this position. She served as assistant commandant of the U.S. Army Military Police School and was later deployed for 18 months as the provost marshal of Multi-National Corps–Iraq. Additionally, she would serve as chief of the Colonels Management Office, Senior Leader Development, Office of the Chief of Staff, Army.

In her last post before receiving her post as the provost marshal general, McGuire served for two years as director of the Senior Leader Development Office, Office of the Chief of Staff of the Army. During her last year in this position, she also served as the head of the Army Suicide Prevention Task Force. After a year and a half in this position, in September 2011, she became director of manpower and personnel for the Joint Chiefs of Staff. As of 2012, she still held this position, which is the highest personnel position at this level.

During her career, McGuire attended several training programs and received two master's degrees—one in military arts and sciences from the Command and General Staff College at Fort Leavenworth, Kansas, and the other in strategic studies from the Army

War College at Carlisle Barracks, Pennsylvania. Her first thesis was on the evolution of relations between the military and the media, and her second project explored the importance of constabulary forces in the aftermath of foreign wars. She has also received numerous awards and decorations, including the Bronze Star Medal, the Defense Meritorious Service Medal, the Legion of Merit with two Oak Leaf Clusters, the Meritorious Service Medal with four Oak Leaf Clusters, the Joint Service Commendation Medal, the Army Commendation Medal with three Oak Leaf Clusters, the Army Achievement Medal with three Oak Leaf Clusters, the Iraqi Campaign Medal, the Senior Parachutist's Badge, and the Army Staff Identification Badge.

McGuire received her positions as provost marshal general and commander of the CID in January 2010. Later that year, she was named distinguished alumni of the University of Montana. The position of provost marshal general of the Army began as a wartime position in 1776, and it was reformed for most eras when significant combat was taking place. The position was reestablished most recently in 2003 as part of the War on Terror.

Andrew K. Frank

See also: Iraq War (2003–2011); Military Police; War on Terror (2001–).

References and Further Reading

Castro, Jeffrey. "First Woman Becomes Army Provost Marshal General." January 15, 2010. http://www.army.mil/article/32999.

McGuire, Colleen L. "Military-Media Relations and the Gulf War: A Compromise between Vietnam and Grenada?" Master's thesis, U.S. Army Command and General Staff College, 1992.

McINTOSH, ELIZABETH P. MacDONALD (1915–)

Elizabeth P. MacDonald McIntosh joined the Office of Strategic Services (OSS) in 1942 and worked as a Morale Branch operations officer in New Delhi and then in Kunming, western China. She was one of hundreds of OSS women stationed abroad in Europe and Asia. After the war, she published an account of her wartime experiences, *Undercover Girl* (1947), and worked for other government organizations. In 1958, she joined the newly formed CIA as an operations officer. In 2007, the OSS Society awarded her its Distinguished Service Award.

Born in Washington, D.C., in 1915 and raised in Hawaii, McIntosh graduated from the University of Washington in 1935 with a master's degree in journalism. She returned to Hawaii, where she worked as a journalist for Scripps Howard, and she was there when the Japanese bombed Pearl Harbor. In 1942, she moved to Washington, D.C., as a White House correspondent and to cover Eleanor Roosevelt.

She had been studying Japanese in Hawaii, so the OSS recruited her, eventually sending her to work in the Pacific theater of war. Initial recruitment for the OSS in 1942 and 1943 drew on personal contacts of William "Wild Bill" Donovan and his staff. It also drew upon a network of college-trained linguists and people, regardless of their politics, who knew other languages and particular regions and cultures. All of these recruits were volunteers. McIntosh fit the requirements. Her husband at the time, Alexander MacDonald, also joined, but regulations prevented them from being in the same area. The marriage later ended in divorce, as did many marriages among OSS couples.

McIntosh worked in the Morale Operations (MO) arm of the OSS. Although the U.S. government worked to curtail rumors and loose talk on the American homefront, it actively promoted gossip that could undermine German and Japanese political and military control. In 1941, the United States set up its own intelligence apparatus, and through MO the OSS promulgated rumors aimed at weakening the resolve of both civilians and soldiers who served the Axis powers. McIntosh was tied to an MO project in the Pacific theater. Her job was to help write and promote rumors and other reports aimed at demoralizing Japanese troops, encouraging surrender, and protecting Allied troops and indigenous insurgents. Her operations influenced actions in Thailand, French Indochina, and Burma.

Both the male and female recruits had to acculturate themselves to their roles in a new, quasimilitary branch of the government. All recruits faced hard work, dangerous travel, and difficult living conditions. Some of their male colleagues thought that women did not belong in these settings, while others recognized their hard work and capabilities. McIntosh's experiences had particular challenges. In addition to finding Japanese prisoners of war who might

aid them, the Americans in the OSS had to find people to help them get material that could pass as authentic—including paper, seals, and ink for their phony letters and leaflets. McIntosh's newspaper experience helped her in the invention of these texts.

McIntosh's memoir, *Undercover Girl* (1947), chronicles her evolution into a well-rounded secret operator in the Pacific theater of war at the same time that the newly formed OSS under the leadership of Donovan became a viable intelligence agency. It was one of the first personal accounts of OSS experiences to be published after the war. In closing this memoir, she argued that the persuasion tools she and her OSS colleagues used could be countered through an informed population—a necessary requirement for citizens after World War II. In 1989, McIntosh published *The Role of Women in Intelligence*. She has remained active, speaking to the news and public about the OSS. As recently as November 2009, at the age of 93, she spoke at the National Archives in Washington, D.C., about her book on women of the OSS and the roles of Marlene Dietrich and Julia Child in the United States' intelligence community.

Sisterhood of Spies: The Women of the OSS, McIntosh's account of women who worked in the OSS in undercover operations overseas, was published in 1998. She has been a chronicler of women's experiences, not only of those behind desks as filers, encoders, secretaries, and assistants, but also of those in undercover, covert, and analytical work in wartime. As such, McIntosh has been a pioneer and an advocate who has reminded the nation that thousands of women served in these obscure but dramatic, important, and often dangerous roles.

Page Dougherty Delano

See also: Child, Julia McWilliams (1912–2004); Dietrich, Marlene (1901–1992); Espionage; Prisoners of War; Roosevelt, Eleanor (1884–1962); World War II (1941–1945).

References and Further Reading

MacDonald (McIntosh), Elizabeth. *Undercover Girl*. Arlington, VA: Time Life Books, 1993. Original publication, 1947.

McIntosh, Elizabeth P. *The Role of Women in Intelligence*. McLean, VA: Association of Former Intelligence Officers, 1989.

McIntosh, Elizabeth P. *Sisterhood of Spies: The Women of the OSS*. New York: Random House, 1998.

Pinck, Dan. "Elizabeth P. McIntosh Receives Distinguished Service Award," *OSS Society Newsletter*, 2007. http://www.osssociety.org/pdfs/oss_summer_fall_07.pdf.

Veterans History Project. Elizabeth McIntosh interview by Leslie Sewell. 2004. http://lcweb2.loc.gov/diglib/vhp/story/loc.natlib.afc2001001.30838/.

McKEE, FRAN (1926–2002)

On June 1, 1976, Fran McKee became the first female line officer to hold the rank of rear admiral in the U.S. Navy. She was also one of the first two women selected to attend the Naval War College and the first woman to command an activity of the Naval Security Group Command.

Born to Thomas Walker and Geneva Lumpkin McKee on September 13, 1926, in Florence, Alabama, Fran McKee was the oldest of three daughters. McKee graduated from Phillips High School in Birmingham, Alabama, at the age of 15. She went on to earn a degree in chemistry from the University of Alabama in 1950; a master's degree in international affairs from George Washington University, Washington, D.C., in 1970; and an honorary doctorate in public administration from the Massachusetts Maritime Academy. Her patriotism prompted her to enlist in the U.S. Navy in 1950 after the outbreak of the Korean War. Her plan was to serve for two years, do her part for the war effort, and then attend medical school.

McKee was commissioned an ensign on December 4, 1950, and reported for duty to the Office of Naval Research in Washington, D.C., in June 1951 after five months of officer indoctrination at the General Line School in Newport, Rhode Island. She served for four years as assistant to the director, Physical Science Division, and then as administrative aide to the chief of Naval research. In May 1954, she became woman procurement officer at the Navy Recruiting Station Office of Naval Officer Procurement in Boston, Massachusetts.

She attended General Line School at the U.S. Naval Postgraduate School in Monterey, California, and in September 1957 was appointed personnel officer at the Naval Air Station at Port Lyautey, Morocco. In September 1958, McKee was training coordinator at the Damage Control School, Treasure Island, San Francisco, California. She served as classification/mobilization officer on the staff of the chief of Naval

Air Reserve training from January 1962; as officer in charge of the Naval Woman Officers School, Newport, Rhode Island, from 1965; and as personnel officer at the Naval Station, Rota, Spain, from 1967. In August 1969, McKee reported to the Naval War College, Newport, Rhode Island, as one of the first two women selected to attend the regular curriculum program. She graduated in June 1970.

Appointed head of the Special Inquiries and Publication Section, Officer Distribution Division of the Bureau of Naval Personnel, in June 1970, she served as deputy assistant chief of naval personnel for human goals starting in September 1972. The commander served as the senior female naval officer on the Committee to Study Equal Rights for Women in the Military. The committee's work resulted in new opportunities for women in the armed services. Promoted to captain, McKee commanded the Naval Security Group Activity at Fort George G. Meade, Maryland, from September 1973 to May 1976. She was the first woman assigned to head an activity of the Naval Security Group Command.

In February 1976, McKee became the first woman to be nominated for flag rank, and on June 1, 1976, she was promoted to rear admiral (lower half). With this promotion she also became an unrestricted line officer. Prior to this she held only command billets within her restricted area of specialization. As an unrestricted flag officer, McKee could command aviation squadrons, carrier strike groups, SEAL teams, and shore installations, facilities, and activities directly supporting the Navy's warfare mission.

She was director of naval education development at the Naval Education and Training Command, Pensacola, Florida. The Training Command was the largest shore command in the U.S. Navy and provided training for all sailors. Her responsibilities included oversight of Navy Junior ROTC units in high schools and the Navy's postgraduate school in California. In 1978, she was made assistant chief of naval personnel for human resource management with the additional duty as assistant deputy chief of naval operations (human resource management). McKee was promoted to rear admiral (upper half) in November 1978. She retired from the Navy in 1981.

During her career, McKee was awarded the Legion of Merit with Gold Star, the Meritorious Service Medal, the National Defense Service Medal with Bronze Star, the Expert Pistol Medal, and the Sharpshooter Rifle Ribbon. After her naval service, she served as chair of the Legislative and Employment Committee of the Veterans Administration Women's Advisory Committee for Veterans Affairs and as a member of the National Advisory Committee for the Women in Military Service for America Memorial Foundation, Inc. She was also an active member of the Episcopal Church.

At age 75, she suffered a cerebral hemorrhage and died on March 2, 2002, in Annandale, Virginia. McKee was buried with full military honors at Arlington National Cemetery on April 8, 2002. McKee was inducted into the Alabama Women's Hall of Fame in 2007, and a bridge on U.S. Highway 43 in Maury County (the location of her family home) was named in her memory by the state of Tennessee.

Thomas Francis Army, Jr.

See also: Cold War (ca. 1947–1991); Korean War (1950–1953); Women in Military Service for America Memorial.

References and Further Reading

Arlington National Cemetery. "Fran McKee: Rear Admiral, United States Navy." March 16, 2002. http://www.arlingtoncemetery .net/fmckee.htm.

McKee, William C. "Biography of Rear Admiral Fran McKee." *Encyclopedia of Alabama*, January 7, 2009. http://www .encyclopediaofalabama.org/face/Article .jsp?id=h-1901 (accessed February 20, 2012).

McKee, William C. "Rear Admiral Fran McKee." *Tennessee Encyclopedia of History and Culture*. Knoxville: University of Tennessee Press, 2010. http://tennesseeencyclopedia.net/ entry.php?rec=1627.

MEYER, MARIE ANNE (1897–1969)

As a cryptologist and a language specialist, Marie Anne Meyer played a critical role at the Signal Security Agency during World War II and, after the war, at the National Security Agency (NSA). Meyer is celebrated as making some of the initial breaks in the Venona code during the Cold War and, as a result, she was also the first person to receive the NSA's Meritorious Civilian Service Award.

Born in Bloomington, Illinois, on April 7, 1897, Meyer showed a penchant for language study early in her life. She took this love of linguistics to the Illinois State Normal University, where she received a bachelor's degree in education in 1919. Although she immediately began to teach school, she continued to study languages at night during the school year and in formal language programs at the University of Chicago during summer breaks. It was at the University of Chicago, however, that she took her language study to the next level, learning both French and Latin and eventually receiving a master's degree in Latin in August 1930. Throughout the 1930s and 1940s, she continued to take classes, adding Sanskrit, German, and Greek to her language repertoire.

When the United States entered World War II, Meyer's knowledge of language became a valuable asset. In 1943, she began to work for the Army's cryptology organization, the Signal Security Agency, as a German linguist. Meyer's involvement was part of a larger trend during the war where more women worked in the field of cryptology than at any other point in history. Women played more formal roles during this conflict in all fields, largely as a result of President Franklin Delano Roosevelt's authorization of women to take noncombatant military roles.

Even while working as a linguist for the Army, Meyer continued her education. She took correspondence courses in Russian. When the war was over, she brought these skills to a new job working on the Venona project. The top-secret Venona project, a collaboration between the United States and the United Kingdom, centered on cryptanalysis of intelligence messages from inside the Soviet Union. Russian linguist and fellow cryptologist Meredith Gardner credited Meyer with making the first code group recovery to effectively exploit KGB codes.

Although the Venona project continued until 1980, Meyer worked on several other cryptology projects through the Armed Forces Security Agency as well as through the NSA. For the rest of her career, she worked on facets of Russian code breaking. She also helped train others, teaching several Russian language classes at the NSA training school.

Meyer retired in 1960. She became the first person to be awarded the NSA's Meritorious Civilian Service Award. Meyer died in December 1969 in Illinois.

Debbie Sharnak

See also: Cold War (ca. 1947–1991); Espionage; World War II (1941–1945).

References and Further Reading

National Security Agency. "Marie Meyer." Women in American Cryptology. http://www.nsa.gov/about/cryptologic_heritage/women/honorees/meyer.shtml (accessed January 24, 2012).

Nigel West. *Venona: The Greatest Secret of the Cold War.* New York: HarperCollins, 2000.

MILITARY AIR TRANSPORT SERVICE (MATS)

The Military Air Transport Service (MATS) was activated on June 1, 1948, as the first joint command between the Navy and Air Force. Created by consolidating the Air Transport Command and the Navy Air Transport Service, the MATS was employed for the transportation of military personnel and cargo internationally, though it later took on additional, more technical services such as the Air Weather Service (AWS), Air Rescue Service (ARS), and Air Photographic and Charting Service (APCS).

Just three weeks after its activation, MATS was called upon to perform the massive airlift operation known as Operation Vittles, which delivered over 2.5 tons of food and fuel to West Berlin after the Soviet Union cut off the city from all other sources of aid. MATS also provided essential transport and aeromedical evacuation services during the Korean War. The Department of Defense deactivated MATS in 1966 due to the demands of the expanding Vietnam War.

During its years of service, MATS proved to be a fruitful service for the employment and advancement of women in the military. Women served as flight attendants in MATS carrier services across both the Atlantic and Pacific, carrying military personnel and their families to and from international military bases. Women also served in more technical positions, especially in the APCS and AWS, where they provided logistical and technical expertise to the commands. Perhaps the greatest contribution by the female military personnel of the MATS occurred in the Korean War. Flight nurses provided essential aid to soldiers in the field and kept those soldiers alive and stable while being transported away from the battlefield. MATS provided over one-third of all aeromedical evacuations during the Korean War, with women providing the majority of care to the soldiers.

Andrew Polk

See also: Air Force Nurse Corps (AFNC); Korean War (1950–1953); Nursing.

References and Further Reading

Ulannoff, Stanley M. *MATS: The Story of the Military Air Transport Service*. New York: Moffa Press, 1964.

Williams, Nicholas M. *Aircraft of the United States' Military Air Transport Service*. Hinckley, UK: Midland Press, 1999.

MILITARY POLICE

The Military Police Corps, officially established in 1941, represents an early branch of the U.S. Army.

Police duties were not new to the mission, however. Mounted soldiers ("Troops of the Marechaussee") served during the American Revolution. Civil War soldiers, including the Veterans Reserve Corps and Provost Corps, also performed military police duties. The insignia of crossed pistols, approved in 1923 for the military police, further distinguished the emerging role. World War I, World War II, and the Korean War would all pass into history before women became full-fledged Military Police Corps members.

President Jimmy Carter abolished the Women's Army Corp (WAC) in October 1978, and the Army discontinued the separate corps effective October 20, 1978. Women shed their goddess Athena insignia and forever forward donned the crossed pistols of the military police. Women would become an integral part of the Military Police Corps.

The first gender-integrated class of military police (One-Station-Unit Training) began on July 8, 1977, at Fort McClellan. During the next several years, each class graduated a generation of enlisted women to serve throughout the Military Police Corps command structure. Their initial service as privates and specialist grades opened new opportunities for career military service. Some of these women continued to acquire considerable expertise, and they achieved senior enlisted noncommissioned officer status. Moreover, some would achieve commissioned officer status and pursue careers as officers.

One of these early pioneers from the WAC was Mary Elizabeth Clarke. She enlisted as a private at age 20 in August 1945. In September 1949, she graduated from the WAC Officer Candidate Course at Fort Lee, Virginia. Maj. Gen. Clarke was the last WAC commandant before women merged into the Regular Army. She was the first woman to command the U.S. Army Military Police School and was the post commander at the same time for Fort McClellan. In addition, Clarke was the motivating energy behind the establishment of the first WAC Museum at Fort McClellan. It was later moved to Fort Lee, one the first WAC training centers.

Brig. Gen. (R) Sherian G. Cadoria originally served in the WAC and then decided to branch transfer to the Military Police Corps. She was the first woman to serve as a military police officer. In addition, she served in the Republic of Vietnam from January 1967 to October 1969. Her service includes commander, MP School Battalion, and first region commander, U.S. Army Criminal Investigation Command.

The appointment of Brig. Gen. Colleen L. McGuire on January 15,

2010, as the first woman provost marshal of the Army and the commander of the U.S. Army Criminal Investigation Department proves her dedication to service. McGuire's accomplishments at the highest levels of the Military Police Corps reflect on her professional contribution, the future of women, and their continuing service to the Army Military Police Corps.

Thomas E. Baker

See also: American Revolution (1775–1783); Cadoria, Sherian Grace (1940–); Civil War (1861–1865); Clarke, Mary E. (1924–); Johnsen, Heather Lynn (1973–); Korean War (1950–1953); McGuire, Colleen L. (n.d.–n.d.); Vietnam War (1965–1973); Women's Army Corps (WAC); World War I (1914–1918); World War II (1941–1945).

References and Further Reading

Depue, Mark R. *Patrolling Baghdad: A Military Police Company and the War in Iraq.* Lawrence: University Press of Kansas, 2007.

Falerios, Kenton. *"Give Me Something I Can't Do": The History of the 82nd Military Police Company from WWI to the Iraq War.* Bloomington, IN: AuthorHouse, 2007.

Young, Richard. *Combat Police: U.S. Army Military Police in Vietnam.* Bloomington, IN: AuthorHouse, 2002.

MILITARY SEA TRANSPORT SERVICE (MSTS)

The Military Sea Transport Service (MSTS) was established in 1949, consolidating the sea transportation services of the Army and Navy. Concerned over the internal competition for the services of the merchant marine in World War II, the newly created Department of Defense sought to prevent such conflicts in future wars. This decision proved to be a shrewd one. Only nine months after the MSTS's official creation, North Korean forces crossed the 38th parallel, and the Korean War began. The MSTS provided essential services during the war, carrying troops and equipment to the peninsula, supplying naval ships with oil and coal, and serving as hospital ships for wounded soldiers. The MSTS continued its service after the war, supplying U.S. bases along with expeditionary and explorative endeavors, while simultaneously supporting nation-building efforts in Europe, Africa, and Asia. The MSTS was again called upon to supply U.S. armed forces in the early years of the Vietnam conflict, but the service was reorganized as the Military Sealift Command in 1970.

Although women had been traditionally barred from most types of naval service, the MSTS's nature as a hybrid between the Navy and merchant marine opened up numerous opportunities for women who wanted to serve on the high seas. Women provided their most critical service during both the Korean and Vietnam conflicts as nurses on board official hospital ships and vessels that became impromptu medical facilities. Navy women from the Women Accepted for Volunteer Emergency Service (WAVES) organization and Hospital Corps were officially allowed on hospital ships in 1953. These women took excellent care of the wounded marines, soldiers, and sailors, but they also served in numerous other support capacities on the ships. In these times of war, the highly capable and courageous women of the MSTS proved that official gender restrictions could not keep them from attending to the many needs of the war effort, both large and small.

Andrew Polk

See also: Korean War (1950–1953); Nursing; Vietnam War (1965–1973); Women Accepted for Volunteer Emergency Service (WAVES); World War II (1941–1945).

References and Further Reading

Godson, Susan H. *Serving Proudly: A History of Women in the U.S. Navy.* Annapolis, MD: U.S. Naval Institute Press, 2002.

Haynes, William F. *Sea Time: Life on Board Supply and Troop Ships during World War II and Its Aftermath.* Princeton, NJ: The Darwin Press, 2007.

MILLIGAN (RASMUSON), MARY LOUISE (1911–)

Col. Mary Louise Milligan Rasmuson was the fifth director of the Women's Army Corps (WAC) from 1957 to 1962. A native of Pennsylvania, Milligan Rasmuson studied at both the Carnegie Institute of Technology and the University of Pittsburgh. She worked in school administration for several years before World War II. Milligan Rasmuson then served in the WAC from 1942 until her retirement in 1962 after she married.

Born Mary Louise Milligan, she had two brothers whom she knew would serve during World War II, given the draft requirements. She believed she was also capable of supporting the war effort, so she traveled to Washington, D.C., to investigate Navy service opportunities for women. However, Milligan learned that the Navy had not yet developed plans for women's wartime service, so she was unable to join that branch of service. When Milligan heard about the newly created Women's Army Auxiliary Corps (WAAC, later the WAC), she selected that service option. Milligan trained in the first WAAC officer candidate class and became a commissioned third officer (then the equivalent of an Army second lieutenant) in late August 1942.

During the war years, Milligan served as director of the First WAAC Training Center in Des Moines, Iowa. At that time, she was a single woman. She also attended several training courses at the Adjutant General's School (1942) and the Command and General Staff School (1945). As a result of her service and training, Milligan received promotion to lieutenant colonel in June 1945.

In 1946, the WAC asked Milligan to transfer to Washington, D.C., to help prepare legislation that would make the WAC permanent. Although she had not initially planned on a career in military service, Milligan believed the legislation was an important step to show Americans that women could play an important part in national defense. After the Women's Armed Services Integration Act passed Congress in 1948, Milligan decided she would remain in the military. She continued to serve at the Pentagon in the chief of staff's office as a WAC officer.

During the 1950s, Milligan was selected as deputy director of the WAC and then served as WAC staff advisor in the European Army Headquarters in Heidelberg, Germany. In 1956, she transferred to Virginia to the Plans and Operations Branch of the Continental Army Command Headquarters. In 1957, the secretary of the Army named Milligan as the next director of the WAC. Upon her appointment to the position on January 3, 1957, Milligan received a temporary promotion to full colonel, which she would hold for the duration of her assignment as director of WAC. At that time, the only WAC member who could hold the rank of colonel was the director. Upon retirement, Milligan Rasmuson and her predecessors reverted to the permanent rank of lieutenant colonel. Although the director of WAC position previously had been a four-year role, before Milligan Rasmuson's term ended the secretary of the Army announced plans to keep Milligan Rasmuson as director for an extra two years, through 1963.

As director of WAC, Milligan Rasmuson made official visits to WAC and other military installations around the world, including sites in Hong Kong, Taiwan, Okinawa, Japan, Panama, and Turkey. Milligan Rasmuson championed efforts to give women credit for their service in the WAAC during 1942 and 1943. She also helped develop the WAC College Junior Officer Procurement Program and worked to secure WAC officers' admittance into the Army's Logistics Officer Career Program. During her tenure as director, WACs also began to serve in the highest enlisted grades of E-8 (master sergeant) and E-9 (sergeant major). Additionally, Milligan Rasmuson helped women gain new career opportunities in electrical and electronics maintenance and operations, including positions at the new Missile Master Unit in Fort Meade, Maryland.

In November 1961, she married Elmer Rasmuson, a prominent Alaskan businessman known for his philanthropy. Upon her marriage, Milligan Rasmuson announced that she would retire in six months to pursue private life.

Milligan Rasmuson's military awards include the Legion of Merit with one Oak Leaf Cluster, the WAC Service Medal, the American Campaign Medal, the World War I Victory Medal, the Army of Occupation Medal, and the National Defense Service Medal. She has also been recognized with an honorary doctor of laws degree from the Carnegie Institute of Technology, one of the first two women to receive the distinction from that institution. In 1960, the state of Pennsylvania recognized her as a Distinguished Daughter of Pennsylvania.

Milligan Rasmuson moved to Alaska to live with her husband, and she has remained active in community service there. She has served on boards for the American Cancer Society in Alaska, children's organizations, and the Historical and Fine Arts Commission. Milligan Rasmuson also served on the Civilian Advisory Board for the Alaskan Command for many years.

Tanya L. Roth

See also: Bailey, Mildred "Inez" Caroon (1919–2009); Hoisington, Elizabeth P. (1918–2007); Korean War (1950–1953); Vietnam War (1965–1973); Women's Armed Services Integration Act of 1948; Women's Army Auxiliary Corps (WAAC); Women's Army Corps (WAC); World War II (1941–1945).

References and Further Reading

Bailey, Beth. *America's Army: Making the All-Volunteer Force*. Cambridge, MA: Belknap Press of Harvard University Press, 2009.

Holm, Jeanne. *In Defense of a Nation: Servicewomen in World War II*. St. Petersburg, FL: Vandamere Press, 1998.

Holm, Jeanne. *Women in the Military: An Unending Revolution*, rev. ed. Novato, CA: Presidio Press, 1993.

Morden, Bettie J. *The Women's Army Corps, 1945–1978*. Washington, D.C.: Center of Military History, 1989.

Witt, Linda, Judith Bellafaire, Britta Granrud, and Mary Jo Binker. *"A Defense Weapon Known to Be of Value": Servicewomen of the Korean War Era*. Hanover, NH: University Press of New England, 2005.

"MISS JENNY"
(CA. 1760–N.D.)

Bilingual and elusive, Loyalist spy "Miss Jenny" kept her identity a secret both during and after the American Revolution.

Information about Miss Jenny's childhood and life after the American Revolution is a mystery. Her real name is not mentioned in any records, though at the time of her work with the British intelligence during the summer of 1781 she appears to have been a young woman, probably in her late teens or early twenties. Details about Miss Jenny come from a letter written by Baron Ottendorf, a German who originally fought with American forces before switching to the British side in 1777. The deposition, a letter written to an unknown recipient, recalled details about Miss Jenny's mission, which took place in early August 1781.

Female spies were somewhat of a paradox in the 18th century. Gender conventions largely discredited women's intelligence. As a result, when soldiers saw women peddling goods in and around army campsites, it rarely aroused suspicion. Girls' education during the mid and late 18th century reinforced notions of female intellectual inferiority. Education for girls included training in domestic duties, such as cooking and household maintenance. Some girls attended local schools to learn reading, writing, and basic arithmetic. Girls of affluent families may have received private instruction from a tutor and gained proficiency in music, singing, and embroidery. Based on the extant information available about Miss Jenny, it appears that she was bilingual, fluent in French and at least proficient in English. Based on this information, Miss Jenny probably received lessons from a private tutor or older family member.

British general Sir Henry Clinton's spy network, to which Miss Jenny belonged, thoroughly penetrated the American landscape. Clinton planted spies within the Continental Army, some serving as officers to American general George Washington. Loyalist civilians scattered throughout the various colonies offered up their homes as "safe houses" to British intelligence. Some female loyalist spies, like Ann Bates, dressed as peddlers and entered Continental Army camps under the pretense of selling useful items to soldiers. Once inside, these spies took note of the number of artillery, food provisions, and number of soldiers. Clinton's spies used small tokens to identify one another.

The deposition taken by Ottendorf provides interesting details of Miss Jenny's mission in August 1781. Unlike Bates, Miss Jenny wore no disguise as she traveled to Kingsbridge, New York, a location near Lt. Gen. Rochambeau's camp. Her mission, it appears, was to discover the strategy for a proposed combined attack of Washington's and Rochambeau's forces on British troops in New York City. Using a forged passport, Miss Jenny approached a French cavalry officer whom she met on the road to Kingsbridge. She asked the officer to escort her into Rochambeau's camp, indicating that she was French. Though the officer helped Miss Jenny enter the camp, his intentions do not appear to be entirely honorable. While recalling her mission to Ottendorf, Miss Jenny explained that the same officer tried to engage her for sex and even threatened to use force on her if she did not comply.

Miss Jenny's troubles increased from there, and she was sent to Rochambeau for questioning. Though he was unsuccessful in extracting information, Rochambeau did not accept Miss Jenny's story that she was searching for her father, a French soldier. The commander ordered Miss Jenny sent to Washington's camp for further questioning. Not caving under pressure, Miss Jenny withstood two days of questioning from two of Washington's men before being transported back to the French camp near Kingsbridge. Rochambeau's men released Miss Jenny on Wednesday, August 15, 1781. Before her release, the chief provost of the French camp ordered Miss Jenny's hair to be cut short as a symbol of public shame.

Miss Jenny's service to Clinton's spy network seems to have ceased after her deposition to Ottendorf in August 1781. Miss Jenny disappears from historical records after this date. Her date and location of death is unknown.

Carrie Glenn

See also: American Revolution (1775–1783); Bates, Ann (1748–1801); Espionage; "355" (n.d.–n.d.).

References and Further Reading

Bakeless, John. *Turncoats, Traitors, and Heroes*. Philadelphia: J. B. Lippincott Company, 1959.

Hastedt, Glenn P. *Spies, Wiretaps, and Secret Operations: A–J*. Santa Barbara, CA: ABC-CLIO, 2011.

MOBILE ARMY SURGICAL HOSPITAL (MASH)

The U.S. Army created the first Mobile Army Surgical Hospital (MASH) units in August 1945. These units were initially deployed in the Korean War. The last MASH unit was deactivated in February 2006. Women played a crucial role in MASH units as front-line nurses. Those who served in a MASH unit were the lead troops in life-saving operations.

Female nurses entered center stage during World War II, as the desperate need for operating room (OR) nurses accelerated to meet the needs of incoming sick and wounded soldiers. The concept of registered nurses as first assistants (RNFA) for doctors in the OR unfolded dramatically. The Korean War, and the MASH units, required the refinement of the role of the RNFA. Fifty-seven army nurses arrived in Pusan, Korea, when the U.S. military forces became engaged in the conflict. The Korean War led to shortages in behind-the-lines health care professionals who could serve close to the battlefield. Soon thereafter, 12 Army nurses arrived in Taejan, Korea, attached to the MASH units. They served alongside male medical personnel throughout the war.

The goal of the MASH units was to save lives by moving medical personnel closer to the front lines where battle casualties were, and where intervention saved lives quickly and successfully. The plan yielded positive results: 97 percent of wounded soldiers who reached a MASH unit survived once treatment was rendered. MASH units were truly mobile; the units' proximity to the battlefield made a significant difference. Standards required that mobile Army surgical hospitals have the capacity to disassemble, be loaded into trucks and ready to depart in six hours, and then reassemble, becoming operational within four hours after arrival at the next destination.

One of the most important and difficult roles of the MASH nurses was to evaluate incoming casualties, conduct triage, determine who required immediate medical treatment, and identify those whose injuries or illness were less critical. One grim reality of war was that it was better to save three lives in the time that it would take to save one. Nurses immediately cut the clothing from wounded soldiers, exposing their wounds, taking vital signs, and documenting their status. A stretcher placed on blocks served as an OR bed.

Five surgical tables and a highly organized triage system moved wounded soldiers to ambulance platoons. Rapid evacuation was a goal once the soldier was stabilized, and generally after postoperative recovery. In addition, nurses cared for soldiers who were classified as nontransferable. Four helicopters supported the efforts by helping to resupply and evacuate the wounded to and from MASH units. Comparatively inactive MASH units repositioned to supplement overburdened units in the theater of operations.

The role of women as doctors and nurses was at the vital core of MASH units. Without them, many more soldiers would have died. The nurses were the central component as primary care providers. During major offensives, the nurses might work 12-hour shifts, six to seven days a week. At the height of a major battle, doctors and nurses often worked 24 hours without a break.

MASH units became firmly entrenched as an essential component in the Vietnam War. The Korean and Vietnam wars served as guideposts for successful helicopter evacuation and timely medical intervention by dedicated MASH nurses and unit personnel. The 1991 Gulf War and the conflicts in Iraq and Afghanistan in the 2000s saw MASH units deployed to the front lines. Advanced methods in the treatment of shock and trauma management developed for MASH units served as standard practice for civilian medical centers in the United States and overseas.

The deliberate process of decommissioning MASH units began in the mid-1990s. As the world changed, so did the demands of combat. The last MASH unit in Korea was decommissioned in 1997, and in October 2006, the 212th MASH (the most decorated combat hospital in the U.S. Army) became the 212th Combat Support Hospital. The 212th MASH's final deployment was to Pakistan to support the 2005 Kashmir earthquake relief operations. The mission accomplished, all tents and the entire hospital were donated to the Pakistani military, a $4.5 million dollar Department of Defense donation. More recently, smaller casualty surgical hospitals (combat support hospitals) deploy even closer to combat operations.

Diane Carlson Evans, a former Vietnam nurse, was the driving force behind the establishment of the Vietnam Women's Memorial, located on the National Mall in Washington, D.C. The women's memorial is near the Vietnam Memorial Wall, north of the Reflecting Pool. The bronze statue, by designer Glenna Goodacre, depicts three female soldiers. A nurse comforts a wounded soldier with an apparent head wound, while another kneels nearby, perhaps in prayer or deliberate meditation. A third soldier stands, her head and eyes turned upward, as if looking for a helicopter that would airlift the wounded soldier to the care of those waiting to render assistance.

Thomas E. Baker

See also: Afghanistan; Gulf War (1991); Iraq War (2003–2011); Korean War (1950–1953); Nursing; Vietnam War (1965–1973); World War II (1941–1945).

References and Further Reading

Norman, Elizabeth. *We Band of Angels: The Untold Story of American Nurses Trapped on Bataan by the Japanese.* New York: Random House, 1999.

Norman, Elizabeth. *Women at War: The Story of Fifty Nurses Who Served in Vietnam.* Harrisburg: University of Pennsylvania Press, 1990.

Sarnecky, Mary T. *A History of the U.S. Army Nurse Corps: Studies in Health, Illness, and Care-giving in America.* Harrisburg: University of Pennsylvania Press, 1999.

MONROE, ROSE LEIGH ABBOTT WILL (1920–1997)

Industrial worker and entrepreneur Rose Will Monroe became the living representation of the iconic "Rosie the Riveter" image during World War II.

Born the third of nine children of a Somerset, Kentucky, farm family on March 12, 1920, Rose was the daughter of Minnie and Walter Leigh. Her father, a construction worker and mason, played a significant role instilling the passion of building and design to his daughter. From a young age, Rose proved herself a handy and versatile helper around the house. Referred to as a "tomboy" as a youth, she was not afraid of using tools. Despite attaining only an eighth-grade education, she channeled her creativity and driven work ethic over the coming decades into a rise to prominence.

Her later successes in life did not originate with a relaxed lifestyle. Married at age 16 in 1936 to Clarence Abbott, she bore two children. Within six years, the couple divorced. Seeking a fresh start, she relocated to Michigan with her daughters. In applying for a ferryboat pilot's position there, she met disappointment again as she was rejected due to her status as a single mother. By this time, however, the United States was at war with the Axis Powers, and women were being accepted into workplaces traditionally reserved for men. The shortage in industrial manpower due to enlistments and conscription permitted women to demonstrate their own mettle on behalf of the war effort.

Like some 20 million other American women, she found employment in one of the thousands of bustling factories churning out war materiel. At the Ford Motor Company's Willow Run Plant in Ypsilanti, Michigan, she labored as a riveter in the production of B-24 bombers. Constructing approximately 9,000 Liberator bombers, one-half of the total made during the war, the plant had the astounding capacity of completing one plane within one hour's time. A massive turntable, 24-hour production schedule, and gigantic facilities allowed for such operations. Although the female workers at such factories were publically celebrated, the war plants in which they toiled did not always embody employee harmony. Women were subjected to the chauvinism typical within labor during the era. The average female worker earned $31.50 per week, some $20 less than men performing similar duties. Yet Rose did not always fall prey to the trickery of her male coworkers. When sarcastically asked by one of the men for a left-handed wrench, she had worked with tools long enough to immediately realize no such instrument existed.

As the war escalated, the image of the enterprising and near-mythic "Rosie the Riveter" was taking form via music, film, and popular art. In 1942, composers Redd Evans and John Jacob Loeb wrote a popular tune celebrating the patriotism and hard work ethic of "Rosies." Meanwhile, the paintings of J. Howard Miller and Norman Rockwell accurately depicted women workers as resilient figures amid tumultuous times. In 1943, movie actor Walter Pidgeon was asked by officials in the War Department to scout for shooting locations for war bond promotional films. While exploring the Willow Run plant, he came into contact with Rose and quickly realized that this real-life "Rosie" offered a human face to the larger-than-life character. Her daughter later recalled that her mother was simply in the right place at the right time. In the following months, Rose appeared in multiple propaganda films and public ceremonies touting the industrial and moral strength of the American homefront.

Amid her new fame, Rose relocated to Indiana, where she reconnected with her first husband. Sadly, Clarence Abbott was killed in an automobile crash only weeks before the couple was to be reunited in marriage. In 1947, she married Calvin Will and gave birth to another daughter. Despite raising a growing family, Rose established a beauty shop and subsequently formed Rose Builders, a company that met success in constructing luxury homes. Turned down to become a pilot during World War II, she at last attained her pilot's license in the 1970s. Her joy of flying nearly claimed her life in a 1978 plane crash resulting in the loss of a kidney and sight in her left eye. After divorcing Will in 1972, she married Clifford Monroe the year following her near-fatal accident.

Monroe passed away in 1997. Her tombstone in New Albany, Indiana, is nostalgically marked "Rosie the Riveter."

Jared Frederick

See also: Rosie the Riveter; World War II (1941–1945).

References and Further Reading

Hastings, Max. *Inferno: The World at War, 1939–1945*. New York: Alfred A. Knopf, 2011.

Jackson, Kenneth T., Karen Markoe, and Arnold Markoe. *The Scribner Encyclopedia of American Lives*, Vol. 5. New York: Charles Scribner's Sons, 2001.

Johnsen, Frederick A. *B-24 Liberator: Rugged but Right*. New York: McGraw-Hill, 1999.

Young, William H., and Nancy K. Young. *World War II and the Postwar Years in America: A Historical and Cultural Encyclopedia*, Vol. 1. Santa Barbara, CA: ABC-CLIO, 2010.

MOODY, JUANITA MORRIS (CA. 1934–)

Signals Intelligence (SIGINT) operations manager Juanita Moody (née Morris) collected information about Cuba during the Cold War that was essential to policy makers dealing with the Cuban Missile Crisis and other emergencies. Moody's work was so important that personal information such as her birth date and details about her work are still considered classified on national security grounds.

Juanita Morris was born in Morven, North Carolina, and spent her childhood there. She enrolled in Western Carolina College in 1942. However, once World War II began and she witnessed many male students leaving for battle overseas, Morris left school after one year to join the war effort as well. She went to the

recruiting office in Charlotte and volunteered with the Signals Intelligence Service (SIS).

Moody arrived at Arlington Hall, a former girls' school and the headquarters of the SIS cryptologic effort, in April 1943. While waiting for her security clearance, Moody began unclassified training in cryptanalysis and quickly became enthralled with the subject. Therefore she was disappointed when her security clearance was granted and she was transferred into the job originally intended for her. Moody's first assignment with the U.S. government placed her in a low-level library position sorting messages and punch cards.

Her personal interest in cryptanalysis led Morris to join a small group that met after work to inspect and study a German code system that remained untouched due to its difficulty. Morris's aptitude for codes was soon noticed, and she was given more challenging assignments. Once the war was over, Morris planned to return to college, but given her talent for cryptanalysis she was asked to remain. She agreed to stay provided she was assigned a more complicated job in the research and development department. It was here that Morris learned about computers, analytic machines, and the need for automating not just codes but communications as well.

In 1948, Juanita married Warren Moody, who was also a government employee. Throughout the 1950s, Juanita Moody continued to be promoted as supervisor of Soviet and other still-classified issues in various analytic organizations. She became in charge of operations running the SIGINT collection of information about Cuba. By the

1960s, this job was becoming increasingly important and demanding. Moody had to deal with many crises and was constantly pushing her workers to reduce the lag time between intercepting and delivering information.

Concern about communist affairs in Cuba began to grow, and in late 1961, National Security Agency (NSA) Deputy Director Louis Tordella came to Moody's office for information on what SIGINT had discovered about Cuba. Final intelligence summary reports were usually created by the Central Intelligence Agency, but high-ranking Department of Defense officials requested a report from Moody herself after witnessing her capabilities and the successful operations she was running. The report Moody prepared went on to play an important role in the creation of policy. In the meantime, she supervised the buildup of a large amount of analytic capacity concerning Cuba and pushed for the information to be passed on as quickly as possible in the wake of dynamic political events.

Her information's most important role came in October 1962 as the United States was on the brink of nuclear war during the Cuban Missile Crisis. She briefed NSA director Lt. Gen. Gordon Blake along with other high-ranking decision makers for presidential meetings, often using ambiguous terms as many telephone lines were not secure. It was Moody who determined the collection, processing, and release of information necessary for managing the crisis. During the Cuban Missile Crisis, Moody did not leave the office for days at a time, often sleeping for only a few hours on a cot in her office. Senior military and political thinkers needed to be able to contact her at any hour for information updates.

Throughout the 1960s and early 1970s, Moody was promoted to increasingly higher NSA positions. Her rise within the government came to an end in 1975 when a Senate committee chaired by Frank Church began investigating abuses of power by intelligence agencies of the federal government. Moody was called to testify before the committee, gaining her a lot of press. The NSA was still a highly secretive organization, so any public reports about it were seen as controversial. According to the NSA's biography of Moody, her associations with abuses of power were false and an unfortunate result of her being a spokesperson in front of Congress. Nevertheless, Moody decided to make things easier for both herself and the NSA by retiring in February 1976 after 33 years of service.

Moody was awarded the National Intelligence Medal of Achievement in December 1975. She was inducted into the NSA's Hall of Honor for her cryptology work in 2003.

Megan Findling

See also: Cold War (ca. 1947–1991); Espionage; World War II (1941–1945).

References and Further Reading

Aid, Matthew. *The Secret Sentry: The Untold History of the National Security Agency.* New York: Bloomsbury Press, 2009.

Frahm, Jill. "From Librarians to Leadership: Women at NSA." *Cryptologic Almanac*, 50th Anniversary Series, March–April 2002.

Hatch, David. "Juanita Moody." *Cryptologic Almanac*, 50th Anniversary Series, May–June 2002.

Johnson, Thomas, and Hatch, David. *NSA and the Cuban Missile Crisis*. Fort Meade, MD: National Security Agency, Center for Cryptologic History, 1998.

MOON, CHARLOTTE "LOTTIE" (1829–1895)

Lottie Moon was the elder of a pair of sisters who served as spies, couriers, and smugglers for the Confederacy during the Civil War.

Born Cynthia Charlotte in Danville, Virginia, on August 10, 1829, to Dr. Robert S. and Cynthia Ann (Sullivan) Moon, Moon was independent and strong-minded from an early age. Her natural proclivity for horsemanship, marksmanship, and acting served her well in her activities on behalf of the Confederacy in later years. Moon's brothers Robert and William served in the Confederate army and navy, respectively, while she and her sister Ginnie did their part on the homefront.

Before marrying Peace Democrat judge James Clark on January 30, 1849, Moon was betrothed to Ambrose Burnside, who later became a general with the Union army. She and Burnside met while she visited Brownsville, Indiana, and he courted her, bringing small gifts to her younger sisters Ginnie and Mary at her family's home at Oxford, Ohio. On their wedding day, June 21, 1848, Moon arrived at the altar and said that she had changed her mind and would not marry Burnside.

As the South withdrew from the Union, Clark avowed states' rights and supported secession. Moon's subterfuge began when she pretended that her son Frank was ill and ordered medical supplies, which she then delivered to wounded Confederate soldiers. Clark and Moon's Jones Station home became the central hub of anti-Union activities in Butler County.

Her first mission was in the summer of 1862. Walker Taylor, a nephew of Zachary Taylor, arrived at Jones Station, Ohio, with a message from Gen. Sterling Price to Col. Edmund Kirby Smith in Lexington, Kentucky. Taylor was too recognizable to carry the message, so Lottie volunteered. Disguising herself as an Irish woman, she easily passed the papers to a Confederate officer, who placed them in Kirby's hands.

On another mission in October 1862, she traveled to Canada disguised as a British woman, and she carried letters from Rev. Stuart Robinson, who tried to convince Jefferson Davis that the Confederacy should unite with the Knights of the Golden Circle. Her acting abilities, flair for costume, and ear for accents, coupled with her uncommon skill at knocking her joints out of place, eased her crossing of lines and supposedly landed her in President Abraham Lincoln's party—though one account places her in his carriage—when he reviewed the Army of the Potomac. She allegedly met Secretary of War Edwin M. Stanton on that occasion.

Finally recognized by Gen. Ambrose Burnside, Moon was caught, and her usefulness to the Confederacy ended. Some scholars suggest that Moon exaggerated her exploits because her movements were logistically impossible and that she was never captured by Burnside but rather created a fictionalized account based on her sister Ginnie's capture.

After the Confederacy's fall, Clark and Moon moved to New York City, where she became a war correspondent for the *World* during the Franco-Prussian War. Returning to Manhattan, she wrote novels under the pseudonym Charles M. Clay. She died of cancer at her son's home in Philadelphia on November 20, 1895.

Rebecca Tolley-Stokes

See also: Civil War (1861–1865); Espionage; Moon, Virginia "Ginnie" (1844–1925); Prisoners of War.

References and Further Reading

Marsh, Thomas O., and Marlene Templin. "The Ballad of Lottie Moon." *Civil War: The Magazine of the Civil War Society* 21 (1988): 40–45.

Marvel, William. *Burnside.* Chapel Hill: University of North Carolina Press, 1991.

Smith, Orphia. *Oxford Spy: Wed at Pistol Point.* Oxford, OH: Cullen Printing, 1962.

MOON, VIRGINIA "GINNIE" (1844–1925)

Ginnie Moon was the younger of a pair of sisters who served as spies, couriers, and smugglers for the Confederacy. She was also the most noted female spy working in Memphis, Tennessee.

Ginnie was born Virginia Bethel in Oxford, Ohio, on June 22, 1844, to Dr. Robert S. and Cynthia Ann (Sullivan) Moon. Unlike the stereotypical Southern belle, Moon was independent and noted for carrying a pearl-handled pistol in her skirts.

When her family moved to Memphis at the beginning of the war, Ginnie stayed behind at Oxford Female College. She soon got around the school rule prohibiting young women from leaving the college unescorted. The school expelled her for shooting the stars out of a U.S. flag flying on campus, and she joined her family in Tennessee.

In Memphis, Moon comforted sick and wounded Confederate soldiers in many ways, including becoming engaged to 16 of them. She prepared bandages and helped in other efforts. When the city fell to Union forces in 1862, Ginnie's beauty and charm beguiled many Union soldiers and officers, who revealed information that she passed to Confederate officials. In the winter of 1863, Ginnie, like her sister Lottie, acted as a courier for Gen. Sterling Price, carrying his message from Jackson, Mississippi, to her brother-in-law, Judge James Clark of Jones Station, Ohio. A young, charming woman, Moon easily slipped into and out of Union territory with sensitive information.

Detained by Union officials as she traveled aboard the *Alice Dean* from Cincinnati to Memphis on April 3, 1863, Moon drew her Colt revolver on Capt. Harrison Rose when he tried to search her without anyone else in the room. After Ginnie threatened to kill him if he touched her and to report his behavior to Gen. Ambrose Burnside, Rose left her in the cabin. She removed sensitive dispatches relating to the Northwest Conspiracy from her corset, wet them, and swallowed them. As Rose accompanied her to the Customs Office, the clanking of her hoop skirt gave her away. Quilted within her clothing were vials of morphine, opium, and camphor, and Moon was charged with smuggling.

Burnside, an old family friend and spurned beau of Lottie's, kept informed of Ginnie's case and released her into her mother's custody. They stayed in Cincinnati for three weeks until Union officials transferred Ginnie to Fort Monroe, Virginia, where she was imprisoned for several months. Eventually, she was paroled to Jones Station, Ohio, home of her sister and brother-in-law.

Moon's version of the events leading to her arrest and detention at Fort Monroe differs significantly from published accounts. In April 1864, she, her sister-in-law Lizzie, along with Lizzie's two children and their nurse, boarded the *Flag of Truce* at Richmond bound for Newport News. They planned to take the steamer to Baltimore and then go on to Europe to join Moon's brother in Liverpool, England. Gen. Benjamin Butler detained the party before they boarded the steamer, demanding that they swear an oath of allegiance to the Union; Ginnie refused. The provost marshal walked her two blocks to Fort Monroe, where she stayed a little over a month. Her mother had not known that Ginnie was imprisoned until she returned to Danville, Virginia, where she corresponded with Confederate president Jefferson Davis. At Danville, Ginnie took charge of a ward at the General Hospital, overseeing the care of 50 soldiers. On one occasion, a seriously wounded charge would not eat the hospital food, so Moon downed two robins, had them cooked, and brought them to him. Before he died, he asked that Moon get his cap and pistol to his family in Kentucky upon his death. Moon attended his funeral as his chief mourner. The soldier's father came for his son's body after the war and heard of Moon's ministrations. In the summer of 1866, the soldier's father

visited Memphis to take her to Kentucky to live as his adopted daughter. Ginnie refused, but she visited the family when coming home from a trip north.

Moon devoted her life to helping others and is remembered in Memphis as the heroine of the yellow fever epidemic of the early 1870s. She appeared in several movies after moving to California to pursue her interests in acting and aviation. Eventually settling in Greenwich Village, New York, she died on September 11, 1925.

Rebecca Tolley-Stokes

See also: Civil War (1861–1864); Espionage; Moon, Charlotte "Lottie" (1829–1895); Nursing.

References and Further Reading

Kinchen, Oscar A. *Women Who Spied for the Blue and the Gray.* Philadelphia: Dorrance & Company, 1972.

Leonard, Elizabeth D. *All the Daring of the Soldier: Women of the Civil War Armies.* New York: W. W. Norton & Company, 1999.

Marvel, William. *Burnside.* Chapel Hill: University of North Carolina Press, 1991.

Moon, Virginia B. "Experiences of Virginia B. Moon, during the War between the States." Moon Collection. Oxford, OH: Smith Library of Regional History, n.d.

Smith, Orphia. *Oxford Spy: Wed at Pistol Point.* Oxford, OH: Cullen Printing, 1962.

MOTTE, REBECCA BREWTON (1737–1815)

Revolutionary War patriot Rebecca Brewton Motte sacrificed her home to help the American cause.

Rebecca Brewton was born on June 15, 1737, the daughter of Robert and Mary Loughton Brewton. The Brewton family was already respected and well established in South Carolina at the time of Rebecca's birth, and she grew up in an atmosphere of privilege and affluence. On June 28, 1758, she married Jacob Motte, a prominent local politician. In August 1775, her brother, Miles Brewton, was lost at sea, and Rebecca became heir to his estate. Five months later, her husband also passed away, and Rebecca found herself one of the richest people in South Carolina. She built an elegant house at her brother's old plantation along the Congaree River, in St. Matthews Parish, which she named Mount Joseph.

Motte was a supporter of the Patriot cause but managed to avoid being personally touched by the Revolutionary War during its first six years. Although she sent all of her male slaves to defend Charleston, armed and equipped at her own expense, and had contributed heavily to the Patriot cause, she had not yet taken an active and individual hand in the war.

However, in January 1781, the hostilities arrived at her doorstep. On May 8, 1781, British forces came to Mount Joseph and took control of Motte's house, which they converted into a fortified military installation by building earthworks around it. Motte and her family were permitted to remain in the house until Patriot forces under the command of Gen. Francis Marion and Col. Henry Lee arrived on the scene in May of 1781. She was then ordered to remove her family and their belongings to a nearby overseer's house.

The works constructed by the British were quite formidable, and the American forces dared not launch a frontal attack against them. So strong were the fortifications that they were referred to as Fort Motte. Marion and Lee attempted to lay siege to the British, but the prospects of starving the enemy out of their stronghold seemed unlikely. The Patriots thought if they could set the manor house on fire, it would force the British outside, where they could be killed or captured. Then the position might be taken.

Lee went to Motte to tell her about the plan and was surprised to find her in complete agreement concerning the destruction of her home, stating that the loss of her property was nothing when compared to the advancement of the cause. She not only endorsed the destruction, she provided the Patriots with the means of bringing it about. Producing a quiver of combustible arrows that a sea captain had brought from the East Indies for her brother, Motte handed over the incendiaries. The arrows were designed to be fired from a musket and would burst into flames when the tip struck against a hard surface. Two of the arrows were fired at the roof of the Motte mansion, but neither one worked properly, and no flames appeared on the house. A third arrow was fired, and shortly thereafter, a small fire could be observed on the wood shingles of the manor house. The British attempted to come out to extinguish the flames, but the only approach to the roof was commanded by a piece of Patriot artillery. Faced with choosing between burning alive in the fire, being blown to bits by Patriot artillery, or surrendering their position, the British opted for the latter, and a white flag was soon to be seen waving from the Motte house. Patriot forces rushed in to take possession of the prisoners and to extinguish the flames on the roof of the house. Motte's devotion to the cause of liberty, regardless of what it cost her personally, made her at once a heroine in South Carolina and across the Colonies.

The end of the Revolutionary War found Motte in a dire position. Her fortune was gone, the plantation was heavily in debt, and it seemed as if she might end her days in poverty and despair. Motte faced her financial problems with the same resolute determination she had shown when deciding the fate of her home. Her strong character and a keen administrative ability enabled her to gradually pay off the debt and accumulate another substantial fortune to leave to her heirs. Along with her son-in-law, Thomas Pinckney, she built a rice plantation, Eldorado, along the South Santee River.

Motte died on January 10, 1815, at her home at Eldorado and was buried in the Saint Philips Episcopal Church Cemetery in Charleston, South Carolina.

Robert P. Broadwater

See also: American Revolution (1775–1783).

References and Further Reading

Booth, Sally Smith. *The Women of '76.* New York: Hastings House, 1973.

Broadwater, Robert P. *Liberty Belles: Women of the American Revolution.* Bellwood, PA: Dixie Dreams Press, 2004.

Kierner, Cynthia A. *Southern Women in Revolution 1776–1800.* Columbia: University of South Carolina Press, 1998.

MOUNTAIN CHARLEY [ELSA JANE GUERIN A.K.A. CHARLES HATFIELD]
(N.D.–N.D.)

Mountain Charley was the name used by Elsa Jane Guerin, a woman who dressed as a man to find work, go westward during the gold rush, and eventually enlist in the Union army. In 1861, she published an autobiography of her pre–Civil War life, *Mountain Charley, or the Adventures of Mrs. E. J. Guerin, Who Was Thirteen Years in Male Attire: An Autobiography Comprising a Period of Thirteen Years Life in the States, California, and Pike's Peak*. Information about her wartime activities was later published in a series of articles in the *Colorado Transcript*.

In *Mountain Charley*, Guerin explained how her early life influenced her strange choice in careers. Her lack of a regular family, her time away at school, and her marriage and young widowhood meant that she had long depended on herself. Widowed with two young children to raise, Guerin searched for a way to survive. She understood the difficulties she would face as a young woman, so she decided to dress as a man to get a job.

Charley soon discovered both the economic and social benefits of being male. She gained freedom as a man who could go wherever he wanted and do as he wished. In the spring of 1855, Charley joined a party of 60 men who were bound for California, the "Land of Gold." By 1859, she was running a bakery and saloon in Colorado, and although several people now knew that she was a woman, she continued dressing as a man. She married her barkeeper, H. L. Guerin.

Although her book ends before the Civil War began, Mountain Charley corresponded with an old friend, newspaper publisher George West, with specific details about her wartime activities. She explained that she had enlisted in Iowa as Charles Hatfield and had served in Western units. In Missouri, she had persuaded the generals that she could spy on the Confederate camp disguised as a woman. She successfully fooled not only the enemy but even some former friends, now also serving in the war, who had known her as a man but who did not recognize her as a woman. At one point, Charley was wounded and her sex discovered, but surprisingly the doctors did not reveal her secret to military officials. She was eventually promoted to first lieutenant and served until the end of the war. Charley delighted in her ability to move back and forth between gender identities.

Although Mountain Charley's adventures were unique, accounts of other Civil War cross-dressers appeared quite regularly in wartime literature, newspapers, and memoirs. It is estimated that as many as 400 women dressed as men to fight in the Civil War.

Tiffany K. Wayne

See also: Civil War (1861–1865); Espionage.

Reference and Further Reading

Guerin, Elsa Jane. *Mountain Charley, or the Adventures of Mrs. E. J. Guerin, Who Was Thirteen Years in Male Attire: An Autobiography Comprising a Period of Thirteen Years Life in the States, California, and Pike's Peak.* With an introduction by Fred W. Mazzulla and William Kostka. Norman: University of Oklahoma Press, 1968.

MUTTER, CAROL ANN SCHNEIDER (1945–)

In April 1996, Lt. Gen. Carol Ann Mutter became the first woman in the history of the U.S. armed forces to be nominated for promotion to lieutenant general.

Born Carol Ann Schneider on December 17, 1945, in Greeley, Colorado, as a young woman she was active in 4-H and was interested in pursuing a career as a mathematics teacher.

Marine Corps Lieutenant General Carol A. Mutter served as the commander of the Marine Corps Systems Command in Quantico, Virginia. She was the first woman promoted to the rank of three-star general. (AP/Wide World Photos)

Inspired by both her former junior high school mathematics teacher, a skilled and dynamic career woman who was also trying to raise a family, and by a female marine recruiting officer, Schneider decided to attend the Marine Corps Woman's Officer Candidate Course in 1966 during the summer of her junior year at the University of Northern Colorado. Upon graduation the following year from the university with a BA in mathematics education, Schneider returned to Quantico, Virginia, completed the Woman Officer Basic Course, was commissioned a second lieutenant, and was assigned to data processing installations at Quantico and Camp Pendleton, California. She expected to remain in the service for three years and then move on to a civilian career.

When Schneider was commissioned a second lieutenant in the Marine Corps in June 1967, federal law stated that women in the armed services could be promoted no higher than colonel. In 1967, during the height of the Vietnam War, however, Congress changed the limits to the number of women in the armed forces and to the rank to which women could be promoted. Schneider discovered that she was effective in her assigned tasks and felt at home in the Marine Corps with its values of discipline, teamwork, family, and patriotism.

In 1971, Schneider returned to Quantico from Camp Pendleton as a platoon commander and instructor for women and officer candidates and by 1973 was promoted to captain. Between 1973 and 1984, she served as project officer for Marine Air Command and Control Systems at Marine Corps Tactical Systems Support Activity at Camp Pendleton. During this time, her other postings included financial management officer at the Development Center Quantico; assistant chief of staff, comptroller, First Marine Aircraft Wing, in Okinawa, Japan; and deputy comptroller at headquarters, Fleet Marine Force, Atlantic, in Norfolk, Virginia. By 1984, she was promoted to lieutenant colonel.

She met and married then marine Maj. James Mutter at the base chapel at Camp Pendleton in May 1977. At the time, it was unusual for marines to marry fellow marines, especially because couples could be separated from each other for significant periods of time. Her relationship with her husband forged lasting ideas about issues regarding family, housing, deployment, recreation, and services for military couples. With these lessons personally learned, Mutter became a powerful voice of support for military families.

In 1985, she was assigned as deputy program manager, and subsequently program manager, for the development of new Marine Corps automated pay and personnel systems for active-duty, retired, and reserve marines. By July 1988, as colonel, she joined the U.S. Space Command J-3 Operations Directorate in Colorado Springs, becoming the first woman to gain qualification as a space director. She served as Command Center crew commander and space director and then as division chief. She was responsible for the operation of the Space Command commander-in-chief's command center.

Transferred to III Marine Expeditionary Force (MEF) on Okinawa in August of 1990, she became the assistant chief of staff, comptroller, for both III MEF and the 3rd Marine Division. One year later, she returned to Quantico,

Virginia, and joined only a handful of women promoted to the rank of brigadier general. After demonstrating her knowledge, training, and leadership, she was transferred to Okinawa in June 1992 as the first woman of general/flag officer rank to command a major deployable tactical command, the Third Force Service Support Group, III MEF, United States Forces, Pacific. Two years later, she was promoted to major general and given charge of the Marine Corps Systems Command at Quantico.

In late March 1996, President Bill Clinton nominated Mutter to the rank of a three-star general. She was the first woman in the history of the U.S. armed forces to be so honored. As the deputy chief of staff, manpower and reserve affairs at Marine Corps headquarters, Washington, D.C., her responsibilities included quality-of-life issues for families in the Marine Corps. This assignment was her last active duty one. She retired in 1999. Modest and unassuming, she described her professional success simply as an "only in America story." Mutter served as an example and role model for women in the armed forces.

Three months after Mutter's nomination to lieutenant general, the U.S. Supreme Court in *United States V. Virginia et al.* ruled that Virginia's solution to allowing women to attend the all-male Virginia Military Institute (VMI)—forming a Virginia Women's Institute for Leadership at Mary Baldwin College—was unconstitutional. Writing for the court, Justice Ruth Bader Ginsberg cited Mutter's successful promotion through the ranks as evidence that fears about training female officers at VMI were ungrounded.

During her career, Mutter received an MA in national security and strategic studies from the Naval War College in Newport, Rhode Island; an MS and honorary doctorate from Salve Regina University, also in Newport; and an honorary doctorate from her alma mater, the University of Northern Colorado. She attended the Amphibious Warfare School and the Marine Corps Command and Staff College, both at Quantico. Her many service awards included the Distinguished Service Medal and the Defense Superior Service Medal.

As a civilian, she served on the Department of Defense Advisory Committee on Women in the Services, advocated for women on a variety of issues, and investigated the effects of deployment on service members and their families. In 2004, her committee recommended codifying the zero-tolerance policy on sexual assault and advocated that a clear definition of sexual assault be incorporated into the Uniform Code of Military Justice. Mutter also served as president of the Women Marines Association, as commissioner on the American Battlefield Monuments Commission, and as a senior fellow of the Joint Forces Staff College. Her nonmilitary awards included the Secretary of Defense Award for Outstanding Public Service, the Living Legacy Patriot Award from the Woman's International Center, and the Margaret Cochran Corbin Award from the Daughters of the American Revolution. She was also inducted into the Colorado Women's Hall of Fame.

Through her extraordinary skill, commitment, dedication, and work ethic, she broke through the "glass ceiling" to demonstrate to women and to men the role women could play in the armed forces. She saw herself not as an activist but as an example. Currently, she works for Carol A. Mutter Associates assisting businesses in their efforts to win government contracts.

Thomas Francis Army, Jr.

See also: Defense Advisory Committee on Women in the Services (DACOWITS); *United States v. Virginia* (1996); Vietnam War (1965–1973); Women in Military Service for America Memorial; Women Marines.

References and Further Reading

Keller, Scott. *Marine Pride: A Salute to America's Elite Fighting Force*. Charleston, SC: Citadel Press, 2004.

Lacy, Linda Cates. *We Are Marines!: World War I to the Present*. Swansboro: Tarheel Chapter, NC-1, Women Marines Association, 2004.

Mutter, Carol A. Interview by Charlayne Hunter-Gault. *Online Newshour: Women in the Military*, April 4, 1996. http://www.pbs .org/newshour/bb/military/mutter_4-04 .html.

Rhem, Kathleen T. "Military Undergoing 'Evolutionary Change' for Women in Service." *American Forces Press Service*, January 2005.

Socha, Rudy. *Above & Beyond: Former Marines Conquer the Civilian World*. Paducah, KY: Turner, 2010.

N

"NANCY HARTS"

During the Civil War, several groups of female militia were raised in the South, calling themselves the Nancy Harts in honor of the Revolutionary War Patriot who had performed numerous acts of bravery to aid the cause. All of these groups were short lived, save one: the Nancy Harts of Lagrange, Georgia.

Located between Atlanta, Georgia, and Montgomery, Alabama, Lagrange became a town of old men, young boys, and women during the Civil War. In the spring of 1861, almost every available man of military age, some 1,300 in number, volunteered for Confederate service and marched off to war. Two of the soldiers' wives, Nancy Hill Morgan and Mary Alford Heard, decided that a women's home guard unit should be formed to protect the town from any possible Union incursions. They called a meeting at the local schoolhouse in May and told all interested women to bring with them whatever muskets or pistols they could find. Some 40 local women responded

to the call, and a militia company was formed. The group decided to call themselves the Nancy Harts in honor of a Georgia heroine who had distinguished herself during the American Revolution. Morgan was elected captain; Heard, Andelia Bull, and Aley Smith became lieutenants; and Augusta Hill and M. E. Colquitt were sergeants.

Dr. Augustus Ware, Lagrange's local physician, was one of the only remaining men in the town. Physically disabled to the extent that he could not perform military service, he was nonetheless experienced in the use of firearms and was familiar with militia drill procedures of the period. The newly formed Nancy Harts approached Ware to ask his assistance in training them, and he readily agreed. Ware used William J. Hardee's *Rifle and Light Infantry Tactics* manual for his instruction and met with the women twice a week for training. Marksmanship was a key focus of Ware's instruction, and the Nancy Harts were drilled extensively in the use of firearms. The officers of the company regularly gave prizes to the top performers, and the women soon gained a reputation of being crack shots.

The Nancy Harts continued to meet twice a week for drill, but the enemy threat they feared failed to materialize. Instead, the town became filled to the brim with Confederate soldiers. Located along a main rail line, Lagrange had become a hospital town for those wounded on the battlefields of Virginia, Tennessee, Mississippi, and Georgia. The Nancy Harts quickly responded and added nursing to their busy schedules of maintaining their homes, raising their families, and participating in the militia.

By the spring of 1865, the military situation in Georgia had become precarious. Atlanta had fallen, and Gen. William T. Sherman had marched his army to Savannah, cutting the state in two. On April 16, 1865, the people of Lagrange received a telegraph from Brig. Gen. Robert Tyler in nearby West Point. Federal forces were approaching the town, and Tyler requested every available able-bodied man to come and help him defend it. Some of the elderly men of Lagrange, as well as a number of walking wounded from the hospital, answered Tyler's call and boarded a train for West Point. Tyler mounted a gallant defense, but he had only 300 men with which to oppose the 3,000 federal troops, and West Point was captured.

On April 17, word arrived that the federal troops were approaching Lagrange, and the Nancy Harts assembled at the home of Heard. Morgan assembled her company and marched the women to the Lagrange Female College, on the outskirts of town, to await the arrival of the enemy. The women were soon met by a small band of Confederate cavalry in the process of fleeing from a full regiment of Union horsemen. Another small band of Confederate troopers followed, but it was soon discovered that these men were federal scouts disguised in Southern uniforms. The Confederate cavalrymen put spurs to their horses and beat a hasty retreat, but not before imploring the Nancy Harts to return to their homes and bar their doors.

The women held firm, however, and when the main body of the Union force, under the command of Col. Oscar Lagrange, came into view, Morgan marched out to meet them. She proclaimed to the colonel that her company was prepared to resist any depredations against their town. Lagrange scanned the line of battle formed behind Heard and complimented the women on their martial bearing and fearless spirit. Lagrange informed the ladies that no depredations would be committed against their town. The town was then surrendered. Before marching off toward Macon, several public buildings, including a tannery, the train depot, and several cotton warehouses, were burned, but none of the homes in Lagrange were molested. The Nancy Harts took credit for successfully defending home and hearth from the invader, and saving Lagrange from destruction.

Robert P. Broadwater

See also: Civil War (1861–1865); Hart, Nancy Morgan (ca. 1735–1830); Nursing.

References and Further Reading

Eggleston, Larry G. *Women in the Civil War: Extraordinary Stories of Soldiers, Spies,*

Nurses, Doctors, Crusaders and Others. Jefferson, NC: McFarland, 2009.

Joslyn, Mauriel. *Confederate Women.* Gretna, LA: Pelican, 2004.

Ott, Victoria E. *Confederate Daughters: Coming of Age during the Civil War.* Carbondale: Southern Illinois University Press, 2008.

NATIVE AMERICAN WOMEN

The roles of Native American women in warfare varied significantly depending on time, place, and cultural affiliation. In Native societies, women were generally responsible for farming and domestic tasks while men engaged in hunting and warfare. Nonetheless, Native women were vital to warfare as they served as intermediaries and peacemakers, influenced decisions to declare war, and occasionally became combatants themselves.

In times of conflict, Native American women played key roles as intermediaries, both facilitating military alliances and preserving peace. When the Spanish conquistador Hernan Cortés marched through Mexico in 1519, he relied on an Aztec woman the Spanish called Dona Maria to serve as his interpreter. Dona Maria became Cortés's mistress and was instrumental in helping the Spanish secure allies among the local Indians, who were eager to overthrow Aztec rule. The internal divisions that resulted from rebellious Aztec subjects joining the Spanish contributed to the collapse of the Aztec Empire in 1521.

While some Native women helped achieve military victories, others worked to avoid war between hostile groups. Pocahontas, the daughter of a powerful Powhatan chief, played a prominent role in smoothing relations between the Natives and English colonists in Virginia. In 1607, Pocahontas participated in a ritual ceremony in which her father adopted colonial leader James Smith and made him a subordinate chieftain. Tensions between the English and the Indians increased, however, and fighting broke out in 1609. Pocahontas served as a diplomatic liaison between the colonists and Natives and in 1614 married English colonist John Rolfe. Her marriage to an English man helped establish peaceful relations between the English and Powhatan. As Dona Maria and Pocahontas demonstrate, many Native American women created alliances between European colonists and Native Americans, at times using sexual relationships and marriage to create kinship ties between groups.

Native American women also held the power to declare war under some circumstances. Throughout the colonial period, women in the Iroquois nation were instrumental in the practice of mourning war. In mourning war, warriors raided neighboring towns and seized captives who were then adopted to replace deceased members of the tribe or executed to ease the grief caused by these deaths. Mourning war parties were formed at the request of women whose relatives had died of sickness or warfare. When the warriors returned with captives, clan matrons decided which captives to adopt and which to execute. Just as women could initiate war, they could also prevent warriors from engaging in battle by refusing to supply the necessary food and supplies. Although women were primarily responsible for agriculture and domestic tasks, they often maintained a significant degree of influence over political and military decisions.

At times, Native women broke with traditional gender roles and engaged in active warfare. During King Philip's War (1675–1676), New England colonists fought against the Wampanoag Indians and their allies. Two of the tribes allied with the Wampanoag, the Sakonnets and the Pocasset, had female chiefs. Awashunkes, *sachem* of the Sakonnets, fought for nearly a year before negotiating peace terms between her people and the Plymouth colony. Wetamoo, leader of the Pocasset, fought alongside the Wampanoag and offered refuge to Metacomet, the Wampanoag chief. Wetamoo led 300 warriors in attacks against 52 English settlements before she died while fleeing an English counterattack.

Not all women who become combatants were tribal leaders, however. Nancy Ward, or Nanye'hi, was a Cherokee who fought alongside her husband against the Creek in the battle of Taliwa in 1775. When her husband fell, Ward took his place on the front line. Native women who participated in armed conflict operated outside of traditional gender norms but were respected within the tribe for their bravery.

The 18th and 19th centuries brought extensive change to Native American societies, although historians continue to debate the extent to which women gained or lost power. Throughout the colonial period, the indigenous inhabitants of North America were devastated by diseases carried to the continent by European colonists, weakened by nearly continuous warfare, and uprooted as white settlers encroached on their land.

After the formation of the United States, Americans attempted to reorganize Native economic life and gender roles around intensive agriculture. White Americans expected Native men to take responsibility for farming, which loosened women's control over the land and challenged their political power. Native Americans resisted change through warfare and by embracing new forms of religion that championed Native power. However, these new religions often stripped women of their traditional roles in political and spiritual matters.

By the 20th century, warfare between Native peoples and the U.S. government had ended. Although many Native Americans questioned their place in American society, Native men served in the major wars of the 20th century. Many volunteered for duty in World War I and World War II, although they were often motivated by loyalty to their homeland rather than to the U.S. government. Native women reclaimed their place in political life and warfare by participating in the Red Power movement and protests of the 1960s and 1970s. Women helped seize Alcatraz Island in 1969 and lived under the 71-day siege at Wounded Knee in 1973.

The way that Native American women participate in warfare continues to evolve. Native women now enlist in the U.S. military alongside their male counterparts and have seen active duty in Afghanistan and Iraq. In 2003, Pvt. Lori Piestewa, a Hopi mother of two small children, became the first enlisted Native American woman to be killed in combat in Iraq.

Jennifer L. Miller

See also: Afghanistan; Brant, Mary "Molly" (ca. 1735–1796); Civil War (1861–1865); Cold War (ca. 1947–1991); Curtis, Namahyoke Sockum (1861–1935); Gulf War (1991); Indian Wars; Iraq War (2003–2011); Korean War (1950–1953); Nonhelema [Grenadier Squaw] (ca. 1720–ca. 1786); North American Colonial Wars (17th–18th centuries); Piestewa, Lori (1979–2003); Prisoners of War; Reserve Officer Training Corps (ROTC); Sacagawea (ca. 1787–1812); Spanish-American War (1898); Tyonajanegen (n.d.–ca. 1820); Vietnam War (1965–1973); War of 1812 (1812–1815); War on Terror (2001–); Ward, Nancy (ca. 1738–ca. 1824); Winema [Tobey Riddle] (ca. 1848–1920); Winnemucca, Sarah [Thocmetony "Shell Flower"] (1844–1891); World War I (1914–1918); World War II (1941–1945).

References and Further Reading

Calloway, Colin G. *First Peoples: A Documentary Survey of American Indian History*, 3rd ed. Boston: Bedford/St. Martin's, 2008.

De Pauw, Linda Grant. *Battle Cries and Lullabies: Women in War from Prehistory to the Present*. Norman: University of Oklahoma Press, 1998.

Horn, James. *Jamestown and the Birth of America*. New York: Basic Books, 2005.

Klein, Laura F., and Lillian A. Ackerman, eds. *Women and Power in Native North America*. Norman: University of Oklahoma Press, 1995.

Richter, Daniel K. "War and Culture: The Iroquois Experience." *William and Mary Quarterly* 40, no. 4 (October 1983): 528–59.

NAVY NURSE CORPS

Female nurses have served in every U.S. war since at least the American Civil War, but it was not until 1908 that they officially served in the U.S. Navy. In that year, Congress authorized the Navy Nurse Corps and named those who were admitted to the exclusively female unit the "Sacred Twenty."

The initial 20 enlistees were stationed at the Naval Hospital in Washington, D.C., and within a year after the Corps was established their numbers grew and they received assignments at other hospitals as well. At first, many hospital administrators had difficulty figuring out what to do with the female nurses without the presence of female patients. They feared that female nurses would be a distraction and not up to the serious tasks at hand. As a result, largely untrained male nurses in the Hospital Corps performed most of the tasks typically assigned to nurses at the time. Within a few years, though, female nurses had largely overcome this obstacle and were stationed overseas in the territories of the Virgin Islands and the Philippines.

The outbreak of World War I provided the greatest impetus for the expansion of the Corps and its mission. In 1916, this expansion was aided when the Navy Medical Department was authorized to recruit nurses under its control. When World War I began, the Corps consisted of 160 nurses, and at its wartime peak it had 1,386. These nurses were largely trained at the Vassar Training Camp. Once they were stationed, the female nurses met the medical needs of their diverse situations. In addition to caring for casualties at various hospitals, the female nurses of the Navy Nurse Corps took on the responsibility of training the otherwise ill-prepared men of the Hospital Corps.

In 1920, the Navy made the Corps part of the "Navy Establishment," and the following year 11 nurses obtained the first commissions for women aboard naval ships. They served aboard USS *Relief*. In 1922, in recognition of the growing role of the Nurse Corps, the Navy Medical Department began a training program for the nurses. In the following years, they obtained retirement benefits, medical services, and disability rights as received by other members of the Navy. By the 1930s, the Corps had shrunk to between 400 and 500 throughout the decade.

The Navy Nurse Corps became part of World War II at its very start. Nurses aboard USS *Relief* tended to the very first casualties of Pearl Harbor. The subsequent war reinvigorated the Corps in the same manner that World War I had done earlier. By serving overseas, women in the Corps became an integral part of the military, and service became more dangerous. Five nurses were captured while they served in Guam in 1941, and the following year 11 nurses were captured in the Philippines and held for more than three years along with 66 other nurses from other branches of the military. As women were increasingly stationed overseas, they also became flight nurses, caring for wounded as they were evacuated. In 1944, women obtained the right to be commissioned as officers. When the war ended, the Navy Nurse Corps had 10,968 nurses.

After the war, the Corps went through significant changes. Perhaps most importantly, it desegregated and welcomed African American Phyllis M. Daley into its ranks. Today, approximately 13 percent of the Corps is African American. In 1947, the Navy Nurse Corps became an official staff corps of the Navy. During the Korean War, naval nurses served throughout the theater of operations. The United States called up the Navy Nurse Corps, Reserve Unit, and they were deployed across the theater of operations and across the globe. With an increased use of air hospitals, members of the Navy Nurse Corps increasingly played a role as flight nurses. At the end of the war, more than 3,000 nurses were serving aboard 93 naval and station hospitals, and on air hospitals, hospital ships, and military transport ships.

The fight for full integration and full equality in the Navy made great headway in the 1960s. In 1961, members of the Corps were assigned to the White House Medical Unit. In 1965, the nursing corps reserve welcomed its first man—George Silver—into its ranks. The outbreak of war in Vietnam also resulted in the building of a medical facility in Danang by the Navy. The facility was staffed with 18 Navy nurses. Navy nurses served elsewhere as well, including in Saigon, where the bombing of an officer's quarters resulted in four nurses being injured and their fellow nurses coming to their rescue. This incident resulted in the first women to receive the Purple Heart for their actions during the Vietnam War. In 1967, the Nurse Corps obtained the right to have the same promotion rights to captain and commander as other members of the Navy.

Members of the Corps have participated in every way since World War I and have had many domestic assignments as well. They helped tend to the wounded after Pearl Harbor, have aided in hurricane relief efforts since 1961, have served on prestigious aircraft carriers since 1971, and have responded to various domestic crises, including the terrorist attacks of September 2001. In addition, for the past four decades, pregnant nurses have been allowed to retain their status in the Navy.

The Navy Nurse Corps remains an important part of the U,S. military efforts overseas. With approximately 2,700 active-duty members and 1,300 reservists, these nurses have played a role in all of the modern overseas and domestic efforts. Most notably, Cmdr. Maureen Pennington earned the Bronze Star for her leadership of a surgical company in the second Iraq conflict.

Andrew K. Frank

See also: Afghanistan; African American Women; Asian American Women; Duerk, Alene Bertha (1920–); Gulf War (1991); Hasson, Esther Voorhees (1867–1942); Hispanic American Women; Iraq War (2003–2011); Korean War (1950–1953); Native American Women; Nursing; USS *Relief*; Vietnam War (1965–1973); War on Terror (2001–); World War I (1914–1918); World War II (1941–1945).

References and Further Reading

Beyea, David. "100 Years and Counting: The Navy Nurse Corps." *All Hands* 1094 (2008): 22–25.

Bowman, Beatrice I. "The History and Development of the Navy Nurse Corps." *American Journal of Nursing* 25 (1925): 356–60.

Godson, Susan H. *Serving Proudly: A History of Women in the U.S. Navy.* Annapolis, MD: Naval Institute Press, 2001.

NELSON, YZETTA L. (1923–2011)

Assigned to the Women's Army Corps (WAC), Yzetta L. Nelson is best known for being the first WAC to be promoted to the rank of command sergeant major. She was promoted during a time of rapid advancement of women in the military.

Born in Shevlin, Minnesota, on September 19, 1923, Nelson enlisted in the WAC in the 1950s. During the 1960s, more voices joined the call for President Lyndon Johnson to support equal promotion opportunities for women officers. Johnson acceded to this pressure in May 1965 and began making promotions. It was on November 8, 1967, however, that he removed any final obstacles, signing Public Law 90-130, which got rid of the legal ceilings on women's promotions that had kept them out of the general and flag ranks for decades. It was shortly after this time, on March 30, 1968, that Nelson became the first woman promoted to the rank of command sergeant major. At the time of her promotion, this was the highest enlisted rank. Nelson's promotion and Johnson's actions ushered in a period of advancement for many women in the armed forces. For example, in the early 1970s, as women actively participated in the military mission in Vietnam, Army regulations changed to permit women in the WAC to request waivers for retention on active duty if they were married or pregnant.

When the military discontinued the WAC in 1978 and integrated women into the armed services, Nelson retired. She had spent 26 years in the Army. After her retirement, she remained deeply devoted to public service. She continued her involvement and leadership, giving speeches about the WAC and about women's role in the military throughout the country. In August 2005, Nelson attended the opening of the Army

Women's Museum, the only museum in the world dedicated to U.S. Army women. Nelson spoke at the event, emphasizing the museum's role in preserving women's history in the military and highlighting female achievements.

In addition, Nelson continued her commitment to public service by serving her community as the Zion Lutheran Church secretary. Nelson was also both an employee and a volunteer for Meals at Home. She continued these activities until her death on May 14, 2011, in Brooklyn Center, Minnesota.

Debbie Sharnak

See also: Korean War (1950–1953); Public Law 90-30 (1967); Vietnam War (1965–1973); Women's Army Corps (WAC).

References and Further Reading

Fisher, Ernest. *Guardians of the Republic: A History of Noncommissioned Officer Corp of the U.S. Army.* Mechanicsburg, PA: Stackpole Books, 2007.

Joseph, Antony. "Honoring Army Women." *Soldiers Magazine,* August 2005, 28–31.

Morden, Bettie J. *The Women's Army Corps, 1945–1978.* Washington, D.C.: Center of Military History, U.S. Army, 1990.

NEWCOM, ELIZABETH [WILLIAM "BILL" NEWCOM] (CA. 1825–N.D.)

A soldier and pioneer of the Mexican War period, Elizabeth Newcom disguised herself as a man and became the first female soldier to cross the Santa Fe Trail and one of a small number of women to receive remuneration and recognition for military service in the mid-19th century.

On September 16, 1847, 22-year-old "William Newcom" strode through the gates of Fort Leavenworth, Kansas, to enlist. The Missouri Volunteers, Santa Fe Trace Battalion, welcomed the arrival of the eager recruit. The United States was in the midst of the Mexican War (1846–1848) and needed fresh troops to settle the territorial dispute. Two days later, Newcom's service was made official. He was officially mustered into service with the other volunteers in Company D. Neither the company's commanding officer, Capt. Paul Holzcheiter, nor any of the 60-odd privates who trained alongside Newcom had any indication that there was something out of the ordinary with this soldier.

William Newcom (also spelled Newcum) was actually Elizabeth Caroline Newcom, a woman hiding her gender with masculine dress and persona. Her deception was necessary; the U.S. Army did not permit women in the armed forces. There is no available documentation regarding Newcom's early life. Even the most basic details—her date of birth, the name of her parents, and where she lived—all remain a mystery. What is known about Newcom comes from primarily military sources.

Military court records show that Newcom's decision to enter the military was for romantic reasons. Amandus V. Schnabel, a German-born immigrant who had immigrated with his family to St. Louis, Missouri, in his teens, had become romantically involved with Newcom. Schnabel induced Newcom to follow him into service by the only means possible, disguising herself as a man. She entered the Army as a private on the same day that Schnabel entered Company D as an officer with the rank of first lieutenant.

Newcom successfully completed initial training in drills, formation, and handling her weapon. She was successfully integrated as part of Company D when they left between the days of October 4 and 6, 1847. Their mission was to protect settlers and travelers along the northern Santa Fe Trail, a passage into California, Colorado, and New Mexico, from attacks by hostile Native American tribes. Keeping this road open and clear also allowed the military to funnel supplies into friendly posts in the Southwest. The Missouri Volunteers made camp along the banks of the Arkansas River near present-day Pueblo, New Mexico. Company D became part of the garrison at Fort Mann, Kansas, during the winter months of 1847.

Specific details about Newcom's activities during this period are absent. She performed her assigned duties and may have participated in armed skirmishes but did nothing to draw attention to her unusual situation. Newcom surfaces in the records in May 1848. She had become pregnant with Schnabel's child, so Schnabel urged her to desert her post. She agreed but soon remorsefully returned to her unit. This incident went unnoticed, but soon afterwards her secret was uncovered. She was sent back to Fort Leavenworth, where she was discharged on May 14, 1848.

Schnabel's complicity in this matter was eventually discovered. He was arrested on October 25, 1848, and court martialed. He was held a prisoner for nearly eight months, until July 7, 1848, when his resignation was accepted. Census records in 1850 place him back with his family, but nothing is known of his life afterwards.

Newcom reappeared in August 1, 1853, five years after her forcible discharge. In the intervening years, she was married to John Smith. The Smiths resided in Platte County, Missouri, and through that county's offices she filed a petition to the U.S. government requesting back pay and the bounty of land due to Mexican War veterans.

A special bill, drafted on her behalf, passed both the House and the Senate. President Franklin Pierce, a fellow veteran of the Mexican War, signed the bill. The issue of her gender was put aside, and Newcom finally gained recognition for her faithful service. She was given eight months of pay with an additional three months and a bounty land warrant of 160 acres of land.

Her activities later in life and the date of her death are unknown.

Michael D. Coker

See also: Republic of Texas.

References and Further Reading

Barile, Mary Collins. *The Santa Fe Trail in Missouri*. Columbia: University of Missouri Press, 2010.

Lookingbill, Brad D., ed. *American Military History: A Documentary Reader*. Malden, MA: John Wiley and Sons, 2010.

Reports of Committees: 30th Congress, 1st session—48th Congress, 2nd session. Washington, D.C.: United States Printing Office, 1874.

NONHELEMA (GRENADIER SQUAW) (CA. 1720–CA. 1786)

Nonhelema, born around 1720, was a Shawnee headwoman and diplomat during the Seven Years War, Pontiac's Rebellion, and the American Revolutionary War. Americans also knew her as Catherine or Katy. Settlers sometimes called her the Grenadier Squaw, possibly because of her tall stature. Nonhelema repeatedly advocated peace with American colonists and became a romanticized figure in the 19th- and 20th-century United States.

Very little is known about Nonhelema's early life until the 1760s. It was during the years between the Seven Years War and the American Revolution that she emerged as an important person among the Maquachake division of the Shawnees. She also led her own town on the Scioto River in Ohio. Nonhelema became a well-known peace advocate at about the same time as her brother, Shawnee leader Cornstalk, began promoting diplomacy with colonists after his experiences fighting the British in the Seven Years War and Pontiac's Rebellion. Nonhelema likely attended diplomatic meetings with Cornstalk as Shawnee women played important roles in relations with outsiders; however, British recorders downplayed women's roles in treaty negotiations. Nonhelema and Cornstalk accompanied Virginia officials home after Cornstalk brokered peace between Shawnees and Virginians in 1774. The following year, a Maquachake headwoman, who may have been Nonhelema, met with congressional agent Richard Butler and warned him of threats and dangers from the more militant Shawnee Piqua and Chillicothe divisions that could again bring Shawnees and whites to war. The headwoman also informed Butler that she had scolded Maquachake men for not reining in the militant Chillicothes and Piquas.

Nonhelema worked with Cornstalk to ensure their people's neutrality at the outset of the American Revolution. Nonhelema frequently informed white settlers of belligerent Shawnees' actions. In 1777, she left most of her possessions and moved away from her town to Fort Randolph in western Virginia, bringing with her approximately 50 cows and horses, which she gave to the fort. She worked as an interpreter and envoy between the fort and other Shawnees. Nonhelema remained dedicated to peace and stayed in the fort even after angry Fort Randolph militiamen murdered Cornstalk in retaliation for Shawnee raids in 1777. The next year, she warned the fort's commander of likely Shawnee attacks in response to Cornstalk's assassination and advised militia leaders of Shawnee war strategies. On another occasion, Nonhelema famously dressed white messengers as Indians so they could reach settlers and inform them of impending attacks. She also guided a French officer from Pittsburgh to Illinois so that he could recruit settlers to help attack British-held Detroit. Toward the end of the Revolutionary War, American leaders noted Nonhelema's importance as a diplomat. Patrick Henry asked her to visit Indians to encourage them to attend peace talks. After the war, Virginians hoped that

Nonhelema could prove to be helpful in obtaining western lands from Shawnees and other Indian groups.

After the American Revolution, Nonhelema moved to a new Maquachake village near Pittsburgh led by Moluntha, another Shawnee peace advocate. In the winter of 1784–1785, Nonhelema petitioned Congress for compensation for her losses in the Revolutionary War, including the livestock given to Fort Randolph. She asked for 2,000 acres of land on the Scioto River in southern Ohio, near the location of her former town. The congressional committee reviewing her claim found that Nonhelema's loyalty should be rewarded, but the United States proposed to compensate her with a set of clothes and daily provisions.

While living in Moluntha's village, Nonhelema continued to work for peace between the Shawnees and the Americans. She used her children, Fanny and Morgan, as messengers between her town and American treaty makers, leading to the controversial Treaty of Fort Finney in 1786. The treaty ceded Shawnee lands in eastern and southern Ohio. Few Shawnee headmen actually signed the treaty, and those that did were in Moluntha and Nonhelema's Maquachake peace-favoring faction. The Fort Finney Treaty outraged most Shawnees, and they rejected the treaty's validity.

That year also saw continued fighting between Shawnees and American settlers that led to the Kentucky militia attacking Nonhelema's peaceful village. Moluntha quickly surrendered to the militiamen, showed them his copy of the Treaty of Fort Finney, and instructed his villagers to raise an American flag. The militia began taking women and children prisoners when a Kentuckian asked Moluntha if he had been involved in a recent Shawnee raid. Not understanding the question, Moluntha enthusiastically nodded and was promptly killed. Nonhelema and the other captives were taken to Kentucky, where they were detained for quite some time. Information about Nonhelema ends after she was taken into custody, and it is believed that she died in captivity or shortly thereafter, in 1786.

J. Hendry Miller

See also: American Revolution (1775–1783); Indian Wars; Native American Women; North American Colonial Wars (17th–18th centuries).

References and Further Reading

Calloway, Colin G. *The Shawnees and the War for America.* New York: Viking, 2007.

Harper, John Robinson. "Revolution and Conquest: Politics, Violence and Social Change in the Ohio Valley, 1765–1795." PhD dissertation, University of Wisconsin–Madison, 2008.

Jefferds, Joseph C., Jr. *Captain Matthew Arbuckle: A Documentary Biography.* Charleston, WV: Education Foundation, 1981.

NORTH AMERICAN COLONIAL WARS (17TH–18TH CENTURIES)

Warfare was a routine occurrence in the colonial era. These conflicts were influenced by imperial prerogatives and European events but were also the direct result of local disputes. Many of these disputes occurred between white settlers and Indians as they fought over land and other resources. The wars impacted colonial women—European and Native American—as they were caught in the crossfire of warring cultures, faced the prospect of captivity, and otherwise dealt with the realities of raids on their homes, food shortages, and other depredations.

The experiences of women differed across the diverse geopolitical space in the colonial era. In areas controlled by the French and Spanish, the desire to create trading alliances and Catholic missions with Native peoples pushed colonial officials to pursue amicable relations. As a result, Europeans and Indians engaged in adaptation and collaboration in areas like New France, Florida, and Louisiana. In addition, these colonies tended to attract more men than women, creating an overwhelming gender imbalance in the European outposts. As a result, Native American women felt the brunt of the wars. Some wars, like the Guale Rebellion in 1597 Spanish Florida (now southeastern Georgia), resulted in the capture of many Native women. Other conflicts, like the Yamassee War in the lower South, similarly brought the reality of war to Native and non-Native women. In this conflict, many Natives were taken captive or killed and countless others unsuccessfully struggled to defend their communities from being destroyed.

In the British colonies, matters differed greatly. Although Anglo-Indian relations also rested on trade, the desire to claim, settle, and then exploit natural resources presented a considerable threat to Indian peoples. Many British newcomers had no interest in adapting to or coexisting with local indigenous populations and instead viewed Indians as a threat to their existence. The two peoples also competed for land and resources, thereby leading to violent and bloody encounters. The British engagement in the Indian slave trade brought additional strains to their relationship, especially in the lower South, where the British encouraged Natives to capture other Indians and then sell them in British markets. Between 1670 and 1715, approximately 30,000 to 50,000 Indians were captured during wars waged primarily for this purpose and sold into slavery. An untold number of those forced into slavery were women.

Captive-taking in the north, although rarely for the Atlantic marketplace, also shaped the wartime of experiences of women. A genre of captivity narratives captured the experiences of some of those forcibly taken by Indian warriors during war. Most captives were taken either to serve as a replacement for a family member killed by the English or to be sold to the French. Native American women, in most instances, made this decision. Mary Rowlandson's narrative describes her ordeals during King Philip's War (1675–1676). Taken in 1675 and held for 11 weeks, Rowlandson detailed her suffering and privations at the hands of the Indians before being ransomed and returned to her family. Other captives chose to stay in their new Native American communities. Mary Jemison, taken captive by Seneca Indians in 1755, married a Seneca man and, despite opportunities to return to her birth family, remained with her adopted tribe until her death in 1833.

Throughout North America, women struggled with the violence inherent in the colonial wars. In these conflicts, Native Americans scalped white women just as European militiamen killed or razed the communities of Native women. Many others were killed or captured in the wars. Women in all communities faced the prospect of violence. In 1637, for example, during the Pequot War (1634–1638), the English militia and its Indian allies attacked the Pequot village at Mystic, burning it to the ground and killing any survivors. Approximately 150 warriors and 350 Native American women and children were slaughtered.

Similar atrocities occurred throughout the colonial wars. At the end of the French and Indian War (1754–1763), violence continued after the Treaty of Paris of 1763. Indeed, the treaty served only to worsen Anglo-Indian relations as promises made by the British to stop the westward flow of settlers went unfulfilled. On December 14, 1763, a group of settlers known as the Paxton Boys massacred 20 Conestoga Indian men, women, and children near Lancaster, Pennsylvania, sparking a rash of revenge attacks on both sides. On May 26, 1764, a party of Indians attacked settlers near a fort in Augusta County, Virginia, killing and wounding 15 and taking 16 settlers prisoner. One of the slain was a pregnant woman, whom they also scalped. Grisly stories such as these inflamed both sides as word of atrocities circulated and created a cycle of mutual aggression.

Women in the 17th and 18th centuries frequently engaged in warfare as participants rather than just victims. The absence of an established national army and scarcity of able-bodied male defenders made it socially acceptable for women to defend themselves through violent means. Many women, especially those in rural outposts, were familiar with firearms and various weapons. When war came, these skills frequently helped them defend themselves. One of the most famous examples of self-defense is that of Hannah Duston (Dustin). In 1697, when Abenaki warriors captured her in New England, she enlisted the help of a captive boy and killed her Abenaki captors. She scalped her Indian captors and took the scalps as trophies back to her village.

Likewise, an Indian attack on an English settlement in New Hampshire in 1705 found the women of the fort without any male defenders. They subsequently donned men's clothes and fired muskets at the Indian attackers, successfully driving them away. The active engagement of women as warriors persisted into the American Revolution and beyond with women's participation in guards and militia. Two famous women of the American Revolution could claim roots in frontier warfare. Margaret "Captain Molly" Corbin, famous for her exploits in the artillery crew at Fort Washington, lost her parents in 1756 at age five to an Indian attack. "Mad" Anne Bailey lost her husband at the Battle of Point Pleasant on October 10, 1774. She then left her child in the care of a neighbor and joined the militia, embarking on what became an illustrious career as a female frontier fighter. Indian women also occasionally fought alongside male warriors. Like their European counterparts, though, they typically confined their participation in military activities to preparing warriors for battle and producing provisions.

Ashley L. Shimer

See also: American Revolution (1775–1783); Bailey, Anne Hennis Trotter "Mad Anne" (1742–1825); Corbin, Margaret Cochran (1751–ca. 1800); Duston, Hannah (1657–1730); Indian Wars; Jemison, Mary (ca. 1742–1833); Johnson, Susannah (ca. 1730–1810); Rowlandson, Mary White (ca. 1635–1711).

References and Further Reading

Gallay, Alan. *The Indian Slave Trade: The Rise of the English Empire in the American South, 1670–1717*. New Haven, CT: Yale University Press, 2003.

Griffin, Patrick. *American Leviathan: Empire, Nation, and Revolutionary Frontier*. New York: Hill and Wang, 2007.

Jones, David E. *Women Warriors: A History*. Dulles, VA: Brassey's, 1997.

Little, Ann M. *Abraham in Arms: War and Gender in Colonial New England*. Philadelphia: University of Pennsylvania Press, 2007.

Ramsey, William L. *The Yamasee War: A Study of Culture, Economy, and Conflict in the Colonial South*. Lincoln: University of Nebraska Press, 2008.

Steele, Ian K. *Warpaths: Invasions of North America*. New York: Oxford University Press, 1994.

NURSING

The care of the sick and wounded has occupied a central place in the history of military planning and organization. After all, the challenges of wartime provisioning, sanitation, and disease have historically been as threatening to soldiers as the battles themselves. The image of the Victorian lady Florence Nightingale touring the British hospitals of the Crimean War (1854–1858) with her reforming zeal and iconic lamp represents women's introduction into the enterprise of military nursing. Nightingale had a profound impact on American women, who used her example to portray nursing as a patriotic, respectable, and professional occupation for women in times of war. However, the actual process of integrating women into the American military has roots much further back and continues to be fraught with notions of femininity and respectability. If progress for female military nurses is marked by visibility, professionalization, and the expansion of their military authority, then the iconic historical images—both real and imagined—of nurses as strong-willed ladies with lamps, battlefield angels, innocent Red Cross "girls," and even not-so-innocent "naughty nurses" have opened doors to recognizing the history of women's patriotic and professional military service at the same time they have often kept nurses segregated and subordinated within it.

During the Revolutionary War, the appearance of female nurses in the military was a sign of desperation. When the military conflict began, low-ranking soldiers unwillingly designated within their regiments to care for the sick or wounded provided nursing services to their comrades in arms. Female nurses fit within the broader category of camp followers, which included women and children following their male kin into war to avoid poverty at home as well as prostitutes and others living off the soldiers' pay. Although these women provided necessary domestic labor for the soldiers at a fraction of the cost of male personnel, military officers regarded them as a nuisance. By 1777, this ad hoc system had come under enough strain and scrutiny to incite congressional action. The hospital staffing plan approved by Congress established military hospitals and included a provision for recruiting women into wartime military nursing at a ratio of 1 nursing matron and 10 staff nurses for every 100 hospitalized soldiers. However, this quota was rarely met. Instead, surgeon's mates continued to perform nursing duties at 100 times the pay of a nurse, and female nurses were often still not recognized (and therefore not recorded) as members of hospital or military staffs. Even in exceptional cases, in which an individual woman might be recognized for some outstanding professional skill or talent in nursing, these reputations rarely survived the short postwar social memories and were voluntarily or forcibly relegated to the necessities of war rather than being an entry point for greater female autonomy, professionalization, or independence. Still, acknowledging the necessity of female nurses to the fledgling U.S. military was an important turning point because it created a precedent for military conflicts to come, in which women would play increasingly prominent historical roles as wartime nurses.

In the antebellum United States, nursing by women continued to be associated with domestic responsibilities; it was not seen as an occupation. When nursing was required outside of the home, it was usually provided by charitable religious organizations or poorly paid nurses of menial social status.

The Civil War prompted the rapid response of a long-planned but newly organized U.S. Sanitary Commission, based upon studies of foreign military operations. Dorothea Dix was appointed to organize an Army nurses' corps for the Sanitary Commission. Dix hoped to emulate the perceived success of Nightingale's nurses in the Crimean War, but her own appointment was due more to her social and political connections than any actual nursing experience. Although her office was flooded with applications from patriotic Union women, her circular specified only healthy, educated, and moral women between 35 and 50 years of age would be considered; personal accounts further indicate that women who were not white, affluent, and plain in appearance were also turned away. These selection criteria were arbitrary and exclusive of the legions of women who provided military nursing services under other titles, but their purpose and effect was to elevate the status and reputation of female nurses from destitute, disreputable, and perhaps promiscuous camp followers and hospital laborers to respectable, self-sacrificing, and competent lady nurses.

The vast majority of hospital and nursing work still occurred outside the authority of Dix's nurses' corps. Convalescing soldiers and male volunteers disqualified from regular military service continued to provide wartime nursing, while preexisting female religious orders and some elite women (such as Clara Barton) refused to take orders from Dix and so operated independently. Southern women also volunteered, but they did so informally as there was no Confederate equivalent to the Sanitary Commission's nursing corps. Black, immigrant, and working women provided a large share of hospital nursing labor but were usually categorized as domestic servants, cooks, laundresses, or other laborers excluded from recognition or pension. Thus, the Civil War tipped the demographics of nursing decisively toward affluent white women, even as many more women and men continued to care for the injured and sick without such respect, remuneration, or remembrance.

With the exception of long, drawn-out negotiations over military nursing pension eligibility, the U.S. government and military showed little inclination to continue military nursing reforms during the remainder of the 19th century. The Geneva Convention of 1864 introduced the idea of Red Cross nursing organizations as a means of rationalizing medical and humanitarian aid during war, but the United States remained skeptical of the ambitious plan, especially its commitment to the neutrality of aid workers. As a result, the U.S. government and military did not move forward in developing such auxiliary nursing organizations even after eventually ratifying the Geneva Convention in 1882. Instead, the U.S. Army founded its own Nurse Corps Division in order to recruit and administer over 1,000 contract nurses for the military in response to the outbreak of the Spanish-American War in 1898. Contract nurses were required to have training school certificates and at least two years' hospital residency. These standards remained in effect after the conflict ended as a small number of contract nurses remained in military service at home and abroad.

Then, in February 1901, the Army Nurse Corps (ANC) was officially founded under Section 19 of the Army Reorganization Act, formalizing the inclusion of 202 (peacetime) contract nurses under the leadership of Dita Hopkins Kinney into the U.S. Army. Kinney had been appointed the first superintendent of the ANC (female), a position designated by the U.S. Senate for a trained, graduate nurse. In 1908, the Navy introduced its own Navy Nurse Corps. The ensuing competition may have elevated the perception of women in both branches in the long term, but the number and status of military nurses remained marginal before World War I. Despite earning higher salaries than the average working American, women's overseas appointments brought practical hardships and limited leave time, and the nursing positions were again restricted to affluent, single, white women. As demand for civilian nurses remained high and women remained marginalized within the military—without official rank or regard for their professional and social status as educated women—the number of military nurses remained small. Still, the institutionalization of a nurse corps in the major military branches promised permanent visibility for women in the armed forces.

The sheer magnitude of destruction at the entrance of the United States into World War I in 1917 challenged the successes and shortcomings of 19th-century military nursing. American women were increasingly well-trained professional nurses serving in both medical and military capacities once unquestionably held by men. Yet it was the glossy images of the young, female voluntary nursing aides in Red Cross uniforms that became the icon of memory, propaganda, and patriotism. In some ways, the glamorizing and sexual objectification of World War I nurses undermined the professional gains institutionalized in nursing prior to the war. However, as the techno-logical advances made in the later years of the war demanded more complex treatments and continuous care, the war also ensured that the next generation of military nurses would require higher educational and training requirements for their work.

By World War II, women were a ubiquitous presence on the front. Professional military uniforms replaced the flowing white Red Cross dresses and headscarves of volunteers. The still very feminine and naïvely angelic representa-tion of military nurses was double-edged as it offered women immediate recogni-tion as military officers at the same time that it segregated, subordinated, and lim-ited any further mobility. Over the course of the American involvement in the war, the number of American military nurses—in both the Army and Navy—rose from only a few thousand to over 70,000 stationed at home and abroad. Yet it was not until the Army-Navy Nurses Act of 1947 that the ANC and Navy Nurse Corps granted women official and permanent officer ranks for their military nursing service.

Proponents of nursing professiona-lization at this time justifiably feared the public's inability to differentiate between trained and undertrained nurses in uniform, but these professionalization advocates also used military rank, pro-fessional association membership, and graduate certificates as barriers against the inclusion of men and African American women. Professional recom-mendations that male nurses be inte-grated into the ANC were not only ignored but also actively opposed by the military medical leadership. African American women were hampered by

segregation and their exclusion from nursing programs, professional organiza-tions, and white soldiers' wards. After four years of American participation in World War II, nursing shortages, which were exacerbated by racial quotas and segregation, came to an impasse, pressur-ing the government to integrate African American nurses rather than face a potential draft of white women. The war ended only a few months later, but when the United States became embroiled in a military conflict on the Korean peninsula, President Harry S Truman implemented a racial desegregation order affecting both male soldiers and female nurses.

In the context of the women's move-ment, Cold War fatigue, and a national nursing shortage, nursing skills and opportunities remained high well after World War II. In fact, about 70 percent of American nurses rejected civilian domesticity to continue working as nurses, and 50 percent of those had plans to take advantage of the G.I. Bill to fur-ther their professional education in the postwar era. The Vietnam War called for a redefinition of the military nurse's image in complex and contradictory ways. Recruitment ads now promised professionalism, safety, gender equality, and personal respect even while empha-sizing the femininity of military nurses and the romantic opportunities military service offered. For the first time, the military recognized that its female mem-bers might be seeking more than mar-riage and motherhood. At the same time, it began making marriage and motherhood permissible for women, allowing male nurses to join the ANC (though not yet the Navy Nurse Corps), and married couples serving in the mili-tary together increased in visibility.

In the 1980s and 1990s, the U.S. military opened its ranks more broadly to women, whose occupations shifted decisively in response. During the Gulf War and various peacekeeping missions, women served as pilots, mechanics, administrative workers, and technical experts. For the first time, just less than half of military women were nurses. At the start of the 21st century, well-educated and licensed professional nurses—male and female—are still in high demand by military recruiters as they continue to provide essential and irreplaceable roles in the modern U.S. military organization. Women and nurses are no longer synonymous in any branch of the military, yet the role of women in combat continues to evoke emotional and political debate rooted in cultural anxieties and contradictions over military women's physical and mental abilities, intoned with fears of uncontrollable male responses (ranging from chivalry to rape) within close, stressful, or dangerous spaces. As the practical lines between combat roles and women's roles continue to blur, the example of nursing serves as a reminder of how the process of integrating women into the U.S. military originally began.

Aeleah Soine

See also: African American Women; Air Force Nurse Corps (AFNC); American Red Cross; American Revolution (1775–1783); Army-Navy Nurses Act of 1947 (Public Law 36-80C); Army Nurse Corps (ANC); Asian American Women; Barton, Clara Harlowe (1821–1912); Bickerdyke, Mary Ann Ball "Mother" (1817–1901); Blackwell, Elizabeth (1821–1910); Cadet Nurse Corps; Camp Followers; Civil War (1861–1865); Cold War (ca. 1947–1991); Daughters of Liberty; Delano, Jane Arminda (1862–1919); Dix, Dorothea Lynde (1802–1887); Gulf War (1991); Hispanic American Women; Indian Wars; Iraq War (2003–2011); Kinney, Dita Hopkins (1855–1921); Korean War (1950–1953); Latin American Military Interventions; McGee, Anita Newcomb (1864–1940); Mobile Army Surgical Hospital (MASH); Native American Women; Navy Nurse Corps; Office of Civilian Defense (OCD); Ott, Elsie S. (1913–2006); Pitcher, Molly (n.d.–n.d.); Public Law 448 (July 2, 1925); Red Cross Volunteer Nurse's Aide Corps; Rodgers, Marie Louise (1926–); Saar, Lisa (1966–); Smith, Genevieve M. (1905–1950); Spanish-American War (1898); Spanish Influenza (Influenza Pandemic); Stimson, Julia Catherine (1881–1948); Tompkins, Sally Louisa (1833–1916); Tower, Ellen May (1868–1898); United States Sanitary Commission (USSC); USS *Benevolence*; USS *Red Rover*; USS *Relief*; USS *Sanctuary*; Vietnam War (1965–1973); War of 1812 (1812–1815); War on Terror (2001–); Women's Medical Specialist Corps (WMSCP); Women's Nursing Corps, Army; World War I (1914–1918); World War II (1941–1945).

References and Further Reading

Enloe, Cynthia. *Maneuvers: The International Politics of Militarizing Women's Lives.* Berkeley: University of California Press, 2000.

Kerber, Linda. *Women of the Republic: Intellect and Ideology in Revolutionary America.* Chapel Hill: University of North Carolina Press, 1980.

Sarnecky, Mary T. *A History of the U.S. Army Nurse Corps (Studies in Health, Illness, and Caregiving).* Philadelphia: University of Pennsylvania Press, 1999.

Schultz, Jane E. *Women at the Front: Hospital Workers in Civil War America.* Chapel Hill: University of North Carolina Press, 2004.

Vuic, Kara Dixon. *Officer, Nurse, Woman: The Army Nurse Corps in the Vietnam War.* Baltimore, MD: Johns Hopkins Press, 2011.

OFFICE OF CIVILIAN DEFENSE (OCD)

The Office of Civilian Defense (OCD) was a federal agency established in May 1941 by executive order and tasked with creating and coordinating national-, state-, and community-level civil defense programs. At its peak it counted more than 10 million volunteer participants. It was abolished in June 1945.

In May 1940, President Franklin Roosevelt revived the World War I–era Council of National Defense (CND) and tasked it with directing the nation's defense program. One important CND unit was the Division of State and Local Cooperation (DSLC). The DSLC's responsibilities included performing wartime emergency functions but also boosting public morale, promoting volunteer services, and running social programs to assist families streaming to cities for employment in war-related industries.

In May 1941, the president issued Executive Order 8757, which transformed the DSLC into the OCD and placed the new division under the direction of energetic New York mayor Fiorello LaGuardia. With the European conflict providing vivid examples of warfare's impact on civilian areas, especially as a result of air attacks, LaGuardia insisted that the primary task of the OCD was protection. Thus he emphasized positions like aircraft and submarine spotters, auxiliary police and fire forces, bomb disposal squads, and air raid wardens and organized large-scale training drills. In late 1941, for example, LaGuardia ordered a practice exercise with 40,000 aircraft spotters on duty the length of the Atlantic coast. However, he paid scant attention to organizing volunteer participation in civilian defense and dismissed OCD social programs such as nutrition, housing, child care, and fitness as "sissy stuff."

Increasing pressure from OCD administrators, the general public, and

First Lady Eleanor Roosevelt, however, forced LaGuardia to reassess the so-called nonprotective services. In September 1941, he appointed the First Lady as assistant director of OCD, hoping her reputation and connections would energize OCD volunteer activities nationwide—especially social programs—and simultaneously mollify his critics. She had a vision of civilian defense as primarily a reform program, which would serve the needs of citizens and get women involved; she organized a national volunteer network with multiple opportunities for women and worked to secure federal funds for child care, nutrition, and maternal health programs.

Although the First Lady's involvement with the OCD raised the profile of the organization, it quickly proved controversial. Critics of the president and of New Deal–style government programs portrayed the OCD as another example of bloated Washington bureaucracy. Some poor personnel decisions in the form of high-profile positions at the agency for friends of the First Lady exacerbated the situation. In February 1942, Roosevelt resigned as OCD assistant director, arguing that the programs that she believed were most important had been launched and stabilized.

The United States' entry into the war suddenly increased OCD's importance and made it imperative to have a full-time director. As a result, James M. Landis replaced LaGuardia, who had been simultaneously serving as director of OCD and mayor of New York. Landis, the former head of the Securities and Exchange Commission (1935–1937), dean of Harvard Law School (1938–1946), and an OCD regional director (1941–1942), served as the chief of OCD from 1942 until August 1943.

Landis directed an extensive reorganization and streamlining of the OCD, and the organization played a significant role in managing the homefront war effort. Armed with a new executive order that strengthened the agency's authority, Landis shifted controversial health and welfare programs to other organizations and squarely focused the OCD on preparing for war. He continued the decentralized model, with a skeleton federal administration overseeing nine regional offices nationwide. National initiatives were explained at this regional level and technical advice was made available. Program implementation, however, remained a responsibility of officials at the state and local levels. A state's Defense Council organized the community volunteer offices. This decentralized model produced varying levels of performance—some communities had engaged leaders and well-developed programs while others lagged behind both in interest and outcomes.

The Landis-era focus on war preparedness meant certain initiatives received greater attention than others. Landis's primary concerns were the Civil Air Patrol (CAP) and the Citizen's Defense Corps (CDC). Founded in December 1941, CAP was envisioned as an all-volunteer method of incorporating civilian aviation, both planes and trained pilots, into the war effort. From 1941 to 1945, CAP assumed many missions, including flying antisubmarine reconnaissance flights, patrolling the U.S. border with Mexico, towing targets for the Army Air Forces, and operating a courier service.

Women were a significant part of CAP during the war years. At first, women served at CAP antisubmarine bases in various administrative roles or as radio operators. As the war progressed, women pilots flew courier missions and also ferried aircraft. As a result, many Women Air Force Service Pilots (WASP) began their military flying careers in the CAP. When the war ended in 1945, fully 20 percent of CAP personnel were women.

Even more opportunities for women existed in the CDC, the national umbrella organization for OCD programs. After December 1941, OCD recruited men for jobs as air-raid wardens and on bomb disposal squads. At the same time, OCD sought to recruit hundreds of thousands of women, primarily for positions in nursing, nutrition programs, and administrative work. In addition, women also served as messengers, fire wardens, and mechanics, and they coordinated community recycling efforts. One wartime OCD publication for neighborhood block leaders prominently featured a uniformed woman block leader on the cover. At its peak during the Landis period, the CDC had approximately 10 million volunteers nationwide, of whom 8,750,000 had a specific job. With millions of men in uniform, women were critical to the success of CDC programs.

However, the initial post–Pearl Harbor enthusiasm and levels of involvement failed to last. New opportunities arose for women in the military services and in well-paying defense jobs, so they had other outlets for their patriotic work. By mid-1943, OCD strained to attract enough women (and also men) to fill volunteer positions. However, with a greatly reduced threat of war reaching American shores, the lack of volunteers did not matter very much. In August 1943, Landis argued that existing state and local organizations could meet a reduced threat of attack and concluded that the OCD was no longer necessary. He then resigned. Several caretaker directors managed OCD subsequently until President Harry Truman abolished the agency in June 1945. State and local organizations gradually closed or ceased operations. Civil defense enjoyed a revival during the Cold War, however, with OCD serving as the model for various organizations.

Thomas Saylor

See also: Civil Air Patrol (CAP); Cold War (ca. 1947–1991); Nursing; Roosevelt, Eleanor (1884–1962); Women Air Force Service Pilots (WASP); World War I (1914–1918); World War II (1941–1945).

References and Further Reading

Jordan, Nehemiah. "U.S. Civil Defense before 1950: The Roots of Public Law 920." n.p.: Institute for Defense Analyses, May 1966.

Kerr, Thomas J. *Civil Defense in the U.S.: Bandaid for a Holocaust?* Boulder, CO: Westview Press, 1983.

Mauck, Elwyn A. "History of Civil Defense in the United States." *Bulletin of the Atomic Scientists* 6, nos. 8–9 (August–September 1950): 265–69.

McEnaney, Laura. *Civil Defense Begins at Home: Militarization Meets Everyday Life in the Fifties.* Princeton, NJ: Princeton University Press, 2000.

OTT, ELSIE S. (1913–2006)

Elsie S. Ott was the first female recipient of the U.S. Army Air Medal. She was also the first credited flight nurse and a pioneer in the air evacuation of wounded and ill military personnel during World War II.

Born on November 5, 1913, in St. James, Long Island, New York, Ott graduated from Smithtown High School in 1933 and the School of Nursing at Lenox Hill Hospital in New York in 1936. Her first positions as a registered nurse were at Kings Park Hospital, Long Island, and St. Francis Hospital, Miami, Florida.

On September 13, 1941, Ott enlisted in the Army Nurse Corps and was commissioned a second lieutenant. She was first assigned to duty as a ward nurse at Barksdale Army Air Field Hospital in Louisiana and later in Fort Story, Virginia. In February 1942, Ott was sent overseas with a large group of nurses and assigned to the 159th Station Hospital located in Karachi, India.

In January 1943, Ott was selected for an experimental 11,000-mile air evacuation mission. This flight was the pioneer intercontinental movement of hospitalized personnel by air, and it initiated the extensive use of flight nurses by the U.S. military. The early years of the war had demonstrated the need for air evacuation. Terrain problems in many overseas locations, such as the mountainous regions of India and China, made the surface transportation of the wounded difficult and impracticable. The ability to transport casualties to medical facilities by air began to be regarded as a way to expedite their evacuation and treatment. Despite some opposition, the ambitious Aeromedical Evacuation program slowly developed. Ott's historic flight was the first test of its application.

Ott was given only hours to prepare for the six-day flight from Karachi, India, to Washington, D.C. She had no training in transporting patients by air and no flight experience. The flight departed on January 17, 1943, and was scheduled to make stops at Salala and Aden, Saudi Arabia; Khartoum and El Fasher, Egyptian Sudan; the Ascension Islands; Natal and Belem, Brazil; Borinquen, Puerto Rico; and Morrison Army Air Field, Florida. With the aid of a medic, Ott served as a nurse for five seriously ill soldiers, consisting of two litter patients and three ambulatory patients. The D-47 transport plane was not equipped to carry patients, and at a number of stops, they were evacuated to nearby medical facilities where Ott assisted in changing dressings, irrigating wounds, and bathing and feeding the patients. The plane arrived at Bolling Army Air Field in Washington at 8:00 p.m. on January 23, 1943. Medical attendants immediately transferred the patients to Walter Reed Army Hospital.

Ott's flight proved the feasibility of long-range air evacuation for wounded patients and revolutionized the traditional chain of evacuation. Her recommendations following the flight were implemented to improve future aeromedical evacuation missions. The success of the flight was highly noted and attributed to Ott's efficiency and professional skill. For her meritorious achievement, Ott received the Air Medal on March 26, 1943, a medal that recognizes the performance of crew members during an aviation mission in a hostile environment. The ceremony was presided over by Brig. Gen. Fred C. Borum and took place at Bowman Army Air Field, Kentucky.

In the spring of 1943, Ott attended the Air Evacuation School at Bowman Field. The program was the first of its kind and consisted of a six-week course of instruction in air evacuation nursing and tactics, aeromedical physiology, survival, climatic conditions, gas-mask drill, and field training in plane-loading procedures. The curriculum also included strenuous physical training with classes in military drill, calisthenics, and physical education. The flight nurses educated in this program were pioneers in a field of nursing that would become a highly specialized branch within the U.S. Air Force Nurse Corps.

In October 1944, Ott returned to India as a member of the 803rd Military Air Evacuation Squadron. She was later promoted to captain before being discharged from the Army Air Force in May of 1946. Ott later married Larry Mandot and settled in Wheaton, Illinois. Twenty-five years after her historic flight, she was selected to christen the new C-9 "Nightingale" aircraft at Scott Air Force Base, Illinois, the first designed specifically for aeromedical evacuations.

Ott died on December 15, 2006, in Cathedral City, California.

Anne M. E. Millar

See also: Air Force Nurse Corps (AFNC); Army Nurse Corps (ANC); Navy Nurse Corps; Nursing; World War II (1941–1945).

References and Further Reading

"Army Nurse Wins Air Medal." *American Journal of Nursing* 43, no. 5 (May 1943): 443–44.

Barger, Judith. "Strategic Aeromedical Evacuation: The Inaugural Flight." *Aviation, Space and Environmental Medicine* 57, no. 6 (June 1986): 613–16.

Barger, Judith. "U.S. Army Air Forces Flight Nurses: Training and Pioneer Flight." *Aviation, Space and Environmental Medicine* 51, no. 3 (April 1980): 414–16.

Jackson, Kathi. *They Called Them Angels: American Military Nurses of World War II.* Lincoln: University of Nebraska Press, 2000.

Sarnecky, Mary T. "Flight Nursing in the Army Nurse Corps in World War II." In *A History of the U.S. Army Nurse Corps*, edited by Mary T. Sarnecky, 250–64. Philadelphia: University of Pennsylvania Press, 1999.

OWENS v. BROWN (1978)

Owens v. Brown became a landmark civil rights case that challenged the validity of federal statutes that restricted women's naval service. In particular, it challenged statute 10 U.S.C. § 6015. Section 6015 prohibited women in the U.S. Navy from being assigned to duty at sea unless they were assigned on hospital ships and transport vessels. This case was brought as a class action on behalf of plaintiff Yona Owens, an interior communications electrician, and all other women in the U.S. Navy. On July 27, 1978, the court determined that the statute violated the due process clause of the Fifth Amendment of the U.S. Constitution, which prohibits the federal government from unfairly or arbitrarily depriving a person of life, liberty, or property.

Section 6015 was initially enacted as a part of the Women's Armed Forces Integration Act of 1948, which was the first federal statute to relax the prohibition of women serving in nonnursing or nonsecretarial positions in the Navy.

Although the act itself was a step towards expansion of career opportunities
for women in the Navy, Section 6015 still
impeded the ability of women to serve at
sea. The statute contained a definitive
prohibition on the assignment of female
personnel to sea vessels and did not allow
the secretary of the Navy to exercise discretion to allow women to serve in this
capacity. The Integration Act was
amended in 1967 and again in 1975, but
none of these amendments modified
Section 6015's blanket prohibition.

In 1978, Owens brought a suit on
behalf of herself and other similarly situ-
ated women in the U.S. Navy in front of
the U.S. District Court for the District
of Columbia. The suit alleged that
Section 6015 was a violation of the due
process clause of the Fifth Amendment
because it did not allow the secretary of
the Navy any discretion to place qualified women in noncombat positions at
sea. The court ultimately agreed with
Owens and the other plaintiffs that
Section 6015 effectively excluded
women from gaining access to the full
range of opportunities and expertise to
be found in the Navy. As a result, this
section worked to deprive women of the
opportunity not only to advance within
the Navy but also in their postmilitary
careers. In essence, sex as opposed to
the abilities of the individual served as
the guiding factor in assigning an individual for naval service. This prohibition
resulted in many women of superior
intelligence, skills, and leadership abilities being passed over for jobs simply
because of the blanket prohibition contained within Section 6015. The court
reasoned that the prohibition contained
in Section 6015 contained unfounded
generalizations about the fitness of

women in a traditionally masculine profession. As these generalizations were
based in stereotype rather than fact,
the statute's original intent to create a
more efficient military was not served.
Because Section 6015 was so broad that
it barred an entire sex from a wide range
of career opportunities for which military authorities had determined them to
be qualified, the court held that it could
not be justified. The court ordered that
military authorities create a policy
regarding the advancement and placement of women without regard to the
prohibition reflected in Section 6015.

Owens v. Brown is significant as part
of a long line of federal equal protection
cases that challenged ongoing assumptions about the suitability of women
for various types of employment,
both in the military and in civilian life.
The federal court for the District of
Columbia, in rendering this decision,
was following precedent that had previously been established by the Supreme
Court of the United States. Beginning in
1971, the Supreme Court began turning
a critical eye toward the question of
unreasonable and arbitrary gender classifications in state and federal laws in nonmilitary circumstances. In 1973, the
Supreme Court began to systematically
strike down military policies that violated the due process clause of the Fifth
Amendment. The court ruled in 1973
that equal housing and medical benefits
could not be denied to families of
servicewomen; in 1975 that women be
allowed to enter military service academies; and in 1978 that women could
not be discharged for pregnancy. The
most important consideration in these
cases was whether or not the classification was substantially related to the

achievement of important government objectives.

Alaina M. Morgan

See also: Women's Armed Forces Integration Act of 1948 (Public Law 80-625)

References and Further Reading

Decew, Judith Wagner. "The Combat Exclusion and the Role of Women in the Military." *Hypatia* 10, no. 1 (Winter 1995): 56–73.

"Due Process Clause." *Black's Law Dictionary*, 9th ed. Minneapolis, MN: Thomson West, 2009.

McSally, Martha E. "Defending America in Mixed Company: Gender in the U.S. Armed Forces." *Daedalus* 140, no. 3 (Summer 2011): 148–64.

Owens v. Brown, 455 F.Supp. 291 (D.D.C. 1978).

P

PARKER, CYNTHIA ANN
(CA. 1824–CA. 1870)

Captured by Comanches when she was a young girl, Cynthia Ann Parker lived with the Comanche for more than 25 years.

Little is known about the birth of Parker, who would live to become legendary in both the Anglo and Comanche societies in the state of Texas during the late 1800s. The only records that shed any light on her birth come from the 1870 census of Anderson County, Texas. According to these records, Parker would have been born somewhere between June 2, 1824, and May 31, 1825. She was born in Crawford County, Illinois, to Lucy (Duty) and Silas M. Parker. She moved to central Texas at the age of 9 or 10 with her family. At the headwaters of the Navasota River, the Parker family constructed what came to be known as Fort Parker, located in what is now Limestone County.

Fort Parker was witness to a fierce Comanche attack on May 19, 1836. These attacks were common throughout the central and western portions of Texas during this time. The Comanche were actively retaliating against the Anglos for what they saw as an outright invasion. Their cunning and combat skills were legendary throughout the state as a result of these attacks. Their Kiowa and Kichai allies aided the Comanche in the raid. The attack resulted in the deaths of several of the Anglo settlers and the capture of five settlers, including Parker.

Over time, the other four captives were either released to other Anglo settlers or traded with other tribes. Parker was the only captive from the Fort Parker raid who remained with the Comanche. For a span of 25 years, Parker lived with the Comanche. She became fully integrated into the Comanche way of life; she saw herself as a Comanche, took a husband (Peta Nocona) from the tribe, and had three children—sons Quanah and Pecos and daughter Topsannah—who were raised in the Comanche way.

In the mid-1840s, Cynthia Ann's brother, John Parker, encountered her and begged her to return to the settlement and live with his family. He recorded that she refused, citing that she had a husband and family that she loved and cared for. Other similar stories, some apocryphal, exist, including one that involves Indian trader Victor Rose. These stories of family members and traders coming into contact with missing and kidnapped settlers, regardless of their basis in truth, spread quickly and evoked strong emotions from other settlers dealing with Native Americans.

It was not until December 18, 1860, that another fateful meeting with whites would have fearful repercussions for Parker. On that date, Lawrence Sullivan Ross led a group of Texas Rangers on an attack of a Comanche hunting camp at Mule Creek. During the raid, the Texas Rangers took three captives whom they believed were Comanche, including Parker and her infant daughter. Ross reported his amazement at Parker's blue eyes. Her uncle, Col. Isaac Parker, identified Cynthia Ann. She subsequently accompanied him to his home in Birdville, Texas, on the condition that, if found, her sons would be sent immediately to her. During a stop in Fort Worth, she was photographed with her daughter at her breast. The photo shows Parker with short hair, a traditional Comanche sign of mourning. She assumed that her husband was dead and feared for the lives of her two sons.

Parker struggled against the white way of life and tried to escape numerous times while living with her uncle in Birdville, as well as when she was living with her brother's family in Van Zandt County. Her troubled life was not eased when the Texas Legislature voted in 1861 to provide her with a $100 annuity for the span of five years along with a league of land in 1861. Parker lived out the rest of her days pining for her dead husband and the two sons she assumed she had lost.

Quanah, her eldest son, became a legendary Comanche chief and a fierce warrior who is remembered for his efforts at the Battle of Adobe Walls in the Panhandle area of Texas. The time of Cynthia Ann's death is uncertain. Some sources put it in 1864, but the 1870 census has her aged 45. She was reinterred with her son Quanah in 1957 at the Fort Sill Post Cemetery.

Ryan C. Davis

See also: Indian Wars.

References and Further Reading

Exley, Jo Ella Powell. *Frontier Blood: The Saga of the Parker Family.* College Station: Texas A&M University Press, 2001.

Jackson, Grace. *Cynthia Ann Parker.* San Antonio, TX: Naylor, 1959.

PERKINS (WILSON), FRANCES (1882–1965)

Frances Perkins was the first woman to serve in a presidential cabinet. She served as secretary of labor from March 1933 to August 1945 under President Franklin D. Roosevelt. Perkins helped design and enact much of the New Deal, including the minimum wage and unemployment

Frances Perkins served as U.S. secretary of labor from 1933 to 1945. As the first woman cabinet member, she was also the first woman to be in line for succession to the presidency. (Library of Congress)

insurance. A firm advocate of fair labor laws and the right of workers to organize, Perkins spent the greater portion of her life fighting to improve the lives of the United States' poor.

Perkins was born on April 10, 1882, in Boston, Massachusetts, to an upper-middle-class family. She was born Fanny Coralie Perkins, but she legally changed her name early in her career. Upon graduation from Mount Holyoke College, Perkins taught school in Massachusetts and Illinois and volunteered at several tenement houses near Chicago, including the famous Hull House, where she learned firsthand the dangerous working and appalling living conditions of the urban poor. By 1909, she had given up teaching science and had moved to New York to study at Columbia University, where she earned a master's degree in economics and sociology in 1910. Perkins became the secretary of the New York Consumers' League, and her zealous lobbying of the state legislature facilitated the passage of a bill limiting the work week for women and children to 54 hours. She also became active in the women's suffrage movement, helping to organize rallies and parades, and even giving street-corner speeches.

One of the more pivotal experiences of Perkins's life occurred in 1911, when she watched helplessly as 146 workers died in the Triangle Shirtwaist fire. The workers, most of them young women, were trapped in a burning building with no fire escapes; many of the women jumped to their deaths to escape the flames. In 1913, Perkins wed Paul Wilson, an economist and budget expert with the New York Bureau of Municipal Research. She gave birth to their only daughter, Susanna, shortly thereafter and withdrew from public life for a time. Perkins soon resumed her advocacy for economic reform and, in 1918, was appointed to the New York State Industrial Commission. In this new position, Perkins expanded factory investigations, reduced the work week for women, and championed minimum wage and unemployment insurance laws. Recognizing Perkins's passion and talent, newly elected governor Franklin D. Roosevelt appointed her as the industrial commissioner of the state of New York, the chief post in the state labor department.

Perkins drew on her New York experiences when Roosevelt chose her as his labor secretary in 1933. Facing the massive unemployment and volatile labor market of the Great Depression, Perkins was an integral part of the New Deal.

She immediately proposed federal aid to the states for direct unemployment relief and an extensive public works program. During her 12 years of service, Perkins' vision and leadership helped shepherd the Wagner Act, which gave workers the right to bargain collectively and organize unions, and the Fair Labor Standards Act, which established a national minimum wage and a maximum workweek for men and women for the first time. Perkins also chaired the Committee on Economic Security, which developed and drafted the legislation that became the Social Security Act in 1935.

After the outbreak of World War II, Perkins was instrumental in the implementation of a wartime economy and the fair assimilation of women into the workforce. She considered the war to be a grave situation but was also committed to ensuring that Americans took their pledge to fight oppression and injustice as seriously at home as they did on the battlefields abroad. She actively lobbied President Roosevelt to exempt women from the military draft, allowing them to remain at home to bolster the much-needed labor force for the industrial war economy. She was also one of the more vocal proponents of allowing Jewish refugees from Europe into the United States. Her tireless efforts to ensure safe working conditions and fair pay did not stop with the coming of the war, and she was able to craft the war economy in such a way as to allow the further progression of her goals in the postwar period.

Perkins also played a crucial role in the many labor uprisings of the era. However, her work with labor unions elicited the ire of numerous conservatives, who actually proposed an impeachment resolution against her after she refused to deport Harry Bridges, the head of the West Coast Longshore Union and an accused communist. The impeachment proceedings were dropped due to a lack of evidence.

Perkins resigned after Roosevelt's death in 1945, but President Harry Truman soon appointed her to the Civil Service Commission in 1946. In the latter part of her life, Perkins continued her endeavors at Cornell University as a professor of industrial and labor relations. In 1965, she died at the age of 85 in New York.

Andrew Polk

See also: World War II (1941–1945).

References and Further Reading

Downey, Kristin. *The Woman behind the New Deal: The Life and Legacy of Frances Perkins—Social Security, Unemployment Insurance, and the Minimum Wage*. New York: Random House, 2009.

Pasachoff, Naomi E. *Frances Perkins: Champion of the New Deal*. New York: Oxford University Press, 1999.

Perkins, Francis. *The Roosevelt I Knew*. New York: Random House, 1946.

PHIPPS, ANITA EVANS (1886–1953)

In the years between the two world wars, Anita Phipps wrote the first complete and workable plan for a women's army corps. She served as the director of women's relations in the U.S. Army from 1921 until 1931.

In 1920, the Nineteenth Amendment to the U.S. Constitution was ratified, giving women the right to vote. The growing political power of women voters, many of whom became active in antimilitary and pacifist movements, was viewed with alarm by the Army. To persuade women voters that a strong military was a necessity, the position of director of women's relations, U.S. Army, was established. The director's job was to maintain a liaison between the War Department and women's organizations to promote the idea of a strong military. After the first appointee resigned, the 35-year-old Phipps was appointed director. Phipps, the daughter of an army general, had served as the director of the Motor Corps Service of the Pennsylvania-Delaware Division of the Red Cross during World War I and had experience in dealing with the military.

Phipps encountered problems from the start. The War Department's failure to give her military status and support for her position caused her to lose credibility with women's organizations. Despite repeated pleas, her job duties were never clearly defined, and her work was dismissed by the War Department. Phipps decided to define her position herself and began planning for what she called a Women's Service Corps, presumably with her as the head. She collected information on the utilization of women by different organizations during World War I, including the British army and the U.S. Navy. She concluded that the policy of enlisting women during World War I but giving them no military training, housing, discipline, or courtesies was a mistake. She proposed that her women's corps should serve in, not auxiliary to, the Army, be fully trained, and serve under the command of women officers. By surveying various army corps, commanders, and branch chiefs, Phipps thought that about 170,000 women could be utilized in wartime.

The General Staff rejected the plan in 1926, citing difficulties in the cost of housing, transportation, and toilet facilities and in the personnel policy involved. Privately, officers in the War Department were fearful that Phipps's plan would establish a powerful organization of women within the Army. Finally, in 1931, Phipps asked the secretary of war to either define her duties and authority or abolish her position. Nothing was done, and in 1931 the new chief of staff, Gen. Douglas MacArthur, informed the War Department that Phipps's duties were of no military value, and the position was eliminated. Although all her efforts seemed to have been in vain, Phipps's study helped lay the groundwork for the creation of the WAC in 1942. Phipps later held the position of head of American Women's Voluntary Services in the District of Columbia during World War II.

Anita Phipps died in 1953.

Vicki L. Friedl

See also: American Red Cross; Women's Army Auxiliary Corps (WAAC); Women's Army Corps (WAC); World War I (1914–1918).

References and Further Reading

Holm, Jeanne. *Women in the Military: An Unfinished Revolution.* Novato, CA: Presidio Press, 1992.

Morden, Bettie J. *The Women's Army Corp, 1945–1978.* Washington, D.C.: U.S. Government Printing Office, 1990.

Treadwell, Mattie E. *The Women's Army Corps.* Washington, D.C.: U.S. Government Printing Office, 1954.

PIESTEWA, LORI (1979–2003)

Pvt. 1st Class Lori Piestewa served in the U.S. Army as a member of the 507th Maintenance Corps during the Iraq War and died in captivity from wounds suffered when her unit was ambushed near Nasiriyah in March 2003. Piestewa, a member of the Hopi tribe, is thought to be the first Native American servicewoman to be killed in combat while fighting for the U.S. armed services.

Hopi Indian Lori Piestewa died in Iraq in March 2003 after being taking captive by the enemy. She is considered to be the first Native American servicewoman killed in combat. (U.S. Army)

Born December 14, 1979, Lori Piestewa grew up in Tuba, Arizona. Her father, Terry Piestewa, is a member of the Hopi tribe, and her mother, Priscilla Baca Piestewa, is of Mexican American descent. Lori was the youngest of four siblings, two boys and two girls, and came from a family with a strong military heritage. Her father served in Vietnam, and her grandfather had fought in World War II. Following in this tradition, Lori acted as the commanding officer of her high school's Junior Reserve Officer Training Corps (ROTC) program.

During her sophomore year of high school, Piestewa met and began a relationship with Bill H. Whiterock, a Navajo and three-sport athlete. While she was still only a senior, they married, and the couple had their first child, Brandon Terry, in 1998. Their second child, Carla Lynn, was born in 1999. However, marital problems caused the couple to separate and eventually divorce shortly thereafter.

In 2001, Piestewa joined the U.S. Army and was assigned to the 507th Maintenance Corps. She acted as the unit's supply clerk, ordering equipment and keeping track of shipments. She quickly became close friends with her roommate, Jessica Lynch, a fellow member of the 507th. In March 2003, the unit was sent to Iraq to participate in Operation Iraqi Freedom. Driving a variety of vehicles from heavy trucks to Humvees, the unit brought up the tail end of a convoy of troops and supplies bound for Baghdad. Many of the 507th's vehicles stalled, overheated, or had trouble keeping up in the difficult terrain. As a result, part of the unit became separated from the convoy.

On March 23, 2003, Piestewa and the other members of the 507th Maintenance Corps who had been separated from the main convoy mistakenly entered the enemy-held city of Nasiriyah, a city they were supposed to bypass. Iraqi soldiers ambushed the unit. During the ensuing firefight, Piestewa was the driver of a Humvee containing Lynch and three other American soldiers. Piestewa successfully maneuvered the vehicle at high speed, avoiding enemy fire and attempting to provide aid and direction to members of the 507th engaged in heavy fighting from stalled vehicles. As Piestewa attempted to drive the Humvee out the ambush, she came to an Iraqi roadblock, and a rocket-propelled grenade hit the Humvee, causing it to crash into a tractor trailer. Piestewa was taken prisoner by Iraqi troops and died in an Iraqi-held hospital from wounds sustained during the crash. Her body was found buried in a shallow grave with the bodies of six other American soldiers near the Tykar military hospital where her friend Lynch was rescued by U.S. forces.

Piestewa became a symbol of Native sacrifice in the war effort. Notably, her family became ardent antiwar activists. Her parents have regularly attended speaking events commemorating their daughter. After it became clear that there were no weapons of mass destruction in Iraq, they became outspoken critics of the global War on Terror.

Numerous efforts have been made to honor the memory of Piestewa. She was posthumously awarded the Purple Heart and Prisoner of War Medal, and in her home state of Arizona, the offensively titled mountain "Squaw Peak" was renamed "Piestewa Peak" in her honor.

David D. Dry

See also: Hispanic American Women; Iraq War (2003–2011); Johnson, Shoshana Nyree (1973–); Lynch, Jessica (1983–); Native American Women; Prisoners of War.

References and Further Reading

Bragg, Rick. *I Am a Soldier, Too: The Jessica Lynch Story.* New York: Alfred A. Knopf, 2003.

Carroll, Al. *Medicine Bags and Dog Tags: American Indian Veterans from Colonial Times to the Second Iraq War.* Lincoln: University of Nebraska Press, 2008.

Lowry, Richard S. *Marines in the Garden of Eden: The True Story of Seven Bloody Days in Iraq.* New York: Berkley Trade, 2007.

Zeinert, Karen, and Mary Miller. *The Brave Women of the Gulf Wars: Operation Desert Storm and Operation Iraqi Freedom.* Minneapolis, MN: Twenty-First Century Books, 2006.

PIGOTT, EMELINE JAMISON (1836–1919)

Emeline Jamison Pigott served as spy for the Confederacy during the American Civil War.

Pigott was born in Harlowe Township of Carteret County, North Carolina, to Levi and Eliza Dennis Pigott. When the Civil War began, Pigott moved with her parents to a farm near Calico Creek in Morehead City. When Confederate troops camped near the family farm, several officers attempted to court Pigott.

However, the 25-year-old Pigott fell in love with a private in the 26th North Carolina named Stokes McRae. When the 26th North Carolina went to New Bern to protect the town from Union troops, Pigott followed McRae's unit. In March 1862, federal troops captured the town of New Bern, North Carolina. Pigott was relieved to discover that McRae was unharmed during the conflict. In late spring of 1863, the 26th North Carolina joined the Army of Northern Virginia. During the Battle of Gettysburg, McRae fought on July 1 under Gen. Henry Heath's assault and on July 3 in the assault on Cemetery Hill. McRae suffered a wound to the upper leg and died of this wound on August 2, 1863. McRae's death devastated Pigott. To ease her suffering, she quickly took action to help his comrades.

Pigott attended to the Confederate wounded until the town of New Bern fell. After fleeing to Kinston, North Carolina, and spending time there, Pigott traveled across Union lines back to her farm on Calico Creek. Upon her return, Pigott discovered that her farm was in the control of Union officers, so she entertained these men while her brother-in-law smuggled food, medicine, and supplies to Confederate soldiers hiding in the surrounding areas. Most notably, Pigott smuggled official correspondence to Confederate posts by hiding letters under her hoop skirt. Pigott pinned letters and tied supplies to her hoop skirt and carried them to secret locations where Confederate soldiers could pick them up. Because she navigated a narrow path between friend and foe, she was careful about whom to trust. Pigott heard rumors that Union officers were aware of her espionage activities.

In 1864, while Pigott was carrying a letter to Confederate officers containing information about the Union army's campaign strategy, she was confronted by a group of Union soldiers. The soldiers took Pigott to a jail in Beaufort where an African American woman searched her for contraband. Pigott protested that only a white woman should touch her, and the Union soldiers obliged. When the men went to find a white woman, Pigott tore the letter into tiny pieces. She then quickly chewed and swallowed as much of the letter as she could. However, both the remaining pieces of the letter and the supplies found hidden in her skirt were enough evidence for the Union soldiers to arrest Pigott. Union personnel held Pigott at a jail in New Bern, where she awaited trial. During the month Pigott spent in jail, she learned that two men had given her a false letter with the intent to inform federal troops of her activities. Pigott summoned the men who set her up and warned them that if she were tried as a spy, at her trial she would reveal their surreptitious involvement in her capture. The men paid for her release. Although she was never tried in a court of law as a spy, Pigott was closely watched and searched by Union troops throughout the remainder of the war.

Although after her arrest Pigott no longer transported supplies and mail to Confederate troops, she continued to help her nation in other ways. Pigott wrote supportive letters to captured and wounded North Carolinian troops who were held in Northern prisons and who were recovering in Northern hospitals. Although none of these men ever caught Pigott's heart as Stokes had, she comforted them through hard times and reminded them of the support they had from those on the homefront.

After the war, Pigott became a member of the New Bern chapter of the United Daughters of the Confederacy. Pigott remained on her family estate and later founded the Morehead City chapter of the United Daughters of the Confederacy. She served as president of the organization until her death at the age of 82 in 1919. Pigott never married but remained loyal to her fallen soldier through her dedication to both the Confederate war effort and those who had died for it.

Lauren K. Thompson

See also: Battle, Mary Frances "Fannie" (1842–1924); Boyd, Marie Isabella "Belle" (1844–1900); Civil War (1861–1865); Edmondson, Isabella "Belle" Buchanan (1840–1873); Espionage; Nursing.

References and Further Reading

Cohn, Scotti. *More Than Petticoats. Remarkable North Carolina Women*. Helena, MT: TwoDot, 2000.

Powell, William Stevens. *Dictionary of North Carolina Biography*. Vol. 5, *P-S*. Chapel Hill: University of North Carolina Press, 1979.

PITCHER, MOLLY
(N.D.–N.D.)

Although an icon of the American Revolution, few definitive details exist regarding the life of the famed "Molly Pitcher," as she has become more of a legend than a historical figure.

Historians agree that Molly Pitcher was most likely Mary "Molly" Ludwig

The actions of patriot "Molly Pitcher" during the American Revolution have become legendary. Historians still debate her identity. (National Archives)

Hays, born to a German family on October 13, 1754, either in New Jersey or Pennsylvania (sources conflict on the location). She married an Irishman named Casper Hays at the age of 15 on July 24, 1769, at St. Michael's and Zion Church in Philadelphia, Pennsylvania. When Casper died, she married William Hays of Bristol, Pennsylvania, who was most likely Casper's brother.

Hays enlisted in the Continental Army from his hometown of Bristol on May 10, 1777. He enlisted in Capt. Francis Proctor's company in the 4th Pennsylvania Artillery. Some sources indicate that Molly left with William and followed him through his initial enlistment through the campaigns of 1777 to include the winter encampment at Valley Forge. According to family lore, the men of the company described her as an illiterate 22-year-old pregnant woman who smoked and chewed tobacco and who swore as well as any of the male soldiers, although this detail may be an extension of the greater myth. Other tales have her leaving Pennsylvania to join her husband in the early summer of 1778 to join Gen. George Washington's forces en route to the Monmouth Campaign. It was this engagement that gave birth to the Molly Pitcher legend.

During the battle on June 28, 1778, with temperatures approaching 100 degrees, she labored tirelessly carrying water in a pitcher (or more likely, a bucket) to quench the soldiers' thirst and to cool the blazing cannons. Soldiers would allegedly cry, "Molly, Pitcher," when they needed a drink; hence the famous moniker. As the British pressed the American position, William was stuck down. Sources

conflict as to whether he fell from heat stroke or as the result of a battle wound. Watching her husband fall, Molly purportedly seized the rammer and continued to assist the cannon crew until the battle concluded. Her conspicuous act of bravery earned her a reputation throughout the army and even gained the attention of Washington, who is said to have bestowed a warrant on her as a noncommissioned officer along with the name of "Sergeant Molly."

Little information exists regarding her life and exploits during the remainder of the war. When the conflict ended, she and her husband moved to Carlisle, Pennsylvania, where William had received 200 acres of bounty land in Westmoreland County for his service in the army. The two had only one child, Johanes Ludwig Hays, who was born in 1783. William Hays died four years later. Molly married John McCauley (also spelled McCalley), who eventually caused her severe financial troubles. The indebted couple sold the original bountied property in 1807, and John passed away three years later. She spent the rest of her days living in Carlisle with her son until she herself died on January 22, 1833, at the age of 78.

On February 21, 1822, McCauley petitioned the state government for and received a soldier's pension of $40 for "services she rendered during the Revolutionary war. It appeared satisfactorily that this heroine had braved the hardships of the camp and dangers of the field with her husband, who was a soldier of the revolution."

Although most historians identify Mary Ludwig Hays McCaulley as the Molly Pitcher of Revolutionary legend, several other women of the period also claim the title. Margaret Corbin, wife of soldier John Corbin in the same artillery company as William Hays, attests to a similar story of assuming her mortally wounded husband's place on the cannon crew during the Battle of Fort Washington. She was then wounded and captured by the British but was soon released and served guard duty at West Point for the remainder of the war. Corbin's regiment petitioned successfully for her to receive both state and federal pensions for her military service.

In addition, Deborah Sampson is sometimes mentioned as a possible Molly Pitcher. Sampson dressed as a soldier and joined the 4th Massachusetts Regiment and served for the duration of the war. Her feminine features led to her fellow male soldiers giving her epithet of "Molly." She, too, successfully petitioned the state government, with the endorsement of the veterans of her regiment and Gov. John Hancock, in 1792 for a pension and back pay as a soldier in the Continental Army.

Regardless of who the real Molly Pitcher was, the story of her exploits has survived over the last two centuries as she maintains her legend as one of the heroes of the American Revolution.

Bradford A. Wineman

See also: American Revolution (1775–1783); Corbin, Margaret Cochran (1751–ca. 1800); Samson [Sampson] (Gannett), Deborah [Robert Shurtliff] (1760–1827).

References and Further Reading

De Pauw, Linda Grant. "Women in Combat: The Revolutionary War Experience." *Armed Forces and Society* 7 (1981): 209–26.

Klaver, Carol. "An Introduction to the Legend of Molly Pitcher." *Minerva: Quarterly Report on Woman and the Military* 12, no. 2 (1994): 35–61.

Martin, David G., ed. *A Molly Pitcher Sourcebook*. Hightstown, NJ: Longstreet House, 2003.

Teipe, Emily J. "Will the Real Molly Pitcher Please Stand Up?" *Prologue: Quarterly of the National Archives Records Administration* 31, no. 2 (1999): 118–26.

PRATHER, MARY LOUISE (1913–1996)

Mary Louise Prather was a prominent American spy and a pioneer in the field of cryptology during World War II and the early Cold War.

Born in 1913, little is known about Prather's early years. She spent her entire life in greater Washington, D.C. In 1938, Prather joined the Signal Intelligence Service (SIS) of the U.S. Army in the position of a civilian stenographer. She attained the position of chief of the Stenographic Section within about two years.

The intelligence activities of the Allies during World War II were headed primarily by two organizations—the British Special Operations Executive (SOE) and the American Office of Strategic Services (OSS), the precursor to the Central Intelligence Agency (CIA). In addition to these organizations, the SIS, the U.S. Army's code-breaking division headquartered at Arlington Hall in Virginia, performed a crucial role. More specifically, the SIS was a part of the U.S. Army Signal Corps, which was responsible for developing, testing, providing, and managing communications and information systems support for the command and control of the combined armed forces. In addition to breaking foreign codes, the SIS was responsible for virtually everything to do with the War Department's code systems. Women working for the SIS worked closely with the 2nd Signal Service Battalion, which provided radio intelligence. The SIS initially worked on an extremely limited budget, lacking the equipment it needed to even intercept messages in order to practice decrypting.

During World War II, Prather was promoted to administrative assistant and personnel officer for the General Cryptographic Branch. In preparation for this position, Prather was trained in cryptographic security, Army and staff organization from a signal intelligence viewpoint, elementary and advanced cryptography, IBM theory and operation, code compilation, and the preparation of cryptanalytic work sheets. She may also have received language instruction in Japanese and German as well as in military cryptanalysis. The SIS valued her training in cryptography as well as her integrity.

Many women like Prather, who were well qualified and deemed to be trustworthy, took advantage of increased career opportunities related to the war effort—including those in highly classified positions—during these years. For example, it was during World War II that President Franklin Delano Roosevelt authorized women to accept noncombatant military roles. Thousands of women took advantage of this reality, which, in turn, freed thousands of men for combat roles. In her position as administrative assistant and personnel officer for the General Cryptographic Branch, Prather was responsible for logging messages in code and for preparing decoded messages for distribution. Undeniably, however, Prather, along with Genevieve Grotjan, is most remembered for her identification of a correlation between two Japanese messages that permitted the decryption of an important new Japanese code system in 1940.

Shortly after the war—in 1946—Prather was awarded the Commendation for Meritorious Civilian Service. Throughout the 1950s, Prather held a number of related positions increasing in responsibility until she was named the chief of the Soviet Information Division in 1960. Upon her retirement as a division chief of the National Security Agency, Prather was recognized again in 1969 with the Meritorious Civilian Service Award.

Prather suffered a stroke and died on December 20, 1996. She was 83.

Katherine Rohrer

See also: Cold War (ca. 1947–1991); Espionage; Feinstein, Genevieve Grotjan (1912–2006); World War II (1941–1945).

References and Further Reading

Budiansky, Stephen. *Battle of Wits: The Complete Story of Codebreaking in World War II*. New York: Free Press, 2000.

Haufler, Hervie. *Codebreakers' Victory: How the Allied Cryptographers Won World War II*. New York: New American Library, 2003.

Obituaries/death notices. *Washington Post*, December 23, 1996.

Wilcox, Jennifer. *Sharing the Burden: Women in Cryptology during World War II* [microform]. Fort George G. Meade, MD: Center for Cryptologic History, National Security Agency, 1998.

PRISONERS OF WAR

Women have served in the U.S. military since its inception and have been captured by the enemy and held as a prisoners of war (POWs).

In the early colonial period and after the American Revolution, Americans clashed with American Indian groups. During these wars, women were often taken captive and held by the Indians. Some remained with the Indians, and others were later "redeemed" and brought home to their families. American colonists also took Indian women as prisoners.

During the American Revolution, some women disguised themselves as men to join the Continental Army while others served in unofficial capacities. Although there is no official record of women being taken as prisoners of war during this conflict, some may have been unwittingly captured by enemy troops. In addition, British troops often seized and burned the homes of colonists, which were being defended by women.

On both sides of the Civil War, women became POWs. During the Civil War more than 250 women disguised themselves as men and served in the armed forces. Several of these disguised women were captured and held as POWs. Many never revealed their sex and accepted their fate and treatment. For example, the Confederate army captured Frances Hook, alias Frank Miller, in December 1863. They released her in a prisoner exchange but recaptured her later in the war and sent her to Andersonville prison. She never revealed her sex and lived in the harsh conditions of the camp.

When female prisoners of war fell victim to the diseases that were rampant in the prisons, their sex often became apparent. While being held as a prisoner at Andersonville, Florena Baldwin became ill with pneumonia. When her sex was revealed in a hospital exam, Baldwin received a private room and the aid of local civilian women, who donated food, medicine, and clothing. In the end, Baldwin died and was buried in Andersonville Cemetery. Many other unknown women were held as prisoners by both sides during the war.

In addition, several female spies were captured and held as prisoners. Two particular female Confederate spies gained fame for their exploits and their time in prison. When Union forces captured spy Belle Boyd, a young teenage girl, in the summer of 1862, they held her as a prisoner in Maryland until she was exchanged in December 1863. Similarly, the Pinkerton Detective Agency arrested Rose O'Neal Greenhow, who ran a Confederate spy ring in Washington, D.C., in August 1861. Initially, Greenhow was kept on house arrest, but in 1862, Union officials moved her and her young daughter to the Old Capitol Prison in Washington. When she was exchanged a few months later, officials sent her to the Confederate capital of Richmond and forbade her to enter Union territory again.

Female Union spies were also captured and held as POWs. Dr. Mary Walker, a contract surgeon for the Union army, served as a spy during the 1864 Atlanta campaign. The Confederate army captured Walker and held her as a POW for four months. For her work, Walker received the Congressional Medal of

Honor. In addition, Harriet Wood, alias Pauline Cushman, worked as a spy for the Union army in the St. Louis, Missouri, and Nashville, Tennessee, areas. When Confederates captured her in 1863, Gen. Braxton Bragg sentenced her to hang. However, when Confederate forces fled the area in the face of advancing Union troops, they abandoned Wood, thus saving her life.

During the Spanish-American War (1898) and World War I, women served with the armed forces as nurses and spies. Some even served in uniform during these conflicts. However, there are no recorded instances of women being taken as prisoners during these wars.

During World War II, the largest number of women serving in the U.S. armed forces were captured and held as POWs. On December 7, 1941, the Japanese attacked Pearl Harbor, a U.S. naval base in Hawaii. A few hours later they began to attack Clark Airfield, a U.S. Army airbase, in the Philippines. Unbeknownst to the Japanese, 99 female Army and Navy nurses, the first unit of American women to ever be sent into a war zone, were stationed on the island at the Fort Stotsenberg hospital outside of Manila. As the bombs dropped and the Japanese invaded, the nurses rushed to evacuate their hospital to find a safer position. Twenty-two nurses managed to escape the island by aircraft or boat ahead of the Japanese invasion. However, on May 6, 1942, the Japanese captured 77 female nurses who had been left behind with their patients at Bataan. For three years the women cared for wounded American POWs on the Philippine peninsula of Bataan. In January 1945, American forces retook the Philippines

and rescued the nurses and other POWs held on the island.

Second Lieutenant Reba Whittle was the only American woman held as a POW in the European theater of operations during World War II. Whittle joined the U.S. Army as a nurse in June 1941 after she had completed nursing school. She served at army posts in New Mexico and California and then volunteered to train as a flight nurse in January 1943. During the war, the Army began using aircraft to evacuate wounded from the battlefield and take them to nearby hospitals for treatment. The medical aircraft were considered noncombatants and were not armed, so women were permitted on them. In January 1944, after months of training, Whittle and 25 other flight nurses with the 813th Medical Air Evacuation Squadron (MAES) arrived in England to begin their work. During her first eight months serving as a flight nurse in the European theater, Whittle flew over 500 hours in missions to Belgium and France. German forces shot down Whittle's plane during an evacuation. The Germans captured the entire crew, including Whittle. They imprisoned Whittle at Luft Stalag IX in Cologne, Germany, in a solitary cell. She was exchanged on January 25, 1945, with 109 other prisoners.

Women continued to serve in all branches of the military in many different capacities after World War II. They served on the battlefields as nurses. None of the women serving with the U.S. military were held as POWs, although the Vietnamese took several American civilian female missionaries prisoner during the Vietnam War.

American women became more active, and accepted, in the armed forces in the late 20th century. In January 1991, the United States and its allies began a war to liberate Kuwait. Approximately 30,000 women served in the U.S. forces during the Gulf War. During the short war, the Iraqi army captured two female American soldiers and held them as POWs. On January 30, 1991, Specialist Melissa Rathbun-Nealy and Specialist David Lockett were taken prisoner after they made a wrong turn with their heavy equipment transfer vehicle and ran into an Iraqi tank unit. Rathbun-Nealy became the first female POW since World War II. She was held for 33 days before her release on March 3, 1991.

Maj. Rhonda Cornum also became a POW during the Gulf War. Cornum, who served as a flight surgeon assigned to the 2/222nd Attack Helicopter Battalion, frequently went out on search-and-rescue missions to care for possible injured downed helicopter crews. On February 27, 1991, during a search-and-rescue mission to locate and recover a downed Air Force F-16 pilot, the Iraqi army shot down the Blackhawk helicopter that Cornum was traveling in. Five of the eight crew members aboard were killed. Suffering from numerous injuries, Cornum and two others were captured by the Iraqis and taken prisoner. The Iraqi government released Cornum on March 6, 1991.

As women's military roles near the front lines increased, so did the possibility of female POWs. In March 2003, the United States led UN forces in an invasion of Iraq. Early in the Iraq War, women became POWs. On March 23, 2003, Jessica Lynch, Lori Piestewa, and Shoshana Johnson traveled with their unit, the 507th Ordnance Maintenance Unit, near Nasiriya, Iraq. The unit's

confusion about which route to take resulted in its driving into an Iraqi unit. After a firefight, the three women were wounded and captured. Piestewa, wounded in the head, died shortly after being captured. U.S. Marines rescued Johnson and Lynch on April 1, 2003. This rescue was the first successful rescue of female POWs since the rescue of prisoners on Bataan during World War II.

Stacy W. Reaves

See also: Afghanistan; American Revolution (1775–1783); Boyd, Marie Isabella "Belle" (1844–1900); Civil War (1861–1865); Cornum, Rhonda (1954–); Cushman, Pauline [Harriet Wood] (1833–1893); Espionage; Greenhow, Rose O'Neal (ca. 1814–1864); Gulf War (1991); Indian Wars; Iraq War (2003–2011); Johnson, Shoshana Nyree (1973–); Korean War (1950–1953); Lynch, Jessica (1983–); North American Colonial Wars (17th–18th centuries); Piestewa, Lori (1979–2003); Rathbun-Nealy (Coleman), Melissa (1970–); Rowlandson, Mary White (ca. 1635–1711); Spanish-American War (1898); Vietnam War (1965–1973); Walker, Mary Edwards (1832–1919); World War I (1914–1918); World War II (1941–1945).

References and Further Reading

Blanton, DeAnne, and Lauren M. Cook. *They Fought Like Demons: Women Soldiers in the American Civil War.* Baton Rouge: Louisiana State University Press, 2002.

Bragg, Rick. *I Am a Soldier, Too: The Jessica Lynch Story.* New York: Alfred A. Knopf, 2003.

Cornum, Rhonda, and Peter Copeland. *She Went to War: The Rhonda Cornum Story.* Novato, CA: Presidio, 1992.

Johnson, Shoshana, and M. L. Doyle. *I'm Still Standing: From Captive U.S. Soldier to*

Free Citizen—My Journey Home. New York: Simon & Schuster, 2010.

Markle, Donald E. *Spies and Spymasters of the Civil War*. New York: Hippocrene Books, 2004.

Norman, Elizabeth M. *We Band of Angels: The Untold Story of American Nurses Trapped on Bataan by the Japanese*. New York: Random House, 1999.

Wise, James E., and Scott Baron. *Women at War: Iraq, Afghanistan, and Other Conflicts*. Annapolis, MD: Naval Institute Press, 2006.

PUBLIC LAW 448 (JULY 2, 1925)

Public Law 448, which passed on July 2, 1925, granted contract nurses who served in the Spanish-American War (1898) full military status as members of the Army Nurse Corps (ANC). In 1922, contract nurses from this war received pensions for their service.

The Spanish-American War increased the need for female nurses to serve American forces in Cuba and the Philippines. Although thousands of women had served as nurses in the Civil War, many did so without training or commission. The Spanish-American War required many certified nursing professionals to care for the wounded soldiers, so in April 1898 Congress authorized Surgeon General George M. Sternberg to employ female nurses under contract and to make appropriation for them at a rate of $30 per month. The decision to employ only certified nurses in this war led to the professionalization of nursing. Nurses had to go through a rigorous examination before being contracted by the military and had to demonstrate their mental, physical, and moral qualifications to serve in the Army.

After receiving their training in religious orders, professional nursing schools, and the Red Cross, approximately 1,500 to 1,700 contract nurses served in the Spanish-American War. Some served on floating hospitals while others served on foreign soil. Soldiers and superiors accepted female nurses as qualified medical workers who had the necessary knowledge and technical skills to help them. The services of female nurses were required after the war ended as well. Some tended to wounded soldiers, while others cared for those who had contracted diseases such as malaria, typhoid, and yellow fever.

The success of female nurses during the Spanish-American War led to the establishment of a nurse corps division. Dr. Anita Newcomb McGee was appointed as acting assistant surgeon general of the U.S. Army on August 29, 1898. Soon after, the surgeon general asked McGee to write a section of the Army Reorganization Act to make nurses a permanent corps of the Medical Department of the Army. As a result, the ANC was established in 1901, making civilian employees into military ones. A Navy Nurse Corps was established in 1908. Women in both branches of the service were seen as now auxiliary to the military, though at the time they had neither rank nor equal pay.

Public Law 448 finally gave the contract nurses who served in the Spanish-American War the recognition they deserved. The passage of the Nineteenth Amendment in 1919, which gave women the vote, helped change the social climate of the nation and paved the way for Public Law 448. The practice of giving women the vote and rewarding them for their service, as with the contract nurses of the Spanish-American War, was indicative of the changing attitude towards women in the 1920s.

Jodie N. Mader

See also: Army Nurse Corps (ANC); Army Reorganization Act (1920); McGee, Anita Newcomb (1864–1940); Spanish-American War (1898).

References and Further Reading

Graf, Mercedes. *On the Field of Mercy: Women Medical Volunteers from the Civil War to the First World War.* Amherst, NY: Humanity Book, 2010.

Kalisch, P. A. "Heroines of '98: Female Army Nurses in the Spanish American War." *Nursing Research* 24, no. 6 (November–December 1974): 411–29.

McGee, Anita Newcome. *List of US Army Nurses Appointment on the Recommendation of the Daughters of the American Revolution Hospital Corps.* Washington, D.C.: National Society of the DAR, 1899.

Sarnecky, Mary T. *A History of the US Army Nurse Corps.* Philadelphia: University of Pennsylvania Press, 1999.

PUBLIC LAW 90-130 (1967)

Public Law 90-130 (PL 90-130), when passed into law in 1967, was a groundbreaking piece of legislation that eliminated many inequities for women's military service in the United States. This legislation improved women officers' career opportunities by opening up flag and general ranks to women, raising retirement ages, and allowing nonmedical female personnel to serve in the Air National Guard. In addition, PL 90-130 eliminated restrictions on how many women could comprise both the officer ranks and the military services in general; prior to 1967, women could make up no more than 2 percent of the total military strength. This law, for which civilian and military women fought for many years, paved the way for greater change in the American servicewoman's status in the 1970s and beyond.

Although PL 90-130 was not signed into law until 1967, the Defense Advisory Committee on Women in the Services (DACOWITS) began recommending in 1960 that the military should eliminate rank limitations on women. However, the leaders of the women's service components, namely the directors of the Women's Army Corps (WAC), the Women in the Air Force (WAF), the WAVES (women in the Navy), and the Women Marines, were concerned about maintaining women's status in the services and worried about pushing the Department of Defense for too much change as women established themselves in national defense.

A year later, things began to change when President John F. Kennedy created the President's Commission on the Status of Women to look at women's opportunities in American society and the workplace. The President's Commission on the Status of Women included a committee on federal employment policies and practices, chaired by former DACOWITS member and *Ladies Home Journal* editor Margaret Hickey. Under Hickey's leadership, the committee partnered with the current DACOWITS members to evaluate the status of servicewomen as employees and citizens.

DACOWITS continued to recommend to the Department of Defense that rank limitations be removed, and the President's Commission on the Status of Women made the same recommendation in its report to the president and the nation. By 1963, the Department of Defense conceded and added a rider to an officer's career bill already in front of Congress. That proposed bill's existing unpopularity, however, made passage difficult. The Department of Defense continued to reevaluate the bill and resubmit it while DACOWITS and women in the services continued to wait. Finally, in 1966, the Department of Defense separated the women's legislation from the current bill. This strategy worked, and House Resolution 5894 (HR 5894) came before Congress in early 1967.

During the four years between the legislation's first appearance in Congress and its actual passage in 1967, military women and members of DACOWITS lobbied in whatever ways they could to support the bill. Although DACOWITS members could not petition Congress in their capacity as DACOWITS members, as private citizens they could still support any legislation they wanted, and HR 5894 was one proposed law DACOWITS women particularly supported.

Part of the reason why female military leaders supported the legislation in the late 1960s was because the rank limitations on women's service became problematic as time went on. Women could not advance beyond lieutenant colonel in the Army, Air Force, or Marine Corps, nor beyond the somewhat equivalent captain rank in the Navy. One woman from each service component, including the Army and Navy Nurse Corps, could hold a temporary rank of colonel or captain while serving as the director of that component, but she then reverted to lieutenant colonel or commander status after stepping down from that role. Moreover, existing regulations limited the number of women who could hold the highest permanent ranks in each of the women's components. As more and more career women advanced through the ranks, too many women were stuck and unable to receive promotions because of the system in place. By the late 1960s, military experts began to estimate that without the removal of rank limitations that PL 90-130 offered, approximately 50 percent of women line officers would have left the services by the early 1970s because they could advance no further in their careers.

President Lyndon B. Johnson signed the legislation into law in the White House's Oval Office on November 8, 1967. In attendance were members of DACOWITS as well as servicewomen from all branches and all ranks. In his speech, Johnson hailed the legislation as an important advance and commented that it might one day be possible to have a woman president who would be commander-in-chief.

PL 90-130 opened positions for women other than nurses and medical specialists to serve in the Air National Guard for the first time. In addition, PL 90-130 removed the 2 percent ceiling on women's military service. Now women would not be limited to filling only a small portion of military openings but could in theory become a much larger part of the nation's defense team. Finally, PL 90-130 opened all officer ranks to women and removed the limitations on how many women could serve in each grade. The law did not assign any women to the general or flag ranks but did open the possibility of doing so in the future.

However, the legislative reports made it clear that the military's need for combat prevented women's total equality in the military: the Department of Defense confirmed that it would not try to use the legislation to remove other restrictions on women's military roles.

PL 90-130 opened the way for women to achieve at higher levels in the armed forces and to serve in a broader capacity than they had previously done. In 1971, the Army and the Army Nurse Corps promoted the first women to the rank of brigadier general, WAC Director Elizabeth Hoisington and Army Nurse Corps Chief Anna Mae Hays. The following year, Jeanne Holm of the Air Force received the same rank, and she would go on to receive promotion to major general in 1973. In November 2008, Ann Dunwoody became the first woman to attain the rank of four-star general, more than 30 years after the legislation passed.

Tanya L. Roth

See also: Air Force Nurse Corps (AFNC); Army Nurse Corps (ANC); Defense Advisory Committee on Women in the Services (DACOWITS); Dunwoody, Ann E. (1953–); Hays, Anna Mae McCabe (1920–); Hoisington, Elizabeth P. (1918–2007); Holm, Jeanne M. (1921–2010); Nursing; Women Accepted for Volunteer Emergency Service (WAVES); Women in the Air Force (WAF); Women Marines; Women's Armed Services Integration Act of 1948; Women's Army Corps (WAC).

References and Further Reading

Holm, Jeanne. *Women in the Military: An Unending Revolution*, rev. ed. Novato, CA: Presidio Press, 1993.

Morden, Bettie J. *The Women's Army Corps, 1945–1978*. Washington, D.C.: Center of Military History, 1989.

Murnane, Linda Strite. "Legal Impediments to Service: Women in the Military and the Rule of Law." *Duke Journal of Gender Law and Policy*, 14 (2007): 1061–96.

R

RATCLIFFE, LAURA (1836–1923)

Confederate nurse and spy Laura Ratcliffe aided Col. John Singleton Mosby and his men.

Ratcliffe was born on May 28, 1836, and attended school in Fairfax, Virginia. After her father died, the family moved to her mother's hometown, a crossroads in Fairfax County only 10 miles west of Washington, D.C., known as Frying Pan. Due to its location, Frying Pan was an area fraught with civil strife and military encounters during the war. Ratcliffe began nursing Confederate soldiers and serving as a spy for Mosby; one of her efforts saved the colonel and his men from a dangerous federal ambush near Frying Pan.

Ratcliffe's devotion to the Confederate soldiers she nursed drew the attention of Gen. J. E. B. Stuart, and they began a friendship. When he departed, he left several precious items in her possession along with two poems that he had written and dedicated to her. Stuart trusted Ratcliffe completely, and he introduced her to Mosby as someone who would be a valuable ally in the conduct of the war in that highly contested area of Virginia.

Mosby frequently used the Ratcliffe farm for his headquarters and for storing confiscated Yankee materials until they could be transferred to Confederate authorities. At Ratcliffe's suggestion, the Confederates used a large rock on the property, nicknamed Mosby's rock, to hide money and important documents or to move messages among troops in the area. In addition, Laura often delivered information in a false-bottomed egg basket. The federals repeatedly searched the farm and questioned Laura, but to no avail.

Ratcliffe saved Mosby's life in February 1863. Federal and Confederate cavalry troops were jockeying for supremacy around Frying Pan. Mosby, who set off to engage a federal picket posted near Frying Pan, walked into a Union trap. Hiding in the pines behind the picket was the 1st Virginia waiting to kill or capture him and his men. Fortunately for him, a talkative young soldier, who had stopped at Ratcliffe's home for milk, had bragged about the trap, dismissing her as a woman who could do no harm. Ratcliffe ran to alert her neighbors to watch for Mosby and warn him, but she found him herself and told him about the trap.

Impoverished after the war, Ratcliffe and her sister were befriended by an older Yankee gentleman, Milton Hanna, who lived nearby. He built them a new home so that he could watch over them, and after her sister died, he married Ratcliffe. Milton died seven years later, leaving Ratcliffe alone and wealthy. She used her inheritance to help the poor and to support local churches. She also took an active interest in managing her estates until an accident left her bedridden for the last nine years of her life.

Laura Ratcliffe Hanna died at the age of 87 in 1923.

Donna Cooper Graves

See also: Civil War (1861–1865); Espionage; Nursing.

References and Further Reading

Bakeless, John. *Spies of the Confederacy.* Philadelphia: J. B. Lippincott, 1970.

Eggleston, Larry G. *Women in the Civil War: Extraordinary Stories of Soldiers, Spies, Nurses, Doctors, Crusaders, and Others.* Jefferson, NC: McFarland, 2003.

Markle, Donald E. *Spies and Spymasters of the Civil War*, rev. ed. New York: Hippocrene Books, 2000.

Massey, Mary Elizabeth. *Women in the Civil War.* Lincoln: University of Nebraska Press, 1994. Original publication 1966 as *Bonnet Brigades.*

Simkins, Francis Butler, and James Welch Patton. *The Women of the Confederacy.* Richmond, VA: Garrett & Massie, 1936.

RATHBUN-NEALY (COLEMAN), MELISSA (1970–)

Melissa Rathbun-Nealy gained fame when she was captured in Iraq in January 1991 and held prisoner for 33 days.

Melissa Rathbun was born March 9, 1970, to Leo and Joan Rathbun. She lived in Grand Rapids, Michigan, where she attended Creston High School before enlisting in the Army in 1988. She married a fellow soldier, but the two divorced after a short time. In the Army, she became a driver in the 233rd Transportation Company.

When the Persian Gulf War began in 1990, Rathbun-Nealy and her company shipped out to Saudi Arabia. On January 30, 1991, Rathbun-Nealy and Specialist David Lockett were assigned to drive a heavy equipment transport (HET) to troops near the border of Kuwait and Saudi Arabia, when they and another vehicle took a wrong turn in the desert. Both vehicles were caught in a firefight near the city of Khafji, Saudi Arabia. The lead car was able to execute a U-turn and escape safely. However, Rathbun-Nealy's vehicle got bogged down in the sand. Iraqi forces later captured Rathbun-Nealy and Lockett. The two soldiers later reported that although their captors wanted to leave the injured Lockett behind, Rathbun-Nealy would not leave without him.

Two miles outside of the city, soldiers in the other vehicle met up with the 1st Marine Division and organized a search effort to find Rathbun-Nealy and Lockett. When they reached the site of the firefight, the Marines reportedly did not find blood or signs of fighting. However, they found scattered personal gear. Later, two captured Iraqi soldiers claimed to have witnessed the transport of an American woman and a black man somewhere near Bashrah, Kuwait, not far from where the firefight had occurred. Despite these reports, Rathbun-Nealy and Lockett were initially listed as "missing" by the Pentagon instead of as prisoners of war (POWs). Following public pressure to declare the two as POWs, on February 12 the Pentagon changed their status to missing in action (MIA). Officials still refused to list them as POWs, fearing public outrage that an American woman had been captured. In fact, their status was not changed to POW until their release on March 3, 1991, along with four other American POWs.

The capture and subsequent release of Rathbun-Nealy was a hot topic during the Gulf War. Out of 400,000 soldiers who served in Operation Desert Storm, 30,000 of these were women. Rathbun-Nealy was the first woman since World War II to be taken as a POW. The Pentagon was concerned that reports of female casualties or POWs would create negative press for the armed forces. In addition, the Pentagon was worried that the capture of these two high-profile targets—one African American and one woman—would raise questions about the armed forces' legacy of race and gender discrimination.

The Pentagon's solution to avoiding public controversy was to deny Rathbun-Nealy and Lockett's status as POWs. Because they were assigned to a noncombat mission, the Pentagon reasoned that they could only be listed as "missing" rather than MIA, a designation for troops missing in the line of combat. In addition, the Pentagon would not list them as POWs because they claimed that the eyewitness reports given by Iraqi POWs did not positively identify Rathbun-Nealy or Lockett. However, given that Rathbun-Nealy and Lockett were the only American woman and African American man thought to be captured together in Iraq, there could have been no doubt of their identification. Ironically, the Pentagon's policy of denial only served to bring the issue more prominently into the public eye.

The Pentagon's denial of the hostile capture of Rathbun-Nealy outraged the American public, which largely supported women's participation in Desert Storm. In addition, Americans questioned why the Pentagon needed to hide female POWs from the public. Concerns about how American women would be treated as POWs coupled with the Pentagon's denials only served to fuel speculation about her capture. The media sympathized with her father, Leo Rathbun, who worked to get the Pentagon to list her as a POW. Americans wanted Rathbun-Nealy to be recognized for her heroism and capture regardless of her gender.

Following Rathbun-Nealy's capture, the U.S. Senate Committee on Foreign Relations released a report on the Pentagon's policy towards POW/MIAs. The Committee charged the Pentagon with being too concerned with artificial restrictions and bureaucratic ideological concerns to find those who were missing. The report speculated that Rathbun-Nealy's and Lockett's absence from an official POW/MIA list would have made their release difficult if the Pentagon had to negotiate with Iraq for the release of POWs.

Tired of the spotlight, Rathbun-Nealy quietly married a fellow veteran, Michael Coleman, in March 1991. The couple has two daughters. They live in San Antonio, Texas.

Cheryl Dong

See also: All-Volunteer Force (AVF); Cornum, Rhonda (1954–); Gulf War (1991); Prisoners of War.

References and Further Reading

Francke, Linda Bird. *Ground Zero: The Gender Wars in the Military.* New York: Simon and Schuster, 1997.

Minority Staff of the U.S. Senate Committee on Foreign Relations. *An Examination of US Policy towards POW/MIAs.* Washington, D.C.: U.S. Senate Committee on Foreign Relations, 1991.

Nantais, Cynthia. "Women in the US Military: Protectors or Protected? The Case of Prisoner of War Melissa Rathbun-Nealy." *Journal of Gender Studies* 8, no. 2 (1999): 181.

Schubert, Frank N. *The Whirlwind War: The United States in Operation Desert Shield and Desert Storm.* Washington, D.C.: CMH Publications, 1995.

RAYE, MARTHA (1916–1994)

Award-winning actress, comedienne, singer, and radio and television performer Martha Raye became one of the first Hollywood entertainers to volunteer to perform for U.S. troops. Her numerous tours in World War II, Korea, and Vietnam earned her an "honorary colonel" designation by the U.S. Army.

The first child born to Irish immigrants and vaudeville couple Peter and Peggy (Hooper) Reed, Martha was born Margaret Teresa Yvonne Reed in a hospital charity ward on August 27, 1916, in Butte, Montana. She appeared in her parents' act when she was only three, dancing with her brother, Bud. Taught to read and write by her mother, she had a sporadic formal education, attending public schools in Montana, Chicago, and New York City.

At age 15, she was singing, dancing, and performing in a children's comedy act. Taking her stage name, Martha Raye, from a telephone book, she toured with her brother, sang as a band vocalist, and performed on radio, in nightclubs, and on Broadway. In 1936, she was signed by Norman Taurog at Paramount to sing the lead opposite Bing Crosby in *Rhythm on the Range*, a role that made her a star.

Nicknamed "Miss Big Mouth" for her wide mouth and raucous personality, her slapstick routines and musical talents landed her a number of roles, usually as a second banana. Married seven times, the last time to Mark Harris from 1991 until her death, Raye was popular on screen, on radio, in cabarets, and on stage for 70 years. She costarred with the best-known comedians and performers of her day, had her own TV show on NBC from 1954 to 1956, and won numerous awards, including a special Oscar in 1969 for her role in entertaining the troops. In 1974, the Screen Actors

Guild bestowed on her a Life Achievement Award.

When the United States entered World War II, Raye devoted much of her time to entertaining the military, even though she had a fear of flying. When her estranged husband, Neal Lang, was commissioned an Army captain, Raye's patriotism led her to volunteer for the first overseas entertainment unit, United Service Organizations (USO)-Camp Shows, Inc. On October 31, 1942, Raye joined fellow entertainers Kay Francis, Mitzi Mayfair, and Carole Landis and did weekly shows in England and North Africa. Their tour was the basis for the movie *Four Jills in a Jeep* (1944). In North Africa, Raye contracted yellow fever, which affected her health for years. Even after she returned to California in 1943, Raye offered room and board in her home to servicemen.

In 1952, Raye again volunteered to entertain the troops in South Korea, but she was so weakened from her previous bout with yellow fever that the tour lasted only a few weeks. The infection forced her to receive blood transfusions, which were gladly offered both by fellow entertainers and a Marine Corp battalion.

During the Vietnam War, Raye went on a number of USO tours in Southeast Asia. From 1964 to 1973, she made eight tours throughout Vietnam, usually for six months at a time and often at her own expense. She won several citations, including the title of honorary military colonel on July 19, 1969. Wounded several times during her visits with the Green Berets, they affectionately called her "Colonel Maggie." In a citation by President Lyndon B. Johnson, she was designated the only one outside the Green Berets allowed to wear their symbol. Though not technically a nurse, Raye used skills she learned as a nurse's aid at Cedars of Lebanon Hospital and in World War II to treat the wounded.

For her work with the troops in Southeast Asia, Raye received numerous awards and medals from such organizations as the American Legion, American Veterans of Foreign Wars, USO, and Freedom Foundation. Her volunteer work in Vietnam also made her unpopular with those in Hollywood who opposed the war. After years of civilian petitions to Congress, President Bill Clinton awarded to Raye the Presidential Medal of Freedom on November 2, 1993.

Raye spent her last years suffering from Alzheimer's disease, strokes, and circulatory problems. She died of pneumonia in Los Angeles, California, on October 19, 1994, and was buried with full military honors at the Fort Bragg Post Cemetery, Fort Bragg, North Carolina. The only woman to receive such an honor, her plaque reads simply "Martha Raye, Civilian."

Gary Kerley

See also: Korean War (1950–1953); Nursing; United Service Organizations (USO); Vietnam War (1965–1973); World War II (1941–1945).

References and Further Reading

Fortin, Noonie. *Memories of Maggie: A Legend Spanning Three Wars.* Austin, TX: Langmarc Publishing, 1995.

"Martha Raye." In *Hollywood Songsters: Singers Who Act and Actors Who Sing: A Biographical Dictionary.* Vol. 3, edited by

James Robert Parrish and Michael Pitts, 712–19. New York: Routledge, 2003.

Pitrone, Jean. *Take It from the Big Mouth: The Life of Martha Raye.* Lexington: University of Kentucky Press, 1999.

RED CROSS VOLUNTEER NURSE'S AIDE CORPS

The American Red Cross established the Volunteer Nurse's Aide Corps in 1941 in response to a request by the Office of Civilian Defense. The Volunteer Nurse's Aide Corps was part of a larger program by the Red Cross to use female volunteers to meet the growing needs of the United States during the war. These organizations included the Gray Lady Corps, which provided for the entertainment of hospital patients, and the Volunteer Dietitian's Aide Corps, which eased the shortage of certified dietitians in both military and civilian hospitals.

As the United States entered World War II, Red Cross and government officials knew that there would not be enough health care professionals to meet the growing health care demands of the military and civilian community. In particular, they were worried about the national shortage of nurses, people who were indispensible to ensuring a high level of care. Consequently, they decided to train and employ nurse's aides, laypeople trained in the basics of health care. The aides could take care of the routine work and thereby allow a nurse to take care of more patients than she normally could.

The Red Cross Volunteer Nurse's Aide Corps was a women's organization that offered opportunities to women with high school degrees and who were between the ages of 20 and 50. These nurse's aides would perform nontechnical work, such as acting as liaisons between nurses or doctors and patients. They would also take care of first aid, personal care of patients, and janitorial work in hospitals. The Red Cross required volunteers to complete an 80-hour training course and to commit to over 150 hours of community service each year. Red Cross officials saw this program not simply as a stopgap measure to provide emergency health care in wartime but also as a larger outreach program that would educate laywomen in public health issues of the day. The Red Cross wanted the Nurse's Aide Corps to be a training ground for future hospital board and committee members as well. Because hospital boards always included a number of upper-class, society women, the Nurse's Aide Corps ultimately provided a valuable introduction for these women into the daily operation of a hospital.

Despite the Red Cross's attempts to portray the fledgling volunteer organization as a controversy-free organization that would not take women outside of their traditional sphere of domestic influence, the Nurse's Aide Corps was a target of general public discontent about the growing role of women in public life. Nurses and women's military auxiliaries had come under conservative fire during World War II with opponents portraying them as loose women who shirked traditional responsibilities to their homes and families. In addition, many politicians worried about the breakdown of traditional gender roles as men left for war and women entered the workforce as their replacements, a concern voiced during all U.S. wars. The Volunteer

Nurse's Aide Corps was one target of this backlash against women's changing gender roles. The leaders of the Volunteer Nurse's Aide Corps were criticized. Again opponents portrayed the volunteers as flighty and loose women, and they criticized the organization for wasting public funds training women who would not commit to their work but would instead take advantage of hospital work to flirt with young soldiers who came to the hospital.

In an effort to head off this criticism, Jane Foster McConnell, assistant to the national director of the Volunteer Nurse's Aide Corps, insisted that most Volunteer Nurse's Aides were older women and that any "flighty" candidates would not be accepted into the program because they were unable to commit to the long hours required of volunteer nurse's aides. These statements sought to assure a wary public that the Red Cross workers were traditional housewives and mothers who did not leave the domestic sphere but merely acted out their domestic responsibilities in a larger space than just the home. Indeed, although many hospitals and hospital directors resisted the establishment of local chapters in their hospitals, thinking that the women would be a waste of precious resources and time, most hospital directors would come to recognize that these female volunteers provided valuable services and were indispensible to the continued success of the American health care system during World War II.

Between 1941 and 1945, 212,000 volunteers offered 42 million hours of service in the Nurse's Aide Corps. This massive turnout of volunteerism was the result of a massive recruitment effort by the American Red Cross, particularly in the closing years of the war as the military recruited more and more nurses from the civilian populations to take care of casualties from the war. Although the Red Cross liked to characterize the nurse's aide volunteers as mainly older women in their forties or fifties who were stay-at-home wives, many younger women also participated in the Nurse's Aide Corps as part of a larger fervor of patriotism and service during World War II. These women sometimes used the opportunity offered by the Red Cross Volunteer Nurse's Aide Corps to further their own careers despite popular belief that a woman's place was in the home. One young woman, Alice Snead, joined the Red Cross Volunteer Nurse's Aide Corps at age 20 and would volunteer at night, sometimes until 12:30 a.m., as she held a steady day job. Snead later used her Red Cross volunteer experience to secure a job as director of the Red Cross chapter in Wilmington, North Carolina.

With the end of the war in 1945, the Red Cross faced the dilemma of what to do with the massive womanpower that it had mobilized during the war. Like many other volunteer agencies, the Red Cross Volunteer Nurse's Aide Corps experienced firsthand wartime demobilization as nurses and doctors returned from military service to take over the positions they had left behind during the war. Suddenly, the volunteer women of the Nurse's Aide Corps were no longer needed. Some media outlets even expressed concern that the continued use of nurse's aides would put nurses and doctors returning from war out of work as hospitals sought to cut personnel costs. However, the Red Cross expressed conservative optimism that the program would continue to support communities that had shortages in nursing staff. The director of the National Volunteer Nurse's Aide Corps, Helen Byrne Lippmann, emphasized the importance of the achievements of the Corps in providing medical care and educating laypeople in the basics of household medicine. She pushed for the continuation in peacetime of a much smaller corps of volunteers that would continue the community building sponsored by the Nurse's Aide Corps. The continuation of the program allowed the Red Cross Nurse's Aide Corps to aid the military in the Korean War and later wars. The Red Cross continues to offer nurse's aide training.

The Red Cross Nurse's Aide Corps was a massive women's volunteer organization that influenced the lives of over 200,000 women during World War II. Despite its prominence and popularity during wartime, historians who study women's work and women's involvement in military service during World War II have largely overlooked the Red Cross Volunteer Nurse's Aide Corps in favor of higher profile women's organizations like the Red Cross nurses and other aide workers who served overseas during World War II. However, the massive participation on the homefront of female volunteers in the Red Cross Nurse's Aide Corps is important to our larger understanding of how World War II affected the depth and scope of women's work.

Cheryl Dong

See also: American Red Cross; American Women's Voluntary Services (AWVS); Gray Lady Corps; "Hello Girls"; Korean War (1950–1953); Nursing; Office of Civilian Defense (OCD); Vietnam War (1965–1973); World War II (1941–1945).

References and Further Reading

Kalisch, Philip A., and Margaret Scobey. "Female Nurses in American Wars: Helplessness Suspended for the Duration." *Armed Forces and Society* 9, no. 2 (1983): 215–44.

Lippmann, Helen Byrne. "The Future of the Red Cross Volunteer Nurse's Aide Corps." *American Journal of Nursing* 45, no. 10 (1945): 811–12.

McConnell, Jane Foster. "Volunteer Nurse's Aides: Six Months Experience with Them." *American Journal of Nursing* 42, no. 5 (1942): 507–510.

National Women's History Museum. "Red Cross." *Partners in Winning the War: American Women in World War II*. Alexandria, VA: National Women's History Museum, 2007.

Rath, Elizabeth H. "ARC Volunteer Nurse's Aides: Their Preparation and Introduction to Service." *American Journal of Nursing* 42, no. 7 (1942): 788–92.

Snead, Alice. Interview by Luann Mims. Transcript. William Madison Randall Library, Wilmington, NC, 2004.

Trott, Lona L. "It's Good That You Want to Help! The Red Cross Nurse's Aide Corps." *American Journal of Nursing* 40, no. 12 (1940): 1355–57.

REED, ESTHER DE BERDT (1746–1780)

Esther de Berdt Reed was a staunch supporter of the American Revolution. She publicly supported the Revolutionary cause and organized donation drives to benefit Continental soldiers. Reed's 1780 broadside, *The Sentiments of an American Woman*, launched Philadelphia women's fund-raising efforts in the Revolutionary War and is an example of early political action by women in America.

Born in London in 1746, Esther de Berdt was the only daughter of Dennis de Berdt, a wealthy merchant who traded with the colonies. As a result of his trading associations, he hosted many Americans at his home, including Joseph Reed, a law student from New Jersey. Esther and Reed met in 1763 and continued writing to each other after Reed finished his legal studies and returned to the colonies two years later. Reed came back to London in 1769 and married de Berdt. The next year, they moved to Philadelphia.

De Berdt Reed's loyalties to the British Crown waned after she moved to Pennsylvania. She likely shared the pro-American sympathies of her merchant father. Joseph Reed supported the Revolution and joined George Washington's staff in 1775. He served first as aide de camp and then as adjutant general. Reed left Washington's staff in late 1778 to become the president of Pennsylvania, a post equivalent to governor.

De Berdt Reed and other women thrust themselves into patriotic action in 1780 after sensing a loss of public morale in wake of the British capture of Charleston. De Berdt Reed spearheaded the effort by publishing *The Sentiments of an American Woman* on June 10. The broadside, which would help lead de Berdt Reed into the presidency of the Ladies' Association of Philadelphia, drew on past examples of women's patriotism and argued that women had an equal duty to men to support the Revolutionary cause. *The Sentiments*

preemptively silenced any potential detractors to the idea of women activists by branding critics unpatriotic.

With the women of Philadelphia called to action by the broadside, de Berdt Reed organized the Ladies' Association to raise funds for Continental soldiers. She suggested that ladies give up unnecessary luxuries and donate the money they saved to the troops. The association garnered much attention because the highest classes of women supported it. In addition, de Berdt Reed received assistance from Benjamin Franklin's daughter, Sarah Franklin Bache. The women divided Philadelphia into 10 districts and went door to door asking women and girls from all levels of society to donate. Loyalists suggested that many donated simply in order to get rid of the women. The association's fund-raising raised nearly $300,000 in paper money. Unfortunately, wartime inflation meant that that amount only converted to about $7,500 in hard specie.

De Berdt Reed originally planned to give the soldiers something that they were not already provided by the army. She suggested to Washington that the converted money be divided up so that each soldier could be given a few dollars worth of gold or silver. Washington did not like this plan for two reasons. First, he feared that discontent would emerge if soldiers accustomed to receiving devalued paper money suddenly had gold in their pockets. Second, Washington worried that soldiers would spend the money on hard liquor. Washington recommended that de Berdt Reed deposit the paper money in the Bank of the United States to be used for soldiers' pay. Donating the money to the bank did not fit with the Ladies' Association's intent of giving the soldiers something that the army could not provide. Washington then proposed that the money be used to furnish linen shirts. De Berdt Reed, realizing the general would not go along with her initial plan for the money, reluctantly agreed to provide shirts to the army.

De Berdt Reed never saw the conclusion of her patriotic fund-raising efforts; she died on September 18, 1780, in a dysentery epidemic. Bache took over the Ladies' Association and completed the delivery of about 2,000 shirts to the army. Although she died before the Revolution's completion, de Berdt Reed inspired similar fund-raising action in New Jersey, Maryland, and Virginia. Originally taking part in unfeminine tasks of political activism and fund-raising, the Ladies' Association ironically led to the formation of sewing circles, which aided the Revolutionary cause but not in the way de Berdt Reed intended. However, historians link *The Sentiments of an American Woman* and its author to subsequent women's political actions such as abolitionist campaigns in the early 19th century.

J. Hendry Miller

See also: American Revolution (1775–1783); Bache, Sarah "Sally" Franklin (1743–1808); Ladies' Association.

References and Further Reading

Diamant, Lincoln, ed. *Revolutionary Women in the War for American Independence: A One Volume Revised Edition of Elizabeth Ellet's 1848 Landmark Series.* Westport, CT: Praeger, 1998.

Kerber, Linda K. *Women of the Republic: Intellect and Ideology in Revolutionary America.* Chapel Hill: University of North Carolina Press, 1980.

Norton, Mary Beth. *Liberty's Daughters: The Revolutionary Experience of American Women, 1750–1800.* Boston: Little, Brown, and Company, 1980.

REPUBLIC OF TEXAS

The Republic of Texas was created after the Mexican War. Women of various backgrounds and races played parts in the fight to create an independent Texas.

Mexico gained independence from Spain in 1821, but the new country's relationship with Native groups to the north was shaky. Native American groups had populated the region long before American migration into Texas. They often raided and fought with local and Native enemies as well as local Hispanic inhabitants. Often, they captured women from rival tribes and communities. Women were valuable to Indian groups as a source of labor, both physical and reproductive. Native Americans required gift giving from their Mexican neighbors, but the fledgling nation of Mexico was financially and politically unable to support the tribute. Native groups, especially the Comanche, encouraged Mexicans living in current-day New Mexico to become semiautonomous and trade with Americans along the Santa Fe Trail to increase the region's success. This alignment with Americans, who illegally and legally settled in modern-day Texas, strengthened northern Mexico's desire to leave Mexico City's domain.

American newcomers to this region, Texans, felt threatened by Mexico's requirements that they convert to Catholicism to become citizens. They also resented Mexico's stance against slavery because many of the American newcomers brought their slaves to the region with them and expected to be able to keep them. In any case, white settlers continued to move to the Texas region and make their mark on the area. After forming their communities, settlers established churches and schools. Although the Mexican government barred Protestants from worshiping in public, settlers built churches and worshiped.

White American women moved to Texas for a number of reasons. They traveled by themselves, with groups, or with their husbands. Their background knowledge of the frontier varied, with some women knowing what to expect and others being ignorant of the conditions of life on the frontier. In addition, many black female slaves migrated to the region with their owners, and most often they had to submit to harsh conditions. Regardless of race, women lived alongside groups or with their husbands in makeshift houses until they could build substantial structures.

In 1832, during the heightening of tensions in northern Mexico, Antonio Lopez de Santa Anna, a military leader and politician, officially took control of Mexico City. Santa Anna seized control by disregarding constitutional law and breaking up Mexico's nation states. Santa Anna refused to grant northern Mexico its independence. In response, Texans adopted their own constitution on November 3, 1835. They hoped to garner assistance from Mexicans upset with Santa Anna and the Mexican government as well as from Native American groups upset with their treatment by the Mexicans.

In 1835, a raid aimed at Mexican rule increased the warfare in northern Mexico until approximately 500 Texans took arms and captured San Antonio's military headquarters. To crush the rebellion, Santa Anna sent his undertrained and underequipped army of 7,000 to San Antonio. Sam Houston, the leader of the Texan army, ordered his men to vacate San Antonio, and they took refuge in the abandoned Spanish mission the Alamo. For 12 days Santa Anna's army besieged the Alamo, and on March 6, 1836, they climbed over the walls and took the fort. However, the Mexican army sustained over 1,000 casualties to gain the victory. Two weeks later, the Mexican army captured 350 Texan soldiers. Instead of taking them prisoners of war, they killed all of them. Houston called for recruits, and his army swelled to 800. On April 21, the now-trained Texan army surprised the Mexican army camped along the San Jacinto River. The next day, the Texans captured Santa Anna and forced him to sign a treaty granting Texas its independence. The Texas Republic created its own constitution, which alienated most Mexicans, and soon began to question its identity as separate from the United States. The issue of annexation would become the biggest debate of the next decade.

During the war, women's roles in the area barely changed. Hispanic women traditionally held loyalties to Mexico. The Texan army occasionally put Hispanic women to work as cooks or laborers. White women aided the war effort in any way they could. Affluent women gave money or cattle, while those with less means made ammunition and donated goods. Regardless of their stance, women of all ethnicities had to take care of their families, livestock, and crops after the men of their family left to join the army. Because they were alone without male protectors in the territory, white women had a particular fear of Santa Anna's army invading Texas. As Santa Anna approached and Houston retreated, women and their families began fleeing their homes to find safety. The mass evacuation of civilians, which began in February 1836, became known as the Runaway Scrape. Texans had to deal with the consequences of the mass dislocations as they worked to create and solidify the newly formed Republic of Texas.

Allyson Perry

See also: Hispanic American Women; Native American Women.

References and Further Reading

DeLay, Brian. *War of a Thousand Deserts: Indian Raids and the U.S.-Mexican War.* New Haven, CT: Yale University Press, 2008.

Howe, Daniel Walker. *What Hath God Wrought: The Transformation of America, 1815–1848.* New York: Oxford University Press, 2007.

Malone, Ann Patton. *Women on the Texas Frontier: A Cross-Culture Perspective.* El Paso: Texas Western Press, 1983.

RESERVE OFFICER TRAINING CORPS (ROTC)

The Reserve Officer Training Corps (ROTC) is a military program that trains college students to become officers for the Air Force, Navy, and Army. Today, ROTC is an elective program open to any male or female student. However, ROTC originally developed in the mid-19th century as a compulsory military training program for all male college students at public institutions receiving federal funds. The initial intent was that training civilians with some military background could be useful in the event of mass wartime mobilization.

Today, some ROTC students receive scholarships to help them pay for their college education, with the expectation that when they graduate from college they will serve for several years in the military. The ROTC program offers the military an alternate source of officer acquisition beyond the federally funded military academies. Students enrolled in ROTC attend one or two extra military science courses each semester in addition to their regular academic course load. They also participate in physical education and weapons training regularly. Although men have participated in ROTC programs around the United States since ROTC's creation, women have only been permitted to be members of the program since the Cold War. In particular, women have been permanent members of ROTC since 1968, aside from a temporary experiment in women's ROTC in the mid-1950s. Before 1968, women could participate only in ROTC "auxiliaries" designed to support men in ROTC.

Following the 1948 Women's Armed Services Integration Act, which admitted women permanently to the military, only the Air Force created an ROTC program for women. In the mid-1950s, the Women in the Air Force (WAF) ROTC was a short-lived experiment designed to help the WAF acquire officer candidates directly from college. This program allowed for the possibility of training women before they graduated rather than simply acquiring them after graduation. The WAF ROTC program was considered experimental and was instituted only at 10 institutions nationwide, including Pennsylvania State University, Butler University, Miami University of Ohio, George Washington University, and six state universities. These institutions were tasked to implement ROTC programs for women who met specific criteria, with a goal of 10 new WAF officers each year.

WAF ROTC members, called "cadettes," did not complete weapons training programs because women were not authorized to carry firearms. However, the members of WAF ROTC pursued the same types of classroom training that women would receive in regular officer training school in the Air Force at that time. Even so, they were not eligible for the types of scholarships that today define ROTC service. In all, the program resulted in only seven new WAF officers, partially because the program allowed women to leave at any time without penalty. The Air Force determined that the program had not been successful and ordered the closure of the WAF ROTC programs in July 1960.

During the 1960s, the ROTC program underwent major changes as a result of pressures from the Vietnam War and the accompanying draft. At select colleges, ROTC stopped being a compulsory program for male students beginning in 1963. To entice students to join the program, the military created new scholarship programs that would help students pay for college. By the end of the decade, other changes in women's status in particular, along with the growing need to develop an officer cadre from the ROTC components, led the Air Force to announce it would open its ROTC program to women once again.

Beginning in 1969, the Air Force ROTC admitted women to ROTC programs around the nation. Initially, these women competed for scholarships on an unequal basis with men, a problem that took several years to work out completely. By the mid-1970s, women were competing equally with men for ROTC scholarships. The Air Force ROTC discovered that, unlike in the 1950s, incorporating women into ROTC worked successfully. Women responded positively to the opportunity of ROTC service and scholarship and began joining ROTC in large numbers. Initially restricted to four schools, by 1972, the Air Force ROTC was training women at 156 schools around the nation.

Once the Air Force opened its program to women, the other branches' ROTC divisions followed suit. In 1972, the Army ROTC and Navy ROTC opened their own test programs. Again, all branches found that women saw the program as attractive and joined eagerly, often competing against men in the scholarship contests. The Army commissioned its first female ROTC graduates in 1975 and 1976. Initially hesitant about how many women to admit to the ROTC programs, primarily because of the more restrictive roles women played in national defense, ROTC ultimately worked well for women because of other changes in women's military status over the course of the decade.

By the end of the 1970s, women could serve at sea in the Navy and the Air Force and were beginning to fly planes. With fewer restrictions on the job opportunities women could hold across the armed forces, ROTC became an increasingly useful means of securing vital officer strength in all military branches nationwide.

During the 1980s and 1990s, ROTC programs continued to grow. The Navy, Air Force, and Army ROTC programs all began to offer nursing scholarships, which also helped increase opportunities for women.

The Army ROTC estimates that women account for 20 percent of its ROTC members and 15 percent of all officers commissioned through the program. ROTC graduates completed at least three years of active military service, or four years for scholarship recipients. Select occupations in the Air Force require service commitments of up to 10 years of active service. In general, the opening of ROTC to women continues to provide an excellent resource for the acquisition of American womanpower.

Tanya L. Roth

See also: Cold War (ca. 1947–1991); Nursing; Vietnam War (1965–1973); Women Accepted for Volunteer Emergency Service (WAVES); Women in the Air Force (WAF); Women Marines; Women's Armed Services Integration Act of 1948; Women's Army Corps (WAC).

References and Further Reading

Holm, Jeanne. *Women in the Military: An Unending Revolution*, rev. ed. Novato, CA: Presidio Press, 1993.

Nieberg, Michael S. *Making Citizen-Soldiers: ROTC and the Ideology of American Military Service.* Cambridge, MA: Harvard University Press, 2000.

REYNOLDS, ARABELLA "BELLE" (1843–1930)

A nurse and "major" during the Civil War, Arabella Reynolds spent much of the war near the front lines.

Arabella Loomis Macomber was born in Shelbourne Falls, Massachusetts, on October 20, 1843, to a well-connected local family. Her hometown was a stop along the Underground Railroad, and she grew up hearing many stories of the horrors of slavery and miraculous escapes from it. These experiences led her to identify strongly with abolitionism and the Union.

In April 1860, Macomber married William S. Reynolds, a druggist, and the couple moved to Peoria, Illinois. In 1861, William Reynolds enlisted in the 17th Illinois Infantry and was moved to the front. In August 1861, Arabella joined her husband at Bird's Point, Missouri, and followed his regiment to various stations, experiencing the same food, general living conditions, and marches as the soldiers.

Belle Reynolds tended wounded soldiers during the October 21, 1861, Battle of Fredericktown, Missouri, regardless of the uniform the soldiers wore. She nursed soldiers again following the Battle at Fort Henry (February 6, 1862). At the start of the Battle of Shiloh (April 6–7, 1862), she began to dress soldiers' wounds. When the wounded were ordered to be moved to ships in the Tennessee River where they could be better attended, she went there. On board the Union steamer *Emerald*, Reynolds worked continuously for 36 hours attending to the needs of 350 wounded men on board. Exhausted and ill, she returned to Illinois on the steamer *Blackhawk*. Her heroism at Shiloh had already made her a local heroine, and several prominent Illinoisans suggested that she deserved to be honored. Upon her return in May 1862, Gov. Richard Yates bestowed upon her the rank of major for her service and bravery during the Battle of Shiloh. Although the title was honorific, she was regarded locally as a heroine.

Not content to remain on the sidelines for long, Reynolds returned to the front to be with her husband. They saw action in Mississippi and at Vicksburg, where she attended to more wounded men. In the spring of 1864, Reynolds and her husband returned to Peoria, where she remained until her death in 1930. For the remainder of her long life, Reynolds was active in the American Red Cross and maintained a public image in an era in which women were normally not allowed such activity.

Rebecca Tolley-Stokes

See also: American Red Cross; Camp Followers; Civil War (1861–1865); Nursing.

References and Further Reading

Leonard, Elizabeth D. *All the Daring of the Soldier: Women of the Civil War Armies.* New York: W. W. Norton, 1999.

"Major Belle Reynolds." *New York Times*, March 15, 1896, 16.

Moore, Frank. *Women of the War: Their Heroism and Self-sacrifice: True Stories of Brave Women in the Civil War.* Alexander, NC: Blue Gray Books, 1997.

Tsui, Bonnie. *She Went to the Field: Women Soldiers of the Civil War.* Guilford, CT: TwoDot, 2003.

RINKER, MOLLY "OLD MOM" (N.D.–N.D.)

Patriot and Philadelphia tavern owner Molly "Old Mom" Rinker served as a spy for the Continental Army during the Revolutionary War.

Although women did not receive permanent status in the U.S. armed forces until the passage of the Women's Armed Service Integration Act in 1948, they have played critical roles in all American wars. During the Revolution, many women served as nurses, cooks, and laundresses for the Continental Army. Some women served as spies, crossing enemy lines to gather intelligence on troop movements.

Rinker was active during the British occupation of the colonial capital of Philadelphia and particularly helpful during the Battle of Germantown on October 4, 1777. Rinker is reported to have taken advantage of the rugged terrain of the Wissahickon Valley to aid Gen. George Washington as he planned his attack on the British position. According to reports, Rinker sat atop a rock overlooking the valley pretending to knit. From time to time she dropped balls of yarn down the steep cliffs that American spies later retrieved. Inside the balls of yarn were messages about

British troop movements. As a result, Rinker's knitting served two purposes. Not only did it allow her to pass concealed messages to the Patriots, but it also demonstrated her dedication to the cause and her support of the boycott of British goods. Rinker also gathered information from the British soldiers who came into her tavern. Her occupation, her gift for observation, and her ability to knit helped to keep her above suspicion and to make her an excellent spy.

Rinker's contributions to the war effort during the crucial Battle of Germantown aided the nation. Gen. John Armstrong, who led troops under Washington that day, is reported as saying he was convinced that without this brave woman his troops would have been doomed. Although the battle ended as a British victory, it proved to be a turning point for the fledgling United States. Washington's bravery and audacity as he led the Continental Army against Sir William Howe and his British troops at Germantown seem to have so impressed France and its foreign minister, Comte de Vergennes, that the French decided after this battle to lend more assistance to the Americans.

Rinker, a patriot, tavern keeper, clandestine scout, and knitter, helped in some way to turn the tide of war in favor of the budding nation. There is a ridge on the eastern side of Philadelphia's Fairmount Park named Mom Rinker's Rock in her honor.

Kathryn A. Broyles

See also: American Revolution (1775–1783); Espionage; Women's Armed Service Integration Act of 1948.

References and Further Reading

Anderson, Laurie H. *Independent Dames: What You Never Knew about the Women and Girls of the American Revolution.* New York: Simon & Schuster, 2008.

Claghorn, Charles Eugene. *Women Patriots of the American Revolution: A Biographical Dictionary.* Metuchen, NJ: Scarecrow Press, 1991.

Fiske, John. *The American Revolution: In Two Volumes.* New York: Houghton, Mifflin and Company, 1892.

Hunter, Darren. "In Search of Molly Rinker." *Philadelphia History Examiner*, Nov. 11, 2010.

McGuire, Thomas J. *The Philadelphia Campaign.* Vol. 2: *Germantown and the Roads to Valley Forge.* Mechanicsburg, PA: Stackpole Books, 2007.

RODGERS, MARIE LOUISE (1926–)

Marie Louise Rodgers is an Army Nurse Corps (ANC) veteran of the Korean and Vietnam Wars and a recipient of the Bronze Star Medal.

Rodgers was born on September 24, 1926, and raised in Birmingham, Alabama, a center of iron and steel production that earned a reputation for racial discord during the civil rights movement. In the Jim Crow era, African American women in that city often found their career opportunities limited to domestic service. Rodgers, however, avoided the low wages, backbreaking labor, and sexual exploitation frequently encountered by African American domestics by enrolling in St. Louis, Missouri's Homer G. Phillips Hospital Nursing School.

Rodgers received a first-rate education at Phillips, one of the few nationally recognized and fully equipped hospitals open to prospective African American doctors, nurses, and technicians. After graduating as a registered nurse, she embarked on a remarkable career. In 1952, Rodgers joined the ANC, a branch of the U.S. Army Medical Department established in 1901. During the Korean War, the first conflict involving U.S. troops after President Harry S. Truman's Executive Order 9981 integrated the armed forces, Rodgers served as an operating room nurse in Puerto Rico. In 1955, Rodgers's committed service earned her a promotion from second lieutenant to first lieutenant. Two years later, she again ascended the officer ranks with a promotion to captain. While gaining valuable experience, Rodgers envied the experiences of her friends who had experienced combat during World War II, and she yearned for a chance to test herself in a similar situation.

The intensification of the Vietnam War afforded Rodgers the opportunity she had long desired. In 1966, after deployments in Paris and elsewhere, Rodgers volunteered for service in Vietnam, where she achieved the rank of major and became a surgical nurse at the 24th Evacuation Hospital at Long Binh Post, the largest U.S. army base in that country. The 24th Evacuation Hospital was particularly busy as its medical staff treated 9,010 patients during its first year of operation and returned 3,782 to active duty. In 1967, such exemplary service earned the hospital a Meritorious Unit Citation, an award that reflects Rodgers's hard work as she ran the operating room for nearly one year.

Due to the unconventional nature of the Vietnam War, many nurses in the ANC faced a significant level of danger and exposure to enemy fire. Although Rodgers escaped injury, as a surgical nurse she confronted the harsh realities of the war. Her unit specialized in cranium, neurological, and facial injuries. She remembers treating fatal cases including the head injuries of a soldier she later placed in a body bag. In September 1967, Rodgers was discharged from duty in Vietnam and returned to the United States, where she took a position at Washington, D.C.'s Walter Reed Army Hospital, the U.S. Army's flagship medical center. Her service in Vietnam, however, was not forgotten.

On November 8, 1967, Rodgers took part in a pivotal moment for women's rights. That day, President Lyndon B. Johnson signed Public Law 90-130, an act that opened advanced military ranks to women and increased the quota for women in the military. While celebrating this event in front of members of Congress, Vice President Hubert Humphrey, and prominent women from across the country, Johnson honored Rodgers by presenting to her the Bronze Star, an award given to military personnel who distinguish themselves in a combat theater. Johnson lauded Rodgers's selfless, compassionate, and professional service in Vietnam.

Rodgers continued to garner professional acclaim in later years. In July 1971, Rodgers, now a lieutenant colonel, began working as the chief of the operating room nursing section at San Francisco, California's Letterman Army Medical Center. At Letterman, Rodgers and other staff helped train approximately one-quarter of the Army's medical personnel and treat hundreds of wounded Vietnam veterans. In 1972, she received the Evangeline G. Bovard Award for being that year's most outstanding Letterman nurse.

Six years later, Rodgers retired with the rank of colonel. Most recently, she volunteered in the pharmacy at the Veteran's Affairs Hospital in El Paso, Texas. In reflecting back on her career, Rodgers notes the unique opportunity afforded to her by the Army and the pride that her career instilled in her father and other African Americans in Birmingham.

Brandon R. Byrd

See also: African American Women; Army Nurse Corps (ANC); Executive Order 9981 (July 26, 1948); Korean War (1950–1953); Nursing; Public Law 90-130 (1967); Vietnam War (1965–1973).

References and Further Reading

Latty, Yvonne. *We Were There: Voices of African American Veterans, from World War II to the War in Iraq.* New York: HarperCollins Publishers, 2004.

Norman, Elizabeth M. *Women at War: The Story of Fifty Military Nurses Who Served in Vietnam.* Philadelphia: University of Pennsylvania Press, 1990.

Vuic, Kara Dixon. *Officer, Nurse, Woman: The Army Nurse Corps in the Vietnam War.* Baltimore, MD: Johns Hopkins University Press, 2009.

ROGERS, EDITH NOURSE (1881–1960)

Edith Nourse Rogers served as a Massachusetts congresswoman from 1925 to 1960. Her 35 years of service made her the longest-serving woman in congressional history.

Edith Nourse was born on March 19, 1881, in Saco, Maine, to Franklin and Frances Riversmith Nourse. Her father managed a textile factory in Lowell, Massachusetts. She was educated in Lowell and France. In 1907, she married attorney John Rogers, and the couple settled in Lowell. Her husband successfully ran for Congress in 1912. Nourse Rogers began her career in public service during World War I as a volunteer inspector of field hospitals for the Women's Overseas Service League and as a Red Cross worker in Washington, D.C. She ran for Congress to fill the seat left vacant by her husband upon his death, winning the election with 72 percent of the vote in a special election in June 1925.

During her years in Congress, Nourse Rogers championed many causes. She represented Massachusetts' Fifth District in the northeastern part of the state, which was the center of the textile industry. Throughout her career, she was especially interested in foreign relations, women's rights, and veterans' affairs. She was an advocate for child labor reform, the 48-hour work week for women, and equal pay for equal work.

The contributions of American men and women during World War I greatly influenced Nourse Rogers's long congressional career. She fought for veterans' benefits for women who had served overseas during the war and helped secure pensions for army nurses after the war. She wanted to ensure that women who served in future wars would be well trained and receive pay and benefits equal to their male counterparts.

She supported the Veterans Administration Act of 1930 and served on the congressional Veterans Affairs committee. Nourse Rogers was instrumental in acquiring major appropriations for Veterans Administration hospitals.

In the spring of 1941, Nourse Rogers planned to introduce a bill in Congress that would establish a women's army corps to give women volunteer opportunities to serve their country during wartime. She wanted full military status for women who served and the same pensions, disability protection, and rights as men. Her actions brought about an immediate reaction from the Army. Chief of staff Gen. George C. Marshall asked her to delay the introduction of the bill so the Army could study the issue. An internal Army memo indicated that Army officials wanted to have control over any women's corps, something that seemed to be an unwelcome inevitability.

In May 1941, Nourse Rogers introduced the bill. It was referred to committee, where it languished. That fall, Marshall and other Army staff, anticipating a shortage of personnel should the United States enter the war, began to change their stance to one favoring the establishment of a women's corps. Shortly after the Japanese bombed Pearl Harbor on December 7, 1941, Nourse Rogers reintroduced her bill to the House Military Affairs Committee. The Women's Army Auxiliary Corps (WAAC) bill proposed to give female volunteers age 21 to 45 the opportunity to volunteer not as part of the Regular Army but as an auxiliary unit. Heated debate ensued. On March 17, the House passed the bill with a 249–86 vote. The Senate passed it on May 14, 1942,

with a 38–27 vote. On May 15, 1942, President Franklin D. Roosevelt signed it into law.

The first women were inducted into the WAAC in July 1942 and began training for noncombat positions that would free male army personnel for combat duties. In 1943, Nourse Rogers introduced the Women's Army Corps (WAC) bill that made women part of the Regular Army and eligible for military benefits.

During and after the war, Nourse Rogers continued her work for soldiers and veterans. She sponsored and helped draft the Servicemen's Readjustment Act of 1944 (the G.I. Bill of Rights Act), which Roosevelt signed into law in June 1944. The program gave veterans up to one year's unemployment compensation and made low-interest loans available for home mortgages or to start businesses. Money for college or vocational training was also part of the G.I. Bill.

Nourse Rogers also worked for women's rights. In 1945, she joined Senator Margaret Chase Smith in authoring an Equal Rights Amendment, which failed to pass Congress. Their Equal Rights Amendment was the first one to be introduced by women.

Following World War II, Nourse Rogers maintained a strong stance against the spread of communism. She supported the work of the House Un-American Activities Committee (HUAC). Although she favored the establishment of the United Nations, she opposed admitting communist China.

Following the Korean War, Nourse Rogers again advocated for veterans when she sponsored the Korean War Veterans Benefits Bill. She was recognized by the

American Legion with its Distinguished Service Medal in appreciation of her work for veterans. It was the first time the award was given to a woman.

In the fall of 1960, Edith Nourse Rogers was engaged in her 19th campaign for Congress but was plagued by poor health. She died on September 10, 1960.

Cheryl Mullenbach

See also: American Red Cross; Cold War (ca. 1947–1991); Korean War (1950–1953); Women's Army Auxiliary Corps (WAAC); Women's Army Corps (WAC); World War I (1914–1918); World War II (1941–1945).

References and Further Reading

Bandel, Betty. *An Officer and a Lady: The World War II Letters of Lt. Col. Betty Bandel, Women's Army Corps*, edited by Sylvia J. Bugbee. Lebanon, NH: University Press of New England, 2004.

Monahan, Evelyn, and Rosemary Neidel Greenlee. *A Few Good Women*. New York: Anchor Books, 2010.

Morden, Bettie J. *The Women's Army Corps, 1945–1978*. Washington, D.C.: Center of Military History, U.S. Army, 2000.

Treadwell, Mattie E. *United States Army in World War II, Special Studies, The Women's Army Corps*. Washington, D.C.: Center of Military History, U.S. Army, 1953.

Yellin, Emily. *Our Mothers' War*. New York: Free Press, 2004.

ROOSEVELT, ELEANOR (1884–1962)

Anna Eleanor Roosevelt Roosevelt was a first lady and social activist who

Eleanor Roosevelt was the first wife of a president to use her unique position to fight for the rights of minorities, women, and the destitute. After her husband died, Roosevelt expanded her responsibilities, serving as U.S. delegate to the United Nations and chairing the committee that drafted the Universal Declaration of Human Rights. (Library of Congress)

campaigned for the rights of women, the poor, and those serving in the United States armed forces.

Born October 11, 1884, to a wealthy family in New York City, Roosevelt had a difficult childhood culminating with the death of her mother and subsequent incarceration of her father in an institution. Roosevelt lived with her grandmother until 1899, when she moved to England to attend the Allenswood Academy. She moved back to the United States in 1901 and became engaged to Franklin Delano Roosevelt (FDR), her fifth cousin once removed, in 1903. The pair had six children, one of whom died in infancy. During the early years of her marriage, Roosevelt's focus was primarily on caring for her family. This focus began to change after World War I broke out in 1914.

Although many other progressive politicians and their families were opposed to the United States building a stronger military, FDR was an interventionist who wanted the United States to join World War I on behalf of the Allies. Therefore, Roosevelt, respectful of her husband's views, also opted not to participate in the antimilitarist movement. When the United States finally entered the war in 1917, Roosevelt immediately became involved. She worked with the local chapter of the American Red Cross, where she balanced the books, served food to soldiers who were leaving from Union Station, and served in any capacity that she could. She was also active in the Navy League's Comfort Committee, which had volunteers knit sweaters, socks, and other items for soldiers serving abroad. Roosevelt also visited the Naval Hospital regularly, attempting to cheer up the wounded and offering to help the families of those impacted by the war appeal for claims. Disturbed by the poor conditions she found in federal hospitals, she began to petition the government to improve them.

During World War I, Roosevelt also did her part within her home, finding ways to cut waste and limit the amount of certain foods that her family consumed, such as meat. Her efforts did not go unnoticed as Herbert Hoover's Food Administration selected her household as a model of how large houses should be run during wartime. Even though Roosevelt often felt fatigue, she reasoned that her sacrifices were worth it when she thought about events in Europe. She had

desperately wanted to volunteer overseas, but having so many young children made it impossible.

Roosevelt's life was transformed in 1921 when FDR contracted polio. Roosevelt became extremely active during the 1920s, vowing to keep her husband's interests and political ambitions alive. She also embraced the 1920s peace movement because she believed that she now understood the true costs of war. In 1932, FDR was elected to the office of president of the United States. Roosevelt transformed the role of first lady. She took her duties seriously. She was always willing to entertain when called upon and always supported and deferred to her husband. However, she was more active than any first lady before her and used her position as a platform for her social activism. She began writing a column six days a week entitled *My Day*, in which she discussed her day-to-day life as well as issues about which she was concerned. Because FDR's disease limited his mobility, she served as his eyes and ears, often traveling throughout the United States for him. She was able to see firsthand the conditions that many Americans were living in during the Great Depression, and she pushed FDR into helping solve the issues that the nation was facing.

Even as the United States was trying to focus on domestic issues during the 1930s, Roosevelt knew what was going on politically in Europe and was especially concerned about Adolf Hitler's many violations of human rights in Germany. Roosevelt was not a proponent of war and had embraced the peace movement of the 1920s, but she came to believe, like most of the country, that war would be necessary to defeat the forces of fascism. Although she always hoped for a world of peace and stability, she recognized that military force was sometimes necessary to achieve these goals. With Germany's invasion of Poland on September 1, 1939, Roosevelt realized that the United States would become entangled in this conflict.

After the Japanese bombed Pearl Harbor on December 7, 1941, the United States entered World War II. Roosevelt immediately began to rally the American people around the war effort. All four of her sons joined the military and were fighting overseas, so she could relate to ordinary Americans who were making sacrifices for the war.

Beginning in 1941, Roosevelt worked with the Office of Civilian Defense (OCD), which was charged with rallying Americans around the war and boosting morale at home. Roosevelt hoped OCD would be able to get millions of volunteers to help with the war effort. However, when she felt that her presence was hurting the OCD rather than helping it, she resigned in February 1942 and concentrated on other ways that she could help the country. Like she had done during the Great Depression, she again traveled throughout the United States, this time visiting defense plants. She used her column *My Day* to promote the war effort and to offer encouragement to those who were fighting the war both at home and abroad. One of the ways in which Roosevelt tried to help was by urging women, both married and single, to take jobs outside of the home. Many women heeded her call, and Roosevelt always made sure to ask when traveling how the female workers were performing. She often wrote about these "Rosie the Riveters" in *My Day*.

Roosevelt also fulfilled her desire to go and support the troops overseas. She traveled to England, Latin America, and the South Pacific hoping to raise morale among troops and boost confidence among the Allies. She was known for making the servicemen feel extremely comfortable and filling them with stories of the homefront. She visited kitchens so that she could see how food was prepared for the troops. She also worked with the Red Cross in her desire to improve facilities for servicemen. Whenever she was overseas, Roosevelt would ask to see how women were contributing to the war effort and suggest ways that their roles could be further expanded.

Roosevelt believed that even though the United States had won the last war, it lost the peace, which is what allowed World War II to occur. She was determined that this would not happen again. She vowed to make the United States a true democracy where everyone had equal rights regardless of sex, race, or religion. If it did not succeed in this way, she thought the sacrifices that the country was making would be in vain. She believed that women workers should not be pushed out of factory and other jobs once the troops returned home and advocated the idea of equal pay for equal work. Roosevelt also supported the efforts of the National Association for the Advancement of Colored People (NAACP) to integrate the armed forces and end discrimination at home, especially in the South where Jim Crow laws regulated that separate was equal. However, Roosevelt refused to support anything that she believed would hurt the war effort, including A. Philip Randolph's proposed 1941 March on Washington.

After FDR died in 1945, Roosevelt retreated to the background to grieve while Harry Truman worked to end the war. In the postwar era, Roosevelt served as a member of the UN delegation (1945–1952), a role that forced her to confront the Soviets about their ideology. Unlike many Americans during the Cold War, Roosevelt insisted that although the Soviet ideology was wrong, so was the American response to it. Throughout the Cold War, Roosevelt continued to make speeches, travel, and write in *My Day* about her views, hoping to garner support from the American public.

After retiring from public life in 1953, Roosevelt kept busy. She remained active in the Democratic Party, supporting the candidacy of Adlai Stevenson in 1952 and 1956. In 1957, she traveled to the Soviet Union and interviewed Nikita Khrushchev, the Soviet premier. In 1961, President John F. Kennedy appointed Roosevelt to the President's Commission on the Status of Women. This was her final public role. On November 7, 1962, she died of tuberculosis at the age of 78.

Elizabeth Ann Bryant

See also: American Red Cross; Cold War (ca. 1947–1991); Office of Civilian Defense (OCD); Rosie the Riveter; World War I (1914–1918); World War II (1941–1945).

References and Further Reading

Beasley, Maurine et al. *The Eleanor Roosevelt Encyclopedia*. Westport, CT: Greenwood Press, 2001.

Roosevelt, Eleanor. *The Autobiography of Eleanor Roosevelt*. New York: De Capo Press, 2000.

Scharf, Lois. *Eleanor Roosevelt: First Lady of American Liberalism*. Boston: Twayne Publishers, 1987.

Youngs, J. William T. *Eleanor Roosevelt: A Personal and Public Life*. New York: Pearson Longman, 2006.

ROSENBERG, ETHEL GREENGLASS (1915–1953)

Ethel Rosenberg was convicted of treason and executed by the United States during the Cold War.

During war or national emergencies, women's roles in society are typically broadened in order to meet the crises. Women become soldiers, factory workers, public speakers, and spies, to name a few. The Cold War, however, was a rather unique crisis: anxiety, paranoia, and xenophobia were major

Ethel and Julius Rosenberg ride to separate prisons following their espionage convictions on March 29, 1951. (Library of Congress)

characteristics of the decades-long conflict in which proxy contests replaced direct combat among the superpowers. Women were occasionally caught up in the national anxiety of the period; such was the story of Ethel Rosenberg.

Born Ethel Greenglass in New York City on September 28, 1915, her childhood was relatively unremarkable. She attended her neighborhood Hebrew school as well as public school. Her Lower East Side neighborhood was predominately Jewish in character, densely populated by dilapidated tenements and crowed with sweatshops. In 1932, Rosenberg was working as a clerk with a shipping company when she began her union activities, including a strike for better pay and shorter working hours. In 1935, she led 150 women who used their bodies to block the entrance to the company's warehouse. Her employer fired her, but the National Labor Relations Board effected her reinstatement with back pay. Her union activism resulted in the establishment of the Ladies Apparel Shipping Clerk's Union. On the eve of World War II, she married Julius Rosenberg, a fellow union activist who had recently received his bachelor's degree in electrical engineering from the City College of New York.

During the war, Rosenberg raised money and supplies for the Allied war effort through the East Side Defense Council. Julius had a job with the Signal Corps but lost his position in 1945 when he was accused of belonging to the U.S. Communist Party. He then established his own machine shop with his brother-in-law, David Greenglass.

Although the Soviet Union was an ally of the United States during most of World War II, after the war the United States and the Soviet Union quickly became opponents following the defeat of Nazi Germany. Their opposing socio-economic systems and objectives in Europe resulted in the Cold War. A critical event in that conflict was the Soviet development of an atomic bomb in 1949. The United States was no longer the sole atomic power. U.S. decision makers were surprised that the Soviets were able to develop nuclear weapons as quickly as they did. There was a concern that spies must have helped the Soviet Union by delivering atomic technology developed in the United States. Klaus Fuchs, a British member of the top-secret Manhattan Project, was accused of being a spy. Hoping to receive a lesser prison sentence for helping to transfer U.S. atomic secrets to the Soviet Union, Fuchs named others involved in the spy ring. The list of names led to David Greenglass, Rosenberg's brother. Greenglass then testified that his brother-in-law was the one who introduced him to the spy ring. On July 17, 1950, the U.S. Federal Bureau of Investigation (FBI) arrested Julius Rosenberg; Ethel Rosenberg was arrested on August 11. With no viable evidence against her, the FBI apprehended Rosenberg hoping that to save his wife Julius would then confess to spying for the Soviet Union.

While on the witness stand, Rosenberg repeatedly denied knowing anything about her family member's work for the Manhattan Project or her brother's espionage activities; she also denied knowing any of the other people that the U.S. and British governments had arrested on charges of selling atomic secrets to the Soviet Union apart from what she learned from the newspapers.

She proclaimed, "We are innocent and to forsake this truth is to pay too high a price for even the priceless gift of life—for life thus purchased we could not live out in dignity and self-respect."

The federal government was never able to produce any evidence that tied Rosenberg into the spy ring (her husband, however, was not as innocent). She was found guilty, primarily on the testimony of her brother. Rosenberg worked to get her two sons, Robert and Michael, into a stable home. Initially, the boys were cared for by Tessie Greenglass (the boys' maternal grandmother), but their spirits quickly soured, leading Michael to contemplate suicide while Robert began grinding his teeth. As most other relatives were either unwilling or unable to take in the boys, Rosenberg had them placed in the Hebrew Children's Home in the Bronx.

The Rosenbergs' death sentences were carried out on June 19, 1953, by electrocution at Sing Sing prison in New York. Ethel Rosenberg was given three jolts of electricity before she finally died. According to Bob Considine, a witness to the executions, she "was given more electricity which started again the kind of ghastly plume of smoke that rose from her head. After two more little jolts, Ethel Rosenberg was dead."

Jim Ross-Nazzal

See also: Cold War (ca. 1947–1991); Espionage; World War II (1941–1945).

References and Further Reading

Detweiler, Robert. "Carnival of Shame: Doctorow and the Rosenbergs." *Religion and American Culture* 6, no. 1 (1996): 63–85.

Meeropol, Robert, and Michael Meeropol. *We Are Your Sons: The Legacy of Ethel and Julius Rosenberg*. New York: Houghton Mifflin, 1986.

Philipson, Ilene. *Ethel Rosenberg: Beyond the Myths*. New York: Franklin Watts, 1988.

Schneir, Walter, and Mirian Schneir. *Invitation to an Inquest*. New York: Doubleday, 1965.

ROSIE THE RIVETER

Rosie the Riveter is the iconic symbol of women who worked outside the home in factory jobs during World War II. She is best characterized by J. Howard Miller's "We Can Do It" picture, which was actually created as a recruiting poster for the Westinghouse Corporation.

"We Can Do It," a poster by J. Howard Miller, is the quintessential image of the female factory worker during World War II. Popularized as "Rosie the Riveter," the image became a national symbol of American unity and patriotism. (National Archives)

World War II changed gender roles. Prior to the entrance of the United States into the war, few white middle-class women worked outside of the home. However, after the Japanese bombed Pearl Harbor on December 7, 1941, millions of women joined the American workforce. Instead of being criticized for taking jobs away from men, as had happened during the Great Depression, during wartime women were actively recruited into the workforce to help the war effort by keeping production numbers high. Factory jobs were seen as unfeminine, so many of the appeals for women workers focused on their femininity. Propaganda pictures of Rosie portrayed her as wearing makeup. Her appearance allowed her to look feminine so that women and the men of their households would not object when they joined the wartime workforce. Even though most women did not take jobs as factory workers but instead took clerical positions, the image of Rosie the Riveter remains the most prevalent icon of wartime women workers.

Much of the attention given to Rosie the Riveter came from the government's concerted effort to recruit women for jobs in war industries so that the United States would not be out-produced by the Axis powers. The ideal of Rosie the Riveter increased in popularity in 1942 when Redd Evans and John Jacob Loeb wrote a song, "Rosie the Riveter." The lyrics extolled the virtues of women who worked in the factories, thus helping the war effort and leading the country to victory. Norman Rockwell painted the first known image of Rosie the Riveter, and it became the cover of the *Saturday Evening Post* on May 29, 1943. Many more depictions followed.

Even though there was a push for women to take the jobs that had been left open by male servicemen, women faced tremendous discrimination upon entering the work force. Most people, including many of the women who took these jobs, saw the positions as temporary and assumed that women would return to their traditional roles after the war ended. Although the government desperately needed these industrial positions to be filled during wartime, factory owners were not eager to hire women. Women continued to be the last hired and first fired in many companies. To combat this problem, both the War Manpower Commission (WMC) and the Office of War Information (OWI) used propaganda for the dual purpose of trying to encourage women to work while helping employers to become receptive to the idea of hiring women. The main strategy of the Rosie the Riveter campaign, which was primarily focused on white housewives, was to use patriotism in ways that reinforced women's traditional images and roles.

Women who chose wartime careers in the defense industry soon learned that Rosie's work was not easy. Factories were often dirty and dangerous. Very few women received anything more than cursory job training. Female workers were consistently paid less than their male counterparts despite the WMC's policy of equal pay for equal work. Consequently, women found that working in the factories was not as glamorous as government propaganda posters made it out to be. Women had to learn how to operate welding machines and rivet guns, read blueprints, maneuver heavy machinery, drive and maintain railroad engines, and even become the "lead man" on assembly lines. Despite all the attention that the fictional Rosie the Riveter received in the media, the real Rosies rarely became foremen, craftsmen, or skilled factory workers. Instead, factories continued to reserve those skilled jobs for men. Even at the wartime production peak, women only held 4.4 percent of the skilled jobs in American industry. In the blue-collar realm, men and their unions reluctantly accepted women as temporary coworkers, but they effectively blocked women from permanent entry into their workplace. In addition to these difficulties, real-life Rosie the Riveters were also forced to deal with sexual harassment from their male coworkers and managers.

Even with all of these obstacles, women continued to enter the wartime workforce in astounding numbers. By March 1944, 2,690,000 women were employed chiefly as unskilled or semi-skilled factory workers. At the end of 1944, one in six female laborers worked in the war sector. The remainder worked in traditionally female jobs; they were employed as wartime secretaries or nurses.

When World War II ended in 1945, many women were relieved that they could leave the workforce and return to their homes. They wanted to return to their prewar lives. Throughout the war, many were faced with the reality of a "double shift" in which they worked at the factory and then had to work at home running the household and taking care of their children. In the postwar era, many Rosies felt that they had done their patriotic duty and were happy to leave the workforce. Other women used the opportunities gained during World War II as a springboard to working outside of the home in peacetime. They enjoyed the money and freedom that working outside the home had given them. As a result, even though many women were forced to give their wartime jobs back to returning servicemen and return to more traditionally female jobs, many willingly made the change in positions to remain in the working world. However, as a whole, in the immediate aftermath of World War II, many women returned to their jobs as housewives. Women did not enter the workforce in such large numbers again until the 1970s. However, the image of Rosie the Riveter, and the evidence that women performed well in traditionally male jobs during World War II helped pave the way for increasing numbers of women in the workforce.

Elizabeth Ann Bryant

See also: Monroe, Rose Leigh Abbott Will (1920–1997); World War II (1941–1945).

References and Further Reading

Ayling, Keith. *Calling All Women.* New York: Harper & Brothers, 1942.

Hartmann, Susan M. *The Home Front and Beyond: American Women in the 1940s.* Boston: Twayne Publishers, 1982.

Rupp, Leila J. *Mobilizing Women for War: German and American Propaganda, 1939–1945.* Princeton, NJ: Princeton University Press, 1978.

ROSS, ELIZABETH "BETSY" GRISCOM (1752–1836)

Betsy Ross is a favorite legendary figure of the American Revolution, popularly credited with sewing, and in part designing, the first U.S. flag. This legend, like most, appears to be a blending of colorful myth and hard facts.

Ross was born Elizabeth Griscom in Philadelphia on January 1, 1752. She was the seventh daughter of the 17 children of Samuel Griscom, a carpenter who helped to build the tower of Independence Hall, and Rebecca James. Betsy was raised in the Quaker religion. She attended her mother's school for Quaker children and later the Friends Public School. She also served as an apprentice to John Webster, an upholsterer, where she met a fellow apprentice and her future husband, John Ross. On November 4, 1773, she married Ross at Huggs Tavern in Gloucester, New Jersey. Because her husband was not a Quaker, the new Mrs. Ross was expelled from her Quaker meeting. The Rosses rented a house on Arch Street in Philadelphia, where they opened an upholstery business. On January 21, 1776, John died from wounds he received from an explosion of gunpowder that he was guarding for the Revolutionary resistance at a Delaware River dock. Ross continued to operate the family business. In addition to upholstery work, she also made flags as part of her business.

Her grandson, William Canby, first told the story of Ross's role in creating the first U.S. flag to a meeting of the Pennsylvania Historical Society in 1870. Canby recounted a visit by Gen. George Washington and Continental Congress members Robert Morris and George Ross in the spring of 1776 to Betsy Ross's shop. Washington showed Ross a drawing of the flag he proposed, and she made suggestions to change the stars to five-pointed ones and to place the stars in a circle instead of in a row as he had drawn. Washington and the committee members agreed, and Ross was given the job of making the first flag of the United States of America. Later that spring, she delivered several flags for use on the ships of the Continental Navy on the Delaware River.

However, little contemporary evidence supports the story of this meeting or of Ross's role in designing the United States' first flag. Washington was with the Continental Army in New York in June 1776, and Congress did not authorize the familiar design for the United States' first national battle flag until June 14, 1777, when it passed the Flag Resolution. This act determined that the naval flag of the United States should have 13 alternating red and white stripes, with 13 white stars on a blue field.

Yet Ross evidently did make battle flags during the Revolutionary War. She is first recorded in this role in May 1777, when she made ship colors for the Pennsylvania State Navy, and she may have made early national flags as well. Perhaps the earliest national flag used in a land battle, at Bennington in August 1777, was of a different pattern from the naval flag, and it took some time for Congress's general design to prevail.

As she continued her upholstery business and made occasional flags, Ross got on with her personal life as well. On June 15, 1777, she married a seaman, Joseph Ashburn, at Gloria Dei Church in Philadelphia and had two daughters, Zillah and Elizabeth. Ashburn was captured by the British while serving as first mate on the brigantine *Patty*. He died on March 3, 1782, at the Old Mill prison in Plymouth, England. Ross learned of her husband's death from John Claypoole, a fellow prisoner and longtime friend of the Ashburns. She married Claypoole on May 8, 1783. Ross later moved her business to another location on Second Street. She and Claypoole had five daughters together, Clarissa Sidney, Susannah, Rachel, Jane, and Harriet. Claypoole died on August 3, 1817, after a long illness.

Ross gave up her business in 1827, turning it over to her daughter Clarissa Sidney Wilson, who operated it until she moved to Fort Madison, Iowa, in 1856. Ross went first to live with her daughter Susannah Satterthwaite in nearby Abington, Pennsylvania, and later returned to Philadelphia and lived in the home of her son-in-law, Caleb Canby, where she died on January 30, 1836, at age 84.

Arthur Holst

See also: American Revolution (1775–1783).

References and Further Reading

Norton, Mary Beth. *Liberty's Daughters: The Revolutionary Experience of American Women, 1750–1800*. Boston: Little, Brown, 1980.

Weigley, Russell F., ed. *Philadelphia: A 300-Year History*. New York: Norton, 1982.

Wulf, Karin A. "Ross, Betsy." In *American National Biography*, Vol. 18, edited by John A. Garraty and Mark C. Carnes, 900–901. New York: Oxford University Press, 1999.

ROSSI, MARIE THERESE (1959–1991)

Maj. Marie Therese Rossi served as an artillery officer and CH-47D Chinook helicopter pilot with the U.S. Army from 1980 until her death on March 1, 1991, in a helicopter crash during mop-up operations after Operation Desert Storm (January 17, 1991–February 28, 1991). She was the first U.S. woman aviation commander to fly in combat.

Rossi was born and raised in Oradell, New Jersey. She was one of four children of Paul and Gertrude Nolan Rossi. Her father was a World War II veteran of the Marine Corps. Rossi graduated from Oradell's River Dell Regional High School in 1976. She earned a bachelor of arts degree in psychology from Dickinson College, in Carlisle, Pennsylvania, in 1980 and a commission as a second lieutenant through the U.S. Army Reserve Officer Training Corps program. Rossi served as an artillery officer at Fort Bliss, Texas, for a number of years before earning her flight wings at the Army's rotary-wing flight program in 1986. Following flight school, she was assigned to an Army aviation unit in South Korea, where she met her future husband, Chief Warrant Officer John A Cayton; Cayton also flew helicopters.

Rossi rose through the ranks of the Army. As a major, she was given command of B Company, 2nd Battalion, 159th Aviation Regiment, 18th Army Aviation Brigade, at Hunter Army Airfield in Savannah, Georgia. In mid-September 1990, at a time when Department of Defense regulations prohibited women from direct combat roles, Rossi led a deployment of 15 Chinook helicopters and approximately 200 officers and enlisted personnel from Hunter Army Airfield to northern Saudi Arabia, where they joined coalition forces defending Saudi Arabia after Iraqi military forces swept into neighboring

Kuwait. For five months, Rossi and her crews flew logistical resupply missions in support of defensive operations.

On February 24, 1991, as coalition forces launched a major ground offensive into Iraq, Rossi led her helicopters 50 miles into enemy territory to ferry troops, ammunition, fuel, and other supplies to U.S. combat forces. She and her unit were among the first aviation units to enter Iraq during the first hours of the ground assault. On the eve of the ground assault, Rossi had become something of a household name to millions of Americans because of a series of media interviews that focused on her proximity to a combat zone and the likelihood that she would become the first U.S. woman to fly in a combat zone if a ground assault became necessary. Rossi downplayed the significance of her position, emphasizing to journalists that she and other military women thought of themselves as well-trained, professional soldiers first and foremost, ready and willing to risk their lives just like their male counterparts. Media interviews with Rossi and other deployed military women energized an ongoing debate in the United States between those who advocated greater opportunities for women in the Department of Defense and those who feared the specter of military women coming home in body bags would dampen the resolve of the American public.

Rossi never had an opportunity to engage further in that debate; on March 1, 1991, the day after Desert Storm officially ended, she and three other crew members died when the helicopter she was piloting crashed into an unlit microwave antenna in northern Saudi Arabia. Her death, widely publicized in television and print media, stunned the nation. She was buried with full military honors in Arlington National Cemetery on March 11, 1991. Hundreds of military and civilian personnel attended her funeral. The epitaph at her grave reads: "First Female Combat Commander To Fly Into Battle." The following year, the U.S. Army honored her by naming its small-arms development and testing facility at Picatinny, New Jersey, the Major Marie Rossi Cayton Armament Technology Facility. Rossi's death and those of five other women killed during operations in the Gulf War did not result in the feared backlash from the American public, nor did it deter the Department of Defense from dramatically expanding opportunities for women in the subsequent decades. Rossi's name and example of courage and sacrifice live on; she is often mentioned in books, articles, and speeches about American military women to this day.

Debra A. Shattuck

See also: Gulf War (1991); Reserve Officer Training Corps (ROTC).

References and Further Reading

Breuer, William B. *War and American Women: Heroism, Deeds, and Controversy.* Westport, CT: Greenwood, 1997.

"Marie Rossi." *People*, May 30, 1991.

Quindlen, Anna. "Public & Private: Women in Combat." *New York Times*, January 8, 1992.

Sullivan, Joseph F. "Army Pilot's Death Stuns Her New Jersey Neighbors." *New York Times*, March 7, 1991.

Zeinert, Karen, and Mary Miller. *The Brave Women of the Gulf Wars: Operation Desert*

Storm and Operation Iraqi Freedom. Minneapolis, MN: Twenty-First Century Books, 2006.

ROUNDTREE, DOVEY MAE JOHNSON (1914–)

Dovey Mae Johnson Roundtree was a member of the first class of black officer candidates in the Women's Army Auxiliary Corps (WAAC). She later became a civil rights attorney and an ordained minister in the African Methodist Episcopal Church (AME).

Raised by her mother and maternal grandparents after the death of her father, Dovey Johnson spent her early years in Charlotte, North Carolina, where she excelled in school. At the urging of her family and a favorite teacher, she applied to Spelman College, the prestigious black college in Atlanta. She entered Spelman in the fall of 1932. At the end of her junior year and the height of the Great Depression, Johnson was forced to make a decision. Finding herself unemployed as a result of a false accusation by her employer and unable to pay her tuition for her final year at Spelman, Johnson planned to leave Spelman to take a teaching position at a small Georgia school. In the end, she did not have to make that decision because an elderly white professor and mentor paid the tuition from her personal savings. Years later Johnson repaid the loan in full.

After graduation, she taught for three years in a small high school in South Carolina. Johnson then moved to Washington, D.C., hoping to find a job in a defense industry. These jobs were open to blacks as a result of the ban on race discrimination in defense industry hiring and the formation of the Fair Employment Practices Committee. Upon her arrival in Washington, Johnson looked up Dr. Mary McLeod Bethune—a family friend, civil rights activist, and founder of the National Council of Negro Women.

Her arrival in 1941 coincided with the move to allow women to enter the military. Bethune, along with First Lady Eleanor Roosevelt, lobbied for the inclusion of black women in the proposed organization. In May 1942, Congress passed, and President Franklin Roosevelt signed, the law that established WAAC. After much debate, black women were allowed to join WAAC, and 40 slots were reserved for African Americans in the first officer candidate class to be trained at Fort Des Moines, Iowa, starting in July 1942.

White and black women were recruited through newspapers and women's magazines. College graduates and professional women were sought to apply for the 440 slots open for officer candidates. With Bethune's encouragement, Johnson attempted to submit her application to officer candidate school to a white army recruiter at a recruitment office in Charlotte. When he refused to take her application, she traveled to Richmond, Virginia, where she was successful.

When Johnson reported to Fort Des Moines, she and the other black officer candidates were assigned to a segregated unit—the 3rd Platoon of the 1st Company. They were housed in separate barracks from their white classmates. Training classes were integrated, but care was taken to prevent the sharing of gas masks and first aid supplies between blacks and whites. Blacks were banned from the service club, and facilities, such as the post swimming pool, were open to blacks only at assigned times.

Johnson graduated and was commissioned as a third officer in August 1942. She was assigned as a recruiter and traveled throughout the South in Georgia, Florida, North and South Carolina, and Texas, as well as north to Ohio. Speaking at black colleges, Young Men's Christian Associations, churches, and black chambers of commerce, she encouraged young black women to join the WAAC despite the open practice of segregation.

Johnson's status as an officer in the WAAC did not shield her from the racism of the 1940s. Soon after being commissioned, she and a group of fellow WAACs—black and white—were eating together in a Des Moines hotel dining room when a white male officer, upon seeing the integrated group, ordered the "darkies" to move to a separate table. Similarly, as a recruiter traveling by bus in Florida, she was ordered to give up her seat for white passengers. When she learned of the Army's plan to form a separate training regiment for blacks under the newly formed Women's Army Corp (WAC) in August 1943, she threatened to resign. Her reactions to these incidents caused her supervisors to label Johnson an agitator and inspired her fellow black WAACs to view her as a spokesperson. Despite the blatant racism and sexism she faced during her time in the WAAC and WAC, Johnson never regretted her decision to serve her country in its time of need.

After her discharge from the WAC, she married Bill Roundtree, her college sweetheart. The marriage was short lived. She then earned her law degree at Howard University and continued the fight for civil rights through her practice in Washington, D.C., where she became the first black member of the D.C. Women's Bar Association. One of her cases, *Sarah Keys v. Carolina Coach Company*, challenged segregation law as it applied to interstate travel. In this landmark civil rights case, a WAC private, Sarah Louise Keys, challenged a bus driver who attempted to remove her from the "white section" of a bus as she traveled home on furlough. As a result, the Interstate Commerce Commission struck down the separate-but-equal doctrine as it applied to interstate public bus transportation.

In 1961, Johnson was ordained a minister in the AME and combined her law expertise with the ministry at Washington's Allen Chapel AME Church. She retired from public life in 1996.

Cheryl Mullenbach

See also: African American Women; Bethune, Mary McLeod (1875–1955); Keys (Evans), Sarah Louise (1929–); Roosevelt, Eleanor (1884–1962); Ten Percenters; Women's Army Auxiliary Corps (WAAC); Women's Army Corps (WAC); Young Men's Christian Association (YMCA).

References and Further Reading

McCabe, Katie, and Dovey Johnson Roundtree. *Justice Older Than the Law: The Life of Dovey Johnson Roundtree.* Jackson: University Press of Mississippi, 2009.

Moore, Brenda L. *To Serve My Country, to Serve My Race: The Story of the Only*

African American WACs Stationed Overseas During World War II. New York: New York University Press, 1996.

Putney, Martha S. *When the Nation Was in Need: Blacks in the Women's Army Corps During World War II*. Metuchen, NJ: Scarecrow Press, 1992.

ROWLANDSON, MARY WHITE (CA. 1635–1711)

One of colonial America's earliest prisoners of war, Mary White Rowlandson is widely known for her 1682 narrative, *The Sovereignty and Goodness of God*. The narrative details her February 10, 1676, capture from Lancaster, Massachusetts, during King Philip's War (1675–1676) and her subsequent three-month captivity among and release from Algonquian-speaking Indians.

Born between the years 1635 and 1637 in England to John White and Joan West White, Mary White and her family traveled to the British colonies during her early childhood and were among the first settlers in Lancaster in 1653. Her father became one of the wealthiest landowners in the settlement. Between the ages of 19 and 21, White married Rev. Joseph Rowlandson in 1656. She bore four children: Mary (1658), who later died in childhood; Joseph (1662); Mary (1665); and Sarah (1669). Sarah would later die in captivity from wounds suffered during the assault on Lancaster. Sometime after hearing rumors in late January of an imminent Indian attack on Lancaster, Reverend Rowlandson went to Boston to request

Algonquins captured Mary Rowlandson in 1676. After her return to her family, Rowlandson wrote the first published account of a woman taken captive by Native Americans. (North Wind Picture Archives)

help. Aid did not arrive in time to prevent the capture of 24 colonists.

Rowlandson recounted in her captivity narrative that on the morning of her capture, she heard gunfire and saw smoke rising from the blazing houses as the Nipmuck Indians massacred her neighbors. Her story of captivity reflected deep-rooted tensions and conflicts between the settlers and the Indians. As Puritans, New England colonists sought to civilize the "untamed" wilderness and Native Americans who inhabited the area by exploiting the land and converting the Indians. Colonists disrupted the tenuous relationship during the spring of 1675 after they hung three Wampanoag Indians for the assumed murder of John Sassamon, a Christian Indian. After nearly two years of gruesome combat beginning in June, the colonists suffered approximately 1,000 casualties and the Algonquian Indians 3,000, one-quarter of their population. The war ended in August 1676 with the death of King Philip, or Metacom, at the hands of a Christian Indian.

Within her narrative, Rowlandson captured the chaos and confusion of war as she reflected on competing ideas. On one hand, Puritan ideology defined Indians as barbaric, but on the other, on some occasions they treated her with kindness while in captivity. After witnessing the murder of her relatives and neighbors, the death of her child in her arms, and the kidnapping of her two other children, Rowlandson attributed her survival and sanity to the will of God. Her pious Puritan devotion is woven into her tale of life among the Indians, including being sold, experiencing near starvation, living in wigwams, and participating in the Indian barter

economy with her knitted items. On one occasion, Rowlandson knitted a shirt for one of King Philip's sons. He gave her a shilling, allowing her the opportunity to purchase valuable horsemeat, a welcomed alternative to her diet of corn, wheat, and ground nuts. Rowlandson was released after nearly 12 weeks of captivity when the English War Council paid a £20 ransom on May 2, 1676. Rowlandson reunited with her husband in Boston, where the two worked diligently on the return of their two captive children.

Rowlandson and the reverend remained in Boston until April 1677, when the couple moved to Wethersfield, Connecticut, where he would deliver his final sermon on November 24, 1678. The reverend died a few days later. Between 1677 and 1678, with the probable encouragement of Puritan minister Increase Mather, Rowlandson wrote her narrative as a testament to the providences of God. The first edition was printed in Boston in March 1682, and within months, Samuel Green published the second and third editions in Cambridge.

Earlier scholars believed Rowlandson died soon after her husband in 1678. New evidence suggests, however, that Rowlandson died much later and after remarrying. On August 6, 1679, Rowlandson married Capt. Samuel Talcott, a widower and one of the prominent colonial leaders from Connecticut. They did not conceive any children. Connecticut records list Mary Talcott's death on January 5, 1711.

The captivity narrative has since been reprinted more than 40 times and deservedly holds its place as a bestselling literary work authored by a woman.

Valerie A. Martinez

See also: Indian Wars; North American Colonial Wars (17th–18th centuries); Prisoners of War.

References and Further Reading

Castiglia, Christopher. *Bound and Determined: Captivity, Culture-Crossing, and White Womanhood from Mary Rowlandson to Patty Hearst.* Chicago: University of Chicago Press, 1996.

Faery, Rebecca Blevins. *Cartographies of Desire: Captivity, Race, and Sex in the Shaping of an American Nation.* Norman: University of Oklahoma Press, 1999.

Greene, David L. "New Light on Mary Rowlandson." *Early American Literature* 20 (1985): 24–38.

Lepore, Jill. *The Name of War: King Philip's War and the Origins of American Identity.* New York: Knopf, 1998.

Rowlandson, Mary. *The Sovereignty & Goodness of God, Together with the Faithfulness of his Promises Displayed: Being a Narrative of the Captivity and Restauration of Mrs. Mary Rowlandson.* Cambridge, MA, 1682. Reprinted as *The Captive* with an introduction by Mark Ludwig. Tucson, AZ: American Eagle Publications, 1990.

Taylor, Alan. *American Colonies.* New York: Penguin Press, 2001.

S

SAAR, LISA
(1966–)

Naval nurse Lisa Saar's service in Iraq saved the lives of many American military personnel.

Born on Long Island, New York, in 1966, Saar spent much of her life in northeastern Pennsylvania. Saar comes from a military family: her father and brother enlisted in the Air Force and her sister serves in the Navy. After graduating high school in 1984, she studied to become a licensed nurse practitioner, and she then enlisted in the Navy three years later. In the Navy, she did not immediately serve as a nurse but instead served as an electrician's mate for eight years until commissioned as a nurse in 1997.

In 2003, Saar was promoted to lieutenant and began the first of her three deployments during the War on Terror. For six months, Saar served on USS *Comfort* while it was stationed in the Persian Gulf during Operation Iraqi Freedom. After its end of operations in 2004, Saar was assigned to Guantanamo Bay for four months to care for detainees. Although Saar served well on these two deployments, it was her deployment to Fallujah, 40 miles west of Baghdad, that challenged her the most.

From August 6, 2006, until March 2007, Saar served in the Fallujah Surgical Unit as part of Combat Logistics Regiment 15 (Forward), 1st Marine Logistical Group (Forward), I Marine Expeditionary Force (Forward). For her service on this deployment, Saar was awarded the Navy and Marine Commendation Medal on April 5, 2007. This medal is awarded to service members of either the Navy or the Marine Corps who distinguish themselves by heroism, outstanding achievement, or meritorious service. Saar was awarded the medal not for any one particular act but for her dedication and good service throughout her deployment. Though not on the front lines of combat, her surgical unit received many wounded marines and Army personnel as well as Iraqi civilians. Although not attendant at every single case, Saar confessed in an interview that she was at the vast majority of the 600 cases that came into her surgical unit during her seven months in Fallujah. Due to the closeness to combat, most of the individuals she and the medical staff treated were driven to the hospital, and many had been injured by sniper bullets and improvised explosive devices.

The dedication she showed to her patients was most visible on the night of November 6, 2006. A marine with a critical head wound was going to die if not transferred to a better equipped medical facility. When he was supposed to be transferred to the main military medical facility in Baghdad, a sandstorm appeared and grounded all flights except for one. A special forces helicopter had been cleared to fly a mission, and the medical staff convinced the team to take the marine and drop him off along the way. Saar volunteered to monitor the marine while on the short trip because she had been the one to initially receive him upon his entrance to the trauma bay. On their way to Baghdad, the helicopter came under intense tracer and rocket-propelled grenade fire that made it impossible for them to continue on, and so the helicopter diverted to Balad Air Force Base north of Baghdad. The marine survived.

For her service on this flight, Saar was nominated for the first inaugural Captain Maria Ortiz Care Award, an award named to honor the first nurse killed by enemy fire since the Vietnam War. Though she did not win the award, Saar was promoted to lieutenant commander in 2008. That year, Saar became the head of the Department of Staff Education and Training at Naval Base Kitsap-Bremerton outside of Seattle, Washington.

Adam M. Carson

See also: Iraq War (2003–2011); Nursing; War on Terror (2001–).

References and Further Reading

Friedrich, Ed. "Nurse Recognized for War Efforts." *Kitsap Sun*, April 11, 2008.

Stutz, Douglas H. "Critical Care Skill in Fallujah Brings NHB Nurse Recognition." *Navy Medicine*, May–June 2008, 17–18.

Women in Military Service for America. "Critical Care: A Navy Nurse Goes Above and Beyond." Voices of Valor, March 2008. http://womensmemorial.org/Education/WHM08KitUSN.html (accessed February 26, 2012).

SACAGAWEA
(CA. 1787–1812)

Sacagawea was a Native American interpreter who was part of the Lewis and Clark Expedition commissioned by President Thomas Jefferson in 1804. Significant controversy exists over almost all aspects of Sacagawea's life, including her birth and death dates as well as the origin of her name. Her name is spelled Sacagawea, Sacajawea, and Sakakawea. Many historians have chosen "Sacagawea" both because of its Hidatsa origin and meaning of "bird woman." In May 1805, Meriwether Lewis recorded the Hidatsa meaning in his journal, the expedition having named a stream after her.

Sacagawea accompanied Lewis and Clark on their western expedition as an interpreter and guide. From a drawing by E. S. Paxson, ca. 1810. (Getty Images)

Sacagawea was born around 1787 to the Lemhi Shoshone tribe, located in the Lemhi Valley in what is now Idaho. Sometime in the fall of 1800, the Shoshone were camped at the Three Forks River in Missouri and were attacked by the Hidatsa. Several prisoners were taken, Sacagawea among them. Fur trader and trapper Toussaint Charbonneau later purchased her, and she moved with him and his other wife to Fort Mandan in present-day North Dakota. Sacagawea was pregnant with her first child when the Corps of Discovery reached the fort in 1804.

A year prior, the Louisiana Purchase had inspired an interest in American expansionism. President Thomas Jefferson commissioned an expedition to the west, the Corps of Discovery, placing it under the command of U.S. Army Capt. Meriwether Lewis and 2nd Lt. William Clark. Jefferson told foreign ambassadors that the mission was purely scientific in nature even as he wrote a secret message to Congress emphasizing the commercial benefits of the expedition. The expedition was also intended to evaluate the strength of British and French Canadian interests already established in the area.

After wintering at Fort Mandan, the Corps of Discovery hired Charbonneau to act as an interpreter between the Hidatsa and the expedition. Upon learning of Sacagawea's Shoshone background, the captains encouraged Charbonneau to bring her and her newborn son, Jean Baptiste, with him. She was needed not only as an interpreter but also as a friendly introduction to the Shoshone people. Lewis considered her important because of the expedition's need for horses to carry the party from the Missouri to the Columbia Rivers—the Shoshone people were the primary traders of horses in that region.

Although Sacagawea has been mythologized as the expedition's guide, she acted in that role relatively few times throughout the expedition. In the summer of 1805, she was able to recognize geographical features that led the group to the Shoshone camps. Once the tribe had been located, she learned that her brother Cameahwait had become its chief. Through her connections, the Corps of Discovery was able to obtain both horses and guides to proceed further west.

One of Sacagawea's important roles was that of translator not only on behalf of the Shoshone but also for other native peoples. The translation process often consisted of passing word through a number of speakers. Due to the presence of Shoshone prisoners taken by Flathead, Walula, and Nez Perce tribes, Sacagawea was able to continue serving as a translator throughout the journey.

A number of other contributions proved Sacagawea's value to the Corps. Sacagawea saved important supplies from the Missouri River during a boat accident, preserving medicines and other goods. She was also familiar with the terrain, supplying the party with medicinal plants and foods as they continued to travel. Her most noted contribution, however, was that of peacemaker. The presence of Sacagawea and her infant son convinced many Native Americans that Lewis and Clark did not intend war on their people, and their presence opened up trade possibilities.

After the conclusion of the expedition, Sacagawea followed her husband to the upper Missouri region. Charbonneau stayed with the Native Americans there, interpreting for explorers and government officials. The couple traveled to St. Louis in 1809 at the invitation of Clark, who had offered to educate their children as thanks for the services that Sacagawea had provided to the expedition. They left Jean Baptiste with Clark and his family to continue his education.

Sacagawea had a second child, Lisette, in 1812 at Fort Manuel, a fur-trading post in what is now South Dakota. Not long after Lisette's birth, Sacagawea grew ill with fever and died. Legends exist that claim Sacagawea lived much longer and died in Wind River Shoshone Reservation in Wyoming in 1884. However, the 1813 adoption of the Charbonneau children by Clark indicates this claim to be unlikely, particularly when coupled with the fact that Sacagawea was listed as deceased on a list compiled by Clark of expedition members in the late 1820s.

Sacagawea is a vital part of the Lewis and Clark story and has become a symbol for a number of progressive movements. The National American Woman Suffrage Association adopted her as a symbol for the suffrage movement, and in 2000 the U.S. Mint placed her image on the Sacagawea dollar coin. Several monuments and natural features across the United States have been named in her honor as well. Of all the figures in the Corps of Discovery, it is Sacagawea whose legacy is most recognizable today.

Gwen Perkins

See also: Indian Wars; Native American Women.

References and Further Reading

Anderson, Irving W. *A Charbonneau Family Portrait: Biographical Sketches of Sacagawea, Jean Baptiste, and Toussaint Charbonneau.* Astoria, OR: Fort Clatsop Historical Association, 1988.

Duncan, Dayton, and Ken Burns. *Lewis and Clark: The Journey of the Corps of Discovery: An Illustrated History.* New York: Knopf Publishing, 1999.

Howard, Harold P. *Sacajawea.* Norman: University of Oklahoma Press, 1971.

Ronda, James P. *Lewis and Clark among the Indians.* Lincoln: University of Nebraska Press, 1988.

SALTER, FANNIE MAE
(1884–1966)

Fannie Mae Salter was the last in a long line of woman keepers of U.S. lighthouses. She retired from active service in 1948, ending nearly 150 years of women's positions in this work.

Most likely born in Chesapeake, Mathews County, Virginia, to Isaac M. Hudgins and Indiana Frances Jarvis, this third of five children was named after her mother but was known to all as Fannie. Nothing is known of her childhood or education. U.S. Census records reveal that Fannie Mae married Clarence W. Salter in 1905. Honeymooning at a lighthouse near Cape Charles, Virginia, set the course for the Salters' life. The Salters' first child, Olga, was born the same year they married. Their second daughter, Mabel, was born in 1906. By 1920, they had moved to Franktown, Northampton County, Virginia, where their son Charles Bradley was born.

In 1922, the Salters moved north to Turkey Point Light in Maryland, where Clarence served as keeper for three short years until his death in 1925. Built in 1833, the Turkey Point Light is the tallest on the Chesapeake Bay, and its light is visible 13 miles given its location on a bluff at the southern peninsula of Elk Neck. The Turkey Point Light is distinguished for being kept by women longer than any other lighthouse in the United States. The Salters lived in a small dwelling adjacent to the lighthouse itself.

The Civil Service declined Salter's request to succeed Clarence due to her age at the time, 42, because it was against Civil Service policy. The record is unclear whether it was Senator O. E. Weller or Senator Harry Arthur Cairtwell who spoke on her behalf to President Calvin Coolidge. Regardless, due to senatorial intervention, in 1925 she became the keeper of the Turkey Point Lighthouse in upper Chesapeake Bay, located in Cecil County, Maryland.

Keeping a lighthouse required that Salter clean and polish the Fresnel lens daily, monitor and change the oil-powered light each night by carrying the oil up the tower's stairs, maintain vigilant ringing of the fog bell, and keep up with general maintenance. There were no sick, vacation, or snow days because Salter's job was essential and so many people relied upon her dependability. Besides these tasks, Salter stocked the lighthouse with supplies and noted the weather and ship traffic in the log she kept.

Her logs indicate the physical stamina required in such a position. In particular, she noted scrubbing lantern floors; cleaning storm panes; mowing the lawn; receiving medicine and stove parts; painting the exterior of the bell house; whitewashing the exterior of the toilet; painting the tower floor, handrail, and ladder; scrubbing the tower steps as well as more painting, scrubbing, and pumping water out of boats; recharging the fire extinguisher; and shellacking the wooden floors.

Located on a four-acre plot, Turkey Point was isolated and essentially self-sufficient. Her life was one of discomfort that was plagued by difficulties. Supplies arrived by boat from Havre de Grace; the nearest town was a dozen miles away by car. The Salters also raised chickens, sheep, and turkeys for meat and eggs and a cow for milk and butter, and planted a garden each year.

Just prior to World War II and during her tenure as lighthouse keeper, the U.S. Coast Guard absorbed the Lighthouse Service. In 1939, Salter, like many lighthouse keepers, faced the choice of opting for a military commission or retiring when her contract ended; Salter decided she would retire. During World War II, the U.S. Coast Guard installed a radio telephone set. With regular supply ships diverted by the war, the Salters foraged from the sea and relied upon their garden, from which they harvested and canned vegetables, which saw them through the winter months. Her four or five daily 50-step trips to the top of the tower were reduced down to one in 1943 when Turkey Point was electrified but the brass oil lamps remained as backups in case the generator failed.

Salter served as lighthouse keeper at Turkey Point until she retired on January 31, 1948, at 65, with several decades of service combining her time alone at Turkey Point and assisting Clarence in his duties at previous lighthouses. Turkey Point guides watercraft into the Chesapeake Bay today.

Initially upon retirement she moved nearby to watch the Turkey Point's light within her nightly view, but eventually she moved to Baltimore, Maryland, where she died in March 1966.

Rebecca Tolley-Stokes

See also: World War II.

References and Further Reading

Clifford, Mary Louise. *Mind the Light, Katie: The History of Thirty-Three Female Lighthouse Keepers.* Alexandria, VA: Cypress Communications, 2006.

Clifford, Mary Louise. *Women Who Kept the Lights: An Illustrated History of Female Lighthouse Keepers.* Williamsburg, VA: Cypress Communications, 1993.

SALVATION ARMY

Best known in the United States for its thrift stores and Red Kettle donation drives during the Christmas holiday season, the Salvation Army (SA) has been serving the needy and fighting for the oppressed since the mid-19th century. First organized as the Christian Mission, the movement began using military parlance to describe its objectives and organization. Envisioning its work as a mission from God, the organization's members called its leader their "general" and thought of themselves as "soldiers of Christ." This concept was standardized with the reorganization of the movement under the name "Salvation Army."

William Booth, a Protestant Christian minister, founded the group in 1865 in London, England. Booth believed that Christian ministers had been focusing so much on gaining converts and maintaining denominational borders that they had blinded themselves to the needs of the poor. Thieves, prostitutes, and drunkards were drawn to Booth's open, informal, and welcoming style of ministry and aid. The organization quickly spread to Ireland, France, the United States, and across the world. Today, the SA is a multinational organization operating in over 100 countries.

Although Booth is officially known as the founder of the SA, his wife, Catherine, can be accurately called its cofounder. William was the organization's general, but Catherine was known as its mother. She was a talented preacher and opened the way for numerous other women to gain leadership roles in the organization. Catherine also influenced her husband's perspective on women's equality. In his 1908 book *Messages to Soldiers*, William wrote of his belief in the equality of women to men. The SA's stance on women's fundamental equality and its practice of female leadership within the organization engendered much of the opposition to the organization in its early years. At the end of the 19th century, there were as many female as male officers in the SA.

Catherine passed down both her intelligence and determination to her daughters, who became exemplary leaders in their own right. Emma became the commander of the SA in the United States, and her sister, Evangeline, became commander in Canada. The SA's work in both countries began with another woman, Eliza Shirley, who migrated to the United States with her family in 1879. A lieutenant in the SA, Shirley convinced William to send an official delegation to begin work on the continent in 1880. The SA's work in North America was progressing splendidly by the opening decade of the 20th century, but tragedy struck when the much admired Emma suddenly died in a train accident in 1903. However, Evangeline soon took her sister's place as the head of the SA's operations in the United States. Her tireless work and gracious spirit won over the American populace, and the SA grew immensely during her 30-year administration. She eventually became the fourth general of the SA, leading the international organization for five years.

Evangeline's most popular work came during World War I. When the United States entered the war in 1917, a few SA officers were sent with the troops to see how the organization could assist the soldiers. Over the next few months, Evangeline specially selected the SA's most committed and industrious men and women to go to France with the American Expeditionary Forces. In France, the SA provided vital services to boost morale. The SA established its famous canteens, where soldiers were served lemonade and pastries and given a place to rest and recuperate. It was at these canteens that the SA also served its famous doughnuts to the troops. The doughnuts reminded the soldiers of home and became incredibly popular among both the officers and enlisted men. The SA also provided restrooms, hostels, and Bible studies to the troops.

The majority of the SA workers were women who sewed the soldiers' clothes, cooked meals, and provided much-needed kindness to the war-weary military. The SA workers followed the soldiers to the front lines, often endangering themselves in the process. The SA's work in the war won the organization the admiration of the American military and civilian population, including that of Gen. John J. Pershing and President Woodrow Wilson. Booth was subsequently awarded the Distinguished Service Medal in 1919. The SA's wartime service continued during World War II, and its advocacy helped establish the United Service Organizations (USO).

The Salvation Army made one of its missions the care and protection of women. William and Catherine Booth were particularly troubled by the abuse of London's prostitutes, women whom they saw as forced into a demeaning and oppressive lifestyle. They also became incensed with the treatment of the thousands of women and children who were forced into dangerous working conditions in England's turn-of-the-century match factories. After lobbying for better conditions and improved pay, the SA eventually opened its own hygienic factory where it paid workers over four times what they were normally paid. This same concern for women was transferred to the operations in the United States. The SA has set up numerous social services specifically for women, including hospitals for unwed mothers as well as daycare centers and affordable housing for single working mothers called Evangeline Houses.

The Salvation Army gained the trust of the American people through its aid to World War I troops. SA soup kitchens, disaster relief work, thrift stores, and homes for the elderly and unemployed encouraged and aided countless people over the decades.

Andrew Polk

See also: United Service Organizations (USO); World War I (1914–1918); World War II (1941–1945).

References and Further Reading

Booth, Catherine, Evangeline Booth, and Kay Radar. *Terms of Empowerment: Salvation Army Women in Ministry*. Atlanta, GA: Salvation Army Printing, 1975.

Hattersley, Roy. *Blood and Fire: The Story of William and Catherine Booth*. New York: Doubleday, 2000.

Merritt, John G. *Historical Dictionary of the Salvation Army*. Lanham, MD: Scarecrow Press, 2006.

Taiz, Lillian. *Hallelujah Lads and Lasses: Remaking the Salvation Army in America, 1880–1930*. Chapel Hill: University of North Carolina Press, 2000.

Winston, Diane H. *Red-Hot and Righteous: The Urban Religion of the Salvation Army*. Cambridge, MA: Harvard University Press, 2000.

SAMSON [SAMPSON] (GANNETT), DEBORAH [ROBERT SHURTLIFF] (1760–1827)

During a period in American history in which women were to be "seen and not heard," Deborah Samson proved that women could, indeed, accomplish the work of a man. Disguised as a man, Pvt.

Deborah Sampson disguised herself as a man and fought in several battles during the American Revolution before her sex was discovered. (Library of Congress)

Robert Shurtliff, Samson had a brief but distinguished career as a soldier in the Revolutionary army.

The daughter of parents who could trace their lineage to the *Mayflower* settlers, Samson grew up in a life of poverty. Abandoned by her father at the age of six in 1766, she was bound out by her mother, who could not provide for her seven children, to a spinster. Samson's father was purported to have died at sea, but recent research suggests that he started a new life in Maine, where he lived as a pauper. Samson eventually ended up in the home of Deacon Jeremiah Thomas in Middleborough, Massachusetts. She spent 10 years at the Thomas home, working in the fields alongside Thomas's sons, which strengthened her physique. Although she did not receive any formal schooling, she was able to review lessons with the Thomas boys each evening after the fieldwork was done. At the age of 18, she became a teacher in Middleborough and supplemented her income by taking on spinning and weaving jobs at home.

During her time in the Thomas household, Samson had observed the growing tension between the British and the colonists, and her desire to assist her country fueled her passion to enlist. Reports indicate that she attempted to join the army as "Timothy Thayer of Carver" in early 1782 but then changed her mind. However, on May 20, 1782, she dressed as a man, walked to Bellingham, Massachusetts, and joined the 4th Massachusetts Regiment as Robert Shurtliff. She marched with 49 other recruits in the company of Capt. George Webb to West Point to receive her uniform.

Although the war had unofficially ended with Gen. Charles Cornwallis's surrender at Yorktown, guerrilla warfare continued, instigated by Loyalists who refused to admit defeat, and the British Army still occupied New York City. During the resulting skirmishes, Samson distinguished herself in hand-to-hand combat. During an engagement in Tarrytown, New York, however, she was wounded in the head by a saber and in the thigh by a musket ball while attempting to retreat. Although a French doctor treated her head wound at a field hospital, he was not notified of the thigh wound. Samson limped out of the hospital while the doctor was with another patient and attempted to extract the musket ball with her knife. She spent some time in recovery but never completely removed the ball, and upon her return to active duty, she came down with a fever. Legend has it that her sex was discovered by Dr. Barnabas Binney, who treated her at his home to protect her secret. After her recovery, however, her true identity was revealed, and Samson received an honorable discharge on October 23, 1783.

Upon her return to Middleborough, she married farmer Benjamin Gannett on April 7, 1785, with whom she had three children. Again a life of poverty ensued, and letters from Samson indicate that she had to borrow money from friends, including Paul Revere. Through his political connections, Revere encouraged Samson to apply for the pension owed to war veterans. She received £34 with interest on January 19, 1792, from Massachusetts governor John Hancock. She also became the subject of a book, *The Female Review; Or, Memoirs of an American Lady*, riddled with factual inaccuracies, published in 1797 by Herman Mann, a distant cousin of educator Horace Mann. Because there is no definitive account of Samson's life, Mann's work has been accepted as a quasi-scholarly work, although Mann himself acknowledged in his introduction that he wrote the book "hurriedly," without complete and accurate knowledge of her experiences. Mann focused on her attempt to protect national liberty. However, he included examples of stories that were not necessarily based in fact but that were popular at the time, such as Native American captivity narratives and instances in which Samson narrowly escaped capture by Native Americans. Furthermore, he misspelled her name, resulting in countless instances of Samson's name as Deborah Sampson.

Mann constantly rewrote his manuscript on Samson, concluding with a final version, published in 1829, two years after Samson's death. His final version told her tale using the first-person narrative. Regardless of the misinformation he presented, Mann was successful in putting Samson on the lecture circuit. Perhaps the first woman to be billed as a professional lecturer, Samson gave lectures about her experience as a soldier, even going so far as to appear in public in her uniform. Advertisements for her lectures described her as the "American Heroine." She spoke throughout Massachusetts, New York, and Rhode Island, thus allowing her and her family to become financially secure. She was awarded a veteran's pension in 1802 of $4 a month that after her death in 1827 was consequently awarded to her husband. Almost two centuries after her death, Michael J. Dukakis, then the governor of Massachusetts, signed a proclamation on May 23, 1983,

declaring Samson as the "Official Heroine of the Commonwealth of Massachusetts," making this the first time any individual had been proclaimed "hero" or "heroine" of any state.

Jennifer Harrison

See also: American Revolution (1775–1783).

References and Further Reading

Evans, Elizabeth. *Weathering the Storm: Women of the American Revolution*. New York: Paragon House, 1989.

Hiltner, Judith. "She Bled in Secret." *Early American Literature* 34, no. 2 (Spring 1999): 190–212.

Mann, Herman. *The Female Review: Life of Deborah Sampson*. New York: Arno, 1972; original publication, 1866.

Norton, Mary Beth. *Liberty's Daughters: The Revolutionary Experience of American Women, 1750–1800*. Boston: Little, Brown, 1980.

SEARS, MARY (1905–1997)

A planktonologist who played a critical role in oceanographic research for the U.S. Navy during World War I, a researcher at the Woods Hole Oceanographic Institute, and a lieutenant commander during the war, Mary Sears was a key player during the years when oceanography was developing into a mature field. Sears played a critical role during World War II when analysts were needed, often on short notice, to synthesize data into useful assessments in the aim of landing troops on enemy beaches during amphibious assaults.

Sears was born in Wayland, Massachusetts, on July 18, 1905. Identified early on by her classmates as a virtual encyclopedia of knowledge about farming, she graduated from the Winsor School in Boston in 1923 at the age of 18. Afterward, Sears entered Radcliffe University with the intention of majoring in Greek; her stepmother, however, suggested she broaden her studies. Two summers in Bermuda investigating marine invertebrates served as the catalyst for what would be a lifelong fascination with and career in studying the sea. Sears graduated magna cum laude in 1927 with a bachelor's degree in zoology and continued at Radcliffe, first in the master's program and then the PhD program, where she completed her dissertation in 1929. It was here that she first came into contact with Dr. Harry Bryant Bigelow and the newly formed Woods Hole Oceanographic Institute (WHOI).

The early 1930s were fruitful years for Sears. During her alternating summers at the Museum of Comparative Zoology at Harvard and winters at WHOI, she not only developed her research interests and skills but also met many who would become major players in marine science—like Columbus O'Donnel Iselin, future wartime director of WHOI—that would dominate both WHOI and the emerging field of oceanography. By 1940, she was a full-time planktonologist. Like so many other academic institutions during World War II, WHOI enjoyed a close relationship with the federal government; it assisted in both offensive and defensive research projects involving oceangoing vessels, including merchant ships and submarines. Sears participated in such projects beginning in 1942, first applying her extensive knowledge of marine biology to investigating causes of and remedies for ship bottom fouling in the aim of increasing ship speed. She interrupted her work at the end of 1942 and attempted to join the Navy's Women Accepted for Volunteer Emergency Service (WAVES) division but was initially rejected for medical reasons; Sears had been the victim of an attack of arthritis early in life. Her acknowledged expertise and the Navy's desperate need for skilled scientists overrode her medical disqualification, however, and she was accepted for service shortly thereafter.

As other oceanographers assisted with the development of instruments, Sears came to play a critical role in the other activity of the Navy's ocean experts: the production of intelligence reports for direct use in high-level strategic planning of all kinds. In 1943, she was commissioned as a lieutenant in the Hydrographic Office in Washington, D.C. Shortly thereafter, consolidation of resources put Sears in charge of the new Oceanographic Unit (OU) in late 1943; simultaneously, OU became the go-to office for all requests for oceanographic intelligence by any branch of the military. Her work on thermoclines, or areas of differing temperature that could be used by U.S. submarines to evade enemy radar, proved critical during the war. Sears's skill at compiling data from myriad sources was also instrumental in providing intelligence for the Navy in the assault on the Philippine island of Luzon in January 1945.

In 1945, Sears received a letter of commendation and the Commendation Ribbon for her work in the OU office, and in October 1945 she was promoted to lieutenant commander. When a permanent Oceanographic Division was created for the Hydrographic Office in February of 1946, Sears was chosen to run it. Sears retired from active duty on June 4, 1946. Thereafter, Sears returned to WHOI. She edited *Oceanography* in 1961, a text that contributed significantly to subsequent research in the field, and was named a senior scientist in the biology department in 1963, where she remained until her retirement in 1970. In 1978, Sears was named scientist emeritus, and she remained an active participant in the WHOI Corporation until 1975.

Sears died in Woods Hole, Massachusetts, in 1997, at the age of 92. In 2000, the Navy named its sixth Pathfinder T-AGS 60 class after her, USNS *Mary Sears*.

Ry Marcattilio-McCracken

See also: Women Accepted for Volunteer Emergency Service (WAVES); World War II (1941–1945).

References and Further Reading

Cutler, T. J., and R. Burgess. "Lest We Forget." *United States Naval Institute Proceedings* 131, no. 12 (2004): 94.

"Navy Names New Ship for Oceanographer Mary Sears." *Bulletin of the American Meteorological Society* 81, no. 2 (February 2000): 340.

Rozwadowski, Helen M., and David K. Van Keuren, eds. *The Machine in Neptune's Garden: Historical Perspectives on Technology and the Marine Environment.* Nantucket, MD: Watson Publications International, 2004.

Sears, Mary, ed. *Oceanography: Invited Lectures Presented at the International Oceanographic Conference.* Washington, D.C.: American Association for the Advancement of Science, 1961.

Sears, Mary, and D. Merriman, eds. *Oceanography: The Past: Proceedings of the Third International Congress on the History of Oceanography.* New York: Springer-Verlag, 1980.

Williams, Kathleen Broome. *Improbable Warriors: Women Scientists and the U.S. Navy in World War II.* Annapolis, MD: Naval Institute Press, 2001.

SEOUL CITY SUE (ANNA WALLACE SUHR) (1898–N.D.)

Anna Wallace Suhr earned the nickname "Seoul City Sue" during the Korean War as an announcer of anti-American propaganda for Radio Seoul in the summer of 1950. She was sometimes referred to as Anna Wallis Suh.

Born in Arkansas in 1898, Anna Wallace was divorced by the age of 22 and living in Johnston County, Oklahoma, with her family. She became a Methodist missionary and schoolteacher and moved to Asia. After settling in Shanghai, China, she taught at the Shanghai American School from 1930 to 1938, where she met and married a Korean man named Suhr.

Although it is unclear whether she went willingly or was forced to go, in 1943 Anna Wallace Suhr entered the Chapei Civilian Assembly Center (CCAC), an internment camp operated by the Japanese just outside of Shanghai. She continued to teach while at the CCAC.

By 1946, Suhr was in Korea tutoring children at the U.S. Diplomatic Mission

School in Seoul, where she remained until the North Korean invasion in June 1950. On June 28, 1950, North Korean forces occupied Seoul, and by July, she and her husband pledged their loyalty to North Korea.

Most sources agree that Suhr first broadcast around August 10, 1950, when members of the 588th Military Police Company first heard her. However, at least one source claims she broadcast as early as July 18, 1950. GIs called her by various names, including Rice Ball Maggie, Rice Bowl Maggie, and Rice Ball Kate; however, Seoul City Sue is the nickname that stuck. The name is perhaps drawn from a popular 1946 song called "Sioux City Sue," by Zeke Manners.

Seoul City Sue played the role of female propagandist radio broadcaster much like Tokyo Rose had during World War II. Seoul City Sue's programs were North Korean propaganda designed to demoralize American troops. Sue read the names of captured or dead American soldiers from their dog tags while tranquil music played in the background. She also welcomed ships by name as a way of illustrating a Korean advantage in the war.

Seoul City Sue went off the air as the result of a U.S. air strike on communications facilities in Seoul on August 13, 1950. Although the station was back on air within two weeks, Seoul City Sue did not return to the airwaves.

On August 27, 1950, the Methodist Missionary Organization identified Suhr as Seoul City Sue. Representatives of the organization claimed her lack of enthusiasm during the broadcasts indicated that she was being forced to participate.

Whether Suhr was forced to make these broadcasts or not remains a mystery, as the details of her life after the August 1950 broadcasts are scarce. Some prisoners of war at Camp 12 near Pyongyang claim to have been indoctrinated by Suhr and her husband in February 1951. A U.S. Army defector claims to have seen her on two occasions in 1965 in North Korea. Others have reported she was executed as a spy for South Korea in 1969. No records have been found to indicate what happened to Suhr, and her fate remains unknown.

Tammy Prater

See also: Espionage; Korean War (1950–1953).

References and Further Reading

Edwards, Paul M. *To Acknowledge a War: The Korean War in American Memory.* Westport, CT: Greenwood Press, 2000.

Lech, Raymond B. *Broken Soldiers.* Urbana: University of Illinois Press, 2000.

SHATTUCK, SARAH HARTWELL (CA. 1737/1738–1798)

Sarah Shattuck supported the Patriot cause in the American Revolution by helping to lead a female brigade to protect Groton and Pepperell, Massachusetts.

Born Sarah Hartwell on March 19, 1737 or 1738, in Massachusetts, she was the daughter of Samuel and Sarah Holden Hartwell. As a young woman, she married Job Shattuck, a veteran of the French and Indian War and a prosperous farmer with large land holdings in Groton, Massachusetts.

Although the records indicate little of her personal attainments and outlooks, her actions reveal a woman firmly committed to American independence and sensible of her roles as wife, household manager, and mother. On one hand, she acted within the proscribed 18th-century bounds for the domestic sphere. She was the mother of nine children—five sons (Job Jr., Ezekiel, William, Daniel, and Noah) and four daughters (Sarah, Rachel, Margaret, and Anna). In her role as the family matron, she supported the participation of her husband and sons in the Patriot cause. Job Shattuck was a lieutenant and later captain of a Groton militia company. As a Minuteman, he took the field at Lexington, Concord, and Bunker Hill. Shattuck and his company also participated in the Battle of Fort Ticonderoga and were present for the surrender of British general John Burgoyne in 1777. On the homefront, Shattuck was a revolutionary leader in Groton. He raised troops and resources for the war effort. Two of the Shattucks' sons, Job Jr. and Ezekiel, also served in the military during the American Revolution.

Shattuck's personal involvement in what would otherwise be considered the male sphere sets her story apart from the thousands of wives and mothers who sent their husbands and sons off to battle the British. When the men of Groton, Pepperell, and neighboring towns marched off toward Concord, the women had their own concerns. As rumors of enemy reinforcements and spies circulated, the women of Groton and Pepperell organized to defend the

bridge over the Nashua River, a main route from Canada to Boston. The 30 or 40 women in this female brigade selected Prudence Wright of Pepperell as their leader and Shattuck as her lieutenant. Dressed in men's clothing, the women armed themselves. Although no enemy troops attempted to pass, the Wright-Shattuck forces intercepted Capt. Leonard Whiting of Hollis, New Hampshire, a British spy. The women unhorsed and detained Whiting. After a careful search, they found incriminating documents hidden in his boot. They conveyed their prisoner to Oliver Prescott in Groton and sent the captured intelligence to the committee of safety. Whiting, perhaps chagrined at being captured by a troop of women, attempted unsuccessfully to charm his way out of the situation.

The Shattuck family survived the Revolution without loss of life. The postwar years were difficult. In 1786, Job Shattuck became embroiled in Shays' Rebellion. As a farmer and civic leader, he was sympathetic to the agricultural dislocation and financial stress that plagued the northwestern counties of Massachusetts. Valueless paper money and high taxes compounded the misery of area farmers. Many lost their lands and livestock to debt collection. Shattuck and others lobbied unsuccessfully for debtor relief. In Middlesex County, he became a leader in efforts to close the courthouse. The attack on the courthouse was the opening volley in the insurgency known as Shays' Rebellion. When disorder spread to other towns, the governor dispatched militia to quell it.

Initially, Shattuck escaped, but a search party dispatched to the Shattuck home found him nearby. In the ensuing skirmish, Shattuck was wounded several times, including a life-threatening sword cut to his knee. Shattuck recovered but walked with a crutch for the remainder of his life. After his capture in December 1786, Shattuck was imprisoned in Boston. Although other rebellion leaders were released on bond, Shattuck spent four months in jail. Tried for treason for his role in the uprising, Shattuck was convicted in May 1787 and sentenced to be hanged on June 28. After several postponements, the governor granted him an unconditional pardon in September. To many, Shays' Rebellion indicated the need for a stronger, centralized national government. As a result, and also in May 1787, the Constitutional Convention convened in Philadelphia.

The available records give no details on Sarah Shattuck's experiences during her husband's imprisonment. Months lived within the shadow of the gallows were difficult for all the Shattuck family.

Shattuck died on May 5, 1798, at age 61. She is buried in Groton.

Alexia Jones Helsley

See also: American Revolution (1775–1783); Wright, Prudence Cummings (1740–1823).

References and Further Reading

Butler, Caleb. *History of the Town of Groton, including Pepperell and Shirley.* Boston: Press of T. R. Marvin, 1848.

De Pauw, Linda Grant. "Women in Combat: The Revolutionary War Experience." *Armed Forces and Society* 7 (1981): 221–22.

Ellet, Elizabeth F. *The Women of the American Revolution*, Vol. 2. New York: Baker and Scribner, 1848.

Kerber, Linda K. *Toward an Intellectual History of Women*. Chapel Hill: University of North Carolina Press, 1997.

SHEEHAN, CINDY LEE MILLER (1957–)

The mother of a fallen soldier, Cindy Sheehan became a prominent antiwar activist whose outspoken opposition to the Iraq War and to the George W. Bush administration in general made her famous.

Born on July 10, 1957, in Los Angeles, California, Cindy Lee Miller (Sheehan) was a Catholic youth pastor and mother of four in suburban California. She entered the national spotlight in 2005 as an audacious and outspoken critic of Operation Iraqi Freedom. Her activism was motivated by the April 2004 death in Iraq of her son, 24-year-old Army specialist Casey Sheehan. Citing his memory, she became a key organizer of Gold Star Families for Peace and founded the "Camp Casey" installation in August 2005 near President Bush's ranch in Crawford, Texas.

Sheehan has stated that she had been a tepid critic of President Bush all along and was immediately skeptical of the invasion of Iraq in March 2003. She claimed that she had been surprised when her son enlisted in the Army in 2000, but it was her grief over his death that galvanized her public dissension. Unable to recover from her loss, Sheehan embarked on a public campaign to challenge the war, demanding more information from Bush and other

After her son's death in Iraq, Cindy Sheehan became an antiwar activist. She set up Camp Casey in Crawford, Texas, near President George W. Bush's ranch. (AP Photo/Waco Tribune-Herald, Duane A. Laverty)

officials about the cause for which her son had died.

In August 2005, Sheehan began a three-week vigil outside the president's Crawford ranch, vowing not to move until he granted her a meeting and an explanation for the war and its aftermath. According to Sheehan, she and her immediate family had met with the president in a condolence visit shortly after Casey's death; he did not, however, agree to meet again. Although her stint at Camp Casey failed to achieve the intended results, it did channel an unprecedented level of media attention onto the antiwar movement. Many argue that Sheehan's actions reinvigorated opposition to the war, which had flagged after its failure to prevent the initial invasion of Iraq.

Camp Casey transformed Sheehan into a highly visible public figure and an internationally recognized speaker and activist. She became a fixture at antiwar demonstrations and secured audiences with a number of celebrities and politicians, including controversial Venezuelan leader Hugo Chavez. Additionally, Sheehan has published two books, *Peace Mom* (2006), an autobiographical account of her development as an activist, and *Dear President Bush* (2006), a collection of essays. Through her work, she has promoted a platform of "matriotism," an antiwar perspective that she deemed the opposite of militaristic patriotism. Matriotism, as Sheehan has articulated it, eschews all war (save for explicitly defensive purposes) on the grounds that it kills other mothers' children. Because everyone has or had a mother, and because motherhood is the essence of caring, Sheehan reasoned, all mothers should oppose war on ethical grounds.

Predictably, Sheehan's philosophy and actions have drawn a great deal of controversy. She has been the subject of multiple arrests, and her husband, who disagreed with activism, filed for divorce while she was entrenched at Camp Casey. Many of the criticisms of Sheehan's work are deeply personal, in large part because her efforts are often couched in and motivated explicitly by her own loss. Some question whether her project is as altruistic as it might appear, while others resent the way in which her actions monopolized the attention of the media and came to represent the entirety of the otherwise diverse peace movement. Perhaps the greatest debate over Sheehan's message is whether or not it has dishonored the war dead; many have argued that describing the war as senseless is disrespectful not only to her son but to all the others who have died in the conflict. Consequently, other "Gold Star" families have undertaken a media campaign proclaiming that Sheehan does not speak for them because they supported the cause for which their loved ones had died.

Despite her early tenacity, Sheehan publicly resigned from the peace movement in May 2007. Citing a need to return to mothering her surviving children and the ineffectiveness of antiwar organizing, Sheehan posted an open letter announcing her departure on the liberal website *DailyKos* and has largely disappeared from the public scene. Although she has formally renounced antiwar activism, Sheehan remains a sharply polarizing figure, a target of criticism for some and a source of inspiration for others.

Rebecca A. Adelman

See also: Iraq War (2003–2011).

References and Further Reading

Abrams, Kathryn. "Women and Antiwar Protest: Rearticulating Gender and Citizenship." *Boston Law Review* 87 (2005): 849–82.

Cockburn, Cynthia. *From Where We Stand: War, Women's Activism, and Feminist Analysis*. London, UK: Zed Book, 2007.

Houppert, Karen. "Cindy Sheehan: Mother of a Movement?" *The Nation* 282 (June 12, 2006): 11–16.

Sheehan, Cindy. *Dear President Bush*. San Francisco, CA: City Lights, 2006.

Sheehan, Cindy. *Peace Mom: A Mother's Journey through Heartache to Activism*. New York: Atria, 2006.

SMITH, GENEVIEVE M. (1905–1950)

At the outset of American involvement in the Korean War, Gen. Douglas MacArthur appointed Genevieve M. Smith as the chief nurse of the Army Nurse Corps (ANC) in Korea. Smith never made it to her post. As she was deploying, her plane crashed. She became the only nurse to lose her life in the Korean War.

Smith was born on April 25, 1905, in Epworth, Iowa. Little is known about Smith's early life. She remained a resident of Epworth until she began active duty in the ANC. Genevieve Smith served in the ANC during World War II, and after the war Smith continued serving her country as the chief nurse of the 155th Station Hospital in Yokohama, Japan.

On June 25, 1950, the United Nations passed Resolution 82, which insisted North Korea cease its invasion of South Korea. The North Korean military continued its pursuit, so the United Nations issued Resolution 83, which asked for military assistance for South Korea. On July 8, 1950, the United Nations appointed Douglas MacArthur as the commander of the UN forces in Korea. MacArthur secured U.S. military involvement in the Korean War and selected Maj. Genevieve Smith as the chief nurse of the ANC in Korea. This appointment came as a surprise because Smith planned to retire the following year, 1951. Even though she planned to retire, Smith felt that it was her duty and graciously accepted the appointment.

Smith's transfer from the 155th Station Hospital in Yokohama, Japan, to Pusan, Korea, began on July 27, 1950. She boarded a dilapidated Douglas C-47D airplane a little before 4:00 a.m., in Haneda, Japan. The plane became airborne at 4:05 a.m., heading toward Pusan, Korea. The plane had difficulty from the beginning of the flight. At approximately 4:21 a.m., the plane had technical difficulties, and shortly thereafter the tail of the plane snapped off. The plane descended, gradually losing altitude until it crashed into the Pacific Ocean. Smith and 24 of her countrymen lost their lives in the crash. Smith was the only Army nurse to lose her life during the Korean War; however, her death was not officially counted as a casualty of the war because it was not due to hostility.

The U.S. government honored Smith and her service to the country by placing a memorial marker in Arlington National Cemetery.

Nancy J. Traylor-Heard

See also: Army Nurse Corps (ANC); Korean War (1950–1953); Nursing; World War II (1941–1945).

References and Further Reading

Bellafaire, Judith. "Called to Duty: Army Women during the Korean War Era." *Army History: The Professional Bulletin of Army History* 52 (2001): 19–27.

Neidel-Greenlee, Rosemary, and Evelyn Monahan. *A Few Good Women: America's Military from World War I to the Wars in Iraq and Afghanistan.* Harpswell, ME: Anchor Publishing, 2010.

Sarnecky, Mary T. *A History of the U.S. Army Nurse Corps.* Philadelphia: University of Pennsylvania Press, 1999.

SPANISH-AMERICAN WAR (1898)

American women played a variety of important roles in the Spanish-American War, from writing about the conflict as journalists to collecting donations for the troops. Women's impressive service as contract nurses for the U.S. Army and Navy during this war led to the establishment of a permanent Army Corps of Nurses in 1901.

Women factored into several of the controversies that precipitated the United States' declaration of war against Spain. Cuba and the Philippines independently began anticolonial insurrections against Spain in 1895 and 1896, respectively. For American reporters, starving women and children emblemized Spain's inhumane policies in putting down the rebellions. In February 1897, Spanish officials strip-searched three Cuban women aboard the *Olivette*, an American passenger ship, before allowing it to leave Havana for Tampa. American newspapers sensationalized the incident, further fanning calls for American intervention on the island. The *New York Journal* tried to rally public opinion against the imprisonment of Evangelina Cisneros, the daughter of a revolutionary; *Journal* reporter Karl Decker helped Cisneros escape from jail in Havana and brought her to New York. Political cartoonists frequently depicted Cuba allegorically as a damsel in distress. These various media representations all appealed to American men's sense of "chivalry" as the reason to "rescue" Cuba from Spain. On April 25, 1898, two months after the mysterious February 15, 1898, explosion of the U.S. battleship *Maine* in Havana harbor, the United States declared war on Spain.

The Spanish-American War lasted less than four months, and most battles were naval engagements. Even so, any initial hopes of maintaining the battlefield as a male preserve were soon revealed to be impractical. At the start of the war, the U.S. military had a hospital corps of 520 men along with 100 stewards and 103 acting stewards. In April, Congress authorized Surgeon General George Sternberg to hire nurses under contract so that there would be adequate numbers of medical staff. A well-connected Washington, D.C., physician, Anita Newcomb McGee, approached Sternberg about recruiting female nurses to serve in the military. Meanwhile, hundreds of letters poured into the secretary of war's office from women wishing to volunteer. These numbered almost 6,000 by September 1898. A large, important professional nurses organization, the Associated Alumnae of Trained Nurses of the United States and Canada, which later became the American Nurses Association, also offered its assistance. However, the telegram the organization sent to Sternberg was so badly garbled in transmission as to render the message incomprehensible. Thus Sternberg accepted McGee's plan instead: to screen applications through a committee within the Daughters of the American Revolution, a hereditary organization of which McGee was an officer. Sternberg was at first reluctant to employ women, and he refused to send out women contract nurses except in response to a specific request for them from the field. However, he came to accept and appreciate women's essential contribution to wartime nursing.

On May 10, 1898, the first contract nurses signed their contracts and proceeded to the embarkation point of Key West, Florida, to serve in the Army's general hospital there. Over 1,700 women, including more than 200 sisters from religious orders, worked as Army nurses during the war. Each received the same compensation: $30 per month and one daily ration. In selecting candidates, McGee emphasized the importance of formal training and experience in nursing as well as commendable character. Sternberg also sought African American women nurses with purported immunity to yellow fever and other tropical diseases. To this end, he sent Namahyoke Curtis to New Orleans to find recruits. A select group of women even worked as contract nurses for the Navy, which was most reluctant to hire female personnel. Esther Voorhees Hasson and five others served aboard the hospital ship *Relief* off the Cuban coast. Eventually women nurses were placed abroad. In mid-July, 129 of them went to Santiago, Cuba. Ellen May Tower became the first American woman to die on foreign soil while in the service of her country. At least 14 other nurses died during the war. As with soldiers, the greatest source of casualties was not combat but disease, particularly typhoid and yellow fever.

The innovation of physical exams upon enlistment kept American women from being able to fight disguised as men, as they had in numerous previous wars. However, some women found other ways to experience the war firsthand. Kathleen "Kit" Blake Watkins, who represented the *Toronto Mail and Express*, is often identified as the first accredited female war correspondent. Journalist Anna Northend Benjamin also covered war news, first from Florida but eventually from Cuba. She, Mabel Clare Craft, and Teresa Howard Dean published stories regularly in *Leslie*'s. Volunteering to nurse gave other women access to material that they then wrote about for newspapers and magazines. After the war, photographer Frances Benjamin Johnston captured images of heroism, from a portrait of Rough Rider and future president Theodore Roosevelt to Adm. George Dewey and his flagship *Olympia* in Manila.

On the homefront, many existing women's organizations rallied in support of the war effort. The General Federation of Women's Clubs expressed the collective spirit well in its resolution that "Like the women of 76 and 61, the women of 98 stand united and ready to aid the government at all times and in all womanly ways." State chapters of the Colonial Dames of America raised funds to collect supplies as well as provide soldiers with books, "delicacies," and other comforts. The Maryland and California chapters, for instance, helped equip the hospital ship *Solace*.

New groups formed specifically for war relief as well. Elite women founded the two largest of these groups: the Women's National War Relief Association (WNWRA) and Auxiliary No. 3 for the Maintenance of Trained Nurses. Politicians' wives played a prominent role in the WNWRA, which formed just weeks after the declaration of war and modeled itself after the U.S. Sanitary Commission from the Civil War. It focused on supporting U.S. troops through fund-raising, collecting, and organizing donations. Auxiliary No. 3, also referred to as the Red Cross Society for the Maintenance of Trained Nurses, aimed to support women nurses at Army field hospitals.

Local war relief headed by women abounded as well. For example, the Women's Emergency Corps in Portland,

Oregon, not only collected sundry donations but also raised funds by selling stationery, badges, and punch. A coalition of women's associations, including the Massachusetts and New England Woman Suffrage Associations, worked with the Volunteer Aid Association in Massachusetts to raise money and gather sheets, shirts, bandages, and dressings. Others near encampments sponsored entertainments for the soldiers; in Nevada, the Carson City Red Cross and Custer Relief Corps organized dances, concerts, and orations at which women themselves often performed. Many such local groups called themselves Red Cross societies even though they had no affiliation with the American Red Cross. The profusion of relief associations often led to duplicated efforts and even rivalries. Appreciation was most often publicly expressed towards the Red Cross as a term for volunteerism without an awareness of what different groups actually accomplished.

The national American Red Cross contributed significantly to war relief within its philosophy of political neutrality. It had distributed food and provided other humanitarian aid in Cuba earlier in the 1890s. After U.S. intervention, the organization continued its broader mission by serving Cuban combatants and refugees and Spanish prisoners of war as well as American soldiers. Clara Barton—a beloved and widely known figure from her Civil War work—nursed troops in Cuba after the battles of El Caney and San Juan Hill (July 1). In addition to sending supplies on the ship *State of Texas*, the American Red Cross conducted relief operations at domestic U.S. military camps, in the Philippines, and in Puerto Rico.

The United States signed an armistice protocol with Spain on August 12, ending hostilities. Despite the swift American victory, critics increasingly questioned the administration of the secretary of war, Russell Alger. Americans were scandalized to learn of poor hygienic practices at camps, unwholesome food rations, and other problems that had led to American fatalities. President William McKinley appointed lawyer and journalist Judith Ellen Foster to inspect mobilization stations. He also created a commission to investigate the conduct of the War Department. Although the collected testimony often indicted the Army's military preparedness and the structure of the medical corps, the work of women nurses won universal praise. The commission concluded that women nurses ought to have been sent sooner to the camps and in greater numbers. As McGee had hoped from the outset, women nurses had proved their value to the military.

The terms of the Treaty of Paris (December 10, 1898) only increased the sense that a permanent Army Nurse Corps would become indispensable. Spain gave the United States possession of the Philippines, Puerto Rico, and Guam. To this new overseas empire, the United States added Hawaii (annexed during the course of the war). In February 1899, nationalist Filipino forces under Emilio Aguinaldo began an open insurrection against American rule. The United States needed to expand its military presence to answer these challenges. Nurses were essential to the success of a standing army in tropical climates. Often women with experience from the war with Spain were the first to gain assignments overseas. Like

Clara Maass, they not only nursed combat wounds—more frequent in the Philippine Insurrection than they had been in the Spanish-American War—but they also participated in medical research on tropical diseases.

Although an earlier bill had failed in 1899, the passage of the Army Reorganization Act in 1901 included provision for a permanent corps of nurses in the Army. Section 19, drafted by McGee, created the Army Nurse Corps as an integral part of the Army. Dita Hopkins Kinney, who had served in the Spanish-American War, became its first superintendent. Trained, graduate nurses could apply for three-year, renewable appointments as active or reserve nurses. For the first time, Army nurses wore uniforms. Though the corps had only about 100 women in its first decade, with over half serving in the Philippines, it marked a turning point in American military history. Women nurses' participation in the Spanish-American War was further commemorated in a veterans organization, the Spanish-American War Nurses, founded in 1900, and by a memorial at Arlington National Cemetery.

Women also authored numerous songs, novels, poems, and other works of art that took the war as their theme, usually but not always from a nationalist point of view. The stalwart, proud soldier of Theo Alice Ruggles Kitson's memorial sculpture, "The Hiker," for example, became iconic. Though collective dissent never coalesced during the war against Spain, some publicly challenged American imperialism and militarism after the start of the Philippine Insurrection. Peace activists and suffragists like Jane Addams and Anna Garlin Spencer thought it hypocritical for the United States to claim it was nurturing democracy in its colonies when the government did not extend equal rights to all of its citizens. Poems like Katherine Lee Bates's "The Pity of It" and Frances E. W. Harper's "The Burdens of All" expressed growing popular discomfort with the atrocities and moral ambiguities of war.

Laura R. Prieto

See also: Addams, Jane (1860–1935); African American Women; American Red Cross; Army Nurse Corps (ANC); Barton, Clara Harlowe (1821–1912); Benjamin, Anna Northend (1874–1902); Civil War (1861–1865); Curtis, Namahyoke Sockum (1861–1935); Hasson, Esther Voorhees (1867–1942); Heavren, Rose (1870–1968); Hispanic American Women; Kinney, Dita Hopkins (1855–1921); Maass, Clara Louise (1876–1901); McGee, Anita Newcomb (1864–1940); Navy Nurse Corps; Nursing; Public Law 448 (July 2, 1925); Republic of Texas; Tower, Ellen May (1868–1898); United States Sanitary Commission (USSC); *USS Relief*; Watkins, Kathleen Blake [Kit Coleman] (1856–1915); Women's Nursing Corps, Army.

References and Further Reading

Graf, Mercedes. "Women Nurses in the Spanish-American War." *Minerva: Quarterly Report on Women and the Military* 19, no. 1 (Spring 2001): 3–38.

Hoganson, Kristin. *Fighting for American Manhood: How Gender Politics Provoked the Spanish-American and Philippine-American Wars.* New Haven, CT: Yale University Press, 1998.

McGraw, Charles. "The Intervention of a Friendly Power: The Transnational Migration of Women's Work and the 1898 Imperial Imagination." *Journal of Women's History* 19, no. 3 (Fall 2007): 137–60.

Sarnecky, Mary. *A History of the United States Army Nurse Corps.* Philadelphia: University of Pennsylvania Press, 1999.

SPANISH INFLUENZA (INFLUENZA PANDEMIC)

There was a major worldwide disease outbreak at the end of World War I. There were more deaths from influenza in the closing months of World War I than from all other causes during the entire war. Estimates of total mortality from the pandemic range from a conservative 20 million to nearly 100 million worldwide, compared to 9.2 million combat fatalities and 15 million total deaths from other causes. The average lifespan in the United States in 1917 and 1919 was 51 years. In 1918, as a result of the pandemic, that average dropped to 39 years. There were 729,381 cases of flu in the U.S. armed forces, with 7.2 percent mortality; 40 percent of the U.S. Navy and 36 percent of the U.S. Army were infected in 1918.

A variant of the influenza A virus caused the 1918 pandemic. The virus has the ability to stick first to the outer surface of the cells lining the lungs and then to penetrate those cells, coopt the intracellular machinery, and cause the cell to manufacture new virus particles that can be egested and coughed up, then infect a new host.

The first written description of what was probably an influenza pandemic was that of Hippocrates, from 412 B.C. Influenza epidemics occur regularly and usually cover a restricted geographic area. Although exposure to a particular variant of the virus confers life-long immunity, the pathogen has the ability to subtly alter its protein structure so that it can appear to be an organism the immune system does not recognize. Occasionally it will develop a whole new gene, allowing it to look like an entirely unique organism to which the body has no immunity whatsoever. These drastic changes, known as antigenic shifts, lead to pandemics, or worldwide disease outbreaks.

The first recorded cases of the influenza pandemic were in the Spanish town of San Sebastian in February 1918, accounting for the disease's most common eponyms—the Spanish Flu or the Spanish Lady. The first military case occurred on March 4 at Camp Funston, Kansas (an adjunct of Fort Riley), and cases were reported in British and French troops on the western front in early April. A curious aspect of the disease was its ability to traverse long distances faster than could be accounted for by existing ground or sea transportation.

In May 1918, the Grand Fleet was confined to port when more than 10,000 British sailors became ill. German general Erich Ludendorff initially thought the flu might be the serendipitous natural intervention that would allow him to triumph. His hopes were dashed when the disease broke out among his own troops and contributed to the failure of his offensive in July. By midsummer the disease mysteriously disappeared, having primarily affected Europe and North America, sparing Asia and the Southern Hemisphere. Although it had caused relatively debilitating illness, the first wave of the pandemic typically caused an illness that abated after about three days and was rarely fatal.

After a brief hiatus, the disease returned with a vengeance in the early fall. This time it seemed to arise in Asia, sweeping through India (where fatalities, though poorly recorded, may have reached 20 million), Southeast Asia, China, Japan, the Pacific Islands, and South America. By September the disease had broken out in Boston and, shortly thereafter, in the eastern Massachusetts military facility at Fort Devens. The second wave was an entirely different disease. Unlike the usual influenza that shows a predilection for the very young and the very old, this pandemic had three peaks of age preference: birth to 5 years, 70–74 years, and, atypically, 20–40 years. Young adults— specifically those of military age—were particularly vulnerable.

The new disease was of remarkably rapid onset. Stories abound of people being unexpectedly found dead sitting in chairs, dying on the subway going home from work, or being well on arising and dying before sundown. The illness started with sudden onset of flushing, chills, and fever followed by a cough with thick, bloody sputum. Within hours the patients would be cyanotic and, unable to move air, would suffocate. Those who survived the early stages would often develop a superimposed bacterial pneumonia a few days later and die from the complication.

There was understandable public panic in reaction to the disease. Cities passed laws mandating stiff fines for citizens venturing out in public without masks. Theaters and churches (but rarely saloons) were closed, and the provost marshal general of the U.S. Army canceled the planned 142,000-man draft for September. Rumors circulated that the disease had been released by a combination of poison gas and rotting bodies from the battlefield, that the Germans had contaminated the U.S. East Coast from submarines, and that Germany's Bayer chemical company had contaminated aspirin with a new germ.

There was no treatment, but, just as it had earlier in the year, the disease spontaneously disappeared. It reemerged in an attenuated form in 1920 before again disappearing, this time for good.

A curious aspect of the epidemic is its relative historical obscurity. When historian Alfred Crosby first became interested in the disease in the mid-1980s, the *Encyclopedia Britannica* accorded it three sentences and the *Encyclopedia Americana* just one. Fielding Garrison's encyclopedic monograph on military medicine, while noting that there were three-quarters of a million cases in the U.S. military in World War I, also gives the disease merely a single sentence. The recent concern about emerging viral diseases has rearoused interest in the disease and generated a handful of books on the pandemic.

The disease has not been seen again, although fear of its recurrence led directly to the swine flu panic and vaccination efforts of 1976 and 2009.

Jack McCallum

See also: World War I (1914–1918).

References and Further Reading

Barry, John M. *The Great Influenza: The Epic Story of the Deadliest Plague in History.* New York: Viking, 2004.

Crosby, Alfred W. *America's Forgotten Pandemic: The Influenza of 1918.* New York: Cambridge University Press, 1989.

Kolata, Gina. *Flu: The Story of the Great Influenza Pandemic of 1918 and the Search for the Virus That Caused It*. New York: Farrar, Strauss and Giroux, 1999.

Levine, Arnold. *Viruses*. New York: Scientific American Library, 1992.

STIMSON, JULIA CATHERINE (1881–1948)

Julia Stimson had a long and distinguished career in nursing. She served as the chief nurse of American Red Cross nursing (1918–1919), director of nursing for the American Expeditionary Forces (AEF; 1918–1919), and dean of the Army School of Nursing and superintendent of the Army Nurse Corps (ANC; 1919–1937).

Julia Catherine Stimson, daughter of Alice Wheaton Bartlett and Henry Albert Stimson, was born in 1881 in Worcester, Massachusetts. Both the Bartletts and the Stimsons were prominent families with ancestors dating back to colonial America. Stimson's early education took place in St. Louis, Missouri, when her father, a Congregational minister, took a pastorate there, and in New York City when the family moved there in 1893. She then attended Vassar College, from which she and her three sisters all graduated. Julia earned a BA degree in 1901. Her desire to enter medical school was forbidden by her family. Instead, after a summer at the Marine Biological Laboratory, Woods Hole, Massachusetts, she studied zoology at Columbia University for two years. She then worked in medical illustration at Cornell University Medical College.

While traveling abroad for health reasons in 1904, Stimson met Annie Goodrich, the superintendent of the New York Hospital Training School for Nurses. This meeting must have made a positive impression on Stimson, as she entered nursing school later that same year at New York Hospital. Even though health problems caused her to take a leave of absence twice while in training, she completed the program in 1908. Her first job, on the recommendation of Goodrich, was that of superintendent of nurses at the Harlem Hospital in New York. Three years later she moved on to Washington University's Barnes Hospital and Children's Hospital in St. Louis, where she was in charge of social services. She became the supervisor of nursing in 1913 at both hospitals and later also the superintendent of the nursing school. During this time period, she also earned an MA in sociology.

Stimson had signed up to be a Red Cross nurse in 1909 and in 1914 had joined the National Committee on Red Cross Nursing. She joined the ANC in 1917 and was named chief nurse of Washington University's Base Hospital 21. Base hospitals were part of a war readiness plan developed by the American Red Cross, in which Red Cross chapters and large hospitals around the country funded and established medical units consisting of physicians, nurses, and orderlies together with all the equipment needed for a 500-bed hospital, ready to deploy with two weeks' notice. When the unit arrived in Rouen, France, Stimson was assigned the same leadership position in the British Expeditionary Forces Hospital No. 12.

In April 1918, Stimson was appointed chief nurse of the American Red Cross in France and in November was named director of nursing of the AEF, supervising and coordinating the demobilization of the over 10,000 nurses serving with the AEF. A year later she became dean of the Army School of Nursing in Washington, D.C., and the fifth superintendent of the ANC, a position which she used to improve opportunities and conditions for Army nurses.

For her work in France she received awards from several governments including the Distinguished Service Medal from the United States; the British Royal Red Cross, First Class; the French *Medaille de la Reconnaissance Francaise;* the *Medaille d'Honneur de l'Hygiene Publique*; as well as the International Red Cross Florence Nightingale Medal. U.S. Army nurses were finally given "relative" rank in 1920, at which time Stimson became the first woman to hold the rank of major. After 20 years of service, Stimson retired from the Army in 1937, but she continued her work on behalf of the profession, serving as president of the American Nursing Association from 1938 to 1944. She returned to active duty from 1942 to 1944 to assist with the recruiting of nurses during World War II, thus providing service during both world wars. When Army nurses were granted full rank by Public Law 810 in August 1948, Stimson was promoted to colonel (retired). She lived just six weeks longer and passed away in Poughkeepsie, New York, on September 30, 1948.

Katherine Burger Johnson

See also: American Red Cross; Army Nurse Corps (ANC); Goodrich, Annie Warburton (1866–1954); Nursing; World War I (1914–1918); World War II (1941–1945).

References and Further Reading

Aynes, Edith A. *From Nightingale to Eagle.* Englewood Cliffs, NJ: Prentice Hall, 1973.

Stimson, Julia C. *Finding Themselves: The Letters of an American Army Chief Nurse in a British Hospital in France.* New York: Macmillan Company, 1918.

U.S. Army Center of Military History. *Highlights in the History of the Army Nurse Corps.* Washington, D.C.: Author, 1995.

STRATTON, DOROTHY CONSTANCE (1899–2006)

Dorothy Stratton became a captain in the U.S. Coast Guard (USCG) and the director of the USCG Women's Reserve, also known as SPAR. Stratton coined the term "SPAR" from the Coast Guard motto *Semper Paratus* (Always Ready).

Stratton was born on March 24, 1899, in Brookfield, Missouri. She grew up the daughter of a Baptist minister in small towns in Missouri and Kansas. In 1920 she graduated with a BA from Ottawa University in Ottawa, Kansas, then worked in various educational positions, including as a high school teacher, vice principal of a junior high school, and dean of girls at a senior high school. Stratton continued her education, earning a master's degree in psychology from the University of Chicago in 1924 and a doctorate in student personnel administration from Columbia University in 1932. Her thesis,

"Problems of Students in a Graduate School," was published in 1933. That same year she was appointed dean of women and associate professor of psychology at Purdue University. Stratton was an active dean, establishing the university's first residence halls for women and an employment placement center for Purdue women. In 1940, she became a full professor.

World War II brought such severe manpower shortages that each military service established a women's reserve. Stratton's first exposure to the military came in 1942 when she served on the selection committee of the Army 5th Corps Area, which met to select the first officer candidate class for the Women's Army Auxiliary Corps (WAAC). Later that same year, Stratton was commissioned as a lieutenant in the Women Accepted for Volunteer Emergency Service (WAVES), joining because "it was a new avenue of service for women, and it seemed important that women give a good account of themselves during the war service and afterward."

She was a member of the first class of WAVES at the Naval Training School at Smith College. The change from college dean to officer trainee was not an easy one to make, evidenced by Stratton's remark to a fellow trainee that she thought she had made "the worst mistake of my life." In September 1942, the newly commissioned Lieutenant Stratton was assigned as the assistant to the commanding officer at the Training Center for Radio Operators at Madison, Wisconsin. She did not serve long in this position; in November 1942, she was ordered to duty in the office of the commandant of the Coast Guard to help develop plans for a women's reserve

corps. The USCG Women's Reserve was established on November 23, 1942, and Stratton was selected as the director by the WAVES director, Lt. Cmdr. Mildred McAfee. She was sworn in on November 24, 1942.

As SPAR director, Stratton was primarily responsible for establishing policies for the procurement, training, utilization, and maintenance of morale of SPAR. At the height of the war, she commanded 1,000 officers and 10,000 enlisted women. Stratton resigned as SPAR director in January 1946, six months before SPAR completed its demobilization. She was appointed to the Retraining and Reemployment Administration to make sure that military women were not overlooked in its mission to help veterans and war workers reintegrate into the civilian community. Stratton served as the director of personnel for the International Monetary Fund (1947–1950) and as the executive director of the Girl Scouts of America (1950–1960).

Stratton received many honors for her service. She was awarded a Legion of Merit for her service as SPAR director. In 2001, a Captain Dorothy Stratton Leadership Award was created in her honor. In addition, the Coast Guard named National Security Cutter WMSL-752 the USCGC *Stratton*. She died on September 17, 2006.

Vicki L. Friedl

See also: McAfee (Horton), Mildred Helen (1900–1994); United States Coast Guard Women's Reserve (SPAR); Women Accepted for Volunteer Emergency Service (WAVES); Women's Army Auxiliary Corps (WAAC); Women's Army Corps (WAC); World War II (1941–1945).

References and Further Reading

Gruhzit-Hoyt, Olga. *They Also Served: American Women in World War II.* Secaucus, NJ: Carol Publishing Group, 1995.

Holm, Jeanne. *Women in the Military: An Unfinished Revolution.* New York: Random House, 1992.

Lyne, Mary C., and Kay Arthur. *Three Years behind the Mast: The Story of the United States Coast Guard SPARS.* Washington, D.C.: n.p., 1946.

Thomson, Robin J. *The Coast Guard and the Women's Reserve in World War II.* Washington, D.C.: Coast Guard, 1992.

Tilley, John A. *A History of Women in the Coast Guard.* Washington, D.C.: Coast Guard, 1996.

STREETER, RUTH CHENEY (1895–1990)

Ruth Cheney Streeter was the first woman to achieve the rank of major in the U.S. Marines and the first commander of the U.S. Marine Corps Women's Reserve (MCWR).

Streeter was born Ruth Cheney on October 2, 1895, in Brookline, Massachusetts. Her parents, Charles and Mary Cheney, were wealthy Episcopalians. After her father's death in 1900, Ruth's mother spent much of the next few years traveling abroad with her children. During her formative years, Ruth attended schools in France, Boston, and Pennsylvania. In 1917, she married Thomas Streeter, a wealthy attorney. Over the course of their marriage, the Streeters would have four children together.

During the United States' involvement in World War I, the Streeters lived in Washington, D.C. While her husband worked for the government, Streeter served in volunteer organizations supporting the soldiers overseas. In memory of her younger brother—a pilot killed in Italy—Streeter and her mother created the Cheney Award, a distinction given annually to a deserving person in the Army Air Corps. The award is still given out in the modern-day Air Force. During the interwar years, the family relocated to New York City and then Morristown, New Jersey. Streeter's philanthropic spirit found many outlets during the Great Depression. She strove to alleviate the suffering of the needy by serving on the Morris County Welfare Board and the State Relief Council.

As the nation mobilized for war and sent men overseas to fight against Nazi Germany and Imperial Japan, the United States' armed services formed women's auxiliary units in an effort to free up men for combat duty. The Army, Army Air Force, Navy, Coast Guard, and Marines all had female reserve organizations. Even before the United States entered World War II, Streeter—sensing that her country would not remain neutral indefinitely—began to take aeronautics courses and flying lessons. In 1942, she earned her pilot's license and joined the New Jersey Civil Air Patrol. Streeter was disappointed to find that because of her age and gender she would be restricted to doing clerical work. Determined to fly, Streeter tried five times to join the Women's Air Force Service Pilots (WASP); however, because of her age she was consistently turned away. She also considered joining the Women Accepted for Volunteer

Emergency Service (WAVES), the Navy's female auxiliary force. Yet once again she learned that she would not be able to fly.

The Marines' female auxiliary was the MCWR. Thanks to her family connections and patriotic willingness to serve, Streeter was offered the command of this organization by President Franklin D. Roosevelt in February 1943. Streeter, still yearning to serve her country during wartime, readily accepted the position and was commissioned a major, making her the first woman to obtain this rank in the Marine Corps. Because she had no experience with the Marines or the military, Maj. C. Brewster Rhodes was attached to Streeter as her adviser throughout the war.

During the war, the MCWR performed a plethora of tasks that contributed to the war effort. Code breakers, radio operators, welders, mechanics, cartographers, drivers, photographers, cooks, and quartermasters were just some of the positions filled by women reservists. Streeter proved so efficient at coordinating these activities that she was promoted to lieutenant colonel on November 12, 1943, and colonel in 1944. Recruitment consumed much of Streeter's workload, and she spent the early portion of her appointment traveling the country giving speeches. She proved especially adept at this, and by the time Japan surrendered in September 1945, 17,640 enlistees and over 800 officers filled the ranks of the MCWR. Streeter also influenced the training of female marines. Although the bulk of MCWR training consisted of desk work, Streeter convinced Marine Corps leadership to put firearms demonstrations in the training program.

On December 7, 1945, three months after the end of World War II, Streeter retired. For her services during World War II, Streeter was awarded the Legion of Merit in 1946. She spent much of her retirement devoting her time to veterans' organizations and historical preservation.

Streeter passed away due to congestive heart failure on September 30, 1990, in Morristown, New Jersey, and was buried in Peterborough, New Hampshire. She was three days shy of her 95th birthday.

Robert L. Glaze

See also: Women Accepted for Volunteer Emergency Service (WAVES); Women Marines; Women's Air Force Service Pilots (WASP); World War I (1914–1918); World War II (1941–1945).

References and Further Reading

Mason, John T. *The Atlantic War Remembered: An Oral History Collection*. Annapolis, MD: Naval Institute Press, 1990.

Stremlow, Mary V. *A History of the Women Marines, 1946–1977*. Washington, D.C.: History and Museum Division Headquarters, U.S. Marine Corps, 1986.

Stremlow, Mary V. *Free a Marine to Fight: Women Marines in World War II*. Washington, D.C.: History and Museum Division Headquarters, U.S. Marine Corps, 1996.

Weatherford, Doris. *American Woman and World War II*. Edison, NJ: Castle Books, 2008.

STRONG, ANNA "NANCY" SMITH (1740–1812)

A member of the Patriot Culper Spy Ring during the Revolutionary War,

Nancy Strong used her clothesline as a signaling device to relay intelligence.

Born Anna Smith on April 14, 1740, in Brookhaven, New York, to prominent New Yorkers Margaret Lloyd and William Henry Smith, she was better known as Nancy to friends and neighbors. She married Judge Selah Strong in 1760.

The Culper Spy Ring was the Revolution's most elaborate espionage operation. Established by Maj. Benjamin Tallmadge in August 1778, the ring provided Gen. George Washington with dispatches concerning British forces in and around New York City. Culper intelligence followed a roundabout route, passing through many sets of hands. At the center of this chain of conveyance was Strong, whose residence at Strong's Neck—a peninsula on the north shore of the Long Island Sound, in Setauket, Long Island—was strategically located to assist Culper traffickers in crossing their most challenging obstacle, the Long Island Sound. Among the many Culper agents, Strong worked most closely with Abraham Woodhull and Capt. Caleb Brewster. Woodhull, Strong's neighbor, received intelligence from messengers leaving New York City. He relied on Strong to signal the arrival of Brewster, the boatman.

Strong covertly signaled to Woodhull by creatively repurposing her outdoor clothesline. A black petticoat hanging on the line indicated that Brewster had landed nearby. The number of handkerchiefs Strong affixed, scattered among other garments, specified in which of the six prearranged landing points Brewster's boat could be found. At nightfall, Woodhull met Brewster in the place indicated by Strong and passed on the intelligence. Brewster then absconded across the sound to American-held Connecticut. Couriers received Brewster and in turn carried the intelligence overland to General Washington's headquarters. Strong was compelled to fulfill these important assignments with extreme stealth in close proximity to her enemies. The British had controlled Long Island since the Battle of Long Island (August 27, 1776), and their troops likely occupied her property.

British counterintelligence officials came perilously close to discovering Strong's activities. A February 4, 1781, report from the double agent William Heron, known to the British as Hiram, suggested that a certain unnamed woman—undoubtedly Strong—might be Brewster's accomplice. The British surely had reason to suspect Strong to be that certain woman. Strong's husband, the judge Selah Strong, was a prominent Patriot who served as captain in Suffolk County's first regiment of Minutemen and represented the town of Brookhaven as a delegate to the First, Second, and Third Provincial Congresses in New York. Moreover, he had been incarcerated since December 29, 1778, for correspondence with rebels while feigning cooperation with loyalists. That Strong avoided suspicion, in light of Hiram's report and her husband's reputation, was at least partly attributable to her gender and the domestic nature of her spy work. Female spies during the war often went unnoticed by their enemies on both sides. Many male military leaders did not perceive women to be capable of espionage, nor did they expect to be outfoxed by petticoats on a clothesline.

Historians have puzzled over the possibility of a second female participant in the Culper Ring, mentioned just once in Culper correspondence by the numeric code "355." She has been the subject of much historical embellishment and speculation. Some insist that the identity of the anonymous agent was actually Strong; they cite the Culper Ring's codebook, in which "355" meant simply "lady," not a specific individual. Strong remains the sole female Culper member identified by name.

Strong reunited with her husband at the end of the war. They named their eighth and last child after George Washington and lived quietly on Strong's Neck thereafter. Strong died on August 12, 1812, in Setauket at the age of 72.

Sonia Hazard

See also: American Revolution (1775–1783); Culper Spy Ring; Espionage; "355" (n.d.–n.d.).

References and Further Reading

Adkins, Edward P. *Setauket: The First Three Hundred Years, 1655–1955*. New York: David McKay Company, 1955.

Currie, Catherine. *Anna Smith Strong and the Setauket Spy Ring*. Port Jefferson Station, NY: C.W. Currie, 1990.

Ford, Corey. *A Peculiar Service*. Boston: Little, Brown and Company, 1965.

Rose, Alexander. *Washington's Spies: The Story of America's First Spy Ring*. New York: Bantam Books, 2006.

SWANTEK, ELIZABETH
(N.D.–N.D.)

Elizabeth Swantek was one of the first women of the Central Intelligence Agency (CIA) to be assigned to special operations overseas. Stationed in Germany for the majority of her career, Swantek was assigned on an equal basis with her male colleagues. Swantek worked for the Office of Strategic Services (OSS) in the unit of the CIA Directorate of Operations from 1951 until her retirement in 1975.

Swantek grew up in West Virginia and graduated as the valedictorian of her high school in 1942. After graduation, Swantek applied for a job with the U.S. Army Signal Corps and worked in Washington, D.C., during World War II. She spent nine years in the Signal Corps learning radio transmission. Toward the end of her time with the Signal Corps, Swantek joined the Navy's Women Accepted for Volunteer Emergency Service (WAVES) and received medical training at Bethesda Naval Hospital. After the end of World War II, Swantek enrolled in school at the University of California at Berkeley, where she majored in political science and foreign languages, with a focus on Russian. The CIA recruited Swantek after her college graduation.

In 1951, Swantek was sent overseas as a part of the Office of Special Operations. Stationed in Germany, Swantek became part of an OSS operation designed to send U.S. agents behind the Iron Curtain during the early years of the Cold War. Swantek was stationed in an isolated chalet in Southern Bavaria, where she and two other male colleagues worked for two years. Swantek's mission was to select, assess, and train potential agents to penetrate the Soviet Union. The potential agents that Swantek worked with were former Soviet citizens who had left the Soviet Union as refugees or defectors. These men were trained to penetrate into Soviet territory and establish themselves as Soviet citizens. They would then remain in their location and serve as long-term assets for the OSS by sending information they had gathered across the Iron Curtain.

Even though the training regimen for these Soviet men was extreme, Swantek took a hands-on approach to her duties to make sure that these assets would be ready for their assignments. Their training consisted of parachute jumps, survival training, drop zone familiarization, and the knowledge of wireless transmission essentials. Swantek was a qualified parachutist, a wireless operator, and an expert in survival skills and thus was well prepared to train and prepare the agents. She participated in every aspect of their training and developed close friendships with the men.

After two years in the field in southern Bavaria, Swantek returned to Washington, D.C., to prepare for additional special operations activities. Throughout her career in the OSS, Swantek filled many roles, including operations director and spy. She went undercover in various disguises. In all of her roles, Swantek successfully provided important information about Soviet intentions during the Cold War. At great personal risk, Swantek and her fellow OSS operatives were able to confirm that the Soviet Union was not planning an all-out attack on Europe, which

was a major concern for the United States and its European allies.

In 1975, at the end of her CIA career, deputy director Gen. Vernon A. Walters presented Swantek with the CIA's Career Intelligence Medal, which is given for a cumulative record of service that reflects exceptional achievements that substantially contributed to the mission of the agency. At the medal ceremony, Walters spoke about Swantek's career at the CIA, discussing how she spent 23 years rising through the ranks and aiding American intelligence efforts.

Swantek and the other pioneer women of the OSS established the groundwork for the many women who came after them in CIA.

Rorie M. Cartier

See also: Army Signal Corps; Cold War (ca. 1947–1991); Espionage; Women Accepted for Volunteer Emergency Service (WAVES); World War II (1941–1945).

References and Further Reading

Hoehling, A. A. *Women Who Spied.* Lanham, MD: Madison, 1993.

Mahoney, M. H. *Women in Espionage: A Biographical Dictionary.* Santa Barbara, CA: ABC-CLIO, 1993.

McIntosh, Elizabeth. *Sisterhood of Spies.* New York: Dell, 1999.

McIntosh, Elizabeth P. *The Role of Women in Intelligence.* Intelligence Profession Series. N.p.: Association of Former Intelligence Officers, 1989.

T

TEN PERCENTERS

"Ten Percenters" was the term used for the first class of African American officer candidates in the Women's Army Auxiliary Corps (WAAC).

When Congress formed the WAAC in May 1942, African American groups lobbied for inclusion of African American women. The War Department agreed to accept African Americans in the WAAC at a proportion of 10 percent of the entire corps—equal to the percentage of African Americans in the U.S. population at the time.

Newspapers and women's magazines advertised to recruit women to the WAAC. Officer candidates were sought at colleges and universities. Mary McLeod Bethune, president of the National Council of Negro Women, helped recruit African American women for the first class of officers. She visited traditional black colleges and garnered names of graduates whom she encouraged to apply to the WAAC.

The application process involved obtaining an official application form from a local recruiting station. Despite problems at some locations where officials refused to issue forms to them, African American women responded overwhelmingly to the call for volunteers. Overall, more than 30,000 women submitted the initial application form. As part of the application process, aptitude tests and physical exams were administered and, as a final stage in the process, interviews were conducted. Women applying to officers' training had to write an essay titled, "Why I Desire Service."

Four hundred forty women were selected to enter the first class of officer candidates at Fort Des Moines, Iowa, in July 1942. Forty were African American. They became known as the Ten Percenters. It is unclear how many African American women actually reported for induction and how many actually graduated. Some reports list 36, others 39, and still others 40. These women came from a wide variety of professions in civilian life, including beautician, college professor, dietician, teacher, secretary, nurse, law student, and musician, among others. Some were recent high school or college graduates and had little work experience.

Upon arrival at Fort Des Moines, the African American candidates were assigned to their own segregated unit—the 3rd Platoon of the 1st Training Regiment, 1st Company. They lived in a separate barrack, marched as a separate unit, and sat in a special section in the classrooms. They were banned from the "whites only" service club. The swimming pool was open to whites during the week and for two hours on Friday nights for African American women. In the mess hall, the African American officer candidates sat at a table labeled "For Coloreds." They obeyed the sign at first. Then they decided to protest. They entered the mess hall, sat down at the "colored table," and turned their plates over, refusing to eat. Eventually, the sign was removed. When questioned about the practice of segregation in the WAAC, officials explained that they were following a policy of the Regular Army and that it had been tested by time and found to work well for everyone.

When graduation day arrived, the roster of officer candidates was arranged to avoid a situation in which an African American woman would be the first WAAC to receive a diploma. Charity Adams would have been the first woman in the alphabetical list of officer candidates. To avoid this, the rosters were broken out by platoon—thereby listing a white woman from the 1st Platoon at the front of the roster.

The Ten Percenters battled racism and sexism to become the first African American women to graduate as officers in the WAAC on August 29, 1942. Racism and sexism in the military did not end with the graduation ceremonies. However, the Ten Percenters were the first to break through the barriers, paving the way for minority women to serve in all branches of the military.

Cheryl Mullenbach

See also: African American Women; Bethune, Mary McLeod (1875–1955); Earley, Charity Adams (1918–2002); Roundtree, Dovey Mae Johnson (1914–); Women's Army Auxiliary Corps (WAAC); Women's Army Corps (WAC); World War II (1941–1945).

References and Further Reading

Earley, Charity Adams. *One Woman's Army: A Black Officer Remembers the WAC*. College Station: Texas A & M University Press, 1989.

McCabe, Katie, and Dovey Johnson Roundtree. *Justice Older Than the Law: The Life of Dovey Johnson Roundtree*. Jackson: University Press of Mississippi, 2009.

Moore, Brenda L. *To Serve My Country, to Serve My Race: The Story of the Only African American WACs Stationed Overseas during World War II*. New York: New York University Press, 1996.

Putney, Martha S. *When the Nation Was in Need: Blacks in the Women's Army Corps during World War II*. Metuchen, NJ: Scarecrow Press, 1992.

THORPE (PACK), AMY ELIZABETH "BETTY" (1910–1963)

Amy Thorpe, codenamed "Cynthia," was an American citizen who served as a spy for the British Security Coordination (BSC) during World War II and purportedly relayed confidential information that shed light on the Axis Powers' Enigma cipher machine.

Born into a relatively privileged family on November 22, 1910, in Minneapolis, Minnesota, her father was a major in the Marine Corps and her grandfather a U.S. senator. She traveled widely with family, and her father eventually left the service in 1923 to study law in Washington, D.C. Having spent much time in the nation's capital as a youth, Thorpe was not one to shy away from vibrant social settings. By her late teens, Thorpe was considered a gorgeous debutante by many in Washington's elite social circles.

She eventually developed a romantic relationship with Arthur Pack, a bureaucrat at the British Embassy who was 20 years older than Thorpe. The two conceived a child together and were subsequently married in 1930, marking the beginning of their strained marriage. Their son was given up to foster parents. Over the ensuing years, Thorpe followed her husband to numerous diplomatic posts across the globe. While he was stationed in Spain, Thorpe became involved in the country's ongoing civil war, possibly as a British operative. There, she smuggled supplies and assisted rebels on numerous occasions. Political and military intrigue seemed to suit the young Minnesotan, and she believed she had discovered her life's calling.

As the Spanish Civil War continued, Pack and his family were ordered to Warsaw, Poland, in 1937. Pack's transfer to Warsaw may have been motivated by the British Secret Intelligence Service (SIS) in order to use Thorpe as an agent there. Despite her own revelations in the realm of foreign intrigue, Thorpe's relationship with her husband continued to deteriorate as he admitted to loving another woman. A year into his new appointment, Pack suffered a severe stroke and had no other option but to return to England. Thorpe remained in Poland. Paid well by British intelligence to obtain confidential information, Thorpe involved herself in a number of affairs with diplomats to access classified material. One such tryst involved Polish official Edward Kulikowski, who informed Thorpe of the Nazis' plan to conquer Czechoslovakia and reclaim the Sudetenland. Although the British government took no affirmative action on the matter, Thorpe proved her ability to obtain intelligence, especially to Cmdr. Jack Shelley of the SIS.

After a brief respite and truce with her husband in London, Thorpe invested herself entirely to the BSC as World War II began in earnest. Now under the guidance of spymaster William Stephenson, codenamed "Intrepid," Thorpe was relocated to her American homeland under the pseudonym "Cynthia." Back in her old stomping grounds of New York and Washington, she reconnected with old family friend Alberto Lais, who also happened to be an admiral and naval consul at the Italian Embassy. By becoming romantically involved with the aged sailor some 30 years her senior, Thorpe obtained secret naval codes and cipher documents that likely helped cripple the lethality of Italian and Axis vessels.

With her superiors looking to gain an inside perspective on the actions of the Nazi-collaborating Vichy France government, Thorpe also worked her way into Washington's French Embassy, posing as a reporter. There, she initiated an affair with public relations officer Charles Brousse in 1941. Only months before the proposed Allied invasion of North Africa in 1942, Thorpe was asked to obtain the naval ciphers used by Vichy French forces and their Axis allies from the embassy. Within time, Brousse himself was at least partially aware of his lover's mission and began feeding her intelligence. After several failed attempts to obtain the multivolume codes, they eventually attained copies with the help of a lock pick and by continuously duping the embassy guard. Although many historians remain unsure whether the cipher codes retrieved by Thorpe were the ones that proved instrumental in the North Africa invasion, her ability to seize and relay confidential information was approvingly noted by superiors.

Believing she had helped save countless Allied lives, Thorpe showed no remorse for sleeping with numerous diplomats and enemy officials. Pack, however, killed himself the same year the war ended. Thorpe married Brousse and lived in a French castle until her untimely death of throat cancer on December 1, 1963. Brousse perished a decade later when an electrical fire devoured part of their mountain home.

Jared Frederick

See also: Espionage; World War II (1941–1945).

References and Further Reading

McIntosh, Elizabeth P. *Sisterhood of Spies: The Women of the OSS.* Annapolis, MD: Naval Institute, 1998.

Miles, Rosalind, and Robin Cross. *Hell Hath No Fury: True Profiles of Women at War from Antiquity to Iraq.* New York: Three Rivers Press, 2008.

Payment, Simone. *American Women Spies of World War II.* New York: Rosen Publishing, 2004.

Stevenson, William. *A Man Called Intrepid: The Incredible WWII Narrative of the Hero Whose Spy Network and Secret Diplomacy Changed the Course of History.* Guilford, CT: Lyons Press, 2000.

West, Nigel. *Historical Dictionary of Sexspionage.* Lanham, MD: Scarecrow, 2009.

"355" (N.D.–N.D.)

Morton Pennypacker, an amateur historian working at the end of the 19th and the early 20th centuries, uncovered a moving tale of an unknown agent, codenamed "355." This woman was caught up in an amorous relationship with a senior spy named Robert Townsend as she gathered data for the Americans while moving in elite British and Tory circles. She was arrested, gave birth to Townsend's love child (whom he raised), and died in childbirth on the British prison ship HMS *Jersey* while it was anchored off New York. Historians, however, question the veracity of this story.

During the American Revolution, the Culper Spy Ring used "355" to indicate a woman. George Washington and Benjamin Tallmadge created the Culper Spy Ring a year after the British drove the Continental Army out of New York City in 1776. Washington managed to keep close tabs on what was going on in New York City, the main base of operations for the British throughout the war, through this ring. The ring was small—only eight names appear on one list of amounts to be reimbursed to individuals—and was based out of Tallmadge's hometown of Setauket, a village on Long Island then about 60 miles from New York City. Messengers would carry the messages of the two primary agents, Abraham Woodhull (codenamed Samuel Culper, Sr.) and Townsend (codenamed Samuel Culper, Jr.), to Setauket. Caleb Brewster would then ferry the messages across Long Island Sound, and they would be delivered to Washington over land by horseback. The two usually sent messages in a code devised by Tallmadge, written in invisible ink between the lines of what appeared to be ordinary correspondence. Washington and the spies possessed the chemicals to write and expose this invisible ink.

The tale of spy 355 was woven from a single sentence in a single letter written by Woodhull to Tallmadge. The number 355 was the Culper code for "woman." The letter in question mentions "a 355," not an agent 355. This particular 355 was to accompany Woodhull to New York City to enable him to "outwit them all." The context may indicate that the "all" he was seeking to outwit would have been the patrols looking for those engaged in rebel activity. It has quite plausibly been suggested that the woman accompanying him was to pose as his wife, as a married couple traveling to see relatives did not match the typical image of solitary spies slinking about clandestinely. The letter states nothing more about this woman or her role in the ring. Furthermore, a woman is not mentioned again in the preserved correspondences playing any tangible role in the ring in the city. In addition, the woman was an acquaintance of Woodhull, not Townsend. Townsend likely had an illegitimate son (some traditions suggest it was actually his

brother's) whom he raised, who was born in 1784 (the war ended the previous year).

It has been reasonably conjectured that the identity of the 355 was Anna Strong (1740–1812). Anna was a cousin and neighbor of Woodhull and would be related by marriage to Tallmadge after the war as well. Her husband, Selah, was an activist for the rebel cause and was imprisoned on the *Jersey* for the duration of the war. Anna, according to legend, was allowed to bring him food. Perhaps her visits to him were the genesis of the "woman spy on the *Jersey*" legend that became part of agent 355 lore. Brewster hid in her house on at least one occasion. He passed on the opportunity to capture a British officer while he was hiding there lest the British become suspicious of Anna's actions, and the loyalties of Setauket, for that matter. Oral tradition holds that she would hang laundry to dry to signal Woodhull (or the primary messenger, Austin Roe) that Brewster and his boat were in town and precisely where he was hiding. Her husband appears on the list of those to be reimbursed mentioned above, though he was in prison, meaning she was actually reimbursed for her expenses on behalf of the ring. Whatever her precise role was in the ring, she did risk her life for her fledgling country.

The legend of 355 grew beyond Pennypacker's imaginative tale. Agent 355 has a life of her own in contemporary literature, comic books, and movies. If one holds that Anna Strong is the identity of Woodhull's companion, then the bravery she displayed is just as worthy of adulation as Pennypacker's fictive femme fatale.

Mark Anthony Phelps

See also: American Revolution (1775–1783); Culper Spy Ring; Espionage; "Miss Jenny" (ca. 1760–n.d.); Strong, Anna "Nancy" Smith (1740–1812).

References and Further Reading

Burke, John, and Andrea Meyer. "Spies of the Revolution." *New York Archives* 9, no. 2 (Fall 2009): 9–13.

Finley, James, ed. *U.S. Army Military Intelligence History: A Sourcebook.* Fort Huachuca, AZ: U.S. Army Intelligence Center, 1995.

Pennypacker, Morton. *General Washington's Spies on Long Island and New York.* New York: Long Island Historical Society, 1939.

Rose, Alexander. *Washington's Spies: The Story of America's First Spy Ring.* New York: Bantam, 2005.

TOMPKINS, SALLY LOUISA (1833–1916)

Sally Tompkins was the only woman to be commissioned as an officer in the army of the Confederate States of America.

Sally Louisa Tompkins was born on November 9, 1833, in Matthews County, Virginia. Her family was a wealthy and religious family with a proud heritage. Her grandfather served as an officer under George Washington in the Revolutionary War and was commended for his bravery at the Battle of Monmouth Courthouse. As a youth, Tompkins discovered her talent for nursing and often volunteered to care for animals and people—both white and black—in her community. Shortly before the beginning of the Civil War, she and her family moved from coastal Virginia to Richmond. Here, she became an active member in St. James Episcopal Church.

After the outbreak of the Civil War, Tompkins devoted herself to the Confederate cause. When the war's first major battle occurred at Manassas (Bull Run) on July 21, 1861, Richmond was flooded with wounded soldiers. In an effort to care for the maimed troops, Tompkins gained the permission of Judge John Robertson, a fellow church member, to use his house as a hospital. In honor of its benefactor, she named her establishment the Robertson Hospital. Relying on other women from St. James, along with other philanthropic Richmonders, Tompkins quickly converted the judge's house into a hospital with a 22-bed capacity. She paid for the majority of the hospital's expenses out of her own pocket. Despite the negative stigma that was attached to female nurses during the 19th century, Tompkins ran her hospital confidently. She was a strict disciplinarian who insisted that her patients and staff abide by her rules.

The Robertson Hospital soon gained a reputation for cleanliness, compassion, and efficiency. Even though germ theory was still not understood, Tompkins insisted that her hospital be exceptionally sanitary. This resulted in the Robertson Hospital achieving the highest survival rate for its patients out of any military hospital—both Union and Confederate—during the Civil War. During its four years of existence, the hospital treated 1,333 wounded soldiers. Of these, only 73 lost their lives. Tompkins's abilities and reputation as a caregiver led famous diarist Mary Chestnut to refer to her as the Confederacy's Florence Nightingale.

The hospital was almost closed down less than a month and a half after its establishment. In an effort to minimize corruption and increase efficiency, the Confederate government ordered that all privately owned hospitals be closed in September 1861. Tompkins, aided by William W. Camp, the assistant secretary of the treasury, appealed to Confederate president Jefferson Davis. Impressed by her accomplishments as a hospital administrator, Davis commissioned Tompkins as a captain in the Confederate cavalry. Thus, Robertson Hospital, now run by an army officer, could remain operational. Tompkins accepted the commission; however, she refused to draw a salary for her position. Tompkins was the first, and only, woman to receive an officer's commission in the Confederate armed forces. Her commission was dated September 9, 1861. Tompkins's rank made it easier for her to acquire much-needed medical supplies for her patients.

"Captain Sally," as Tompkins came to be affectionately referred to by her patients, labored for the rest of the war to care for wounded Confederate soldiers. Because of her hospital's reputation, many wounded soldiers begged to be sent to Tompkins's facility. As she often carried her Bible with her, Tompkins provided for the spiritual as well as physical comfort of her patients. As the war progressed and medicines became scarcer, Tompkins sometimes used herbal remedies to treat her patients. On June 13, 1865, two months after Robert E. Lee surrendered to Ulysses S. Grant at Appomattox Court House, Tompkins closed Robertson Hospital.

Despite numerous romantic proposals both during and after the war, Tompkins never married. Even after closing her hospital, she remained in Richmond, where she continued to do charitable work, assisting widows and orphans of Confederate soldiers. Having exhausted her fortune helping others, Tompkins entered Richmond's Home for Confederate Women in 1905. There she remained for 11 years until she passed away on July 25, 1916. Because of her years of selfless service to the soldiers of the Confederacy, Tompkins was buried with full military honors at Christ Episcopal Church in Matthews County, Virginia.

Robert L. Glaze

See also: Civil War (1861–1865); Nursing.

References and Further Reading

Furgurson, Ernest B. *Ashes of Glory: Richmond at War.* New York: Alfred A. Knopf, 1996.

Hagerman, George. "Confederate Captain Sally Tompkins Was the Only Woman to Be Commissioned an Officer in the Civil War." *America's Civil War* 10, no. 2 (1997): 10–12.

Maggiono, Ron. "Captain Sally Tompkins: Angel of the Confederacy." *OAH Magazine of History* 16, no. 2 (2002): 32–38.

Waugh, Charles G., and Martin H. Greenberg, eds. *The Women's War in the South: Recollections and Reflections of the American Civil War.* Nashville, TN: Cumberland House, 1999.

TOWER, ELLEN MAY (1868–1898)

Spanish-American War nurse Ellen May Tower was the first woman to die on foreign soil while serving the United States.

Nicknamed the Camp Wikoff Angel, she was also one of the first women to receive a military funeral.

Tower was born in Byron, Michigan, on May 8, 1968, to Justice Samuel Spruce Tower and Sarah Bigelow Tower. Patriotic duty ran in the family, as her father had been captain of the 10th Michigan Infantry during the Civil War. Throughout her childhood, Tower dreamed of becoming a nurse. She studied at the Chaffee School and the Byron Village School before her mother's death caused the family to move to Onaway in 1880. Tower's devotion to helping others led her to become a schoolteacher. Her first job was with students in Bancroft, Michigan. She then began work for Dr. Whealock, a female physician. This work quickly brought back her childhood passion for nursing.

Tower pursued her goals by enrolling in a nurse's training program at Grace Hospital in Detroit. On January 17, 1894, at age 26, Tower graduated and began her career at the Michigan School for the Blind in Lansing. However, it was not long before her job was interrupted by political conflict. As relations between the United States and Spain deteriorated in the late 1890s, the county began preparing for war. Tower, too, prepared for the possibility of war, and after four years at the Michigan School for the Blind, she returned to Grace Hospital to train as a war nurse. On April 21, 1898, she became the first nurse to volunteer for duty should the war come. Just three days later war was declared on Spain.

To ensure that nurses serving in the war were the most competent ones available, the Daughters of the American Revolution Hospital Corps was set up. Tower sent multiple letters to the surgeon general's advisor, Dr. Anita Newcomb McGee, requesting to join the prestigious unit, and she was finally accepted. On September 1, 1898, Tower took her oath of service. She then went to Montauk Point, New York, home of Camp Wikoff.

Tower spent her time there caring for soldiers who had become either injured or sick and had been sent back to the United States to recover. Medical care was particularly essential during the Spanish-American War because 90 percent of deaths were a result of disease, not battle wounds. She soon became known as the Camp Wikoff Angel for her dedication to her gruesome tasks and her kind care of soldiers. Tower made sure that soldiers' families were kept informed of their condition at a time when the military did not regularly keep loved ones notified. In late September, Tower volunteered to help soldiers fight disease in Puerto Rico.

Tower spent less than 10 weeks in Puerto Rico before she came down with typhoid fever and succumbed to acute pericarditis. Tireless work nursing the soldiers day and night had significantly weakened her body's disease resistance. She died on December 9, 1898, the day the Treaty of Paris effectively ended the war. She was the first nurse to die during the Spanish-American War and the first woman ever to die on foreign soil in the service of the United States.

The following month her body was returned to Michigan, and on January 15, 1899, a funeral was held in Byron's Cass Avenue Methodist Episcopal Church. It had been five years to the day since Tower had been awarded her nursing diploma. Dr. Sterling delivered her eulogy just as he had been the one to present her nursing diploma. Stores were closed, and 4,000 family members, friends, servicemen, and dignitaries attended. Her body lay at the Light Guard Armory in Detroit before she was buried on January 17 followed by taps and a military salute. It was the first military funeral for a woman ever held in Michigan and only the third in the entire country's history.

Tower's dedication to her country and her life-saving efforts were remembered in her town long after her death. When a new village was founded in 1899, it was named Tower in honor of Ellen May Tower. On May 30, 1903, a 10-foot monument was erected over her grave. The statue depicts a young lady with long hair wearing gray robes and with flowers around her wrist. The people of Byron and the Women's Relief Corps raised funds, and the Michigan State Legislature appropriated $1,000 for the monument honoring her service to others.

Megan Findling

See also: McGee, Anita Newcomb (1864–1940); Nursing; Spanish-American War (1898).

References and Further Reading

Ashlee, Laura Rose. *Traveling through Time: A Guide to Michigan's Historical Markers.* Ann Arbor: University of Michigan Press, 2005.

Graf, Mercedes H. "Women Nurses in the Spanish-American War." *Minerva: Quarterly Report on Women and the Military* 19, no. 1 (Spring 2001): 3–27.

Michigan Legislature House of Representatives. *Journal of the House of Representatives of the State of Michigan*, Vol. 2. Lansing, MI: Wynkoop Hallenbeck Crawford, 1901.

TOWLE, KATHERINE A. (1898–1986)

Col. Katherine A. Towle served as the second director of the U.S. Marine Corps Women's Reserve (MCWR) during World War II and went on to be the first director of the Women Marines beginning in 1948. She served for nearly nine years in the MCWR and Women Marines before retirement and then continued with her education career at the University of California, where she had worked before the war.

Born in 1898 in Towle, California, a town founded by her grandfather in the mid-19th century, Towle moved with her parents to Berkeley in 1908, and in 1915 she graduated from Berkeley High. She went on to attend the University of California between 1916 and her graduation with a bachelor's degree in political science in 1920. During her undergraduate years, she was active in a number of student organizations. Towle briefly continued her graduate education at Berkeley before moving to Columbia University in New York, where she completed additional studies during 1922 and 1923. She ultimately returned to the Berkeley area to work for several years at the University of California as an assistant in admissions, then as resident dean and headmistress of Miss Ransom and Miss Bridges School. In 1933, she resumed her graduate studies and completed a master of arts in political science from the University of California in 1935, with a master's thesis that analyzed the presidential veto since 1889. Although she was interested in pursuing a doctoral degree, she instead became the assistant to the manager and senior editor of the University of California Press from 1935 to 1943.

When she joined the MCWR in 1943, Towle became one of the first eight women officers of the organization. By the time she returned to the University of California in 1946, she had become a colonel in the MCWR and had spent the last six months of her military service as director of the MCWR. Towle succeeded Col. Ruth Cheney Streeter, the original director of the MCWR, in this position.

With the end of the war, Towle became assistant dean of women at the University of California–Berkeley. However, when the Women's Armed Services Integration Act of 1948 passed, creating the Women Marines, Marine Corps commandant Gen. Clifton B. Cates asked Towle to become the first director of the Women Marines. She accepted the position and returned to active military duty in late 1948.

As the director of Women Marines from 1948 to 1953, Towle helped the organization with recruiting efforts, with great success in recruiting that focused on colleges and universities. During her tenure, the Women Marines established its policies and began to grow its numbers. The Women Marines adopted new uniforms designed by Mainbocher, which would become its signature attire in future years. In 1952, Mills College awarded Towle the doctor of laws degree as an honorary award. In her time as director, Towle established a reputation for herself and the Women Marines that fostered respect from male marines, particularly senior officers.

According to provisions of the Women's Armed Services Integration Act, Towle retired from military service in 1953 because she had reached age 55. Upon retirement, Towle received a Legion of Merit from the president, a Letter of Commendation from the Marine Corps commandant, and the Naval Commendation Medal.

Although Towle's military career had ended, she went back to the University of California at Berkeley, where she spent another 13 years in academic administration roles. From 1953 to 1960, Towle was the dean of women, only the fourth to hold this role in the university's history. During the first half of the 1960s (1961–1965), Towle served as the assistant dean of students. In her final year before retirement, Towle was dean of students (1965–1966). When Towle left the university in 1966, she did so once again under institutional age requirements for retirement. During her final years as dean, the free speech movement came to Berkeley, and Towle had some interaction with movement leaders as they presented their petitions to the administration. However, in her position Towle did not have the authority to authorize some of the campus changes desired by the student activists.

Towle received many honors in her lifetime in addition to honors in her name. In 1962, the first director of the MCWR from World War II, Ruth Cheney Streeter, endowed a $20,000 scholarship at the University of California–Berkeley in Towle's name. In 1968, the University of California honored Towle with an honorary doctor of laws degree, and she was selected as a charter member of the Berkeley Fellows that year, an organization formed in recognition of the university's

100th anniversary. In 2005, the University of California named a residence hall after Towle.

In her retirement years, Towle volunteered occasionally and traveled. She died on March 1, 1986, in Pacific Grove, California.

Tanya L. Roth

See also: Dulinsky, Barbara J. (n.d.–n.d.); Johnson, Opha Mae (1900–1976); Streeter, Ruth Cheney (1895–1990); Women Marines; Women's Armed Services Integration Act of 1948; World War II (1941–1945).

References and Further Reading

Holm, Jeanne. *In Defense of a Nation: Servicewomen in World War II*. St. Petersburg, FL: Vandamere Press, 1998.

Holm, Jeanne. *Women in the Military: An Unfinished Revolution,* rev. ed. Novato, CA: Presidio Press, 1993.

Kerr, Clark. *The Gold and the Blue: A Personal Memoir of the University of California, 1949–1967.* Vol. 2: *Political Turmoil.* Berkeley: University of California Press, 2003.

Monahan, Evelyn, and Rosemary Neidel-Greenlee. *A Few Good Women: America's Military Women from World War I to the War in Iraq and Afghanistan.* New York: Alfred A. Knopf, 2010.

Nathan, Harriet. "Administration and Leadership: Katherine A. Towle." Interview. University History Series. Berkeley: University of California, 2007. http://content.cdlib.org/ark:/13030/kt000000gm/ (accessed May 20, 2010).

Stremlow, Mary. *A History of the Women Marines, 1946–1977.* Washington, D.C.: History and Museums Division, U.S. Marine Corps, 1986.

Witt, Linda, Judith Bellafaire, Britta Granrud, and Mary Jo Binker. *"A Defense Weapon Known to Be of Value": Servicewomen of the Korean War Era.* Hanover, NH: University Press of New England, 2005.

TRACEY, PATRICIA ANN (1950–)

In 1996, Patricia Ann Tracey became the first woman to achieve the rank of vice admiral in the Navy.

Tracey was born in the Bronx, New York, on November 30, 1950. She graduated from the Academy of Mount St. Ursula High School in 1966. Tracey, then age 15, enrolled in the College of New Rochelle, where she earned a bachelor's of arts degree in mathematics within five years. Upon completing college, she fought for a waiver in order to enter the Navy at such a young age. In 1970, she completed the Women's Officers School and was commissioned as an ensign. She also earned a master's degree in operations research from the Naval Postgraduate School. Tracey has also been awarded an honorary doctorate of letters from Wilson College.

Tracey began her career at the Naval Space Surveillance System located in Dahlgren, Virginia, where she qualified as a command center officer and orbital analyst. After her tour on the staff of the commander of the Pacific Fleet, she moved to the Bureau of Naval Personnel, where she served as the placement officer for graduate education and service college students.

From 1980 to 1982, Tracey served as an extended planning analyst in the Systems Analysis Division on the chief of naval operations' staff. Following this position, her career moved her back to New York where, in Buffalo, she served as the executive officer at the Naval Recruiting District for the next two years. In 1984, she was then transferred to the Program Appraisal Division of the chief of naval operations' staff, where she was assigned as a manpower and personnel analyst.

In 1986, Tracey was given her first command when she was named commander of the Naval Technical Training Command at Treasure Island. Following her two-year tour there, she was transferred to the Enlisted Plans and Community Management Branch of the chief of naval personnel's staff. Once again she found herself in command in 1990 when she assumed command of Naval Station Long Beach, California. At the end of this assignment, Tracey reported as a fellow with the Chief of Naval Operations' Strategic Group at the Naval War College.

From 1993 to 1995, Tracey was assigned to be the director for manpower and personnel on the Joint Staff. From the Joint Staff, Vice Admiral Tracey once again assumed command when she was appointed commander at the Naval Training Center, Great Lakes. Following this position she became the chief of naval education and training, and director of naval training for the chief of naval operations from July 1996 to December 1998. Also in 1996, she became the first woman in naval history to achieve the rank of vice admiral.

From December 1998 to August 2001, she served as the deputy assistant secretary of defense (military manpower and personnel policy) in Washington, D.C. She was responsible for the establishment of all policies concerning military personnel matters including accessions and retention programs; compensation and benefits; and policies governing classification, assignment, and career development for over 1 million servicemembers of the Department of Defense.

In 2001, Tracey was assigned as director, Navy staff, Office of the Chief of Naval Operations at the Pentagon. Here she was in command of a 1,400-person headquarters, with nine individual flag-level directorates and a budget of $90 million. During this assignment, the Pentagon was attacked during the September 11, 2001, terrorist attacks. This attack destroyed 89 percent of the Navy staff space within the Pentagon, yet Tracey led the emergency reconstitution efforts. Tracey was also instrumental in taking the staff to wartime footing within 15 hours of the attack. Following the attack, she directed the design and construction of the new workspace, which enabled the Navy staff to be back in its offices and back at work in just two-and-a-half months.

Tracey retired in 2004 after a 34-year career that earned her many honors and awards. These include, but are not limited to, two Defense Distinguished Service Medals, two Navy Distinguished Service Medals, the Legion of Merit (third award), the Meritorious Service Medal (third award) and the French Légion d'Honneur. After retirement, the recognition did not end. In December 2010, Tracey was inducted into the Naval Postgraduate School Hall of Fame.

Since retirement, Tracey has served as a consultant of the U.S. Navy from 2004 to 2005 and then to the Department of Defense from 2005 to 2006. Also in 2006, Tracey began serving as a senior fellow at the Center for Naval Analysis. In 2007, she became a director of U.S. Steel Corporation. She also serves on the Armed Forces Benefit Association and United States Naval Institute. Tracey is also a trustee of Wilson College in Chambersburg, Pennsylvania.

Sharon Michelle Courmier

See also: War on Terror (2001–).

References and Further Reading

Gaytan, Peter S., and Marian Edelman Borden. *For Service to Your Country: The Essential Guide to Getting the Veterans' Benefits You've Earned.* New York: Citadel Press, 2011.

Goldberg, Alfred. *Pentagon 9/11.* Washington, D.C.: Historical Office, Office of the Secretary of Defense, 2007.

Sweetman, Jack. *American Naval History: An Illustrated Chronology of the U.S. Navy and Marine Corps, 1775–Present.* Annapolis, MD: Naval Institute Press, 2002.

Wise, James E., and Scott Baron. *Women at War: Iraq, Afghanistan, and Other Conflicts.* Annapolis, MD: Naval Institute Press, 2006.

Hailed as "the Moses of her people" because of her courageous rescues of hundreds of slaves through the Underground Railroad, Harriet Tubman also served as a Union scout during the Civil War. (Library of Congress)

TUBMAN, HARRIET [ARAMINTA ROSS] (CA. 1820–1913)

Ex-slave Harriet Tubman became active in the abolitionist movement and the Underground Railroad. She also served as a Union scout during the Civil War.

Tubman was born Araminta Ross in Dorchester County, Maryland. Her date of birth is a point of contention, being noted as early as 1815 and as late as 1825. Like many African American slaves in the United States, Ross was kept in a state of illiteracy, physically abused, and separated from portions of her family. In one incident, an angry overseer struck her on the head with a two-pound weight. Consequently, Ross suffered from seizures, hallucinations, headaches, and slowed speech for the remainder of her life.

In 1844, Ross married John Tubman, a free African American. Shortly thereafter, she changed her first name to Harriet in honor of her mother. Five years later, without her husband, who refused to follow her, Tubman escaped to freedom by fleeing to Philadelphia. Here, Tubman became involved in the Underground Railroad—a covert network of free African Americans and abolitionists who shepherded slaves escaping from the South to freedom in the North and Canada.

After gaining her freedom, Tubman made numerous trips back to Maryland to lead other slaves out of bondage. Although the purpose of her earliest trips south was to free her family, she soon began shepherding friends, acquaintances, and strangers to freedom. During one of her expeditions, she attempted to bring her husband north, only to find that he had married another woman. Tubman quickly earned a reputation as a strict disciplinarian on her missions. She always carried a pistol both for protection and to prevent runaway slaves from abandoning the expedition and compromising the safety of the group. During the antebellum years, she made over a dozen trips back into Maryland, freeing a total of about 300 slaves. Tubman's willingness to risk her own safety to lead her people to freedom—coupled with her devout Christianity—earned her the nickname "Moses."

Despite Tubman's nonviolent methods, she found a kindred spirit in the radical abolitionist John Brown. Both individuals dedicated their lives to freeing slaves, and both believed that they were ordained by God to carry out their missions. Recognizing her prestige within the African American community, Brown asked Tubman to begin recruiting slaves and ex-slaves for his impending war on the peculiar institution. Tubman began recruiting for this purpose and gave every indication that she intended to accompany Brown on his crusade. For reasons that are still unclear, Tubman did not join Brown for his raid on Harper's Ferry. Brown's mission failed, and he was subsequently executed.

When the Civil War broke out in 1861, Tubman devoted herself to the Union war effort. Like most African Americans—slave and free—Tubman saw a Northern victory over the Confederacy as a necessary precursor to the abolition of slavery. Even though she was discouraged over the federal government's reluctance to initially make abolition one of its war aims, Tubman became a nurse in Port Royal, South Carolina—a Union-occupied region of that Confederate state. Here she cared for Northern soldiers as well as for the community's slaves.

As the war progressed, Tubman expanded her involvement beyond nursing. President Abraham Lincoln's Emancipation Proclamation—issued on January 1, 1863—provided Tubman with new opportunities to aid the Union. African Americans could now enlist in the U.S. Army. Like her fellow abolitionist Frederick Douglass, Tubman was active in recruiting former slaves into the Union's armed forces. Moreover, Tubman organized networks of spies and scouts among recently liberated slaves. With their knowledge of local geography and infrastructure, slaves were a valuable resource in the planning of many Union operations. Tubman served as a guide for multiple expeditions herself. During the Combahee River Raid in June 1863, Union troops—including a regiment of former slaves—under Col. James Montgomery and guided by Tubman succeeded in destroying several plantations and their stockpiles of cotton. More importantly, the expedition liberated over 700 slaves. Tubman continued her nursing and scouting activities for the remainder of the conflict.

After the war, Tubman returned to her home in Auburn, New York, and continued her social activism. In addition to her continued pleas for racial justice, she adopted the cause of gender equality, campaigning for women's suffrage. She traveled to numerous major Northern cities during the waning decades of the 19th century giving speeches and attending conferences for equality. In 1869, Tubman married Nelson Davis, a black veteran of the Civil War. The couple remained married until his death.

On March 10, 1913, Tubman died of pneumonia in New York.

Robert L. Glaze

See also: African American Women; Civil War (1861–1865); Espionage; Nursing.

References and Further Reading

Bordewich, Fergus M. *Bound for Canaan: The Epic Story of the Underground Railroad, America's First Civil Rights Movement.* New York: Harper Collins, 2005.

Clinton, Catherine. *Harriet Tubman: The Road to Freedom.* New York: Back Bay Books, 2004.

Larson, Kate Clifford. *Bound for the Promised Land: Harriet Tubman, Portrait of an American Hero.* New York: Ballantine Books, 2004.

Lowry, Beverly. *Harriet Tubman: Imagining a Life.* New York: Random House, 2007.

TURCHIN, NADINE [NEDEZHDA] LVOVA (1826–1904)

Nadine Lvova Turchin's diary of 1863 and 1864 presents details of her travels with the Union army as a nurse and the wife of a commander. Conveying thoughts about military strategies, everyday life, and descriptions of the people she knew, her diary is unique in that an educated immigrant woman with a military background wrote it.

Born in Russia as Nedezhda Lvova in 1826, Nadine Lvova Turchin was the daughter of a colonel in the czar's army. She was brought up in military camps, and, as a member of the aristocracy, she received a solid education. Her husband, born Ivan Vasilvetich Turcheninov and known as John Basil Turchin in the United States, was a graduate of the military academy in St. Petersburg and a veteran of the Crimean War.

The couple immigrated to the United States in 1856, living briefly in Long Island and Philadelphia before settling in Mattoon, Illinois, in the late 1850s, where John found work as a topographical engineer for the Illinois Central Railroad.

In 1861, John Turchin was appointed colonel, commanding the 19th Illinois Infantry. Nadine went with him on his campaigns in Missouri, Kentucky, Tennessee, and Alabama. An 1862 account tells of John becoming ill and Nadine taking his place as head of the regiment while nursing him. In 1863, John was ordered to report to the commander of the Army of the Cumberland, where he commanded a cavalry division. Again, Nadine accompanied him, and, after she was designated as a nurse, she nursed the men on the front lines of battle.

The only diary of Nadine's that has been found begins May 26, 1863, and ends on April 26, 1864. Written in French, it provides accounts of battles such as Missionary Ridge, Chattanooga, and Chickamauga. It also conveys Nadine's thoughts about the war, her acquaintances, and the infantry. She often complained about the incompetence of the American army and the army marshals' ignorance of military operations, implying that her husband's military accomplishments were underappreciated. She also recorded her frustration at being dependent on commanders whom she saw as unqualified, even writing that the commanding general ought to make her his chief of staff or personal advisor. At other times, she wrote of the boredom and monotony of military life. Despite the complaints in her diary, accounts by the men in the army lauded Nadine for her loyalty to the United States and to the troops as well as for her bravery.

The Turchins settled in Radom, Illinois, after the Civil War, and little is known of their life there. Nadine died in Radom in 1904.

Sigrid Kelsey

See also: Civil War (1861–1865); Nursing.

References and Further Reading

De Pauw, Linda Grant. *Battle Cries and Lullabies: Women in War from Prehistory to the Present.* Norman: University of Oklahoma Press, 1998.

Leonard, Elizabeth D. *All the Daring of the Soldier: Women of the Civil War Armies.* New York: W. W. Norton & Company, 1999.

McElligott, Mary Ellen, ed. " 'A Monotony Full of Sadness': The Diary of Nadine Turchin, May, 1863–April 1864." *Journal of the Illinois State Historical Society* 70 (1977): 27–89.

TYONAJANEGEN
(N.D.–CA. 1820)

Tyonajanegen (Two Kettles Together) was an Oneida Indian woman who fought on the side of the colonists in a number of key battles in the American Revolution.

Not much is known of the life of Tyonajanegen before her marriage to Han Yerry sometime in the 1750s. Her husband, who was of part Mohawk and part German descent, was the chief warrior of the Wolf Clan branch of the Oneida. Yerry was known by Natives as Tewahangarahken (He Who Takes Up the Snow Shoe) and by local whites as Han Yerry Doxtader, reflecting his supposed German heritage.

The couple settled at Oriska, a Native village in upstate New York, and maintained a substantial farm. They had a house, a barn, 15 horses, 60 hogs, and 100 chickens. They also possessed both a wagon and a sleigh. Together they had four children, three sons and a daughter, and Tyonajanegen made meals for her family and guests, using brass and copper cooking implements and pewter plates.

Tyonajanegen, her husband, and their sons all favored and fought for the rebel cause during the Revolutionary War. The Oneidas of Oriska resented the coercive tactics used by William Johnson, a British diplomat, in negotiating the treaty of Fort Stanwix (1768). The treaty forced the Oneida to open their eastern territory, including Oriska, to future white settlement. By 1777, the Oneida were prepared to break with the majority of the other tribes of the Iroquois Confederacy and join the rebels.

Tyonajanegen played an integral role in the fight against the British army besieging Fort Schuyler (formally Fort Stanwix) during the Saratoga campaign. The British, under Col. Barry St. Leger, attempted to take the fort in support of Gen. John Burgoyne's campaign to gain control of the Hudson River Valley. After the fort was surrounded by British troops and communications with the outside were broken, Tyonajanegen was sent out to inform American officials of the siege and seek assistance. She stealthily maneuvered past the British lines, then rode on horseback to Fort Dayton. Tyonajanegen, along with her husband, her son Cornelius, and many other Oneidas, joined the expedition to relieve the besieged fortress. In the ensuing fight, the Battle of Oriskany, the rebels were ambushed by a combined force of British and Native troops and suffered heavy losses.

For much of the battle, Tyonajanegen fought on horseback armed with two pistols. However, when her husband was shot in the right wrist, she took the responsibility of loading his gun for him while he continued to fire. After the six-hour battle, Tyonajanegen rode to notify nearby rebels of the outcome. Because of their participation in the battle, Tyonajanegen and Yerry's Oriska frame home was burned to the ground by a pro-British Iroquois war party. Nevertheless, Tyonajanegen continued to support the rebel cause. During the battle of Saratoga, Tyonajanegen served as a messenger for the rebels, an act of service Gen. Horatio Gates rewarded with a gift of three gallons of rum. After the war, Tyonajanegen largely disappeared from the historical record, but she is known to have died in the early 1820s, outliving her husband by almost three decades.

David D. Dry

See also: American Revolution (1775–1783); Native American Women.

References and Further Reading

Glatthaar, Joseph T., and James K. Martin. *Forgotten Allies: The Oneida Indians and the American Revolution*. New York: Hill and Wang, 2006.

Norton, David J. *Rebellious Younger Brother: Oneida Leadership and Diplomacy, 1750–1800*. DeKalb: Northern Illinois University Press, 2009.

Robinson, Guy, and Phil Lucas. *From Warriors to Soldiers: The History of Native American Service in the United States Military*. Bloomington, IN: iUniverse, 2010.

Viola, Herman, and Ben N. Campbell. *Warriors in Uniform: The Legacy of American Indian Heroism*. New York: National Geographic, 2008.

U

UNITED SERVICE ORGANIZATIONS (USO)

The United Service Organizations (USO) and its subsidiary Camp Shows, Inc., is a private nonprofit entity that provides morale, entertainment, and recreational services to members of the United States' armed forces and their families. Although it is not a U.S. government agency, it has been chartered by Congress and works closely with the Department of Defense (DOD). It relies heavily on private donations as well as on funding and support services from the DOD. The USO is best known for the clubs it runs in the continental United States and overseas (mostly near U.S. military bases) and for the "Camp Shows" it puts on for American servicemen.

The USO's origins date back to American participation in World War I. During that conflict, the War Department relied on a number of organizations to provide recreational and morale services for American soldiers, sailors, and marines—the Young Men's Christian Association (YMCA), the Young Women's Christian Association (YWCA), the Salvation Army, the Jewish Welfare Board, the National Catholic Community Service, and the Traveler's Aid Society. These organizations often duplicated services and worked at cross-purposes with each other.

The outbreak of a new war in 1939 and the growing likelihood of American belligerency led to rapid growth in the military establishment. This growth made apparent the need for improved coordination among civilian service organizations. In February 1941, at President Franklin D. Roosevelt's request, their leaders met in New York and decided to set up an umbrella agency to further their common mission of supporting the morale and recreational needs of service personnel and their families.

On February 4, 1941, after getting a charter from the U.S. Congress, these organizations created the USO. The new organization expanded rapidly. By the following September, the USO had opened 89 clubs. One year later, with the United States in the war, the number of clubs had expanded to 967. In late 1944, at its height, the USO operated 3,035 clubs and canteens in the United States.

During World War II, both men and women volunteered for the USO. However, women's labor provided the foundation for most of its activities and kept the clubs open throughout the war years. To most servicemen, who had to live in an essentially masculine environment at their duty stations, the women in the clubs provided a welcome change. Moreover, the USO provided an outlet that channeled women's passion to help the war effort into functions that did not challenge traditional notions about women's role in society. Through their work, USO hostesses made their normally private domestic roles as nurturers and caretakers visible. They also incorporated their vital roles as mothers and sweethearts into their service to the nation and the state.

Although not as extensive a program as the clubs and the canteens, the Camp Shows became the USO's main claim to fame. These shows were live performances put on both in the United States and overseas. They often featured celebrities such as Bing Crosby, Judy Garland, Betty Grable, Lauren Bacall, the Andrews Sisters, Marlene Dietrich, Lucille Ball, and the best-known and most active USO performer, Bob Hope. The Hollywood studio heads and their stars were always eager to show their patriotism, and these shows gave them an excellent opportunity to do so.

As was the case for the clubs and canteens, women constituted the heart and soul of the Camp Show program. For the female entertainers in the camp shows, traveling with the USO, especially when sent overseas, helped them to be patriots and adventurers as well as professionals. For the servicemen in the audiences, the women in the shows served as reminders of, and substitutes for, their girlfriends back home, as rewards for their sacrifices in fighting the war, and as embodiments of the society they were defending.

The USO was disbanded at the end of World War II. Private contributions, which made up all of the organization's funding, dried up. Furthermore, the contraction in the size of the American military establishment made such a large agency unnecessary. However, the onset of the Cold War and growing overseas military commitments in both Europe and Asia made the need for an organization like the USO apparent. When the Korean War broke out in June 1950, the Truman Administration asked that the USO be reconstituted to provide social, recreational, and entertainment services for American servicemen.

As they had during World War II, women again provided the overwhelming majority of USO volunteers. Female workers in the clubs, canteens, and touring Camp Shows provided relief from the stresses of combat, life in the predominantly male barracks and bases, and living in an alien Asian culture. Once again, both the USO Camp Shows and the network of clubs proved immensely popular among members of the armed forces.

The end of the Korean War did not mean the end of the USO. The United States' growing overseas commitments and the large network of military bases both in the United States and overseas meant that servicemen far from home would continue to need its morale and recreational services. Following the Korean War, the USO instituted organizational changes to reflect changing social values in the United States. It dropped chaperoned dances with volunteer hostesses and gave priority to overseas entertainment for the troops—a focus that it has maintained to the present day.

The Vietnam War stretched the USO's resources. Antiwar feeling in the United States impacted USO operations by resulting in declining contributions and numbers of volunteers. Hollywood celebrities, many of whom were antiwar activists, refused to go on tour in Vietnam. Nevertheless, the USO maintained a large presence in Southeast Asia throughout the United States' involvement in Vietnam. The USO was in Vietnam as early as April 1963—two years before the arrival of the first American combat units. Eventually, the USO established 23 clubs in Vietnam and Thailand, which served up to a million members of the American armed forces each month.

The USO sought to bring a little bit of home to soldiers in Vietnam. Most USO workers were women. They served 18-month tours and provided everything from food service to help in writing letters home. Although the organization discouraged romantic liaisons between servicemen and workers, these women were expected to look attractive. The young women who worked in the clubs were required to wear miniskirts. This tension between maintaining chastity and keeping the traditional "good girl" image of the hostesses while also

projecting sex appeal led to continuing gender tension in USO clubs. Stresses over changing codes of sexual conduct manifested themselves in the activities of many junior hostesses who sought pleasure through casual socializing and frequent sexual experimentation with men they met through the USO.

The USO also did its best to provide entertainment. Led by Hope, USO troupes, including female celebrities such as Ann Margaret, Joey Heatherton, and Martha Raye, helped relieve the stresses of war. The presence of these women meant a lot to American servicemen overseas.

The end of the Vietnam War did not signal an end to USO activity. The United States continued to maintain bases overseas, and all of them required some kind of USO presence. New challenges confronted the USO as growing American military involvement in the Middle East and the Persian Gulf led the organization to expand its presence there. Increasingly, the USO was obliged to observe and respect the sensibilities of the Muslim governments and peoples in the Persian Gulf area. When Hope took his Christmas show to the Gulf area during Operation Desert Shield in December 1990, he was faced with unprecedented restrictions. The State Department monitored Hope's jokes to avoid offending the government of Saudi Arabia. The media was restricted from covering the shows. Because local custom requires that women wear veils in public, a number of female performers, including Ann Jillian, Marie Osmond, and the Pointer Sisters, were left off of Hope's Christmas Eve show. Despite these new restrictions on the USO's Camp Show component, the organization maintained clubs on every major American base in the Persian Gulf area during Operations Desert Shield and Desert Storm.

The terrorist attacks of September 11, 2001, on New York and Washington, D.C., and the American military operations in Afghanistan and Iraq undertaken in response to them once again signaled the need to expand USO services. To provide support for troops participating in Operation Iraqi Storm, the USO opened centers in Kabul, Afghanistan, and Balad Air Base, Iraq, as well as more centers in Qatar and Kuwait. The USO has also maintained Internet and e-mail stations at its centers. It also has expanded the centers it has at major international airports in the United States. There remain a large number of celebrities willing to venture into war zones to provide entertainment, including Carrie Underwood, Steven Colbert, Trace Adkins, and World Wrestling Entertainment.

For all of the organizational changes, the USO's basic mission remains the same as when it began. The driving force behind its operations is the need of civilian society to offer emotional and material support for service personnel and their families. This urge gave rise to the organization during World War II and remains in force today. The American military relies on the USO and other auxiliary organizations as well as families and communities to supply troops with essential personal supplies and to meet the troops' recreational and morale needs.

Walter F. Bell

See also: Afghanistan; Dietrich, Marlene (1901–1992); Gulf War (1991); Iraq War

(2003–2011); Korean War (1950–1953); Raye, Martha (1916–1994); Salvation Army; Vietnam War (1965–1973); War on Terror (2001–); World War I (1914–1918); World War II (1941–1945); Young Men's Christian Association (YMCA); Young Women's Christian Association (YWCA).

References and Further Reading

Weatherford, Doris. *American Women and World War II*. New York: Facts on File, 1990.

Winchell, Meghan K. *Good Girls, Good Food, Good Fun: The Story of the USO Hostesses during World War II*. Chapel Hill: University of North Carolina Press, 2008.

UNITED STATES COAST GUARD WOMEN'S RESERVE (SPAR)

President Franklin D. Roosevelt signed Public Law 772 on November 23, 1942, officially establishing the U.S. Coast Guard Women's Reserve. SPAR was the moniker given to members of this new unit. It was a play on words taken from the Coast Guard's motto *Semper Paratus* or *Always Ready*. Approximately 10,000 enlisted personnel and 1,000 officers served in this all-female corps during World War II.

Candidates were required to be women between the ages of 20 and 36, and they signed on for the duration of the war plus six months. Enlisted personnel had to complete a minimum of two years of high school; officers needed at least two years of college. A married woman was permitted to join as long as her husband was not a member of the Coast Guard. Single women were allowed to marry only after completing their initial training, and again their spouses could not be Coast Guardsmen. SPARs were compelled to resign immediately upon becoming pregnant. Beginning in October 1944, African Americans were allowed to join SPAR.

Members of the Coast Guard's Women's Reserve were forbidden to give orders to any male servicemembers. This precedent was established in the SPAR's sister organization in the Navy, the WAVES (Women Accepted for Volunteer Emergency Service). This restriction caused problems at times, especially when SPAR officers were placed in charge of male subordinates. These issues were circumvented when the judge advocate general ruled that women could issue orders as long as their commanding officer was male, which was usually the case. The female guardsmen were originally required to serve only in the continental United States. On September 27, 1944, this policy was reversed and SPARs were permitted to transfer overseas, as well as to Alaska and Hawaii.

Navy lieutenant Dorothy Stratton, a former dean of women at Purdue University, transferred to the newly created military branch and was named director with the rank of lieutenant commander. She would achieve the rank of captain in February 1944. It was Stratton who devised the name SPAR from the Coast Guard motto. She also noted that a spar was a support beam for ships, just as the new unit would provide an invaluable support role to the service. Many of the first recruits also transferred from the WAVES into the new Coast Guard contingent. Officers trained at Smith College in Northampton, Massachusetts, and at Mount Holyoke College in South Hadley, Massachusetts. Eventually, officer training was conducted at the U.S. Coast Guard Academy in New London, Connecticut, where the women were commissioned as ensigns.

Enlisted women went through boot camp at Oklahoma A & M Teachers College at Stillwater, Iowa State Teachers College at Cedar Falls, and Hunter College in the Bronx. At Hunter College, they trained alongside WAVES who had already established a training facility. On June 14, 1943, a Coast Guard training depot was established at the Palm Beach Biltmore Hotel in Florida. SPAR recruits were indoctrinated here until early 1945, when many trained at Manhattan Beach, Brooklyn. Boot camp for women was much the same as that for their male counterparts—a monotonous routine of physical and classroom training combined with rigid military discipline that transformed civilians into their new role of service. The volunteers were given the rank of seaman second class upon completion of their training.

The Women's Reserve was created to augment the Coast Guard's shore operations and to allow more men to serve at sea. Thus their official slogan was "Release a Man to Fight at Sea." Recruitment challenges were daunting at first. Convincing women to join any branch of the armed forces was difficult enough and especially so with the Coast Guard, which was not as popular as the Army or Navy. Higher wages in the civilian sector also hampered efforts, so a strategy was developed to appeal to patriotism. Recruitment posters read, "Make a date with Uncle Sam and enlist in the Coast Guard SPARs." *Tars and Spars* was a popular song-and-dance show that helped push up recruitment numbers. Jeeps were used in parades with the slogan "Don't be a spare—be a SPAR" painted on the spare tires.

SPARs served throughout the ranks in over 43 different Coast Guard ratings from yeomen, air traffic controllers, and clerks to cooks, pharmacist mates, and coxswains. A majority of these women were trained in communications to deal with the tremendous amount of signals sent to ships at sea. A number of sea-women stationed at Florida were charged with the vital mission of directing sub-marines on their way from training at Groton, Connecticut, to the Pacific Theater. Some were placed in charge of a new and highly secret technology called the LORAN Navigation System.

Ensign Jan Thorpe's experience demonstrates just how quickly the new female corps released men for sea duty. Thorpe signed on as an officer in January 1943 and was assigned to New York City in the Code Board office that May. When she arrived, the staff was entirely male, and a total of three female officers were stationed in the district. By November, Ensign Thorpe was in charge of the Code Board, and all male officers had shipped out.

Another officer, Ensign Martha Vaughn, illustrates the extent of responsibility placed on SPAR personnel. Vaughn joined in January 1943 and was sent on a brief stint in Washington, D.C., before being assigned to Florida. Here she reviewed and edited classified documents and was sent to Coast Guard bases throughout Florida to teach other members how to decode and handle sensitive information. Vaughn was then put in charge of communications at Key West, Florida. In addition to being responsible for a large number of enlisted women arriving at the base, she oversaw communications between Navy minesweepers along the coast and the top-secret ship signals housed in a safe in the communications office.

Enlisted personnel also carried a lot of responsibility, as in the case of Doris McMillan. McMillan enlisted in January 1943 and was assigned to the busy port of New Orleans, Louisiana. Upon arrival, approximately 20 percent of the staff was female, but within two months nearly all the staff was SPARs. McMillan experienced a rather unusual form of gender discrimination. While on leave, an older woman began screaming and hitting her with an umbrella. Apparently she was upset at her son being sent to sea and blamed young McMillan. By early 1944, McMillan was a yeoman second class, supervising 16 clerks and working five-and-a-half days a week until the end of the war.

Florence Finch became the only SPAR decorated for combat during World War II. Born in the Philippines to an American father and Philippine mother, Finch worked with the resistance during the Japanese occupation and was captured, tortured, and imprisoned before being liberated by U.S. forces. In July 1945, Finch enlisted in the SPARs at Buffalo, New York, and was awarded the Asiatic-Pacific campaign ribbon for her services. After the war, she was presented with the Medal of Freedom.

The Women's Reserve was disbanded in June 1946. However, these women paved the way for future generations of women in military service. On December 3, 1973, women were permitted to serve as regular, active-duty members of the U.S. Coast Guard, and in 1976 the U.S. Coast Guard Academy became the first service academy to admit women.

William E. Whyte

See also: African American Women; Asian American Women; Finch, Florence Ebersole Smith (1915–); Stratton, Dorothy Constance (1899–2006); Women Accepted for Volunteer Emergency Service (WAVES); World War II (1941–1945).

References and Further Reading

Gruhzit-Hoyt, Olga. *They Also Served: American Women in World War II.* New York: Carol Publishing Group, 1995.

Lyne, Mary C., and Kay Arthur. *Three Years behind the Mast: The Story of the United States Coast Guard SPARs.* Washington, D.C.: U.S. Coast Guard, 1946.

Tilley, John A. *A History of Women in the Coast Guard.* Washington, D.C.: U.S. Coast Guard, 1996.

UNITED STATES SANITARY COMMISSION (USSC)

The United States Sanitary Commission (USSC) was a privately run philanthropic organization established during the American Civil War to collect and distribute supplies, to assist the federal government in the management of military hospitals, and to make inquiries and give advice on issues of sanitation and medicine. The USSC was the only civilian-run organization to receive official recognition from the federal government. Middle- and upper-class men, who sought to reassert their social and political status after the expansion of the franchise and the advent of machine politics, comprised the executive board of the Commission. Northern women of various socioeconomic backgrounds comprised the leadership of the Commission branches and the bulk of the volunteers. The wartime relationship between these men and women provided much-needed battlefield assistance, along with conflict over the place and value of women's work.

The USSC emerged from the Women's Central Association of Relief (WCAR) in response to the U.S. Army's failure to maintain adequate sanitation and supply sufficient medicine in the aftermath of the Battle of Bull Run in the spring of 1861. Elizabeth Blackwell, the first female doctor in the United States, founded the WCAR in the spring of 1861 to manage relief work, communicate directly with the U.S. Army Medical Department, and select and train women nurses. WCAR vice president Henry W. Bellows traveled to Washington, D.C., to establish political connections, but he shifted his thinking regarding the nature of a wartime relief organization after visiting army camps and military hospitals. Rather than presenting the proposal laid out by the WCAR, Bellows informed Secretary of War Simon Cameron that a wartime relief agency, based in the capital, would improve and maintain the physical and mental health of the army, manage the organization of military hospitals and camps, and advise the transportation of the wounded. The USSC received executive approval in June 1861.

The USSC had a hierarchical structure, with an executive board, inspectors, and field agents in Washington, D.C.; branches located in major Northern cities; and soldiers' aid societies dispersed in smaller towns. Unitarian minister Bellows served as president, New York lawyer George Templeton Strong as treasurer, landscape architect Frederick Law Olmsted as general secretary, and architect Alfred J. Bloor as corresponding secretary. Due to exhaustion, disagreements with other board members, and money difficulties, Olmsted resigned in 1863 and was replaced by John Foster Jenkins. Bloor maintained connections with the Northern homefront through direct correspondence with regional branches and local aid societies. Unlike his colleagues on the executive board, Bloor was convinced that the Commission needed to respond to the needs of Northern women. He was let go from his position in October 1864.

The USSC was supported by the grassroots efforts of Commission branches, including the WCAR, and by localized soldiers' aid societies. In September 1862, the USSC recognized the WCAR as an auxiliary branch, but it continued to function independently from the parent organization. Twelve regional branches located in New York City, Boston, Philadelphia, Cincinnati, Louisville, Cleveland, Pittsburgh, Chicago, New Albany, Detroit, Buffalo, and Columbus supported the USSC throughout the war. The regional branches existed and functioned under the authority and direction of the USSC, but they also initiated programs accepted by the parent organization. The establishment of female associate managers, who communicated supply requests to the homefront and provided reports on the conditions of the homefront and battlefront, provided branch managers with more time for recruitment activities. Local soldiers' aid societies provided the bulk of the support for the USSC

coming from the Northern homefront. By late fall 1862, over 1,400 soldiers' aid societies were associated with the USSC, and, over the course of the war, nearly 7,000 aid societies were created. Both the regional branch offices of the USSC and the local soldiers' aid societies were managed, worked, and sustained primarily by women.

To counter what the Commission saw as the inefficiency and confusion of federal government action and the lack of order or benevolence at the local level, the USSC emphasized centralized efforts and philanthropy based on scientific principles to effectively carry out wartime needs. The USSC fulfilled this goal through fund-raising, inquiries, advice, transportation, and distribution. One of the Commission's first tasks included raising the necessary money to hire field agents and to transport supplies to the front. Money initially came from insurance companies, businesses, and property holders. Early donations allowed the Commission to begin its work, but the organization would be plagued by a lack of sufficient funds and supply shortages throughout the war. The course of the war and Northern sympathy toward the war influenced the amount of money and supplies held by the USSC at any given moment. Inspectors thoroughly investigated and reported the conditions of camps and troops, including sewage disposal, cleanliness, clothing, cooking, and diets, and advisors made recommendations to the War Department. The USSC advised the War Department to improve the diets of soldiers to include greater nutritional variety, to reorganize the Medical Bureau to better care for the sick and wounded in hospitals, and to allow the

Commission to participate in the transportation of supplies and of the wounded and sick to hospitals.

In the first year of the war, the USSC focused on persuading the government to reorganize the Medical Bureau, which the Commission saw as plagued by poor management, bureaucracy, and the demands of special interests. In April 1862, Congress passed a reorganization bill, which provided for an increase in the number of medical and nonmedical personnel, establishment of inspectors, an increase in the requirements in sanitation reports, as well as the dismissal of Dr. Clement Finely from the post of surgeon general and the appointment of William Hammond.

The USSC remained in communication with its branches to ensure the continual flow of supplies to the troops and the battlefront. Women on the Northern homefront provided over $15 million worth of supplies over the course of the war, including ice, bandages, lint, pens, paper, clothing, and food. When the USSC was unable to obtain supplies from local aid societies, it bought goods on the market. To keep the Northern homefront abreast of its supply and distribution activities, the USSC began publishing the *Sanitary Commission Bulletin* in November 1863, along with giving lecture tours in USSC regions. Both attempts at improved communication with the homefront were suggestions of female branch managers. The Commission used the publication to advance the organizational themes of centralization and a scientific basis for philanthropy. The *Bulletin* was published twice a month and circulated to local aid societies and troops.

Due to wartime cooperation with the federal government and the Northern homefront, the USSC experienced conflict and controversy. Advice offered by the USSC to the federal government was not always welcome. While the USSC criticized the Medical Bureau for failing in its duties to the troops, the Bureau believed the Commission exaggerated its concerns about sickness and sanitation. The appointment of Edwin M. Stanton as secretary of war in 1862 also placed strains on the Commission's influence in the War Department because Stanton accused the Commission of engaging in trade rather than philanthropy. Although the Commission was called on by the armies of George B. McClellan and John C. Frémont, in early 1864 Gen. William T. Sherman refused to let the Commission use military transportation for supplies.

The USSC clashed with other philanthropic organizations, including the United States Christian Commission (USCC) and the Western Sanitary Commission (WSC). Both the USCC and the WSC were perceived by the Commission to be threats to its success in gaining the support and contributions of the homefront and in the push for centralized and efficient work. The USCC functioned as a philanthropic organization and provided religious tracts and materials to soldiers, while the WSC provided supplies for the trans-Mississippi region including Texas, Kansas, Missouri, Arkansas, Mississippi, Tennessee, Louisiana, and Kentucky. Unlike the USSC, the WSC relied on local leaders and solutions to meet supply and distribution needs. The executive board believed the methods of the WSC were inefficient, bred repetitiveness, and undermined the USSC's role as a national benevolent organization.

The women of the Northern home-front proved to be the Commission's most formidable foe during the course of the war. At the beginning of the war, the executive board believed that it could easily gain the support and participation of women and that women would naturally and dutifully carry out benevolent activity, while the structure and centralized organization of the USSC would bring direction and efficiency to their activities. The wartime assistance of women on the Northern homefront depended on local circumstances like child care, family illness, and community welfare. As became increasingly evident in branch-issued questionnaires, Northern women held both the USSC and the federal government responsible for the requests for and the distribution of supplies. Women questioned why the federal government was unable to provide the necessary supplies for war, particularly in light of rising taxes. They indicated their anger over supposed corrupt and fraudulent practices on the part of the USSC. Specifically, women feared that the supplies they provided were not getting to the battlefront or were being sold.

Certain activities carried out by the women on the Northern homefront went against the directions of the USSC and earned its dissatisfaction. Some women sent supplies directly to the battlefront rather than to the USSC as instructed. Sanitary fairs, which were successful fund-raising activities for Commission branches, were seen by the Commission to be violations of its emphasis on centralization. Despite the success of sanitary fairs—the Northwestern Sanitary Commission's fair raised $100,000 in 1863—the Commission believed that the fairs benefited the parent organization very little and provoked unnecessary emotion and localized activity.

The USSC chose not to involve itself directly in the process of demobilization, although Commission women sought to continue their activities by assisting returning soldiers and families. At the conclusion of the war, the USSC informed branches to continue operating until July 4, 1865, after which they needed to forward remaining supplies and money to the Commission. The last official act of the USSC came with the publication of its official history in 1866, entitled *History of the United States Sanitary Commission.*

Sarah K. Nytroe

See also: Blackwell, Elizabeth (1821–1910); Civil War (1861–1865); Nursing.

References and Further Reading

Attie, Jeanie. *Patriotic Toil: Northern Women and the American Civil War.* Ithaca, NY: Cornell University Press, 1998.

Cassedy, James H. "Numbering the North's Medical Events: Humanitarianism and Science in Civil War Statistics." *Bulletin of the History of Medicine* 66, no. 2 (1992): 210–33.

Frederickson, George M. *The Inner Civil War: Northern Intellectuals and the Crisis of the Union.* Urbana: University of Illinois Press, 1965.

Giesberg, Judith Ann. *Civil War Sisterhood: The U.S. Sanitary Commission and Women's Politics in Transition.* Boston: Northeastern University Press, 2000.

Giesberg, Judith Ann. "In Service to the Fifth Wheel: Katharine Prescott Wormeley and Her Experiences in the United States Sanitary Commission." *Nursing History Review* 3 (1995): 43–53.

Leonard, Elizabeth D. *Yankee Women: Gender Battles in the Civil War.* New York: W. W. Norton & Company, 1994.

Maxwell, William Quentin. *Lincoln's Fifth Wheel: The Political History of the United States Sanitary Commission.* New York: Longmans, Green & Company, 1956.

UNITED STATES v. VIRGINIA (1996)

The U.S. Supreme Court decision that opened the doors of state-supported military colleges to women, *United States v. Virginia* held that women were as able as men to complete and benefit from a military education.

The case began in 1989, when a young woman asked the Virginia Military Institute (VMI) for an application. VMI replied that it did not accept women. The U.S. Constitution's equal protection clause says, "No state shall ... deny to any person within its jurisdiction the equal protection of the laws," and the federal Department of Justice, arguing that denying women equal access to a state-funded military education was a violation of it, sued VMI.

Founded in 1839 as an institution that would turn young men into citizen-

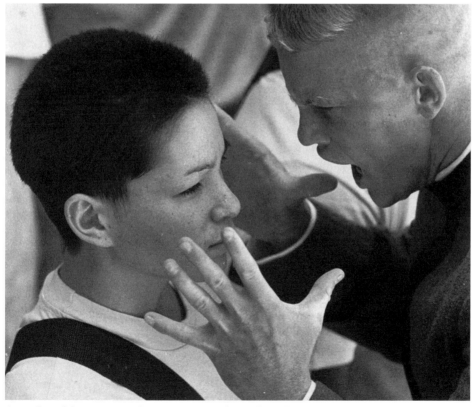

A member of the Virginia Military Institute Cadre, right, yells at a female freshman during the "Meet the Cadre" ceremony in the barracks area of the school in Lexington, Virginia, August 19, 1998. (AP/Wide World Photos)

soldiers, over the years VMI became a fully accredited military college supported by the state's money. It produced many members of Virginia's political, legal, and economic elite. Gen. George Marshall, the World War II hero and secretary of state, graduated from VMI. So did luminaries such as Supreme Court Justice Tom Clark.

The distinguishing feature of VMI was its adversative system, and the heart of the system was the "rat line." Freshmen were dubbed "rats." As VMI's witnesses testified during *United States v. Virginia*, the purpose of the rat line was to put maximum physical and mental stress on new students, breaking them down so that they could be rebuilt as VMI men. Their heads were shaved. In addition, at all times, they had to walk at rigid attention, chins tucked into their collarbones and eyes straight ahead. Any upperclassman could order rats to perform errands or drop down to do pushups as punishment for alleged infractions. The Institute prided itself on treating all students equally during their four years and felt that the absence of privacy assured each student that he was being treated that way. The spartan four-student dormitory bedrooms had unlocked doors with shadeless windows facing the hallways. Bathrooms were communal, without partitions or stalls.

That equality, VMI believed, would be destroyed if women were admitted to the Institute. Women would need privacy. They would not be able to stand the stress of VMI or its physical fitness demands, so its standards for them would have to be different. Women, VMI claimed, learned through cooperation rather than competition. They would not benefit from the kind of rigorous,

competitive military education that the institute offered.

By 1989, however, all of the federal military academies admitted women and had given up the adversative system as unnecessary. As their representatives testified, there was no resultant lowering of standards. The academies' admission of women reflected late-20th-century changes in attitudes, and those in turn were reflected in American law.

Many of the legal changes could be attributed to the advocacy of Ruth Bader Ginsburg, an attorney with the American Civil Liberties Union. During the 1970s, Ginsburg worked on numerous gender equality cases, arguing six before the U.S. Supreme Court and winning five of them. Ginsburg maintained that if the government treated women differently from men on the basis of outmoded stereotypes, it was denying them the equal protection of the laws. In 1982, Sandra Day O'Connor, the first female Supreme Court justice, wrote for the Court that a state had to have an "exceedingly persuasive justification" for providing any benefit to only one sex. A single-sex classification could be validated "only by showing at least that the classification serves 'important governmental objectives and that the discriminatory means employed' are 'substantially related to the achievement of those objectives.' " In addition, classifications could not be justified by reference to "fixed notions" or "archaic and stereotypic notions" about men and women.

Faced with the suit against VMI and in the absence of an "extremely persuasive justification" for denying women a military education, the state of Virginia quickly organized a supposedly comparable military program at a nearby private women's college. It offered far fewer courses and training facilities than VMI and substituted what it called a gentle "cooperative method which reinforces self-esteem" for the tough adversative method.

In 1996, the Supreme Court said in *United States v. Virginia* that such a program was inadequate. Ginsburg, who had been appointed to the Court in 1993, wrote for it that there was no "exceedingly persuasive justification" for treating women differently from men. Even VMI agreed that some women, like some men, might want and be able to profit from the adversative method of education.

The assumption that women would benefit from being excluded from VMI because they learned differently could not be maintained, Ginsburg continued. She compared VMI's assertion of "gender-based developmental differences" to the way medical "authorities" in the past had justified excluding women from all higher education on the basis of its supposed detrimental effect on their ability to reproduce. The Constitution not only prohibits treating groups of people unequally but also forbids treating individuals unequally on the basis of characteristics of groups, Ginsburg stated. So-called " 'inherent differences' between men and women," she admonished, did not constitute adequate justification "for artificial constraints on an individual's opportunity." Changing the Court's standard for assessing gender-specific classifications to one of "skeptical scrutiny," she declared that such classifications could not be used to perpetuate the historic discrimination against women. Courts had

an obligation to assess "actual state purposes" behind such classifications, and the purposes of Virginia, based as they were on outmoded stereotypes, were constitutionally unacceptable.

VMI was ordered to admit women. The Citadel, South Carolina's comparable military institute, read the decision and quickly admitted women as well. Women were now officially welcome in all the nation's military colleges.

Philippa Strum

See also: Faulkner, Shannon Richey (1975–).

References and Further Reading

Brodie, Laura Fairchild. *Breaking Out: VMI and the Coming of Women*. New York: Vintage Books, 2001.

Diamond, Diane, and Michael Kimmel. " 'Toxic Virus' or Lady Virtue: Gender Integration and Assimilation at West Point and VMI." In *Going Coed: Women's Experiences in Formerly Men's Colleges and Universities, 1950–2000*, edited by Leslie Miller-Bernal and Susan L. Poulson, 263–86. Nashville, TN: Vanderbilt University Press, 2004.

Strum, Philippa. *Women in the Barracks: The VMI Case and Equal Rights*. Lawrence: University Press of Kansas, 2002.

URDANG, CONSTANCE (1922–1996)

Writer Constant Urdang worked as a military intelligence analyst during World War II. Her poetry, novellas, prose, and contributions to numerous periodicals explored two major themes: the meaning of womanhood and the serendipity of accidents.

Born in New York City on December 26, 1922, to Annabel Schfran and Harry Rudman, Urdang was educated at the Fieldston School founded by Felix Alder in 1878. The Fieldston School sought students from a variety of racial, economic, religious, and cultural backgrounds. She received a BA from Smith College in Northampton, Massachusetts, where she graduated cum laude in 1943.

Following her graduation from Smith, Urdang moved to Washington, D.C., where she worked for the U.S. Department of the Army as a military intelligence analyst from 1944 to 1946. The major duties of an intelligence analyst include supervision, coordination, collection, analysis, processing, and dissemination of strategic and tactical intelligence. Most of Urdang's work as an intelligence analyst consisted mainly of reviewing documents and information in order to seek connections so that the Army could predict events or establish associations between people, places, and events. Intelligence analysis breaks into two classes, tactical and strategic. Tactical analysis focuses on short term, time-sensitive activities of known offenders or groups of individuals while strategic intelligence analysis has a long-term focus allowing the Army to develop tactics for the future and contingency plans.

Urdang's language skills and ability to analyze, recall, reformulate, and make connections between many pieces of data was essential to her work as an intelligence analyst. Another aspect of her responsibilities was drafting regular intelligence report, plans, and briefings to communicate her findings to superiors higher up the chain of command. Though her work kept her mostly in the office and relied on her scrutiny of documents and some typical and clerical skills, prior to the mobilization of women workers during World War II, women working in intelligence and military fields were generally viewed as anomalies.

Urdang was one of more than 1 million "government girls" who worked in jobs previously occupied by men who had enlisted or been drafted during World War II. Government girls understood that men would reclaim these high-paying jobs once the war ended. By 1944, a full one-third of all civil service jobs in the nation were filled by women.

After her service to the Army ended, Urdang returned to New York City, where she worked as a copy editor at Bellas Hess, Inc., and later as an editor for P. F. Collier & Son Publishers. Urdang met Donald Finkel in Iowa. They fell in love and graduated from the University of Iowa's Writers Workshop in 1956, earning MFAs. The two poets headed south to Mexico, where they spent the year writing in Mexico City and San Miguel de Allende. They had three children: two daughters and one son.

Beginning in 1957, Urdang coedited *Prize Stories '57* with Paul Engle. They edited a subsequent edition of the series in 1959. In 1960, Urdang and her family moved to Missouri when her husband accepted a faculty position at Washington University in St. Louis. He was also the University's poet-in-residence. Critics compared poems in her first book of poetry, *Charades and Celebrations* (1965), to W. H. Auden. Urdang experimented with elements of collage in *Natural History* (1969) by blending clippings, old photos, and excerpts from letters in the narrative of her protagonist, a St. Louis, Missouri, housewife.

Urdang taught advanced exposition, in which writers inform but do not persuade their audience on a certain topic, in 1974 at Washington University. She also instructed in the Writing Workshops for Women program at the University's School of Continuing Education. She published another book of poetry in the 1970s, *The Picnic in the Cemetery* (1975). Three years later, in 1977, she and her husband developed and coordinated the University's Writers Program, which evolved into the Graduate Writers Program. They both taught in the program from 1977 to 1984. She was a visiting lecturer at Princeton University during the spring of 1985.

She published several works, including poems and novellas, throughout the 1980s: *The Lone Woman and Others* (1980), *Only the World* (1983), *Lucha* (1986), *American Earthquakes* (1998), *Alternative Lives* (1990), and *The Women Who Read Novels; and Peacetime (Two Novellas)* (1990), several of which draw upon landscapes as various as Mexico, Brazil, and the Ozarks.

Urdang died of lung cancer on October 8, 1996, in St. Louis, Missouri. Her manuscripts and correspondence are collected within the Constance Urdang Papers at Washington University Libraries.

Rebecca Tolley-Stokes

See also: Espionage; Government Girls; World War II (1941–1945).

References and Further Reading

Augustine, Jane. "Constance (Henriette) Urdang." In *Contemporary Women Poets*, edited by Pamela L. Shelton, 341–42. Detroit, MI: St. James Press, 1998.

Proctor, Tammy. *Female Intelligence: Women and Espionage in the First World War.* New York: New York University Press, 2003.

United States Department of the Army. *Pamphlet 611-21. Personnel Selection and Classification. Military Occupational Classification and Structure.* Washington, D.C.: Department of the Army, 2007. http://www.apd.army.mil/pdffiles/p611_21_v1.pdf.

USS *BENEVOLENCE*

USS *Benevolence* is a Haven-class naval hospital ship that served during and after World War II from 1945 to 1950. Many Navy Nurse Corps women worked on board.

The *Benevolence* was initially a merchant ship, the *Marine Lion*, and was built and accommodated for naval service in Chester, Pennsylvania. After being refitted and renamed, the *Benevolence* joined other ships stationed on the Pacific front in 1945. The *Benevolence* could house more than 800 patients, and its crew was made up of members from the Naval Nurse Corps, doctors, and other officers and soldiers. Members of the Naval Nurse Corps were not only responsible for tending to the sick and injured but also for training Hospital Corpsmen for emergency triage on the battlefield and on battle ships, where these women were not permitted to go.

When it arrived, the *Benevolence* was the first hospital ship in the Tokyo area. As a result, it served more than 8,000 recently released Allied prisoners of war (POWs). The *Benevolence* made many trips to bring home the sick and injured veterans. On August 20, 1945, the ship anchored off of Yokosuka,

Japan, and processed more than 1,500 Allied POWs. Many nurses aboard the *Benevolence* described the state of many POWs as particularly shocking. The *Benevolence* returned to San Francisco at the end of November to return veterans to American ports. Between 1945 and 1946, the *Benevolence* traveled between Pearl Harbor, China, Japan, and the American West Coast returning POWs and other evacuees to American ports.

In the summer of 1950, the U.S. Navy began to ready the *Benevolence* and a handful of other ships to return to active duty as Navy hospital ships during the Korean War. On August 25, 1950, while returning from a shakedown cruise off of the Farallon Islands in poor weather, the *Benevolence* was rammed mid-ship by a freighter, the SS *Mary Luckenbach*. Within a half-hour the ship was completely submerged and the ship's crew and passengers, more than 500 people, were forced to evacuate and wait for rescue. Twenty-three people died as a result of the sunken *Benevolence*, including the prospective captain of the hospital ship and one Navy nurse, Lt. Wilma Ledbetter from Chillicothe, Texas.

Elizabeth Dean Worley

See also: Duerk, Alene Bertha (1920–); Korean War (1950–1953); Navy Nurse Corps; Nursing; Prisoners of War; Women Accepted for Volunteer Emergency Service (WAVES); World War II (1941–1945).

References and Further Reading

Monahan, Evelyn M., and Rosemary Neidel-Greenlee. *A Few Good Women: America's Military Women from World War I to the Wars in Iraq and Afghanistan*. New York: Alfred A. Knopf Press, 2010.

Wise, James E., Jr., and Scott Baron. *Women at War: Iraq, Afghanistan, and Other Conflict.* Annapolis, MD: Naval Institute Press, 2006.

USS *RED ROVER*

The first hospital ship in the Navy, USS *Red Rover* served on the Mississippi River during the Civil War. It was also the first Navy ship to have women serve aboard in official capacities. Women aboard the ship served as nurses or other caretakers and did not possess Navy rank.

The *Red Rover* was a civilian-made side-wheel steamer built in 1859. *Red Rover* displaced 786 tons at a length of 256 feet and a draft of 8 feet and had a speed of 8 knots. The ship carried a naval complement of 47 as well as a medical department of over 30. Additionally the ship carried one 32-pound cannon for defense.

Initially used as a floating barracks for the Confederacy, the *Red Rover* was captured by the Union Army on April 7, 1862, at Island Number 10 near New Madrid, Missouri, and converted for use as a hospital ship. On June 10, 1862, *Red Rover* entered service in the Union Army. Assistant Surgeon George H. Bixby served as senior surgeon supervising a complement of male nurses. The medical staff aboard *Red Rover* assisted in evacuating and caring for the wounded throughout the summer of 1862. In September, the ship arrived in St. Louis to be outfitted for the winter but was still under the jurisdiction of an Illinois prize court. It was subsequently sold to the U.S. Navy on September 30, 1862, and commissioned in the Navy on December 26, 1862.

The Navy allowed four nuns from the Sisters of the Holy Cross to serve on board as nurses. The sisters had been serving at various shore hospitals, and one had served previously on *Red Rover*. Sisters Veronica, Adela, and Callista arrived onboard on Christmas Eve while Sister St. John of the Cross joined them in February. Additionally, five African American women assisted the nurses: Alice Kennedy, Sarah Kinno, Ellen Campbell, Betsy Young, and Dennis Downs. The *Red Rover* became an integral part of the Mississippi Squadron, always staying near the flagship and the scene of operations. The ship carried 2,497 patients, both Union and Confederate, to shore hospitals. *Red Rover* continued to serve up and down the river until late 1864, when it moored permanently at Mound City. Bixby and two sisters remained aboard until the ship was decommissioned on November 17, 1865, and then sold at public auction. Despite *Red Rover*'s success as a hospital ship, the Navy would remain without another hospital ship until the Spanish-American War.

More than 12 members of the Sisters of the Holy Cross served aboard *Red Rover* throughout the war. They demonstrated the ability of women to serve aboard naval ships during wartime and the advantages of the virtues of gentleness and compassion. Unknowingly, these women served as the forerunners to the Navy Nurse Corps. In recognition of their service, Congress voted to authorize a pension for the Sisters in 1892, but only 63 were still alive.

Glenn A. Conley

See also: African American Women; Civil War (1861–1865); Nursing; Spanish-American War (1898).

References and Further Reading

Godson, Susan. *Serving Proudly: A History of Women in the U.S. Navy.* Annapolis, MD: Naval Institute Press, 2001.

Roca, Steven Louis. "Presence and Precedents: The USS *Red Rover* during the American Civil War, 1861–1865." *Civil War History* 44, no. 2 (June 1998): 91–110.

USS *RELIEF*

During the Spanish-American War, female nurses served on the hospital ship USS *Relief*.

First built as the steam-driven passenger liner SS *John Englis* in 1896 by the Delaware River Ship Building Co. in Chester, Pennsylvania, the ship was acquired by the U.S. Army in 1898 to serve as a mobile military hospital during the Spanish-American War. The vessel was designated as the U.S. Army Hospital Ship *Relief*. During the Spanish-American War, the *Relief* served the injured in the Cuban and Pacific theaters and transported out-of-action soldiers from ports as widely separate as San Juan, Puerto Rico, and Manila, the Philippines, to mainland hospitals on both the East and West Coasts.

Active combat duty demands for men resulted in a shortage of trained men capable of serving as nurses and medical specialists aboard naval vessels like the *Relief*. Consequently, the government incorporated female nurses into the military apparatus. Although there were no official military nursing positions for women until Congress created the Army Nurse Corps (1901), the inclusion and acceptance of female nursing staff aboard military vessels became the status quo during wartime. In part, women's acceptance as military nurses resulted from their service on the *Relief* between 1898 and 1901 as well as from earlier examples of women's work on hospital ships during the Civil War.

Following the conclusion of operations in the Spanish-American War, the *Relief* was transferred to the U.S. Navy on November 13, 1902. Because of the ongoing controversy over who should command hospital ships—military line officers or medical officers—the *Relief* did not see active service again until 1908. President Theodore Roosevelt decided that medical ships should be commanded by medical personnel in order to ensure that a hospital ship would accompany the Great White Fleet on its circumnavigation of the globe. Therefore, on February 6, 1908, at the Mare Island Navy Yard, the ship was commissioned as USS *Relief* under the command of Surgeon Charles F. Stokes, U.S. Navy. Stokes was the first medical officer to command a hospital ship.

Upon completion of the Great White Fleet's around-the-world tour, the *Relief* was damaged during a typhoon while leaving the Philippine Islands on November 18 and 19, 1909. As a result, it had to return to Olongapo, Philippine Islands. The ship was deemed not seaworthy and was docked as a stationary hospital ship for the next decade. On April 11, 1918, the ship was renamed USS *Repose* so that the U.S. Navy could use the name on a new hospital ship. It was sold May 15, 1919, and used as a

merchant vessel. Registry information after 1937 is unavailable.

Jeremy L. Piercy

See also: Army Nurse Corps (ANC); Civil War (1861–1865); Nursing; Spanish-American War (1898).

References and Further Reading

Devilbiss, Margaret Conrad. *Women and Military Service: A History, Analysis, and Overview of Key Issues.* Ft. Belvoir, VA: Defense Technical Information Center, 1990.

Mooney, James L. *Dictionary of American Naval Fighting Ships*, Vol. 6. Washington, D.C.: Navy Department, Office of the Chief of Naval Operations, Naval History Division, 1976.

Wright, Marcus. *Wright's Official History of the Spanish-American War: A Pictorial and Descriptive Record of the Cuban Rebellion, the Causes that Involved the United States, and a Complete Narrative of Our Conflict with Spain, on Land and Sea.* Washington, D.C.: War Records Office, 1900.

USS *SANCTUARY*

USS *Sanctuary* is a haven-class hospital ship that served in both World War II and the Vietnam War. Many female nurses from the Navy Nurse Corps served on board the ship during these wars.

The Sun Shipbuilding and Dry Dock Co. of Chester, Pennsylvania, built the *Sanctuary* in 1944. The Todd Shipbuilding Co. of Hoboken, New Jersey, converted the *Sanctuary* to a hospital ship. The goal of turning the *Sanctuary* into a haven-class hospital ship was accomplished in large part by the citizens of Hoboken who matched the cost of conversion through the purchase of war bonds in order for the conversion to be completed.

Members of the Navy Nurse Corps and doctors made up most of the ship's officers and crew. They were not only responsible for tending to the sick and injured, but they were also responsible for training Hospital Corpsmen for emergency triage on the battlefield. This responsibility was especially important because corpsmen served in places where women were technically not permitted, such as in battles on the beaches and on fighting ships.

In August 1945, the crew of the *Sanctuary* arrived at Pearl Harbor. It was immediately sent to the Japanese coast. By September 13, 1945, the *Sanctuary* was taking aboard American and British wounded. It also took in Japanese prisoners of war (POWs). Within a matter of days, the ship's capacity was exceeded. Consequently, the ship proceeded to Okinawa with more than 1,300 POWs and brought them to Naha, where the POWs were delivered to Army personnel. Between 1945 and 1946, the *Sanctuary* continued traveling various routes between Japan, Guam, Hawaii, and California, retrieving POWs and other soldiers and returning them to American ports.

In 1967, the *Sanctuary* began her participation in the Vietnam War as a hospital ship, with the crew on board tending to wounded soldiers and personnel. Between 1967 and 1970, the ship aided mostly marines while rotating between Danang, Chu Hai, and other ports. After 1970, the *Sanctuary* was the only Navy haven-class hospital ship to remain off the coast of Vietnam. On April 23, 1971, the ship left Danang for the last time before returning to California.

After its use in the Vietnam War, the *Sanctuary* played an important role in the process of preparing women in the Navy for sea duty and, ultimately, opportunities for professional advancement. Traditionally, women in the Navy had been excluded from sea duty. This restriction prevented many women from receiving promotions and building a naval career, as sea duty is a pivotal part of that process. In 1972, Adm. Elmo Zumwalt, chief of naval operations, began to allow some women to serve aboard Navy ships, training for seagoing specialties. The Navy assigned a crew to the former hospital ship to give women a chance to develop skills in areas other than as nurses, corpsmembers, and other health-related fields. Some women worked in supply, operations, and administration aboard the *Sanctuary*. Initially plans were to use the ship to provide medical services to military dependents overseas, but it shortly thereafter anchored in Florida. The *Sanctuary* was removed from service in 1975.

Elizabeth Dean Worley

See also: Navy Nurse Corps; Nursing; Prisoners of War; Vietnam War (1965–1973); Women Accepted for Volunteer Emergency Service (WAVES); World War II (1941–1945).

References and Further Reading

Monahan, Evelyn M., and Rosemary Neidel-Greenlee. *A Few Good Women: America's Military Women from World War I to the Wars in Iraq and Afghanistan.* New York: Alfred A. Knopf Press, 2010.

Wise, James E., Jr., and Scott Baron. *Women at War: Iraq, Afghanistan, and Other Conflicts.* Annapolis, MD: Naval Institute Press, 2006.

V

VALDEZ, RAMONA M.
(1984–2005)

Cpl. Ramona Valdez served in Iraq as a communications specialist and on the Female Search Force. She was killed in action by a suicide bomber in June 2005.

Ramona M. Valdez was born on June 26, 1984, in the Dominican Republic. Valdez's mother, Elida Nuñez, immigrated to the United States, leaving Valdez and her sister Fiorela with their grandparents. At age six, Ramona and Fiorela joined their mother in the Bronx, New York. At age 14, she began working at the Statue of Liberty. By age 15, Valdez graduated from Jane Addams High School and began attending community college.

In early 2002, at age 17, Valdez joined the U.S. Marine Corps to help financially support her family. She completed basic training at Marine Corps Recruit Depot in Parris Island, South Carolina, and became a communications specialist at the Marine Corps Base Camp in LeJeune, North Carolina. That year Corporal Valdez also met Cpl. Armando Guzman, a fellow Bronx native and marine. In 2003, Valdez and Guzman married.

Valdez was assigned to the Counter Improvised Explosive Device Working Group of the Headquarters Battalion, 2nd Marine Division, II Marine Expeditionary Force. By February 2005, Valdez was deployed to Iraq in support of Operation Iraqi Freedom as a communication specialist.

In Iraq, Valdez was also part of the Female Search Force, a team responsible for guarding checkpoints and searching Iraqi women and children. Female search forces were implemented in order to calm concerns around male soldiers searching Iraqi women, violating local customs. Checkpoints were very dangerous because they were places where U.S. servicemembers and Iraqis interacted, making them targets for attacks by suicide bombers. On June 23, 2005, a convoy of Female Search Force members was returning to

Camp Fallujah when a suicide bomber attacked the convoy. The suicide bomber's truck rammed into one of the convoy trucks. The impact caused an enormous fire and explosion, killing Valdez and five other marines as well as severely burning seven other marines. Valdez was killed in action four days short of her 21st birthday and eight months from the end of her four-year enlistment.

On June 1, 2007, the U.S. Marine Corps honored the memory of Valdez. The II Marine Expeditionary Force Communications Training Center at the Marine Corps Base Camp in LeJeune, North Carolina, was named the Valdez Training Facility during a building dedication ceremony.

Valdez's awards and decorations include the Purple Heart (posthumously awarded), the National Defense Service Medal, the Global War on Terrorism Service Medal, and the Iraq Campaign Medal.

Estefania Ponti

See also: Hispanic American Women; Iraq War (2003–2011); War on Terror (2001–).

References and Further Reading

Alt, Betty Sowers. *Following the Flag: Marriage and the Modern Military.* Westport, CT: Greenwood, 2006.

Ballard, John R. *Fighting for Fallujah: A New Dawn for Iraq.* Westport, CT: Greenwood, 2006.

Ryan, Cheyney. *The Chickenhawk Syndrome: War, Sacrifice, and Personal Responsibility.* Lanham, MD: Rowman & Littlefield, 2009.

VAN DEVANTER (BUCKLEY), LYNDA MARGARET (1947–2002)

Lynda Van Devanter Buckley was one of the first women to write critically about the experiences of American nurses in Vietnam. In 1983, she published her memoir, *Home before Morning*, written with Christopher Morgan. She played an active role in female veterans' affairs, addressing issues of post-traumatic stress disorder, gender discrimination, and serious health issues that veterans, including women like herself, and Vietnamese civilians developed due to exposure to chemicals such as Agent Orange. She served as the founding executive director of the Women's Project of the Vietnam Veterans of America from 1979 to 1984.

Born in Arlington, Virginia, in 1947, Lynda Van Devanter responded as many did to President John F. Kennedy's 1961 inaugural address—she was eager to serve her country. After she finished nursing school in 1968, she joined the U.S. Army, which commissioned her as a second lieutenant in the Army Nurse Corps. She served as an Army surgical nurse in Vietnam from June 8, 1969, until June 7, 1970, first with the 71st Evacuation Hospital in Pleiku, near the Cambodian border, and later with the 67th Evacuation Hospital. Like many of her fellow nurses, she was ill prepared for the horrific realities of caring for battle-maimed soldiers or the constraints of a male-dominated military system.

Her experiences in Vietnam included nights frequently disturbed by the call to care for incoming wounded, greeting the med-evac helicopters. Because of rocket attacks, she often slept under her bunk. Her operating room patients included not only young GIs but also Vietnamese civilians. Van Devanter found short-term relief and release from the rarified and strained world of the battlefield hospital in affairs with doctors, some of whom were married. When she returned to the United States, she nursed in a civilian hospital. However, her struggles with post-traumatic stress disorder led her to give up nursing. She suffered with nightmares, alcoholism, drug abuse, and psychological problems.

In 1979, Van Devanter founded the Vietnam Veterans of America's Women's Project. She served as its director from 1979 until 1984. She wrote her memoir, *Home before Morning: The True Story of an Army Nurse in Vietnam*, as part of therapy. The memoir grew out of Van Devanter's need come to terms with her time in Vietnam by returning to those experiences and laying claim to the strengths that she had gained while there. She also drew on and honored the community of women, soldiers, and reporters who endured similar difficulties and losses. As a result, she reinforced the idea that sharing the sorrow, pain, and knowledge were necessary steps to well-being. In addition, Van Devanter played an important role in legitimizing women's experiences as warriors. Although only one-fifth of GIs in Vietnam were involved in actual combat, while the majority engaged in logistics and supply roles, all male veterans could lay claim to the heroic role of soldier. This was not the case for women returning from the war zone. Van Devanter explored this exclusion. She not only confronted the government's failure to support women who had served in the war, but also addressed their fellow veterans' refusal to accept them as "vets." As a result, she helped to reform the image of what it meant to look like a veteran.

In addition, the memoir explored Van Devanter's own ordeals with post-traumatic stress disorder, which included excessive drinking, drug abuse, nightmares, and unbearable memories of the gore and emotional upheavals experienced in Vietnam. Her memoir spoke to the collective experiences of many women who had dealt with similar dislocations, which had not yet been discussed or examined, and galvanized these women. *Home before Morning* also challenged the docile, placid, innocent images of women who served in Vietnam. They were not "girls" or "donut dollies." Instead, these Army nurses had to deal with a gruesome, sexually loose world where male chauvinism, racism, trauma, and military authoritarianism influenced everyone's behavior. Upon its publication, she faced both disapprobation and support. The popular TV show *China Beach* was drawn in part from Van Devanter's memoir.

In 1991, Van Devanter and Joan A. Furey edited a collection, *Visions of War, Dreams of Peace: Writings of Women in the Vietnam War*. Van Devanter characterized this book as an important process of sharing and healing for women, many of whom had survived their postwar years by silencing, or trying to silence, their memories of Vietnam.

Van Devanter died at the age of 55 from a vascular disease that she attributed to chemical exposure in Vietnam.

Page Dougherty Delano

See also: Army Nurse Corps (ANC); Nursing; Vietnam War (1965–1973).

References and Further Reading

Bates, Milton J. *Wars We Took to Vietnam: Cultural Conflict and Storytelling.* Berkeley: University of California Press, 1996.

Marshall, Kathryn. *In the Combat Zone.* New York: Penguin, 1987.

Mithers, Carol Lynn. "Missing in Action: Women Warriors in Vietnam." *Cultural Critique*, no. 3 (Spring 1986): 79–90.

O'Neil, Susan. *Don't Meaning Nothing.* Amherst: University of Massachusetts Press, 2004.

Van Devanter, Lynda. *Home before Morning: The Story of an Army Nurse in Vietnam.* Amherst: University of Massachusetts Press, 2001. Original publication, 1983.

Van Devanter, Lynda, and Joan A. Furey, eds. *Visions of War, Dreams of Peace: Writings of Women in the Vietnam War.* New York: Warner Books, 1991.

VAN LEW, ELIZABETH (1818–1900)

A native Virginian who served as a Union spy in the Confederate capital of Richmond, Virginia, Elizabeth Van Lew was often referred to as Crazy Bet. Van Lew's efforts on behalf of the Union during the Civil War led to the escape of dozens of Union prisoners from Libby Prison in Richmond, the collection of vital intelligence on Confederate military positions in and around the city, and other successful activities of the Union underground throughout the war.

Van Lew was born October 15, 1818, in Richmond, Virginia, the first child of John Van Lew and Eliza Louise Baker Van Lew. In the 1830s, her parents sent her to Philadelphia to live with relatives while she received her education. Although the Van Lews owned slaves, Elizabeth developed a strong abolitionist stance that provided a foundation for her actions during the Civil War. She believed not only that slavery had corrupted Southern society but also that its immoral nature made it a national sin.

As the war began, Confederate women in their Church Hill neighborhood asked Van Lew and her mother to join them in providing sustenance and supplies to the growing Confederate armies that flocked to Richmond. The Van Lew women refused the requests, creating suspicion about the family's loyalty that would follow them throughout the conflict. In an effort to deflect the criticism, occasionally Van Lew would minister to the Confederate wounded and encamped soldiers. She also became an accomplished hostess, entertaining Confederate officers and government officials in the family's home, as well as boarding a Confederate captain and his family for a time. She even explained her desire to visit Union prisoners as a reflection of a proper Confederate woman's Christian duty to minister to those deemed most unworthy. This public persona was simply a way for Van Lew to gain access to people and information that would further the Union cause while raising the least suspicion.

The public perception of her as crazy may have developed from the odd clothing she wore and nonsensical mutterings she uttered as she walked through the streets of the city during the war. However, the most recent biography contends that factual evidence does not exist to support such contentions; instead, resentment for her Unionism, her radical stance on slavery, and her lifelong spinsterhood and reclusive lifestyle may be more the cause of the nickname.

The majority of Van Lew's early war work related to providing for and assisting in the escape of Union prisoners held in Richmond. Both personally and with the aid of free blacks, slaves, and other Unionists, Van Lew sent prisoners messages that were hidden in the spines of books, in the false bottoms of food platters, in the soles of her servants' shoes, or in a hollow egg in a basket of eggs. She had her own encryption code, composed of letters and numbers, which she kept secure in the back of her watch, and she used the family property around the city as relay stations to pass on information to Union officials. She also used much of her family's finances to bribe Confederate guards and clerks.

Van Lew supervised an extensive spy network that may have included Mary Elizabeth Bowser, believed to be Van Lew's former black servant, who gained a maid position in the Confederate White House and sent information back to Van Lew. Some doubt exists about her identity and relationship to Van Lew, but the extent and success of the Union underground led by Van Lew, including the 1864 escape of 103 prisoners from Libby Prison, makes the story plausible.

By 1864, Van Lew began to work as chief correspondent of the Unionist spy network, sending information to Gens. George H. Sharpe (chief of the Secret Service), Benjamin F. Butler (Army of the James), George G. Meade (Army of the Potomac), and Ulysses S. Grant (overall Union commander). The information coming from Unionists in Richmond led to a failed raid by Gen. Judson Kilpatrick and Col. Ulrich Dahlgren to free more prisoners and to the successful final Union assault by Grant's forces on Richmond. Gratitude for her services during the war eventually led to a government payment of $5,000 in 1867 and her appointment as postmaster of Richmond by President Ulysses Grant in 1869, a post she held for eight years. Community resentment toward Van Lew continued for the remainder of her life due to her Republican politics, her advocacy for African American equality, and her perpetual association with Southern disloyalty and the conquering Union.

Van Lew died September 25, 1900, in Richmond, Virginia.

Kristen L. Streater

See also: Bowser, Mary Elizabeth (ca. 1839–n.d.); Civil War (1861–1865); Espionage.

References and Further Reading

Leonard, Elizabeth D. *All the Daring of the Soldier: Women of the Civil War Armies.* New York: W. W. Norton & Company, 1999.

Ryan, David, ed. *A Yankee Spy in Richmond: The Civil War Diary of "Crazy Bet" Van Lew.* Mechanicsburg, PA: Stackpole Books, 1996.

Varon, Elizabeth R. *Southern Lady, Yankee Spy: The True Story of Elizabeth Van Lew, A Union Agent in the Heart of the Confederacy.* New York: Oxford University Press, 2003.

VAUGHT, WILMA L. (1930–)

Wilma L. Vaught, the first woman in the U.S. Air Force to deploy with a bomber unit, was also the first woman from the comptroller field to reach the rank of brigadier general in the Air Force.

Vaught was born on March 15, 1930, in Pontiac, Illinois. She was raised on a farm in rural Scotland, Illinois, and was the eldest of two daughters. Vaught attended the University of Illinois at Urbana-Champaign College of Business, graduating with a bachelor of science degree in 1952.

Vaught soon found a job in the corporate sector. However, she quickly realized few advancement opportunities existed for women. A military recruitment advertisement promising all recruits the possibility of becoming a manager and supervisor caught Vaught's attention and ultimately led to her decision to join the Air Force.

In January 1957, Vaught was commissioned as a second lieutenant in the Air Force. She completed the Officer's Basic Military Training Course at Lackland Air Force Base in Texas. She then studied at the Statistical Services Officers' Course, located at Texas's Sheppard Air Force Base, for three months. Despite the strong restrictions at that time on both the number of women who could serve in the military and the capacities in which they could serve, Vaught soon rose to leadership positions. In September 1957, she reported to the 805th Air Base Group at Barksdale Air Force Base in Louisiana as chief of the Data Services branch and commander of the Women in the Air Force Squadron Section. Her service took her abroad in April 1959, when she went to Zaragoza Air Base in Spain. Vaught served there until April 1963 as the chief of the Management Analysis Division of the 3974th Combat Support Group.

When Vaught returned stateside, she served as chief of the Management Analysis Division for the 306th Bombardment Wing while assigned to the 306th Combat Support Group at McCoy Air Force Base in Florida. Shortly thereafter she became the first woman to deploy with a Strategic Air Command operational unit. This honor occurred when Vaught was serving on a temporary tour of duty at Andersen Air Force Base in Guam. This service, in which Vaught was the executive officer and chief of the Management Analysis Division of the 4133rd Provisional Bombardment Wing, was during Operation ARC Light.

Vaught continued her education at the University of Alabama at Tuscaloosa, completing a master's program in business administration in 1968. The Vietnam War was escalating, and Vaught would soon enter the conflict herself, serving as a management analyst in the Office of the Deputy Chief of Staff, Comptroller, Military Assistance Command, in Saigon. She was stationed close to the front lines, and rocket strikes often hit within two blocks of her quarters.

As one of the first women to serve in such a capacity, Vaught faced substantial resistance from male colleagues. Although the Johnson administration's changing regulations during the Vietnam War lessened the restrictions on women serving in the military and created more opportunities for their advancement, attitudes in the field did not necessarily change. Vaught herself was outspoken about women's rights to serve in these new capacities and was eager to take advantage of the opportunities.

Upon completing her tour of duty in Vietnam, Vaught once again returned stateside. This time she was stationed in Ohio as part of the Headquarters Air Force Logistics Command at Wright-Patterson Air Force Base. She served as chief of the Advanced Logistics Systems Plans and Management Group until summer 1972, when she became the first female officer to attend the Industrial College of the Armed Forces. Also after Vaught left Wright-Patterson, she was assigned to the Directorate of Management Analysis, Office of the Comptroller, Headquarters U.S. Air Force, in Washington, D.C. There she served as chief of the Cost Factors Branch and later as chief of the Security Assistance Division until 1977, when she was assigned to the Air Force Systems Command Headquarters. At the headquarters, she was the director of programs and budget in the Office of the Deputy Chief of Staff, Comptroller, and became the deputy chief of staff in March 1980.

Vaught broke more barriers on September 8, 1980, when she became the first woman in the comptroller field to become a brigadier general. She was appointed commander of the U.S. Military Entrance Processing Command headquartered at Great Lakes, Illinois, in 1982, and retired as one of only three female generals in the Air Force and one of seven female generals in the U.S. armed forces in 1985. Before her retirement, Vaught also chaired NATO's Women in the Allied Forces Committee and was the senior woman military representative to the Secretary of Defense's Advisory Committee on Women in the Service.

After her retirement, Vaught remained active in pursuing the interests of military women, presiding over the Women's Memorial Foundation board of directors and from this position working to establish a memorial to honor military women. The foundation raised over $20 million to create the Women in Military Service for America Memorial, which was dedicated on October 18, 1997.

Vaught experienced many "firsts" for women in the Air Force and is one of the most decorated women in military history. Her honors include the Defense and Air Force Distinguished Service Medals, the Air Force Legion of Merit, the Bronze Star, and the Vietnam Service Award with four stars. She was the first woman to command a unit that received the Joint Meritorious Unit Award and was inducted into the National Women's Hall of Fame in 2000.

Jamie L. Huber

See also: Vietnam War (1965–1973); Women in Military Service for America Memorial; Women in the Air Force (WAF).

References and Further Reading

Ashabranner, Brent. *A Date with Destiny: Women in Military Service for America Memorial*. Brookfield, CT: 21st Century Press, 2000.

Lewis, Vicki, and Wilma L. Vaught. *Side-by-Side: A Photo History of American Women in the Military*. New York: Stewart, Tabori, and Chang, 1999.

Vaught, Wilma L. *The Day the Nation Said "Thanks!" A History and Dedication Scrapbook of the Women in Military Service for America Memorial*. Washington, D.C.: Military Women's Press, 1999.

Waisman, Charlotte S., and Jill S. Tietjen. *Her Story: A Timeline of the Women Who Changed America*. New York: Harper, 2008.

VEGA, SARAH
(1981–)

Petty Officer Sarah Vega, a first class marine science technician with the U.S. Coast Guard (USCG), served two voluntary deployments in the War on Terror. She spent time in Iraq, Kuwait, and Afghanistan in support of Operation Iraqi Freedom (OIF). She has been awarded several medals for her service.

Born in 1981 in Bitburg, Germany, where her parents were stationed at the time, Vega grew up in Kodiak, Alaska. She is the great-granddaughter of an Army World War II veteran and the daughter of Air Force personnel. Her daughter, Izabella, was born in 2002.

In 2000, Vega joined the USCG. According to statistics from the Department of Defense (DOD) and the USCG, as of September 2011, a total of 6,790 or 15 percent of active-duty USCG personnel were women.

In 2005, when she was a second class marine science technician (MST2), Vega volunteered to join the Coast Guard Redeployment Assistance Inspection Detachment (RAID) team IV. The RAID IV team consisted of nine members. She was one of two women in the group. The Army trained MST2 Vega and her fellow team members for their overseas duties. The RAID team prepared to assist with inspections of hazardous materials in Iraq. The team deployed in October 2005 and spent five months on the ground inspecting vehicles and training army units in various areas of Iraq. RAID IV also assisted U.S. Navy Customs officials in Iraq with the shipment and inspections of military equipment. This joint effort between the RAID IV team and Navy Customs facilitated the inspection of equipment that in turn allowed troops to return home quickly. As a result of the RAID IV team's work, some soldiers were able to return home a month ahead of their scheduled arrival.

The RAID IV team briefly deployed to Iraq, where the team faced various and constant attacks from insurgents. The team made it out of Iraq, in February 2006, without any casualties. Upon their return home, five RAID IV Coast Guard team members, including MST2 Vega, were awarded the Army's Combat Action Badge for their combat action. In addition, on February 3, 2006, MST2 Vega received the Coast Guard Commendation Medal with Operational Distinguishing Device ("O"). The medal with "O" recognizes her heroism, patriotism, voluntarism, and service with the RAID IV team.

Twelve months after her return home, the then 25-year-old MST2 Vega volunteered once again for a second phase of the RAID team, now the RAID V team. The team deployed for Afghanistan in October 2006. RAID V conducted customs inspections and training for military personnel in Afghanistan. The deployment lasted five months. Members of RAID V returned home in March 2007. That month, while the team was still deployed, MST1 Vega received the League of United Latin American Citizens Excellence Military Service Award for Active Duty Personnel. The award is an annual recognition to one active-duty member of each branch of the military. The award recognizes one male and one female member who demonstrate excellence in their military service.

In May 2008, the Women's Memorial Foundation featured then MST1 Vega as one of five women highlighted in their Mother's Day issue. According to the Foundation, as of 2007, an estimated 7,000 mothers were deployed in active duty military. Vega was praised and commended as an excellent role model for her then six-year-old daughter, Izabella.

After her tour in Afghanistan, MST1 Vega has not volunteered for any other deployments or RAID missions. Instead, she was reassigned from the Kodiak, Alaska, USCG division to the Marine Safety Detachment unit in Cape Canaveral, Florida. Her work in Florida is far less dangerous. The USCG Marine Safety Detachment works closely with the crab fishing industry in an effort to make crab fishing a safer industry. The team conducts inspections of fishing vessels and offers safety training for the crewmen. First Lady Michelle Obama also recognized MST1 Vega's devotion and patriotism to her military duty in a March 3, 2009, speech to American servicewomen.

Lizeth Elizondo

See also: Afghanistan; Iraq War (2003–2011); War on Terror (2001–); Women in Military Service for America Memorial.

References and Further Reading

Francis, Sara. "U.S. Coast Guard and Industry Work Together to Make Fisheries Safer." *Proceedings: The Coast Guard Journal of Safety at Sea of the Marine Safety and Security Council*, Winter 2005–2006, 42–44.

Voices of Valor. "Semper Paratus: Coast Guard Woman Is Always Ready—Even in a War Zone." Washington, D.C.: Women in Military Service for America Memorial Foundation, March 2008.

White House. "Remarks by the First Lady at the Women in Military Service for America Memorial Center." Arlington, VA: White House, March 3, 2009.

VELAZQUEZ, LORETA JANETA [HARRY T. BUFORD] (1842–1897)

Disguised as Lt. Harry T. Buford, complete with a glued-on beard and moustache, Loreta Janeta Velazquez recruited a group of Confederate soldiers and served as their commander during the American Civil War. In her memoirs, Velazquez claimed that she disguised herself as a man to fulfill her desire for adventure.

Born in Havana, Cuba, on June 26, 1842, Velazquez claimed to have been born to a wealthy family in Cuba and raised in New Orleans by an aunt, where as a girl she thrilled to the exploits of Joan of Arc and fantasized about a military career. Nevertheless, her life seemed destined to follow a path typical for 19th-century women—she married young and bore three children. After the deaths of her children and her husband's decision to join the Confederate forces, however, Velazquez revived her memories of "military glory" and her desire "to win fame on the battle-field." Her attempts to enlist her husband's approval for a scheme to disguise herself as a soldier were unsuccessful, so she waited until his departure to implement her plan.

She wrote that she began her career in disguise as a Confederate officer, Lt. Harry T. Buford, in order to raise a regiment to deliver to her husband's command. He was killed early in the war; despite her grief, Velazquez decided to continue her own military career. She claimed to have fought in the First Battle of Bull Run and afterwards to have decided that she could better serve the Confederate cause as a spy. After being wounded, arrested, unmasked, imprisoned, and released, Velazquez promptly redonned her male disguise and enlisted in the 21st Louisiana Regiment but soon secured a commission in the cavalry. What followed were many patrols, and Velazquez often demonstrated her military competence and courage.

Velazquez wrote that she married her second husband during the war, a Thomas C. DeCaulp (the only one of four husbands whom she named in her memoirs). She claimed that like her first husband, DeCaulp was killed in the war, but historical records show that he survived. Some historians believe that the couple had a falling-out or that DeCaulp deserted Velazquez, and in hiding this fact she introduced one of many discrepancies in her story. In any event, Velazquez wrote that after being badly wounded, being unmasked again, feeling frustrated with the war, and becoming widowed for the second time, she took on the more lucrative job of managing blockade-running operations. She also wrote that at various points she performed espionage duties, sometimes in female guise as "Mrs. Alice Williams." After the war, she claims to have married and been widowed a third time before marrying her fourth husband and giving birth to a son. Around 1880, Velazquez was lost to the historical record, and no information on her later life or death is known.

She published her memoirs, *The Woman in Battle: A Narrative of the Exploits, Adventures, and Travels of Madame Loreta Janeta Velazquez, Otherwise Known as Lieutenant Harry T. Buford, Confederate States Army*, in 1876 and was immediately labeled a fraud because of the apparent exaggeration and contradictions. Jubal Early, a former Confederate general, was among those who denounced the book. The sensational tone of the book makes it difficult for today's readers to accept, although it was consistent with similar memoirs of its time. However, many of the details of actual battles, weather, and daily life ring true. Most likely, her story contains both elements of truth and fiction.

Velazquez is interesting as a typical example of the several dozen women who gained fame based on a memoir or autobiography detailing their supposed exploits disguised as male soldiers. Copies of these books have been preserved, but verifying the truth of the stories is extremely challenging to the historian. In Velazquez's case, as in many others, there is no evidence to prove that she was not a soldier, and the discrepancies and exaggerations could be categorized as not untypical in the memoirs of war veterans. It is possible, or even probable, that Velazquez did serve in the army, although the true nature of her achievements cannot be determined. What is perhaps even more interesting is the likelihood that for every woman like Velazquez who lived to publish her tale and thus come to public recognition, there were many others who were killed in action or who kept their experiences forever secret, returning to traditional female roles or even maintaining their disguise long after the war had ended.

Gayle Veronica Fischer

See also: Civil War (1861–1865); Espionage.

References and Further Reading

Hall, Richard. *Patriots in Disguise: Women Warriors of the Civil War.* New York: Marlowe & Company, 1993.

Leonard, Elizabeth. *All the Daring of the Soldier: Women of the Civil War Armies.* New York: W. W. Norton & Company, 1999.

Massey, Mary Elizabeth. *Women in the Civil War.* Lincoln: University of Nebraska Press, 1994. Reprint of *Bonnet Brigades*, 1966.

Seeley, Charlotte Palmer. *American Women and the U.S. Armed Forces: A Guide to the Records of Military Agencies in the National Archive Relating to Women.* Washington, D.C.: National Archives and Records Administration, 1992.

Velazquez, Loreta Janeta. *The Woman in Battle: The Civil War Narrative of Loreta Janeta Velazquez, Cuban Woman and Confederate Soldier*, edited by Jesse Aleman. Madison: University of Wisconsin Press, 2003.

VICTORY GARDENS

The American government encouraged citizens to plant "victory gardens" during the world wars to support the war efforts. Subsequently, Americans planted victory gardens to supplement their diets because of the scarcity of necessities and to show their support for servicemembers and the nation-state. Victory gardens were also popular during the wars in other countries such as Canada, England, and Germany.

To promote victory gardens during wartime, the government used posters like this one created during World War II. (Library of Congress)

Victory gardens are often associated with World War II, but they actually were popularized during World War I when the federal government encouraged private citizens to plant what they originally called "war gardens." At the end of World War I, the government persuaded people to maintain their wartime gardens and changed the name to "victory gardens" to celebrate the end of the war.

First Lady Eleanor Roosevelt encouraged Americans to begin planting victory gardens again in 1943 when she planted one at the White House. The federal government, especially the Department of Agriculture, individual state governments, and voluntary societies such as the American Women's

Voluntary Services, Inc., also encouraged the planting of gardens as the country faced a growing food shortage and increased rationing. By the end of the war, approximately 20 million Americans had planted gardens and were producing approximately 40 percent of the country's vegetables. Beyond supplementing diets, these gardens helped citizens save on transportation costs and on materials used for canning and distributing goods.

Planting a victory garden was also a way to boost morale. It gave citizens on the homefront a way to participate in the war effort and gave them something concrete and useful to do for their country. Ads in magazines as well as propaganda urged people to do their part through victory gardens. The media further encouraged people to eat more nutritious meals in order to preserve their strength to better serve the war effort and argued that self-interest served national interest.

There were several reasons given to encourage people to plant victory gardens. Many people believed that planting and tending gardens improved psychological health. Gardens brought order to a world that because of war seemed increasingly chaotic. Victory gardens also reinforced a feeling of natural order or the human control of nature. Unlike during World War I, when people tore out flowers to make room for vegetables, during World War II propagandists and magazine writers encouraged people to maintain flower gardens in addition to vegetable gardens. Flowers expressed patriotism, especially red, white, and blue flowers, and offered a space for peaceful contemplation for returning servicemembers. Propaganda also encouraged women to act as heads of household in the absence of men and suggested that women could properly provide for their families by ensuring that they had a nutritious diet. Therefore, victory gardens were a way to serve their families' needs and their country's needs in a time when patriotism was at a peak.

By 2009, victory gardens were making another comeback in response to the economic recession. In addition to the gardens helping people save money, many Americans were concerned about the quality and safety of produce available and about global warming, and wanted to live healthier lives.

M. Michaele Smith

See also: Roosevelt, Eleanor (1884–1962); World War I (1914–1918); World War II (1941–1945).

References and Further Reading

Bentley, Amy. *Eating for Victory: Food Rationing and the Politics of Domesticity.* Urbana: University of Illinois Press, 1998.

"Digging Their Way Out of Recession." *Economist* 390, no. 8620 (2009): 36.

Miller, Char. "In the Sweat of Our Brow: Citizenship in American Domestic Practice during WWII—Victory Gardens." *Journal of American Culture* 26, no. 3 (2003): 395–409.

VIETNAM WAR (1965–1973)

American women's roles in the Vietnam War varied widely. They acted in a variety of noncombat military and civilian roles. Women were also prominent in the antiwar movement in the United States. Whatever their role, many women found the Vietnam War to be a transformative experience that forced radical changes in the way society viewed gender roles.

Although restricted by law from serving in combat positions, thousands of women served in the American military during the Vietnam War. During the Vietnam era, female members of the U.S. armed forces belonged to separate women's branches—the Women's Army Corps (WAC), the Navy's Women Accepted for Volunteer Emergency Service (WAVES), and the Air Force's Women's Auxiliary Ferrying Squadron (WAFS). These separate branches allowed women to take part in the military effort but restricted them to administrative fields, aid to servicemen, nursing, and health services.

The vast majority of women who served in the American military in Vietnam, numbering nearly 8,000, served as nurses. Most of the female nurses served in the Army. They worked in either Mobile Army Surgical Hospital (MASH) units or in evacuation hospitals in large cities such as Saigon, Danang, or Chu Lai. Navy nurses, who provided care for marines, had similar assignments or were stationed on hospital ships offshore.

In 1963, two years before direct American entry into the war, nurses in the armed forces numbered only 3,000. As the war escalated, all branches of service, but particularly the Army, stepped up their recruiting efforts. Many women signed up to serve as wartime nurses in exchange for having the Army, Navy, or Air Force pay their tuition.

In 1956, the Army had initiated a student nurse program, which paid for the final years of nursing education for recruits. In return, the nurse graduates agreed to serve for two years. These women had to be at least 21 years old when they entered the service and were all awarded commissions in the medical corps. The degree of preparation varied among the services. Before being assigned to Vietnam, Army nurses underwent 8 to 10 weeks of training at Fort Sam Houston, Texas. Navy nurses had no specific training but were required to serve for two years before being assigned overseas. Air Force nurses received two months of flight training.

Despite the intensive education and training, nothing could prepare them for the experience of working in a hospital in a war zone. Most of the recruits had recently graduated from college and had less than two years of practical nursing experience. None of the services provided information on the conditions or dangers the recruits would face in the war zone.

In Vietnam, the young women were thrust into situations where they had to care for massive numbers of casualties during periods of heavy fighting. They worked physically and mentally demanding shifts that often ran as long as 72 hours. Frequently, these young women were assigned to perform triage —deciding which casualties needed immediate attention, which could wait, and which were beyond help. In a war without distinct front lines, nurses faced danger from mortar, rocket, and sapper attacks, particularly if they served in MASH units. These emotional and physical pressures often resulted in physical and mental exhaustion as well as occasional breakdowns.

In addition to the pressures involved in caring for casualties, nurses faced gendered expectations and discrimination. Both their superiors in the care facilities and the men they met as casualties or coworkers expected nurses to provide emotional support and nurturing as well as medical care. Female nurses also experienced a great deal of sexual pressure. In a survey conducted on 137 Vietnam nurse veterans in 1984, 63 percent of those questioned reported some form of sexual harassment. Many men assumed that nurses were available for dating and sex. Indeed, many nurse veterans reported incidents of rape. In addition, the emotional bonds forged between men and women who saw the horrors of war every day often evolved into romantic or sexual liaisons that could lead to resentments or conflicts within the medical unit. Female nurses who had sexual relationships often found themselves facing the same double standards that existed in wider American society. They found their reputations damaged, which could reflect on all women in the armed services and which reinforced the enduring myth that women who joined the military held lower moral standards and looser values than did civilian women.

After returning to the United States, many nurse veterans, like many of their male counterparts, suffered from depression, anger, anxiety, nightmares, feelings of alienation, and other symptoms that fell into the category of post-traumatic stress disorder. Many found family and friends unwilling to talk about the war. Because they were classified as noncombatants, they initially received no public recognition for their service or their resulting problems. Most veterans

organizations excluded them, and the Veterans Administration (VA) neither extended any support services nor provided much information on educational or financial benefits.

In response, female veterans got together to call attention to the problems and discrimination they faced. Led by Lynda Van Devanter, a former Army nurse, they launched the Vietnam Veterans Association Women's Project. Van Devanter became the project's first spokesperson. Intense publicity campaigns led to a 1983 congressional investigation into the VA for lack of services for women. These measures led to improvements in VA services and benefits for women by the 1990s.

In addition to those who served as nurses, 700 women served in Vietnam in the WAC, 500 in the WAF, a lesser number in the WAVES, and 36 in the Women Marines. Enlisted women worked in administrative capacities as secretaries, clerks, and stenographers while female officers worked in more technical capacities in communications, logistics, and information services. WAC advisors first appeared in Vietnam as advisors to the South Vietnamese Army in the planning and development of the Women's Armed Forces Corps concerning organization, recruitment, training, and administration. Subsequently, WAC officers and enlisted personnel served in the Headquarters of the Military Assistance Command Vietnam in Saigon, in the Headquarters, U.S. Army; at Tan Son Nhut Air Base; and in the Army Central Support Command facilities at Qui Nhon and Cam Ranh Bay. WAF personnel worked at air bases in Thailand and at Danang, and WAVES worked in the Naval

Communications Information Center in Saigon and with the Naval Supply Activity Unit in Cam Ranh Bay. Most Women Marines served in Japan or Okinawa.

Senior male commanders in Vietnam in all four of the services expressed reservations over the propriety of women serving in the combat area of South Vietnam. They were concerned about living and working conditions for female military personnel. In addition, they feared that, in a war without a front in a conventional sense, women would be targets for attack by the communists. In addition, they expressed concerns about the distractions these women would pose for their male coworkers. Manpower demands resulting from mobilization following the 1965 expansion of the American military presence in Vietnam plus directives from the Department of Defense overcame this resistance. All of the military commands in Vietnam relaxed restrictions on the assignment of women solely to support facilities in Saigon and other large urban areas or support bases.

American civilian women also worked directly with the U.S. armed forces in Vietnam. The American Red Cross had a predominately female field service staff that assisted servicemen with emergency leaves and worked as liaisons between soldiers and their families. The Red Cross also sponsored the Supplemental Recreational Activities Overseas organization that—along with Army Special Services—ran clubs and canteens in rear areas and often greeted soldiers returning from operations with coffee, food, and soft drinks. The United Service Organizations, the best-known of the military support

organizations, hired singers and dancers to tour with major entertainers such as Bob Hope, Martha Raye, and Racquel Welch.

In Saigon and other major cities in South Vietnam, civilian women worked as secretaries and receptionists in diplomatic facilities such as the U.S. Embassy in Saigon and consulates in other urban areas as well as other government offices. They also served in a variety of relief organizations, affiliated both with the government and private religious groups, that helped the Vietnamese in schools, orphanages, kitchens, and hospitals.

Women were also active in the antiwar movement in the United States. Many women who had been active in the civil rights movement in the early 1960s, most prominent among them Coretta King, the wife of Martin Luther King Jr., and Angela Davis, expanded their activities into the antiwar movement. Women were also prominent in student opposition to the war. For example, students Bettina Aptheker, the daughter of American communist Herbert Apthecker; Bernadine Dorn, a founder of Students for a Democratic Society and later a member of the Weather Underground; and Diane Oughton, another member of the Weather Underground who was killed when a bomb she was helping to assemble accidentally exploded, were all antiwar activists.

Other American women became antiwar activists internationally. Mary Clarke and Lorraine Gordon organized Women Strike for Peace in the spring of 1965 and were among the first Americans to visit Hanoi in May. They attended a peace conference in Moscow where they met with a number of female officials from North Vietnam. In Hanoi, Clarke, Gordon, and their hosts planned a general peace conference that was to meet in Jakarta, Indonesia, the following year. Plans for the conference fell through when the government was overthrown by the Indonesian military.

A string of antiwar women, as well as other prominent American peace activists, visited North Vietnam during the course of American involvement in the war. None was more notable or more controversial than actress Jane Fonda. In itself, there was nothing exceptional about her July 1972 visit except for her celebrity and the fact that she was photographed visiting a North Vietnamese antiaircraft battery. However, rumors surrounding Fonda's visits with American prisoners of war and radio broadcasts to troops combined to generate accusations of treason that led to the loss of American lives. Even though these stories were more imagined than real, they became a part of public memory. They were used by the right wing to argue that Fonda and other antiwar dissenters prevented the United States from winning in Vietnam.

Vietnam proved a transformative experience for women in the military and on the homefront. Although female military personnel served primarily in administrative or clerical jobs in Vietnam, the war set in motion a process that helped to transform women's roles in the armed forces over the following decade. The demands of mobilization opened new opportunities for military women worldwide. The abolition of the draft in 1973 forced the services to make more effective use of the skills of female volunteers. These dynamics were enhanced by the rise of the women's movement and by federal court rulings barring sexual discrimination in the military. By the close of the 1970s, separate women's services in all four branches of the American military were abolished and women fully integrated into the armed forces.

Walter F. Bell

See also: Abzug, Bella (1920–1998); African American Women; American Red Cross; Asian American Women; Bailey, Mildred "Inez" Caroon (1919–2009); Cadoria, Sherian Grace (1940–); Cammermeyer, Margarethe (1942–); Clarke, Mary E. (1924–); Dulinsky, Barbara J. (n.d.–n.d.); Fonda, Jane [Lady Jayne Seymour Fonda] (1937–); Foote, Evelyn Patricia "Pat" (1930–); Gellhorn, Martha (1908–1988); Harris, Marcelite Jordan (1943–); Hays, Anna Mae McCabe (1920–); Herz, Alice (1883–1965); Higgins (Hall), Marguerite (1920–1966); Hispanic American Women; Hoefly, E. Ann (1919–2003); Jackson, Gilda A. (1950–); Kennedy, Claudia J. (1947–); Mobile Army Surgical Hospital (MASH); Native American Women; Nelson, Yzetta L. (1923–2011); Nursing; Raye, Martha (1916–1994); Rodgers, Marie Louise (1926–); United Service Organizations (USO); USS *Sanctuary*; Van Devanter (Buckley), Lynda Margaret (1947–2002); Vaught, Wilma L. (1930–); Weiss, Cora Rubin (1934–); Women Accepted for Volunteer Emergency Service (WAVES); Women in the Air Force (WAF); Women Marines; Women Strike for Peace (WSP); Women's Army Corps (WAC); Women's Auxiliary Ferrying Squadron (WAFS).

References and Further Reading

Holm, Jeanne. *Women in the Military: An Unfinished Revolution*. Novato, CA: Presidio Press, 1982.

Lembcke, Jerry. *Hanoi Jane: War, Sex, and Fantasies of Betrayal*. Amherst: University of Massachusetts Press, 2010.

Marshall, Kathryn. *In the Combat Zone: An Oral History of American Women in Vietnam, 1966–1975*. Boston: Little, Brown, 1987.

Norman, Elizabeth. *Women at War: The Story of Fifty Military Nurses Who Served in Vietnam*. Philadelphia: University of Pennsylvania Press, 1990.

Tischler, Barbara. "The Antiwar Movement." In *A Companion to the Vietnam War*, edited by Marilyn B. Young and Robert Buzzanco, 384–402. Oxford, UK: Blackwell, 2006.

Van Devanter, Lynda. *Home before Morning: The Story of an Army Nurse in Vietnam*. New York: Warner Books, 1983.

VIVANDIERES

The term *vivandieres* is used to designate a type of female sutler that first rose to prominent usage in the armies of Napoleonic France. The term was used to describe women who accompanied their husbands and fathers in the French army during the wars of the French Revolution. These women differed from camp followers in that they held an official position in the regiment. The concept was adopted by numerous American military organizations on both the Union and Confederate sides during the American Civil War, in which they were often referred to as "cantinieres" as well.

In the American Civil War, the official designation of *vivandiere* was applied to women who served with Zouave units or other ethnically derived organizations. These women were often wives or daughters of the soldiers of the regiment. Oftentimes, they were also referred to as "daughters of the regiment." They were considered to be respectable women and were often admired by the troops. They

During the Civil War, vivandieres served with ethnic units on both sides of the conflict. These women traveled with units as mascots, sutlers, and nurses. (Library of Congress)

traveled with the unit to which they were attached and received no pay. These women performed a number of important activities within the regiment. They acted as mascots, sutlers, and nurses. In their role as mascot, these women often marched with the regiment on parade, appearing in uniforms that resembled those of the parent organization. As sutlers, they sold materials to the men that they could not procure through the usual supply channels. The most common substance vivandieres dispensed was alcohol, and their identifying emblem was the round or oval flask that contained brandy or wine that the men could purchase for a fee. However, during battle, and to wounded soldiers, alcohol was given out free of charge. In addition, vivandieres helped with the wounded during battle, essentially performing triage. Finally, some even took a place alongside the men, on occasion fighting in the line in battle. Most vivandieres were removed from the service of the Union and Confederate armies after the first year of the war.

Because they were considered members of the regiment, vivandieres had their own uniforms. These uniforms usually consisted of jackets that were close approximations of those of the units to which they belonged. Many times, these were enhanced with the addition of vanity features such as extra braid or lace. In addition, they wore men's pants under a knee-length skirt. In this respect, their attire was similar to the bathing and gymnastic outfits of the period. Interestingly, the pants of their uniforms were often modified for comfort, being sewn in two sections. They were composed of cotton from the waist to just above the hem of the skirt, and then made of wool from the hemline down. In this manner they would appear as if they were wearing the same pants as the male members of the regiment.

James McIntyre

See also: Brownell, Kady (1842–1915); Camp Followers; Civil War (1861–1865); Divers, Bridget (ca. 1840–n.d.).

References and Further Reading

Broadwater, Robert P. *Daughters of the Cause: Women of the Civil War*. Altoona, PA: Daisy Publications, 1998.

Massey, Mary Elizabeth. *Women in the Civil War*. Lincoln: University of Nebraska Press, 1994. Original publication, 1966.

Middleton, Lee. *Hearts of Fire: Soldier Women of the Civil War*. Franklin, NC: Genealogy Publishing Service, 1993.

W

WAKEMAN, SARAH ROSETTA [LYONS WAKEMAN] (1843–1864)

Sarah Rosetta Wakeman was one of the several hundred women who fought in the American Civil War disguised as a man. Enlisting in a regiment of New York volunteers on August 30, 1862, under the name Lyons Wakeman, she fought undetected for nearly two years until her death from dysentery on June 19, 1864. The collection of letters to her family she left behind provides unusual insight into the experience of a disguised woman soldier. Unlike narratives prepared for publication by other women soldiers, including Sarah Emma Edmonds and Loretta Janeta Velazquez, Wakeman's letters present a simple and unembellished account of her experience.

Born on January 16, 1843, in Afton, New York, Wakeman was the oldest of Harvey Anable and Emily Hale Wakeman's nine children. After some schooling and work as a domestic, she left home in early August 1862. Masquerading as a man under the name Lyons Wakeman, she became a boatman on the Chenango Canal but enlisted in the 153rd Regiment of New York State Volunteers on August 30, 1862. Although Wakeman's letters do not indicate clear motivations behind her decision to take on the role of a man, the motivations of women soldiers could include patriotism, a search for adventure, the desire to stay close to a loved one, or economic pressures. Her letters, however, attest to her enjoyment of the soldier's life. She also clearly appreciated the independence gained through army life.

Mustered into the Union army in October 1862, Wakeman's regiment served guard duty in Alexandria, Virginia, and in Washington, D.C. The 153rd Regiment joined Maj. Gen. Nathaniel P. Bank's Red River campaign in Louisiana in February 1864, and in April Wakeman had her first engagement with the enemy. Falling ill with dysentery during the retreat to Alexandria after the failure of the campaign, Wakeman was admitted to the regimental hospital on May 3, 1864. By May 22, 1864, she had been sent to a larger hospital in New Orleans, Louisiana. Although she lingered for nearly a month before her death on June 19, 1864, medical personnel never recorded the secret of her sex on her records, and her headstone in the Chalmette National Cemetery of New Orleans reads simply Lyons Wakeman.

Juliana Kuipers

See also: Civil War (1861–1865); Edmonds (Seelye), Sarah Emma [Franklin Thompson] (1841–1898); Velazquez, Loreta Janeta [Harry T. Buford] (1842–1897).

References and Further Reading

Blanton, DeAnne, and Lauren M. Cook. *They Fought Like Demons: Women Soldiers in the American Civil War*. Baton Rouge: Louisiana State University Press, 2002.

Burgess, Lauren Cook, ed. *An Uncommon Soldier: The Civil War Letters of Sarah Rosetta Wakeman, Alias Private Lyons Wakeman, 153rd Regiment, New York State Volunteers*. New York: Oxford University Press, 1995.

Leonard, Elizabeth D. *All the Daring of the Soldier: Women of the Civil War Armies*. New York: W. W. Norton & Company, 1999.

WALKER, ANNA NANCY SLAUGHTER (N.D.–N.D)

Nancy Slaughter Walker is known for her involvement with Capt. William Clarke Quantrill's Missouri Raiders during and after the Civil War. Slaughter was supposedly a raider, but her role is often confused because her identity remained questionable until recent scholarship on Quantrill and his unit revealed her history.

Anna Walker was the daughter of Morgan Walker, who owned a plantation in Blue Springs, Missouri. Anna married a merchant, Dr. Riley Slaughter, and went by the alias "Nancy Slaughter." When a visiting physician stayed at the Slaughters' home, her husband awoke to find Anna getting back in their bed. The next evening, he pretended to sleep and saw her leave their bed and return to bed with the physician. This event led to a divorce, and she went back to her father's house in Jackson County.

Anna's brother, Andrew Walker, rode with Quantrill. During the Civil War, "Quantrill's Raiders" protected the Missouri homefront against Northern guerillas. Quantrill's unit engaged in controversial acts against Union troops, raided farmland, and acted independently from the Confederate government. After the Confederate surrender, the government labeled Quantrill's men as outlaws. Quantrill's Raiders continued their pursuits through Indian Territory and Texas.

Walker quickly caught the eye of Quantrill, and she became his mistress; thus her involvement with the Raiders' expeditions began. Quantrill fell madly in love with Walker. Instead of going to Arkansas to protect Indian Territory from federal invasion, Quantrill enlisted in the Confederate army as a private so that he could be closer to Walker. However, after some time, Walker became the love interest of Bill Anderson and then the mistress of Quantrill's chief lieutenant

George Todd. Finally, she fell for another guerilla leader, Joe Vaughn. Walker married Vaughn in 1862, infuriating Quantrill.

Quantrill's anger about Walker's marriage prompted him to betray his friends and raid the Walker farm. Quantrill knew that she was the heir to the land, home, and slaves that belonged to her father. As a result, Quantrill raided the Walker plantation, claiming to do it in the name of abolition. He and his band killed livestock. His attack on the Walkers sent residents in Jackson Country into a panic. The subsequent hysteria of Quantrill's first famous guerilla expedition on the Walker plantation fueled both the frequency of his raids and his legacy.

When her father died near the end of the war, Walker inherited a portion of the land. She sold this land to fund and open a brothel in Baxter Springs, Missouri. Now in control of her own money and livelihood, and confident of the income from her new business, Walker divorced Vaughn on the grounds that she had no further use for him.

Because of Walker's alias "Nancy Slaughter," she is often categorized as a woman who rode with and fought alongside Quantrill's Raiders. However, her involvement with the guerilla outlaw group was as a serial mistress rather than as a female vigilante.

Lauren K. Thompson

See also: Civil War (1861–1865).

References and Further Reading

Berry, Stephen William. *Weirding the War: Stories from the Civil War's Ragged Edges*. Athens: University of Georgia Press, 2011.

Brown, Dee Alexander. *The Gentle Tamers; Women of the Old Wild West*. New York: Putnam, 1958.

Castel, Albert E. *William Clarke Quantrill: His Life and Times*. New York: F. Fell, 1962.

Connelley, William Elsey. *Quantrill and the Border Wars*. New York: Pageant Book Co, 1956.

Jones, David E. *Women Warriors: A History*. Washington, D.C.: Brassey's, 1997.

WALKER, MARY EDWARDS (1832–1919)

Born in New York on November 26, 1832, Mary Edwards Walker became a Civil War surgeon, prisoner of war, and Medal of Honor recipient.

The child of free-thinking abolitionists, Walker had an unconventional childhood. Her parents raised her and her sisters to be as independent as their only son. The intellectual atmosphere

Dr. Mary Walker volunteered her medical services during the Civil War, tending to soldiers in Washington, D.C., and Virginia. (National Archives)

surrounding Walker during her youth became heightened as a result of the Seneca Falls Convention on Women's Suffrage in 1848, John Humphrey Noye's Oneida Commune, and the bloomer movement, as well as the spiritualism awakening, temperance, and abolitionism movements. Walker attended Falley Seminary and taught at the Muretto Village, a short distance from her home. Throughout his life, her father voraciously read medical books in search of a cure for his recurring illness. Years later, those same books prompted Mary to seriously consider medical school. Her parents prohibited the fashionable tight clothing, such as corsets, that restricted movement and circulation. They agreed with some medical professionals who believed that snug-fitting dress caused permanent and irreversible damage to women's bodies, sentiments Walker advocated her entire life. In addition, Walker found long hoopskirts and crinoline bothersome and unnecessary. After acceptance to Syracuse Medical College in December 1853, she experimented with clothing design, permanently deciding on a uniform of shortened skirt with trousers underneath. Due to her choice of garments, Walker endured a life of ridicule, police arrests, and taunting by the press. Walker graduated with her medical degree in June 1855 and a few months later married classmate Dr. Albert Miller.

The marriage had a rocky start. Ignoring traditional wedding attire at the ceremony, Mary donned her usual uniform, had the word "obey" stricken from the vows, and preferred to hyphenate her last name, never acknowledging the title of "Mrs." After a few years of marriage and a shared medical practice, rumors of Albert's infidelities reached Mary. He confessed after she confronted him. Although she left him and set up her own medical practice, she could not secure a divorce until after the Civil War.

Caught up in the dress reform movement in 1857, Walker published articles in *Sibyl*, a fashion reform magazine. Additionally, she lectured about temperance and women's suffrage. Throughout her life she remained dedicated to women's rights, serving on boards, speaking, and confronting Congress on an array of issues including pensions for Civil War nurses. Walker authored two books: *Hit* and *Unmasked, or the Science of Immortality*. Both covered a variety of topics including marriage, social diseases, and women's health issues. She headed to Washington, D.C., a few months after the war began to answer the Union call for physicians in October 1861.

Walker initially served voluntarily as assistant surgeon for Dr. J. N. Green while she worked to secure a paid commission from the Union army. As assistant surgeon, she met ambulances, prescribed medications, made diagnoses, and administered treatment. Walker left Washington in January 1862 to attend medical classes, but in November she raced to Virginia to help Gen. Ambrose Burnside and his troops. After escorting sick soldiers by rail to Washington, she headed for Fredericksburg to help in the field. In Washington, she established free lodging for women looking for wounded loved ones, escorted mortally wounded soldiers to their homes, searched for missing soldiers, and advocated against amputation when she deemed it unnecessary.

In January 1864, Walker received an official appointment to the 52nd Ohio Volunteer Infantry under Gen. George H.

Thomas at Gordon's Mills. On April 10, 1864, she was taken prisoner of war and incarcerated in Castle Thunder Prison for four months. Then, in October 1864, she obtained an official contract as acting assistant surgeon, U.S. Army. She served the rest of the war in a female military prison in Louisville. On January 24, 1866, Walker received the Congressional Medal of Honor from President Andrew Johnson for meritorious service, but the U.S. Congress later rescinded the decoration. Walker unsuccessfully petitioned Congress for reinstatement of the medal. Refusing to return the award as requested, she defiantly wore the medal until her death on February 21, 1919. Congress reinstated Walker's medal posthumously on June 10, 1950.

Adriana G. Schroeder

See also: Civil War (1861–1865); Prisoners of War.

References and Further Reading

Graf, Mercedes. *A Woman of Honor: Dr. Mary E. Walker and the Civil War.* Gettysburg, PA: Thomas Publications, 2001.

Poynter, Lida. "Dr. Mary Walker, M.D. Pioneer Woman Physician." *Medical Woman's Journal* 53, no. 10 (1946): 43–51.

Snyder, Charles McCool. *Dr. Mary Walker: The Little Lady in Pants.* New York: Arno Press, 1974.

WALSH, LORETTA PERFECTUS (1896–1925)

Loretta Perfectus Walsh served as the first enlisted woman in the U.S. Navy.

Loretta Walsh, the first female naval recruit, was sworn in on March 21, 1917, in Philadelphia as a chief yeoman in the U.S. Navy. (Corbis)

Born on April 22, 1896, in Philadelphia, Walsh was raised in Olyphant, Pennsylvania, and educated at the Scranton Lackawanna Business College in Scranton, Pennsylvania. In 1915, she began working as a clerical assistant for the Philadelphia Navy League, a civilian support organization for the U.S. Navy. It was from that office that she was recruited to enlist in the Navy during World War I.

Struggling with personnel shortages in Navy administrative offices during World War I as enlisted men went into combat, Secretary of the Navy Josephus Daniels took advantage of a loophole in Navy regulations and authorized the enlistment of women into the Naval Coast Defense Reserve on March 19, 1917. Daniels made the announcement public two days later on March 21, 1917. Ultimately, over 12,000 women would enlist and serve in the armed forces during World War I. These women were popularly referred to as yeomanettes in reference to the rating of yeoman (F) given by the Navy, short for yeoman female. Basic requirements for female recruits included that they be between 18 and 35 years old, of good character and neat appearance, and able to pass a basic physical examination. Although there were no strict education requirements, there was a preference for high school graduates with business or office experience. Almost all of the enlisted women were given the rank of yeoman (F) but received no formal training from the military. Serving in the Navy, Marine Corps, and Coast Guard, these women worked exclusively in administrative, clerical, and supply positions.

Walsh had been working in a clerical position in the office of the Navy League for two years as the administrative assistant to the wife of Lt. Cmdr. Frederick Payne of the Fourth Naval District in Philadelphia. As soon as the authorization to enlist women for administrative positions was announced, Payne immediately recruited Walsh. She responded with enthusiastic interest. Within hours, Walsh submitted her written application and underwent a basic physical examination by a doctor and nurse on staff at the station. On the afternoon of March 21, 1917, Walsh was admitted and sworn in as the first female Navy petty officer at the rank of chief yeoman.

During her active duty, Walsh worked as a recruiter in Philadelphia and Atlantic City, New Jersey, and sold liberty bonds. She was noted to be especially successful at garnering both support and recruits for the Navy by emphasizing the willingness and enthusiasm shown by women who were eager to serve as encouragement for male recruits. Only one-and-a-half years into her service, Walsh became ill with influenza in the fall of 1918 during the national flu epidemic. She entered the Naval Hospital as a patient and there continued working by helping to nurse other patients. However, her condition worsened, and she was discharged for disability in 1919. She was accorded veteran's benefits and entered a government hospital in Denver, Colorado. She was later transferred to a private sanatorium near her hometown in Pennsylvania, where she remained hospitalized until her death at the age of 29 on August 6, 1925. She was buried in St. Patrick's Cemetery in Olyphant, Pennsylvania.

Over a decade after her death, the National Yeoman F, an organization created by veteran yeomanettes, requested that the War Department reinter Walsh at Arlington Cemetery and provide space for a memorial dedicated to commemorating all U.S. Navy yeomen (F) who served during World War I. The War Department granted Walsh a burial plot in accordance with her veteran status but did not approve the space for a memorial. Undeterred, the National Yeoman F partnered with the Olyphant, Pennsylvania, American Legion post to raise the necessary funds to erect a memorial at Walsh's burial place in her hometown. The memorial was dedicated in October 1937 with over 2,000 attendees, including many yeomanettes. Upon her gravestone is engraved the following: "Woman and Patriot, first of those enrolled in the United States Naval Service, her comrades dedicate this monument to keep alive forever memories of the sacrifice and devotion of womanhood."

In recognition of her service and achievement as the first enlisted woman in the U.S. Navy, the Naval Historical Center has identified the date of Walsh's enlistment on March 21, 1917, as an important date in American naval history.

Kate Wells

See also: Nursing; Spanish Influenza (Influenza Pandemic); World War I (1914–1918); Yeoman (F).

References and Further Reading

Ebbert, Jean, Marie-Beth Hall. *Crossed Currents: Navy Women in a Century of Change.* Washington, D.C.: Brassey's, 1999.

Ebbert, Jean, and Marie-Beth Hall. *The First, the Few, the Forgotten: Navy and Marine Corps Women in World War I.* Annapolis, MD: Naval Institute Press, 2002.

Gavin, Lettie. *American Women in World War I: They Also Served.* Niwot: University Press of Colorado, 1997.

WAR OF 1812 (1812–1815)

The War of 1812 lasted from the American declaration of war on June 18, 1812, until March 23, 1815. As they had in previous wars, women played important roles in the conflict, both on and off the field of battle. The war was largely a response to the trade restrictions imposed by England to isolate Napoleon from overseas support. Britain boarded American ships, impressed crews to work in the Royal Navy, and tried to block American relations with France. It also supported American Indian raids along the frontier. The British refused to cease hostilities until it was too late, only agreeing to stop interfering with American shipping two days before the declaration of war. The declaration of war and the war's greatest battle might have been prevented by faster communication.

The American military was unprepared for conflict, with only 6,700 regular soldiers and 16 ships at the outset. It had to make up for its numerical weakness with militias, but these proved unreliable and were responsible for many defeats early in the war. Some militias refused to follow orders or showed more loyalty to their state than to the country. For example, the New York militia under Gen. William Dearborn was in position to take Montreal in 1812 but ignored orders to move because it was only raised to defend the state.

For Britain, the war was only a small diversion from the campaigns against Napoleon; the number of British soldiers sent into the conflict reflected this attitude. With both armies committing few soldiers, the battles were much smaller and less organized than those on the continent. To compensate for its numerical weakness, the British Army went on the defensive for the first two years of the war. However, the Royal Navy, which had already decisively beaten the French at sea, used its superiority to blockade the coast and raid American ports.

The campaigns of 1812 accomplished little for either side. Gen. William Hull led an expedition into Canada four days after the declaration of war but withdrew to Fort Detroit. He later surrendered the fort without a fight to what he wrongly believed was a large force. Gen. Stephen van Rensselaer's force was also defeated at Queenston Heights during its expedition into Canada. The American campaigns of 1813 were more successful. Andrew Jackson captured much of Alabama from the Creeks, who were supported by Britain. Operations against Canada also improved, though they continued to fall short of major objectives. Cdre. Oliver Hazard Perry built a fleet on Lake Erie, which facilitated the recapture of Detroit. American forces also captured York and defeated the British at the Battle of the Thames. None of these actions was decisive because continued problems among officers and with the militia prevented further action.

In 1814, Britain moved more soldiers into Canada and prepared for an invasion, but American forces under Winfield Scott delayed them with a brief incursion into Canada. In September, the invasion was decisively blocked by the Battle of Lake Champlain, which eliminated the Royal Navy's presence in the Great Lakes. However, the British continued to dominate the Atlantic and moved veterans of the Napoleonic wars into Maryland where they raided Washington, burned the Capitol and White House, and laid siege to Baltimore.

Women were rarely directly involved in the fighting during the War of 1812, but they performed essential logistical work. On the battlefield, women carried water and provisions to the men engaged in combat. While serving in this capacity, they were exposed to the same dangers as the men in ranks. Women also followed the armies on the march and lived in the forts to perform the work necessary for the combatants' welfare. Soldiers' wives accompanied them to serve as cooks, seamstresses, laundresses, and nurses. Perhaps the most important of women's wartime functions was nursing. Field medicine was primitive, and many Americans, around 17,000 in all, died from disease. The prevalence of disease and high rate of infection from wounds suffered in combat made medical care a priority.

Women also served a valuable historical role, as many accompanying the army kept detailed diaries. Few women were allowed to travel with the army; usually only around six were selected for every hundred men, and these were chosen by lottery. Those who were not selected maintained their homes while their husbands and sons were at war—a task that put them in charge of household management and defense.

Some women reported fighting in the war disguised as men. However, it is difficult to determine the facts of such cases because they served under pseudonyms and the military kept little documentation. Lucy Brewer, possibly the first female marine, claimed that she served aboard USS *Constitution* and fought in three battles. Her story and those like it are difficult to corroborate based on limited historical records.

The war officially ended on December 24, 1814, with the signing of the Treaty of Ghent. Because Britain and France were at peace, Britain no longer needed to interfere with trade, nor did it need to capture American sailors to replace its losses. Neither side had much to gain from the war, so they agreed to reestablish the prewar boundaries. Around 2,260 Americans were killed and 4,505 wounded. The British suffered losses of 1,600 killed and 3,679 wounded.

The Battle of New Orleans, perhaps the most famous battle of the war, continued until over a month after the war's formal resolution. British general Edward Pakenham tried to capture the city in October with a force of 7,500 men. Andrew Jackson, who held a strong defensive position along the Mississippi River, blocked Pakenham's assault. On January 8, Pakenham's army launched a frontal assault that was repelled and ended the British ambitions in the South. The losses were disproportionate, with the Americans inflicting around 2,000 casualties while only suffering 71, of which 13 were fatalities. Despite the battle having no effect on the resolution of the war, it became a source of national pride and played a major role in Jackson's election as president. More importantly, it gave Americans a sense of victory even though the war concluded without achieving any significant political gains.

Marcus Schulzke

See also: Asian American Women; Brewer, Lucy [Louisa Baker, George Baker, Lucy West, Eliza Bowen] (ca. 1793–n.d.); Cole, Mary Ann (n.d.–n.d.); Indian Wars; Nursing.

References and Further Reading

Adams, Henry. *The War of 1812*. Lanham, MD: Cooper Square Press, 1999.

Benn, Carl. *The War of 1812, Essential Histories*. New York: Routledge, 2003.

Borneman, Walter R. *1812: The War That Forged a Nation*. New York: Harper Perennial, 2005.

Langguth, A. J. *Union 1812: The Americans Who Fought the Second War of Independence*. New York: Simon & Schuster, 2007.

WAR ON TERROR (2001–)

In response to the September 11, 2001, attacks, U.S. president George W. Bush declared a global War on Terror on September 20, 2001. It is difficult to determine what exactly counts as part of this war as it is a fight that is not limited by national barriers or any specific enemy. It is also a politically contested name; Republicans continually invoke it as a justification of foreign policy, while Democrats prefer to reframe counterterrorism operations in more diplomatic terms. The debate over the definition of the war, and the extent to which it constitutes a war, is central to its history; it also shapes the means used to wage the war because the terrorists' status as enemy combatants dictates how they should be treated. Bush provided loose guidelines: the war's goal is the global defeat of terrorism, foreign states aiding terrorists must be attacked, and the war will last longer than conventional engagements. The second of these points is part of what became known as the "Bush Doctrine," reflecting the president's assertion that every country is either an ally or a supporter of terrorism. This objective is a particularly important one because the terrorists' evasiveness leads the United States and its allies to focus on states that support them.

Al Qaeda and its affiliates have been the primary targets of the War on Terror. Most of the major operations in the War on Terror were attacks against regimes that supported Al Qaeda or that were suspected of doing so. The first major act of the War on Terror was the invasion of Afghanistan, Operation Enduring Freedom, which was launched on October 8, 2001. It was a direct response to the 9/11 attacks, as the Taliban government was a supporter of Al Qaeda, sheltered many of its leaders, and refused to cooperate with American efforts to investigate the attacks. The invasion met with mixed results. Coalition forces managed to take control of the country's major cities and install a new government, but many of the top Al Qaeda leaders, including Osama bin Laden, fled into Pakistan. The occupying force lacked the numerical strength to maintain security throughout the country and protect the borders. Consequently, the invasion became a long-term struggle to eliminate insurgent forces and prevent Al Qaeda from establishing new bases in Pakistan. Since 2004, the United States has supported attacks in the Waziristan region of Afghanistan, where the Taliban have sought to reestablish themselves.

Just as contentious as the name of the war and its objectives is the proper treatment of enemy combatants. Following the invasion of Afghanistan, hundreds of suspected Al Qaeda operatives were captured and imprisoned in Guantanamo Bay, Cuba, without trial. Later, it was revealed that many of those at the base were tortured. Suspected terrorists captured elsewhere were likewise tortured, often being taken to foreign countries to avoid American law as part of a program called extraordinary rendition.

Iraq became the second major front in the war after coalition forces took control of the country in April 2003. In the years following, mujahideen from Afghanistan, Chechnya, and other Muslim countries moved into the country to fuel the insurgency started by remaining Saddam Hussein loyalists. Although there is little evidence that Iraq had a connection with terrorists before the invasion, it has since become one of their primary battlegrounds. Like Afghanistan, the War in Iraq became a protracted counterinsurgency operation.

The War on Terror is also fought on several minor fronts. The United States gives financial and military aid to a number of countries fighting against Islamic insurgents. For example, around 1,200 advisors were sent to the Philippines to help the armed forces of the Philippines fight against Islamic separatists on Mindanao and Sulu. In each of these minor fronts, American forces do not fight directly, but they provide advice, training, and civilian outreach programs. Capturing terrorists' resources is also a central objective. Following the 9/11 attacks, agents seized Al Qaeda assets, depriving the group of finances and a means of safely transferring funds. In Afghanistan, coalition soldiers worked to stop the production and sale of opium, which is one of the insurgents' major sources of income.

Domestically, the War on Terror is primarily an effort to increase security. Following the 9/11 attacks, the Department of Homeland Security (DHS) was created by consolidating 22 formerly independent government agencies. The new DHS was put under the command of former governor of Pennsylvania Tom Ridge, and new steps were also taken to increase communication among U.S. security services. Many new safety precautions were implemented, like the color-coded alert system and the creation of the Transportation Security Administration. Among the most controversial of the new security measures was the USA PATRIOT Act (the Uniting and Strengthening America by Providing Appropriate Tools Required to Intercept and Obstruct Terrorism Act) of 2001. This bill gave government agencies far more discretion over surveillance than they had in the past, including the ability to wiretap without a search warrant. Critics condemned the bill as a breach of civil liberties, but many of its provisions remained in effect when the bill was renewed in 2005.

The War on Terror marks a turning point for women in the U.S. military. Women have been allowed to serve in the military for decades, but even as recently as the Gulf War, they were only given support roles. Faced with declining recruiting numbers and two major foreign operations, the Army and Marine Corps gave female soldiers a larger role in the fighting. The emphasis on counterinsurgency has also brought more women into combat; with no front lines, personnel in all units are potential combatants. Despite the formal ban on women serving in combat, female soldiers routinely serve as checkpoint guards and members of search teams.

Marcus Schulzke

See also: Afghanistan; African American Women; Asian American Women; Brown, Monica Lin (1988–); Campbell, Kim Reed (1975–); Charette, Holly A. (1983–2005); Clark, Regina Renee (1962–2005); Crea, Vivien S. (1952–); Dunwoody, Ann E. (1953–); Espionage; Gulf War (1991); Hester, Leigh Ann (1982–); Hispanic American Women; Howard, Michelle (1960–); Iraq War (2003–2011); Johnson, Shoshana Nyree (1973–); Lynch, Jessica (1983–); Mariner, Rosemary Bryant (1953–); Native American Women; Piestewa, Lori (1979–2003); Rathbun-Nealy (Coleman), Melissa (1970–); Saar, Lisa (1966–); Sheehan, Cindy Lee Miller (1957–); Tracey, Patricia Ann (1950–); Valdez, Ramona M. (1984–2005); Vega, Sarah (1981–).

References and Further Reading

Cassidy, Robert. *Counterinsurgency and the Global War on Terror: Military Culture and Irregular War.* Stanford, CA: Stanford University Press, 2008.

Jones, Seth G. *In the Graveyard of Empires: America's War in Afghanistan.* New York: W. W. Norton & Company, 2010.

Keegan, John. *The Iraq War.* New York: Vintage Books, 2005.

Lustick, Ian S. *Trapped in the War on Terror.* Philadelphia: University of Pennsylvania Press, 2006.

WARD, NANCY
(CA. 1738–CA. 1824)

A prominent leader among the Cherokee people for nearly 30 years, Nancy Ward sought to keep her people out of conflicts with the white colonists during the American Revolution. At an early age, Ward took part in a skirmish with the enemies of her tribe, the Creeks. Her participation in this campaign won her a seat on the Council of Chiefs. In addition, she is credited with introducing dairy farming to the Cherokee people. In later years, she could not stop the younger leaders of her tribe from selling large areas of their ancestral lands to white settlers.

Nancy Ward—an anglicized version of her actual name, Nanye'il—was most likely born at the village of Chota on the Little Tennessee River in the modern state of Tennessee. At an early age, she married a Cherokee named King Fisher and bore him a son, Fivekiller, and a daughter, Catherine. Ward first came to prominence in 1775 when she took the place of her husband in a skirmish with the Creeks at Taliwa (near present-day Canton, Georgia). Her act of bravery won her great respect among the other members of the Cherokee tribe—they gave her the title of War Woman—and she was made head of the Cherokee Women's Council. In this role, she also attained a seat on the Council of Chiefs.

Soon thereafter she remarried to a white trader by the name of Brian Ward. She bore a daughter by Ward, Elizabeth. The trader eventually returned to his home and another wife in South Carolina. Nancy is said to have visited the couple occasionally, and there appears to have existed an amicable arrangement between the three. Through her numerous contacts with whites, she seems to have maintained good relations with the settlers who were making their way into western Tennessee. These amiable contacts were to prove important during the early stages of the American Revolution.

During the early stages of the conflict, some of the more militant factions of the Cherokee followed British entreaties and went to war with the colonists along the frontier. Ward was a member of a faction that opposed this policy. She is credited with warning John Sevier, a leader of the Tennessee settlers, of an impending raid in 1776. This warning allowed the settlers to successfully defend themselves against the raid. As the colonists reacted to the Cherokee attacks, they sent numerous military forces into the Indian territories. These expeditions routinely burned Cherokee crops and towns. Such was the gratitude towards

Ward, however, that Chota was spared from the reprisals. During this period, the Cherokee captured a Mrs. William Bean, and Nancy personally intervened to ensure the woman's life was spared. It is from her association with this woman that Ward learned the production of butter and cheese, and she soon introduced dairy farming to her people.

In 1780, a similar sequence of events occurred. Once again Ward warned settlers of an impending raid. Likewise, when the inevitable counteroffensive came to Cherokee territory, she again met the settlers with an offer of peace from the chiefs. Although her efforts were in vain and the Cherokee villages were pillaged, her property was once more spared.

In the aftermath of the American Revolution, Ward worked to stave off the increasing encroachment of whites onto Cherokee lands. Ward perceived that much of her people's chances for survival depended on their economic well-being. She consequently lobbied for intensive agriculture and cattle ranching to maintain a stable economy among her people. In this realm, her efforts were quite successful. However, her efforts to preserve the integrity of Cherokee lands were not crowned with the same triumph.

Although she was too ill to attend, Ward sent a strong message to the Cherokee Council in May 1817 urging the tribe not to part with any more of its land. Her entreaties were unsuccessful, however, as that year a new government based on a republican model supplanted the old hierarchy among the Cherokee. One of the first acts of this government was to approve the Hiwasee Purchase of 1817, under which they renounced their title to all land north of the Hiwasee River.

Forced in her old age to move from Chota, Nancy Ward responded by opening an inn overlooking the Ocoee river in the southeaster corner of Tennessee, near the present town of Benton. It was here that she died and was buried on her property in 1822. Thirteen years later, the Cherokee surrendered this land as well and were removed to new lands in the Southwest.

James McIntyre

See also: American Revolution (1775–1783); Native American Women; North American Colonial Wars (17th–18th centuries).

References and Further Reading

McClary, Ben Harris. *Nancy Ward: The Last Beloved Woman of the Cherokee*. Benton, TN: Polk County Publishers, 1996.

Perdue, Theda. *Cherokee Women: Gender and Culture Change, 1700–1835*. Lincoln: University of Nebraska Press, 1998.

Williams, Samuel C. *Tennessee during the Revolutionary War*. Knoxville: University of Tennessee Press, 1974.

WARNER, JEMIMA
(N.D.–1775)

A young woman who joined the Pennsylvania Rifle Battalion of the Continental Army as a camp follower, Jemima Warner participated in Benedict Arnold's campaign against Quebec in 1775. After leaving her husband's dead body in the Maine wilderness, she rejoined the expedition and took part in several attempts to secure the city's surrender. She was killed during the siege of the city on December 11, 1775.

No data is available concerning Warner's early life. There is no record of her birth or her marriage. The first record of her life commences when her husband, James Warner, joined Captain Smith's Company of Pennsylvania Riflemen at Harris's Ferry (now Harrisburg) in July 1775. At this time, his teenaged bride Jemima followed him. Smith raised his unit in response to a call for expert riflemen issued by the Second Continental Congress on June 14. As the number of volunteers far exceeded the quantity sought in the initial call, this company, as well as several others, were amalgamated into what became known as William Thompson's Pennsylvania Rifle Battalion. The unit marched to Cambridge, where it was brigaded with the other Pennsylvania recruits, creating an organization known as the Pennsylvania Rifle Battalion. The battalion fell under the overall command of Col. William Thompson. Smith's company served in the siege of Boston during August, and Jemima Warner served as a camp follower, aiding her husband and other troops by cooking and doing laundry.

On September 11, 1775, two companies of Pennsylvania riflemen, including the one in which Warner and her husband served, were dispatched on a special mission under the overall command of Arnold. The men were to take part in an invasion of Canada. As before, Warner followed her husband. She accompanied him with his unit on the march from Cambridge to Kennebec in what would later become Maine, and then on across the wilderness. As Arnold's troops traversed the wilds of Maine, their supplies began to run short. In addition, the weather turned cold. As a result of these factors, sickness began to set in among the troops. Her husband succumbed to what appears to have been pneumonia. After staying by his side in his final moments as he lay propped against a tree, she buried his body under some leaves. She then took up his rifle and powder and made her away alone for some 20 miles to rejoin the American column as it advanced to Quebec. Some accounts have her running the entire distance to catch up with the tail of the column.

Upon reaching Quebec with the rest of Arnold's forces, Warner took part in several attempts to secure the surrender of the city. In the first of these, she attempted to gain entrance into the city with a document calling on the local populace to surrender. She was barred admittance by the guards at the St. John's Gate. The second attempt was much more elaborate than the first. In this attempt, Warner dressed in the gown of a lady and approached the town. This time, sentries permitted her to enter the town. She then proceeded with a document giving Arnold's terms for the surrender of the city to the governor, Guy Carleton. Carleton tore up the document and ordered Warner imprisoned. A short time later, Carleton had her ejected from the city with a message rejecting the proposed terms. She rejoined the lines of Arnold's invasion force, still aiding with care of the sick and wounded, helping to prepare food, and cleaning clothes.

In addition, Warner likely took her husband's rifle and stood in the firing line with the troops blockading Quebec. This possibility emerges from the fact that on December 11, 1775, a cannon ball fired from the city killed her. Due to these circumstances, Warner is often considered to be one of the first women to die in combat in the service of the United States of America.

James McIntyre

See also: American Revolution (1775–1783); Camp Followers.

References and Further Reading

Lefkowitz, Arthur S. *Benedict Arnold's Army: The 1775 American Invasion of Canada during the Revolutionary War.* New York: Savas Beatie, 2008.

Stroh, Oscar. *Thompson's Battalion and/or the First Continental Regiment.* Harrisburg, PA: Graphic Services, 1975.

WATKINS, KATHLEEN BLAKE [KIT COLEMAN] (1856–1915)

Journalist and war correspondent Kathleen Watkins, also known as Kit Coleman, became the first officially sanctioned female war correspondent during the Spanish-American War.

Kathleen Blake was born on February 20, 1856, in Castleblakeney, Ireland, to a middle-class farming family. She received a classical education and completed her studies in her late teens at a finishing school in Belgium. From an early age, she was transfixed by literature and writing. At the age of 20, she married a well-to-do man who was many years older. The marriage was an unhappy one, and when her husband died, his family refused to grant her his estate. Now without funds, she immigrated to Canada in 1884.

In Canada, Blake met and married Thomas Watkins, a Toronto businessman. Kathleen Watkins taught French and music to augment the family's income, but when it became clear that her second husband was an incorrigible philanderer, she left him and took a job as the women's editor for the Toronto *Daily Mail*. To pursue her writing passion and to augment her salary, she also published numerous short stories, the first one appearing in print in 1889.

Watkins's work on the newspaper eventually earned her a daily column, which also began in 1889. Writing under the pen name "Kit," she explored many topics including politics, religion, science, and business. Her superiors at first winced at such topics for a section ostensibly aimed at women, but as readership of her work increased dramatically, they did not dissuade her from such writing.

A naturally restless and curious individual, Watkins began to travel, reporting on what she saw and the people she met. Beginning in 1892, she essentially became a traveling correspondent and regaled her readers with stories about her travels to England, Ireland, the West Indies, and nearly every state in the United States. Indeed, by the mid-1890s, her reporting had made her a household name in Canada and the United States, particularly among women. By 1894, she was without doubt the most influential woman journalist in North America and one of the top reporters for any English-language newspaper. When the Toronto *Daily Mail* and *Empire* merged in 1895, she remained as the women's page editor. This combination increased her visibility and readership.

Watkins gained her greatest fame during the Spanish-American War. Anxious to report on the situation in Cuba and to cover hostilities there, she convinced her newspaper to allow her to go to Cuba and report from that island. She faced an uphill battle, however, in persuading the U.S. War Department to classify her as an official war correspondent. Her persistence paid off, however, for she became the first officially sanctioned female war correspondent. Her superiors at the newspaper had instructed her to write features and interest stories, with the implication that the tough from-the-front reporting should be left to male journalists. Watkins would hear none of that, however. As it turned out, she almost did not make it to Cuba, as male correspondents and military officials, disgruntled by her presence, tried to prevent her passage.

Watkins left Tampa, Florida, in late June 1898, arriving in Cuba in July just prior to the cessation of hostilities there. Characteristically, she made the best of the situation and wrote a long series of reports that detailed the after-effects of the war in Cuba. Both heart-wrenching and compelling, her reporting from the front made her even more of a celebrity. The human cost of war was a frequent focus of her stories.

Watkins returned to Canada later that year, stopping in Washington, D.C., to speak to a congress of international female journalists. While in Washington, she also met and married Theobold Coleman, a Canadian physician.

Not surprisingly, Watkins was a champion of women's rights and believed that it was foolhardy for women to depend exclusively on men for their economic well-being. In 1911, the *Daily*

Mail and Empire revamped its contents and cut back on Watkins's space. She promptly resigned and began writing her own column independently, which was rapidly picked up by newspapers in Canada and the United States on a syndicated basis. Due to fear of retribution from her employers, it was not until 1910 that she publicly voiced her support for women's suffrage. Indeed, the *Daily Mail and Empire* had vociferously opposed women's suffrage. Watkins continued to write until her death in Hamilton, Ontario, Canada, on May 16, 1915.

Paul G. Pierpaoli Jr.

See also: Spanish-American War (1898).

References and Further Reading

Freeman, Barbara M. *Kit's Kingdom: The Journalism of Kathleen Blake Coleman.* Ottawa, ON: Carleton University Press, 1989.

Smith-Rosenberg, Carroll. *Disorderly Conduct: Visions of Gender in Victorian America.* New York: Oxford University Press, 1986.

WEISS, CORA RUBIN (1934–)

Social worker Cora Weiss became a peace activist and an advocate for civil rights and women's rights.

Weiss was born in Harlem, New York, on October 2, 1934, to Vera Dourmashkin and Samuel Rubin, a Russian émigré businessman who founded Faberge Perfumes in 1937 and later formed the Samuel Rubin Foundation, which founded the Institute for Policy Studies in 1963. At the University of Wisconsin in 1952, Weiss organized fellow students against Wisconsin senator Joseph McCarthy's anticommunist witch hunt in the United States. Here she learned valuable lessons about grassroots organizing that she would employ in subsequent crusades. Weiss studied law and social work but risked expulsion by handing out birth-control devices to her classmates. Weiss graduated in 1956 with a BA in anthropology.

Weiss then began graduate work at Hunter College School of Social Work in New York City, specializing in psychiatric social work. Part of her training involved working with returning Korean War veterans at the Louis M. Rabinowitz School of Social Work.

In the early 1960s, the Weiss family offered civil right workers, primarily Student Nonviolent Coordinating Committee members, a vacation on Martha's Vineyard where they could rest and recuperate from the brutalizing experience of working in the South. Weiss was a founder, along with fellow activists Bella Abzug and Dagmar Wilson, of Women Strike for Peace (WSP). WSP mobilized against the U.S. government's nuclear testing programs by demanding that magazine and newspaper editors give publicity to the dangers of nuclear war. Most WSP members were married, middle-class, white women who used consensus methods in their decision making. In 1964, the WSP was the first of the era's peace groups to approach the Pentagon and demand to speak to Secretary of Defense Robert McNamara. This action resulted in the closing of Pentagon doors to the public, a first.

In an integrative effort to involve women of color in the antiwar movement, Weiss and others formed the Jeanette Rankin Brigade in 1969. Named for the first pacifist woman in Congress, the group developed ties with other organizations to march on Washington, D.C., in an attempt to end the war in Vietnam. Weiss had a major role in organizing the largest antiwar demonstration of the decade, which took place on November 16, 1969, in Washington, D.C. Many consider this demonstration a turning point in the Vietnam War and the antiwar movement.

Weiss also cochaired the Committee of Liaison with Families of Prisoners Detained in Vietnam. As such, she helped orchestrate the exchange of mail between American prisoners of war (POWs) and their families. This exchange helped reveal the names and locations of POWs, which in turn helped in their repatriation. In 1972, amid heavy U.S. air attacks, Weiss flew to the Democratic Republic of Vietnam (North Vietnam) with family members of POWs. They returned home with three prisoners of war.

Since then, Weiss has remained committed to the advancement of peace, civil and human rights, and women's rights in the United States and around the world. For many years, she has directed the Samuel Rubin Foundation. Weiss's work, however, has not been without controversy. Some have labeled her efforts as little more than flimsy fronts for the Communist Party or the extreme left, while others describe her efforts to locate and release POWs during Vietnam as traitorous because they engaged the enemy and bypassed official government channels.

Rebecca Tolley-Stokes

See also: Abzug, Bella (1920–1988); Korean War (1950–1953); Prisoners of War; Vietnam War (1965–1973); Women Strike for Peace (WSP).

References and Further Reading

DeBenedetti, Charles. *An American Ordeal: The Antiwar Movement of the Vietnam Era.* Syracuse, NY: Syracuse University Press, 1990.

Weiss, Cora. *There's Hope.* New York: Pilgrim Press, 1981.

WIDNALL, SHEILA EVANS (1938–)

Sheila E. Widnall was President Bill Clinton's secretary of the Air Force from 1993 until 1997, the first woman to head a military service. A gifted scientist, she spent 30 years studying and teaching aeronautics and astronautics at the Massachusetts Institute of Technology (MIT) before going to Washington, D.C., to sit in the Cabinet. After leaving office, she returned to the university and the work she loves.

Sheila Evans was born on July 13, 1938, in Tacoma, Washington. She attended MIT, where she earned a bachelor of science degree in aerospace and astronautics in 1960, a master of science in 1961, and a doctor of science in 1964. She worked at the Boeing Company in 1957, 1959, and 1961 and at the Aeronautical Research Institute of Sweden in 1960. That same year, she married William Soule Widnall.

Widnall worked as a research staff engineer in the department of aeronautics and astronautics at MIT in 1961 and

As secretary of the Air Force from 1993 until 1997, Sheila Widnall became the first woman to head a military service. (AP/Wide World Photos)

1962. She remained at MIT, working as a research assistant from 1962 to 1964, assistant professor from 1964 to 1970, associate professor from 1970 to 1974, and full professor from 1974 to 1986. She was director of university research for the Department of Transportation from 1974 to 1975. She was promoted to Abby Rockefeller Mauze professor in 1986 and kept that post until 1993. She served as associate provost for the 1992–1993 academic year and was the first woman to chair a department at MIT.

Widnall is internationally known for her work in fluid dynamics, specifically in the areas of aircraft turbulence and spiraling air flows. Her research activities in fluid dynamics have included such complex subjects as boundary layer stability; unsteady hydrodynamic loads on fully wetted and supercavitating hydrofoils of finite span; unsteady lifting-surface theory; unsteady air forces on oscillating cylinders in subsonic and supersonic flow; unsteady leading-edge vortex separation from slender delta wings; tip-vortex aerodynamics; helicopter noise; aerodynamics of high-speed ground transportation vehicles; vortex stability; aircraft-wake studies; turbulence; and transition. She taught undergraduate dynamics and aerodynamics, graduate-level aerodynamics of wings and bodies, aeroelasticity, acoustics and aerodynamic noise, and aerospace vehicle vibration.

After 30 years at MIT, Widnall was chosen in 1993 by President Clinton for the position of secretary of the Air Force. In that role, she was responsible for the U.S. Air Force's current and future readiness to accomplish its missions. She concentrated on quality-of-life issues, modernization and acquisition reform, and scientific and technological development. She oversaw the recruiting, training, and equipping of the 380,000 men and women on active duty, 251,000 members of the Air National Guard and the Air Reserve, and 184,000 civilians of the total force. She was in charge of planning, justifying, and allocating the service's annual budget of approximately $62 billion, and her department oversaw logistical support, maintenance, research and development, and welfare of personnel. During Widnall's tenure, the Air Force issued its long-range vision statement, called "Global Engagement: A Vision for the 21st Century Air Force." She implemented research and development project requests by the president or the secretary of defense and cochaired the Department of Defense Task Force on Sexual Harassment and Discrimination.

Widnall left the Cabinet in 1997 and returned to MIT, where she resumed her career in astronautics. Since returning, she has worked with the space and policy teams of the Lean Aerospace Initiative.

Widnall has been a member of the board of directors for Chemical Fabrics, Inc., since 1984. She was a member of the editorial board for *Science* magazine from 1985 to 1987, president of the board from 1987 to 1988, and chairman 1988 to 1989. She sat on the board of trustees of the Carnegie Corporation from 1984 to 1992 and has been a trustee of the Aerospace Corporation since 1986, the ANSER Corporation since 1988, and the Boston Museum of Science since 1989. She was a member of the Smithsonian Council from 1986 to 1989 and a member of the board of directors and a fellow of the American International Academy of Astronautics from 1975 to 1977. She sat on the board of directors of the American Academy of Arts and Sciences from 1982 to 1989. She has published more than 60 papers and lectures, often in her field. She has received honorary doctorates from several colleges and universities, including Smith College, Mt. Holyoke College, Columbia University, and Princeton University. In 1998, she received the Living Legacy Award from the Women's International Center.

Amy Blackwell

Reference and Further Reading

Perl, Peter. "Affairs of State." *Working Woman* 21, no. 11 (November–December 1996): 32.

WILLIAMS, CATHAY [WILLIAM CATHEY] (CA. 1844–N.D.)

Cathay Williams was the first documented African American woman to serve in the Regular Army in the 19th century. Dressed as a man, Williams enlisted in the 38th Infantry on November 15, 1866, in St. Louis, Missouri, as "William Cathey," a cook, aged 22.

Williams was familiar with army life before she enlisted with the 38th Infantry. Born in Independence, Missouri, sometime around 1844 to an enslaved mother and free father, Williams was a house slave to William Johnson, a wealthy farmer who lived near Independence. Johnson, who died sometime before the outbreak of the Civil War in 1861, moved his slaves and household to Jefferson City, Missouri, when Williams was a child.

At the start of the Civil War, Williams and the other slaves in the area were taken as contraband by Brig. Gen. William P. Benton of the 13th Army Corps to Little Rock, Arkansas. Benton pressed the inexperienced Williams into cooking for the officers. As a servant for the 13th Army Corps, she witnessed the Battle of Pea Ridge (or Elkhorn Tavern), in Benton County, Arkansas, on March 7 to 8, 1862; the Red River Campaign at Shreveport, Louisiana, March 10 to May 22, 1864; and accompanied the troops on their marches to New Orleans; the Gulf of Savannah, Georgia; and then to Macon, Georgia. She was subsequently cook and washerwoman to Maj. Gen. Philip Sheridan as he laid waste to the Shenandoah Valley in Virginia during August and

September of 1864. Towards the end of the war, Williams was sent on to Virginia, Iowa, and, finally, back west to Jefferson Barracks, Missouri.

After the Civil War, Congress created the 38th, 39th, 40th, and 41st Infantry Regiments (Colored). These African American soldiers serving in the Western territories of the United States were commonly referred to as Buffalo Soldiers, a descriptive name originating from Native Americans.

Williams was mustered into Company A of the 38th Infantry and served as a private in the Army from February 13, 1867, until she was given a certificate of discharge for disability on October 14, 1868, at Fort Bayard, New Mexico. On her enlistment papers, Williams is described as 5 feet 9 inches tall, with a black complexion, eyes, and hair. She was illiterate, so officials signed her name on documents inconsistently. Although a medical examination was required prior to enlistment, the surgeon apparently gave Williams a brief and cursory inspection. Moreover, Williams's army career was complicated by diseases such as smallpox and cholera, so she had often been sick and hospitalized during her service. Williams's gender was discovered only during the last examination, this time based on feigned sickness, before her discharge.

Williams told a reporter for a *St. Louis Daily Times* article published January 2, 1876, that she joined the Army to be near a cousin and a special friend who had also enlisted and because she wanted to be self-reliant with a reliable income. Williams marched with her comrades from Fort Riley, Kansas, to Fort Cummings, New Mexico, arriving October 1, 1867, where she resumed her assigned duties. According to her own account to the *Times* reporter, she had an unremarkable military career and was a good soldier. Violent conflicts commonly erupted between the solders and the surrounding white communities, so Williams was proud of having avoided unbecoming behavior. Growing tired of the military life, she admitted to the *Times* reporter that she lied about being ill and, upon a more thorough examination, she was issued a discharge after the doctor discovered her ruse. Upon returning to civilian life, she resumed her life as a woman and settled in Trinidad, Colorado.

Williams was not the first woman to dress as a man in order to serve. During the Civil War alone, historians estimate that nearly 400 women disguised themselves as men in order to fight. Even after being discharged upon discovery, some women received pensions for their service. Williams filed for an invalid pension in June 1891 based on military service and her complaints of persistent, vague chronic pains and her deafness. She was examined on September 9, 1891, in Trinidad, Colorado, by the Pension Bureau doctor, who reported her as 5 feet 7 inches tall, 160 pounds, large, stout, aged 49, with toes on both feet amputated. Nevertheless, her claim was denied February 1892 because the doctor observed no disability. Denied a pension based on disability, Williams still expected to receive a land grant as a reward for her military service. Because her name does not appear on the Trinidad federal census schedule for the year 1900, historians assume Williams was deceased by then.

Karen Mason

See also: African American Women; Civil War (1861–1865).

References and Further Reading

Blanton, Deanne. "Cathay Williams: Black Woman Soldier, 1866–68." In *Buffalo Soldiers in the West: A Black Soldiers Anthology*, edited by Bruce A. Glasrud and Michael N. Searles, 101–13. College Station: Texas A&M University Press, 2007.

Tucker, Phillip Thomas. *Cathy Williams: From Slave to Buffalo Soldier*. Mechanicsburg, PA: Stackpole Books, 2002.

WILSON, RUTH WILLSON

(N.D.—N.D.)

Ruth Willson Wilson was an American cryptanalyst beginning during World War I and through the late 1920s. She is considered one of the early pioneers in the field of cryptology for women. Wilson was a cryptanalyst for the Cipher Bureau, commonly called MI-8 or the "Black Chamber," in New York City.

Born in the latter half of the 1880s, very little is known about Willson's early life. Upon graduating from Syracuse University, Willson worked in a number of New York schools teaching Spanish and other Romance languages.

In 1917, the British intercepted a coded message, sent from Germany to Mexico, petitioning the country to attack the United States. If Mexico complied, the German government would reward the country for its efforts and return the territory Mexico had previously ceded to the United States after it won the war. This telegram, known as the Zimmermann Telegram, prompted the United States to enter World War I on April 6, 1917, as a member of the Allies. In June 1917, the State Department and U.S. Army jointly established and funded the U.S. Army Code and Cipher Section, designated MI-8.

Distinctly Edwardian in her appearance, Willson was hired in 1918, at the age of 30, as a linguist for the Cipher Bureau, headed by chief of the organization, Herbert Yardley. Initially, using her Spanish language skills, her work concentrated on analyzing and deciphering Spanish codes received from Latin America.

A dedicated and ambitious employee, Willson soon took it upon herself to learn Japanese and read the plaintext codes. She often worked side by side with Yardley as one of his closest assistants. Together with Yardley and their fellow cryptanalyst Frederick Livesey, Willson helped decipher many Japanese codes. After deciphering the code, Yardley designated the code as "Ja," in which the *J* stood for Japanese, and the *a* designated the code as the first Japanese code deciphered. After completion, Willson and Livesey turned in the decoded messages to the typists to turn into "fair copies." During her time working on the Japanese codes, it was not uncommon for Willson and other staff members to work around the clock in 12-hour shifts. Nor was it uncommon for the staff to work until midnight.

In 1925, Willson married Howard L. Wilson, legally changing her surname and resulting in frequent confusion. During this time she commuted to the MI-8 building in New York from the wealthy, northern suburb of Scarsdale in Westchester County.

MI-8 struggled with financial support throughout the 1920s and was forced to lay off members of its staff until only six of the staff remained, including Wilson. Wilson, in addition to Victor Weiskopf and another cryptanalyst, worked secretively in the back of the building and away from the public view. In 1929, under Secretary of State Henry L. Stimson, MI-8 was shut down.

Yardley and his five remaining employees, including Wilson, were given three months of pay upon the closure of MI-8. Immediately after the closure, Wilson and Weiskopf were offered positions in Washington, D.C., with the Signal Corps. Wilson declined, having no desire to move to the nation's capital. At the time of MI-8's closure, Wilson received a higher wage than Weiskopf. In fact, after Yardley, she was the second highest paid staff member, earning $3,750 per year.

In 1931, Yardley published *The American Black Chamber*, a book that explicitly divulged the work of the staff at the Cipher Bureau. As a result of Yardley's disclosure of confidential information, the U.S. government never trusted him again. He did, however, escape prosecution. In spite of his withered reputation, he received praise from Wilson, who is rarely referenced directly in the book. As colleagues and former coworkers, the pair remained in contact. In the latter half of the 1930s, Yardley discovered that the Japanese were using more than 20 different codes. He sent samples of each of the codes to Wilson for her analysis.

Little information about Ruth Willson Wilson outside of her career with the Cipher Bureau survives. Following her career in the Cipher Bureau, she

continued her education, studying Chinese and Japanese at Columbia University. She graduated in 1947 with a master's degree in Far Eastern affairs.

Alison Vick

See also: Army Signal Corps; Espionage; World War I (1914–1918).

References and Further Reading

Kahn, David. *The Reader of Gentlemen's Mail: Herbert O. Yardley and the Birth of American Codebreaking*. New Haven, CT: Yale University Press, 2004.

Yardley, Herbert O. *The American Black Chamber*. Annapolis, MD: Naval Institute Press, 1931.

WINEMA [TOBEY RIDDLE] (CA. 1848–1920)

Winema (Tobey Riddle) was a Modoc Indian from either southern Oregon or northern California. Winema is best known for her role as a translator and advisor during the Modoc War of 1872–1873.

She married an American settler, Frank Riddle, in 1862 and had a son, Jefferson C. D. Riddle, in 1863. Although some reports claim that Riddle bought Winema from her father, it is more likely that Euroamerican men had to follow Modoc marriage customs centered on reciprocal gift exchange. Winema's marriage placed her in an important position as cultural intermediary between Modocs and the United States.

The Modoc Indians lived in an area around the California and Oregon border.

Winema, also known as Tobey Riddle, acted as an interpreter during negotiations in the Modoc War. In this photograph, she is standing between an Indian agent and her husband, Frank (left), with four Modoc women in front, ca. 1873. (National Archives)

Facing the increasing presence of white settlers in their territory, the Modocs reluctantly agreed to move to a reservation during the 1860s. U.S. treaty negotiators viewed them as part of the Klamath tribe and placed the Modocs onto the Klamath Reservation. Some Modocs settled among the numerically superior Klamaths while others refused to move or left due to abuses they suffered at the hands of Klamaths or from American agents. Kintpuash, also known as Captain Jack and a cousin of Winema, led the Modocs that remained off the reservation.

In late 1869, newly appointed Oregon Indian Superintendent Alfred Meacham employed Winema and Frank Riddle as interpreters in negotiations with Kintpuash that intended to persuade the Modoc leader to return to the reservation. The negotiations proceeded peacefully. The only exception was a misunderstanding when another Modoc proclaimed that he would not return to the reservation. Several Modocs drew weapons before Winema dissolved tensions by shouting to the men to withhold fire and advised them to consider Meacham's proposals. Eventually, Meacham convinced Kintpuash and his followers to return to the Klamath reservation.

Kintpuash's stay among the Klamath was brief. He and approximately 150 followers established residence on the Lost River in 1870. The Modocs remained there peacefully for the next two years. The U.S. Army did little about the Lost River Modocs until late 1872, when a military force descended on Kintpuash's settlement with the intention of forcing them back to the reservation. A fight ensued, and the Modocs fled to the easily defendable lava beds surrounding Tule Lake.

After failing to dislodge Kintpuash's Modocs in December 1872 and January 1873, American officials decided negotiation would be cheaper than war and again dispatched Meacham to negotiate as head of the Peace Commission. Meacham enlisted Winema as an interpreter and advisor based on her knowledge and previous service. Gen. Edward Canby also served on the commission to show the Modocs that the United States would use force. The commission members did not agree on strategy for much of February and March 1873.

Kintpuash met with the commission on April 2, though no agreement was made. The commission, only authorized to accept surrender from the warriors, refused the Modocs' desire for a Lost River reservation and amnesty. During a break in the talks, Winema cautioned Meacham to be wary of attacks on the commission. Meacham passed the warning on to Canby, who ignored it. Meacham met again unsuccessfully with Kintpuash on April 5. The Modocs then sent for Winema, who carried to the lava beds the message that any Modoc wishing to surrender would receive protection. This caused dissention among Kintpuash's followers, and on her way back to the commission's camp, a Modoc warned Winema of imminent combat. Winema notified the commission, but they ignored her information until the next day when scouts spotted a possible trap. Kintpuash again sent for Winema, who reluctantly returned to the lava beds, where the men demanded to know who informed her of the ambush. Winema refused to divulge her informant but returned safely to the commission.

On April 10, Kintpuash's followers convinced him to cease talks and attack the Peace Commission on the following day. Meacham urged Canby to heed Winema's warnings, but to no avail, as Canby and others doubted her allegiance. Winema went with the party fearful for her life, though unbeknownst to her at the time, Kintpuash told the other Modocs that she was not to be harmed. During negotiations, Kintpuash signaled to two concealed Modocs who emerged with weapons and distributed them. Kintpuash himself shot and killed Canby. Meacham tried to flee but was grazed by a bullet and mistaken for dead. As Modocs began to scalp Meacham, Winema shouted that soldiers were attacking, thus frightening away Kintpuash's party and saving Meacham's life.

After the ensuing war, Winema served as an interpreter at Kintpuash's trial. Winema and her family accompanied Meacham on speaking tours throughout the United States about their exploits in the Modoc War, though the tours were largely unsuccessful. She returned to Oregon and stayed on the Klamath Reservation, where she received a government pension until her death in 1920, though some sources say 1932.

J. Hendry Miller

See also: Indian Wars; Native American Women.

References and Further Reading

Bales, Rebecca. " 'You Will Be the Bravest of All:' The Modoc Nation to 1909." PhD dissertation, Arizona State University. 2001.

Meacham, Alfred B. *Wi-ne-ma (The Woman Chief) and Her People*. Hartford, CT: American Publishing Company, 1876.

Murray, Keith A. *The Modocs and Their War*. Norman: University of Oklahoma Press, 1959.

Riddle, Jeff C. *The Indian History of the Modoc War and the Causes That Led to It*. San Francisco, CA: Marnell and Co., 1914.

WINNEMUCCA, SARAH [THOCMETONY "SHELL FLOWER"] (1844–1891)

Sarah Winnemucca, a Paiute Indian, served as a military scout and guide for the U.S. Army during the Bannock Indian war.

She was born to Paiute tribal leader Winnemucca in 1844 along the Truckee River in Nevada. Sarah's parents named her Thocmetony, which means "shell

During the Bannock Indian War, Paiute Indian Sarah Winnemucca served as a military scout and guide for the U.S. Army. (Nevada Historical Society)

flower." It is unknown when she took the name Sarah Winnemucca. She became an important spokesperson for her people during the late 19th century. Working as an interpreter for the U.S. Army, she tried to maintain peace between white settlers and the Native tribes in Nevada. After peace was achieved, Sarah traveled throughout the United States lecturing to audiences about the poor living conditions of Indians and the inadequacies of the reservation system.

During the late 1850s, white settlers, looking for land for ranching and mining, were taking over land in the peaceful Truckee River valley where Sarah and the Paiutes lived. The Native tribes found themselves in conflict with the white settlers over the use of the land and resources. In 1866, violence from white ranchers forced Sarah's tribe, the Paiutes, north to join the warring Bannock tribe. Gen. George Crook led U.S. troops against the Bannocks and Paiutes in what was to become known as the Pyramid Lake War. Crook's mission was to subdue the hostiles and force them onto the newly created reservations. Wanting peace and protection, Winnemucca and her brother Natches led a band of peace-seeking Paiutes to Fort McDermitt.

When the Pyramid Lake war ended, the U.S. government resettled Winnemucca's band of Paiutes, along with other members of the tribe, onto the Malhern reservation. In 1869, Winnemucca's command of English and understanding of white culture led to her employment as an interpreter at Fort McDermitt. In this position, Winnemucca worked to persuade those tribal bands that had not moved to the reservation to seek peace and resettle there. Although she encouraged the Paiutes to move to the reservation, she did not agree with the reservation system. She found the agents corrupt and felt that her people received poor or little food and supplies. In 1870, she beseeched Maj. Henry Douglas, superintendent of Indian affairs of Nevada, to allow her people to leave the reservation and to be given better supplies. Unfortunately, her letters detailing the plight of her people did not result in better living conditions on the reservation or permission for the Paiutes to leave.

By the late 1870s, the Paiute and Bannock tribes found themselves surrounded by white ranchers, miners, and settlers. The growing white presence, the restriction of the reservation, and the Indian agent's inability to provide sufficient rations led to widespread hunger among the tribes. In May 1878, a

Bannock shot two white men. This violent event brought tensions between the whites and Indians to a climax. Bannock leader Buffalo Horn led a war party on a raid of white ranches. White volunteer soldiers and ranchers killed Buffalo Horn in a skirmish. Fearing that the Paiutes would join the hostile Bannocks, Gen. Oliver Otis Howard, charged with bringing in the hostiles and keeping peace, sent Winnemucca to the Paiutes to convince them to remain peaceful. She was able to convince some of her tribesmen to remain peaceful; however, a band of Paiutes decided to follow the warring Bannocks and their new leader Egan. Howard hired Winnemucca as a guide and scout to help him track Egan and his hostile band of Indians through mountainous terrain in Nevada and Idaho. Winnemucca's knowledge of the environment and of the Indians helped Howard and his 480 men gain a victory over the hostiles at Birch Creek. The war finally ended with the death of Egan at the hands of another Indian.

Howard remembered the valuable aid Winnemucca supplied to the army during the campaign against the Bannocks. He requested that she report to Camp Harney where the Indian prisoners were held and act as an interpreter for the army. Eventually the Paiutes and Bannocks were sent back to the reservation. Howard then hired her as an interpreter at Fort Vancouver, Washington, and as a teacher to a group of Sheep-eater Indian children living nearby.

By 1882, Winnemucca had ended her job as an interpreter and schoolteacher for the army. Saddened by the hunger and deplorable living conditions that plagued her people on the reservation, she began giving lectures around the country about the reservation and her adventures as a scout during the Bannock War. Wealthy easterners supported her lectures and often sent money to help the Paiutes get food and other supplies. In 1884, Winnemucca had given up on the lecture circuit and moved to Montana with her brother Natches, where she started a school for Indian children.

On October 17, 1891, Winnemucca died of tuberculosis at Henry's Lake, Montana.

Stacy Reaves

See also: Indian Wars; Native American Women.

References and Further Reading

Canfield, Gae Whitney. *Sarah Winnemucca of the Northern Paiutes.* Norman: University of Oklahoma Press, 1988.

Hopkins, Sarah Winnemucca. *Life among the Paiutes: Their Wrongs and Claims.* Reno: University of Nevada Press, 1994. Original publication, 1883.

Seagrave, Ann. *High Spirited Women of the West.* Lakeport, CA: Wesanne Publishers, 1992.

Stewart, Patricia. "Sarah Winnemucca." *Nevada Historical Quarterly,* Winter 1971, 23–37.

Zanjani, Sally. *Sarah Winnemucca.* Lincoln: University of Nebraska Press, 2001.

WOMEN ACCEPTED FOR VOLUNTEER EMERGENCY SERVICE (WAVES)

The WAVES, a division of the U.S. Navy established during World War II, allowed a large number of women to serve in

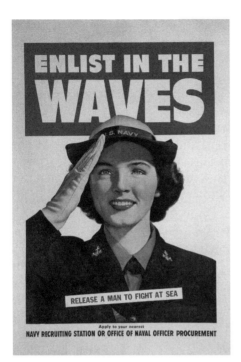

A World War II poster encourages women to join the WAVES (Women Accepted for Volunteer Emergency Service), the first female division of the U.S. Navy. (Library of Congress)

the reserve component of the Navy. The word "emergency" highlighted the necessity and temporary nature of introducing women into widespread naval service during wartime to free male sailors for sea duty. Although women had served as yeomen (F) during World War I, at the start of World War II only a small number of women remained in the Navy, and those were serving in the Nurse Corps without permanent officer status. With the establishment of the WAVES, the Navy prepared not only to allow women to enlist, as they had during World War I, but also to commission women as officers.

Establishing the WAVES was not a simple effort. The Naval Reserve Act of 1938 limited service to men so new

legislation was necessary to authorize the service of women. In addition to the legislative challenge, within the naval establishment there was significant opposition to bringing women into the Navy.

Similar debates over the role of women in the military existed throughout the service branches. For example, to incorporate women and channel their efforts for the war, the Army established the Women's Army Auxiliary Corps (WAAC) in 1941. The "auxiliary" designation meant that the women served "with" the Army but not "in" the Army. This distinction led to differences in pay and difficulty with enforcing regulations and orders.

Seeking to avoid similar problems, Navy leaders sought a way for women to be included within the regular Navy. Giving the Navy the ability to regulate women involved in the war effort helped to calm some of the concerns and opposition of leaders. On July 30, 1942, President Franklin Delano Roosevelt signed into law an amendment to the Naval Reserve Act of 1938 that established the Women's Reserve branch of the Naval Reserve. The official name of the new organization was the U.S. Naval Reserve (Women's Reserve); however, the term WAVES continued to be the one most commonly used to describe the female sailors. In the next several months, the Navy commissioned Mildred McAfee, president of Wellesley College, as a lieutenant commander and appointed her the first director of the WAVES. Consequently, McAfee became the first woman to hold a commission as an officer in the U.S. Navy. The Navy also commissioned several other prominent female educators and professionals to lead the new organization.

The first major effort for the new leaders of the WAVES was the task of establishing a structure for recruiting and training. Female officers, and eventually enlisted recruiters, were assigned to recruiting offices throughout the country. The WAVES established high entrance requirements. Candidates for officers had to be between 20 and 49 years of age and possess a college degree or have two years of college education combined with professional or business experience. Enlisted candidates had to be between 20 and 35 years of age and possess a high school or business school diploma or have related work experience. These entrance requirements resulted in Navy women having higher levels of education and work experience than their male Navy counterparts.

The Navy chose college campuses to conduct enlisted and officer training for the WAVES. The existing facilities and the academic atmosphere were naturally accommodating to military indoctrination. Initially, officer training took place at Smith College in Northampton, Massachusetts. Within months, officer training was also conducted at nearby Mount Holyoke College. At these western Massachusetts centers, the military trained officers not only for the WAVES but also for the Coast Guard Women's Reserve (SPARS) and Marine Corps Women's Reserve.

Training for enlisted women also took place on college campuses; the first three training sites were located at Oklahoma A&M (now Oklahoma State University), University of Wisconsin, and Indiana University. Several other colleges also became the locations of basic training or specialized training. The SPARS and Women Marines also used the WAVES enlisted training sites until those two branches established their own training sites in 1943. The WAVES recruiting and training efforts proved successful. By the end of 1942, only four months after the authorizing legislation, there were 770 officers and 3,109 enlisted women in the WAVES.

During their service, members of the WAVES served in a wider range of occupations than had their World War I predecessors, the yeomen (F). Most of the women served in secretarial and clerical positions, but thousands also served in jobs that had previously been limited to men. These nontraditional jobs included roles in the aviation community, Judge Advocate General Corps, medical profession, communications field, and intelligence department as well as in science and technology fields.

The military justified the wide range of jobs that WAVES did as necessary because they took these previously male roles so that the men could then leave to serve aboard combat ships, combat aircraft, or overseas, where women's service was not allowed. Late in World War II, the military authorized WAVES to serve in certain overseas U.S. possessions, and a number were sent to Hawaii. The war ended before women could be sent to other overseas locations.

Keeping with the rules of the regular Navy, the WAVES did not initially accept African American women. At this point in time, the Navy only allowed African American men to serve as mess attendants and stewards. Under increasing pressure, however, Roosevelt approved the acceptance of African American women into the reserves in October 1944. In November 1944, Harriet Ida Pickens and Frances Wills completed officer training and became the first female African American WAVES officers. African American women did not begin serving in the enlisted ranks until January 1945.

As the United States fought battles in the European and Pacific theaters of World War II, the Navy's demand for personnel increased. As a result, the number of WAVES continued to grow throughout the war. On July 31, 1945, the WAVES reached its peak at 86,291 members, including 8,475 officers, 73,816 enlisted, and another 4,000 in training. The WAVES constituted about 2-1/2 percent of the Navy's total strength. As the WAVES size grew, so did the authorized rank structure. The director of the Women's Reserve became a captain position that McAfee held until 1946. At the end of the war, the WAVES drew down rapidly along with the Navy and the rest of the armed forces. Despite its initial "emergency" designation, the WAVES remained a part of the Naval Reserve even after the conflict ended.

The third director of the Women's Reserve, Joy Bright Hancock, led the charge for establishing women as a permanent part of the Navy. Hancock had served as a yeoman (F) during World War I and had entered the WAVES in 1942 as a lieutenant. After much effort and with the full support of military leaders, the Women's Armed Services Integration Act (Public Law 625) was passed on June 12, 1948. This act granted women permanent status in the regular and reserve components of all the armed services. The director of the Women's Reserve became the assistant to the chief of naval personnel for women and retained the captain rank. Although the WAVES officially ceased to exist once women had permanent status in the Navy, the acronym was in common use well into the 1970s. In 1972, with the continued integration of women, the Navy eliminated the position of assistant to the chief of naval personnel for women.

The WAVES were established to meet an urgent manpower shortfall during a time of crisis. Through exceptional leadership this group organized, recruited, and trained many women to support the Navy's mission during World War II. In recognition of their valued service they were granted permanent status three years after the end of the war. The WAVES served as examples of the contributions that women could make in the Navy and the armed forces. Their dedicated service changed many preconceived ideas concerning women in the military and paved the way for future changes and integration.

Glenn A. Conley

See also: African American Women; Espionage; Hancock, Joy Bright (1898–1996); Hopper, Grace Murray (1906–1992); McAfee (Horton), Mildred Helen (1900–1994); Sears, Mary (1905–1997); United States Coast Guard Women's Reserve (SPAR); Women Air Force Service Pilots (WASP); Women Marines; Women's Armed Services Integration Act of 1948; Women's Army Auxiliary Corps (WAAC); Women's Army Corps (WAC); Women's Army Corps (WAC) Officer Basic Course; World War I (1914–1918); World War II (1941–1945); Yeoman (F).

References and Further Reading

Bachner, Evan. *Making WAVES: Navy Women of World War II*. New York: Abrams, 2008.

Ebbert, Jean, and Marie-Beth Hall. *Crossed Currents: Navy Women in a Century of Change*. Washington, D.C.: Batsford Brassey, 1999.

Godson, Susan. *Serving Proudly: A History of Women in the U.S. Navy*. Annapolis, MD: Naval Institute Press, 2001.

Gruhzit-Hoyt, Olga. *They Also Served: American Women in World War II*. Secaucus, NJ: Carol Publishing Group, 1995.

Hancock, Joy Bright. *Lady in the Navy: A Personal Reminiscence*. Annapolis, MD: Naval Institute Press, 1972.

Wingo, Josette Dermody. *Mother Was a Gunner's Mate: World War II in the WAVES*. Annapolis, MD: Naval Institute Press, 1994.

WOMEN AIR FORCE SERVICE PILOTS (WASP)

A World War II program to train women pilots to fly military aircraft during World War II, the Women Air Force Service Pilots (WASP) program was designed to free men for combat duty overseas. After training, the WASP worked in a variety of capacities at over 120 Army Air Force (AAF) bases in the continental United States during the course of the war. These pilots were the first women in American history to fly military aircraft. They flew every type of aircraft in the AAF, flew over 60 million miles, and proved women could be capable and successful military pilots, thereby contradicting gendered assumptions about them.

The Women's Auxiliary Ferrying Squadron (WAFS) and Women's Flying Training Detachment (WFTD) combined to form the WASP in July 1943. The AAF used "Airforce" as one word in the acronym. AAF general Henry H. "Hap" Arnold named Jacqueline Cochran director of the WASP, and Nancy Harkness Love maintained her position overseeing the ferrying pilots. The WASP program started as an experiment to see whether women had the physical, emotional, and intellectual capabilities to fly military aircraft. Approximately 25,000 applicants applied to the program, 1,830 women were accepted, and 1,074 graduated. The program initially required 200 hours of flying experience to qualify, but as the number of women pilots with a high number of flying hours dwindled, the military reduced this requirement to 35 hours. To enter the program, the women also needed a high school diploma, letters of recommendation, and an interview with Cochran or one of her administrative officers. Almost all the women accepted were white, with the exception of two Chinese American women and one Native American woman. African American women were not admitted into the program because Cochran feared the public's reaction to their admittance.

The AAF trained the WASP at Avenger Field in Sweetwater, Texas, for between five and seven-and-a-half months. Each WASP class flew the same type of aircraft and received training almost identical to the men in the AAF, with the exclusion of combat. Training included ground school, cross-country flying, night flying, instrument flying, daily calisthenics, and practice in link trainers. Women took courses in subjects that included physics, navigation, math, meteorology, and Morse code. After

A group of Women's Air Force Service Pilots (WASP) at New Castle Army Base in Delaware. (Corbis)

each of the three phases of training (primary, basic, and advanced), they were given check rides by AAF officers and other pilots. Instructors were required to eliminate pilots who were not of the highest caliber; the washout rate was the same for both men and women trainees.

WASP trainees went to the field for training at their own expense and were responsible for finding transportation home if they washed out of the program. They received $150 a month during training, minus 5 percent for retirement deductions. The women used this salary to pay $30 for gym clothes and $1.65 a day for room and board. The women paid for these expenses because the program was an experiment and the women

were civilian pilots. Because the AAF planned on militarizing the WASP program, which would give the female pilots military benefits, the WASP abided by the same rules as male military pilots. In addition, they were bound by rules Cochran assigned. Trainees could not eat at certain restaurants in Sweetwater, Texas, because of the establishments' association with drinking. A WASP could not stay overnight in a hotel unless it was with her husband or parents. As a result of public fears surrounding military women, Cochran assigned these additional rules, among others, to protect the pure, feminine image of the WASP.

After graduating, each WASP received $250 a month. She then used a portion of her salary to pay for uniforms, which were partially covered by the AAF. As civilian pilots, the women had only some of their medical expenses covered by the AAF. Dental appointments with a medical officer were provided. The Air Force also offered the WASP insurance packages for purchase. However, they had to pay for hospitalization when ill or injured, even for service-related accidents. The military did little to aid the families in the event of a WASP's death. For the 38 WASP deaths during the war (11 of whom died during training), the Air Force sent only a cheap pine box and an occasional small payment to assist with burial costs. Families of these WASP were responsible for paying to ship the women's bodies home, so often WASP classmates would contribute financial assistance. Furthermore, the families of the deceased were not allowed to display a Gold Star, which symbolized the death of a family member in wartime service, or drape an American flag over the coffin. Thus, although the WASP performed the same duties as military men, with the exclusion of combat, their civilian status kept them from receiving full military benefits or honors.

WASP director Jacqueline Cochran gave the women pilots various assignments throughout the United States, including testing aircraft returned from overseas duty, copiloting bombers, transporting confidential military equipment, and flying radio-controlled drone planes. One WASP, Ann B. Carl, flew experimental jet aircraft. Many of these assignments were dangerous. War-weary aircraft often had malfunctioning instruments or broken parts that failed in midflight. WASP also demonstrated the

safety of certain aircraft, including the B-26 or B-29, to male AAF pilots. In a demonstration, women pilots would fly aircraft deemed unsafe by male pilots. If the WASP could fly a plane effectively, then male pilots assumed they were safe and easy to fly, even if they had previously found the aircraft dangerous or difficult to pilot. WASP towed targets behind planes so male cadets on the ground could practice shooting live ammunition. WASP ferrying duties included flying planes from factories to military bases and from the East and West Coasts to military bases. The planes coming out of the factories had never been flown before, and many had mechanical defects. Some WASP assignments included searchlight tracking missions. In these missions, the women flew planes in the same pattern at different altitudes while men on the ground pointed lights at the plane. Instrument flying was necessary for this task because looking outside the plane caused temporary blindness.

At the conclusion of the program, Cochran published a report on WASP performance. The result of medical studies conducted on the WASP, including aptitude and psychological tests, showed that the women pilots had equivalent endurance and flew as consistently and for the same number of hours as male pilots. WASP test scores and performance, as well as elimination and graduation rates, were comparable to those of the male pilots. At times, the WASP even had lower elimination rates than male pilots.

The WASP program disbanded on December 20, 1944, after Congress failed to grant militarization. Most of the WASP desperately wanted to fly after the war, and many offered to fly for just $1 a year, although the AAF declined their offer. Women were not allowed to fly military aircraft again until the 1970s. Shortly after World War II, the Air Force began including jet experience in their training. With a few minor exceptions, women were excluded from progressing to the next stage of aviation—jet flight. The WASP finally received veteran status and limited benefits in 1977. The success of the program made possible the training of future women pilots in the Air Force.

The WASP again received recognition for their wartime service on March 10, 2010, when they received the Congressional Gold Medal in Emancipation Hall at the Capitol in Washington, D.C. Speaker of the House Nancy Pelosi, journalist Tom Brokaw, Texas senator Kay Bailey Hutchison, Air Force major Nicole Malachowski, and other members of Congress spoke at the ceremony and praised these women pilots for their work. WASP Deanie Parrish accepted the Congressional Gold Medal on behalf of the women pilots. With this medal awarded 65 years after World War II, the WASP finally received the honor they were due.

Sarah Parry Myers

See also: African American Women; Asian American Women; Cochran, Jacqueline (ca. 1910-1980); Love, Nancy Harkness (1914–1976); Native American Women; Women in the Air Force (WAF); Women's Auxiliary Ferrying Squadron (WAFS); Women's Flying Training Detachment (WFTD); World War II (1941–1945).

References and Further Reading

Douglas, Deborah G. *American Women and Flight since 1940*. Lexington: University Press of Kentucky, 2004.

Keil, Sally Van Wagenen. *Those Wonderful Women in Their Flying Machines*. New York: Rawson, Wade, 1979.

Landdeck, Katherine Sharp. "Experiment in the Cockpit: The Women Airforce Service Pilots of World War II." In *The Airplane in American Culture*, edited by Dominick A. Pisano, 165–98. Ann Arbor: University of Michigan Press, 2003.

Merryman, Molly. *Clipped Wings: The Rise and Fall of the Women Airforce Service Pilots (WASP) of World War II*. New York: New York University Press, 1998.

Stallman, David A. *Women in the Wild Blue: Target-Towing WASP at Camp Davis*. Sugarcreek, OH: Carlisle Printing, 2006.

WOMEN IN MILITARY SERVICE FOR AMERICA MEMORIAL

The only memorial in the world dedicated to the military service of all women throughout one nation's entire history, the Women in Military Service for America Memorial occupies 4.2 acres adjacent to Arlington National Cemetery's ceremonial entrance in Virginia, directly across the Potomac River from Washington, D.C.

In 1982, the American Veterans Committee, a national organization of veterans in the United States, proposed a memorial to honor the military service of American women. Three years later, Representative Mary Rose Oakar, a Democrat from Ohio and chair of the House Subcommittee on Libraries and Memorials, and Senator Frank Murkowski, a Republican from Alaska and chair of the Senate Committee on Veterans' Affairs, introduced a resolution to establish a privately funded memorial on federal land in the vicinity of Washington, D.C. Congress enacted the resolution, known as Public Law 99-610, which was signed by President Ronald Reagan on November 6, 1986. The Women in Military Service for America Memorial Foundation, headed by retired Air Force brigadier general Wilma L. Vaught, selected the design of architects Marion Gail Weiss and Michael Manfredi in November 1989 from more than 130 proposals submitted and raised roughly $22 million to support the construction of the memorial. The official groundbreaking took place on June 22, 1995, with remarks by President Bill Clinton. The memorial was finally dedicated on October 18, 1997, before approximately 40,000 women veterans, active-duty servicewomen, and their friends and families.

The design of the Women in Military Service for America Memorial incorporates the 31-foot-tall neoclassical, semicircular wall—known as the hemicycle—built by the architectural firm of McKim, Mead, and White in the late 1920s to serve as the eastern gateway to Arlington National Cemetery from the Lincoln Memorial and the Arlington Memorial Bridge. The memorial features two outdoor settings: an upper terrace that offers panoramic views of Arlington National Cemetery and Washington, D.C., as well as large glass panels onto which quotations from and about American servicewomen are etched; and a plaza, known as the Court of Valor, with a reflecting pool and 200 jets of water symbolizing the collective voices of servicewomen. A 33,000-square-foot education center, located behind the hemicycle, contains permanent and temporary exhibitions on the history of women in the armed forces of the United States; a computerized register of names, photographs, and service records from some 250,000 individual servicewomen as of February 2012 (out of perhaps 2.5 million women who are eligible); a 196-seat theater for film screenings, conferences, lectures, and other events; a hall of honor that recognizes those women who died in service, were prisoners of war, or received the nation's highest awards for service and bravery; and a shop selling memorabilia and books written by and about women in military service.

The metropolitan Washington, D.C., area is also home to the U.S. Marine Corps War Memorial (dedicated in 1954), Vietnam Veterans Memorial (1982), U.S. Navy Memorial (1991), Vietnam Women's Memorial (1993), Korean War Veterans Memorial (1995), National World War II Memorial (2004), and U.S. Air Force Memorial (2006). The National Monument to the Women of World War II in central London (dedicated in 2005) honors the work of women of the United Kingdom—both in uniform and on the homefront. The Rosie the Riveter Memorial in Richmond, California (dedicated in 2000), honors the women who worked in the defense industry during World War II. Moreover, many war memorials—from the Motherland monument in Volgograd, Russia (dedicated in 1967), to statues of winged victory around the world—feature female personifications. The Women in Military Service for America Memorial, however, remains distinctive in its commitment to recognize and honor the contributions of all women who have served in the armed forces of one nation—past, present, and future.

James I. Deutsch

See also: American Revolution (1775–1783); Civil War (1861–1865); Gulf War (1991); Iraq War (2003–2011); Korean War (1950–1953); Rosie the Riveter; Spanish-American War (1898); Vaught, Wilma L. (1930–); Vietnam War (1965–1973); War of 1812 (1812–1815); World War I (1914–1918); World War II (1941–1945).

References and Further Reading

Ashabranner, Brent K. *A Date with Destiny: The Women in Military Service for America Memorial.* Brookfield, CT: Twenty-First Century Books, 2000.

Bellafaire, Judith Lawrence. "Women in Military Service for America Memorial Foundation, Inc. (WIMSA)." In *Gender Camouflage: Women and the U.S. Military,* edited by Francine D'Amico and Laurie Weinstein, 176–81. New York: New York University Press, 1999.

Vaught, Wilma L. *The Day the Nation Said "Thanks!": A History and Dedication Scrapbook of the Women in Military Service for America Memorial.* Washington, D.C.: Military Women's Press, 1999.

"Women in Military Service for America Memorial," *Army Magazine* 59 (August 2009): 66–69.

WOMEN IN THE AIR FORCE (WAF)

The Women in the Air Force (WAF) component of the U.S. Air Force was a loose, administrative umbrella structure for all Air Force women between 1948 and 1976. Unlike the Army, which formalized women's service within a separate corps (the Women's Army Corps, WAC), the WAF was not technically separate from the U.S. Air Force. The WAF organization existed as a way to administer women's roles within the Air Force and was led by women who advised the Air Force on women's utilization, including a director of WAF at the head of the component. As the youngest branch of the military service, the Air Force decided it would keep women as fully integrated with men as possible.

During World War II, a number of WACs performed jobs with the Army Air Forces, which was part of the Army at that time. In 1947, the Air Force became a new branch of the military, separate from the Army. Although still part of the Army as WACs, small numbers of women worked in the new Air Force prior to the passage of the 1948 Women's Armed Services Integration Act. Title III of this act created the provisions for women's service in the Air Force and specifically prohibited women from serving in aircraft performing in combat missions. As a result of this regulation, the Air Force decided that women could not hold any pilot positions because pilots could potentially be tasked to fly in combat situations unexpectedly. The Air Force also decided to restrict women from many flight crew and navigational positions.

Overall, however, Title III offered vague outlines of how women would be integrated into the Air Force. Unique out of all of the other women's service components created from the Women's Armed Services Integration Act, the Air Force was the only branch where female officers would compete with male officers for promotions. Although utilized under the title of WAF and known as WAFs, Air Force women officers were fully integrated for rank promotion processes up to the rank of colonel, the highest rank any woman could achieve according to the 1948 law.

In the 1950s, the Air Force initially struggled as it sought to define how the WAF structure and administration would work, including other matters such as women's utilization, training, and recruiting. Fewer than 2,000 women elected to transition to the WAF from other areas of military service, although the law allowed for more than double that number to serve in the WAF in its first two years of existence.

The WAF began by establishing itself as an elite service opportunity that would accept only the best young women as enlisted personnel or officers. Initially, the Air Force also demonstrated its commitment to sexual integration by admitting women to the Officer Candidate School at Lackland Air Force Base, Texas. The program provided only small numbers of women officers, however, because the training was primarily for enlisted personnel with at least some college background and WAF numbers were so small at that time. WAF basic training remained separate from men's, although all new Air Force members also trained at Lackland, regardless of gender.

With the onset of the Korean War, all of the women's components set high recruiting goals, but the WAF created the highest level of such goals beginning in 1951. When recruiting efforts did not come even close to these goals, however, the Air Force reevaluated these targets and director of the WAF Mary Shelly recommended that quality remain the most important emphasis for recruiters. At the same time, male Air Force leaders began to question whether the WAF

provided the service with any useful benefits because there were so few women in the organization and because their roles were so limited.

In 1956, a small pilot program for a WAF Reserve Officer Training Corps (ROTC) began on several select college campuses. The intent of the program was to assess whether ROTC for WAFs would offer a good option for officer procurement. The program resulted in relatively few commissioned WAF officers.

By 1958, overall personnel reductions in the military led to a closer evaluation of the WAF. The Air Force determined that women should be utilized in traditionally feminine roles and removed women from nontraditional jobs and fields that had only a few WAFs overall. The WAF ROTC program ended in 1958 as well, and a number of bases became closed to WAFs. The size of the WAF continued to get smaller through the first part of the 1960s, reflecting the ongoing recruitment problems, disinterest in the WAF from male Air Force leaders, and increasingly, WAF dissatisfaction with career options. By 1965, WAF numbers reached their lowest point ever.

After 1965, the status and numbers of WAF began to improve dramatically, beginning with the selection of Jeanne Holm to the role of director of WAF in that year. The growth of the Vietnam War and reliance on male troops through the draft helped expand recruiting for the women's services to provide the support needed for the military strength increase. By 1967, all of the women's services committed to efforts to expand their numbers.

In November 1967, President Lyndon B. Johnson signed Public Law 90-130, which offered two key benefits for WAF personnel. First, the act removed rank restrictions for female officers in all branches. This provision allowed for the possibility of more equitable competition between men and women on the Air Force promotion lists, which continued to be the only gender-integrated officer promotion process across the U.S. armed forces. Before the passage of Public Law 90-130, a number of female officers had been passed over for promotion year after year because of gender-based restrictions that did not account for their actual capability or experience. With the new law in place, WAFs could compete for rank promotion at any level. Yet although more than 20 WAF lieutenant colonels were eligible to receive promotions to colonel in 1968, only 1 attained that honor.

By 1968, the Air Force began to assess the possibility of opening ROTC to women once again. Beginning in early 1969, coeducational ROTC began at several campuses, and seven women participated in summer field training required for them to enroll in the program in the fall. Starting in fall 1969, the Air Force ROTC opened its doors to more than 500 women at 81 colleges across the nation. At some institutions, the Air Force ROTC program had more women than men, and enrollments doubled nationwide for WAF ROTC members within two years. Not until 1972 would the other service branches begin to admit women to their ROTC programs.

Altogether, WAF numbers doubled in the late 1960s under Holm's leadership, and job and training opportunities expanded as WAF presence increased. The other changes late in that decade, including Public Law 90-130 and the opening of Air Force ROTC to women, also created a foundation for further changes and expansion in the 1970s. Holm held the director of WAF position for eight years, longer than any of her predecessors and two times the normal length of time in that position.

Only two more women would serve as director of WAF before the position was formally dissolved in 1976. Col. Billie Bobbitt succeeded Holm from 1973 to 1975, and Col. Bianca Trimeloni became the last director of WAF from 1975 to 1976. Upon Trimeloni's retirement, she recommended that the office of the director of WAF be discontinued.

The WAF became somewhat unnecessary by the middle of the 1970s in light of women's continued integration into the Air Force and all areas of the U.S. military. Overall, policies that guided women's enlistment, commissioning, and training became more uniform with those that applied to men, for example. The Air Force created one enlistment standard for all recruits, regardless of gender, and began to train men and women together. In particular, the decision to admit women to all service academies beginning in the fall of 1976 provided additional impetus for ending the WAF administrative structure.

At the same time, the Air Force continued to exclude women from pilot and navigation roles. Bobbitt recommended a reevaluation of the flight exclusion policies when she left the director of WAF position in 1975, and the Air Force began a test program for women pilots soon after. During these tests and studies, the Air Force determined that nearly one third of all pilot positions could be opened to women, in addition to a substantial number of navigation and aircraft support roles. However, Section 6015 of U.S. Title 10, the provisions from the 1948 Women's Armed Services Integration Act, continued to bar women from flying in combat. Thus, as some roles began to open to women, still other flight-related positions remained off limits.

In the years after the WAF ended in 1976, Air Force women continued to expand their roles and opportunities year after year. During the 1980s, Air Force women deployed to Grenada to provide air crew and other support. A female Air Force Reserve officer became the first female reserve member promoted to brigadier general in 1983, and the 1986 top graduate of the Air Force Academy was a woman. More than a decade after women began to serve in flight roles, Congress eliminated Title 10 laws that prohibited women from flying in combat following Operations Desert Shield and Desert Storm in 1990 and 1991.

Tanya L. Roth

See also: Cold War (ca. 1947–1991); Gulf War (1991); Holm, Jeanne M. (1921–2010); Iraq War (2003–2011); Korean War (1950–1953); May, Geraldine Pratt (1895–1997); Public Law 90-130 (1967); Reserve Officer Training Corps (ROTC); Vietnam War (1965–1973); Women's Armed Services Integration Act of 1948 (Public Law 80-625); Women's Army Corps (WAC); World War II (1941–1945).

References and Further Reading

Holm, Jeanne. *In Defense of a Nation: Servicewomen in World War II*. St. Petersburg, FL: Vandamere Press, 1998.

Holm, Jeanne. *Women in the Military: An Unfinished Revolution*, rev. ed. Novato, CA: Presidio Press, 1993.

Monahan, Evelyn, and Rosemary Neidel-Greenlee. *A Few Good Women: America's Military Women from World War I to the War in Iraq and Afghanistan*. New York: Alfred A. Knopf, 2010.

Witt, Linda, Judith Bellafaire, Britta Granrud, and Mary Jo Binker. *"A Defense Weapon Known to Be of Value": Servicewomen of the Korean War Era*. Hanover, NH: University Press of New England, 2005.

WOMEN IN THE COAST GUARD STUDY

On August 14, 1989, the commandant of the Coast Guard, anticipating that women would reach 50 percent of the workforce by 2000, chartered a report on the study of women in the Coast Guard. The report investigated more than 20 general areas of concern for women that ranged from recruiting to pregnancy. Overall, the commandant hoped to determine the current utilization of women in the Coast Guard and to then provide areas of improvement for military service.

To conduct the study, the chief of staff gathered members of various rank, race, parental, and marital statuses, in addition to including both men and women. This team conducted personal interviews of about 2,600 members of both sexes and sent an 85-item questionnaire to all women in the Coast Guard and a comparable number of male servicemen.

The team found sexist attitudes and the lack of attention toward misogyny at the top as the most identified barrier to women in the Coast Guard. The second and third concerns were a lack of total equal opportunity for women and the male-dominated upper echelon. Consequently, the theme of gender equity that links each of these top three concerns together was found throughout the team's conclusions. Current cadets and graduates revealed during their training that their teachers, peers, and the overall Academy immersed the cadets in a high-stress, male-centered environment. At the Academy, attrition rates for women were higher than those of men and were also higher than attrition rates at any other service academy. Likewise in recruit training, women's attrition was approximately 50 percent higher than that for men.

The team stated reasons for the recruit attrition rate, including General Educational Development (GED) scores and physical ability, but they hinted that all attrition rates were indicative of the high number of sexual harassments reported. According to the study, more than 50 percent of women felt sexual harassment was a problem for the Coast Guard, and 58 percent of women and 9 percent of men stated they had been sexually harassed between 1987 and 1989 during training.

To combat sexual harassment and the androcentric atmosphere, the team recommended the Coast Guard reevaluate its sexual harassment training, the commandant must affirm the value of women and support a nontolerance stance toward sexual harassment, and the Coast Guard must provide more female role models who hold leadership positions. Along with feeling undervalued in the Coast Guard, women sought pregnancy and child care options, despite some servicemen's critique of pregnant women who seemed to shirk duties. On a final note, a major expectation outlined in the study was to increase the number of recruited women to 20 percent to continue the branch's growth without compromising its organization.

Allyson Perry

See also: Women's Advisory Council (Coast Guard).

References and Further Reading

D'Amico, Francine, and Laurie Weinstein, eds. *Gender Camouflage: Women in the U.S. Military.* New York: New York University Press, 1999.

U.S. Coast Guard. *Women in the Coast Guard Study.* Prepared by the U.S. Coast Guard in cooperation with the Defense Advisory Committee on Women in the Services and the Department of Transportation. Commandant Publication 5312.17, 1990.

WOMEN MARINES

The Women Marines component of the U.S. military existed from 1946 to 1977, when the component was formally dissolved and female marines became fully integrated into the U.S. Marine Corps. Although the Women Marines became an administrative component of the U.S. military beginning in 1946, during World War I and World War II the Marines utilized women as a reserve force to support the war efforts. The creation of the Women Marines as an organization with both regular and reserve service opportunities represented the culmination of women's contributions to the war efforts. Because Women Marines could not serve at sea, and because of the Marine Corps' primary focus in serving at sea and in combat, Women Marines were traditionally the smallest of the women's service components and often considered the most elite.

Marine Corps legend holds that the first Woman Marine was Lucy Brewer, who fought in the War of 1812. Disguised as a man, Brewer served on board USS *Constitution*. Often regarded as legend, the Marine Corps has nonetheless recognized Brewer as the first Woman Marine.

The first woman formally recruited into the Marine Corps was Opha M. Johnson, who enlisted in the Women Marine Reserves in 1918. Approximately 300 women joined the Women Marine Reserves that year to support the war effort.

In February 1943, to provide for a way to utilize womanpower in support of World War II, the Marine Corps established the Marine Corps Women's Reserve. Under the direction of Col. Ruth Cheney Streeter, more than 1,000 officers and 18,000 enlisted women served as women reservists (WRs) across the continental United States. By the end of the war, 85 percent of all enlisted personnel at the Marine Corps headquarters were women, and up to two-thirds of the permanent staff at large Marine Corps posts and stations were women. Women also worked in 16 out of 21 career fields to support the war cause. Classified as members of the reserve component, WRs received military benefits on the same basis as men.

When the war ended in 1945, Streeter drafted a plan to maintain women on a reserve, but inactive, basis in case of future need. Because she felt that women should only be in the military when the nation needed them, Streeter resigned at the end of that year. Beginning in 1946, the new WR director, Katherine Towle, oversaw demobilization efforts and the planning for a postwar women's reserve in the Marines. Although the Army and Navy planned to pursue regular status for their women's components, the commandant of the Marine Corps wanted to keep women as inactive reserves only, with the exception of approximately 10 officers who would oversee personnel matters, training, recruiting, and general direction activities. During 1946 and 1947, the Marines continued to work with reserve women in small numbers and to plan for the future of the reserve organization.

In June 1948, however, Congress approved the Women's Armed Services Integration Act. When President Harry S. Truman signed this act into law on June 12, it became Public Law 80-625, which authorized women as permanent regular and reserve members of the Army, Air Force, Navy, and Marine Corps. The law allowed the Marine Corps to utilize as many women in the reserves as it wished, but the number of women with regular service status in the Marine Corps could be no more than 2 percent of the nation's total military strength. By June 1950, the Women Marines were authorized to reach 100 officers, 10 warrant officers, and 1,000 enlisted women.

However, this allotment also represented a proportion of the total strength that the Marine Corps could have. The more women the Marines recruited, the fewer men it could have. Thus, the Women Marines had no plans to actually attain those numeric goals. The Marine Corps, instead, planned to keep women at no more than 1 percent of its overall strength.

The law provided for a director of Women Marines, whose job would be to help the commandant of the Marine Corps administer women's service. Col. Katherine Towle became the first director of the permanent Women Marines. The first enlisted women of the Women Marines were sworn in to the component in November 1948, on the 173rd anniversary of the Marine Corps. Seven of those women had served in the Marines since the war, and the eighth had enlisted in the reserves in 1947. These women became the first to be known as Women Marines.

Enlisted Women Marines trained at Parris Island, South Carolina, while Women Marines officers completed training at Quantico, Virginia. The first African American Women Marines joined the organization in 1949. Although at that time black and white male marines trained in segregated units, the Women Marines integrated black and white recruits from the beginning.

With the beginning of the Korean War in 1951, the Women Marines and its reserve units experienced a number of changes. In particular, the Women Marines began admitting enlisted women at the age of 18, as well as women who could pass a high school equivalency exam if they did not have a diploma. Partially as a result of these changes and the increased need for women, the Women Marines began to be younger and less experienced. Beginning in the early 1950s, enlisted Women Marines could serve in 27 out of the Marine Corps's 43 occupational fields. However, 95 percent of all Women Marines were concentrated in six fields: personnel administration, supply, communications, disbursing, data processing, post exchange, and public information. Women Marines officers could fill only nine positions in four fields, primarily in personnel, administration, and accounting.

Numbers of Women Marines remained small through the 1950s and into the 1960s. However, several changes and opportunities for Women Marines also emerged in the 1960s. In particular, the Pepper Board of 1964 reevaluated the status and roles of the Women Marines to better understand how the Marines could utilize Women Marines effectively. Subsequently, the Women Marines began to expand women's occupational opportunities and training, increase where women could be stationed (including more overseas opportunities), and call for more male instructors in basic training, more personal development and grooming classes in basic training, and new incentives to qualified enlisted women.

Until late 1966, no more than 9 or 10 women served in Europe at any one time, and the only overseas station in the Pacific that was open to women was Hawaii. In 1967, Master Sgt. Barbara Jean Dulinksy became the first Woman Marine to serve in a combat zone when she received her assignment to Vietnam. Between 1967 and 1973, 8 to 10 enlisted women and one or two officers served in Vietnam at any one time. By the end of the war, approximately 28 enlisted women and eight officers total completed tours in Vietnam. Women Marines also began to serve in Okinawa, Japan, and Hong Kong during those years.

The passage of Public Law 90-130 in 1967 lifted rank restrictions on Women Marines officers, which meant that Women Marines could now serve above the rank of colonel. Beginning in 1973, the Snell Committee began to prepare equal opportunity plans for the Women Marines. In 1975, the commandant of the Marine Corps authorized women to be assigned to all fields, except for the four classified as combat-related: infantry, artillery, armor, and flight crews. As the Women Marines began to evaluate how to improve women's access to jobs and opportunities, the Women Marines also planned to increase their strength by nearly one-third between 1973 and 1977. Sometimes in small numbers, women began to move into new positions such as military police.

As part of the changes in expanding women's roles in the Marine Corps, the director of the Women Marines position became less focused on direct administration and began to operate more as an advisor or consultant. In line with the other changes authorized over the course of the 1970s, in June 1977 the Marine Corps decided to remove the position of director of Women Marines. The dissolution of this position on June 30, 1977, marked the end of the formal organization of the Women Marines. From then on out, women would be Marines. Although the Marines continue to enforce some sex-based policies that exclude women from participating in certain areas, by and large women are subject to the same policies and opportunities as men.

In 1978, Margaret Brewer became the first female marine to receive promotion to general. In 1994, Gen. Carol Mutter became the first two-star general in the Marine Corps. Two years later, Mutter became the first woman in any military branch to be promoted to three-star general (lieutenant general).

Although the Women Marines as a formal component within the Marine Corps ceased to exist, women continue to serve proudly in the Marine Corps

alongside men. Women currently account for more than 6 percent of the total Marine Corps and serve in nearly all roles, aside from combat. Today, women in the Marine Corps serve all over the world and are no longer limited to certain geographic locations.

Tanya L. Roth

See also: African American Women; Brewer, Lucy [Louisa Baker, George Baker, Lucy West, Eliza Bowen] (ca. 1793–n.d.); Brewer, Margaret A. (1930–); Dulinsky, Barbara J. (n.d.–n.d.); Johnson, Opha Mae (1900–1976); Korean War (1950–1953); Mutter, Carol Ann Schneider (1945–); Public Law 90-130 (1967); Streeter, Ruth Cheney (1895–1990); Towle, Katherine A. (1898–1986); Vietnam War (1965–1973); Women's Armed Services Integration Act of 1948 (Public Law 80-625); World War I (1914–1918); World War II (1941–1945).

References and Further Reading

Holm, Jeanne. *In Defense of a Nation: Servicewomen in World War II*. St. Petersburg, FL: Vandamere Press, 1998.

Holm, Jeanne. *Women in the Military: An Unending Revolution*, rev. ed. Novato, CA: Presidio Press, 1993.

Stremlow, Mary. *A History of the Women Marines, 1946–1977*. Washington, D.C.: History and Museums Division, U.S. Marine Corps, 1986.

West, Lucy Brewer. *The Female Marine; or, Adventures of Miss Lucy Brewer.* New York: Da Capo Press, 1966.

WOMEN STRIKE FOR PEACE (WSP)

Women Strike for Peace (WSP) was a civilian organization created in the early

A group of women from Women Strike for Peace holding signs warning against an escalation of the Cuban Missile Crisis and promoting peace. (Library of Congress)

1960s in protest of the United States' nuclear proliferation and nuclear weapons preparation drills. The original strike took place on November 1, 1961, when approximately 50,000 women formed protests and struck in cities around the nation. The organization eventually gained international recognition and influence. WSP's mission was to secure a ban on nuclear weapons and testing, drawing from a pacifist background that argued that war was an extraneous,

unnecessary lethal system. WSP emphasized women's maternal roles in protecting their children rather than the state
using weapons to do so. WSP also
expanded its protests beyond nuclear
weapons to contest the United States'
expansion of its role in Vietnam during
the 1960s.

The planning for the first strike began
in September 1961 in Washington, D.C.,
when a small group of pacifist activists
began to assess how women could contest nuclear weapons by using their
social roles as women. These individuals
included Dagmar Wilson and other early
WSP members Jeanne Bagby, Folly
Fodor, Eleanor Garst, and Margaret
Russell. The next day, the group began
to spread word of the plans to strike from
their usual family and work obligations
for one day. The strike would occur in
the name of ending the arms race. In five
weeks, women organized protests in
nearly 70 cities around the nation. In the
weeks that followed, the Washington
group learned that American women
were interested in continuing the protest
activity, and WSP began its transition
from a one-day event to a peace organization. In addition, the organization soon
became international in scope: on
January 15, 1962, WSP helped lead a
number of peace events in the United
States, Europe, Africa, and Asia.

As a national organization, WSP
maintained a very loose structure that
allowed members to pursue action as
they saw fit in their communities. WSP
developed a strong communications system that enabled the organization to
keep interested women apprised of
events and actions effectively. Just one
year after the first strike, the organization had helped initiate a number of

demonstrations, rallies, protests, and
other activities through local chapters
that developed. WSP members also
wrote regularly to government representatives to advocate for the end of the
arms race and peace. Primarily composed of white, middle-class, college-
educated women, WSP members
emphasized traditional feminine appearances that highlighted their identities as
wives and mothers. In 1962, a WSP delegation traveled to Geneva to lobby the
Conference of the Seventeen-Nation
Committee on Disarmament. Coretta
Scott King, the wife of Rev. Martin
Luther King Jr., participated in the
group of 50 women.

WSP drew attention to the problems
of nuclear war, and members saw success in a number of ways. The organization played an important role in the
adoption of the 1963 Limited Test Ban
Treaty, signed by the United States,
the Soviet Union, and the United
Kingdom. Along with the shift towards
protesting the Vietnam War in the mid-
1960s, the organization joined with
international women's peace groups to
end war.

Tanya L. Roth

See also: Vietnam War (1965–1973).

References and Further Reading

Alonso, Harriet Hyman. *Peace as a Woman's Issue: A History of the US Movement for World Peace and Women's Rights.* Syracuse, NY: Syracuse University Press, 1993.

Swerdlow, Amy. *Women Strike for Peace: Traditional Motherhood and Radical Politics in the 1960s.* Chicago: University of Chicago Press, 1993.

Taylor, Ethel Barol. "Women Strike for Peace." In *Modern American Women: A Documentary History*, compiled by Susan Ware. New York: McGraw-Hill, 1996.

WOMEN'S ADVISORY COMMITTEE OF THE WAR MANPOWER COMMISSION (1942–1945)

The Women's Advisory Committee of the War Manpower Commission (WMC) advised the WMC on matters of policy regarding women in war industry, employment of youth under 18 years of age, and employment in industries of women with young children. Under chairmanship of the federal security administrator, WMC was formed as a World War II agency under the Office for Emergency Management (OEM) by Executive Order 9139 on April 18, 1942, and consisted of representatives from the War Department; departments of agriculture, labor, and the Navy; Federal Security Agency (FSA); War Production Board (WPB); Selective Service System (SSS); and Civil Service Commission (CSC). The Women's Advisory Committee was established by WMC order on August 31, 1942, and was later confirmed by Executive Order 9279 on December 5, 1942. The committee originally comprised 14 women—12 full-fledged members and 2 alternates—who were actively engaged in various fields, including education, labor, management, farm groups, and social welfare organizations. The committee first studied a problem bearing upon the utilization of women in the war effort, then acquainted the WMC with its findings,

and lastly made suggestions for government policy affecting women and youths.

At its first meeting in October 1942, the committee made its basic recommendations to WMC, which the organization accepted as policy. The committee called for the removal of all barriers to the employment of women in any occupation that they could satisfactorily fulfill. They further requested the admittance of women on a basis of equality with men in all forms of training and wage rates on the basis of work performance rather than gender. Another early policy adopted by WMC based on Women's Advisory Committee recommendations provides safeguards for the protection of the physical and intellectual development of persons under the age of 18 whose services might be required during the war. Groundbreaking in its proposals, the committee continuously urged the increased utilization of older women in the war effort as well as an adoption of a wide-scale system of part-time and split shifts for women workers.

The Women's Advisory Committee of the WMC did not confine its activities to the boardroom. WMC published a series of pamphlets and training manuals, including "Training Women for War Work: Methods and Suggestions for Expediting the Job" and "Training Womanpower," targeted to women workers and the companies with a large female workforce. The 1944 pamphlet, "The Wartime Responsibility of Women's Organizations," greatly urged women to educate themselves about current wartime policies. Before WMC's termination on September 19, 1945, the Women's Advisory Committee recommended postwar planning that called for a fair, accurate definition of full employment and positive planning for the placement of all workers, regardless of sex.

Ashanti White

See also: World War II (1941–1945).

References and Further Reading

Price, Virginia. "Advisors on Woman Power." *Independent Women*, June 1944.

"The Wartime Responsibility of Women's Organizations." Washington, D.C.: U.S. War Manpower Commission: Women's Advisory Committee, January 1944.

WOMEN'S ADVISORY COUNCIL (COAST GUARD)

The Coast Guard established the Women's Advisory Council (WAC) in 1991 to address women's concerns on issues such as the recruiting, retention, and advancement of active-duty and reserve women.

In May 1977, more than a year before Judge John J. Sirica ruled in *Owens v. Brown* that Navy ships should take "measured steps" to sexually integrate shipboard crews, two high-endurance cutters, USCGC *Morgenthau* and USCGC *Gallantin*, were selected as the first Coast Guard ships to operate with women assigned as permanent crew. Later that year, 10 enlisted women and 2 women officers arrived on board, and by 1983, 35 of 129 women officers in the Coast Guard were serving aboard seagoing vessels. Five of those 129 officers were aircraft pilots. Female enlistment in the same year stood at 1,747, including 85 enlisted women at sea. Despite integration, women still acknowledged the persistent gender gap, and it was noted that women were under-represented in high-visibility and command-cadre positions. This imbalance led to a systematic effort to identify gender-related concerns and problems.

Like its predecessor, the Minority Officer Advisory Council, later named the Minority Advisory Council, which was established to systematically obtain input for utilization in the management of the branch's equal opportunity concerns following the recommendation from the 1987 study entitled "Ascension and Retention of Minority Coast Guard Officers," WAC was chartered after the release of the 1990 study "Women in the Coast Guard." The Council originally consisted of nine officers and senior enlisted women who advised senior officers and civilian administrators on policy matters. WAC's recommendations, along with the efforts of the Defense Advisory Committee on Women in the Services (DACOWITS), led to the passing of the Care of New Born Children Program, which allows new mothers and fathers the option of taking one year's leave with the assurance of retaining their rank and rating upon return. In September 1998, WAC was consolidated with the Minority Advisory Council to form the Diversity Advisory Council (DAC), creating a single organizational entity to review, coordinate, and provide advice and recommendations across diversity initiatives, including generational diversity and religious tolerance training.

The DAC has five permanent members, including the gender policy advisor and military civil rights coordinator. Twenty other councilmembers are selected to represent a cross section of occupational levels and include civilians, active-duty and reserve officers, enlisted personnel, and auxiliarists. Members attend the biannual meetings in Washington, D.C., where the council reviews new issues for applicability, conducts initial issue research, and presents past research to the commandant. Between meetings, DAC members perform research on specific issues to determine their impact on the fleet and to draft recommendations. Members are also expected to liaise with other organizations regarding DAC findings and solicit for concerns that Coast Guard members feel should be addressed by the DAC. Council members are charged with monitoring the climate of the Coast Guard environment in their geographic areas and bringing forward issues of concern. Upon returning to their units, members help convey the commandant's feedback to the field.

Ashanti White

See also: Defense Advisory Committee on Women in the Services (DACOWITS); Women in the Coast Guard Study.

References and Further Reading

D'Amico, Francine, and Laurie Weinstein, eds. *Gender Camouflage: Women and the Military.* New York: New York University, 1999.

Holm, Jeanne. *Women in the Military: An Unfinished Revolution.* Novato, CA: Presidio Press, 1993.

Tilley, John A. "A History of Women in the Coast Guard." *Commandant's Bulletin.* Washington, D.C.: U.S. Coast Guard, 1998.

WOMEN'S ARMED SERVICES INTEGRATION ACT OF 1948 (PUBLIC LAW 80-625)

The Women's Armed Services Integration Act of 1948, also known as Public Law 80-625, granted women a permanent role in the four regular branches of the U.S. military: the Army, the Navy, the Marines, and the newly created Air Force. This legislation established the guidelines that determined which women could serve and, in particular, affirmed that women would participate in national defense as a noncombat labor resource only. The regulations contained within Public Law 80-625 have been modified periodically since 1948, but this legislation served as the foundation for much of women's status in the military even into the early 21st century. In the 1950s, 1960s, and 1970s, Congress eliminated or revised elements of the Women's Armed Services Integration Act to expand women's military status and service opportunities even further.

Although women have participated in all American wars, they could not legally serve in the U.S. military until the 20th century. The creation of the Army Nurse Corps in 1901 and the Navy Nurse Corps in 1908 offered women the first opportunity to participate in the United States' formal military structure. In World War I, the Navy and Marine Corps allowed a few women to serve in very select roles, but World War II represented a major turning point in women's military service. During that conflict, the nation began to see womanpower as

Secretary of Defense James Forrestal (center) congratulates (left to right) Col. Geraldine May, Col. Mary A. Hallaren, Cpt. Joy Bright Hancock, and Maj. Julia E. Hamblet after the passage of the Women's Armed Services Integration Act in Washington, D.C., 1948. (Library of Congress)

an important resource for helping the nation fight and win wars. In a total war environment, the American military could utilize women not just as nurses but also in administrative jobs and other supportive functions so that men could be free to perform duties such as combat and combat support roles.

Approximately 350,000 to somewhere over 400,000 women served in the U.S. military during World War II. The Army first admitted women with auxiliary status with the creation of the Women's Army Auxiliary Corps (WAAC), which meant women served alongside the Army but not in it. Thus, women were ineligible for military benefits. The Navy and Marine Corps admitted women to their ranks as reservists, which meant that the Navy's Women Accepted for Volunteer Emergency Service (WAVES) and Women Marines received the same benefits as male reservists. In 1943, the Army upgraded women's status to full military membership and converted the WAAC into the Women's Army Corps (WAC). WACs, WAVES, and Women Marines filled a variety of job roles, mostly within the United States. Some women served overseas in Europe and North Africa, and many nurses went to the front lines in all war theaters, including the Pacific.

During World War II, women demonstrated they could be an excellent source of personnel strength in wartime.

Because of this success, and because of the difficulties that the service branches had experienced in securing women's military participation, military officials began submitting legislation that asked Congress to authorize a permanent place for women in the services after the war's end. Under wartime legislation, women could serve only for the length of the war, plus six months to allow for demobilization efforts as the war ended. From 1946 through early 1948, Congress debated whether to admit women to the military permanently, at times seeming unconvinced that the nation needed to rely on women in the military during peacetime. The Army, in particular, however, argued that keeping women in the services would allow for the development of a small corps of women that could be expanded in case a future war occurred.

Ultimately, the armed forces convinced Congress that being prepared for a future war was a good idea. The House and Senate approved the legislation in early 1948, but with particular stipulations. Women could make up only 2 percent of the total armed forces strength, which was at that time approximately the amount of women used in World War II. Women were not to serve in combat, which the law very clearly designated by noting that WAVES and Women Marines could serve only on transport and hospital ships but no other sailing vessels. Women in the Air Force (WAF), members of the newest branch of the military, could not serve on planes. Women were also not to command men but only to command women.

President Harry Truman signed the Women's Armed Services Integration Act into law on June 12, 1948. The final

version of the legislation required that women be at least 18 to enlist and 21 to become an officer in any branch. Women under the age of 21 would have to have parental permission in order to join the services. Public Law 80-625 also mandated that married women could only join the services if they had prior military service. Otherwise, the services could recruit only unmarried women, although servicewomen could marry once they were in the military.

Women with children under the age of 18 could not serve in the military, according to the Women's Armed Services Integration Act. The military needed women who could quickly and easily be reassigned to new posts anywhere in the world as the services required. Women with children could not move so easily, and Congress and military leaders believed there was thus no need for them.

Aside from the stipulations that women could not serve in combat or combat support roles, the legislation did not say anything about the jobs women could or could not perform. They were, however, limited in rank. Women officers could be promoted no further than lieutenant colonel in the Army, Air Force, and Marine Corps, or commander in the Navy. The only exception to this was that each of the service branches, including the Army Nurse Corps and Navy Nurse Corps, would have one woman serve as director. The director would receive a temporary rank of colonel or captain (Navy) but upon retirement or the end of that position would become a lieutenant colonel or commander permanently. Despite the limitations that the Women's Armed Services Integration Act placed on women, the legislation granted women a permanent foothold in the services, from which they would expand their opportunities and roles in the decades to come.

Tanya L. Roth

See also: Army Nurse Corps (ANC); Hallaren, Mary (1907–2005); Navy Nurse Corps; Public Law 90-130 (1967); Women Accepted for Volunteer Emergency Service (WAVES); Women in the Air Force (WAF); Women Marines; Women's Army Auxiliary Corps (WAAC); Women's Army Corps (WAC); World War I (1914–1918); World War II (1941–1945).

References and Further Reading

Holm, Jeanne. *Women in the Military: An Unending Revolution*, rev. ed. Novato, CA: Presidio Press, 1993.

Morden, Bettie J. *The Women's Army Corps, 1945–1978*. Washington, D.C.: Center of Military History, 1989.

Witt, Linda, Judith Bellafaire, Britta Granrud, and Mary Jo Binker. *"A Defense Weapon Known to Be of Value": Servicewomen of the Korean War Era*. Hanover, NH: University Press of New England, 2005.

WOMEN'S ARMY AUXILIARY CORPS (WAAC)

The volunteer women's auxiliary to the U.S. Army, the Women's Army Auxiliary Corps (WAAC) served as the precursor to the Women's Army Corps (WAC). It existed from May 1942 until September 1943.

In May 1941, U.S. congresswoman Edith Nourse Rogers from Massachusetts introduced a bill to establish a women's auxiliary corps for service with the Army of the United States. The attack on Pearl Harbor by the Japanese in December 1941 provided the impetus for Congress to seriously consider the establishment of a women's corps. With the United States at war, every man was needed for combat. The idea of women in noncombat positions was a viable solution to an anticipated manpower shortage. After months of debate, Congress passed the bill establishing the Women's Army Auxiliary Corp (WAAC) on May 14, 1942. President Franklin D. Roosevelt signed it into law on May 15, 1942.

Oveta Culp Hobby was appointed director of the WAAC. Recruitment of officers and auxiliaries (enlisted women) began immediately. Officer candidates were recruited at colleges and universities. Auxiliaries were recruited in large cities and small towns across the United States. Ads were placed in newspapers and women's magazines. Application forms were available at local recruiting stations. Women between the ages of 21 and 45 who were at least 5 feet tall and weighed at least 100 pounds could apply. Married women were accepted provided they signed an affidavit stating that they had arranged for the care of any dependents. Enrollment numbers were set at 150,000. Within the first few weeks, 35,000 applications had been submitted.

A WAAC training center was established at Fort Des Moines, Iowa. The first class of officer candidates began six weeks of training on July 20, 1942. The first auxiliary class started its four-week basic training, led by male Army officers, at Fort Des Moines on August 17. Subsequent classes received training by newly commissioned WAAC

Women in the first Women's Army Auxiliary Corps (WAAC) unit in overseas service, 149th Post Headquarters Company, as they leave for their assignment in North Africa in 1943. (R. Gates/ Archive Photos/Getty Images)

officers. Additional WAAC training centers were opened in Florida, Georgia, Massachusetts, Louisiana, and Arkansas.

Training consisted of classes in military courtesy and customs, first aid, hygiene, physical fitness, marching, current events, and map reading. After basic training, auxiliaries were given training in special areas. Upon completion of training, recruits were prepared to free men for combat duty.

By fall of 1942 WAACs began replacing male soldiers as typists, clerks, cooks, and drivers. Some were assigned as recruiters to ensure a steady stream of WAAC recruits. Others were assigned to the Aircraft Warning Service (AWS), where they monitored aircraft flying along the coastlines, or to the Ordnance Department, where they handled bullets, gunpowder, and loaded shells. They also processed men for overseas assignments, issuing weapons and maintaining personnel files.

In November 1942, the first WAACs were sent overseas when five WAACs were requested to serve as secretaries on Lt. Gen. Dwight D. Eisenhower's staff in North Africa. The first WAAC unit was assigned overseas in January 1943, also to Eisenhower's headquarters in North Africa. They served as postal workers, secretaries, clerks, typists, switchboard operators, radio operators, teletypists, and cryptographers. In addition, WAACs served with Lt. Gen. Mark

W. Clark's Fifth Army in North Africa and the Mediterranean. They followed closely behind the front-line units, working as communications specialists, telephone operators, clerks, typists, and stenographers.

As auxiliaries to the Regular Army who served under a separate command structure, all WAACs served without Army rank, officer status, or military benefits. Furthermore, WAACs serving overseas were not eligible for overseas pay, government life insurance, veterans' medical coverage, and death benefits—all benefits of the Regular Army. If the enemy captured a WAAC, she was not protected by the international laws governing prisoners of war.

These circumstances reinforced the need to replace the WAAC with a women's corps within the Regular Army. However, before Congress began hearings to make the WAAC part of the Regular Army, a public relations crisis occurred for WAAC officials. Controversy had followed the WAAC from its inception. Debate in Congress when the original WAAC bill was introduced had centered on the appropriateness of women in the military. Some congresspeople opposed the use of women in traditional male roles. The public was also divided on the issue.

Early in 1943, questions were raised about the moral integrity of the women serving in the WAAC. Rumors abounded that pregnancy was rampant. Disgruntled servicemen and newspaper reporters were blamed for the hints of moral indiscretion among the WAACs. The rumors became so persistent that a congressional investigation by a Joint House and Senate Military Affairs Committee was formed to address the problem.

Secretary of War Henry Stimson and WAAC Director Hobby were called to testify. The committee was satisfied with the testimony of the two and dropped the investigation. But the rumors affected morale within the WAAC and impacted recruitment efforts.

Hearings began in March 1943 on the conversion of the WAAC into the Regular Army, and in July 1943, Congress established the WAC. Women who were in the WAAC could leave service or transfer to the WAC. About 75 percent of the women in the WAAC transferred to the WAC. As members of the WAC, women were part of the regular U.S. Army. They now received full military status, including regular Army ranks, full pay, and benefits.

Cheryl Mullenbach

See also: Earley, Charity Adams (1918–2002); Espionage; Hobby, Oveta Culp (1905–1996); Prisoners of War; Rogers, Edith Nourse (1881–1960); Roundtree, Dovey Mae Johnson (1914–); Ten Percenters; Women's Army Corps (WAC); World War II (1941–1945).

References and Further Reading

Allen, Ann. "The News Media and the Women's Army Auxiliary Corps: Protagonists for a Cause." *Military Affairs* 50, no. 2 (April 1986): 77–83.

Bandel, Betty. *An Officer and a Lady: The World War II Letters of Lt. Col. Betty Bandel, Women's Army Corps*, edited by Sylvia J. Bugbee. Lebanon, NH: University Press of New England, 2004.

Treadwell, Mattie E. *The United States Army in World War II: Special Studies: The Women's Army Corps*. Washington, D.C.: Office of the Chief of Military History, Department of the Army, 1954.

U.S. Congress. *Congressional Record.* 77th Cong., 2nd sess., 1942. Vol. 87.

WOMEN'S ARMY BAND

The Women's Army Band, or the 14th Army Women's Army Corps Band, is the only army band to be comprised entirely of women. On July 20, 1942, the first contingent of women was inducted into the Women's Army Auxiliary Corps (WAAC) at Fort Des Moines, Iowa. Recognizing the importance of army bands in promoting morale, enhancing public relations and recruitment efforts, and performing at ceremonial and recreational events, the Army sanctioned the formation of women's bands to serve the WAAC. By early 1943, five bands—the 400th Army Band, 401st Army Band, 402nd Army Band, 403nd Army Band, and 404th Army Band—were composed entirely of women. WAAC bands were later reorganized and officially activated in the Women's Army Corps (WAC) on January 21, 1944.

The Women's Army Band, led by WAC sergeant MaryBelle Nissly, was organized at Fort Des Moines in 1942. It received title to the lineage and honors of the 400th Army Service Forces Bands upon its activation at Fort Meade, Maryland, in August 1948. Until Nissly's tenure, only warrant officers had served as band conductors. However, as a result of special legislation in 1944, WAC Nissly became the first woman in military history to win a warrant officer band leader appointment. Despite its progressiveness, the Women's Army Band fell under the segregated umbrella of the American

military. Only white women were accepted into the band because of the military's fear of angering Southern audiences.

Upon its redesignation, the 14th Army WAC Band reported to the WAC Training Center the following year to serve alongside the 392nd Band at Camp (now Fort) Lee. The commander was Warrant Officer Junior Grade Katherine V. Allen, a graduate of the Julliard School of Music. Under Allen's command, the 14th Army WAC Band toured many different regions including the Fifth Army area of responsibility; Hollywood, California; and the Rose Bowl Parade in 1951. Its special trips ranged from appearances at the World's Fair in New York in 1956 to marching in the 1953, 1957, and 1961 presidential inaugural parades. After the 269th Army Band at Fort McClellan was deactivated in September 1960, the 14th functioned as the post band. Initially, members were housed in a combined barracks and rehearsal hall in the basic training area. In 1973, it moved to a four-level building on the main post where, for the first time, it had adequate space for a rehearsal hall, practice rooms, and comfortable living quarters. It was during this time that the band integrated racially.

The band continued to flourish but eventually fell victim to the women's movement that called into question the necessity of gender-separated services. In July 1972, the WAC Center commander, Col. Dorotha Garrison, moved to preserve its all-female status by requesting that it be designated a special band; the Army staff disapproved. Although WAC was officially inactivated in 1978, the Army ended the 32-year tradition of an all-female band in 1975. The band did not disband but allowed men to join its ranks. Now fully integrated, the 14th Army Band continues to play today.

Ashanti White

See also: Baldenecker, Donna-Mae (1920–2010); Women's Army Auxiliary Corps (WAAC); Women's Army Corps (WAC); Women's Army Corps (WAC) Training Center; World War II (1941–1945).

References and Further Reading

Holm, Jeanne. *Women in the Military: An Unfinished Revolution.* Novato, CA: Presidio Press, 1993.

Morden, Bettie J. *The Women's Army Corps, 1945–1978.* Washington, D.C.: Center of Military History, U.S. Army, 2000.

Treadwell, Mattie. *The Women's Army Corps.* Washington, D.C.: Center of Military History, United States Army, 1991.

World War II poster encouraging women to show their patriotism by joining the Women's Army Corps (WAC). (Library of Congress)

WOMEN'S ARMY CORPS (WAC)

As the likelihood that the United States would join World War II intensified, many American women expressed an interest in assisting the U.S. military. By the spring of 1941, Edith Nourse Rogers, a U.S. congresswoman from Massachusetts, had prepared legislation that outlined the formation of a women's military corps. She sought legal benefits and protection that had been denied to contract and volunteer nurses in previous wars. However, reluctant to give women military recognition equivalent to that granted to men, the War Department

ensured that the bill under consideration did not entitle women to full military benefits.

The Japanese attack on Pearl Harbor on December 7, 1941, and the U.S. entry into the war underscored the need for women who could perform routine non-combat work and thereby free men for combat duties. Army chief of staff Gen. George C. Marshall encouraged a resistant Congress to pass a bill creating the Women's Army Auxiliary Corps (WAAC) in May 1942.

Oveta Culp Hobby, head of the Women's Interest Section in the War Department's Bureau of Public Relations, became the WAAC commanding officer. Assigned the rank of major, she oversaw the enlistment of qualified applicants. Recruitment posters for the WAAC featured a uniformed woman standing in front of an American flag and above it the statement "This Is My War Too!" The WAAC was open to women who were 21 to 45 years of age without dependents and who met minimum height and weight requirements. Marital status was not a factor. Applicants went to Army recruitment stations, where interviewers evaluated their abilities and skills. The women also took aptitude tests and had to pass physical examinations.

Every applicant wrote an essay to explain her motivation to join the corps. Many sought service for patriotic reasons and to help bring the war to an earlier end because they had a boyfriend, a spouse, or another relative in service. Economic incentives motivated many as women enjoyed having employment and professional opportunities unavailable to them in peacetime. Some considered wartime service a valuable work experience that would be helpful in acquiring jobs in the future. The potential for adventure lured many as well.

Initial WAAC officer candidates trained at Fort Des Moines, Iowa, and were commissioned in September 1942. The officers then trained the first 12,200 enlistees for the 150,000 WAAC positions authorized by Congress. Instructors taught the enlistees basic military skills, such as map reading and defense against air attack, as well as military customs and protocol. Women also practiced first-aid techniques and drilled to acquire discipline and physical fitness. WAACs perfected administrative procedures for assignments to supply and company positions.

At first, WAACs were deployed to assignments such as translation and folding parachutes. Although many WAACs served in nursing or clerical roles, some utilized mechanical skills for radio operation and motor pool duties. Later, WAACs were trained at specialist schools and sent to assignments where their skills were needed. Some attended officer candidate school. Officials often assigned WAACs to U.S. military bases where they could perform routine tasks so that male soldiers could be sent overseas more quickly. WAACs were assigned to such specialty units as the Transportation Corps, Chemical Warfare Service, Signal Corps, Army Medical Department (where they served on land and in hospital ships), Army Ground Forces, and Corps of Engineers (where some worked on the Manhattan Project). Some WAACs were sent overseas. The 149th Post Headquarters Company, assigned to Lt. Gen. Dwight D. Eisenhower at Algiers, was the first to go, in January 1943. Women also served with Lt. Gen. Mark W. Clark's Fifth Army in Africa and Italy, often near the front lines.

WAACs encountered varying attitudes toward their service. Many male officers and soldiers accepted their presence, but some men disliked them and attempted to make their service difficult and force them to quit. WAACs occasionally faced unfair disciplinary actions or endured verbal abuse and hostility. Such treatment, health concerns, fear, disillusionment with military service, or family pressure led some WAACs to ask to be discharged. Others deserted. Military officials could not court-martial these women because the WAACs did not have full military status.

In July 1943, legislation reorganized the WAAC into the Women's Army Corps (WAC), granting women the same military status as male troops. WAACs who wanted to transfer to the WAC as soldiers were expected to meet more demanding standards, including more thorough medical examinations. Each also had to secure the recommendation of her commander. Approximately 75 percent of the WAACs transferred. Hobby held the highest WAC rank, that of colonel.

Soon after the establishment of the WAC, the U.S. Eighth Air Force asked for the services of a WAC battalion. The first WACs assigned there went to London in July 1943. Notable WAC service included providing assistance to the 1944 Normandy Invasion. WACs plotted bomber positions, collected intelligence, censored soldiers' mail, and served as cryptographers. Only women considered sufficiently mature and stable were selected to serve in Europe.

Most commanders recognized the competence and efficiency of the WACs. Ultimately, the Army requested as many as 600,000 women in the corps. That demand was never met because many women preferred higher-paying jobs on the homefront or joined rival military auxiliaries. Overall, approximately 150,000 served in the corps. WACs were stationed in the United States, in Europe, in North Africa, in the Middle East, in the China-India-Burma Theater, and in the southwest Pacific. Many were awarded Purple Hearts for wounds they received from bombings and artillery fire. Others received Air Medals, Bronze Stars, and other citations.

Although it consisted primarily of whites (94%), the corps also represented the diverse population of the United States. Some 4,000 African American as well as Hispanic American, Asian American, and Native American women served in the corps. As with other military units at that time, African American units were segregated, but Hobby sought improvements such as the integration of black officers and equitable salaries for WACs.

An estimated 2,000 WACs chose to enlist after World War II. Most of the women, however, were honorably discharged at the end of the conflict. Hobby retired in July 1945, and Lt. Col. Westray B. Boyce became WAC director. The public reception given to returning WACs was generally apathetic and unappreciative: men, not women, were regarded as war heroes. Because of their military status, WAC veterans were, like their male colleagues, eligible for such benefits as the G.I. Bill, but they often had to fight legally to receive health care from the Veterans Administration.

The WAC enabled women to seek careers in the postwar military, although many initially encountered difficulties in achieving rank and pay equivalent to their service achievements. In 1948, the Women's Armed Services Integration Act incorporated the WAC as a corps within the U.S. Army. Thirty years later, the separate corps came to an end and female soldiers joined the Army directly instead of the WAC. The Army Women's Museum, located at Fort Lee, Virginia, preserves artifacts and materials documenting the WAC's history.

Elizabeth D. Schafer

See also: African American Women; Army Signal Corps; Asian American Women; Brion, Irene (1920-); Earley, Charity Adams (1918–2002); Hispanic American Women; Hobby, Oveta Culp (1905–1996); Native American Women; Nursing; Reserve Officer Training Corps (ROTC); Rogers, Edith Nourse (1881–1960); Women's Armed Services Integration Act of 1948 (Public Law 80-625); Women's Army Auxiliary Corps (WAAC); Women's Army Corps (WAC) Officer Basic Course; World War II (1941–1945).

References and Further Reading

Brion, Irene. *Lady GI: A Woman's War in the South Pacific: The Memoir of Irene Brion.* Novato, CA: Presidio, 1997.

Earley, Charity Adams. *One Woman's Army: A Black Officer Remembers the WAC.* College Station: Texas A&M University Press, 1989.

Green, Anne Bosanko. *One Woman's War: Letters Home from the Women's Army Corps, 1944–1946.* Foreword by D'Ann Campbell. Saint Paul: Minnesota Historical Society Press, 1989.

Henderson, Aileen Kilgore. *Stateside Soldier: Life in the Women's Army Corps, 1944–1945.* Columbia: University of South Carolina Press, 2001.

Meyer, Leisa D. *Creating GI Jane: Sexuality and Power in the Women's Army Corps during World War II.* New York: Columbia University Press, 1996.

Miller, Grace Porter. *Call of Duty: A Montana Girl in World War II.* Baton Rouge: Louisiana State University Press, 1999.

Moore, Brenda L. *Serving Our Country: Japanese American Women in the Military during World War II.* New Brunswick, NJ: Rutgers University Press, 2003.

Putney, Martha S. *When the Nation Was in Need: Blacks in the Women's Army Corps during World War II.* Metuchen, NJ: Scarecrow Press, 1992.

Treadwell, Mattie E. *The Women's Army Corps.* Washington, D.C.: Office of the Chief of Military History, Department of the Army, 1954.

Weise, Selene H. C. *The Good Soldier: A Story of a Southwest Pacific Signal Corps WAC.* Shippensburg, PA: Burd Street Press, 1999.

WOMEN'S ARMY CORPS (WAC) OFFICER BASIC COURSE

The Women's Army Corps (WAC) Officer Basic Course prepared female officer candidates for service in the WAC.

The WAC was formed in July 1943. It replaced the Women's Army Auxiliary Corp (WAAC), which had been established by Congress in May 1942. The WAC consisted of officers and enlisted women. Officer candidates had high school or college educations, and many had work experience. Women between the ages of 21 and 45 who were at least 5 feet tall and weighed 100 pounds could apply. Applicants were tested on intelligence, personality, mental alertness, and physical condition. The application process included an interview and a written test consisting of questions on math, grammar, and reasoning.

The eight-week officer training course was offered at Army installations around the country. Upon arrival, officer candidates were issued military clothing, including uniforms, underclothes, coats, shoes, hats, galoshes, pajamas, robes, and slippers. Shortly after their arrival they received typhoid, smallpox, and tetanus shots.

The officer candidates' day began with reveille and roll call around 6:00 a.m. Breakfast was at the mess hall soon after. They then returned to their barracks to make their beds and clean. The first drill of the day occurred before classes began at 8:00 a.m. There was a break for lunch at about noon. Classes ended at 5:00 p.m. After supper, an hour was set aside for study. The rest of the evening was "free" time usually spent washing and ironing uniforms and shining shoes. Lights were out at 9:30 p.m., and a bed check took place at 11:00 p.m.

The officer candidates' basic course consisted of both physical training and classroom studies. The physical training included handsprings and pushups, as well as saluting, drilling, marching in formation, and issuing commands in strong, loud voices. Classroom time was spent learning military discipline and organization, rules and regulations, courtesy and customs, first aid, hygiene, and map reading. The candidates studied current events and practiced how to survive enemy attacks by air or with chemicals. They learned "property accountability"—the Army's way of keeping track of supplies and its bookkeeping system. The female candidates also studied "mess management"—how to feed an army on a budget.

Inspections were a regular part of the candidates' training course. Officers were expected to look professional, and their living quarters were expected to be spotless. Pristine uniforms and polished shoes were compulsory. Dust balls under cots, unpolished latrines, smudges on walls, or dirt on floors were unacceptable. Items in lockers were expected to be in order. Beds had to be made according to Army regulations.

At the end of the officers' training course, candidates were tested on leadership, military rules and customs, care of equipment, first aid, sanitation, and physical drills. Upon graduation from the officer candidates' course, the new officers oversaw the schooling of auxiliaries who were training to replace men in noncombat positions as cooks, bakers, truck and ambulance drivers, record keepers, stenographers, telephone operators, and messengers.

Cheryl Mullenbach

See also: Women's Army Auxiliary Corps (WAAC); Women's Army Corps (WAC); World War II (1941–1945).

References and Further Reading

Bandel, Betty. *An Officer and a Lady: The World War II Letters of Lt. Col. Betty Bandel, Women's Army Corps*, edited by Sylvia J. Bugbee. Lebanon, NH: University Press of New England, 2004.

Earley, Charity Adams. *One Woman's Army: A Black Officer Remembers the WAC*. College Station: Texas A & M University Press, 1939.

Treadwell, Mattie E. *United States Army in World War II, Special Studies, The Women's Army Corps*. Washington, D.C.: Center of Military History, U.S. Army, 1953.

WOMEN'S ARMY CORPS (WAC) TRAINING CENTER (1948–1954)

The military used the Women's Army Corps (WAC) Training Center in Fort Lee, Virginia, to prepare female soldiers for life in the ranks.

In 1943, the government disbanded the Women's Army Auxiliary Corps

(WAAC), an assisting branch of the Army, and created the WAC. The WAC provided gender equality in pay and privilege for female soldiers, while the WAAC had placed women in a subordinate role. After World War II ended, the Army demobilized and closed many WAC training facilities. However, the Army requested that the corps become permanent in 1946. The WAC became a permanent corps within the U.S. Army on June 12, 1948. Three days later, June 15, 1948, the WAC Training Center was established at Fort Lee, Virginia.

The WAC Training Center opened on October 4, 1948, under the direction of Col. Mary A. Hallaren and commanded by Lt. Col. Elizabeth C. Smith. Women of the WAC operated the entire facility. The WAC Training Center's mission was "to prepare the woman soldier for the job she will be assigned in the Army; to indoctrinate her into the elements of military life and customs; and to imbue her with the high moral and ethical standards which the Army demands." The center offered an eight-week basic training course to prepare WAC recruits. The training included physical training, first-aid courses, map-reading courses, and administration training. Recruits were not trained to shoot carbine rifles unless they volunteered for special training. The facility also offered an additional six-week training course to outstanding recruits. The Leader's Corps further trained the recruits academically and with on-the-job training. The outstanding recruits learned leadership strategies.

Recruits were not the only WAC soldiers who received training at the WAC Training Center; reenlistees from World War II retrained and noncommissioned officers also trained at the Officer Candidate School there. The school offered potential officers on-the-job training as training staff and company officers for six months. After graduating from Officer Candidate School, the soldiers were promoted to a commissioned officer as second lieutenant. The Officer Candidate School at the WAC Training Center provided the majority of the WAC leadership. The WAC Training Center could train up to 1,547 female recruits and potential officers at a time. The WAC Training Center was also the home of the only all-WAC band, the 14th Army Band. The band relocated from Fort Meade to the training center at Fort Lee in 1949 and included 26 talented WAC musicians.

In 1954, the WAC Training Center at Fort Lee closed when training relocated to Fort McClellan, Alabama, the new home of the WAC. The WAC disbanded on October 20, 1978, when female soldiers were integrated into Regular Army units, which had previously been all male.

Nancy J. Traylor-Heard

See also: Hallaren, Mary (1907–2005); Women's Army Auxiliary Corps (WAAC); Women's Army Corps (WAC); Women's Army Band; World War II (1941–1945).

References and Further Reading

Morden, Bettie J. *Women's Army Corps, 1945–1978*. Washington, D.C.: Government Printing Office, 1990.

U.S. Army Women's Museum. "WAC Training Center at Fort Lee, Virginia, 1948–1954." http://www.awm.lee.army.mil/research_pages/wac_lee.htm (accessed February 16, 2012).

WOMEN'S AUXILIARY FERRYING SQUADRON (WAFS)

Created in 1942 to deal with the wartime shortage of male pilots on the home-front, the Women's Auxiliary Ferrying Squadron (WAFS) was designed to allow civilian women to ferry planes throughout the United States. It was later merged with the Women's Flying Training Detachment (WFTD) to create the Women Air Force Service Pilots (WASP).

When faced with a need for more male combat pilots to send abroad during World War II, the U.S. Army Air Force began to consider seriously using experienced female pilots to fly aircraft within the United States. The War Department had considered creating units of female pilots since 1930, but at that time the chief of the U.S. Army Air Force (AAF) gave the idea little heed. Still, the idea remained in consideration. In 1939, Jacqueline Cochran, a famed woman aviator, wrote to First Lady Eleanor Roosevelt suggesting that women pilots could be used in the case of a national emergency. In 1940, Nancy Harkness Love, another famed aviatrix, stated a similar proposal to Maj. Gen. Robert Olds of the Air Corps Ferry Command. Finally, with a growing need for more "manpower" in 1942, Olds determined it was time to implement such a program.

The WAFS was created on September 10, 1942, within the Air Transport Command as one of two women's aviator units. Both the WAFS and the WFTD were later merged in August 1943 to create the WASP program. The WAFS were under the leadership of Love, who had proposed the creation of the unit to Olds two years prior. Love's appointment as commander of the WAFS did not go uncontested as U.S. AAF chief of staff Henry "Hap" Arnold had promised Cochran and the White House that Cochran would have command of any women's aviation unit that was created. Cochran had petitioned for a women's aviation unit in 1939. After her proposals went unheeded, she took a group of women pilots to England to fly with the British Air Transport Auxiliary, which had been using women pilots since January 1940. In a politically based decision, command of the WAFS was given to Love, while, in a peace offering, Cochran was given command of the newly organized WFTD to train women pilots.

Before the two groups were merged into the WASP program under Cochran's command, 232 women were trained as part of the WFTD program, first in Houston, Texas, and later at Avenger Field in Sweetwater, Texas, which serves as the current home to the WASP Museum. Despite politically imbued competitions for leadership, pilots of the WAFS program began arriving at New Castle Air Base in Delaware, and after an intensive screening process and a brief orientation consisting of flight training and ground school, they began ferrying planes on October 20, 1942. The female civilian pilots were soon flying military planes on noncombat missions throughout the contiguous United States.

The creation of the WAFS was based upon need but also upon the success of similar programs in the Soviet Union and Great Britain. In addition, similar programs in other armed forces branches were opening up for women in the United States. The Women's Army Auxiliary Corps (WAAC) program began in 1942 and was changed to the Women's Army Corps (WAC) when the program was militarized in 1943. The Navy also established the Women Accepted for Volunteer Emergency Service (WAVES) in 1942. Women excelled in these new positions. Yet the WAFS (and later the WASP) were not recognized as a militarized program. WAFS were civilian employees and were paid $250 a month. They were not provided with any benefits, even in the case of injury or death, and were required to buy their own uniforms, which consisted of an open-collared light gray shirt, slacks, and a gray-green belted jacket.

Stringent requirements were in place for those desiring to enter the WAFS program. Love insisted on requirements that were far stricter than those in place for men who were being recruited at the same time. Pilots for the WAFS were recruited from among commercially licensed women pilots who had at least 500 hours flying time and a 200-horsepower engine rating. The women also had to be between 21 and 35, high school graduates, and have had a recent cross-country flying experience. On average, women who joined the WAFS averaged about 1,100 hours of flying experience at the time of their recruitment. Love recruited women to the WAFS by sending telegrams to 83 of the United States' best women pilots. Twenty-seven of them met the rigorous requirements and answered her call to serve. These women, along with Love herself, would come to be known as "The Originals."

At first, per the organization's original mission, WAFS ferried AAF primary trainers and light aircraft from the factories, such as Stearmans and PT-19 Fairchilds. Later duties also included delivering fighters, bombers, and transports, including pursuit planes such as the P-38 and P-51. WAFS were not allowed to fly combat missions, but their noncombat missions were often grueling and dangerous because both ferrying and towing were risky activities. Many WAFS, and later WASP, pilots suffered serious injuries during their course of duty, and some were even killed in the course of duty.

When the WAFS and the WFTD were merged into the WASP program, the WAFS were ultimately reassigned to Cochran. Love continued to head the WAFS section of the program. By June 1944, all pilots assigned to the WAFS section of the program transferred back to the training command, with the exception of 123 women who were qualified to fly pursuit aircraft. Because all of the original WAFS were commercially trained pilots and did not undergo the same military-style training as most in the WASP program, many of them never fully considered themselves members of the WASP program. Cochran lobbied for a one-day militarization when an announcement was made on December 20, 1944, that the WASP program would be deactivated. This militarization would have given the pilots veteran status and access to G.I. Bill benefits, but it was denied. It was not until 1977, after much lobbying of Congress, that the WASP, including its WAFS component, finally achieved military active-duty status for the service of its pilots. On July 1, 2009,

President Barack Obama and the U.S. Congress awarded the WASP the Congressional Gold Medal. Three of the roughly 300 surviving WASPs were on hand to witness the event.

Though their numbers never rose over 28, the WAFS had a tremendous impact both on military history and in broadening acceptable roles for women. First as pilots in their own program, and later as pilots in the WASP program, these women demonstrated they could fly all of the same aircraft as men, just as well as men. While it took a great deal of time for their service to be officially recognized, their service had an astounding effect on the country.

Jamie L. Huber

See also: Cochran, Jacqueline (ca. 1910–1980); Love, Nancy Harkness (1914–1976); Roosevelt, Eleanor (1884–1962); Women Accepted for Volunteer Emergency Service (WAVES); Women Air Force Service Pilots (WASP); Women's Army Auxiliary Corps (WAAC); Women's Army Corps (WAC); Women's Flying Training Detachment (WFTD); World War II (1941–1945).

References and Further Reading

Cole, Jean Hascall. *Women Pilots of World War II*. Salt Lake City: University of Utah Press, 1992.

Haynsworth, Leslie, and David Toomey. *Amelia Earhart's Daughters*. New York: William Morrow and Company, 1998.

Keil, Sally Van Wagenen. *Those Wonderful Women in Their Flying Machines: The Unknown Heroines of World War II*. New York: Four Directions Press, 1990.

Merryman, Molly. *Clipped Wings: The Rise and Fall of the Women Airforce Service Pilots (WASPs) of World War II*. New York: New York University Press, 1998.

Rickman, Sarah Byrn. *The Originals: The Women's Auxiliary Ferrying Squadron of World War II*. Sarasota, FL: Disc-Us Books, 2001.

Rickman, Sarah Byrn, and Deborah G. Douglas. *Nancy Love and the WASP Ferry Pilots of World War II*. Denton: University of North Texas Press, 2008.

Schrader, Helena. *Sisters in Arms: British and American Women Pilots during World War II*. Barnsley, South Yorkshire, UK: Pen and Sword Books, 2006.

Strebe, Amy Goodpaster. *Flying for Her Country: The American and Soviet Women Military Pilots of World War II*. Dulles, VA: Potomac Books, 2009.

WOMEN'S FLYING TRAINING DETACHMENT (WFTD)

A program designed to train women pilots during World War II in order to see if women were capable of flying military aircraft and also to free men for combat duty overseas, the Women's Flying Training Detachment (WFTD) combined with the Women's Auxiliary Ferrying Squadron (WAFS) in July 1943 to become the Women's Air Force Service Pilots (WASP). These women pilots were the first in American history to fly military aircraft. The success of the WFTD program led the Army Air Force to continue utilizing women pilots until December 1944.

The Army Air Force started these two women's pilot programs in 1942. As early as May 1940, experienced pilot Nancy Harkness Love approached the Army Air Force with a plan to utilize women for ferrying planes. Similarly, Jacqueline Cochran began making plans and talking to Army Air Force general

Henry H. "Hap" Arnold about an American women's pilot program. Arnold first declined both of these original plans. In 1941, instead of giving her a program, Arnold asked Cochran to select and supervise a group of American women to fly in the British Air Transport Auxiliary, a branch of the Royal Air Force. When Cochran returned to the United States after this assignment, she read in the newspapers on September 10, 1942, that Love had started the WAFS. She was upset because she said Arnold had given her permission to start a program first. When Cochran met with Arnold on September 12, he gave her permission to start the WFTD, which was officially approved on September 14, 1942. Historians debate the origins of the WAFS and WFTD programs. Some argue Arnold knew about the plans to start the WAFS but kept the information from Cochran. Others say he had no knowledge of it because he had recently been in the hospital, and therefore he was just as upset by the situation as Cochran.

To qualify for the WFTD program, women pilots needed to be between the ages of 21 and 35, have around 200 hours of flying experience, and possess a high school diploma. They also needed to present letters of recommendation and attend an interview with Cochran or one of her administrative officers.

On November 16, 1942, the first class of 30 women pilots started training at the Howard Hughes Air Field in Houston, Texas. These and later trainees went to the field for training at their own expense and were also responsible for their own transportation home if they washed out of the program. The women paid for these and other expenses, including room and board, because the program was an experiment and the women were civilian pilots.

Army Air Force officials and WFTD director Cochran restricted the media's access to the program, and many people living in Houston did not even know about the WFTD program. Cochran also assigned additional rules to the trainees in order to present a moral, feminine image of the women pilots. For example, trainees could not eat at certain restaurants because of the establishments' association with drinking. They could also not stay overnight in a hotel unless they were with their husband or their parents.

Training lasted between five and seven-and-a-half months. These female pilots flew the same type of aircraft as and received training almost identical to the men in the Army Air Force, with the exclusion of combat training. Training included ground school, cross-country flying, night flying, instrument flying, daily calisthenics, and, for later classes, practice in link trainers. They took courses in subjects including physics, navigation, math, meteorology, and Morse code. In January 1943, training was divided into three phases—primary, basic, and advanced. After each of these phases, the female pilots took check rides with Army Air Force officers and sometimes civilian pilots. The washout rate was the same for both male and female trainees because it was the job of instructors to eliminate pilots who were not of the highest caliber.

The first WFTD class of 23 female pilots graduated on April 24, 1943. This class was designated as 43-1, based on the year of graduation and class number.

In the meantime, three other WFTD classes (43-2, 43-3, and 43-4) had started training. Unlike the first class, these classes and all subsequent classes trained at Avenger Field in Sweetwater, Texas. After graduation, the first WFTD class was assigned to duty with the WAFS pilots ferrying planes. Later classes were placed in assignments at over 120 Army Air Force bases around the United States. These assignments including testing aircraft returned from overseas duty, copiloting bombers, transporting confidential military equipment, and flying radio-controlled drone planes. Much of this work was dangerous. Aircraft returned to the United States after overseas duty often had malfunctioning instruments or broken parts that failed in midflight. Ferrying duties included flying planes from factories to military bases and from the East and West Coasts to military bases. The planes coming out of the factories had never been flown before, and many had mechanical defects.

The WFTD program started as an experiment to see whether women had the physical, emotional, and intellectual capabilities to fly military aircraft. The success of the WAFS and the first few WFTD classes led to the continuation of the programs. The female pilots in the WFTD had similar elimination and graduation rates to male pilots. If these women had not met success, the Army Air Force would have ended the programs. In July 1943, the Army Air Force combined the WAFS and WFTD programs in order to form the Women's Air Force Service Pilots (WASP).

Sarah Parry Myers

See also: Cochran, Jacqueline (ca. 1910–1980); Love, Nancy Harkness (1914–1976); Women Accepted for Volunteer Emergency Service (WAVES); Women Air Force Service Pilots (WASP); Women's Army Auxiliary Corps (WAAC); Women's Army Corps (WAC); Women's Flying Training Detachment (WFTD); Women's Auxiliary Ferrying Squadron (WAFS); World War II (1941–1945).

References and Further Reading

Keil, Sally Van Wagenen. *Those Wonderful Women in Their Flying Machines*. New York: Rawson, Wade Publishers, 1979.

Landdeck, Katherine Sharp. "Experiment in the Cockpit: The Women Airforce Service Pilots of World War II." In *The Airplane in American Culture*, edited by Dominick A. Pisano, 165–98. Ann Arbor: University of Michigan Press, 2003.

Merryman, Molly. *Clipped Wings: The Rise and Fall of the Women Airforce Service Pilots (WASP) of World War II*. New York: New York University Press, 1998.

Rich, Doris L. *Jackie Cochran: Pilot in the Fastest Lane*. Gainesville: University Press of Florida, 2007.

Rickman, Sarah Byrn. *Nancy Love and the WASP Ferry Pilots of World War II*. Denton: University of North Texas Press, 2008.

WOMEN'S LAND ARMY

The Women's Land Army (WLA) was created during World War II to assist American farmers who were burdened by the lack of male agricultural workers due to wartime enlistments. The first federal agricultural program for women, the WLA was responsible for recruiting, training, and placing over 2 million women, known as "farmerettes," in farm jobs across the country from 1943 through 1945. Women, along with foreign workers, military personnel, convicts, prisoners of war, migrant workers, and high school students, ensured that farmers exceeded agricultural yield expectations.

Even before the United States' official entry into World War II in 1941, American farmers struggled with labor shortages. As many as 2 million men left farming jobs between 1940 and 1942 as industrial war work enticed former agricultural workers into more lucrative jobs in urban centers just as war production required increasing food production. As early as 1940, the Women's National Farm and Garden Association began pushing to create a federally sponsored WLA. In November 1941, First Lady Eleanor Roosevelt announced that she would push the Office of Civilian Defense to recruit for a WLA. Meanwhile, to address existing agricultural harvests and labor shortages, college programs and several states began to organize female farm workers. New York, Vermont, and California were especially successful at enlisting women to assist with fruit and vegetable harvests and dairy work.

Despite a clear push from farmers for additional labor and several successful organizational models, several challenges existed for the creation of a federal WLA. The secretary of agriculture, Claude Wickard, spoke explicitly against the idea of the WLA. Additionally, leaders in farm organizations, especially in the South and Midwest, were vocal that urban women without agricultural experience could lead to potentially more work for farmers; they feared that the women would not have

the training, stamina, or attitude to cope with the work. Despite resistance, in the fall of 1942, President Franklin D. Roosevelt urged Wickard to consider the idea. It was only after U.S. Department of Agriculture (USDA) officials began making plans independently to operationalize female workers that Wickard agreed to create the WLA. In April 1943, the War Food Administration formally announced the formation of the WLA under the umbrella of the U.S. Crop Corps. Florence Hall, a nationally renowned home economist with a rural background, was appointed head of the organization.

The WLA was modeled after a number of previously successful organizations, including the private Women's Land Army of America formed during World War I, Works Progress Administration (WPA) projects, the British Women's Land Army, and successful state farm efforts. Like earlier WPA projects, WLA organization was decentralized in order to be most effective for local farmers. The WLA was administered by the federal government through the Emergency Farm Labor Program under the jurisdiction of the USDA but was operated by state extension services. In 1943, 43 states appointed WLA state supervisors in either full- or part-time positions. Large states also had county supervisors. Supervisors were charged with recruiting and organizing workers, establishing housing, providing training opportunities and child care options, and reporting back to the federal level. The WLA partnered with agricultural and women's colleges, local women's clubs, and voluntary organizations to recruit, train, and house women workers.

Basic requirements for recruits stated that women must be over 18 years old and be physically fit to do difficult labor. The USDA suggested that workers be motivated primarily by patriotism, enjoy outdoor activity, as well as be adaptable, patient, and dependable. There was no requirement for workers to have farm experience, though rural women more familiar with the types of work needed were asked to take on longer, more complex assignments. Assignments through the WLA were designed to be flexible for the wide variety of recruits that applied. Volunteers included women from agricultural backgrounds who left professional positions to come back to the family farm, college women who worked during school breaks, professional women who used one or two weeks of vacation time, and homemakers who worked part-time days.

The established WLA uniform included navy blue denim overalls, a tailored sports shirt, denim jacket, and hat. The uniform was priced at $6. Given the low agricultural wages, many women found the price prohibitive and chose not to purchase the uniform, wearing their own clothes instead. Additionally problematic for enforcing the uniform was that a denim shortage existed soon into the war as many textile manufacturers converted their factories for military uniforms.

Workers were primarily trained on the job, but many states offered short training courses for specific skills such as driving and maintaining tractors, pruning fruit trees, and performing dairy and poultry work. Women were usually assigned to jobs according to their experience and the length of their service. Those with long-term assignments lived with local farmers whenever possible. Short-term workers with assignments such as harvesting that required a great number of workers were most often placed in group camps. Often women lived in dormitories at local colleges, in function halls, or in cabins meant for migrant workers.

At the start of the program, women were used primarily for harvesting, specifically fruits and vegetables. However, as the WLA proved successful and farmers reported satisfaction with female workers, they were increasingly used for a wide variety of farming tasks such as haying, irrigation, grain production, pruning trees, driving tractors and trucks, and dairy and poultry farming. After the first year produced large-yield crop harvests for those farmers who utilized WLA workers, the WLA garnered a particularly good reputation for providing workers who had a strong work ethic and patriotic spirit. Very few farmers complained about the workers that were provided them. After the success of 1943, many farmers who had not hired WLA workers were convinced to hire them for subsequent seasons.

The WLA faced significant challenges to its organization and success. Two major problems surfaced immediately. First, recruitment efforts were stymied by strong biases by farmers in the Midwest and the South. Midwestern farmers were resistant to using urban women with no previous farm experience. They were concerned that these women would be physically unable to do the work and would be too proud to do the types of jobs that would be asked of them on the farm and in the farmhouse. Additionally, many Southern farmers objected to using white women for fieldwork that had traditionally been done by African Americans and migrant workers. After the successes of other farmers in 1943, the WLA made inroads into these regions but never saw the same amount of support as it had in the West Coast and Northeast regions.

The second major challenge for the WLA was related to the lack of standards for wages, housing, and sanitation. While the WLA set minimum wages, rates of pay were established locally between the farmer and the workers. The pay was often very low, especially when compared to the wages available for women in industrial war work, and did not cover additional expenses such as housing, food, transportation, and uniforms. Many women reported that they required supplemental help from family in order to participate in the WLA. Additionally, a lack of standards for housing and sanitation meant that women often had a wide range of experiences. Many of the housing camps were poorly managed and received complaints about unsanitary conditions. By 1944, the WLA had begun to address these concerns and set standards for sanitation, child care, and even entertainment for women living in camps.

Overall, the majority of female WLA workers and the farmers who hired them noted that working with the WLA was a very positive experience. During its operation, the WLA offered work opportunities for more than 2 million women across the United States. The number of enlisted women in the WLA exceeded initial expectations for the program. In 1943, the Extension Service planned to hire 300,000 women for emergency harvesting work, 10,000 women for annual labor, and 50,000 for seasonal work. By the end of 1943, over 600,000 women had enlisted. Estimates are that women made up over 25 percent of all agricultural workers in 1943, that from 1943 to 1945 the Extension Service had placed approximately 1.5 million nonfarm women in agricultural jobs, and that an equal number of women worked on farms independently of the federal program. Making up a large segment of agricultural workers during the war, women were a major contributor to the success of the largest crop yields farmers had seen in years.

The WLA was discontinued at the conclusion of the war in 1945; however, women who were interested in continuing work in agriculture were able to do so through the U.S. Crop Corps under the Emergency Farm Labor Program. The postwar years saw a continued rise in the number of women in the workforce, including in the rates of women working in agriculture. Without an iconic image like "Rosie the Riveter," WLA farmerettes received less popular recognition than other female war workers. However, they made an invaluable contribution to maintaining the American homefront and supporting the war effort during World War II.

Kate Wells

See also: African American Women; Hall, Florence Louise (1888–1983); Office of Civilian Defense (OCD); Roosevelt, Eleanor (1884–1962); Rosie the Riveter; World War I (1914–1918); World War II (1941–1945).

References and Further Reading

Carpenter, Stephanie. " 'Regular Farm Girl': The Women's Land Army in World

War II." *Agricultural History* 71, no. 2 (1997): 162–85.

Carpenter, Stephanie. *On the Farm Front: The Women's Land Army in World War II.* DeKalb: Northern Illinois University Press, 2003.

Litoff, Judy Barrett, and David C. Smith. " 'To the Rescue of the Crops': The Women's Land Army during World War II." *Prologue* 25 (Winter 1993): 346–61.

Weiss, Elaine F. *Fruits of Victory: The Woman's Land Army of America in the Great War.* Washington, D.C.: Potomac Books, 2008.

WOMEN'S MEDICAL SPECIALIST CORPS (WMSCP)

On April 16, 1947, the Army-Navy Nurses Act established the Women's Medical Specialist Corps (WMSCP).

Before the creation of the WMSCP, dietitians, occupational therapists, and physical therapists worked in the Army as civilian employees. During World War I, these specialists served in the United States and Europe, and most of them were women. These specialists provided professional care and rehabilitative support to soldiers. They worked under Army regulations even though they were civilian employees, and they did not have military rank and benefits. Because they did not have military rank, they had no authority and frequently faced personnel challenges in the Army. In addition, they did not have war risk insurance. These specialists could not receive compensation for disability, and their families received no compensation if they died during service. They did not get a discharge bonus or even lower fares when they traveled. In addition, those specialists who acquired work-connected illness during World War I were not entitled to receive treatments in the federal hospitals after the end of the war.

Although the problems facing civilian specialists in the military had surfaced during World War I, the War Department did not fix the problems. When World War II began, the government faced similar problems. The Medical Department recognized these specialists' contributions and services during World War I. In addition, the professional services these specialists provided won compliments from some medical military officers. One of these grateful officers was Maj. Gen. Norman T. Kirk, who later became the surgeon general of the Army. Kirk played an important role in supporting the establishment of the WMSCP in 1947.

During World War II, these specialists worked side by side with nurses and other medical professionals. In 1942, dietitians and physical therapists received relative rank in the Medical Department before their deployment overseas. They held the relative rank during the war and for six months after the war. Only dietitians and physical therapists served with commissioned status and received overseas assignment. Occupational therapists did not receive commissioned military status and had no overseas assignments because there was little need for this kind of treatment before the wounded soldiers' transfer to Veterans Administration hospitals. In addition, one of the changes made during World War II was to have the mess officers in place. The mess officers had no background in nutritional care and only worked as administrators. They could not see the nutritional need of duty personnel or a patient from a professional perspective.

On June 22, 1944, Congress passed Public Law 78-350. Under this law, dietitians and physical therapists received commissioned status and the same benefits as other commissioned officers. During World War II, more than 1,640 dietitians and over 1,600 physical therapists served in the Army. Their presence benefited the Army hospitals' operation, especially if these professional personnel stayed after the war. Their contributions and services were critical during World War II.

After World War II, other institutions and government agencies recruited these civilian professionals to work for them. If the Army wanted to keep these professionals in the Army, it needed to do something. In 1946, Surgeon General Kirk recommended the formation of the WMSCP in the Regular Army. He stated that militarizing these civilian employees in the Regular Army would not cost more than keeping them as civilian employees. In addition, he stressed that dietitians and physical therapists had relative ranks in the Army during the war and that arrangement proved successful to the Army hospitals' operations.

In February 1947, the elimination of the mess officers from the hospital's food service operation proved a good change. After the removal of the mess officers, a dietitian supervised and was responsible for all food service operations in the hospitals. This change showed a public recognition of the dietitians' professional knowledge. During the Korean War, dietitians managed food service operations. They took care of staff and patient food service. Another organizational innovation was to create centralized food services, eliminating the final preparation of food in ward kitchens.

On April 16, 1947, the WMSCP was created under the Army-Navy Nurses Act. The newly formed corps was a female-only corps in the Regular Army. The corps members received full commissioned rank. The law authorized the corps to establish its strength as nine-tenths of one WMSCP member for every 1,000 members of the Regular Army. The corps contained a dietitian section, an occupational therapist section, and a physical therapist section. Each section had an assistant chief who reported to the chief of the corps.

The first chief of the WMSCP was Col. Emma E. Vogel. The first assistant chief of the dietitian section was Lt. Col. Helen C. Burns. The physical therapist section's first assistant chief was Lt. Col. Edna Lura. The occupational therapist section's first assistant chief was Lt. Col. Ruth A. Robinson. In the corps, 39 percent of officers worked in the dietitian section, 33 percent worked in the physical therapist section, and 28 percent served in the occupational therapist section. These specialists received Regular Army status. The law also established a WMSCP section in the Officers' Reserve Corps. The corps' specialists served in Army hospitals and provided professional care, therapies, and rehabilitative support to the soldiers. In July 1949, members of WMSCP could transfer to the Air Force.

Each section in the corps had its area of focus and contribution to the Army. Dietitians focused on providing professional care related to diet to staff, soldiers, and patients in the Army hospitals. The physical therapist sections' professional physical therapy also played a critical role in helping war-injured patients to recover. Physical therapists served in the United States and overseas. In the United States, each general hospital had a chief physical therapist in charge of all physical therapy activities, and a number of physical therapists worked under the chief. Physical therapists ran treatment clinics in the hospital or at a facility that was a subdivision of the hospital. The clinic provided heat and cold treatments, electrotherapy, and massage.

When WMSCP officers began serving in Europe under the European Command, they needed to strengthen their connections at professional meetings. Starting from 1953, professional meetings were available for them to attend in Europe. During the Korean War, the WMSCP physical therapists helped to train the South Korean Army's medical personnel in rehabilitative support. The Army also offered in-service educational programs and special courses for dietitians, physical therapists, and occupational therapists. In addition to serving in the Army during the wars, corps members also served as members of medical teams overseas for humanitarian missions.

The Korean War was the first war in which dietitians and physical and occupational therapists served as members of the WMSCP in the Army. Recruiting these specialists had been a problem. There were not enough graduates in these three professional areas, but the need for these specialists had been high in the industries and other civilian areas. As a result, the Army had to compete with other civilian institutions for such specialists. As did the Army Nurse Corps, the WMSCP also kept a small number of these specialists

on active duty. The WMSCP kept between 180 and 220 officers on active duty in the Regular Army. Although the Army needed 1,075 corps professionals based on the total strength of 1,532,000 Army personnel in 1951, it never reached that level despite the calling of reserve officers to active duty. In 1952, the number went up to 630, with two-thirds of them being reserve officers; the number dropped down to 607 in 1953. During wartime, more WMSCP specialists served on active duty.

In May 1953, WMSCP officers' appointment in the Regular Army could be in the grade of first lieutenant instead of second lieutenant. On August 5, 1955, under Public Law 84-294, male dietitians as well as physical and occupational therapists could serve in the corps' reserve. The WMSCP then changed its name to the Army Medical Specialist Corps (AMSC). As of 1966, these male AMSC specialists could also serve in the Regular Army. This integration brought a new dimension to the corps. During the Vietnam War, both male and female members of AMSC served in military hospitals in Vietnam, Japan, Hawaii, and the continental United States. In February 1973, the last group of AMSC specialists left Vietnam. Since its establishment in 1947, the contribution of WMSCP was a significant component in the Army.

Edy Parsons

See also: Army-Navy Nurses Act of 1947 (Public Law 36-80C); Army Nurse Corps (ANC); Korean War (1950–1953); Navy Nurse Corps; Nursing; Vietnam War (1965–1973); World War I (1914–1918); World War II (1941–1945).

References and Further Reading

Anderson, Robert S. *Army Medical Specialist Corps.* Washington, D.C.: U.S. Government Printing Office, 1968.

Hartwick, Ann M. Ritchie. *The Army Medical Specialist Corps: The 45th Anniversary.* Washington, D.C.: U.S. Government Printing Office, 1995.

Lynch, Richard F. *The Past, Present and Future of Army Dietetics.* Carlisle Barracks, PA: U.S. Army War College, 1989.

Standage, L. Sue. *A Role for the Army Medical Specialist Corps in Nation Assistance.* Carlisle Barracks, PA: U.S. Army War College, 1993.

United States Army Medical Specialist Corps. *The Army Medical Specialist Corps, 1917–1971.* Washington, D.C.: U.S. Government Printing Office, 1972.

United States, Department of the Army. *Army Medical Specialist Corps: The Army Health Care Team.* Washington, D.C.: Department of the Army, 1990.

WOMEN'S NURSING CORPS, ARMY

Founded on February 2, 1901, the Women's Nursing Corps (WNC) became a permanent component of the Army Medical Department under the Army Organization Act of 1901. The corps contained both regular and reserve female nurses. The idea behind the formation of a nursing corps was to have trained nurses providing qualified nursing care to the soldiers who were sick or wounded in the Army and to have them on a permanent basis. In 1918, under the Army Reorganization Act, the Nurse Corps (female) was renamed to the Army Nurse Corps (ANC).

Anita Newcomb McGee pushed for a permanent female nurse corps. In 1900, she drafted the legislation that was later incorporated into the Army Organization Act's Section 19. In addition to standard nursing training, WNC nurses also received military nursing training, which required them to support and handle the wounded soldiers quickly. They needed to work close to the combat zones, to move from place to place as needed, and often to put their lives at risk.

To join the WNC, a nurse had to graduate from a hospital training school that had provided her a thorough education in both theoretical and practical training. A nurse then had to do a residency for at least two years at a hospital accepted by the Army. The nurse needed to submit a certificate of health issued by a physician with her application. In addition, the superintendent of that nurse's training school had to write a letter of recommendation, which included information about the nurse's professional qualifications and moral character. By 1912, more states had nurse registration laws. The WNC preferred to choose those nurses coming from states with high standards. The WNC kept a list of qualified candidates who agreed to serve for at least three years. When vacancies were available, the WNC notified the nurse.

The WNC had a superintendent, chief nurses, nurses, and reserve nurses. Dita Hopkins Kinney, the first superintendent of the WNC, was paid $1,800 per year. Army nurses received $40 per month if they served in the United States, and $10 more if they served outside of the United States. The Army nurses had a three-year appointment that could be renewed for three more years if their performance was satisfactory.

The WNC only kept a few hundred Regular Army nurses on active duty during peacetime and called reserve nurses on active duty during times of war. For example, in March 1917, the WNC had 403 Regular Army nurses on active duty. After the United States declared war in April 1917, the number rose higher. By November 1918, the ANC provided 21,480 nurses, including reserve nurses on active duty, to military installments. After the war, the number of nurses on active duty dropped back to only a few hundred. Similar staffing numbers emerged during World War II, the Korean War, and the Vietnam War.

During World War I, approximately 100 nurses died of disease and other causes. No Army nurses died as a direct result of enemy action. The Army recognized the contribution of the ANC during World War I, awarding medals for outstanding service to more than 100 Army nurses. Although Army nurses had made a significant contribution during the war, they were not given ranks in the Army.

The Army Reorganization Act of 1920 authorized relative rank for Army nurses. For instance, the superintendent received the rank of major, and all other Army nurses received the rank of second lieutenant. The superintendent's office was no longer part of the Personnel Division and had to report to the surgeon general instead of the chief of the Personnel Division. The new ANC Division handled personnel, discharges, and records. In 1925, the maximum age for joining the ANC fell from 35 to 32 years old. In 1926, a new law allowed Army nurses to retire after serving for 30 years.

World War II demonstrated the significance of the ANC. At the peak of World War II, over 57,000 Army nurses were on active duty. They served in general and field hospitals, on hospital ships, and on hospital trains. They also helped to evacuate the wounded. During World War II, the ANC pioneered the use of the flight nurses. In 1943, the first class of ANC flight nurses graduated. They evaluated and prepared the patient before air evacuation and helped to transport and take care of the patient during air evacuation. During World War II, 201 Army nurses were killed, 16 of whom died as a direct result of enemy action. After World War II, over 1,600 nurses received medals for their bravery and service. Following World War II, Army nurses were also eligible to receive veterans' benefits. In 1947, the Army-Navy Nurses Act authorized full commissioned rank to members of the ANC. In 1949, the Air Force Nurse Corps (AFNC) was established, and some Army flight nurses transferred to the AFNC as core members.

Starting in August 1955, the corps accepted male nurses to the ANC Reserve. The decision to include male nurses was a response to the shortages faced by the ANC. In 1963, the corps only had 2,918 nurses even though it was supposed to have 5,000 during peacetime. During the Vietnam War, the ANC needed more nurses. The continuous shortage of female nurses made the ANC accept male nurses. In September 1966, the ANC allowed male nurses to serve as Regular Army nurses in the ANC. From then on, the ANC was no longer an all-female corps.

Edy Parsons

See also: Air Force Nurse Corps (AFNC); Army-Navy Nurses Act of 1947 (Public Law 36-80C); Army Nurse Corps (ANC); Army Reorganization Act (1920); Kinney, Dita Hopkins (1855–1921); Korean War (1950–1953); McGee, Anita Newcomb (1864–1940); Navy Nurse Corps; Nursing; Spanish-American War (1898); Vietnam War (1965–1973); World War I (1914–1918); World War II (1941–1945).

References and Further Reading

Feller, Carolyn M., and Constance J. Moore, eds. *Highlights in the History of the Army Nurse Corps.* Washington, D.C.: U.S. Army Center of Military History, 1996.

Sarnecky, Mary T. *A History of the U.S. Army Nurse Corps.* Philadelphia: University of Pennsylvania Press, 1999.

Tomblin, Barbara Brooks. *G.I. Nightingales: The Army Nurse Corps in World War II.* Lexington: University Press of Kentucky, 1996.

Vuic, Kara Dixon. *Officer, Nurse, Woman: The Army Nurse Corps in the Vietnam War.* Baltimore, MD: Johns Hopkins University Press, 2009.

WORLD WAR I (1914–1918)

The outbreak of World War I in the summer of 1914 in the Balkan area of Eastern Europe initially appeared to be a small local squabble. This dispute quickly escalated to a full-scale war that involved most European countries, the entire British Empire, parts of the Middle East and Africa, and, almost three years later, the United States. From its beginning in the summer of 1914 to the Armistice in November 1918, over 65 million men were mobilized worldwide, over 8 million were killed, and over 21 million were wounded. In the United States alone, over 4 million men were mobilized, 2 million were sent overseas, and about 116,000 died. Civilian casualties across Europe, Russia, and the Middle East amounted to over 6 million. Women and other civilians in every country participated in the war in some way, risking their lives and well-being as well.

By the time the United States entered the war in April 1917, there were already civilian and military volunteers in place who were ready to serve their country. Women, like men, were eager to use their talents but had a much harder time being accepted, whether as nonmilitary workers or as true members of the military establishment. As a result, most women served as civilian volunteers, although there was one group of women who was considered part of the U.S. Navy as well as large groups who served with the military while not being considered part of it.

Dr. Anita McGee urged the government to create a permanent nursing corps and drafted legislation that was incorporated into the Army Reorganization Act in 1901. That act established the precursor to the Army Nurse Corps (ANC). McGee had worked in the office of the U.S. Surgeon General during the Spanish-American War and had experienced a nursing shortage. As a result, she recognized the necessity of military nurses. However, at the time of its organization, the ANC was considered an auxiliary of the Army, and its members had only quasimilitary status. Army nurses were given no military rank, benefits, retirement, or equal pay. The Navy followed with the Navy Nurse Corps (NNC) in 1908, in which the nurses also served with the Navy but not in the Navy. Neither group was actually granted full military status with benefits, pay, and rank equal to the men until 1944.

Even before American entry into the conflict, the U.S. Navy became the first branch of the military service to fully accept female members, granting them pay and rank equal to the men. This acceptance resulted from the non-gender-specific language in the Naval Act of 1916, which created the Naval Coastal Defense Reserve Force. Because the act used the word "citizens" rather than "males," a supportive secretary of the Navy, Josephus S. Daniels, decreed that positions in the Navy such as clerks or yeomen were not limited to men. This omission was rectified in 1925 by adding the work "male" before the word "citizens." Daniels, anticipating a great need for recruits due to a large increase in warships, insisted that the Navy should recruit and fully accept women into the Naval Reserve for certain noncombat positions. A call went out for female volunteers, with the first woman enrolling in March 1917, just a few weeks before the United States entered the war. The enrollment of women did not occur without a great deal of public criticism, as the idea of women in the military was considered completely outlandish by many military men and by society in general.

These female recruits needed to be proficient in typing, shorthand, plain copying, spelling, and letter writing. There were also physical requirements such as having good vision and speech, a healthy heart and lungs, and good oral health. Virtuous character and a neat appearance were also must-haves.

Applicants were to be 60 to 70 inches tall and weigh between 112 and 150 pounds, although these limits were overlooked for exceptionally well-qualified candidates.

When the United States declared war on the Axis Powers on April 6, 1917, there were already 200 young women serving as yeomen (F), sometimes called "yeomanettes," a diminutive term that sounded disparaging and was not very popular with the women. During the war years of 1917 through 1918, over 11,000 women enlisted in the Navy, mainly to do clerical work. However, they were also in other lines of work, taking jobs as messengers and couriers, in naval intelligence, as telephone operators, as munitions workers, as drivers, and as recruiters. Every state in the union, as well as Hawaii, Alaska, and Puerto Rico, was represented with women in the Navy. And although most of the recruits came from a middle-class background, there were women from every socioeconomic level. Unlike their male counterparts, these new recruits received no formal preparation and were often on the job the day after they enlisted.

By the end of 1917, there were yeoman (F) clerks serving in every naval district in the country. They usually labored from 8:00 a.m. to 5:00 p.m., six days a week, doing work that had to be precise and speedy. They needed to type at least 25 words per minute and learn military language, rank, and designations to do their job well. Typists had to make six copies of every document— the original and five carbon copies. Some couriers delivered items from office to office, while others traveled to more exciting locations such as the workplaces of high-ranking officers or even the White House. Those with particularly interesting work were the almost 50 women who worked in military intelligence. The women processed fingerprints, broke codes, censored cables, and monitored all ship-to-shore messages. They, along with the telephone operators, who had to work with speed and dexterity, had to be loyal as well as very close-mouthed.

The naval women who worked in munitions did so side by side with civilian women, and although the work was dirty and grueling, the women soon surpassed the men's productivity. Very few women could drive a motor vehicle in 1917, which makes it even more surprising that the Navy recruited women to drive light trucks delivering materials to ships anchored in Norfolk Navy Yard. Yeomen (F) also worked recruiting for the Navy, a job they did with flair, especially the ones who had bubbly personalities.

The Navy had no intention of putting women on board ships and thus added no specific policies to cover the newest recruits. There was nothing stated about women who were married or had children, and the few who did have children had to make their own child care arrangements. However, the few yeomen (F) who became pregnant were immediately discharged. There appear to have been few discipline problems with the women; most of those recorded were minor and usually stemmed from not knowing or not understanding unique military policies. In some ways the women had it easier than the men as they were not required to wear their uniforms when off duty and thus were not nearly as visible when out in the community.

The U.S. Marine Corps was not as quick to use the services of women, and it was August 1918 before the Corps decided to recruit them as clerks, using the now-famous slogan "Free a Man to Fight." The official title of the approximately 300 women who served was marine reserve (F), but the women were widely known by another diminutive, "Marinettes." The Coast Guard also opened some positions to women, and a few transferred from their naval assignments to ones with the Coast Guard, retaining the rank of yeoman (F). The women who served as yeoman (F) and marine reserve (F) were the only women to actually receive honorable military discharges with full veterans' benefits after World War I. The actions of these women paved the way for other women in later wars.

Most of the American women who served during World War I were nurses, but again they had no rank or authority, nor equal pay. They were not officers, nor were they noncommissioned officers. It was not until after the war ended that they received what was called "relative rank," but that meant rank with no benefits or privileges. They did not get complete equal status with male soldiers until another war, in 1944.

The American Red Cross (ARC) officially served as the reserve for the ANC and recruited over 21,000 nurses from 1914 to 1918, with over 10,000 of these serving at or near the front, while the others served at base and camp hospitals all over the United States. Years earlier, the National Committee on Red Cross Nursing Service created a plan to register nurses who would be available in case of a natural disaster or war. In 1916, in anticipation of American involvement in the war, the ARC implemented a plan to establish medical units, called base hospitals, that would function just as hospitals in the United States, with a group of medical personnel that could work together, would have equipment and supplies for a predetermined number of patients, and would be trained to mobilize and set up a hospital as quickly as possible. It began with 500-bed mobile hospitals and staffs of 20 doctors, 46 nurses, and 153 enlisted men each. Later the size was enlarged to 1,000-bed hospitals with an increase of personnel to 35 doctors, 100 nurses, 200 enlisted, and some civilian employees.

Local organizations such as the Daughters of the American Revolution or the Order of the Eastern Star would raise money for equipment and supplies for the hospital units. These units remained under ARC civilian control until mobilized, at which time they became part of the Navy or the Army. When the United States declared war in April 1917, 33 hospital units had already been authorized and were in the process of organizing. Six of the base hospital units, including the nurses, departed for Europe in May 1917, arriving before Gen. John J. Pershing and the American Expeditionary Forces (AEF), and many more followed.

Even with the ARC registry, there was a great need for Army and Navy nurses. There was heavy recruiting for nurses; the surgeon general requested 1,000 each month in August 1918, then he raised that number to 1,000 a week the next month. The demand for professional nurses was so great that the need would not be met for the duration of the war. There was a shortage of over 1,000 American nurses in Europe in

July 1918; that shortage increased to almost 7,000 by November. Articles appeared in professional journals, magazines, and newspapers with titles such as "Nurses of America, Your Country Needs You!" Many of the nurses were decorated, both by the United States and foreign governments. Even though these women were sworn into the U.S. Army, they were not given any rank nor were they considered veterans after they returned home.

Although McGee gets credit for starting the Nursing Corps, another woman really nurtured it into existence. Nurse Jane A. Delano was superintendent of the Nursing Corps from 1909 to 1912 and served as founding chair of the ARC Nursing Service. During her years with the Nursing Corps, she worked out of the U.S. surgeon general's office and maintained the Nursing Corps as a viable entity. From 1912 on, she concentrated on working with the ARC and deserves most of the credit for recruiting the thousands of nurses who served in World War I. She died in France five months after the Armistice while on an inspection tour.

Dora E. Thompson served as superintendent of the ANC throughout the war years. She joined the Nursing Corps in 1902 and had served with the Nursing Corps for 12 years before being promoted to this position. She oversaw the increase in the Nursing Corps from its prewar numbers of about 400 to over 21,000 in 1918. But the long hours and hard work had a price, and she spent most of 1919 recuperating before her next assignment. She retired from the ANC in 1932.

Julia Catherine Stimson joined the Nursing Corps in 1917 and was chief nurse of Base Hospital No. 21 in France. In April 1918, she was appointed chief nurse of the ARC in France and director of nursing for the AEF. She went on to become the dean of the Army School of Nursing in Washington, D.C., and superintendent of the ANC in 1919. She was made a major when the nurses were given relative rank in 1920. She retired from the ANC in 1937 but returned to active duty during World War II. She died just six weeks after being granted full rank, as a colonel, in 1948.

Despite a great need for doctors, the U.S. Army Medical Department refused to allow female physicians to enlist, although it did allow women to serve as "contract surgeons," another term for hired civilians. Some female physicians who were determined to serve signed on in this capacity, serving at base hospital units and performing the same work as their male counterparts. Others served as nurses, relief workers, dieticians, or anesthetists. The War Department also turned down an offer of a mobile hospital fully staffed by women, so the Women's Overseas Hospital and the American Women's Hospitals formed and sent all-female staffed units to the front. Over 350 women doctors were affiliated with these two organizations that had no connection to the military. When the surgeon general requested that female physicians be commissioned due to the great need, he was told that they were not "physically qualified." Women were finally granted temporary commissions in the U.S. Army Medical Corps in April 1943, but only for the duration of the war plus six months. This change in policy was not made permanent until 1952.

Although it has been a long-held rule that the United States does not send women into combat, American women have served near and at the front in many wars. It has been estimated that between 25,000 and 35,000 American women served in the war zone during World War I. Although the majority of these women served as nurses, women filled a myriad of other positions, either as civilians or as nurses with the military but not in the military. And although the chiefs of the various Army branches wanted to establish a women's corps, the secretary of war, Newton D. Baker, did not support this idea.

Early in World War I, General Pershing, commander of the AEF, recognized the need for a new communications system in France as well as for skilled workers to operate it. French telephone operators did not fit the bill, so in October 1917, Pershing asked for 100 French-speaking telephone operators to be sent to him, especially those with experience from working for the telephone company. It was soon clear that bilingual telephone operators were a necessity, and they were placed under the authority of the Signal Corps. Authorized as civilian employees of the Army, the women were led to believe they were enlisting as members of the Army. With the time it took to cull through applicants and then provide training, the first unit of 33 did not sail until March 1918. A total of five units went over before the Armistice. Known as the "Hello Girls," they served all over France and England. They were paid the same as male soldiers in comparative jobs but were required to pay for their own uniforms, at a cost equal to several months' pay. Over 7,500 women applied for these jobs, about 450 were sworn in, and 223 of them served in Europe, again under the rule of the Army but not considered members of it. Over the next several years, over 50 bills were introduced in Congress to grant them veteran status. However, as it was for most of the other women who served, it was not until 1977 that the remaining 18 still living of those who served were granted veteran status, and it was 1979 before they received their certificates, medals, and full veterans' benefits.

In August 1917, the U.S. surgeon general, Maj. Gen. William C. Gorgas, established the Division of Special Hospitals and Physical Reconstruction using those trained in the newly emerging fields of physical and occupational therapy to help disabled soldiers. Women and men known as reconstruction aides (RAs) were used to teach and assist these men to recover some of their physical and mental abilities or learn new ones. The RAs provided training to the wounded so they could return home to productive lives. They, like the nurses, were considered civilians who served with the Army but not in the Army. Other women trained in psychology assisted in the treatment of those soldiers suffering from shell shock. Nearly 2,000 women served as RAs in 1917 and 1918, with over 300 of them at 20 base hospitals overseas. Unfortunately, the U.S. Army Medical Department was not as enthusiastic about this new profession. After the war, the RAs organized in 1921 as the World War Reconstruction Aides Association and spent years trying to gain recognition for their veteran status, pointing out that they had taken the same oath of office as military enlistees, yet their discharge papers identified them as civilians who served with the military. By the next world war in the 1940s, these occupational and physical therapists, along with dieticians, became members of divisions in the surgeon general's office, but not until the G.I. Bill Improvement Act of 1977 were they recognized as veterans.

Women of color also wanted to do something to support the United States during wartime. African American men were drafted during World War I while black women demonstrated their patriotism through raising funds, working in war production, and knitting and sewing for the soldiers. They volunteered en masse, but their service was turned down. Only 14 of the over 11,000 enlisted women in the U.S. Navy were African American, and even this number appears to be due mainly to a black civilian male employee of the Navy who was authorized to choose his own staff of yeomen. Approximately 1,800 black trained nurses signed up with the ARC awaiting ANC assignments, but none were sent to base or camp hospitals, either in the United States or abroad, until after the Armistice in November 1918. The issue of separate quarters and mess for these women was the problem that was overridden only by the immediate need for their services during the flu pandemic of 1918 and 1919. Finally, on November 22, 1918, eighteen black nurses were assigned to active duty in the ANC at hospitals in the United States, a history-making event. They could only nurse the black soldiers, and they had no benefits, rank, or equal pay.

Thousands of American women served in and with the U.S. Army, Navy, Marines, and Coast Guard during World War I. Most of them were given lower pay than their male counterparts, no rank nor benefits, and no veterans' status until decades later. Yet, despite all of this, they volunteered and served honorably. Their sacrifices, made in the second decade of the 20th century, were finally recognized after American involvement in three more wars in which female service proved vital as well as a major women's liberation movement. It was not until near the end of the century that books and articles were written about them and their work.

Katherine Burger Johnson

See also: African American Women; American Red Cross; Army Nurse Corps (ANC); Army Reorganization Act (1920); Army Signal Corps; Ayres, Clara Edith Work (1880–1917); Baker (Steffen), Cecilia Genevieve "Lucille" (1900–1968) and Baker (French), Genevieve Cecilia (1900–1999); Bolton, Frances Payne Bingham (1885–1977); Delano, Jane Arminda (1862–1919); Driscoll, Agnes Meyer (1889–1971); Espionage; Friedman, (Clara) Elizebeth Smith (1892–1980); Gold Star Mothers' Pilgrimages (1930s); Goodrich, Annie Warburton (1866–1954); Hancock, Joy Bright (1898–1986); Hasson, Esther Voorhees (1867–1942); Heavren, Rose (1870–1968); "Hello Girls"; Hitt, Genevieve Young (1885–1963); Hunton, Addie Waites (1866–1943); Johnson, Opha Mae (1900–1976); Keichline, Anna Wagner (1889–1943); McClelland, Helen Grace (1887–1984); McGee, Anita Newcomb (1864–1940); Navy Nurse Corps; Nursing; Spanish-American War (1898); Spanish Influenza (Influenza Pandemic); Stimson, Julia Catherine (1881–1948); Streeter, Ruth Cheney (1895–1990); Victory Gardens; Walsh, Loretta Perfectus (1896–1925); Wilson, Ruth Willson (n.d.–n.d.); Yeoman (F).

References and Further Reading

Ebbert, Jean, and Marie-Beth Hall. *The First, the Few, the Forgotten: Navy and Marine Corps Women in World War I.* Annapolis, MD: Naval Institute Press, 2002.

Gavin, Lettie. *American Women in World War I: They Also Served.* Niwot: University Press of Colorado, 1997.

Holm, Jeanne. *Women in the Military: An Unfinished Revolution.* Novato, CA: Presidio Press, 1982. Revised edition, 1993.

Kennedy, David M. *Over There: The First World War and American Society.* New York: Oxford University Press, 1980.

Sarnecky, Mary T. *A History of the U.S. Army Nurse Corps.* Philadelphia: University of Pennsylvania Press, 1999.

Schneider, Dorothy, and Carl J Schneider. *Into the Breach: American Women Overseas in World War I.* New York: Viking, 1991.

Steinson, Barbara J. *American Women's Activism in World War I.* New York: Garland Publishing, 1982.

Stimson, Julia C. *Finding Themselves: The Letters of an American Army Chief Nurse in a British Hospital in France.* New York: Macmillan, 1918.

U.S. Army Center of Military History. *Highlights in the History of the Army Nurse Corps.* Washington, D.C.: U.S. Army Center of Military History, 1995.

WORLD WAR II (1941–1945)

Approximately 45 million people died in World War II, a conflict that spanned the globe. The war touched every continent and every ocean. The United States entered the war relatively late, in December 1941, after the Japanese attacked Pearl Harbor. The United States mobilized 16.4 million men and women into the armed forces for the war. More than 405,000 Americans died and 670,000 were injured in the war. During World War II, women officially entered the military for the first time. Women had been affiliated with the military before, usually as nurses, unpaid volunteers, or civilian employees, but for the first time they were included in more nontraditional roles and achieved regular military status. The labor shortage caused by the war also gave many women on the homefront an opportunity to secure higher-paying civilian jobs or to break into the labor market for the first time. The female labor force grew by over 50 percent, reaching 19.5 million by 1945. The biggest change was that for the first time married women, instead of single women, became the majority of female wage earners.

Japanese forces completely surprised Americans when they bombed Pearl Harbor, Hawaii, early on the morning of December 7, 1941. Although the Japanese did not accomplish all they had hoped in the attack, the results were devastating to Americans. The bombs destroyed or damaged 187 aircraft and 18 naval vessels. The attack also killed over 2,000 American servicemembers. The next day the United States declared war on Japan, and on December 11, 1941, Hitler declared war on the United States. The United States joined the other Allied nations and became known as one of the "Big Three"—the United States, the United Kingdom, and the Union of Soviet Socialist Republics—in the fight against the Axis Powers of Germany, Italy, and Japan.

Even before the United States' entry into the war, Americans watched events in Europe and Asia with growing alarm. The Sino-Japanese War began in 1937, and Germany invaded Poland in 1939. Both the Japanese and the Germans were brutally aggressive as they sought to expand their military and economic power over neighboring countries. The United States president, Franklin Delano Roosevelt, wanted to help the Allied Powers stop German and Japanese aggression, but most Americans were strongly isolationist and wary of getting involved in another conflict that seemed remote from them, especially after American involvement in World War I. Even reports of both the German and Japanese atrocities did not sway most Americans, who thought that these reports were either greatly exaggerated or completely fabricated for war propaganda as had been done during World War I.

Consequently, Roosevelt prodded Congress to support the Allied Powers without officially declaring war. In 1940, Congress passed the first peacetime draft in an attempt to rebuild the military, which had been quickly demobilized after World War I. In 1941, Congress passed the Lend-Lease Act, which allowed the United States to supply arms to Britain, China, and the Soviet Union, even though none of these countries were in the position to pay for them. Roosevelt also froze Japan's assets in the United States and stopped trade with Japan, which severely limited Japan's access to much-needed oil. In the end, it took the Japanese attack on Pearl Harbor to bring the United States fully into the war.

After the United States officially entered the war, the peacetime industry, which produced mostly civilian consumer goods, shifted into full-scale military production. As industry expanded, 17 million new jobs opened during the war. Factories were retooled and began producing military-related items such as tanks, aircraft carriers, guns, bombs, planes, and ammunition, not only to supply the U.S. military but also to continue supplying the other Allied countries. With the military draining manpower into services, factories began looking to new populations to replace those men in the factories and to meet the incredible wartime demands. In response to this demand, Americans poured out of rural communities and into cities in search of high-paying jobs in the war industry.

African Americans, both men and women, helped fill the gap left in the workforce by white men leaving for the military. This is not to say that all African Americans worked in factories; on the contrary approximately, 1 million African Americans served in the military, enlisting at a rate 60 percent above their proportion of the general population. In addition, the number of black workers increased from 2.9 million to 3.8 million during World War II.

Stateside, African Americans also flocked to the cities; 700,000 left the South and moved to the North and the West looking for improved opportunities. African Americans faced extreme racism both in and out of the military. The military was still segregated, and blacks were usually given the most menial jobs available and given all jobs at lower pay. They were denied service in markets, restaurants, hotels, and other public accommodations and had even more difficulty than most people in finding housing. However, black men made considerable gains during the war; they were employed in higher numbers at higher-paying jobs than had been available to them before the war. In addition, they held on to these gains after the war. African American women faced the toughest discrimination of any group. Black women had fewer opportunities than either white women or black men, and they continued to be relegated to the lowest-paying jobs. The female African American labor force did not change much. Prior to the war, 90 percent of African American women had been in the work force, and that did not change during the war. However, the war allowed many of these women the opportunity to leave domestic work for higher-paying manufacturing jobs or positions in the American military.

The other previously untapped labor force that gained new opportunities during World War II was comprised of married white women. Historically, single women had worked in the public sector, but married women had not worked in great numbers before World War II. During the war, however, their labor was needed to support the nation and also to support their families. The trend of working married women continued after the war, and this group never fully retreated into the private sphere. The inclusion of married women in the workforce was the biggest and most lasting change to the numbers of women in the workforce. Women were employed in jobs that had previously been barred to them, and they changed the face of industry.

However, working women remained in the minority. The majority of married white women continued to stay in the home even during World War II. Historians have often focused on the wartime creation of "Rosie the Riveter," and they minimize other roles women played during the war. This trend diminished the role of homemakers. During the war, women received praise when they did "men's work," but they did not when they did traditional "women's work." Women who did not enter the workforce were still expected to contribute to the war effort. They could do this work through volunteer work with organizations like the Red Cross, the United Service Organizations (USO), or at hospitals or day care centers. The work of these women is often forgotten in the rush to acknowledge the path-breaking work of other women in war industry and the military.

Although during wartime women were encouraged to do "men's work," they were still expected to look and act like women. Furthermore, women were expected to want to maintain their femininity and to worry about the effects work would have on them. Because of the intense labor shortage, the federal government as well as industry created an advertising campaign to persuade women to enter the workforce and fill jobs that had been previously barred to them. Through these campaigns, employers tried to appeal to women and alleviate some of the gender anxieties created by women's entrance into these jobs. To do so, they pointed out that women could remain feminine and that they would hold these jobs only for the duration of the war. Propaganda often focused on the femininity of workers.

Women made incredible advances during the war but were unable to maintain most of them. According to a poll taken near the end of the war, 75 percent of women wanted to keep their jobs after the war. Propaganda and newspapers constantly reminded women that their new roles were only temporary, that they were there only for the duration, and that they should be glad that they would be able to return to their more traditional roles as mothers and wives. Many employers tried to hire female family members of employees who had entered

the service. They believed that it would be easier to convince these women to give up wartime jobs for their husband, brother, or father when those men returned. There were some lasting changes to women's status as the government and larger public acknowledged that women could make important contributions to American society. In response to women's wartime work, Congress seriously considered passing the equal rights amendment and an equal pay act, and several states passed equal pay acts during the war, allowed women to serve on juries, and passed laws to protect married women from discriminatory policies that existed during the Depression to keep married women out of the workplace.

Women, whether working or not, faced many difficulties during the war. The massive influx of people into cities with war industries and military bases over a short period of time led to a lack of sufficient housing as well as to transportation problems. In order to deal with the housing shortage, many families doubled up in houses, apartments, or trailers. Some workers even shared beds in shifts. The school systems were quickly overwhelmed with new students, so some schools had double school days so they could move twice as many students through. Local grocery stores could not keep up with demand to meet the new population's food needs.

The rapid influx of people, combined with the demands of the military and industry for materials, led to skyrocketing costs of necessities and to the need for rationing. The overcrowding of cities also led to higher crime rates. As the government rationed necessities, women on the homefront had to come up with inventive ways to take care of themselves and their family members. Many planted "victory gardens" to supplement their families' diet. Workers had to cut back on their automobile use because gas and rubber were rationed, so existing public transportation systems were also overwhelmed. Women also tried to come up with inventive ways to take care of their children while holding down jobs as single parents while their husbands were serving overseas. The government tried to provide child care or to encourage factories to do so, but they only achieved limited results, and the few child care facilities created were quickly overwhelmed. To deal with the problem, many women shared child care responsibilities with other women, and many women left their children behind with family members when they moved to cities for jobs in the war industry.

Women could also serve the American war effort through military service. Although women had been affiliated with the military before, usually as nurses, World War II was the first time that they could officially enlist in the military and receive full military status. Women's participation in the American military went through many transitions. The first women's auxiliary was the Women's Army Auxiliary Corps (WAAC), which was created in 1942 and was later changed to the Women's Army Corps (WAC). Soon all of the other services had women's corps: the Navy WAVES; the Women's Air Force Service Pilots (WASPs); the SPARS, which were the women in the Coast Guard; and the Marine Corps Women's Reserve (MCWR). The WAC was the largest of the women's corps with 140,000 women, followed by

the WAVES, who enlisted 100,000 women, and the Army Nurse Corps (ANC) with 60,000 women. The MCWR enlisted 23,000, the Navy Nurse Corps (NNC) had 14,000 enlistees, 13,000 women enlisted in the SPARs, and about 1,000 female aviators served as WASPs.

Women in the military were intended to replace men in support roles so that more men would be freed for combat. The women filled various occupations in the military, including office, service, communications, and mechanical work; food preparation; technical and professional work; and trade and manual labor. As was also true of women who worked in the war industry, these women would later lose many of the professional gains that they had made during the war. At the end of the war, around 260,000 women were in uniform, but only about 14,000 remained in 1948.

Both the ANC and the NNC predated the war; the Army created a Nursing Corps in 1901, and the Navy soon followed when it established the NNC in 1908. During World War II, nurses served in every theater and experienced combat as they cared for wounded soldiers, and some were taken prisoner. For example, 66 nurses spent the entire war as POWs in the Pacific. By the end of the war, female nurses finally received equal pay and full military rank.

African American nurses faced more difficulties than their white counterparts. Both the ANC and the NNC were originally all-white organizations. A small number of black women served as nurses during World War I with the ANC, but it returned to its all-white status shortly after that war. Furthermore, it was difficult for black women to become nurses because most nursing schools would not admit them. The nursing shortage finally compelled the military to change its policy. By the end of World War II, there were 500 black nurses in the ANC, but only 4 in the NNC. Only a few black nursing units served overseas; most served stateside and were only allowed to care for black patients and prisoners of war.

There was much debate over how to bring women into the armed forces during World War II. The Army was the first military branch to create a women's auxiliary. In doing so, it was not necessarily responding to the desires of women for equal opportunities but rather to its own manpower needs. The other services were even less enthusiastic about utilizing women and resisted creating women's auxiliaries until their manpower needs overwhelmed their reluctance. There was also much debate on how women should be brought into the military. For example, the Navy was concerned about the creation of a separate auxiliary, like the Army had created, because the women would then be outside the hierarchy and therefore outside the direct control and discipline of the Navy. Consequently, the Navy decided it was best not to create an auxiliary and instead brought women into its ranks. The Army also decided to streamline its command over women and, in 1943, the WAAC became the WAC. Women of the WAC were integrated into the Army's chain of command. The other female services inspired similar debates and looked to each other and to similar female services in Allied countries to try to navigate the groundbreaking creation of a permanent place in the military for women in uniform to respond to the incredible manpower needs of a massive global conflict.

The supporters of women's entrance into the military had another major obstacle—public opinion. One of the major concerns expressed by the public over the entrance of women into the military was the possibility of sexual exploitation and the common misperception that these women would serve as prostitutes for the men in the military. In response, the female leadership of the WAAC enforced a sexual double standard; they tightened restrictions on women even while the Army was loosening its policies on male servicemembers' sexual activity. The WAAC felt pressure to create these restrictions because of the controversy around admitting women into the military. The WAAC wanted to legitimize women's place in the service and felt the best way to accomplish legitimacy was to keep these women above any suspicion.

Another common concern expressed by the public over women's entrance in to the military was that their femininity would be diminished. Lesbianism or perceived lesbianism was seen as a major threat to the future of women in the military. Although there was concern in the larger military about gay men in the ranks, these men were not seen as a threat to the military establishment. On the other hand, lesbianism was viewed as a threat to the female services like the WAC. If the public perception of the WAC was that it cultivated mannishness in women, the legitimacy of the service could be called into question and the future of women in the military would be undermined. The appearances of individual WACs were policed to ensure that the WAC maintained a feminine image.

Once the war wound down and the manpower crises eased, the military began dishonorably discharging both men and women suspected of being homosexuals.

Like the rest of the military, women's corps were segregated. African American women, like their male counterparts, were most often delegated menial assignments and were largely excluded from clerical positions. The Army prohibited female African American officers from commanding white WACs. However, when black officers were not available, white women could command black units, although most African American officers commanded most African American units. African American units were also underutilized as a result of the larger military segregation policies. Black WACs faced more difficulties than their white counterparts as a result. For example, because black men throughout the military were largely relegated to menial jobs, jobs often seen as too difficult for women, African American WACs were underutilized. Although some women served overseas, most of them served on bases in the United States and had to deal with American racism. For example, within the Army there was an informal policy of assigning African American women from the South to bases in the South with the assumption that these women would be prepared to handle Southern attitudes toward blacks.

The war also gave many American women the opportunity to explore and express their sexuality in new, more overt ways. The most obvious example is the pin-up girl. The pin-up genre dates back to at least the 1910s, but pin-ups in the United States became defined by their development during World War II. During the war, the pin-up offered pleasure and escape to servicemen far from the comforts of home. Pin-ups, especially those taken by Alberto Vargas Y. Chavez, which appeared regularly in *Esquire*, established new standards of beauty for American women. Some historians have argued that the 1940s pin-ups expressed a greater acceptance of women's sexuality as well as women's ownership of their sexuality. Others argue that although women enjoyed their sexuality, some men still felt like they had the right to control the sexuality of women. Pin-ups may have allowed women to redefine and embrace their sexuality, but they also produced a higher and narrower, if not impossible, standard of physical beauty for women. They also reinforced the idea that a woman's sexuality existed for the pleasure of men.

World War II was an especially brutal and horrific conflict. First, the waging by both sides of total war—targeting enemy civilian populations in order to demoralize the enemy and to interfere with war production—resulted in devastating consequences for those involved. Although many American civilians did not have to deal on a daily basis with the horrors of war, they heard the news and adapted their lives accordingly.

World War II also revealed the horrors of genocide. Soon after Adolph Hitler came to power in Germany, his regime began instituting anti-Jewish legislation that severely limited where Jews could work or live and who they could marry. Jews were forced to wear a yellow star to signify their status. Eventually the Nazi government revoked the citizenship of Jews. Then, in November of 1938, the Nazis orchestrated a series of pogroms against Jews in Germany. During

Kristallnacht, or the "night of broken glass," many Jews were murdered and many more arrested. Soon Nazi leadership began instituting its "Final Solution" to the "Jewish problem." The government created a work- and death-camp system to systematically exterminate Jews and others deemed undesirable by Hitler, including communists, homosexuals, and gypsies. By the end of the war, more then 6 million people lost their lives to the Nazi program of ethnic cleansing.

Debates exist over whether the Allies knew of the Holocaust and could have stopped it sooner than they did. American immigration policy, as well as domestic anti-Semitism, restricted the number of Jews who could escape to the United States. Furthermore, disbelief over reports of horrific war crimes in Germany prevented these atrocities from getting wide media attention during the war.

World War II also saw the first use of the atomic bomb. In 1940, Roosevelt authorized the Manhattan Project, and American scientists began work building the first atomic bomb. This "most terrible weapon" was first tested successfully in July 1945 in the state of New Mexico. President Harry S Truman authorized its use against Japan on August 6, 1945. The first atomic bomb was dropped by the *Enola Gay* and detonated over the Japanese city of Hiroshima. Three days later, a second atomic bomb was dropped on Nagasaki. Both cities were leveled. Combined, about 140,000 people were killed instantly, and because of the radiation unleashed by the bombs that number nearly doubled in the next year; thousands more died from the fallout in the next five years. Images of the effects of the atomic bomb would haunt Americans for generations.

At the end of World War II there was a new world order. The United States and the Soviet Union, wartime allies, emerged as competing world powers and descended into another global conflict, the Cold War. In the United States, the combination of increased incomes, rationing, and lack of consumer products during the war lead to postwar prosperity. In addition, the G.I. Bill contributed to a housing boom and made college educations accessible for a wider population. The G.I. Bill widened the gap between men and women; women who served in the military received G.I. benefits; however, they only made up about 2 percent of the military, so men were the overwhelming beneficiaries.

Labor and industry leaders and the government also encouraged women to return to more traditional feminine pursuits—the home and the family. Although many women felt pushed out of the workforce, others left willingly. Some women remained in the military. The marriage rate skyrocketed during and after the war; the divorce rate also increased, especially among returning veterans. Wartime separation from male family members and the demands of working and caring for children during a time when there was limited access to necessities meant that many women were eager to rid themselves of part of their burden. Many women were also eager to reestablish family bonds that had been stretched by the war.

However, contrary to the popular perception of the postwar period, many married women found it necessary to secure jobs after the war in order for their families to maintain a middle-class lifestyle, which was now largely focused on consumption. Furthermore, as a result of the postwar economic prosperity, women could find jobs, especially in the service sector, but these jobs certainly did not offer women the same opportunities or pay that had been available during the war; the labor force continued to be sex-segregated, so women were usually limited to "pink-collar," and therefore low-paying, jobs.

M. Michaele Smith

See also: African American Women; Air Force Nurse Corps (AFNC); American Red Cross; American Women's Voluntary Services (AWVS); Anderson, Elda Emma "Andy" (1899–1961); Army Nurse Corps (ANC); Army Signal Corps; Asian American Women; Baker, Josephine (1906–1975); Baldenecker, Donna-Mae (1920–2010); Bethune, Mary McLeod (1875–1955); Blake, Esther McGowin (1897–1979); Blodgett, Katharine Burr (1898–1979); Bolton, Frances Payne Bingham (1885–1977); Bourke-White, Margaret (1904–1971); Brion, Irene (1920–); Cadet Nurse Corps; Caracristi, Ann Zeilinger (1921–); Child, Julia McWilliams (1912–2004); Civil Air Patrol (CAP); Cochran, Jaqueline (ca. 1910–1980); Cold War (ca. 1947–1991); Cook, Cordelia Elizabeth "Betty" (n.d.–n.d.); Dietrich, Marlene (1901–1992); Driscoll, Agnes Meyer (1889–1971); Duerk, Alene Bertha (1920–); Earley, Charity Adams (1918–2002); Espionage; Feinstein, Genevieve Grotjan (1912–2006); Finch, Florence Ebersole Smith (1915–); Fox, Annie G. (1893–1987); Galloway, Irene O. (1908–1963); Gang, Jeanne Hamby (1921–2006); Gellhorn, Martha (1908–1998); Government Girls; Gray Lady Corps; Greenwood, Edith Ellen (1920–); Gulovich, Maria (1921–2009); Hall (Goillot), Virginia (1906–1982); Hall, Florence Louise (1888–1983); Hays, Anna Mae McCabe (1920–); Higgins (Hall); Marguerite (1920–1966); Hispanic American Women; Hobby, Oveta Culp (1905–1995); Hoefly, E. Ann (1919–2003); Hoisington, Elizabeth P. (1918–2007); Holm, Jeanne M. (1921–2010); Hopper, Grace Murray (1906–1992); Lamarr, Hedy (1914–2000); Lauwers, Barbara (1914–2009); Lee, Hazel Ying (1912–1944); Leftenant Colon, Nancy (1921–); Love, Nancy Harkness (1914–1976); May, Geraldine Pratt (1895–1997); McAfee (Horton), Mildred Helen (1900–1994); McIntosh, Elizabeth P. McDonald (1915–); Milligan (Rasmuson) Mary Louise (1911–); Monroe, Rose Leigh Abbott Will (1920–1997); Native American Women; Navy Nurse Corps; Nursing; Office of Civilian Defense (OCD); Ott, Elsie S. (1913–2006); Perkins (Wilson), Frances (1882–1965); Prather, Mary Louise (1913–1996); Prisoners of War; Red Cross Volunteer Nurse's Aide Corps; Rogers, Edith Nourse (1881–1960); Roosevelt, Eleanor (1884–1962); Rosie the Riveter; Roundtree, Dovey May Johnson (1914–); Salvation Army; Sears, Mary (1905–1997); Stimson, Julia Catherine (1881–1948); Stratton, Dorothy Constance (1899–2006); Streeter, Ruth Cheney (1895–1990); Thorpe (Pack), Amy Elizabeth "Betty" (1910–1963); Towle, Katherine A. (1898–1986); United Service Organizations (USO); United States Coast Guard Women's Reserve (SPAR); Urdang, Constance (1922–); USS *Sanctuary*; Victory Gardens; Women Accepted for Volunteer Emergency Services (WAVES); Women Air Force Service Pilots (WASP); Women in Military Service for America Memorial; Women in the Air Force (WAF); Women Marines; Women's Advisory Committee of the War Manpower Commission (1942–1945); Women's Army Auxiliary Corps (WAAC); Women's Army Band; Women's Army Corps (WAC); Women's Army Corps (WAC) Officer Basic Course; Women's Auxiliary Ferrying Squadron (WAFS); Women's Flying Training Detachment (WFTD); World War I (1914–1918); Wu, Chien-Shiung (1912–1997); Young Men's Christian Association (YMCA); Young Women's Christian Association (YWCA).

References and Further Reading

Buszek, Maria Elena. *Pin-Up Grrrls: Feminism, Sexuality, Popular Culture.* Durham, NC: Duke University Press, 2006.

Foner, Eric. *Give Me Liberty! An American History*. New York: W. W. Norton & Company, 2006.

Hall, Jean Ebbert Marie-Beth. *Crossed Currents: Navy Women from World War I to Tailhook*. Washington, D.C.: Brassey's, 1993.

Hartmann, Susan M. *The Home Front and Beyond: American Women in the 1940s*. Boston: Twayne Publishers, 1982.

May, Elaine Tyler. *Homeward Bound: American Families in the Cold War Era*. New York: Basic Books, 1988.

Meyer, Leisa D. *Creating GI Jane: Sexuality and Power in the Women's Army Corps during World War II*. New York: Columbia University Press, 1996.

Milkman, Ruth. *Gender at Work: The Dynamics of Job Segregation by Sex during World War II*. Urbana: University of Illinois Press, 1987.

Stiehm, Judith Hicks. "Women, Men, and Military Service: Is Protection Necessarily a Racket?" In *Women Power and Policy*, edited by Ellen Boneparth, 282–95. New York: Pergamon Press, 1982.

WRIGHT, PRUDENCE CUMMINGS (1740–1823)

Soon after the outbreak of the American Revolutionary War in April 1775, Prudence Cummings Wright was elected commander of a Pepperell, Massachusetts, women's militia known as Mrs. David Wright's Guard. The group, which she herself decided to gather, managed to prevent Hollis Loyalists from exchanging information with British regulars. As Pepperell men were away on duty fighting British troops in Concord, Mrs. David Wright's Guard arrested the spies at Jewett's Bridge over the Nashua River, between Pepperell and Groton, and took them to the Committee of Safety in Groton.

Born on November 26, 1740, in Hollis, Hillsborough County, New Hampshire, Prudence Cummings was the daughter of Samuel Cummings and Prudence Lawrence Cummings. The Hollis town clerk for 22 years, her father was a respected local figure and active representative in municipal and church affairs. Prudence had two sisters, Mary and Sibbell. She also had three brothers, Samuel, Thomas, and Benjamin. All of the Cummings children were born in Hollis. Prudence grew up in Hollis and left for Pepperell, Massachusetts, on December 28, 1761, at age 21, when she married 26-year-old David Wright, a private in the militia. She gave birth to their first child, David, in 1763. She then had 10 other children: Prudence (1764), Cummings (1766), Mary (1767), Wilkes (1769), Caroline Matilda (1772), Liberty (1774), Deverd (1776), Liberty (1778), and Artemas (1780). The last one, Daniel, was born in 1783. Prudence suffered two tragedies in her personal life. She lost two children. On July 1, 1774, she lost six-year-old Mary to fever. The next year, on March 11, 1775, her seven-month-old boy, Liberty, suddenly died. She later gave the same name to another baby boy born in 1778.

Though she had left Hollis for the neighboring town of Pepperell, Wright regularly visited her friends and family in Hollis, and especially her mother. In Pepperell, she also regularly gathered with the other women of the community and was known as a hard-willed woman who was devoted to her family and her town.

The Cummings family was split in its political engagements. Prudence Wright was a Patriot, assuming that the colony of Massachusetts should, as the other 12 British colonies in North America, be represented at the British Parliament and taxed also according to representation. However, her brothers Samuel and Thomas were Tories, Loyalists who supported King George III and the British government. They were very close to British army officer Leonard Whiting and Benjamin Whiting, the first sheriff of Hillsborough County.

When the Revolutionary War broke out in April 1775, 35-year-old Wright was the mother of five children. Her husband and the Pepperell men were ready to fight for the Revolutionary cause and waited for the first call, which came in April as British troops entered Lexington and Concord. As the British retreated back to Boston, rumors circulated about spies who were passing information to the British from Canada to Boston, crossing the town of Pepperell.

When she visited her mother in Hollis after the death of her son, Wright heard a conversation between her brother Samuel and his friend Leonard Whiting, who planned to deliver information to British regulars. On her return to Pepperell, Wright exposed the situation to the local women, who gathered in a company known as Mrs. David Wright's Guard. Numbering between 30 and 40 women, the guard was determined to stop any enemy to the democracy and decided to take action as their husbands and brothers had already left for battle. Wright was chosen as company commander. Dressed in their husbands' clothes and armed with anything that would serve as a potential weapon, including muskets and pitchforks, the company gathered one night a couple of days after April 19 at Jewett's Bridge over the Nashua River in Pepperell. They knew that because the enemy was coming from the north, the bridge was the only possible way to cross the town. They waited until they finally heard two men approaching on horseback. Those men were Whiting and Cummings, Wright's brother. The women arrested the men and compelled them to dismount, looking for proof of hidden information meant for the British. They found papers in Whiting's boots. The women held the men prisoner until morning and then sent to jail in Groton. The documents were sent to the Committee of Safety in Groton.

In March 19, 1777, a town meeting voted to form a Committee of Estimation to pay Wright's Guard for their services during the Revolutionary War. As women could not be paid to serve in the militia, the women's group was referred to as Leonard Whiting's Guard.

Prudence Cummings Wright died on December 2, 1823, in Pepperell, at age 83.

Florence Dupré

See also: American Revolution (1775–1783); Shattuck, Sarah Hartwell (ca. 1737/1738–1798).

References and Further Reading

New England Historic Genealogical Society. *The New England Historical and Genealogical Register for the Year 1860*, vol. 14. Boston: Samuel G. Drake Publisher, 1860, p. 90.

Ryan, Michael D. *Concord and the Dawn of Revolution: The Hidden Truths.* Charleston, SC: History Press, 2007.

Shattuck, Lemuel. *Memorials of the Descendants of William Shattuck*. Boston: Dutton and Wentworth, 1855.

Shattuck, Mary L. P. *Prudence Wright and the Women Who Guarded the Bridge: The Story of Jewett's Bridge*. Nashua, NH: Wheeler Press, 1899.

WU, CHIEN-SHIUNG (1912–1997)

Chinese American physicist, researcher, and university professor Chien-Shiung Wu performed important research in the United States as part of the Manhattan Project. Following World War II, she served as a professor at Princeton, working and publishing for more than three decades in the area of atomic physics.

Wu, born May 29, 1912, was raised in the small town of Liuhe, Jiangsu province, some 40 miles north of Shanghai. Her father, Zhongyi Wu, founder and

Atomic physicist Chien-Shiung Wu worked on the Manhattan Project. (Library of Congress)

principal of a local vocational high school for women, encouraged Chien-Shiung to pursue education. She attended local schools through primary school age, then left home for high school in Suzhou, also in Jiangsu province. Here Wu studied English and sciences. After completing high school and working for one year as a teacher, in 1930 Wu enrolled at National Central University in Nanjing, where she continued her studies in the sciences, in 1934 earning a BS degree in physics.

Following two years at National Central University as a research assistant, in 1936 Wu moved to the United States to continue her studies in the field of physics. Enrolling at the University of California–Berkeley, then a leading center for experimental as well as theoretical physics, Wu worked under 1939 Nobel laureate Ernest O. Lawrence, inventor of the cyclotron atom smasher. Wu earned a PhD in physics in 1940, with a dissertation on nuclear interactions of noble gases, then remained two additional years at Berkeley as a resident fellow and lecturer.

In May 1942, Wu married Luke Chia Liu Yuan, a Chinese PhD physicist then working at the California Institute of Technology. The couple relocated to the East Coast, and Wu taught at Smith College, a small liberal arts institution in Massachusetts, in 1942 and 1943. But Wu wanted greater opportunities for research, and this led her to move in the fall of 1943 to Princeton, and then in March 1944 to Columbia, in New York City. Here she joined the scientific staff of the Division of War Research, an integral part of the wartime Manhattan Project.

The Manhattan Project, so named because it was first headquartered in Manhattan, a New York City borough, was a secret military project of the U.S. government, established in 1942 to manufacture a nuclear weapon. Project directors recruited top U.S. scientists and engineers to work on the initiative and from the outset employed faculty from leading American universities. Here Columbia played a significant role: already by the late 1930s, Columbia scientists were attempting atomic fission in order to produce energy. This made the university a logical center for Manhattan Project research activities and, indeed, at its peak the project employed some 700 men and women at Columbia.

Wu's work for the Division of War Research helped to solve the important question of fuel for an atomic reaction, and thus a bomb. When the Manhattan Project began, the only known fuel options were uranium and plutonium. But to use uranium, first its U-235 isotope needed to be extracted from the more common U-238—only the former can sustain the fission chain reaction needed for a bomb. Columbia scientists, including Wu, employed the gaseous diffusion technique to accomplish the separation. Specifically, Wu was among a small group that labored in the instrumentation group; these scientists utilized ionization chambers and Geiger counters to observe and document the diffusion process. Once completed in these laboratory experiments, the separation process was continued from 1944 on a massive scale at the Oak Ridge facility in Tennessee, one of the three primary Manhattan Project sites. Although there were some 300 women among the tens of thousands of scientists and workers at Manhattan Project locations nationwide, the overwhelming majority of these women were white, making Wu's wartime contributions even more significant.

Wu remained with the Division of War Research until 1946; she then returned to a regular faculty role at Columbia, first as research associate (1946–1952), then as associate professor (1952–1957), and finally as professor from 1958 until her retirement in 1980. Wu's work in the field of physics gained international recognition, including such awards as election to both the National Academy of Sciences (1958) and the American Academy of Arts and Sciences (1972). Wu also received honorary degrees from several universities, both in the United States and abroad. Wu died February 16, 1997, in New York City.

Thomas Saylor

See also: Asian American Women; World War II (1941–1945).

References and Further Reading

Grinstein, Louise S., Rose K. Rose, and Miriam H. Rafailoivch. *Women in Chemistry and Physics: A Bibliographic Sourcebook.* Westport, CT: Greenwood Press, 1993.

Howes, Ruth H., and Caroline L. Herzenberg. *Their Day in the Sun: Women of the Manhattan Project.* Philadelphia, PA: Temple University Press, 1999.

Jack, Jordynn. *Science on the Home Front: American Women Scientists in World War II.* Urbana: University of Illinois Press, 2009.

Y

YEOMAN (F)

Yeoman (F) was the designation for women accepted for enlisted service in the Navy, who performed mainly clerical work during World War I.

The Navy was unprepared for the onslaught of female yeomen who enlisted during World War I and did not have a method in place for recording the gender of a recruit; it had never had to deal with this issue before. Initially some women mistakenly found themselves with orders to serve on combatant vessels due to a lack of gender identification in paperwork, which was not part of the Navy's intention for women. To clarify their gender on paper, the Navy clarified women sailors' status with an "F" for female.

The growth of the Navy created a demand for male yeomen stationed ashore to be reassigned to the new ships. Secretary of the Navy Josephus Daniels felt that enlisting women in the Navy as yeomen stationed ashore would relieve some of the personnel shortage the Navy was facing. The Naval Act of 1916 provided the loophole that Daniels needed in order to permit the enlistment of women. The act created a naval reserve force. Eligibility for the first three components of the force was restricted to former members of the Navy or Merchant Marine. However, the fourth component, the Naval Coast Defense Reserve Force, had open eligibility for individuals without prior military service without any reference to gender. On March 19, 1917, the Bureau of Navigation sent a letter to the commandants of all naval districts authorizing them to enroll women in the Naval Coast Defense Reserve Force as yeomen.

The recruiting stations faced two problems initially among the wave of women volunteers: how to test their aptitude and how to conduct a medical examination. The recruiters often called upon civilian sources such as the Clark Shorthand Institute in Boston to

Navy yeomen (F) line up for a department inspection in 1919. (Library of Congress)

administer tests to determine applicants' aptitude in shorthand, typewriting, plain copying, letter writing, and spelling. The problem of the medical exam was solved by Lt. Cmdr. Frederick Payne in Philadelphia. He came up with the solution of asking a Navy nurse to assist the Navy physician in conducting the exam. In mid-March, the Navy Department issued directives indicating that women could be disqualified for the same physical reasons as men and provided a size and weight chart.

Perhaps the largest discrepancy among the "yeomanettes," as the women became known, was their uniforms. The Navy Department had not designed a uniform for the women at the time it announced that enlistment was open for women. It was not until April 17, 1917, that the Navy Department issued direction on women's uniforms, and then only specified a service coat and skirt. This open-ended directive led initially to local variations of the uniform until a more specific uniform was directed.

Even once standardized uniform regulations for women emerged, many women continued to customize their uniforms. Hats were the most widely varied uniform component. Some women wore a beret or "tam-o'-shanter"; others wore a fore-and-aft or "overseas" cap (today known as a flight cap or garrison cap), while others chose the traditional "Dixie cup" hat. It was not until

September 1918 that the Navy prescribed an overcoat and then a cape as outerwear with the uniform. The uniforms issued to women were conservative interpretations of the male equivalents that suited the work that the women did.

Most of the yeomen (F) performed the standard clerical tasks associated with the rate; however, some ended up doing other jobs. Even the most experienced typists found it difficult to learn the Navy's language. The list of acronyms and unique vocabulary could seem unending. However, it helped the women to feel that they were truly contributing to the war effort. About 134 yeomanettes worked at the Headquarters of the Navy Bureau of Supplies and Accounts. There, work was anything but the stereotypical clerk work. One yeoman (F) assisted the officer in charge of clothing, overseeing the manufacturers' production of clothing for a quarter of a million enlisted men. Another yeoman (F) routinely signed $4 million vouchers in the disbursing department.

Yeomen (F) also served in Naval Intelligence. Others worked as messengers and couriers or as telephone operators. Yeomen (F) with little prior office experience would often be assigned as messengers relaying messages and paperwork between offices. In Naval Intelligence, the yeomen (F) processed fingerprints, helped break codes, and monitored radio transmissions. Nearly 50 yeomen (F) worked in the Naval Intelligence office in New York, which dealt with cases of actual or suspected espionage and monitored the sailors' favorite hangouts where alcohol loosened lips. Many women became telephone operators in order to free men for the war effort. The yeomen (F) are credited with increasing the efficiency of the switchboards at many installations. The impact of women serving ashore in the Navy during World War I surprised many and allowed more men to be pulled to sea duty.

Eventually, 11,880 women served in the Navy during World War I. The greatest number in service at one time was on December 1, 1918: 11,275, or approximately 2 percent of the Navy's total manpower. Just prior to the war's end, the Navy stopped accepting women enlistees. However, the Navy did not move to discharge the women who were currently serving. Eventually all women's enlistment dates were cut to October 1920 by the Naval Appropriations Act of 1919. Many women continued to work in the civil service, and all who had served were considered veterans. They received the World War I Victory Medal, the Good Conduct Medal, and benefits such as burial at Arlington National Cemetery, government insurance, and Veterans Administration medical care for service-related disabilities. No other women served in the Navy, outside of the Nurse Corps, until World War II.

Glenn A. Conley

See also: Baker (Steffen), Cecelia Genevieve "Lucille" (1900–1968) and Baker (French), Genevieve Cecilia (1900–1999); Driscoll, Agnes Meyer (1889–1971); Hancock, Joy Bright (1898–1986); Navy Nurse Corps; Walsh, Loretta Perfectus (1896–1925); Women Accepted for Volunteer Emergency Service (WAVES); World War I (1914–1918).

References and Further Reading

Ebbert, Jean, and Marie-Beth Hall. *Crossed Currents: Navy Women in a Century of*

Change. Washington, D.C.: Batsford Brassey, 1999.

Ebbert, Jean, and Marie-Beth Hall. *The First, the few, the Forgotten: Navy and Marine Corps Women in World War I*. Annapolis, MD: Naval Institute Press, 2002.

Godson, Susan. *Serving Proudly: A History of Women in the U.S. Navy*. Annapolis, MD: Naval Institute Press, 2001.

Rielage, Lisa. "Enlisting the Aid of Yeoma-nettes." *Cobblestone* 27, no. 3 (March 2006): 16–18.

YOUNG MEN'S CHRISTIAN ASSOCIATION (YMCA)

Beginning with the Civil War, the Young Men's Christian Association (YMCA) found ways to support American soldiers during wartime. The YMCA helped form the U.S. Christian Commission (USCC) and the United Service Organizations (USO). It also ran canteens and post exchanges. Although a male organization, women worked for and supported the YMCA from its inception.

The YMCA formed in Britain in 1844. It then spread from England to North America in 1851, first to Montreal, Canada, then to Boston, Massachusetts. During this early antebellum period, prayer meetings, church attendance, and an emphasis on Bible study—and less an emphasis on physical education—were the defining interests of the association concerned with the evils connected with the emerging urbanization. By the end of the decade, just one YMCA had a bowling alley and not one had a gymnasium. Starting in 1856, the YMCA began supplying U.S. Navy training ships with books in such places as Portsmouth, New Hampshire, and a short time later in Boston. However, many people in and around Boston had begun to articulate a profound need to attend to "the total man," or to address the spiritual aspects of the mind, the body, and the nation.

At the outset of the Civil War, many members of the fledgling American YMCA joined the war effort. In addition, many Northern members who did not enlist formed the USCC, a group that organized aid workers and chaplains for Union soldiers as well as ministries for Confederate prisoners of war. The USCC sent nurses to military hospitals and supplies to Union troops. The YMCA programs established during the Civil War would expand and continue in later wars.

The years between the Civil War and 1880 laid the groundwork for "the total man" emphasis in the YMCA. During this period, YMCAs became synonymous with sports programs as well as reading rooms, reflecting the push to combine spirit, mind, and physical strength. By the Spanish-American War, the YMCA, confident that the United States represented God's divine plan, sent members abroad to aid in the war effort, and correspondence from Teddy Roosevelt and his Rough Riders came back to the United States on YMCA letterhead.

At the outset of the United States' entry into World War I, the YMCA offered optimistic enthusiasm and support for "the war to end war." Luther Gulick, the YMCA's wartime consultant during the war, issued a manual that prescribed the organization's intertwined commitments to God and country as critical to the United States' success in the Great War. During the war, the YMCA not only offered support at home through considerable fund-raising efforts, but it also managed most of the U.S. Army canteens and post exchanges in the United States and abroad. Both male and female YMCA workers operated the canteens. During the war, the YMCA modified its evangelistic message to better fit the soldiers' needs—a "religion of the trenches"—and kept the names of combatants who converted to Christianity on a "war roll."

YMCA aid efforts during World War II included an international effort to help prisoners of war. In addition, the YMCA worked with the Young Women's Christian Association (YWCA), National Catholic Community Service, National Jewish Welfare Board, Traveler's Aid Association, and Salvation Army to form the USO, which sent entertainers overseas to perform for American troops. They also set up centers for members of the military on the homefront. In addition, the YMCA worked with Japanese internment camps in the United States, supporting those who had belonged to YMCAs before internment. By 1946, more than 10 percent of YMCA members were women.

John R. Mott, who served as head of the YMCA through both world wars, was awarded the Distinguished Service Medal for his role as general secretary of the National War Work Council. In addition, after World War II, Mott won the 1946 Nobel Peace Prize for his contributions to relief work and recreational activities for prisoners of war. The YMCA continues to emphasize the quaternary of spirit, mind, body, and nation.

Joshua Fleer

See also: Civil War (1861–1865); Korean War (1950–1953); Prisoners of War; Spanish-American War (1898); United Service Organizations (USO); Vietnam War (1965–1973); World War I (1914–1918); World War II (1941–1945); Young Womens' Christian Association (YWCA).

References and Further Reading

Johnson, Elmer L. *The History of YMCA Physical Education.* Chicago: Association Press, 1979.

Lancaster, Richard C. *Serving the U.S. Armed Forces, 1861–1986: The Story of the YMCA's Ministry to Military Personnel for 125 Years.* Springfield, VA: Armed Services YMCA, 1987.

Putney, Clifford. *Missionaries in Hawai'i: The Lives of Peter and Fanny Gulick, 1797–1883.* Amherst: University of Massachusetts Press, 2010.

Putney, Clifford. *Muscular Christianity: Manhood and Sports in Protestant America, 1880–1920.* Cambridge, MA: Harvard University Press, 2001.

YOUNG WOMEN'S CHRISTIAN ASSOCIATION (YWCA)

The Young Women's Christian Association (YWCA) has been connected to the battlefield from its outset. But that connection is intimately linked to the rise of industrialization and the divide between home and work that proceeded from it. The YWCA traces its origin back to two British groups founded in 1855: one, the Prayer Union, which directed its focus toward heavenly things, and the other, the General Female Training Institute, which focused its concerns on the earthly obligation to help nurses returning from the Crimean war. In contrast to Young Men's Christian Association's (YMCA) emphasis on manly work, the YWCA emphasized middle-class virtuousness through wholesome pursuits and respectable behavior. The YWCA in the United States first began using the moniker in 1866 in Boston. By 1907, many disparate groups throughout the United States coalesced as under a single YWCA national board.

However, not all autonomous YWCAs were included under the national umbrella. The YWCA's mission to "bring about the kingdom of God among young women" has been interpreted differently by different members. Prior to the 1907 consolidation, African American women had formed YWCAs that would find ways to continue despite segregation policies implemented under the national board. Social Gospel tendencies carried over into YWCA associations through which African American women, especially, emphasized social justice and racial uplift. Involvement in the YWCA provided agency for these African American women.

At the outset of World War I, African American sentiment over U.S. entry into the war was ambivalent. In the summer of 1917, prior to the U.S. declaration of war, many members of the New York City YWCA marched in protest of President Woodrow Wilson's limited definition of democracy that included interested parties overseas but did not include some of its own citizens.

Nevertheless, mobilization for World War I created growth in the YWCA, both in terms of members and in terms of associations to accommodate them. As membership increased by almost 40 percent nationally, the YWCA made unprecedented inroads in the South. The YWCA was transformed into a relief agency on the homefront and abroad, establishing such programs as the Hostess Houses that provided supervised rest and recreation for soldiers. And with war contracts, the YWCA experienced significant economic growth. Wilson's War Department chairman, Raymond Fosdick, invited the YWCA, among select other groups, to serve overseas on the Commission on Training Camp Activities to keep morale high among soldiers stationed both at home and abroad.

The world war brought a heightened sense of racial and gender distinctions as the categories of both "American" and "women" were brought into sharp relief. Stereotypes that men fought and women provided support remained strong, even as the country increasingly depended on women to fulfill new homefront responsibilities. The YWCA focused its attention on women war workers serving as U.S. Army nurses and as bilingual switchboard operators, known as the "Hello Girls." The YWCA further emphasized a homelike atmosphere for women war workers and stressed evangelical Christian morals such as sex education, calling on the "power of spiritual forces" to help the women in these public wartime jobs resist sexual advances. Indeed, the YWCA stressed the idea that women held a unique responsibility to withhold from sexual temptation. In order to move freely in and out of the army camps and hospitals, the YWCA created an insignia for recognition among guards and other security personnel. Both the American and British YWCAs chose the blue triangle, with the three sides representing body, mind, and spirit.

After World War I, African American women in the YWCA who had met the urgent sense of national duty to the war effort as voluntary citizens sought to carry the association's slogan, "An Equal Chance for the Colored Girl," into the postwar boom. At the conclusion of World War II, the YWCA national board reintegrated in 1946, but during the interwar period, in such places as New York City, the YWCA offered African American women a community center where they could highlight religion, education, and culture through social activism.

Joshua Fleer

See also: African American Women; "Hello Girls"; Nursing; World War I (1914–1918); World War II (1941–1945); Young Men's Christian Association (YMCA).

References and Further Reading

Mjagkij, Nina, and Margaret Spratt, eds. *Men and Women Adrift: The YMCA and the YWCA in the City.* New York: New York University, 1997.

Putney, Clifford. *Muscular Christianity: Manhood and Sports in Protestant America, 1880–1920.* Cambridge, MA: Harvard University Press, 2001.

Robertson, Nancy Marie. *Christian Sisterhood, Race Relations, and the YWCA, 1906–1946.* Urbana: University of Illinois Press, 2007.

Weisenfeld, Judith. *African American Women and Christian Activism: New York's Black YWCA, 1905–1945.* Cambridge, MA: Harvard University Press, 1997.

World Young Women's Christian Association. *The Girl Reserve Movement: A Manual for Advisors.* N.p.: National Board of the Young Women's Christian Associations, 1918. Reprint, 1921.

Z

Z-116 (AUGUST 7, 1972)

Z-gram number 116 (Z-116), part of the "Equal Rights and Opportunities," was a naval policy enacted in the 1970s that offered women better service opportunities and access than they previously had.

For decades, women had been allowed to join the Navy. However, the military limited their enlistment in numbers and the duties they could perform. The Z-116 stated that "we can do far more than we have in the past in according women equal opportunity to contribute their extensive talents to achieve full professional status."

The Z-116 was part of the more than 120 proclamations issued by Elmo Zumwalt, chief of naval operations (CNO). The youngest CNO in naval history, Zumwalt set out a series of policies designed to reduce racism and sexism in the Navy. After researching the problems, he published numerous "Z-grams" as statements of naval policy regarding Navy personnel.

Zumwalt's first goal with Z-116 was to "utilize officer and enlisted women on board ships" at sea. The first ship that women would be assigned to was USS *Sanctuary*, a noncombatant hospital naval ship. Through this pilot program, the Navy would garner "valuable planning information regarding the prospective increased utilization of women at sea." In addition, women would have new access to all Naval Reserve Officers Training Corps (NROTC) programs nationwide. Also, women could now be potentially selected to attend joint-service colleges. Furthermore, the Z-gram opened to naval women access to all staff corps, such as the Chaplain Corps and the Civil Engineer Corps. Women were offered various "paths of progression to flag rank within the technical and managerial spectrum," as had already been done with male officers. Some of these opportunities included promotion to the rank of rear admiral. Naval women could now also enter the fields of intelligence, cryptology, public affairs, and maintenance.

The timing of Z-116 coincided with a national push for women's rights and the congressional debates over the Equal Rights Amendment (ERA), an amendment that would guarantee equal rights regardless of sex under any federal, state, or local law. In this environment, Zumwalt convened two study groups of women who concluded that women's talent was being underutilized in the Navy. In addition, Z-116 came out after the end of the draft (1973), and therefore at a time when an all-volunteer service force was needed for all branches of the military. In order to fill the gaps left by the draft's elimination, a plan was set to expand women's roles in the service and to improve their overall numbers. Zumwalt's changes in the Navy reflect these social and political changes in the United States in the 1970s.

This Z-gram had immense results. Adm. Alene B. Duerk was the first woman to be promoted to rank of rear admiral in 1972 as a result of the Z-116.

Jodie N. Mader

See also: Duerk, Alene Bertha (1920–); Reserve Officer Training Corps (ROTC); USS *Sanctuary.*

References and Further Reading

Disher, Sharon Hanley. *First Class: Women Join the Ranks at the Naval Academy.* Annapolis, MD: Naval Institute Press, 1998.

Ebbert, Jean, and Mary-Beth Hill. *Crossed Currents: Navy Women from World War I to Tailhook.* Washington, D.C.: Brassey's, 1993.

Ebbert, Jean, Mary-Beth Hill, and Edward Beach. *Crossed Currents: Navy Women in a Century of Change.* Washington, D.C.: Brassey's, 1999.

Zumwalt, Elmo. *On Watch: A Memoir.* New York: Quadrangle, 1976.

ZANE, ELIZABETH "BETTY" (c. 1759–c. 1847)

Elizabeth, or Betty, Zane was seen as a hero for her actions during the Revolutionary War. She achieved fame by transporting gunpowder to the beleaguered defenders of her brother's fort, Fort Henry, when his supply ran out. Little detail is available concerning Zane's personal life, and what is known of her chief exploit remains controversial.

She was the daughter of William Zane and is claimed by both Hardy and Berkley Counties in the current state of West Virginia. Her father was a descendant of Robert Zane, a Quaker who emigrated from Ireland to New Jersey in 1677. It seems that William may have married outside of the Quaker community, and this possibly motivated him to move south to Virginia. There he and his wife had four sons and a daughter, Elizabeth. She was the youngest of the five children. One of her brothers, Ebenezer, is sometimes credited with founding the town of Wheeling on the Virginia frontier (now in West Virginia). Three of her brothers moved to the small trading post growing in the area in 1769. In 1774, they built a fort, really a fortified house, named Fincastle. In essence, the fort consisted of a fortified house with a powder magazine some 50 yards away. This architecture was standard procedure at the time in order to protect the main living quarters in case of an accident in the powder magazine. In 1776, with revolutionary ferment gaining momentum on the frontier, they renamed the fort after Virginia patriot Patrick Henry. Over the course of the American Revolution, Native Americans often attacked frontier outposts such as this in an attempt to turn back the encroachment of white settlement. Fort Henry was no exception; Indians attacked it in 1777 and 1782. Likewise, Indians burned sections of the fort in 1781, but these were rebuilt.

Only vague information is available concerning the other aspects of Elizabeth's life. She had two marriages. The first was to a John or Henry McGloughlin (alternately spelled McGlaughlin or McLaughlin). This marriage produced five children: Mary, Rebecca, Nancy, Catherine, and Hannah. Sometime after the death of her first husband, Elizabeth married a Jacob or John Clark. This marriage yielded another two children, Catherine and Ebenezer. The family lived on a farm just west of Martin's Ferry, located just inside the Ohio boundary from Wheeling.

Zane achieved fame for her actions on September 11, 1782. She had only recently returned to the Virginia frontier from Philadelphia, where she had been living with relatives while attending school, when a group of Indians attacked the fort. The attack came on so quickly that the settlers barely possessed enough time to reach safety inside. Consequently, they had only removed a portion of the powder from the magazine for the defense of the fort. After the initial onslaught, the attacking Native Americans settled in and laid siege to Fort Henry. During the fighting, the powder supply ran dangerously low. At this point, Elizabeth, who had taken refuge inside with her brother and several others, volunteered to go to the powder magazine. Removing her excess clothing, she covered the distance between the two structures exceedingly quickly. The dash of a woman from the fort caught the attackers off guard as well, and they were so distracted at the spectacle that they did not attempt to harm her on the way to the magazine. On her return trip, some of the Indians had regained their focus on the assault. Realizing the nature of her mission, the Indians began to shoot at Zane. She made the return trip to the fort unscathed. Her actions provided the defenders with enough powder to withstand the remainder of the siege.

The details of Zane's actions remain controversial. The chief source of information is an account that was written down by Noah Zane, Ebenezer's son, for a family history. A fictionalized version appeared in the novel *Betty Zane* (1903) by Zane Grey, one of Elizabeth Zane's descendents. The controversy about the event stems from an 1849 deposition given by 84-year-old Lydia (Boggs) Cruger. Cruger named Molly Scott as the actual heroine of the battle at Fort Henry.

Although the exact date of her death is unknown, Zane died sometime prior to 1831 at approximately age 65. She is buried in the Walnut Grove Cemetery. A monument detailing her exploits at Fort Henry was erected there in 1928.

James McIntyre

See also: American Revolution (1775–1783); Indian Wars; North American Colonial Wars (17th–18th centuries).

References and Further Reading

Diamante, Lincoln, ed. *Revolutionary Women in the War for American Independence.* Westport, CT: Praeger, 1998.

O'Hammon, Neal, and Richard Taylor. *Virginia's Western War.* Mechanicsburg, PA: Stackpole Books, 2002.

Withers, Alexander S. *Chronicles of Border Warfare.* Cincinnati, OH: Robert Clarke Company, 1895.

Chronology

1676   Mary Rowlandson is captured by Indians in Massachusetts. She is later ransomed back to her family.

1776   The American War of Independence begins.
Patriot Margaret Corbin helps to defend Fort Washington. When her husband is killed, she takes his place firing one of two Patriot cannons until she is wounded.

1778   "Molly Pitcher," possibly the nickname of Mary Ludwig Hays McCauley, goes from camp follower to cannon operator in the Continental Army when her husband collapses on the battlefield in Monmouth, New Jersey.

1782   Deborah Samson, disguised as a man, serves in Gen. George Washington's army.

1783   The Treaty of Paris ends the War of Independence.

1812   The United States and Great Britain fight the War of 1812. It lasts until 1815. Mary Marshall and Mary Allen serve as nurses aboard USS *United States*.

1830s   After decades of women unofficially serving as lighthouse keepers when their husbands or fathers became ill, the Coast Guard officially assigns women as keepers in the Lighthouse Service.

1846   The United States and Mexico fight the Mexican-American War from 1846 to 1848.
Elizabeth Newcom disguises herself as Bill Newcom in order to fight in the Missouri Volunteer Infantry during the Mexican War. She is dismissed when her identity is discovered.

1859   Maria Andreu (a.k.a. Maria Mestre de los Dolores) serves as the keeper of the St. Augustine Lighthouse in Florida (1859–1862). She is the first Hispanic woman to serve in the Coast Guard and to oversee a federal shore installation.

1861   The American Civil War begins.
Dorothea Dix is appointed superintendent of the U.S. Army Nurses.

1862   Dr. Mary E. Walker works as an assistant surgeon with General Burnside's Union troops, a service that will earn her a Medal of Honor.
Four white Catholic nuns and five African American women provide medical care aboard the Union Navy's *Red Rover*.

1865   The American Civil War ends.

1881   Civil War nurse Clara Barton forms the American Red Cross.
Lime Rock Lighthouse keeper Ida Lewis becomes the first woman to be awarded a Gold Lifesaving Medal in the Coast Guard.

1898   The United States deploys 1,500 civilian women, mostly nurses, in the Spanish-American War. A few dozen are African Americans, specifically chosen to serve in Cuba because it was believed they were immune to yellow fever.

1901   A women's Army Nursing Corps is established as part of the Medical Department. It officially becomes the Army Nurse Corps (ANC) in 1918.

1908   The Navy Nurse Corps (NNC) is established.

1913   Navy nurses serve aboard the transport ships USS *Mayflower* and USS *Dolphin*.

1917   The United States enters World War I.
The Navy authorizes the enlistment of women as "yeoman (F)." They become widely known as yeomanettes.
Loretta Perfectus Walsh becomes the first woman to serve as chief petty officer in the Navy.
More than 10,000 nurses serve in World War I.

1918   Twin sisters Genevieve and Lucille Baker serve in the Naval Coastal Defense Reserve, becoming the first uniformed women to serve in the Coast Guard.
Opha Mae Johnson becomes the first woman to enlist in the Marine Corps Reserve.
World War I comes to an end, and more than 11,000 Navy yeomanettes and 300 female marines are asked to resign.

1920   The Army Reorganization Act grants military nurses the status of officers with relative rank from second lieutenant to major.

1941   The United States enters World War II.
Women receive 1,619 medal, citations, and commendations during World War II.
The Coast Guard hires its first civilian women to fill secretarial and clerical positions.

1942   The Women's Army Auxiliary Corps (WAAC) is created with Oveta Culp Hobby as its first director. It is not considered an official part of the Army.

The highly secretive Battery X project uses women to crew antiaircraft artillery in the Military District of Washington.

The Women's Auxiliary Ferrying Squadron (WAFS) is founded.

The Women's Flying Training Detachment (WFTD) is founded.

SPARS, the Coast Guard Women's Reserve, is established with Dorothy Stratton as its director and Dorothy Tuttle as its first enlistee.

Women Accepted for Volunteer Emergency Service (WAVES) is created as an official part of the Navy.

At the fall of Corregidor, the Japanese take American female nurses prisoner.

A total of 81 nurses are taken prisoner during the Pacific campaign.

1943   The Cadet Nurse Corps is created to train women for military service.

The 149th WAAC Post Headquarters Company becomes the first WAAC unit to serve overseas.

Congresswoman Edith Nourse Rogers introduces legislation to change the name of the WAAC to Women's Army Corps (WAC).

WAC special troops are deployed overseas in Italy.

WAFS member Cornelia Fort is killed while flying for the United States. Her death is considered a civilian casualty.

The WAFS and WFTD are combined to create the Women Air Force Service Pilots (WASP).

The U.S. Marine Corps creates the Marine Corps Women's Reserve with Col. Ruth Cheney Streeter as its first director.

Capt. Anne Lents is the first commissioned officer in the Women Marines.

Pvt. Lucille McClarren is the first enlisted woman in the Women Marines.

1944   Army nurses land at Normandy on June 10, 1944.

WASP is ended, but women are allowed to finish their training.

1945   The 6888th Central Postal Directory Battalion, an African American WAC unit, is deployed in Europe.

The female nurses who were captured at the fall of Corregidor are released by the Japanese.

The first five African American women—Olivia Hooker, D. Winifred Byrd, Julia Mosley, Yvonne Cumberbatch, and Aileen Cooke—become SPARs.

Marjorie Bell Stewart becomes the first SPAR to be was awarded the Silver Lifesaving Medal.

The first detachment of female marines arrives in Hawaii for duty.

World War II ends.

1946   WACs are included in the Regular Army and the Organized Reserve Corps.

WAC officers arrive in Japan for assignment to the 8000th WAC Battalion.

Congress provides reemployment rights for WAAC and WAC.

1947   The Army-Navy Nurse Act makes the ANC and the Women's Medical Specialist Corps (WMSCP) part of the Regular Army and gives permanent commissioned officer status to Army and Navy nurses.

The SPARs are deactivated.

The U.S. military makes the U.S. Air Force a separate branch of the armed forces. It was previously an arm of the Army as the Army Air Force (AAF).

1948   The Women's Armed Service Integration Act of 1948 (Public Law 80-625) grants women permanent status in the regular and reserve forces of the Army, Navy, Marine Corps, and Air Force.

Executive Order 9981 ends racial segregation in the armed forces.

WACs with prior service become enlisted in the Regular Army.

Col. Katherine A. Towle becomes the first director of the Women Marines.

1949   WAC, Army of the United States, is terminated, and its members reenlist in the WAC Regular Army.

The Air Force Nurse Corps is established.

The Women's Reserve of the U.S. Coast Guard Reserves (SPAR) is reestablished.

The first African American woman, Annie E. Graham (Gillard), enlists in the Marines.

1950   The Korean War begins.

The U.S. Coast Guard Women's Volunteer Reserve is opened to all eligible veteran SPAR officers.

Nurse Genevieve Smith is killed in a plane crash en route to her assignment in Korea. Eleven more nurses die in a single plane crash heading to a U.S. naval hospital in Yokosuka, Japan.

1951   The Defense Advisory Committee on Women in the Services (DACOWITS) is created to advise on the recruitment of military women for the Korean War.

President Harry S Truman authorizes the armed forces to discharge women who become pregnant or adopt minor children.

1953   The Korean War ends.

The first female physician is commissioned as a medical officer in the Regular Army.

Women in the Navy Hospital Corps receive positions aboard Military Sea Transportation Service (MSTS) ships for the first time.

Staff Sgt. Barbara Olive Barnwell becomes the first Woman Marine to be awarded the Navy and Marine Corps Medal for Heroism.

1955   Military advisors begin U.S. involvement in Vietnam.

Men are accepted into the formerly all-female Army and Air Force Nurse Corps and the Army Medical Specialist Corps.

1957   Virginia H. Schroeder becomes the first woman in Coast Guard history to qualify for the Expert Pistol Medal.

1958 Elizabeth Splaine becomes the first Coast Guard SPAR to become warrant officer.

1960 Master Gunnery Sergeant Geraldine M. Moran becomes the first Woman Marine to be promoted to the rank of E-9.

1961 Bertha Peters becomes the first Woman Marine to be promoted to sergeant major (E-9).

1962 Pearl Faurie becomes the first SPAR to be promoted to E-9.

1965 Approximately 75 women enlist in the U.S. Coast Guard Reserve.
Men are accepted into the previously all-women Navy Nurse Corps.
The Marine Corps assigns Master Sgt. Josephine Davis to be the first woman to have attaché duty. She will later become the first Woman Marine to serve under hostile fire.
Rose Franco becomes the first Hispanic American woman to be promoted to chief warrant officer in the Woman Marines.

1967 The United States repeals legal provisions that placed a 2 percent cap on the number of women serving in the military and ceilings on the highest grade women can achieve.
Master Sgt. Barbara Jean Dulinsky becomes the first Woman Marine to serve in a combat zone.

1968 The first woman is sworn into the Air National Guard (ANG) after Public Law 90-130 allows women to enlist.
Lt. Col. Jenny Wren becomes the first Woman Marine to attend Command and Staff College.

1969 The Air Force Reserve Officers Training Corps (AFROTC) is opened to women.

1970 Anna Mae Hays (ANC) and Elizabeth Hoisington (WAC) are promoted to brigadier general. Hays is the first woman in the U.S. military to wear a star.
1st Lt. Patricia Murphy becomes the first Woman Marine to be a certified military judge.

1971 The Air Force experiences a series of firsts, with women being promoted to brigadier general (Jeanne M. Holm), completing Aircraft Maintenance Officer's School, becoming the first female aircraft maintenance officer, becoming a flight surgeon in the Air Force and the Air Force Reserve, and serving as the first female technician in the Air Force Reserve.

1972 Women are allowed to serve in the Reserve Officer Training Corps (ROTC).
The chief of naval operations, Adm. Elmo R. Zumwalt, publishes Z-116, which declares the Navy's commitment to equal rights and opportunities for women.
USS *Sanctuary*, a hospital ship, is the first naval vessel to sail with a mixed male and female crew.
The House of Representatives hears and fails to pass a bill that authorizes the appointment of women to "any military service academy." The restriction will be lifted in 1975.

1973 The U.S. military ends its policy of conscription.

The first Navy women earn military pilot wings.

Jeanne M. Holm is promoted to major general, the first woman in the history of the armed forces to wear two stars.

The U.S. Navy accepts its first female chaplain.

The Supreme Court rules that the dependents of military women are entitled to the same benefits as those of military men.

The Coast Guard Women's Reserve is ended and women are officially integrated into active duty and the Coast Guard Reserve. Alice Jefferson becomes the first SPAR to be sworn into the regular Coast Guard.

The Coast Guard ends combat exclusion for women.

1974 An Army woman becomes the first female military helicopter pilot.

The Coast Guard begins mixed-sex basic training.

Eleanor L'Ecuyer becomes the first woman on active duty in the Coast Guard to be promoted to captain since World War II.

1975 The Department of Defense offers pregnant women an option to remain on active duty rather than be discharged.

The Air Force places the first woman on operational crew status.

The Coast Guard announces that it will admit women to the Academy in New London.

1976 Women are admitted to the service academies for the first time. The Coast Guard's incoming class includes three women out of a total of 50 cadets.

The Navy promotes Rear Adm. Fran McKee, the first woman of one-star rank in the military branch.

The Air Force selects the first woman reservist for the undergraduate pilot training program.

1977 The Air Force grants military veteran status to Women Air Force Service Pilots (WASP) who flew during World War II.

The Coast Guard deploys the first mixed-gender crews on board the *Gallatin* and *Morgenthau*.

1978 The Navy and Marines allow women to serve on noncombat ships as technicians, nurses, and officers.

The Coast Guard opens all officer career fields and enlisted ratings to women.

The Marine Corps promotes Margaret A. Brewer to brigadier general, the first woman in the corps to achieve one-star rank.

The Army promotes a woman to two-star general for the first time.

The courts determine that the ban on women serving on Navy ships is unconstitutional. Congress amends a law to open noncombat ships to women.

The WAC is disestablished and its members integrated into the Regular Army.

Jeanette Roberts Burr becomes the first uniformed Coast Guard woman to be a lightkeeper when she obtains the post at the New Dungeness Light Station.

1979   Hazel Johnson-Brown becomes the first African American woman to be promoted to general.

Beverly Kelley becomes the first woman to command a military vessel aboard the Coast Guard cutter *Cape Newagen*.

The first female naval aviator obtains carrier qualification.

The Marine Corps begins to assign women to serve as embassy guards.

1980   Fourteen women graduate from the Coast Guard Academy. They are the first to graduate from any service academy.

Roberta Hazard is the first woman to be assigned to command a naval training command.

Susan Helms, of the Air Force, becomes the first woman from the military to go into space.

1981   First Class Storekeeper Mary Alice "Mike" Shaffer, the last World War II–era SPAR, retires from the Coast Guard Reserve.

1982   The Air Force selects Jacqueline Susan Parker to be the first female aviator for Test Pilot School.

The Marine Corps prohibits women from serving as embassy guards as a reaction to the seizing of the U.S. Embassy in Iran from 1979 to 1981.

When her HH-52 airplane crashes, Lt. Colleen Cain becomes the first woman killed in the line of duty.

1983   Colleen Nevius is the first woman in the Navy to complete Test Pilot School.

Approximately 200 Army and Air Force women are deployed to Grenada in Operation Urgent Fury.

Jacqueline A. Ball and Deborah R. Winnie are the first Hispanic women to graduate from the Coast Guard Academy.

1984   Kristine Holderied becomes the first woman to graduate at the top of the class of the Naval Academy.

Linda Moroz is the first woman to complete Navy Dive School.

1985   Denise Matthews graduates at the top of her class at the Coast Guard Academy, becoming the first woman to earn this distinction.

1986   Six women serve as Air Force pilots, copilots, and boom operators on the KC-135 and KC-10 tankers that refuel FB-111s during the raid on Libya.

Terrie A. McLaughlin becomes the first woman to graduate from the Air Force Academy at the top of her class.

Beth E. Hubert of the Navy becomes the first female jet test pilot in any service.

1988   NASA selects Kathryn Sullivan to be an astronaut, the first Navy woman to earn this distinction.

The Marines reverse policy and allow women to be assigned as embassy guards once again.

Grace Parmalee becomes the first Asian American female warrant officer in the Coast Guard.

1989   The United States deploys 770 women to Panama as part of Operation Just Cause.

The U.S. Military Academy at West Point names Kristin M. Baker as its brigade commander and first captain. She is the first woman to hold this post.

The Navy assigns Janice Ayers as its first female command master chief at sea.

1990   The Navy makes sexual harassment a formal offense in Article 1166 of its regulations.

Operation Desert Shield begins with 14 Coast Guard reservists serving in the Persian Gulf.

Kristin Baker becomes the first female captain at the U.S. Marine Academy.

1991   The Gulf War is waged.

Congress repeals the law that bans women from flying combat missions.

The first Navy woman to do so, Darlene Iskra assumes command of a ship.

Juliane Gallina becomes the first woman to be named brigade commander at the Naval Academy.

Marilyn Melendez Dykman becomes the first Hispanic woman to be a Coast Guard aviator.

1993   Congress repeals the law that bans women from serving on combat ships. Women deploy with USS *Fox*.

The Marine Corps opens all pilot positions to women.

The Army names Jill Henderson its Drill Sergeant of the Year, the first time a woman wins the competition in its 24-year history.

The Army makes African American Vernice Armour its first female combat pilot.

Lt. Shannon Workman becomes the first female pilot to qualify for night landings on aircraft carriers.

Adm. Louise Wilmost becomes the first woman to command a naval base.

The Coast Guard makes Lane McClelland its first female chief judge.

1994   USS *Eisenhower* is the first aircraft carrier to have permanent female crewmembers.

Eileen Collins, an Air Force officer, becomes the first woman to copilot the space shuttle.

The Air Force Reserve gets its first woman fighter pilot.

Lt. Kara Hultgreen becomes the first female Navy pilot to be killed on duty when she crashes during flight operations off USS *Abraham Lincoln*.

Two female pilots fly the first combat missions by women when they help enforce the no-fly zone over southern Iraq.

1995   Eileen Collins becomes the first female space shuttle pilot.

Marcelite J. Harris, of the Air Force, becomes the first African American woman to be promoted to major general.

Gilda Jackson becomes the first African American marine to be promoted to colonel.

Rebecca Marier graduates as valedictorian at the U.S. Military Academy at West Point, the first woman to achieve this distinction.

The United States launches USS *Benfold*, the first ship in the Navy that was specifically modified for full gender integration.

1996 Coast Guard vice admiral Patricia Tracey is promoted to three-star rank.

Lt. Gen. Carol A. Mutter becomes the first female marine to attain three-star rank.

For the first time, women fire Tomahawk cruise missiles from a warship in a combat zone when they launch a multiservice strike against the regime of Saddam Hussein. Lt. Erica Niedermeier is one of two officers to oversee the strike team.

Heather Johnsen becomes the first woman to be assigned to guard the Tomb of the Unknown Soldier at Arlington Cemetary.

1997 The Army promotes Claudia Kennedy as the first woman to become lieutenant general and achieve three-star status.

1998 Female fighter pilots participate in Operation Desert Fox in Iraq, firing missiles and laser-guided bombs during the earliest strikes of the campaign.

Sally Brice-O'Hara becomes the first female commanding officer of a Coast Guard Training Center.

1999 The Air Force promotes Leslie F. Kenne, its first woman to become lieutenant general, a three-star rank.

Air Force colonel Eileen Collins becomes the first woman to command the space shuttle.

The first women graduate from the Virginia Military Institute and the Citadel.

The first African American woman is selected to command a Navy ship.

2000 A suicide bomber attacks USS *Cole* in Yemen. Female members of the military are among the victims.

Rear Adm. Vivien S. Crea becomes the first woman to be promoted to admiral in the Coast Guard.

Capt. Kathleen McGrath becomes the first woman to command a Navy warship at sea when it is deployed to the Persian Gulf.

The Army National Guard promotes the first woman to major general.

2001 The Army promotes Coral Wong Pietsch, the first woman to become brigadier general in the Judge Advocate General's Corps.

The U.S. Army Women's Museum opens at Fort Lee, Virginia.

Terrorists highjack four commercial aircraft and crash two into the World Trade Center, one into a field in Pennsylvania, and one into the Pentagon.

The United States initiates a global War on Terror.

War in Afghanistan begins.

Capt. Vernice Armour becomes the first female African American pilot in the Marine Corps.

2002 The Army National Guard promotes its first African American woman brigadier general.

Sgt. Jeannette L. Winters, a marine, becomes the first U.S. servicewoman to
die in the global War on Terror.

2003 Operation Iraqi Freedom (Iraq War) begins with the invasion by the U.S. military and overthrow of the regime of Saddam Hussein.

Lori Piestewa is killed in battle, the first Native American servicewoman to
die in combat. She is one of three women who are taken prisoners of war
during the first days of the war in Iraq.

Lt. Holly Harrison becomes the first Coast Guard woman to command a cutter
in a combat zone. She later becomes the first woman in the Coast Guard to
receive the Bronze Star Medal.

Capt. Vernice Armour becomes the first African American woman to be a
combat pilot after several missions in Iraq.

2004 Col. Linda McTague takes command of a fighter squadron, the first woman in
U.S. Air Force history to do so.

Meredith Austin commands the National Strike Force Coordination Center,
becoming the first woman to be commanding officer of the center.

Theresa Tierney becomes the first female commanding officer of the Coast
Guard Institute.

2005 Sgt. Leigh Ann Hester becomes the first woman to be awarded the Silver Star
for combat action.

Susan Y. Desjardins becomes the Air Force Academy's commandant of
cadets, the first woman to hold this position at any of the military academies.
She comes to office just after a sexual assault scandal (2003–2005).

Nicole Malachowski becomes the first woman in Air Force history to join the
prestigious U.S. Air Force Air Demonstration Squadron "Thunderbirds."

Cpl. Ramona M. Valdez and Lance Cpl. Holly A. Charette become the first
female marines to be killed in the Iraq War.

2006 The Coast Guard appoints Vivien Crea to be the first female vice commandant
of the Coast Guard, making her the first woman to serve as a deputy service
chief in any branch of the armed forces.

Maj. Megan McClung becomes the first female marine officer to be killed in
the Iraq War.

2007 Martha McSally becomes the first woman to command a Navy fighter
squadron.

2008 Ann Dunwoody becomes the first woman to be promoted to four-star general
by the U.S. Army.

2009 Maj. Teresa King becomes the first woman to be the commandant of the Drill
Sergeant School at Fort Jackson, South Carolina.

2010 President Barack Obama awards the WASP the Congressional Gold Medal.

Rear Adm. Nora Tyson becomes the first woman in the Navy to command a carrier strike group.

2011   Rear Adm. Sandra Stosz assumes command of the U.S. Coast Guard Academy, becoming the first woman to command a U.S. service academy.
Marcia M. Anderson becomes the first female African American to obtain the rank of major general in the Army.
Patricia D. Honoro is named surgeon general of the Army, becoming the first woman or nurse to hold the position.
War in Iraq officially ends.

2012   President Barack Obama nominates Air Force Lieutenant General Janet Wolfenbarger to become that service's first female four-star general.

Bibliography

Abzug, Bella. *Bella!: Ms. Abzug Goes to Washington*. New York: Saturday Review Press, 1972.

Ackmann, Martha. *The Mercury 13: The Untold Story of Thirteen American Women and the Dream of Space Flight*. New York: Random House, 2003.

Adams, Henry. *The War of 1812*. Lanham, MD: Cooper Square Press, 1999.

Addams, Jane. *Newer Ideal of Peace*. New York: Macmillan Co., 1907.

Addams, Jane. *Peace and Bread in Time of War*. New York: Macmillan Co., 1922.

Addams, Jane, Emily G. Balch, and Alice Hamilton. *Women at The Hague: The International Congress of Women and Its Results, with Introduction by Harriet Hyman Alonso*. Urbana: University of Illinois Press, 2003.

Adkins, Edward P. *Setauket: The First Three Hundred Years, 1655–1955*. New York: David McKay Company, 1955.

Aid, Matthew. *The Secret Sentry: The Untold History of the National Security Agency*. New York: Bloomsbury Press, 2009.

"The Air Force's First Black Female General." *Ebony Magazine*, October 1992, 62–66.

Albright, Madeleine. *Madam Secretary: A Memoir*. New York: Miramax, 2003.

Albright, Madeleine. *Memo to the President Elect: How We Can Restore America's Reputation and Leadership*. New York: HarperCollins, 2008.

Albright, Madeleine. *The Mighty and the Almighty: Reflections on America, God, and World Affairs*. New York: HarperCollins, 2006.

Alfonso, Kristal L. M. *Femme Fatale: An Examination of the Role of Women in Combat and the Policy Implications for Future American Military Operations*. Maxwell Air Force Base, AL: Air University Press, 2009.

Allawi, Ali. *The Occupation of Iraq: Winning the War, Losing the Peace*. New Haven, CT: Yale University Press, 2008.

Allen, Ann. "The News Media and the Women's Army Auxiliary Corps:

Protagonists for a Cause." *Military Affairs* 50, no. 2 (1986): 77–83.

Alonso, Harriet Hyman. *Peace as a Woman's Issue: A History of the US Movement for World Peace and Women's Rights*. Syracuse, NY: Syracuse University Press, 1993.

Alsmeyer, Marie Bennett. *The Way of the WAVES: Women in the Navy*. Conway, AR: HAMBA Books, 1981.

Alt, Betty Sowers. *Following the Flag: Marriage and the Modern Military*. Westport, CT: Greenwood Publishing Group, 2006.

Amendments to Army-Navy Nurses Act of 1947: Hearings before the United States Senate Committee on Armed Services, 81st Cong. 2 (February 6, 1950). Microfiche. Westport, CT: Greenwood Press, 1973.

American Expeditionary Forces Base Hospital No. 10, United States. *History of the Pennsylvania Hospital Unit: The Great War*. New York: P.B. Hoeber, 1921.

American Nurses Association. *American Journal of Nursing* 19, no. 2 (1919): 887.

Andersen, Timothy P. *Citizen Jane: The Turbulent Life of Jane Fonda*. New York: Henry Holt, 1990.

Anderson, Irving W. *A Charbonneau Family Portrait: Biographical Sketches of Sacagawea, Jean Baptiste, and Toussaint Charbonneau*. Astoria, OR: Fort Clatsop Historical Association, 1988.

Anderson, Laurie H. *Independent Dames: What You Never Knew about the Women and Girls of the American Revolution*. New York: Simon & Schuster, 2008.

Anderson, Martin. "Meeting with the President's Commission on An All-Volunteer Armed Force: Memorandum for the President's File." Washington, D.C., February 21, 1970.

Anderson, Robert S. *Army Medical Specialist Corps*. Washington, D.C.: U.S. Government Printing Office, 1968.

Arlington National Cemetery. http://www.arlingtoncemetery.net/fmckee.htm, accessed March 13, 2012.

Army-Navy Nurses Act of 1947: Bulletin 6. Washington, D.C.: War Department, May 5, 1947.

Army News Service, March 23, 1998.

"Army Nurse Wins Air Medal." *American Journal of Nursing* 43, no. 2 (1943): 443–44.

"Army Nurses Receive Medals for Heroism." *New York Times*, July 16, 1943, 4.

"Around the Corps: North Carolina." *Marines* 27 (February 1998): 6–7.

Ashabranner, Brent K. *A Date with Destiny: The Women in Military Service for America Memorial*. Brookfield, CT: Twenty-First Century Books, 2000.

Ashlee, Laura Rose. *Traveling through Time: A Guide to Michigan's Historical Markers*. Ann Arbor: University of Michigan Press, 2005.

Attie, Jeanie. *Patriotic Toil: Northern Women and the American Civil War*. Ithaca, NY: Cornell University Press, 1998.

Atwood, Kathryn J. *Women Heroes of World War II: 26 Stories of Espionage, Sabotage, Resistance, and Rescue*. Chicago, IL: Chicago Review, 2011.

Augustine, Jane. "Constance (Henriette) Urdang." In *Contemporary Women Poets*, edited by Pamela L. Shelton, 341–42. Detroit, MI: St. James Press, 1998.

Axelrod, Alan. *The War between the Spies: A History of Espionage during the American Civil War*. New York: Atlantic Monthly Press, 1992.

Ayling, Keith. *Calling All Women*. New York: Harper & Brothers, 1942.

Aynes, Edith A. *From Nightingale to Eagle*. Englewood Cliffs, NJ: Prentice Hall, 1973.

Bachner, Evan. *Making WAVES: Navy Women of World War II*. New York: Abrams, 2008.

Bailey, Beth. *America's Army: Making the All-Volunteer Force*. Cambridge, MA: Belknap Press of Harvard University Press, 2009.

Bailey, Margaret E. *The Challenge: Autobiography of Colonel Margaret E. Bailey*. Lisle, IL: Tucker Publications, 1999.

Bakeless, John. *Spies of the Confederacy*. Mineola, NY: Dover Publications, 1970.

Bakeless, John. *Turncoats, Traitors, and Heroes*. Philadelphia: J.B. Lippincott Company, 1959.

Baker, Jean-Claude, and Chris Chase. *Josephine: The Hungry Heart*. New York: Random House, 1993.

Baker, Josephine, and Jo Bouillon. *Josephine*. Translated from the French by Mariana Fitzpatrick. New York: Harper & Row, 1977.

Baker, Rachel. *The First Woman Doctor: The Story of Elizabeth Blackwell, M.D.* New York: J. Messner, 1944.

Bales, Rebecca. " 'You Will Be the Bravest of All': The Modoc Nation to 1909." PhD dissertation, Arizona State University, 2001.

Ballard, John R. *Fighting for Fallujah: A New Dawn for Iraq*. Westport, CT: Greenwood Publishing Group, 2006.

Bandel, Betty. *An Officer and a Lady: The World War II Letters of Lt. Col. Betty Bandel, Women's Army Corps*, edited by Sylvia J. Bugbee. Lebanon, NH: University Press of New England, 2004.

Barbuto, Richard V. *Niagara 1814: America Invades Canada*. Lawrence: University Press of Kansas, 2000.

Barfield, Thomas J. *Afghanistan: A Cultural and Political History.*

Princeton, NJ: Princeton University Press, 2010.

Barger, Judith. "Strategic Aeromedical Evacuation: The Inaugural Flight." *Aviation, Space and Environmental Medicine* 57, no. 6 (1986): 613–16.

Barger, Judith. "U.S. Army Air Forces Flight Nurses: Training and Pioneer Flight." *Aviation, Space and Environmental Medicine* 51, no. 3 (1980): 414–16.

Barile, Mary Collins. *The Santa Fe Trail in Missouri*. Columbia: University of Missouri Press, 2010.

Barkalow, Carol. *In the Men's House*. New York: Poseidon Press, 1990.

Baron, Scott. *They Also Served: Military Biographies of Uncommon Americans*. Spartanburg, SC: Military Information Enterprises, 1997.

Barry, John M. *The Great Influenza: The Epic Story of the Deadliest Plague in History*. New York: Viking, 2004.

Barton, Clara. *The Story of My Childhood*. New York: Baker and Taylor Company, 1907.

Basic, Christine. "Strict Scrutiny and the Sexual Revolution: *Frontiero v. Richardson*." *Journal of Contemporary Legal Issues* 14 (2004): 117.

Bates, Milton J. *Wars We Took to Vietnam: Cultural Conflict and Storytelling*. Berkeley: University of California Press, 1996.

Bauer, Friedrich Ludwig. *Decrypted Secrets: Methods and Maxims of Cryptology*. Berlin: Springer-Verlag, 2007.

Beach, Edward L. *The United States Navy: 200 Years*. New York: Henry Holt and Co., 1986.

Beall, C. C. "The Heroine on the Cover." *Collier's Illustrated Weekly* 113, no. 6 (April 15, 1944): 65.

Bearden, Jim, and Linda Jean Butler. *Shadd: The Life and Times of Mary Shadd Cary*. Toronto, ON: N. C. Press, 1977.

Beasley, Maurine H., Holly C. Shulman, and Henry R. Beasley, eds. *The Eleanor Roosevelt Encyclopedia.* Westport, CT: Greenwood Press, 2001.

Beck, Joan. "She's Gone, but the Issue Hangs in the Air." *Chicago Tribune,* May 25, 1997.

Bellafaire, Judith A. *The Army Nurse Corps: A Commemoration of World War II Service.* Washington, D.C.: U.S. Army Center for Military History, 2001.

Bellafaire, Judith, and Mercedes Herrera Graf. *Women Doctors in War.* College Station: Texas A&M University Press, 2009.

Bellafaire, Judith Lawrence. "Called to Duty: Army Women during the Korean War Era." *Army History: The Professional Bulletin of Army History* 52 (2011): 19–27.

Bellafaire, Judith Lawrence. "Women in Military Service for America Memorial Foundation, Inc. (WIMSA)." In *Gender Camouflage: Women and the U.S. Military,* edited by Francine D'Amico and Laurie Weinstein, 176–81. New York: New York University Press, 1999.

Bellafaire, Judith Lawrence. *Women in the United States Military: An Annotated Bibliography.* New York: Routledge Press, 2011.

Bender, Kristin. "Woman Aviator among the Best Ever." *Oakland* (CA) *Tribune,* January 20, 2004.

Benedict, Helen. *The Lonely Soldier: The Private War of Women Serving in Iraq.* Boston, MA: Beacon Press, 2010.

Benn, Carl. *The War of 1812: Essential Histories.* New York: Routledge, 2003.

Bentley, Amy. *Eating for Victory: Food Rationing and the Politics of Domesticity.* Urbana: University of Illinois Press, 1998.

Bentley, Elizabeth. *Out of Bondage: The Story of Elizabeth Bentley.* New York: Ballantine Books, 1951, repr. 1988.

Bergerud, Eric M. *Fire in the Sky: The Air War in the South Pacific.* Boulder, CO: Westview Press, 2001.

Berkin, Carol. *Revolutionary Mothers: Women in the Struggle for American Independence.* New York: Alfred Knopf, 2005.

Berlin, Ira, Barbara J. Fields, Steven F. Miller, Joseph P. Reidy, and Leslie S. Rowland, eds. *Free at Last: A Documentary History of Slavery, Freedom, and the Civil War.* New York: New Press, 1992.

Berner, Brad K. *The Spanish-American War: A Historical Dictionary.* Lanham, MD: Scarecrow Press, 1998.

Berry, Stephen William, ed. *Weirding the War: Stories from the Civil War's Ragged Edges.* Athens: University of Georgia Press, 2011.

Berson, Robin Kadison. *Young Heroes in World History.* Westport, CT: Greenwood Press, 1999.

Beyea, David. "100 Years and Counting: The Navy Nurse Corps." *All Hands* 1094 (2008): 22–25.

Bidwell, Bruce W. *History of the Military Intelligence Division, Department of the Army General Staff: 1775–1941.* Frederick, MD: University Publications of America, 1986.

Billings, Charlene W. *Grace Hopper: Navy Admiral and Computer Pioneer.* Hillside, NJ: Enslow, 1989.

Billings, Eliza. *The Female Volunteer; or the Life and Wonderful Adventures of Miss Eliza Allen, a Young Lady of Eastport, Maine.* Cincinnati, OH: H. M. Rulison, 1851.

Bjornstad, Randi. "Call of the Bugle: First Female U.S. Military Bugler Has a Place in the Hall of Fame." *The Register-Guard,* August 2, 2009.

Blackman, Ann. *Seasons of Her Life: A Biography of Madeleine Korbel Albright.* New York: Scribners, 1998.

Blackman, Ann. *Wild Rose: The True Story a Civil War Spy.* New York: Random House, 2006.

Blackwell, Elizabeth. *Work in Opening the Medical Profession to Women.* London: Longmans, Green, and Co., 1895.

Blanton, DeAnne. "Cathay Williams: Black Woman Soldier, 1866–68." In *Buffalo Soldiers in the West: A Black Soldiers Anthology*, edited by Bruce A. Glasrud and Michael N. Searles, 101–13. College Station: Texas A&M University Press, 2007.

Blanton, DeAnne, and Lauren McCook. *They Fought like Demons: Women Soldiers in the American Civil War.* Baton Rouge: Louisiana University Press, 2002.

Blatch, Harriet Stanton, and Alma Lutz. *Challenging Years: The Memoirs of Harriot Stanton Blatch.* Westport, CT: Hyperion Press, 1976.

Bohrer, Melissa Lukeman. *Glory, Passion, and Principles: The Story of Eight Remarkable Women at the Core of the American Revolution.* New York: Atria Books, 2003.

Bolton, Frances P. "Nursing Answers." *American Journal of Nursing* 42, no. 2 (1942): 138–40.

Booth, Catherine, Evangeline Booth, and Kay Radar. *Terms of Empowerment: Salvation Army Women in Ministry.* Atlanta, GA: Salvation Army Printing, 1975.

Booth, Sally Smith. *The Women of '76.* New York: Hastings House, 1973.

Bordewich, Fergus M. *Bound for Canaan: The Epic Story of the Underground Railroad, America's First Civil Rights Movement.* New York: Harper Collins, 2005.

Borneman, Walter R. *1812: The War That Forged a Nation.* New York: Harper Perennial, 2005.

Boulware, Dorothy S. "Gilda Jackson Becomes 'First' Colonel." *Baltimore Afro-American*, October 25, 1997.

Boumil, Marcia Mobilia, Stephen C. Hicks, and Joel Friedman. *Women and the Law.* Littleton, CO: Fred B. Rothman & Co., 1992.

Bourke-White, Margaret. *Portrait of Myself.* Boston, MA: G. K. Hall & Co., 1985.

Bourke-White, Margaret. *They Called It "Purple Heart Valley": A Combat Chronicle of the War in Italy.* New York: Simon and Schuster, 1994.

Bowman, Beatrice I. "The History and Development of the Navy Nurse Corps." *American Journal of Nursing* 25 (1925): 356–60.

Boyd, Belle. *Belle Boyd in Camp and Prison.* London: Saunders, Otley, and Co., 1865.

Bragg, Rick. *I Am a Soldier, Too: The Jessica Lynch Story.* New York: Alfred A. Knopf, 2003.

Branson, Susan. "From Daughters of Liberty to Women of the Republic: American Women in the Era of the American Revolution." In *The Practice of U.S. Women's History*, edited by S. Jay Kleinberg, Eileen Boris, and Vicki L. Ruiz, 50–66. New Brunswick, NJ: Rutgers University Press, 2007.

Braun, Hans-Joachim. "Advanced Weaponry of the Stars." *American Heritage* 12, no. 4 (1990): 10–16.

Breuer, William B. *War and American Women: Heroism, Deeds, and Controversy.* Westport, CT: Greenwood Press, 1997.

"Brigadier General Anna Mae Hays." *Army Heritage Center Foundation.* 2010. http://www.armyheritage.org/education-and-programs/educational-resources/soldier-stories/214-brigadier-general-anna-mae-hays.html, accessed February 20, 2012.

Brinkley, David. *Washington Goes to War.* New York: Knopf, 1988.

Brion, Irene. *Lady GI: A Woman's War in the South Pacific: The Memoir of*

Irene Brion. Novato, CA: Presidio Press, 1997.

Broadwater, Robert P. *Daughters of the Cause: Women in the "Civil War."* Santa Clarita, CA: Daisy Publishing Company, 1993.

Broadwater, Robert P. *Liberty Belles: Women of the American Revolution.* Bellwood, PA: Dixie Dreams Press, 2004.

Brodie, Laura Fairchild. *Breaking Out: VMI and the Coming of Women.* New York: Vintage Books, 2001.

Brokaw, Tom. *The Greatest Generation.* New York: Random House, 1998.

Brown, Charles B. "A Woman's Odyssey: The War Correspondence of Anna Benjamin." *Journalism Quarterly* (Fall 1969): 522–30.

Brown, Dee Alexander. *The Gentle Tamers: Women of the Old Wild West.* New York: Putnam, 1958.

Brown, Theodore M. *Margaret Bourke-White, Photojournalist.* Ithaca, NY: Cornell University Press, 1972.

Brown, Thomas J. *Dorothea Dix: New England Reformer.* Cambridge, MA: Belknap Press of Harvard University Press, 1997.

Budiansky, Stephen. *Battle of Wits: The Complete Story of Codebreaking in World War II.* New York: Simon and Schuster, 2000.

Bumiller, Elisabeth. "Letting Women Reach Women in Afghan War." *New York Times*, March 6, 2010.

Burgan, Michael. *Great Women of the American Revolution.* Mankato, MN: Compass Point Books, 2005.

Burgess, Lauren Cook, ed. *An Uncommon Soldier: The Civil War Letters of Sarah Rosetta Wakeman, alias Private Lyons Wakeman, 153rd Regiment, New York State Volunteers.* New York: Oxford University Press, 1994.

Burke, Carol. *Camp All-American, Hanoi Jane, and the High-and-Tight.* Boston, MA: Beacon, 2004.

Burke, John, and Andrea Meyer. "Spies of the Revolution." *New York Archives* 9, no. 2 (2009): 9–13.

Burns, Thomas L. *United States Cryptologic History.* Vol. 6, *The Quest for Cryptologic Centralization and the Establishment of NSA: 1940–1952.* Fort George G. Meade, MD: Center for Cryptologic History, National Security Agency, 2005.

Burton, David H. *Clara Barton: In the Service of Humanity.* Westport, CT: Praeger, 1995.

Bush, George, and Brent Scowcroft. *A World Transformed.* New York: Knopf, 1998.

Bussey, Gertrude, and Margaret Tims. *Pioneers for Peace: Women's International League for Peace and Freedom, 1915–1965.* Oxford, UK: Alden Press, 1980.

Buszek, Maria Elena. *Pin-Up Grrrls: Feminism, Sexuality, Popular Culture.* Durham, NC: Duke University Press, 2006.

Butler, Caleb. *History of the Town of Groton, including Pepperell and Shirley.* Boston: Press of T. R. Marvin, 1848.

Callahan, Sean. *Margaret Bourke-White, Photographer.* Boston: Little, Brown and Company, 1998.

Calloway, Colin G. *First Peoples: A Documentary Survey of American Indian History*, 3rd ed. Boston, MA: Bedford/St. Martin's, 2008.

Calloway, Colin G. *The Shawnees and the War for America.* New York: Viking, 2007.

Cammermeyer, Margarethe, with Chris Fisher. *Serving in Silence.* New York: Penguin, 1994.

Cammermeyer v. Aspin, 850 F.Supp. 910, 924 (1994).

Campbell, D'Ann. *Women at War with America: Private Lives in a Patriotic Era.* Cambridge, MA: Harvard University Press, 1984.

Campbell, Robin D. *Mistresses of the Transient Hearth: American Army Officers' Wives and Material Culture, 1840–1880*. New York: Routledge, 2005.

Canfield, Gae Whitney. *Sarah Winnemucca of the Northern Paiutes*. Norman: University of Oklahoma Press, 1988.

Cannon, Jill. *Heroines of the American Revolution*. Santa Barbara, CA: Bellerophon Books, 1995.

Canwell, Diane, and Jon Sutherland. *American Women in the Vietnam War*. Milwaukee, WI: World Almanac Library, 2005.

"Capt. Kathleen McGrath, 50, Pioneering Warship Commander." *New York Times*, October 1, 2002, B8.

Carbaugh, Marsha Wilson, and Lorraine Cook White. *The Barbour Collection of Connecticut Town Vital Records*. Baltimore, MD: Genealogical Publishing Company, 1999.

Carnegie, Mary Elizabeth. *The Path We Tread: Blacks in Nursing Worldwide, 1854–1994*, 3rd ed. New York: National League for Nursing Press, 1995.

Carpenter, Stephanie A. *On the Farm Front: The Women's Land Army in World War II*. DeKalb: Northern Illinois University Press, 2003.

Carpenter, Stephanie A. " 'Regular Farm Girl': The Women's Land Army in World War II." *Agricultural History* 71, no. 2 (1997): 162–85.

Carroll, Al. *Medicine Bags and Dog Tags: American Indian Veterans from Colonial Times to the Second Iraq War*. Lincoln: University of Nebraska Press, 2008.

Carroll, Anna Ella. *Reply to the Speech of Hon. J. C. Breckinridge*. Washington, D.C.: Henry Polkinhorn, 1861.

Carroll, Anna Ella. *The War Powers of the General Government*.

Washington, D.C.: Henry Polkinhorn, 1861.

Cashman, Diane Cobb. *Headstrong: The Biography of Amy Morris Bradley, 1823–1904*. Wilmington, NC: Broadfoot, 1990.

Cassedy, James H. "Numbering the North's Medical Events: Humanitarianism and Science in Civil War Statistics." *Bulletin of the History of Medicine* 66, no. 2 (1992): 210–33.

Cassidy, Robert. *Counterinsurgency and the Global War on Terror: Military Culture and Irregular War*. Stanford, CA: Stanford University Press, 2008.

Castel, Albert E. *William Clarke Quantrill: His Life and Times*. New York: F. Fell, 1962.

Castiglia, Christopher. *Bound and Determined: Captivity, Culture-Crossing, and White Womanhood from Mary Rowlandson to Patty Hearst*. Chicago, IL: University of Chicago Press, 1996.

Castro, Jeffrey. "First Woman Becomes Army Provost Marshal General." January 15, 2010. http://www.army .mil/article/32999, accessed March 15, 2012.

Cave, Damien. "Women at Arms: A Combat Role, and Anguish, Too." *New York Times*, November 1, 2009.

Cavit, Christina M. "Donna-Mae Baldenecker Burr Smith, the U.S. Military's First Female Bugler." *Noteworthy: Official Newsletter of the IWBC. Lady Brass Series* 15, no. 2 (2009): 12–14.

Center for Cryptologic History. *The Friedman Legacy*. Fort George G. Meade, MD: National Security Agency, 2006.

Central Intelligence Agency. *A Look Back . . . : Maria Gulovich: Sweetheart of the OSS*. Langley, VA: Central Intelligence Agency, 2010.

Chafe, William. *The American Woman: Her Changing Social, Economic and*

Political Roles, 1920–1970. New York: Oxford University Press, 1972.

Chalou, George C. "Women in the American Revolution: Vignettes or Profiles?" In *Clio Was a Woman: Studies in the History of American Women,* edited by Mabel E. Deutrich and Virginia C. Purdy, 73–90. Washington, D.C.: Howard University Press, 1980.

Chandler, Susan. "Addie Hunton and the Construction of an African American Female Peace Prospective." *Affilia* 20, no. 3 (2005): 270–83.

Chiles, James R. "Breaking Codes Was This Couple's Lifetime Career." *Smithsonian* 18, no. 3 (1987): 128–44.

Cirillo, Vincent J. *Bullets and Bacilli: The Spanish-American War and Military Medicine.* New Brunswick, NJ: Rutgers University Press, 1999.

Claghorn, Charles Eugene. *Women Patriots of the American Revolution: A Biographical Dictionary.* Metuchen, NJ: Scarecrow Press, 1991.

Clare, Micah E. "Face of Defense: Woman Soldier Receives Silver Star." *American Forces Press Service,* March 24, 2008.

Clarke, Mary A. *Memories of Jane A. Delano.* New York: Lakeside, 1934.

Clifford, Mary Louise. *Mind the Light, Katie: The History of Thirty-Three Female Lighthouse Keepers.* Alexandria, VA: Cypress Communications, 2006.

Clifford, Mary Louise. *Women Who Kept the Lights: An Illustrated History of Female Lighthouse Keepers.* Williamsburg, VA: Cypress, Communications, 1993.

Clinton, Catherine. *Harriet Tubman: The Road to Freedom.* New York: Back Bay Books, 2004.

Clinton, Catherine, and Nina Silber, eds. *Divided Houses: Gender and the Civil War.* New York: Oxford University Press, 1992.

Cob, Edna. "She Won't Leave G.I.s: Utica Nurse Brings Healing Hand—and Heart—to Pain-Wracked Korean Front." *Utica Observer-Dispatch,* April 29, 1951.

Cochran, Jacqueline, and Floyd Odlum. *The Stars at Noon.* Boston, MA: Little, Brown and Company, 1954.

Cohen, Daniel A., ed. *The Female Marine and Related Works: Narratives of Cross-Dressing and Urban Vice in America's Early Republic.* Amherst: University of Massachusetts Press, 1998.

Cohn, Scotti. *More Than Petticoats: Remarkable North Carolina Women.* Helena, MT: TwoDot, 2000.

Cole, Jean Hascall. *Women Pilots of World War II.* Salt Lake City: University of Utah Press, 1992.

Coleman, Penny. *Spies!: Women in the Civil War.* White Hall, VA: Shoe Tree Press, 1992.

Collier, Richard. *America's Forgotten Pandemic.* London: Allison and Busby, 1996.

Colonel Eileen M. Collins: Leadership Lessons from Apollo to Discovery. Video. Chicago, IL: Chicago Humanities Festival, 1998.

Committee of Naval Affairs. *Casualties aboard Steamship "Mongolia."* New York: Government Printing Office, 1917.

Connelley, William Elsey. *Quantrill and the Border Wars.* New York: Pageant Book Co., 1956.

Cooney, Robert, and Helen Michalowski. *The Power of the People: Active Nonviolence in the United States.* Philadelphia, PA: New Society Publishers, 1987.

Cornum, Rhonda, and Peter Copeland. *She Went to War: The Rhonda Cornum Story.* Novato, CA: Presidio, 1992.

Coryell, Janet L. *Neither Heroine nor Fool: Anna Ella Carroll of Maryland.*

Kent, OH: Kent State University Press, 1990.

Coski, John M. *Capital Navy: The Men, Ships, and Operations of the James River Squadron*. Campbell, CA: Savas Woodbury, 1996.

Crapol, Edward, ed. *Women and American Foreign Policy: Lobbyists, Critics, and Insiders*. Westport, CT: Greenwood Press, 1987.

Crosby, Alfred W. *America's Forgotten Pandemic: The Influenza of 1918*. New York: Cambridge University Press, 1989.

Cunningham, John T. *Clara Maass: A Nurse, a Hospital, a Spirit*. Belleville, NJ: Rae Publishing, 1968.

Currie, Catherine. *Anna Smith Strong and the Setauket Spy Ring*. Port Jefferson Station, NY: C. W. Currie, 1990.

Cutler, Thomas J., and Rick Burgess. "Lest We Forget." *United States Naval Institute Proceedings* 131, no. 12 (2005): 94.

D'Amico, Francine. "Tailhook: Deinstitutionalizing the Military's 'Women Problem.' " In *Wives and Warriors: Women in the Military in the United States and Canada*, edited by Laurie Weinstein and Christie C. White, 235–43. Westport, CT: Bergin and Garvey, 1997.

D'Amico, Francine, and Laurie Weinstein, eds. *Gender Camouflage: Women in the U.S. Military*. New York: New York University Press, 1999.

Darrach, Henry. *Lydia Darragh: One of the Heroines of the Revolution*. Philadelphia, PA: City History Society, 1916.

Daughan, George C. *1812: The Navy's War*. New York: Basic Books, 2011.

Davis, Allen F. *American Heroine: The Life and Legend of Jane Addams*. New York: Oxford University Press, 1973.

Davis, William Watts Hart. *History of Bucks County, Pennsylvania: From the Discovery of the Delaware to the Present Time*, Vol. 3. New York: Lewish Historical Publishing Company, 1905.

Davison, Henry P. *The American Red Cross in the Great War: 1919*. Ithaca, NY: Cornell University Library, 2009.

Davol, Leslie T. "Shifting Mores: Esther Bubley's World War II Boarding House Photos." *Washington History* 10, no. 2 (1998/1999): 44–62.

De Leeuw, Karl, and Jan Bergstra. *The History of Information Security: A Comprehensive Handbook*. Amsterdam, NLD: Elsevier, 2007.

De Pauw, Linda Grant. *Battle Cries and Lullabies: Women in War from Prehistory to the Present*. Norman: University of Oklahoma Press, 1998.

De Pauw, Linda Grant. "Women in Combat: The Revolutionary War Experience." *Armed Forces and Society* 7 (1981): 209–226.

DeBenedetti, Charles, and Charles Chatfield. *An American Ordeal: The Anti-War Movement of the Vietnam Era*. Syracuse, NY: Syracuse University Press, 1990.

Decew, Judith Wagner. "The Combat Exclusion and the Role of Women in the Military." *Hypatia* 10, no. 1 (1995): 56–73.

Decker, Evelyn. *Stella's Girl: The Autobiography of Captain Evelyn Decker, a World War II and Korean War Veteran*. New York: iUniverse, 2008.

DeLay, Brian. *War of a Thousand Deserts: Indian Raids and the U.S.-Mexican War*. New Haven, CT: Yale University Press, 2008.

Department of the Army. *Margaret C. Corbin Award*. TRADOC Regulation 672-8. Fort Monroe, VA: United States Army, 2008.

Depue, Mark R. *Patrolling Baghdad: A Military Police Company and the War in Iraq*. Lawrence: University Press of Kansas, 2007.

Devilbiss, Margaret Conrad. *Women and Military Service: A History, Analysis, and Overview of Key Issues*. Ft. Belvoir, VA: Defense Technical Information Center, 1990.

Diamant, Lincoln, ed. *Revolutionary Women in the War for American Independence: A One Volume Revised Edition of Elizabeth Ellet's 1848 Landmark Series*. Westport, CT: Praeger, 1998.

Diamond, Diane, and Michael Kimmel. " 'Toxic Virus' or Lady Virtue: Gender Integration and Assimilation at West Point and VMI." In *Going Coed: Women's Experiences in Formerly Men's Colleges and Universities, 1950–2000*, edited by Leslie Miller-Bernal and Susan L. Poulson, 263–86. Nashville, TN: Vanderbilt University Press, 2004.

Dickason, Elizabeth. "Remembering Grace Murray Hopper: A Legend in Her Own Time." *Chips* 12, no. 2 (1992): 4–7.

"Digging Their Way out of Recession." *Economist* 390 (February 26, 2009): 36.

Dix, Dorothea L. *Asylum, Prison, and Poorhouse: The Writings and Reform Work of Dorothea Dix in Illinois*, edited by David L. Lightener. Carbondale: Southern Illinois University Press, 1999.

Dix, Dorothea L. *On Behalf of the Insane Poor: Selected Reports 1842–1862*. North Stratford, NH: Ayer Company, 1975.

Dobbs, Michael. *Madeleine Albright: A Twentieth-Century Odyssey*. New York: Henry Holt, 1999.

Dock, Lavinia L., Sarah Elizabeth Pickett, and Clara Dutton Noyes. *History of American Red Cross Nursing*. New York: Macmillan Company, 1922.

Doubler, Michael D. *The National Guard and Reserve: A Reference Handbook*. Westport, CT: Praeger, 2008.

Douglas, Deborah G., and Amy Foster. *American Women and Flight since 1940*. Lexington: University Press of Kentucky, 2004.

Downey, Kristin. *The Woman behind the New Deal: The Life and Legacy of Frances Perkins—Social Security, Unemployment Insurance, and the Minimum Wage*. New York: Random House, 2009.

Dubois, Ellen Carol. "Harriot Stanton Blatch and the Transformation of Class Relations among Woman Suffragists." In *Gender, Class, Race, and Reform in the Progressive Era*, edited by Noralee Frankel and Nancy Schrom Dye, 162–79. Lexington: University Press of Kentucky, 1991.

Dubois, Ellen Carol. *Harriot Stanton Blatch and the Winning of Woman Suffrage*. New Haven, CT: Yale University Press, 1997.

Duncan, Dayton, and Ken Burns. *Lewis and Clark: The Journey of the Corps of Discovery: An Illustrated History*. New York: Knopf Publishing, 1999.

Earley, Charity Adams. *One Woman's Army: A Black Officer Remembers the WAC*. College Station: Texas A&M University Press, 1989.

Ebbert, Jean, and Marie-Beth Hall. *Crossed Currents: Navy Women from World War I to Tailhook*. Washington, D.C.: Batsford Brassey, 1993.

Ebbert, Jean, and Marie-Beth Hall. *The First, the Few, the Forgotten: Navy and Marine Corps Women in World War I*. Annapolis, MD: Naval Institute Press, 2002.

Edgar, Walter B. *Partisans and Redcoats: The Southern Conflict That Turned the Tide of the American Revolution*. New York: Harper Perennial, 2003.

Edmonds, Sarah Emma. *Memoirs of a Soldier, Nurse, and Spy: A Woman's Adventures in the Union Army*, edited by Elizabeth D. Leonard. DeKalb: Northern Illinois University Press, 1999.

Edwards, Julia. *Women of the World: The Great Foreign Correspondents.* Boston, MA: Houghton Mifflin, 1988.

Edwards, Paul M. *To Acknowledge a War: The Korean War in American Memory.* Westport, CT: Greenwood Press, 2000.

Eggleston, Larry G. *Women in the Civil War: Extraordinary Stories of Soldiers, Spies, Nurses, Doctors, Crusaders and Others.* Jefferson, NC: McFarland, 2009.

"Elizabeth Friedman." In *Contemporary Authors*, Vol. 102, pp. 202. Detroit, MI: Gale Research Company, 1981.

Ellet, Elizabeth Fries. *The Women of the American Revolution.* Charleston, SC: Nabu Press, 2010.

Ellington, Charlotte Jane. *Beloved Mother: The Story of Nancy Ward.* Johnson City, TN: Over Mountain Press, 1994.

Ellis, Lee. "Collins, Eileen Marie (Colonel, USAF), NASA Astronaut." In *Who's Who of NASA Astronauts*, 46–47. River Falls, WI: Americana Group Publishing, 2004.

Elwood-Akers, Virginia. *Women War Correspondents in the Vietnam War, 1961–1975.* Metuchen, NJ: Scarecrow Press, 1988.

Enloe, Cynthia. *Maneuvers: The International Politics of Militarizing Women's Lives.* Berkeley: University of California Press, 2000.

Enloe, Cynthia. *The Morning After: Sexual Politics at the End of the Cold War.* Berkeley: University of California Press, 2000.

Erkkila, Betsy. "Revolutionary Women." *Tulsa Studies in Women's Literature* 6, no. 2 (1987): 189–223.

Exley, Jo Ella Powell. *Frontier Blood: The Saga of the Parker Family.*

College Station: Texas A&M University Press, 2001.

Faber, Doris. *Bella Abzug.* New York: William Morrow, 1976.

Faery, Rebecca Blevins. *Cartographies of Desire: Captivity, Race, and Sex in the Shaping of an American Nation.* Norman: University of Oklahoma Press, 1999.

Fainaru, Steve. "Silver Stars Affirm One Unit's Mettle." *Washington Post*, June 26, 2005.

Falerios, Kenton. *"Give Me Something I Can't Do:" The History of the 82nd Military Police Company from WWI to the Iraq War.* Bloomington, IN: AuthorHouse, 2007.

Farolan, Ramon. "From Stewards to Admirals: Filipinos in the U.S. Navy." *Asian Journal*, July 21, 2003.

Faust, Drew Gilpin. *Mothers of Invention: Women of the Slaveholding South in the American Civil War.* New York: Vintage Books, 1996.

Feinman, Ilene Rose. *Citizenship Rites: Feminist Soldiers and Feminist Antimilitarists.* New York: New York University Press, 2000.

Feller, Carolyn M., and Constance J. Moore, eds. *Highlights in the History of the Army Nurse Corps.* Washington, D.C.: U.S. Army Center of Military History, 1996.

Feller, Carolyn M., and Debora R. Cox, eds. *Highlights in the History of the Army Nurse Corps.* Washington, D.C.: U.S. Army Center of Military History, 2001.

Fennelly, Catherine. *Connecticut Women in the Revolutionary Era.* Chester, CT: Pequot, 1975.

Ferrell, John. *Beloved Lady: A History of Jane Addams' Ideas on Reform and Peace.* Baltimore, MD: Johns Hopkins University Press, 1967.

Fessler, Diane Burke. *No Time for Fear: Voices of American Military Nurses in*

World War II. East Lansing: Michigan State University Press, 1996.

Fickeissen, Janet L. "Clara Louise Maass." In *American Nursing: A Biographical Dictionary*, edited by Vern L. Bullough, Olga Maranjian Church, and Alice Stein. New York: Garland Publishers, 1988.

Finch, Florence E. S. Oral history interview by William Thiesen. United States Coast Guard, January 28, 2008.

Finger, Seymour Maxwell. *American Ambassadors at the UN: People, Politics, and Bureaucracy in Making Foreign Policy*. New York: Holmes and Meier, 1988.

Finley, James, ed. *U.S. Army Military Intelligence History: A Sourcebook*. Fort Huachuca, AZ: U.S. Army Intelligence Center, 1995.

Fiore, Faye. "They All See Me as a Soldier Now." *Los Angeles Times*, July 26, 1996, 3.

Fishel, Edwin C. *The Secret War for the Union: The Untold Story of Military Intelligence in the Civil War*. New York: Houghton Mifflin, 1996.

Fisher, Ernest. *Guardians of the Republic: A History of Noncommissioned Officer Corp of the U.S. Army*. Mechanicsburg, PA: Stackpole Books, 2007.

Fiske, John. *The American Revolution: In Two Volumes*. New York: Houghton, Mifflin and Company, 1892.

Fitch, Noel Riley. *Appetite for Life: The Biography of Julia Child*. New York: Doubleday, 1999.

Flinn, Kelly. *Proud to Be: My Life, the Air Force, the Controversy*. New York: Random House, 1998.

Foner, Eric. *Give Me Liberty! An American History*. New York: W. W. Norton & Company, 2006.

Foote, Evelyn P. "War Is No Time to Make Changes." *Washington Post*, February 19, 1991, 17A.

Ford, Corey. *A Peculiar Service*. Boston, MA: Little, Brown and Company, 1965.

Fortin, Noonie. *Memories of Maggie: A Legend Spanning Three Wars*. Austin, TX: Langmarc Publishing, 1995.

Foster, Carrie. *Women for All Seasons: The Story of the Women's International League for Peace and Freedom*. Athens: University of Georgia Press, 1989.

Foster, Carrie. *The Women and the Warriors: The U.S. Section of the Women's International League for Peace and Freedom, 1915–1946*. Syracuse, NY: Syracuse University Press, 1995.

Foster, Rhea Dulles. *The American Red Cross: A History*. New York: Harper and Brothers, 1950.

Frahm, Jill. "From Librarians to Leadership: Women at NSA." Cryptologic Almanac 50th Anniversary Series, 2002. http://www.nsa.gov/ public_info/_files/crypto_almanac _50th/From_Librarians_to_Leadership .pdf, accessed March 15, 2012.

Frahm, Jill. "The Hello Girls: Women Telephone Operators with the American Expeditionary Forces during World War I." *Journal of the Gilded Age and Progressive Era* 3 (2004): 33–42.

Frahm, Jill. *Venona: An Overview*. Cryptologic Almanac 50th Anniversary Series. N.p.: National Security Agency, 2000.

Frahm, Jill. *Wilma Davis*. Cryptologic Almanac 50th Anniversary Series. N.p.: National Security Agency, 2000.

Francis, Sara. "U.S. Coast Guard and Industry Work Together to Make Fisheries Safer." *Proceedings: The Coast Guard Journal of Safety at Sea of the Marine Safety and Security Council* 62 (Winter 2005): 42–44.

Francke, Linda Bird. *Ground Zero: The Gender Wars in the Military*. New York: Simon and Schuster, 1997.

Frederickson, George M. *The Inner Civil War: Northern Intellectuals and the Crisis of the Union.* Urbana: University of Illinois Press, 1965.

Freedman, Lawrence, and Efraim Karsh. *The Gulf Conflict, 1990–1991: Diplomacy and War in the New World Order.* Princeton, NJ: Princeton University Press, 1993.

Freeman, Lucy, and Alma Halbert Bond. *America's First Woman Warrior: The Courage of Deborah Sampson.* New York: Continuum, 1992.

Friedrich, Ed. "Nurse Recognized for War Efforts." *Kitsap Sun*, April 11, 2008.

Furgurson, Ernest B. *Ashes of Glory: Richmond at War.* New York: Alfred A. Knopf, 1996.

Furguson, Ernest B. *Freedom Rising: Washington in the Civil War.* New York: Alfred A. Knopf, 2004.

Galbraith, William, and Loretta, eds. *A Lost Heroine of the Confederacy: The Diaries and Letters of Belle Edmondson.* Jackson: University Press of Mississippi, 1990.

Gallay, Alan. *The Indian Slave Trade: The Rise of the English Empire in the American South, 1670–1717.* New Haven, CT: Yale University Press, 2003.

Gardner, Michael R. 2002. *Harry Truman and Civil Rights: Moral Courage and Political Risks.* Carbondale: Southern Illinois University Press.

Garner, Bryan A., ed. "Due Process Clause." In *Black's Law Dictionary*, 9th ed. Minneapolis, MN: Thomson West, 2009.

Gavin, Lettie. 1997. *American Women in World War I: They Also Served.* Niwot: University Press of Colorado.

Gaytan, Peter S., and Marian Edelman Borden. *For Service to Your Country: The Essential Guide to Getting the Veterans' Benefits You've Earned.*

Updated Edition. New York: Citadel Press, 2011.

Gellhorn, Martha. *The Face of War.* New York: Atlantic Monthly Press, 1959; repr. 1988.

Gellhorn, Martha. *Point of No Return.* Lincoln: University of Nebraska Press, 1948; repr. 1989.

Gellhorn, Martha. *Selected Letters of Martha Gellhorn*, edited by Caroline Moorhead. New York: Henry Holt and Company, 2006.

Gellhorn, Martha. *Travels with Myself and Another.* New York: Jeremy P. Tacher/Putnam, 1978.

Gellhorn, Martha. *The View from the Ground.* New York: Atlantic Monthly Press, 1988.

Giesberg, Judith Ann. *Army at Home: Women and the Civil War on the Northern Home Front.* Chapel Hill: University of North Carolina Press, 2009.

Giesberg, Judith Ann. *Civil War Sisterhood: The U.S. Sanitary Commission and Women's Politics in Transition.* Boston, MA: Northeastern University Press, 2000.

Giesberg, Judith Ann. "In Service to the Fifth Wheel: Katharine Prescott Wormeley and Her Experiences in the United States Sanitary Commission." *Nursing History Review* 3 (1995): 43–53.

Gilbo, Patrick F. *The American Red Cross: The First Century.* New York: Harper & Row, 1981.

Gladwin, Mary Elizabeth. *The Red Cross and Jane Arminda Delano.* Philadelphia, PA: W. B. Saunders, 1931.

Glatthaar, Joseph T., and James K. Martin. *Forgotten Allies: The Oneida Indians and the American Revolution.* New York: Hill and Wang, 2006.

Glines, Carroll V. *Minutemen of the Air: The Valiant Exploits of the Civil Air Patrol in Peace and War.* New York: Random House, 1966.

Godson, Susan H. *Serving Proudly: A History of Women in the U.S. Navy.* Annapolis, MD: Naval Institute Press, 2001.

Goldberg, Alfred. *Pentagon 9/11.* Washington, D.C.: Historical Office, Office of the Secretary of Defense, 2007.

Goldberg, Vicki. *Margaret Bourke-White: A Biography.* New York: Harper & Row, 1986.

Goldstein, Joshua S. *War and Gender.* New York: Cambridge University Press, 2001.

Goodrich, Annie Warburton. *The Social and Ethical Significance of Nursing: A Series of Addresses.* New Haven, CT: Yale University School of Nursing, repr. 1973.

Graf, Mercedes. *A Woman of Honor: Dr. Mary E. Walker and the Civil War.* Gettysburg, PA: Thomas Publications, 2001.

Graf, Mercedes. "Women Nurses in the Spanish-American War." *Minerva: Quarterly Report on Women and the Military* 19, no. 1 (2001): 3–38.

Graham, John. *The Gold Star Mother Pilgrimages of the 1930s.* Jefferson, NC: McFarland, 2005.

Green, Harry Clinton, and Mary Wolcott Green. *The Pioneer Mothers of America: A Record of the More Notable Women of the Early Days of the Country, and Particularly of the Colonial and Revolutionary Periods.* Whitefish, MT: Kessinger Publishing, 2007.

Greene, David L. "New Light on Mary Rowlandson." *Early American Literature* 20 (1985): 24–38.

Greene, Julie. *The Canal Builders: Making America's Empire at the Panama Canal.* New York: Penguin Press, 2009.

Greenhow, Rose O'Neal. *My Imprisonment and the First Year of Abolition Rule at Washington.* London: Richard Bentley, 1863.

Gregory, Chester W. *Women in Defense Work during World War II: An Analysis of the Labor Problem and Women's Rights.* New York: Exposition Press, 1974.

Griffin, Patrick. *American Leviathan: Empire, Nation, and Revolutionary Frontier.* New York: Hill and Wang, 2007.

Grinstein, Louise S., Rose K. Rose, and Miriam H. Rafailoivch. *Women in Chemistry and Physics: A Bibliographic Sourcebook.* Westport, CT: Greenwood Press, 1993.

Groh, Lynn. *The Culper Spy Ring.* Philadelphia, PA: Westminster Press, 1969.

Gruhzit-Hoyt, Olga. *They Also Served: American Women in World War II.* New York: Carol Publishing Group, 1995.

Grunwald, Lisa, and Stephen J. Adler. *Women's Letters: America from the Revolutionary War to the Present.* New York: Dial, 2005.

Guerin, Elsa Jane. *Mountain Charley, or the Adventures of Mrs. E. J. Guerin, Who Was Thirteen Years in Male Attire: An Autobiography Comprising a Period of Thirteen Years Life in the States, California, and Pike's Peak,* with an introduction by Fred W. Mazzulla and William Kostka. Norman: University of Oklahoma Press, 1968.

Gundersen, Joan R. *To Be Useful in the World: Women in Revolutionary America, 1740–1790.* Chapel Hill: University of North Carolina Press, 2006.

Gurin, Patricia, and Louise Tilley, eds. *Women, Politics and Change.* New York: Russell Sage Foundation Publication, 1992.

Gwinn, Kristen E. *Emily Greene Balch: The Long Road to Internationalism.* Urbana: University of Illinois Press, 2010.

Hagerman, George. "Confederate Captain Sally Tompkins Was the Only

Woman to Be Commissioned an Officer in the Civil War." *America's Civil War* 10, no. 2 (1997): 10–12.

Hall, Richard. *Women on the Civil War Battlefront.* Lawrence: University Press of Kansas, 2006.

Hancock, Joy Bright. *Lady in the Navy: A Personal Reminiscence.* Annapolis, MD: Naval Institute Press,1972; repr. 2002.

Hanson, Joyce. *Mary McLeod Bethune and Black Women's Political Activism.* Columbia: University of Missouri Press, 2003.

Hardy, Michael C. *Remembering Avery County: Old Tales from North Carolina's Youngest County.* Charleston, SC: The History Press, 2007.

Harper, John Robinson. "Revolution and Conquest: Politics, Violence and Social Change in the Ohio Valley, 1765–1795." PhD dissertation, University of Wisconsin-Madison, 2008.

Harris, Gail, and Pamela J. McLaughlin. *A Woman's War: The Professional and Personal Journey of the Navy's First African American Female Intelligence Officer.* Lanham, MD: Scarecrow Press, 2010.

Harrison, Todd. "Analysis of the Fy 2011 Defense Budget." Washington, D.C.: Center for Strategic and Budgetary Assessments, 2011.

Hartmann, Susan M. *The Home Front and Beyond: American Women in the 1940s.* Boston, MA: Twayne, 1982.

Hartwick, Ann M. Ritchie. *The Army Medical Specialist Corps: The 45th Anniversary.* Washington, D.C.: U.S. Government Printing Office, 1995.

Haskins, Jim. *African American Military Heroes.* New York: John Wiley and Sons, 1998.

Hastedt, Glenn P. *Spies, Wiretaps, and Secret Operations.* Santa Barbara, CA: ABC-CLIO, 2011.

Hastings, Max. *Inferno: The World at War, 1939–1945.* New York: Alfred A. Knopf, 2011.

Hatch, David A. "Juanita Moody." Cryptologic Almanac 50th Anniversary Series, May–June 2002.

Hatch, David A. "The Punitive Expedition Military Reform and Communications Intelligence." *Cryptologia* 31, no. 1 (2007): 38–45.

Hattersley, Roy. *Blood and Fire: The Story of William and Catherine Booth.* New York: Doubleday, 2000.

Haufler, Hervie. *Codebreakers' Victory: How the Allied Cryptographers Won World War II.* New York: New American Library, 2003.

Hawkins, Walter L. *African American Generals and Flag Officers: Biographies of over 120 Blacks in the United States Military.* Jefferson, NC: McFarland & Company, 1992.

Haynes, John Earl, and Harvey Klehr. *Early Cold War Spies: The Espionage Trials That Shaped American Politics.* New York: Cambridge University Press, 2006.

Haynes, John Earl, and Harvey Klehr. *Venona: Decoding Soviet Espionage in America.* New Haven, CT: Yale University Press, 1999.

Haynes, William F. *Sea Time: Life on Board Supply and Troop Ships during World War II and Its Aftermath.* Princeton, NJ: Darwin Press, 2007.

Haynsworth, Leslie, and David Toomey. *Amelia Earhart's Daughters: The Wild and Glorious Story of American Women Aviators from World War II to the Dawn of the Space Age.* New York: Harper, 2000.

Hays, Anna Mae. "Hays on Enlisting," "Hays on Korea," "Hays on the Draft," "Hays on India and Ledo Road," "Hays on Opportunities for Women in the Army," and "Hays on Vietnam." *Voices of the Past*, edited by Amelia J. Carson. Washington, D.C.: U.S. Army Senior Officer Oral History Program, 1983.

Heinemann, Sue. *Timelines of American Women's History.* New York: Penguin Group, 1996.

Henderson, Ashyia N., ed. *Contemporary Black Biography,* Vol. 27. Detroit, MI: Gale Group, 2001.

Hershberger, Mary. *Jane Fonda's War: A Political Biography of an Antiwar Icon.* New York: New Press, 2005.

Hershberger, Mary. *Jane Fonda's Words of Politics and Passion.* New York: New Press, 2006.

Higgins, Marguerite. *Our Vietnam Nightmare: The Story of U.S. Involvement in the Vietnamese Tragedy, with Thoughts on a Future Policy.* New York: Harper & Row, 1965.

Higgins, Marguerite, and Carl Mydans. *Red Plush and Black Bead.* Garden City, NY: Doubleday, 1955.

Higgins, Marguerite, and Carl Mydans. *War in Korea: The Report of a Woman Combat Correspondent.* Garden City, NY: Doubleday, 1951.

Hine, Darlene Clark. *Black Women in White: Racial Conflict and Cooperation in the Nursing Profession, 1890–1950.* Bloomington: Indiana University Press, 1989.

The History Project. *Improper Bostonians: Lesbian and Gay History from the Puritans to Playland.* Boston: Beacon Press, 1998.

Hoehling, A. A. *Women Who Spied.* Lanham, MD: Madison, 1993.

Hoganson, Kristin L. *Fighting for American Manhood: How Gender Politics Provoked the Spanish-American and Philippine-American Wars.* New Haven, CT: Yale University Press, 1998.

Holm, Jeanne. *In Defense of a Nation: Servicewomen in World War II.* St. Petersburg, FL: Vandamere Press, 1998.

Holm, Jeanne. *Women in the Military: An Unfinished Revolution.* Novato,

CA: Presidio Press, 1993; original publication, 1982.

Holmstedt, Kristen. *Band of Sisters: American Women at War in Iraq.* Mechanicsburg, PA: Stackpole Books, 2008.

Hopkins, Sarah Winnemucca. *Life among the Paiutes Their Wrongs and Claims.* Reno: University of Nevada Press, 1994; original publication, 1883.

Hopkins, Stella M. "Marine Officer Managing to Push Stereotypes Aside: Corps' First Woman Colonel Commands Largest Industrial Employer East of I-95." *The State,* April 28, 2000.

Hoppin, Christopher J. *Same Date of Rank: Grads from the Top and Bottom from West Point, Annapolis, and the Air Force Academy.* Bloomington, IN: Xlibris, 2010.

Horn, James. *A Land as God Made It: Jamestown and the Birth of America.* New York: Basic Books, 2005.

Horton, Mildred McAfee, et al. *The Reminiscences of the WAVES.* Annapolis, MD: U.S. Naval Institute, 1971–1979.

Howard, George. "The Desert Training Center/California-Arizona Maneuver Area." *Journal of Arizona History* 26, no. 3 (1985): 273–94.

Howard, Harold P. *Sacajawea.* Norman: University of Oklahoma Press, 1971.

Howe, Daniel Walker. *What Hath God Wrought: The Transformation of America, 1815–1848.* New York: Oxford University Press, 2007.

Howes, Ruth H., and Caroline L. Herzenberg. *Their Day in the Sun: Women of the Manhattan Project.* Philadelphia: Temple University Press, 1999.

Howlett, Charles, and Ian Harris. *Books, Not Bombs: Teaching Peace since the Dawn of the Republic*. Charlotte, NC: Information Age Publishing, 2010.

Howton, Elizabeth, "Page 4: One Woman's War." *Palo Alto Online*, August 9, 1995. http://www. paloaltoonline.com/weekly/morgue/ page4/1995_Aug_9.NOTES09.html, accessed March 15, 2012.

Hughes, Langston. *Famous American Negroes*. New York: Dodd, Mead & Company, 1954.

Hunt, Harold. *Transforming the Ranks: Black Female Sergeants Major*. Hanover, MD: Hunt Enterprises, 2008.

Hunter, Darren. "In Search of Molly Rinker." *Philadelphia History Examiner*, November 11, 2010.

Hunton, Addie W., and Kathryn M. Johnson. *Two Colored Women with the American Expeditionary Forces*. New York: G.K. Hall and Co., 1997.

Hurd, Charles. *The Compact History of the American Red Cross*. New York: Hawthorn Press, 1959.

Hutchinson, Kay Bailey. *Leading Ladies: American Trailblazers*. New York: Harper Collins, 2007.

Jack, Jordynn. *Science on the Home Front: American Women Scientists in World War II*. Urbana: University of Illinois Press, 2009.

Jackson, Grace. *Cynthia Ann Parker*. San Antonio, TX: Naylor, 1959.

Jackson, Kathi. *They Called Them Angels: American Military Nurses of World War II*. Lincoln: University of Nebraska Press, 2000.

Jackson, Kenneth T., Karen Markoe, and Arnold Markoe. *The Scribner Encyclopedia of American Lives*, Vol. 5. New York: Charles Scribner's Sons, 2001.

Jakobson, Pia Katarina. "Daughters of Liberty: Women and the American Revolution." In *Women's Rights: People and Perspectives*, edited by Christa DeLuzio, 35–56. Santa Barbara, CA: ABC-CLIO, 2010.

Jason, Sonya. *Maria Gulovich, OSS Heroine of World War II: The Schoolteacher Who Saved American Lives in Slovakia*. Jefferson, NC: McFarland, 2009.

Jefferds, Joseph C., Jr. *Captain Matthew Arbuckle: A Documentary Biography*. Charleston, WV: Education Foundation, 1981.

Jeffreys-Jones, Rhodri. *American Espionage*. New York: Free Press, 1977.

Jensen, Kimberly. "A Base Hospital Is Not a Coney Island Dance Hall." *Frontiers: A Journal of Women Studies* 26, no. 2 (2005): 206–35.

Jensen, Kimberly. *Mobilizing Minerva: American Women in the First World War*. Urbana: University of Illinois Press, 2008.

Johannsen, Robert Walter. *To the Halls of Montezumas: The Mexican War in American Imagination*. New York: Oxford University Press, 1998.

Johnsen, Frederick A. *B-24 Liberator: Rugged but Right*. New York: McGraw-Hill, 1999.

Johnson, Elmer L. *The History of YMCA Physical Education*. Chicago, IL: Association Press, 1979.

Johnson, Shoshana. *I'm Still Standing: From Captive U.S. Soldier to Free Citizen—My Journey Home*. New York: Touchstone, 2010.

Johnson, Shoshana, and M. L. Doyle. *I'm Still Standing: From Captive U.S. Soldier to Free Citizen—My Journey Home*. New York: Simon & Schuster, 2010.

Johnson, Susannah. *A Narrative of the Captivity of Mrs. Johnson*. Bowie, MD: Heritage Classic, 1990; original publication, 1796.

Johnson, Thomas, and Hatch, David. *NSA and the Cuban Missile Crisis*. Washington, D.C.: National Security Agency Center for Cryptologic History, 1998.

Jones, David E. *Women Warriors: A History.* Washington, D.C.: Brassey's, 1997.

Jones, Seth G. *In the Graveyard of Empires: America's War in Afghanistan.* New York: W. W. Norton & Co., 2009.

Jordan, Nehemiah. "U.S. Civil Defense before 1950: The Roots of Public Law 920." N.p.: Institute for Defense Analyses, May 1966.

Joseph, Antony. "Honoring Army Women." *Soldiers Magazine* 60, no. 8 (2005): 28–31.

Joslyn, Mauriel. *Confederate Women.* Gretna, LA: Pelican, 2004.

Kahn, David. *The Codebreakers: The Story of Secret Writing.* New York: Macmillan, 1967.

Kahn, David. *The Reader of Gentlemen's Mail: Herbert O. Yardley and the Birth of American Codebreaking.* New Haven, CT: Yale University Press, 2004.

Kalisch, Philip A. "Why Not Launch a New Cadet Nurse Corps?" *American Journal of Nursing* 88, no. 3 (1998): 316–17.

Kalisch, Philip A., and Margaret Scobey. "Female Nurses in American Wars: Helplessness Suspended for the Duration." *Armed Forces and Society* 9, no. 2 (1983): 215–44.

Katzenstein, Mary F. *Faithful and Fearless: Moving Feminist Protest inside the Church and Military.* Princeton, NJ: Princeton University Press, 1999.

Keegan, John. *The Iraq War.* New York: Vintage Books, 2005.

Keil, Sally Van Wagenen. *Those Wonderful Women in Their Flying Machines.* New York: Rawson, Wade, 1979.

Keller, Scott. *Marine Pride: A Salute to America's Elite Fighting Force.* Charleston, SC: Citadel Press, 2004.

Kennedy, Claudia J. "Redefining the Warrior Mentality: Women in the Military." In *Sisterhood Is Forever: The Women's Anthology for the New Millennium,* edited by Robin Morgan, 409–17. New York: Washington Square Press, 2003.

Kennedy, Claudia J., and Malcolm McConnell. *Generally Speaking.* New York: Warner Books, 2001.

Kennedy, David M. *Over There: The First World War and American Society.* New York: Oxford University Press, 1980.

Kephart-Sulit, Beth. "Anna Wagner Keichline: A Portrait of Pennsylvania's First Registered Female Architect." *Pennsylvania Architect* 5, no. 1 (Winter 1992).

Kerber, Linda. *No Constitutional Right to Be Ladies: Women and Obligations of Citizenship.* New York: Hill and Wang, 1998.

Kerber, Linda K. 1997. *Toward an Intellectual History of Women.* Chapel Hill: University of North Carolina Press.

Kerber, Linda K. *Women of the Republic: Intellect and Ideology in Revolutionary America.* Chapel Hill: University of North Carolina Press, 1980.

Kernodle, Portia B. *The Red Cross Nurse in Action 1882–1948.* New York: Harper and Brothers, 1949.

Kerr, Barbara. *Glimpses of Medford: Selections from the Historical Register.* Charleston, SC: History Press, 2007.

Kerr, Clark. *The Gold and the Blue: A Personal Memoir of the University of California, 1949–1967.* Vol. II, *Political Turmoil.* Berkeley: University of California Press, 2003.

Kerr, Thomas J. *Civil Defense in the U.S.: Bandaid for a Holocaust?* Boulder, CO: Westview Press, 1983.

Kessler, Lauren. *Clever Girl: Elizabeth Bentley, the Spy Who Ushered in the*

McCarthy Era. New York: Harper Collins, 2003.

Kierner, Cynthia A. *Southern Women in the Revolution, 1776–1800: Personal and Political Narratives*. Columbia: University of South Carolina Press, 1998.

Kilian, Michael. "Air Force, Lt. Flinn Put End to Ordeal, General Discharge Averts Court-Martial, Ends Military Career." *Chicago Tribune*, May 23, 1997.

Kimmel, Elizabeth Cody. *Ladies First: 40 Daring American Women Who Were Second to None*. Des Moines, IA: National Geographic Books, 2006.

Kinchen, Oscar A. *Women Who Spied for the Blue and the Gray*. Philadelphia: Dorrance & Company, 1972.

Klaver, Carol. "An Introduction to the Legend of Molly Pitcher." *Minerva: Quarterly Report on Woman and the Military* 12, no. 2 (1994): 35–61.

Klein, Laura F., and Lillian A. Ackerman, eds. *Women and Power in Native North America*. Norman: University of Oklahoma Press, 1995.

Kluger, Richard. *The Paper: The Life and Death of the New York Tribune*. New York: Alfred A. Knopf, 1986.

Knight, Louise W. *Jane Addams and the Struggle for Democracy*. Chicago, IL: University of Chicago Press, 2005.

Koch, Harriet Berger. *Militant Angel*. New York: Macmillan, 1951.

Kolata, Gina. *Flu: The Story of the Great Influenza Pandemic of 1918 and the Search for the Virus That Caused It*. New York: Farrar, Strauss and Giroux, 1999.

Kotcher, Joann P. *Donut Dolly: An American Red Cross Girl's War in Vietnam*. Denton: University of North Texas Press, 2011.

Lacy, Linda Cates. *We Are Marines!: World War I to the Present*. Swansboro, NC: Tarheel Chapter,

NC-1, Women Marines Association, 2004.

Lamarr, Hedy. *Ecstasy and Me: My Life as a Woman*. New York: Fawcett Crest Books, 1967.

Lancaster, Richard C. *Serving the U.S. Armed Forces, 1861–1986: The Story of the YMCA's Ministry to Military Personnel for 125 Years*. Springfield, VA: Armed Services YMCA, 1987.

"Land Army Described: Head of Women's Program Also Shows Model of Uniform." *New York Times*, May 11, 1943, 18.

Landdeck, Katherine Sharp. "Experiment in the Cockpit: The Women Airforce Service Pilots of World War II." In *The Airplane in American Culture*, edited by Dominick A. Pisano, 165–98. Ann Arbor: University of Michigan Press, 2003.

Langguth, A. J. *Union 1812: The Americans Who Fought the Second War of Independence*. New York: Simon & Schuster, 2007.

Lanker, Brian. *I Dream a World: Portraits of Black Women Who Changed America*. New York: Stewart, Tabori & Chang, 1989.

Larner, Brad, and Adrian Blow. "A Model of Meaning-Making Coping and Growth in Combat Veterans." *Review of General Psychology* 15, no. 3 (2011): 187–97.

Larson, C. Kay. "Bonnie Yank and Ginny Reb." *Minerva: Quarterly Report on Women and the Military* 8, no. 1 (1990): 35–61.

Larson, Kate Clifford. *Bound for the Promised Land: Harriet Tubman, Portrait of an American Hero*. New York: Ballantine Books, 2004.

Latty, Yvonne. *We Were There: Voices of African American Veterans, from World War II to the War in Iraq*. New York: HarperCollins, 2004.

Layton, Edwin. *And I Was There*. New York: William Morrow, 1985.

Lech, Raymond B. *Broken Soldiers.* Urbana: University of Illinois Press, 2000.

Lefkowitz, Arthur S. *Benedict Arnold's Army: The 1775 American Invasion of Canada during the Revolutionary War.* New York: Savas Beatie, 2008.

Lembcke, Jerry. *Hanoi Jane: War, Sex, and Fantasies of Betrayal.* Amherst: University of Massachusetts Press, 2010.

Leonard, Elizabeth D. *All the Daring of the Soldier: Women of the Civil War Armies.* New York: W. W. Norton & Company, 1999.

Leonard, Elizabeth D. *Yankee Women: Gender Battles in the Civil War.* New York: W. W. Norton & Company, 1994.

Leonard, Patrick J. "Ann Bailey: Mystery Woman Warrior of 1777." *Minerva* 11, no. 3 (1993): 1.

Lepore, Jill. *The Name of War: King Philip's War and the Origins of American Identity.* New York: Knopf, 1998.

Levine, Arnold. *Viruses.* New York: Scientific American Library, 1992.

Levine, Daniel. *Jane Addams and the Liberal Tradition.* Madison: Wisconsin History Society, 1971.

Levine, Suzanne Braun, and Mary Thom. *Bella Abzug.* New York: Farrar, Straus and Giroux, 2007.

Lewin, Ronald. *The American Magic: Codes, Ciphers, and the Defeat of Japan.* New York: Farrar, Strauss and Giroux, 1982.

Lewis, Ted. *Critical Infrastructure Protection in Homeland Security: Defending a Networked Nation.* Hoboken, NJ: John Wiley & Sons, 2006.

Lewis, Vicki, and Wilma L. Vaught. *Side-by-Side: A Photo History of American Women in the Military.* New York: Stewart, Tabori, and Chang, 1999.

Lewis, Virgil Anson. *Life and Times of Anne Bailey: The Pioneer Heroine of the Great Kanawha Valley.* Charleston, WV: Butler Printing Co., 1891.

Library of Congress. "Alene Duerk Collection." Veterans History Project. http://lcweb2.loc.gov/diglib/vhp/story/loc.natlib.afc2001001.28852/.

Lindberg, Kerrie G. "The History of the Air Force Nurse Corps from 1984 to 1998, a Research Paper." Maxwell Air Force Base, AL: Air War College, 1999.

Lippman, Thomas W. *Madeleine Albright and the New American Diplomacy.* Boulder, CO: Westview Press, 2000.

Lippmann, Helen Byrne. "The Future of the Red Cross Volunteer Nurse's Aide Corps." *American Journal of Nursing* 45, no. 10 (1945): 811–12.

Liptak, Eugene, and Richard Hook. *Office of Strategic Services, 1942–45: The World War II Origins of the CIA.* New York: Osprey Publishing, 2009.

Litoff, Judy Barrett, and David Clayton Smith. " 'To the Rescue of the Crops': The Women's Land Army during World War II." *Prologue* 25 (Winter 1993): 346–61.

Litoff, Judy Barrett, and David Clayton Smith, eds. *American Women in a World at War: Contemporary Accounts from World War II.* Lanham, MD: Rowman and Littlefield, 1997.

Little, Ann M. *Abraham in Arms: War and Gender in Colonial New England.* Philadelphia: University of Pennsylvania Press, 2007.

Loane, Nancy K. *Following the Drum: Women at the Valley Forge Encampment.* Dulles, VA: Potomac Books, 2009.

Long, Nancy Ann Zrinyi. *Life and Legacy of Mary McLeod Bethune.* Boston: Pearson, 2006.

Lookingbill, Brad D. *American Military History: A Documentary Reader.*

Malden, MA: John Wiley and Sons, 2010.

Loth, David. *A Long Way Forward: The Biography of Congresswoman Frances P. Bolton*. New York: Longmans, Green and Co., 1957.

Lowry, Beverly. *Harriet Tubman: Imagining a Life*. New York: Random House, 2007.

Lowry, Richard S. *Marines in the Garden of Eden: The True Story of Seven Bloody Days in Iraq*. New York: Berkley Trade, 2007.

Lowry, Thomas P. *Confederate Heroines: 120 Southern Women Convicted by Union Military Justice*. Baton Rouge: Louisiana State University Press, 2006.

Lujan, Susan. "Agnes Meyer Driscoll." *Cryptologia* 15 (January 1991): 47–56.

Lustick, Ian S. *Trapped in the War on Terror*. Philadelphia: University of Pennsylvania Press, 2006.

Lutz, Christine. "Addie W. Hunton: Crusader for Pan-Africanism and Peace." In *Portraits in African-American Life Since 1865*, edited by Nina Mjagkij, 109–27. Wilmington, DE: Scholarly Resources, 2003.

Lynch, Richard F. *The Past, Present and Future of Army Dietetics*. Carlisle Barracks, PA: U.S. Army War College, 1989.

Lyne, Mary C., and Kay Arthur. *Three Years behind the Mast: The Story of the United States Coast Guard SPARs*. Washington, D.C.: U.S. Coast Guard, 1946.

MacDonald, Anne M. *Feminine Ingenuity: Women and Invention in America*. New York: Ballantine Books, 1992.

MacDonald (McIntosh), Elizabeth. *Undercover Girl*. Arlington, VA: Time Life Books, 1993; original publication, 1947.

Mace, Nancy Mace. *In the Company of Men: A Woman at The Citadel*. New York: Simon and Schuster, 2002.

Maggiono, Ron. "Captain Sally Tompkins: Angel of the Confederacy." *OAH Magazine of History* 16, no. 2 (2002): 32–38.

Mahle, Melissa Boyle. *Denial and Deception: An Insider's View of the CIA from Iran-Contra to 9/11*. New York: Nation Books, 2004.

Mahoney, M. H. *Women in Espionage: A Biographical Dictionary*. Santa Barbara, CA: ABC-CLIO, 1993.

"Major Belle Reynolds." *New York Times*, March 15, 1896, 16.

Malone, Ann Patton. *Women on the Texas Frontier: A Cross-Culture Perspective*. El Paso: Texas Western Press, 1983.

Manegold, Catherine S. *In Glory's Shadow: The Citadel, Shannon Faulkner, and a Changing America*. New York: Random House, 2001.

"Marching into History." *Washington Times*, March 23, 1996 1.

"Marie Rossi." *People*, May 30, 1991.

Mariner, Rosemary. "The Military Needs Women." *Washington Post*, May 11, 1997, 7C.

Markle, Donald E. *Spies and Spymasters of the Civil War*, rev. ed. New York: Hippocrene Books, 2000.

Marsh, Thomas O., and Marlene Templin. "The Ballad of Lottie Moon." *Civil War: The Magazine of the Civil War Society* 21 (1988): 40–45.

Marshall, H. E. *Dorothea Dix, Forgotten Samaritan*. Chapel Hill: University of North Carolina Press, 1937.

Marshall, Kathryn. *In the Combat Zone: An Oral History of American Women in Vietnam, 1966–1975*. Boston, MA: Little, Brown, 1987.

Marshall, Max L. *The Story of the U.S. Army Signal Corps*. New York: F. Watts, 1965.

Marston, Daniel. *Essential Histories: The American Revolution, 1774–1783*. New York: Routledge, 2002.

"Martha Raye." In *Hollywood Songsters: Singers Who Act and Actors Who Sing: A Biographical Dictionary*, vol. 3, edited by James Robert Parrish and Michael Pitts, 712–19. New York: Routledge, 2003.

Martin, David G., ed. *A Molly Pitcher Sourcebook*. Hightstown, NJ: Longstreet House, 2003.

Marvel, William. *Burnside*. Chapel Hill: University of North Carolina Press, 1991.

"Mary Louise Prather." *Washington Post*, December 23, 1996.

Mason, John T. *The Atlantic War Remembered: An Oral History Collection*. Annapolis, MD: Naval Institute Press, 1990.

Massey, Mary Elizabeth. *Women in the Civil War*. Lincoln: University of Nebraska Press, 1993; original publication, 1966 as *Bonnet Brigades*.

Mather, Cotton. *Magnalia Christi Americana; or, The Ecclesiastical History of New-England from Its First Planting in the Year 1620, unto the Year of Our Lord, 1698: In Seven Books*. London: n.p., 1702.

Mauch, Christof. *The Shadow War against Hitler: The Covert Operations of America's Wartime Secret Intelligence Service*. New York: Columbia University Press, 2003.

Mauck, Elwyn A. "History of Civil Defense in the United States." *Bulletin of the Atomic Scientists* 6, nos. 8–9 (1950): 265–69.

Maxwell, William Quentin. *Lincoln's Fifth Wheel: The Political History of the United States Sanitary Commission*. New York: Longmans, Green & Company, 1956.

May, Antoinette. *Witness to War: A Biography of Marguerite Higgins*. New York: Penguin Books, 1985.

May, Elaine Tyler. *Homeward Bound: American Families in the Cold War Era*. New York: Basic Books, 1988.

Mayer, Holly A. *Belonging to the Army: Camp Followers and Community during the American Revolution*. Columbia: University of South Carolina Press, 1996.

McCabe, Katie, and Dovey Johnson Roundtree. *Justice Older Than the Law: The Life of Dovey Johnson Roundtree*. Jackson: University Press of Mississippi, 2009.

McClary, Ben Harris. "Nancy Ward, Beloved Woman." *Tennessee Historical Quarterly* 21 (December 1962): 352–64.

McClary, Ben Harris. *Nancy Ward: The Last Beloved Woman of the Cherokee*. Benton, TN: Polk County Publishers, 1996.

McConnell. Jane Foster. "Volunteer Nurse's Aides: Six Months Experience with Them." *American Journal of Nursing* 42, no. 5 (1942): 507–10.

McDoniel, Estelle. *Registered Nurse to Rear Admiral: A First for Navy Women*. Austin, TX: Eakin Press, 2003.

McElligott, Mary Ellen, ed. " 'A Monotony Full of Sadness': The Diary of Nadine Turchin, May, 1863–April 1864." *Journal of the Illinois State Historical Society* 70 (1977): 27–89.

McEnaney, Laura. *Civil Defense Begins at Home: Militarization Meets Everyday Life in the Fifties*. Princeton, NJ: Princeton University Press, 2000.

McGraw, Charles. "The Intervention of a Friendly Power: The Transnational Migration of Women's Work and the 1898 Imperial Imagination." *Journal of Women's History* 19, no. 3 (2007): 137–60.

McGuire, Colleen L. "Military-Media Relations and the Gulf War: A Compromise between Vietnam and Grenada?" Master's thesis, U.S. Army Command and General Staff College, 1992.

McGuire, Thomas J. *The Philadelphia Campaign*. Vol. 2, *Germantown and the Roads to Valley Forge*. Mechanicsburg, PA: Stackpole Books, 2007.

McIntosh, Elizabeth P. *The Role of Women in Intelligence*. McLean, VA: Association of Former Intelligence Officers, 1989.

McIntosh, Elizabeth P. *Sisterhood of Spies: The Women of the OSS*. New York: Random House, 1998.

McKee, William C. "Rear Admiral Fran McKee." In *Tennessee Encyclopedia of History and Culture*. Knoxville: University of Tennessee Press, 2010.

McKee, William C. "Fran McKee." In *Encyclopedia of Alabama*. January 7, 2009. http://www.encyclopediaofalabama .org/face/Article.jsp?id=h-1901, accessed February 20, 2012.

McSally, Martha E. "Defending America in Mixed Company: Gender in the U.S. Armed Forces." *Daedalus* 140, no. 3 (2011): 148–64.

Meacham, Alfred B. *Wi-ne-ma (The Woman Chief) and Her People*. Hartford, CT: American Publishing Company, 1876.

Meckling, William H. "Comment on 'Women and Minorities in the All-Volunteer Force.' " In *The All-Volunteer Force after a Decade: Retrospect and Prospect*, edited by Rodger Little, G. Thomas Sicilia, and William Bowman, 112. New York: Pergamon-Brassey's, 1986.

Medina, Jun. "Florence Ebersole Finch, a Living Fil-Am WWII Hero." *Philippine Mabuhay News* 19, no. 11 (March 11–17, 2011).

Medlicott., Alexander, Jr. "The Legend of Lucy Brewer: An Early American Novel." *New England Quarterly* 39, no. 4 (1966): 461–73.

Merritt, John G. *Historical Dictionary of the Salvation Army*. Lanham, MD: Scarecrow Press, 2006.

Merry, Lois K. *Women Military Pilots of World War II : A History with Biographies of American, British, Russian and German Aviators*. Jefferson, NC: McFarland & Company, 2010.

Merryman, Molly. *Clipped Wings: The Rise and Fall of the Women Airforce Service Pilots (WASP) of World War II*. New York: New York University Press, 1998.

Mershon, Sherie, and Steven Schlossman. *Foxholes and Color Lines: Desegregating the U.S. Armed Forces*. Baltimore, MD: Johns Hopkins University Press, 1998.

Meyer, Leisa D. *Creating GI Jane: Sexuality and Power in the Women's Army Corps during World War II*. New York: Columbia University Press, 1996.

Michigan Legislature House of Representatives. *Journal of the House of Representatives of the State of Michigan*. Volume 2. Lansing, MI: Wynkoop Hallenbeck Crawford Co., 1901

Middleton, Lee. *Hearts of Fire: Soldier Women of the Civil War*. Franklin, NC: Genealogy Publishing Service, 1993.

"Mildred McAfee Horton Dies; First Head of WAVES Was 94." *New York Times*, September 4, 1994.

Miles, Rosalind, and Robin Cross. *Hell Hath No Fury: True Profiles of Women at War from Antiquity to Iraq*. New York: Three Rivers Press, 2008.

Milkman, Ruth. *Gender at Work: The Dynamics of Job Segregation by Sex during World War II*. Urbana: University of Illinois Press, 1987.

Milks, Keith A. "Brewer Made Corps History When She Made General." *Army Times*, May 21, 2003.

Miller, Char. "In the Sweat of Our Brow: Citizenship in American Domestic Practice during WWII—Victory

Gardens." *Journal of American Culture* 26, no. 3 (2003): 395–409.

Minority Staff of the U.S. Senate Committee on Foreign Relations. *An Examination of US Policy towards POW/MIAs.* Washington, D.C.: U.S. Senate Committee on Foreign Relations, 1991.

Mithers, Carol Lynn Mithers. "Missing in Action: Women Warriors in Vietnam." *Cultural Critique* 3 (Spring 1986): 79–90.

Mjagkij, Nina, and Margaret Spratt, eds. *Men and Women Adrift: The YMCA and the YWCA in the City.* New York: New York University, 1997.

Moldow, Gloria. *Women Doctors in Gilded-Age Washington: Race, Gender, and Professionalization.* Urbana: University of Illinois Press, 1987.

Monahan, Evelyn M., and Rosemary Neidel-Greenlee. *A Few Good Women: America's Military Women from World War I to the Wars in Iraq and Afghanistan.* New York: Alfred A. Knopf, 2010.

Montag, C. J. "SSG Timothy Nein and the Convoy 678N Engagement." Fort Bliss, TX: United States Army Sergeants Major Academy, 2008–2009.

Moon, Virginia B. "Experiences of Virginia B. Moon, during the War between the States." Moon Collection. Oxford, OH: Smith Library of Regional History, n.d.

Mooney, James L. *Dictionary of American Naval Fighting Ships,* Volume 6. Washington, D.C.: Navy Department, Office of the Chief of Naval Operations, Naval History Division, 1976.

Moore, Brenda L. "African-American Women in the U.S. Military." *Armed Forces and Society* 17 (April 1991): 363–84.

Moore, Brenda L. *To Serve My Country, to Serve My Race: The Story of the Only African American WACS Stationed Overseas during WWII.* New York: New York University Press, 1996.

Moore, Frank. *Women of the War: Their Heroism and Self-sacrifice: True Stories of Brave Women in the Civil War.* Alexander, NC: Blue Gray Books, 1997; original publication, 1866.

Moorhead, Caroline. *Gellhorn: A Twentieth-Century Life.* New York: Henry Holt and Company, 2003.

Morden, Bettie J. *The Women's Army Corps, 1945–1978.* Washington, D.C.: Center of Military History, 1989.

Morgan, Paul W., Jr. "The Role of North-American Women in U.S. Cultural Chauvinism in the Panama Canal Zone, 1904–1945." PhD dissertation, Florida State University, 2000.

Mosher, Andy. "Blast Kills at Least 2 Marines, Injures 13." *Washington Post,* June 25, 2005, A16.

Mulhall, Erin. "Women Warriors: Supporting She 'Who Has Borne the Battle.' " *IAVA Issue Reports,* October 2009.

Murnane, Linda Strite. "Legal Impediments to Service: Women in the Military and the Rule of Law." *Duke Journal of Gender Law and Policy* 14 (2007): 1061–96.

Murray, Keith A. *The Modocs and Their War.* Norman: University of Oklahoma Press, 1959.

Murray, Pauli. *Song in a Weary Throat: An American Pilgrimage.* New York: Harper and Row, 1987.

Murray, Williamson, and Robert H. Scales Jr. *The Iraq War: A Military History.* Cambridge, MA: Belknap Press of Harvard University Press, 2005.

Mutter, Carol A. Interview by Charlayne Hunter-Gault. *Online Newshour: Women in the Military,* April 4, 1996. http://www.pbs.org/newshour/bb/

military/mutter_4-04.html, accessed March 15, 2012.

Namias, June. *White Captives: Gender and Ethnicity on the American Frontier.* Chapel Hill: University of North Carolina Press, 1993.

Nantais, Cynthia. "Women in the US Military: Protectors or Protected? The Case of Prisoner of War Melissa Rathbun-Nealy." *Journal of Gender Studies* 8, no. 2 (1999): 181.

Nathan, Amy. *Count on Us: American Women in the Military.* Washington, D.C.: National Geographic Society, 2004.

Nathan, Amy. *Take a Seat, Make a Stand: A Hero in the Family.* New York: iUniverse, 2006.

Nathan, Harriet. *Administration and Leadership: Katherine A. Towle.* Interview. University History Series. Berkeley: University of California, 2007. http://content.cdlib.org/ark:/13030/kt000000gm/, accessed May 20, 2010.

National Archives. "RG 15, Records of the Veterans Administration, Albert D.J. Cashier Pension File." Washington, D.C.: National Archives.

National Archives. "RG 94, Military Service Records and Medical Records of Albert Cashier." Washington, D.C.: National Archives.

National Security Agency. "Marie Meyer." Women in American Cryptology. http://www.nsa.gov/about/cryptologic_heritage/women/honorees/meyer.shtml, accessed January 24, 2012.

National Security Agency Central Security Service. "Elizebeth S. Friedman (1892–1980) 1999 Inductee." Hall of Honor, 2009. http://www.nsa.gov/about/cryptologic_heritage/hall_of_honor/1999/friedman_e.shtml, accessed March 13, 2012.

National Women's History Museum. "Red Cross." *Partners in Winning the War: American Women in World War II.* 2007. http://www.nwhm.org/online-exhibits/partners/exhibitentrance.html.

"Navy Names New Ship for Oceanographer Mary Sears." *Bulletin of the American Meteorological Society* 81, no. 2 (2000): 340.

Neidel-Greenlee, Rosemary, and Evelyn Monahan. *A Few Good Women: America's Military from World War I to the Wars in Iraq and Afghanistan.* Harpswell, ME: Anchor, 2010.

Neprud, Robert E. *Flying Minute Men: The Story of the Civil Air Patrol.* New York: Dell Sloan and Pierce, 1948.

New England Historic Genealogical Society. *The New England Historical and Genealogical Register for the Year 1860.* Boston, MA: Samuel G. Drake, 1860.

Nieberg, Michael S. *Making Citizen-Soldiers: ROTC and the Ideology of American Military Service.* Cambridge, MA: Harvard University Press, 2000.

Norman, Elizabeth M. *We Band of Angels: The Untold Story of American Nurses Trapped on Bataan by the Japanese.* New York: Random House, 1999.

Norman, Elizabeth M. *Women at War: The Story of Fifty Military Nurses Who Served in Vietnam.* Philadelphia: University of Pennsylvania Press, 1990.

Norton, David J. *Rebellious Younger Brother: Oneida Leadership and Diplomacy, 1750–1800.* DeKalb: Northern Illinois University Press, 2009.

Norton, Mary Beth. *Liberty's Daughters: The Revolutionary Experience of American Women, 1750–1800.* Boston, MA: Little, Brown, and Company, 1980.

Nouzille, Vincent. *L'espionne: Virginia Hall, une Americaine dans la guerre.* Paris, France: Fayard, 2007.

O'Hammon, Neal, and Richard Taylor. *Virginia's Western War.*

Mechanicsburg, PA: Stackpole Books, 2002.

O'Neil, Susan. *Don't Meaning Nothing.* Amherst: University of Massachusetts Press, 2004.

O'Neill, Ann Marie, et al. "Collins, Eileen (Eileen Marie), 1956." *People* 49, no. 18 (May 1998): 225.

O'Toole, G. J. A. *The Encyclopedia of American Intelligence and Espionage: From the Revolutionary War to the Present.* New York: Facts on File, 1988.

Oates, Stephen B. *Woman of Valor: Clara Barton and the Civil War.* New York: Free Press, 1995.

Obama, Barack. "Address to the Nation on the Way Forward in Afghanistan and Pakistan." West Point, NY, December 1, 2009.

Oberg, Barbara, ed. *The Papers of Benjamin Franklin*, 39 vols. New Haven, CT: Yale University Press, 1999.

Oberlin Alumni Magazine 14 (1917): 292.

O'Donnell, Patrick K. *Operatives, Spies, and Saboteurs: The Unknown Story of the Men and Women of World War II's OSS.* New York: Free Press, 2004.

Official WASP archive. Woman's Collection, Texas Woman's University, Denton.

Oliver, Kelly. *Women as Weapons of War: Iraq, Sex, and the Media.* New York: Columbia University Press, 2010.

Olmsted, Kathryn S. *Red Spy Queen: A Biography of Elizabeth Bentley.* Chapel Hill: University of North Carolina Press, 2002.

Opfell, Olga S. *The Lady Laureates: Women Who Have Won the Nobel Prize.* Metuchen, NJ: Scarecrow Press, 1977.

Ott, Victoria E. *Confederate Daughters: Coming of Age during the Civil War.* Carbondale: Southern Illinois University Press, 2008.

Owens v. Brown. 455 F.Supp. 291 (D.D.C. 1978).

Oxtra, Cristina. "Asian-Americans Have Long, Proud History in U.S. Military." *US Air Force Press Releases*, May 28, 2002.

Palmisano, Joseph M. *Notable Hispanic American Women.* Detroit, MI: Gale Research, 1998.

Pasachoff, Naomi E. *Frances Perkins: Champion of the New Deal.* New York: Oxford University Press, 1999.

Payment, Simone. *American Women Spies of World War II.* New York: Rosen Publishing, 2004.

Peare, Catherine Owens. *Mary McLeod Bethune.* New York: Vanguard Press, 1951.

Pearson, Judith L. *The Wolves at the Door: The True Story of America's Greatest Female Spy.* Guilford, CT: Lyon Press, 2005.

Pember, Phoebe Yates. *A Southern Woman's Story: Life in Confederate Richmond*, edited by Bell Irvin Wiley. Marietta, GA: McCowat-Mercer Press, 1954.

Pennypacker, Morton. *General Washington's Spies on Long Island and New York.* New York: Long Island Historical Society, 1939.

Perdue, Theda. *Cherokee Women: Gender and Culture Change, 1700–1835.* Lincoln: University of Nebraska Press, 1998.

Pérez, Louis A., Jr. *The War of 1898: The United States and Cuba in History and Historiography.* Chapel Hill: University of North Carolina Press, 1998.

Perkins, Francis. *The Roosevelt I Knew.* New York: Random House, 1946.

Perkins, Nancy J. "It's Already Been Done: Contexts of Achievement." *Innovation: Quarterly of the Industrial Designers Society of America*, Summer 2000.

Perry, Joellen. "We Must Find and Destroy Her." *US News and World Report*, January 27, 2003.

Petry, Lucile. "The U.S. Cadet Nurse Corps: A Summing Up." *American Journal of Nursing* 45, no. 12 (1945): 1027–28.

Petry, Lucile. "The U.S. Cadet Nurse Corps: Established under the Bolton Act." *American Journal of Nursing* 43, no. 8 (1943): 704–8.

Pfeiffer, Susan, and Ronald F. Williamson, eds. *Snake Hill: An Investigation of a Military Cemetery from the War of 1812*. Toronto, ON: Dundurn Press, 1991.

Piehler, G. Kurt. "The War Dead and the Gold Star: American Commemoration of the First World War." In *Commemorations: The Politics of National Identity*, edited by John R. Gillis, 168–85. Princeton, NJ: Princeton University Press, 1994.

Pinck, Dan. "Elizabeth P. McIntosh Receives Distinguished Service Award." *OSS Society Newsletter*, 2007. http://www.osssociety.org/pdfs/oss_summer_fall_07.pdf, accessed March 15, 2012.

Pinkerton, Allan. *The Spy of the Rebellion; Being a True History of the Spy System of the United States Army during the Late Rebellion*. New York: G. W. Carleton, 1883.

Pisano, Dominick. *To Fill the Skies with Pilots: The Civilian Pilot Training Program, 1939–46*. Urbana: University of Illinois Press, 1993.

Pitrone, Jean. *Take It from the Big Mouth: The Life of Martha Raye*. Lexington: University of Kentucky Press, 1999.

Plant, Rebecca Jo. *Mom: The Transformation of Motherhood in Modern America*. Chicago, IL: University of Chicago Press, 2010.

Plastas, Melinda. *A Band of Noble Women: Racial Politics in the Women's Peace Movement*. Syracuse, NY: Syracuse University Press, 2011.

Polimar, Norman. *The Naval Institute Guide to Ships and Aircraft of the U.S. Fleet*, 18th ed. Annapolis, MD: US Naval Institute, 2005.

Pope, Virginia. "Out of Uniform . . ." *New York Times*, November 8, 1942, SM30.

Poulos, Paula Nassen, ed. *A Woman's War, Too: U.S. Women in the Military in World War II*. Washington, D.C.: National Archives and Records Administration, 1996.

Powell, William Stevens. *Dictionary of North Carolina Biography*. Chapel Hill: University of North Carolina Press, 1979.

Poynter, Lida. "Dr. Mary Walker, M.D. Pioneer Woman Physician." *Medical Woman's Journal* 53, no. 10 (1946): 43–51.

Prados, John. *Combined Fleet Decoded*. New York: Random House, 1995.

"President Bush's Speech on Terrorism." *New York Times*, September 6, 2006.

Price, Virginia. "Advisors on Woman Power." *Independent Women*, June 1944.

Proctor, Tammy M. *Female Intelligence: Women and Intelligence in the First World War*. New York: New York University Press, 2003.

Pryor, Elizabeth Brown. *Clara Barton: Professional Angel*. Philadelphia: University of Pennsylvania Press, 1987.

Putney, Clifford. *Missionaries in Hawai'i: The Lives of Peter and Fanny Gulick, 1797–1883*. Amherst: University of Massachusetts Press, 2010.

Putney, Clifford. *Muscular Christianity: Manhood and Sports in Protestant America, 1880–1920*. Cambridge, MA: Harvard University Press, 2001.

Putney, Martha S. *When the Nation Was in Need: Blacks in the Women's Army*

Corps during World War II. Metuchen, NJ: Scarecrow Press, 1992.

Quindlen, Anna. "Public & Private: Women in Combat." *New York Times*, January 8, 1992.

Quinn, Arthur. *Hell with the Fire Out: A History of the Modoc War*. Boston, MA: Faber & Faber, 1997.

Raines, Rebecca Robbins. *Getting the Message Through: A Branch History of the U.S. Army Signal Corps*. Washington, D.C.: Center of Military History, 1996.

Ramsey, William L. *The Yamasee War: A Study of Culture, Economy, and Conflict in the Colonial South*. Lincoln: University of Nebraska Press, 2008.

Randall, Mercedes M. *Improper Bostonian: Emily Greene Balch*. New York: Twayne, 1964.

Randall, Mercedes M., ed. *Beyond Nationalism: The Social Thought of Emily Greene Balch*. New York: Twayne, 1972.

Rank, Melissa A. *What Influenced the Development of the Air Force Nurse Corps from 1969 through 1983*. Maxwell Air Force Base, AL: Air War College, 1999.

Rath, Elizabeth H. "ARC Volunteer Nurse's Aides: Their Preparation and Introduction to Service." *American Journal of Nursing* 42, no. 7 (1942): 788–92.

Read, Phyllis J., and Bernard L. Witlieb. *The Book of Women's Firsts: Breakthrough Achievements of Almost 1,000 American Women*. New York: Random House, 1992.

Reef, Catherine ed. *African Americans in the Military*, rev. ed. New York: Facts on File, 2010.

Reeves, Connie. *The History of the Air Force Nurse Corps*. N.p.: Amazon Digital Services, 2011.

Reports of Committees: 30th Congress, 1st Session–48th Congress, 2nd Session. Washington, D.C.: United States Printing Office, 1874.

Rhem, Kathleen T. "Military Undergoing 'Evolutionary Change' for Women in Service." *American Forces Press Service*, January 2005.

Rhodes, Jane. *Mary Ann Shadd Cary: The Black Press and Protest in the Nineteenth Century*. Bloomington: Indiana University Press, 1998.

Rich, Doris L. *Jackie Cochran: Pilot in the Fastest Lane*. Gainesville: University Press of Florida, 2007.

Richter, Daniel K. "War and Culture: The Iroquois Experience." *William and Mary Quarterly* 40, no. 4 (1983): 528–59.

Rickman, Sarah Byrn. *Nancy Love and the WASP Ferry Pilots of World War II*. Denton: University of North Texas Press, 2008.

Rickman, Sarah Byrn. *The Originals: The Women's Auxiliary Ferrying Squadron of World War II*. Sarasota, FL: Disc-Us Books, 2001.

Ricks, Thomas. *Fiasco: The American Military Adventure in Iraq, 2003 to 2005*. New York: Penguin, 2007.

Riddle, Jeff C. *The Indian History of the Modoc War and the Causes That Led to It*. San Francisco, CA: Marnell and Co., 1914.

Rielage, Lisa. "Enlisting the Aid of Yeomanettes." *Cobblestone* 27, no. 3 (2006): 16–18.

Riva, Maria. *Marlene Dietrich*. New York: Alfred A. Knopf, 1993.

Robertson, Nancy Marie. *Christian Sisterhood, Race Relations, and the YWCA, 1906–1946*. Urbana: University of Illinois Press, 2007.

Robinson, Guy, and Phil Lucas. *From Warriors to Soldiers: The History of Native American Service in the United States Military*. Bloomington, IN: iUniverse, 2010.

Robinson, Thelma M. *Your Country Needs You: Cadet Nurses of World War II*. Bloomington, IN: Xlibris Corporation, 2009.

Roca, Steven Louis. "Presence and Precedents: The USS *Red Rover* during the American Civil War, 1861–1865." *Civil War History* 44, no. 2 (1998): 91–110.

Rollyson, Carl. *Beautiful Exile: The Life of Martha Gellhorn*. Lincoln, NE: iUniverse, 2001.

Ronda, James P. *Lewis and Clark among the Indians*. Lincoln: University of Nebraska Press, 1988.

Roosevelt, Eleanor. *The Autobiography of Eleanor Roosevelt*. New York: De Capo Press, 2000.

Rose, Alexander. *Washington's Spies: The Story of America's First Spy Ring*. New York: Bantam, 2006.

Rosenberg-Naparsteck, Ruth. "The Legacy of Mary Jemison." *Rochester History* 68, no. 1 (2006): 1–32.

Rossiter, Margaret W. *Women Scientists in America: Struggles and Strategies to 1940*. Baltimore, MD: Johns Hopkins University Press, 1984.

Rostker, Bernard D. *I Want You!: The Evolution of the All-Volunteer Force*. Santa Monica, CA: RAND, 2006.

Roth, Michael. *Historical Dictionary of War Journalism*. Westport, CT: Greenwood Press, 1997.

Rowlandson, Mary. *The Sovereignty & Goodness of God, Together with the Faithfulness of His Promises Displayed: Being a Narrative of the Captivity and Restoration of Mrs. Mary Rowlandson, ...* Cambridge, MA: 1682. Reprinted as *The Captive* with an introduction by Mark Ludwig. Tucson, AZ: American Eagle Publications, 1992.

Rozwadowski, Helen M., and David K. Van Keuren, eds. *The Machine in Neptune's Garden: Historical Perspectives on Technology and the Marine Environment*. Nantucket, MD: Watson Publications International, 2004.

Ruíz, Vicki, and Virginia Sánchez Korrol, eds. *Latina Legacies: Identity, Biography, and Community*. New York: Oxford University Press, 2005.

Rupp, Leila J. *Mobilizing Women for War: German and American Propaganda, 1939–1945*. Princeton, NJ: Princeton University Press, 1978.

Ryan, Cheyney. *The Chickenhawk Syndrome: War, Sacrifice, and Personal Responsibility*. Lanham, MD: Rowman & Littlefield, 2009.

Ryan, David, ed. *A Yankee Spy in Richmond: The Civil War Diary of "Crazy Bet" Van Lew*. Mechanicsburg, PA: Stackpole Books, 1996.

Ryan, Kathy L., Jack A. Loeppky, and Donald E. Kilgore Jr. "A Forgotten Moment in Physiology: The Lovelace Woman in Space Program." *Advances in Physiology Education* 33 (September 2009): 157–64.

Ryan, Maria. " 'War in Countries We Are Not at War With': The 'War on Terror' on the Periphery from Bush to Obama." *International Politics* 48, nos. 2–3 (2011): 364–89.

Ryan, Michael D. *Concord and the Dawn of Revolution: The Hidden Truths*. Charleston, SC: History Press, 2007.

Sadler, Christine. "Nurses' Morale Bubbling Over." *Washington Post*, August 15, 1943, B4.

Sadler, Georgia Clark. "Women in Combat: The U.S. Military and the Impact of the Persian Gulf War." In *Wives and Warriors: Women in the Military in the United States and Canada*, edited by Laurie Weinstein and Christie C. White, 79–97. Westport, CT: Bergin and Garvey, 1997.

Sandwich, Brian. *The Great Western: Legendary Lady of the Southwest.* El Paso: Texas Western, 1921.

Sarmiento, Ferdinand L. *Life of Pauline Cushman, the Celebrated Union Spy and Scout.* Philadelphia, PA: John E. Potter and Company, 1865.

Sarnecky, Mary T. *A Contemporary History of the U.S. Army Nursing Corps.* Washington, D.C.: Government Printing Office, 2010.

Sarnecky, Mary T. *A History of the U.S. Army Nurse Corps: Studies in Health, Illness, and Care-giving in America.* Philadelphia: University of Pennsylvania Press, 1999.

Scharf, Lois. *Eleanor Roosevelt: First Lady of American Liberalism.* Boston, MA: Twayne, 1987.

Scheller, Robert John, Jr., and Mary Strange. *Breaking the Color Barrier: The US Naval Academy's First Black Midshipmen and the Struggle for Racial Equality.* New York: New York University Press, 2005.

Schneider, Dorothy, and Carl J. Schneider. *Into the Breach: American Women Overseas in World War I.* New York: Viking, 1991.

Schoultz, Lars. *Beneath the United States: A History of U.S. Policy towards Latin America.* Cambridge, MA: Harvard University Press, 1998.

Schrader, Helena. *Sisters in Arms: British and American Women Pilots during World War II.* Barnsley, South Yorkshire, UK: Pen and Sword Books, 2006.

Schubert, Frank N. *The Whirlwind War: The United States in Operation Desert Shield and Desert Storm.* Washington, D.C.: CMH Publications, 1995.

Schultz, Jane E. *Women at the Front: Hospital Workers in Civil War America.* Chapel Hill: University of North Carolina Press, 2004.

Schuyler, Constance B. "Clara Louise Maass." In *Past and Promise: Lives of New Jersey Women*, edited by Joan Burstyn, 166–67. Syracuse, NY: Syracuse University Press, 1997.

Schwartz, Heather E. *Women of the U.S. Air Force: Aiming High.* North Mankato, MN: Capstone Press, 2011.

Sciolino, Elaine, and Shenon, Philip. "Much Anguish on Both Sides in Pilot's Case." *New York Times*, May 25, 1997.

Scoggins, Michael C. *The Day It Rained Militia: Huck's Defeat and the Revolution in the South Carolina Backcountry, May–July 1780.* Charleston, SC: History Press, 2005.

Scott, Robert N. *The War of the Rebellion: A Compilation of the Official Records of the Union and Confederate Armies*, Series II, Vol. 5. Harrisburg, PA: National Historical Society, 1985.

Seagrave, Ann. *High Spirited Women of the West.* Lakeport, CA: Wesanne Publishers, 1992.

Sears, Mary, ed. *Oceanography: Invited Lectures Presented at the International Oceanographic Conference.* Washington, D.C.: American Association for the Advancement of Science, 1961.

Sears, Mary, and Daniel Merriman, eds. *Oceanography: The Past: Proceedings of the Third International Congress on the History of Oceanography.* New York: Springer-Verlag, 1980.

Seaver, James. *A Narrative of the Life of Mrs. Mary Jemison*, edited and with introduction by June Namias. Norman: University of Oklahoma Press, 1992.

Serving in Silence: The Margarethe Cammermeyer Story. Culver City, CA: Sony Pictures Home Entertainment, 2006.

Sewell, Leslie, dir. *The Government Girls of World War II.* Documentary film, 2004.

Shapiro, Laura. *Julia Child.* New York: Lipper, Viking Group, 2007.

Shattuck, Lemuel. *Memorials of the Descendants of William Shattuck.* Boston, MA: Dutton and Wentworth, 1855.

Shattuck, Mary L. P. *Prudence Wright and the Women Who Guarded the Bridge: The Story of Jewett's Bridge.* Nashua, NH: Wheeler Press, 1899.

Shearer, Benjamin F. *Home Front Heroes: A Biographical Dictionary of Americans during Wartime.* Westport, CT: Greenwood Press, 2007.

Sheffield, Suzanne Le-May. *Women and Science: Social Impact and Interaction.* Santa Barbara, CA: ABC-CLIO, 2004.

Sherrow, Victoria. *Women and the Military: An Encyclopedia.* Santa Barbara, CA: ABC-CLIO, 1996.

Shibata, Shingo. *Phoenix: Letters and Documents of Alice Herz: Thought and Practice of a Modern-day Activist.* New York: Bruce Publishing Co., 1969.

Shields, Elizabeth A. *Highlights in the History of the Army Nurse Corps.* Washington, D.C.: Government Printing Office, 1981.

Shilts, Randy. *Conduct Unbecoming: Lesbians and Gays in the U.S. Military—Vietnam to the Persian Gulf.* New York: St. Martin's Press, 1993.

Shockley, Megan Taylor. *"We, Too, Are Americans": African American Women in Detroit and Richmond, 1940–1954.* Urbana: University of Illinois Press, 2004.

Shrady, George Frederick, and Thomas Lathrop Stedman. *Medical Record 91.* New York: William Wood and Company, 1917.

Sicherman, Barbara, and Carol Hurd Green. *Notable American Women: The Modern Period: A Biographical Dictionary*, Vol. 4. Cambridge, MA: Radcliffe College, 1980.

Sifry, Micah, and Christopher Cerf, eds. *The Gulf War Reader.* New York: Three Rivers Press, 1991.

Silber, Nina. *Daughters of the Union: Northern Women Fight the Civil War.* Cambridge, MA: Harvard University Press, 2005.

Silverman, Jonathan. *For the World to See: The Life of Margaret Bourke-White.* New York: The Viking Press, 1983.

Simkins, Francis Butler, and James Welch Patton. *The Women of the Confederacy.* Richmond, VA: Garrett & Massie, 1936.

"Six Hello Girls Help First Army." *Stars and Stripes*, October 4, 1918.

Skaine, Rosemarie. *Women at War: Gender Issues of Americans in Combat.* Jefferson, NC: McFarland & Company, 1999.

Smith, Alfred Emanuel, Francis Rufus Bellamy, and Harold Trowbridge Pulsifer, eds. *The Outlook.* New York: Outlook, 1917.

Smith, Donald George Jr. "A Study of the Persian Gulf War as a Catalyst for Change in the Air Force Nurse Corps' Clinical and Deployment Readiness." PhD dissertation, New York University, 2003.

Smith, Jill Halcomb. *Dressed for Duty: America's Women in Uniform 1898–1973*, Vol 1. San Jose, CA: R. J. Bender, 2001.

Smith, Orphia. *Oxford Spy: Wed at Pistol Point.* Oxford, OH: Cullen Printing Co., 1962.

Smolenski, Mary C., Donald G. Smith Jr., and James Nanney. "A Fit, Fighting Force: The Air Force Nursing Services Chronology." Washington, D.C.: Office of the Air Force Surgeon General, 2005.

Smoot, Betsy R. "An Accidental Cryptologist: The Brief Career of Genevieve Young Hitt." *Cryptologia* 35, no. 2 (2011): 164–75.

Smoot, Betsy R. "Pioneers of U.S. Military Cryptology: Colonel Parker Hitt and His Wife, Genevieve Young

Hitt." *Federal History* 4 (2012): 87–100.

Snead, Alice. Interview by Luann Mims. Transcript. William Madison Randall Library, Wilmington, NC, 2004.

Snyder, Charles McCool. *Dr. Mary Walker: The Little Lady in Pants*. New York: Arno Press, 1974.

Socha, Rudy. *Above & Beyond: Former Marines Conquer the Civilian World*. Paducah, KY: Turner Publishing Company, 2010.

Southall, Sally. *Hold the Line Please: The Story of the Hello Girls*. Studley, UK: Brewin Books, 2003.

Spoto, Donald. *Blue Angel: The Life of Marlene Dietrich*. New York: Doubleday, 1992.

St. George, Judith. *Sacagawea*. New York: Putnam, 1997.

Stallard, Patricia Y. *Glittering Misery: Dependents of the Indian Fighting Army*. Norman: University of Oklahoma Press, 1992.

Stallings, William. *Data and Computer Communications*. Upper Saddle River, NJ: Pearson Communications, 2007.

Stallman, David A. *Women in the Wild Blue: Target-Towing WASP at Camp Davis*. Sugarcreek, OH: Carlisle Printing, 2006.

Standage, L. Sue. *A Role for the Army Medical Specialist Corps in Nation Assistance*. Carlisle Barracks, PA: U.S. Army War College, 1993.

Stanton, Edward F. *Contemporary Hispanic Quotations*. Westport, CT: Greenwood, 2003.

Steele, Ian K. "Susannah Johnson, Captive." In *The Human Tradition in Colonial America*, edited by Ian K. Steele and Nancy L. Rhoden, 257–71. Wilmington, DE: Scholarly Resources, 1999.

Steele, Ian K. *Warpaths: Invasions of North America*. New York: Oxford University Press, 1994.

Steinson, Barbara J. *American Women's Activism in World War I*. New York: Garland, 1982.

Stevens, Peter F. *Rebels in Blue: The Story of Keith and Malinda Blalock*. Dallas, TX: Taylor, 2000.

Stevenson, William. *A Man Called Intrepid: The Incredible WWII Narrative of the Hero Whose Spy Network and Secret Diplomacy Changed the Course of History*. Guilford, CT: Lyons Press, 2000.

Stewart, Patricia. "Sarah Winnemucca." *Nevada Historical Society Quarterly* 14 (Winter 1971): 23–37.

Stiehm, Judith Hicks. "Women, Men, and Military Service: Is Protection Necessarily a Racket?" In *Women Power and Policy*, edited by Ellen Boneparth, 282–95. New York: Pergamon Press, 1982.

Stiehm, Judith Hicks. *Arms and the Enlisted Woman*. Philadelphia, PA: Temple University Press, 1989.

Stimson, Julia C. *Finding Themselves: The Letters of an American Army Chief Nurse in a British Hospital in France*. New York: Macmillan Company, 1918.

Strebe, Amy Goodpaster. *Flying for Her Country: The American and Soviet Women Military Pilots of World War II*. Dulles, VA: Potomac Books, 2009.

Stremlow, Mary V. *A History of the Women Marines, 1946–1977*. Washington, D.C.: Government Printing Office, 1986.

Stremlow, Mary V. *Free a Marine to Fight: Women Marines in World War II*. Washington, D.C.: History and Museum Division Headquarters, U.S. Marine Corps, 1996.

Stremlow, Mary V. *U.S. Marine Corps Women's Reserve: A History of the Women Marines, 1946–1977*. Washington, D.C.: U.S. Marine Corps, 1986.

Stroh, Oscar. *Thompson's Battalion and/ or the First Continental Regiment*.

Harrisburg, PA: Graphic Services, 1975.

Strum, Philippa. *Women in the Barracks: The VMI Case and Equal Rights.* Lawrence: University Press of Kansas, 2002.

Stuart, Nancy Rubin. *Muse of the Revolution: The Secret Pen of Mercy Otis Warren and the Founding of a Nation.* Boston, MA: Beacon Press, 2006.

Stutz, Douglas H. "Critical Care Skill in Fallujah Brings NHB Nurse Recognition." *Navy Medicine* 99, no. 3 (2008): 17–18.

Sudlow, Lynda L. *The Fifth Maine Regiment Community Building: A History.* Portland, ME: Arlington Street Press, 1992.

Sullivan, Jill M. *Bands of Sisters: U.S. Women's Military Bands during World War II.* Lanham, MD: Scarecrow Press, 2011.

Sullivan, Joseph F. "Army Pilot's Death Stuns Her New Jersey Neighbors." *New York Times*, March 7, 1991.

Sullivan, Regina Diane. "Woman with a Mission: Remembering Lottie Moon and the Woman's Missionary Union." PhD dissertation, University of North Carolina, Chapel Hill, 2002.

Swarns, Rachel L. "Commanding a Role for Women in the Military." *New York Times*, June 30, 2008.

Swarns, Rachel L. "A Step Up for Women in the U.S. Military." *International Herald Tribune*, November 22, 2008.

Sweetman, Jack. *American Naval History: An Illustrated Chronology of the U.S. Navy and Marine Corps, 1775–Present.* Annapolis, MD: Naval Institute Press, 2002.

Swerdlow, Amy. *Women Strike for Peace: Traditional Motherhood and Radical Politics in the 1960s.* Chicago, IL: University of Chicago Press, 1993.

Taiz, Lillian. *Hallelujah Lads and Lasses: Remaking the Salvation Army in America, 1880–1930.* Chapel Hill: University of North Carolina Press, 2000.

Tanner, Stephen. *Afghanistan: A Military History from Alexander the Great to the War against the Taliban.* New York: Da Capo Press, 2009.

Taylor, Alan. *American Colonies.* New York: Penguin Press, 2001.

Taylor, Amy Murrell. *The Divided Family in Civil War America.* Chapel Hill: University of North Carolina Press, 2005.

Taylor, Ethel Barol. "Women Strike for Peace." In *Modern American Women: A Documentary History*, edited by Susan Ware, 217–19. New York: McGraw-Hill, 1996.

Taylor, Susie King. *Reminiscences of My Life in Camp.* New York: Arno Press & New York Times, 1968.

Teipe, Emily J. "Will the Real Molly Pitcher Please Stand Up?" *Prologue: Quarterly of the National Archives Records Administration* 31, no. 2 (1999): 118–26.

Telgen, Diane, and Jim Kamp, eds. *Notable Hispanic American Women*, Vol. 68. Detroit, MI: Gale Research, 1993.

Thomas, Earle. *The Three Faces of Molly Brant.* Kingston, ON: Quarry Press, 1996.

Thompson, Mark. "Aye, Aye, Ma'am." *TIME*, March 2000.

Thomson, Robin J. *The Coast Guard and the Women's Reserve in World War II.* Washington, D.C.: Coast Guard, 1992.

Tilley, John A. *A History of Women in the Coast Guard.* Washington, D.C.: U.S. Coast Guard, 1996.

Tischler, Barbara. "The Antiwar Movement." In *A Companion to the Vietnam War*, edited by Marilyn B.

Young and Robert Buzzanco, 384–402. Malden, MA: Blackwell, 2006.

Tomblin, Barbara Brooks. *G.I. Nightingales: The Army Nurse Corps in World War II*. Lexington: University Press of Kentucky, 1996.

Tousignant, Marylou. "A New Era for the Old Guard: Woman Joins Elite Ranks of Soldiers Tending Tomb of the Unknowns." *Washington Post*, March 23, 1996, C01.

Treadway, Sandra Gioia. "Anna Maria Lane: An Uncommon Common Soldier of the American Revolution." *Virginia Cavalcade* 37, no. 3 (1988): 134–43.

Treadwell, Mattie E. *United States Army in World War II, Special Studies: The Women's Army Corps*. Washington, D.C.: Center of Military History, United States Army, 1953.

Treadwell, Mattie E. *The Women's Army Corps: United States Army in World War II*. Washington, D.C.: Office of the Chief of Military History, Department of the Army, 1954.

Trott, Lona L. "It's Good that You Want to Help! The Red Cross Nurse's Aide Corps." *American Journal of Nursing* 40, no. 12 (1940): 1355–57.

Tsui, Bonnie. *She Went to the Field: Women Soldiers of the Civil War*. Guildford, CT: TwoDot, 2003.

Tucker, Eric. "Rhode Island Marine Killed in Iraq Bombing." Associated Press. http://militarytimes.com/valor/marine-lance-cpl-holly-a-charette/941127, accessed March 15, 2012.

Tucker, Phillip Thomas. *Cathy Williams: From Slave to Buffalo Soldier*. Mechanicsburg, PA: Stackpole Books, 2002.

Tufty, Esther Van Wagoner. "Durand's Margaret Brewer Will Retire from Marines." *Argus-Press*, June 9, 1980, 13.

Turner, Bernice. Interview. Savannah, GA, October 9, 2010.

Tyson, Ann Scott. "Army Promotes Its First Female Four-Star General." *Washington Post*, November 15, 2008.

Tyson, Ann Scott. "Woman Gains Silver Star—and Removal from Combat." *Washington Post*, May 1, 2008.

U.S. Army. *Army Medical Specialist Corps: The Army Health Care Team*. Washington, D.C.: Department of the Army, 1990.

U.S. Army. *Pamphlet 611-21. Personnel Selection and Classification. Military Occupational Classification and Structure*. Washington, D.C.: Department of the Army, 2007.

U.S. Army Center of Military History. *Highlights in the History of the Army Nurse Corps*. Washington, D.C.: U.S. Army Center of Military History, 1995.

U.S. Army Medical Department, Office of Medical History. "Embracing the Past: First Chief, Army Nurse Corps Turns 90! Brigadier General Anna Mae V. McCabe Hays." U.S. Army Medical Department Office of Medical History, March 11, 2011. http://history.amedd.army.mil/HaysBio/HayesBio.html, accessed February 20, 2012.

U.S. Army Medical Specialist Corps. *The Army Medical Specialist Corps, 1917–1971*. Washington, D.C.: U.S. Government Printing Office, 1972.

U.S. Army Women's Museum. "WAC Training Center at Fort Lee, Virginia, 1948–1954." http://www.awm.lee.army.mil/research_pages/wac_lee.htm, accessed February 16, 2012.

U.S. Center for Cryptologic History. *The Origins of NSA*. Fort George G. Meade, MD: Center for Cryptologic History, 1996.

U.S. Coast Guard. *Women in the Coast Guard Study*. Commandant Publication 5312.17. Prepared by the U.S. Coast Guard in cooperation with the Defense Advisory Committee on

Women in the Services and the Department of Transportation, 1990.

U.S. Coast Guard Historian's Office. "Florence Ebersole Smith Finch, USCGR (W): Coast Guard SPAR Decorated for Combat Operations during World War II." United States Coast Guard, January 26, 2012.

U.S. Congress. *Congressional Record.* 77th Cong., 2nd sess. (1942), Vol. 87.

U.S. Congress. House. *Honoring Brigadier General Hazel Winifred Johnson-Brown.* 112th Cong., H.R. 88, 2005.

U.S. General Accounting Office. *Women in the Military: Deployment in the Persian Gulf War.* NSIAD-93-93. Washington, D.C.: General Accounting Office, July 1993.

U.S. War Manpower. Commission, Women's Advisory Committee. *The Wartime Responsibility of Women's Organizations.* January 1994.

Ulannoff, Stanley M. *MATS: The Story of the Military Air Transport Service.* New York: Moffa Press, 1964.

Ulrich, Laurel Thatcher. *The Age of Homespun.* New York: Alfred A. Knopf, 2001.

Ulrich, Laurel Thatcher. " 'Daughters of Liberty': Religious Women in Revolutionary New England." In *Women in the Age of the American Revolution*, edited by Ronald Hoffman and Peter J. Albert, 211–43. Charlottesville: University Press of Virginia, 1989.

Ulrich, Laurel Thatcher. *Good Wives: Image and Reality in the Lives of Women in Northern New England, 1650–1750.* New York: Knopf, 1982.

"Uncle Sam Presents 'Hello Girls!' " *Stars and Stripes*, March 29, 1918.

Utley, Robert Marshall. *Frontier Regulars: The United States Army and the Indian, 1866–1891.* New York: Macmillan, 1974.

Utley, Robert Marshall. *Frontiersmen in Blue: The United States Army and the Indian, 1848–1865.* Lincoln: University of Nebraska Press, 1981.

Vairo, Sharon A. "History of the United States Air Force Nurse Corps, 1949–1954." Doctor of Nursing Science dissertation, University of San Diego, Philip Y. Hahn School of Nursing, 1998.

Van Devanter, Lynda. *Home before Morning: The Story of an Army Nurse in Vietnam.* New York: Warner Books, 1983.

Van Devanter, Lynda, and Joan A. Furey, eds. *Visions of War, Dreams of Peace: Writings of Women in the Vietnam War.* New York: Warner Books, 1991.

Van Vugt, William E. *British Buckeyes: The English, Scots, and Welsh in Ohio, 1700–1900.* Kent, OH: Kent State University Press, 2006.

Varon, Elizabeth R. *Southern Lady, Yankee Spy: The True Story of Elizabeth Van Lew, a Union Agent in the Heart of the Confederacy.* New York: Oxford University Press, 2003.

Vaught, Wilma L. *The Day the Nation Said "Thanks!" A History and Dedication Scrapbook of the Women in Military Service for America Memorial.* Washington, D.C.: Military Women's Press, 1999.

Verges, Marianne. *On Silver Wings: The Women Airforce Service Pilots of World War II.* New York: Ballantine Books, 1991.

Veterans History Project. Elizabeth McIntosh interview by Leslie Sewell. 2004. http://lcweb2.loc.gov/diglib/vhp/story/loc.natlib.afc2001001.30838/, accessed February 1, 2012.

Vietor, Agnes C. *A Woman's Quest: The Life of Marie E. Zakrzewska, M.D.* New York: D. Appleton & Co., 1924.

Villahermosa, Gilberto. "America's Hispanics in America's Wars." *Army Magazine*, September 2002.

Viola, Herman, and Ben N. Campbell. *Warriors in Uniform: The Legacy of American Indian Heroism.* New York: National Geographic, 2008.

"Virginia Goillot, of French Resistance, Dies." *Baltimore Sun*, July 13, 1982.

Vistica, Gregory L. "Sex and Lies." *Newsweek*, June 2, 1997.

Voices of Valor. "Semper Paratus: Coast Guard Woman Is Always Ready— Even in a War Zone." Washington, D.C.: Women in Military Service for America Memorial Foundation, March 2008.

Vuic, Kara Dixon. *Officer, Nurse, Woman: The Army Nurse Corps in the Vietnam War*. Baltimore, MD: Johns Hopkins University Press, 2009.

Waisman, Charlotte S., and Jill S. Tietjen. *Her Story: A Timeline of the Women Who Changed America*. New York: Harper, 2008.

Walker, Keith. *A Piece of My Heart: The Stories of 26 American Women Who Served in Vietnam*. Novato, CA: Presidio Press, 1997.

Walters, Rob. *Spread Spectrum: Hedy Lamarr and the Mobile Phone*. Seattle, WA: BookSurge, 2006.

Ward, Harry M. *For Virginia and for Independence: Twenty-Eight Revolutionary War Soldiers from the Old Dominion*. Jefferson, NC: McFarland & Company, 2011.

Warren, Edward. *A Doctor's Experiences in Three Continents*. Baltimore, MD: Cushings and Bailey, 1885.

Waugh, Charles G., and Martin H. Greenberg, eds. *The Women's War in the South: Recollections and Reflections of the American Civil War*. Nashville, TN: Cumberland House, 1999.

Weatherford, Doris. *American Woman and World War II*. Edison, NJ: Castle Books, 1990; reprint, 2008.

Webster, Raymond. *African American Firsts in Science and Technology*. Detroit, MI: Gale Cengage, 1999.

Weinstein, Laurie Lee, and Christie C. White, eds. *Wives and Warriors:*

Women in the Military in the United States and Canada. Westport, CT: Bergin and Garvey, 1997.

Weisenfeld, Judith. *African American Women and Christian Activism: New York's Black YWCA, 1905–1945*. Cambridge, MA: Harvard University Press, 1997.

Weiss, Cora. *There's Hope*. New York: Pilgrim Press, 1981.

Weiss, Elaine F. *Fruits of Victory: The Woman's Land Army of America in the Great War*. Washington, D.C.: Potomac Books, 2008.

Weitekamp, Margaret A. *Right Stuff, Wrong Sex: America's First Women in Space Program*. Baltimore, MD: Johns Hopkins University Press, 2004.

Wensyl, James. "Captain Molly." *Army* 31 (November 1981): 48–53.

West, Lucy Brewer. *The Female Marine, or Adventures of Miss Lucy Brewer*. Boston: n.p., 1817; reprint 1966.

West, Nigel. *Historical Dictionary of Sexspionage*. Lanham, MD: Scarecrow, 2009.

West, Nigel. *Venona: The Greatest Secret of the Cold War*. New York: HarperCollins, 2000.

WETA TV. "Homefront: World War II in Washington." Documentary film. 2007.

White House. "Remarks by the First Lady at the Women in Military Service for America Memorial Center." Arlington, VA: White House, March 3, 2009.

Whitehorne, Joseph. *While Washington Burned: The Battle for Fort Erie 1814*. Baltimore, MD: Nautical and Aviation Publishing Company of America, 1992.

Whites, LeeAnn, and Alecia P. Long, eds. *Occupied Women: Gender, Military Occupation, and the American Civil War*. Baton Rouge: Louisiana State University Press, 2009.

Wilcox, Jennifer. *Sharing the Burden: Women in Cryptology during World War II*. Fort George G. Meade, MD: Center for Cryptologic History, National Security Agency, 1998.

Willever, Heather, and John Parascandola. "The Cadet Nurse Corps: 1943–48." *Association of Schools of Public Health* 109, no. 3 (1994): 455–57.

"Will Head Women in New Crop Corps: Miss Florence Hall, Senior Home Economist in Agricultural Extension Service, Is Named." *Washington Post*, April 13, 1943, 22.

Williams, Gary A. "Katharine Burr Blodgett (1898–1979)." In *Out of the Shadows: Contributions of Twentieth-Century Women to Physics*, edited by Nina Byers and Gary Williams, 149–57. New York: Cambridge University Press, 2006.

Williams, Kathleen Broome. *Grace Hopper: Admiral of the Cyber Sea*. Annapolis, MD: Naval Institute Press, 2004.

Williams, Kathleen Broome. *Improbable Warriors: Women Scientists and the U.S. Navy in World War II*. Annapolis, MD: Naval Institute Press, 2001.

Williams, Kenneth P. "The Tennessee River Campaign and Anna Ella Carroll." *Indiana Magazine of History* 46 (1950): 221–48.

Williams, Nicholas M. *Aircraft of the United States' Military Air Transport Service*. Hinckley, UK: Midland Press, 1999.

Williams, Rudi. "Asian Pacific American Women Served in World War II, Too." *American Forces Press Service*, May 27, 1999.

Williams, Rudi. "DoD's Personnel Chief Gives Asian-Pacific American History Lesson." *American Forces Press Service*, June 3, 2005.

Williams, Samuel C. *Tennessee during the Revolutionary War*. Knoxville: University of Tennessee Press, 1974.

Wilson, Dorothy Clarke. *Lone Woman: The Story of Elizabeth Blackwell, the First Female Doctor*. Boston: Little, Brown and Company, 1970.

Wilson, Dorothy Clarke. *Stranger and Traveler*. Boston: Little, Brown and Company, 1975.

Wilson, Gill Robb. *I Walked with Giants*. New York: Vantage Press, 1968.

Winchell, Meghan K. *Good Girls, Good Food, Good Fun: The Story of the USO Hostesses during World War II*. Chapel Hill: University of North Carolina Press, 2008.

Wingo, Josette Dermody. *Mother Was a Gunner's Mate: World War II in the WAVES*. Annapolis, MD: Naval Institute Press, 1994.

Winston, Diane H. *Red-Hot and Righteous: The Urban Religion of the Salvation Army*. Boston, MA: Harvard University Press, 1999.

Wise, James E., and Scott Baron. *Women at War: Iraq, Afghanistan, and Other Conflicts*. Annapolis, MD: Naval Institute Press, 2006.

Wiser, William. *The Great Good Place: American Expatriate Women in Paris*. New York: W. W. Norton & Company, 1991.

Withers, Alexander S. *Chronicles of Border Warfare*. Cincinnati, OH: Robert Clarke Company, 1895.

Witt, Linda, Judith Bellafaire, Britta Granrud, and Mary Jo Binker. *"A Defense Weapon Known to Be of Value": Servicewomen of the Korean War Era*. Hanover, NH: University Press of New England, 2005.

Wolfe, Margaret Ripley. *Daughters of Canaan: A Saga of Southern Women*. Lexington: University Press of Kentucky, 1995.

Women in Military Service for America. "Critical Care: A Navy Nurse Goes Above and Beyond." Voices of Valor, March 2008. http://womensmemorial

.org/Education/WHM08KitUSN. html, accessed February 26, 2012.

"Women in Military Service for America Memorial." *Army Magazine* 59 (August 2009): 66–69.

Women in Military Service for America Memorial. "1950s." http://www .womensmemorial.org, accessed January 21, 2005.

Women in Military Service for America Memorial Foundation. "Margaret Zane Fleming." http://www .womensmemorial.org/H&C/ Collections/collectionsarkorea.html, accessed March 15, 2012.

Women Marine's Association. *The History of the U.S. Women Marines.* Nashville, TN: Turner, 1992.

"Women of Color Award Winners." *Women of Color* 9, no. 2 (2010): 33.

Wood, Sara Wood. "Woman Soldier Receives Silver Star for Valor in Iraq." *American Forces Press Service*, June 16, 2005.

Woodmansee, Laura S. *Women Astronauts.* Burlington, ON: Apogee Books, 2002.

World Young Women's Christian Association. *The Girl Reserve Movement: A Manual for Advisers. Y.W.C.A.* New York: National Board of the Young Women's Christian Associations, 1918; repr. 1921.

Wright, Marcus. *Wright's Official History of the Spanish-American War: A Pictorial and Descriptive Record of the Cuban Rebellion, the Causes that Involved the United States, and a Complete Narrative of Our Conflict with Spain, on Land and Sea.* Washington, D.C.: War Records Office, 1900.

Wright, Mary. *Elizabeth Blackwell of Bristol, the First Female Doctor.* Bristol, UK: Bristol Branch of the Historical Association, 1995.

Yardley, Herbert O. *The American Black Chamber.* Annapolis, MD: Naval Institute Press, 1931.

Yellin, Emily. *Our Mothers' War: American Women at Home and the Front during World War II.* New York: Free Press, 2004.

Yost, Edna. *American Women of Science.* Philadelphia, PA: J.B. Lippincott Company, 1943.

Young, Alfred F. *Masquerade: The Life and Times of Deborah Sampson, Continental Soldier.* New York: Vintage Books, 2004.

Young, Alfred F. *The Shoemaker and the Tea Party.* Boston: Beacon Press, 1999.

Young, Richard. *Combat Police: U.S. Army Military Police in Vietnam.* Bloomington, IN: AuthorHouse, 2002.

Young, William H., and Nancy K. Young. *World War II and the Postwar Years in America: A Historical and Cultural Encyclopedia.* Santa Barbara, CA: ABC-CLIO, 2010.

Youngs, J. William T. *Eleanor Roosevelt: A Personal and Public Life.* New York: Pearson Longman, 2006.

Yount, Lisa. *American Profiles: Women Aviators.* New York: Facts on File, 1995.

Zanjani Sally. *Sarah Winnemucca.* Lincoln: University of Nebraska Press, 2001.

Zeiger, Susan. *In Uncle Sam's Service: Women Workers with the American Expeditionary Force, 1917–1919.* Ithaca, NY: Cornell University Press, 1999.

Zeinert, Karen. *Those Courageous Women of the Civil War.* Millbrook, CT: Millbrook Press, 1998.

Zeinert, Karen, and Mary Miller. *The Brave Women of the Gulf Wars:*

Operation Desert Storm and Operation Iraqi Freedom. Minneapolis, MN: Twenty-First Century Books, 2006.

Zenor-Lafond, Holly. "Women and Combat: Why They Serve." *Inquiry Journal* 4 (Spring 2008): 32–38.

Zimmerman, Jean. *Tailspin: Women at War in the Wake of Tailhook.* New York: Doubleday, 1995.

Zumwalt, Elmo. *On Watch: A Memoir.* New York: Quadrangle, 1976.

Categorical Index

Dietrich, Marlene (1901–1992), 188–89,
 208, 386, 544

Divers, Bridget (CA. 1840–N.D.), 189–90

Dix, Dorothea Lynde (1802–1887),
 190–93, 352, 425

Driscoll, Agnes Meyer (1889–1971),
 193–94

Duerk, Alene Bertha (1920–),
 194–95, 682

Dulinsky, Barbara J. (N.D.–N.D.), 195–96,
 330, 621

Dunwoody, Ann E. (1953–), xix,
 197–98, 455

Duston, Hannah (1657–1730),
 198–99, 423

Earley, Charity Adams (1918–2002),
 10, 201–2

Edmonds (Seelye), Sarah Emma
 [Franklin Thompson] (1841–1898),
 139, 140, 145, 203–5, 207

Edmondson, Isabella "Belle" Buchanan
 (1840–1873), 205–6

Faulkner, Shannon Richey (1975–),
 213–15

Feinstein, Genevieve Grotjan
 (1912–2006), 215–17

Fields, Evelyn Juanita (1949–), 217–19

Finch, Florence Ebersole Smith (1915–),
 44–45, 219–20, 548

Fleming, Margaret Zane (1917–1997),
 221–22

Flinn, Kelly (1970–), 222–24

Fonda, Jane [Lady Jayne Seymour
 Fonda] (1937–), 224–26, 578

Foote, Evelyn Patricia "Pat" (1930–),
 226–27

Ford (Willard), Antonia (1838–1871),
 207, 227–29

Fox, Annie G. (1893–1987), xix, 39,
 229–30

Friedman, (Clara) Elizebeth Smith
 (1892–1980), 230–32

Fulton, Sarah Bradlee (1740–1835), 207,
 234–36

Galloway, Irene O. (1908–1963),
 237–39, 302

Gang, Jeanne Hamby (1921–2006),
 239–40

Gay, Samuel [Ann Bailey] (N.D.–N.D.),
 240–42

Gellhorn, Martha (1908–1998), 242–44

Glaspie, April Catherine (1942–),
 244–45

Goodrich, Annie Warburton
 (1866–1954), 247–49, 517

Greenhow, Rose O'Neal
 (CA. 1814–1864), 140, 207,
 228, 254–56, 449

Greenwood, Edith Ellen (1920–),
 256–57

Gulovich, Maria (1921–2009), 261–63

Hall (Goillot), Virginia (1906–1982),
 265–67

Hall, Florence Louise (1888–1983),
 267–68, 645

Hallaren, Mary (1907–2005), 268–70,
 302, 628, 639

Hancock, Joy Bright (1898–1986),
 270–71, 343, 609, 628

Harris, Marcelite Jordan (1943–),
 272–73

Hart, Nancy (CA. 1843–1902), 207,
 273–74

Hart, Nancy Morgan (CA. 1735–1830),
 275–77

Hasson, Esther Voorhees (1867–1942),
 277–79, 512

Hays, Anna Mae McCabe (1920–), xix,
 279–81, 455

Heavren, Rose (1870–1968), 281–82

Herz, Alice (1883–1965), 285–87

Hester, Leigh Ann (1982–), 287–88

Higgins (Hall), Marguerite (1920–1966),
 288–91, 344

Hitt, Genevieve Young (1885–1963),
 293–95

Hobby, Oveta Culp (1905–1995),
 295–98, 630, 634, 636

CONFLICTS AND THEATERS OF OPERATION

COURT CASES AND LEGISLATION

ORGANIZATIONS AND GROUPS

MINORITIES

MISCELLANEOUS

Index

Note: Page numbers in **bold** indicate main entries in the encyclopedia.

Darragh, Lydia Barrington, 28,
177–79, 207
Daughters of Liberty, **179–80**
Daughters of the American Revolution
(DAR), 163, 381, 511, 532
Hospital Corps, 381, 532
Daughters of the regiment, 81, 110–11,
139, 189, 579
Divers, Bridget, 189–90
Davis, Angela, 577
Davis, Ann Simpson, **180–82**
Davis, Benjamin O., 246
Davis, Jefferson, 96, 255, 402, 404, 531
Davis, John, 181
Davis, John L., 183
Davis, Nelson, 539
Davis, Wilma Zimmerman, **182–83**
Dawes team, 262
Daytona Normal and Industrial Institute
for Negro Girls. *See* Bethune-
Cookman College
Dean, Teresa Howard, 512
Dearborn, William, 587
Dear Fatherland, Rest Quietly
(Bourke-White), 95
Dear President Bush (Sheehan), 508–9
DeCaulp, Thomas C., 572
Decision in Africa (Hunton), 312
Decker, Evelyn, 342–43
Decker, Karl, 511
The Defeat (Warren), 27
Defense, Department of, 184–85
Defense Advisory Committee on
Women in the Services
(DACOWITS), **183–86**, 305, 344,
409, 453–54, 626
Defense Authorization Acts, 259
Defense industries, 482–83
African American women, 661
Hispanic American women, 292
Monroe, Rose Leigh Abbott Will,
398–400
World War II, 660–62
De Gaulle, Charles, 60

De Havilland, Olivia, 251
Delano, Jane Arminda, 20–21,
186–88, 656
Delany, Martin, 128
Dependent benefits. *See Frontiero v.
Richardson*
Desegregation of military, 211–12,
360, 427
Desertion, 203, 240–42
Destry Rides Again (film), 189
Diaries, 539–40
Dickinson, Charles, 173
Dickinson, Velvalee, 231–32
Dickson, Henry, 80
Dickson, John, 80
Dietitians, 648–50
Dietrich, Marlene, **188–89**, 208,
386, 544
Digital Equipment Corporation, 308
Discovery shuttle, 160
Discrimination, racial
in defense industries, 661
in public transportation, 338–39, 488
YMCAs in World War I, 311–12
See also Segregation, racial
Distinguished Flying Cross, 12, 121–22
Distinguished Service Cross, 208, 266,
379–80
Distinguished Service Medal, 152, 187,
248, 334, 378, 385, 409, 499, 518
Divelbess, Diane, 121
Divers, Bridget, **189–90**
Diversity Advisory Council (DAC),
626–27
Division of Special Hospitals and
Physical Reconstruction, 658
Division of State and Local Cooperation
(DSLC), 429
Dix, Dorothea Lynde, **190–93**, 352, 425
Dona Maria, 413
Donovan, William, 134, 263, 266,
385–86
"Don't Ask, Don't Tell" policy, 120.
See also Homosexuality

Contributors

EDITOR

Lisa Tendrich Frank
Independent Scholar
Tallahassee, Florida

CONTRIBUTORS

Rebecca A. Adelman
University of Maryland–Baltimore
County

Thomas Francis Army, Jr.
University of Massachusetts at Amherst

Siobhan Elise Ausberry
U.S. Army Center of Military History
Washington, D.C.

Gustavo Adolfo Aybar
Freelance Writer
Kansas City, Missouri

Barbara Bair
Manuscript Division, Library of Congress

Thomas E. Baker
University of Scranton

Walter F. Bell
Aurora, Illinois

Amy Blackwell
Clemson University

Marcia Schmidt Blaine
Plymouth State University

Robert D. Bohanan
Independent Scholar

Ilouise S. Bradford
University of North Carolina
at Chapel Hill

Kevin M. Brady
Tidewater Community
College

Robert P. Broadwater
Freelance Writer
Bellwood, Pennsylvania

Stefan Brooks
Lindsey Wilson College

Kathryn A. Broyles
American Public University System

Mitzi M. Brunsdale
Mayville State University

Elizabeth Ann Bryant
Florida State University

L. Bao Bui
University of Illinois, Urbana-
Champaign

Brandon R. Byrd
University of North Carolina
at Chapel Hill

Robin D. Campbell
Excelsior College

David M. Carletta
John Jay College

Adam M. Carson
University of Arkansas

Rorie M. Cartier
University of North Carolina
at Greensboro

Michael D. Coker
Old Exchange and Provost
Building
Charleston, South Carolina

Glenn A. Conley
Clark State Community College

David M. Corlett
College of William and Mary

Janet L. Coryell
Western Michigan University

Sharon Michelle Courmier
Lamar University

Ryan C. Davis
Freelance Writer
Temple, Texas

Amanda de la Garza
Zephic Productions

Page Dougherty Delano
Borough of Manhattan Community
College

James I. Deutsch
Center for Folklife and Cultural
Heritage, Smithsonian Institution

Cheryl Dong
University of North Carolina
at Chapel Hill

David D. Dry
Miami Dade Virtual College

Blake A. Duffield
University of Arkansas

Florence Dupré
Independent Scholar
Reunion, France

Angela Esco Elder
University of Georgia

Lizeth Elizondo
University of Texas–Austin

Brittany Erin Elwood
Indiana State University

Megan Findling
New York University

Gayle Veronica Fischer
Salem State University

Joshua Fleer
Florida State University

Andrew K. Frank
Florida State University

Jared Frederick
West Virginia University

Vicki L. Friedl
Independent Scholar

Sarah J. Gavison
University of Colorado at Boulder

Jessica L. Ghilani
University of Pittsburgh

Betty J. Glass
Special Collections and Archives
University of Nevada, Reno

Robert L. Glaze
University of Tennessee at Knoxville

Carrie Glenn
California State University,
Los Angeles

Donna Cooper Graves
University of Tennessee, Martin

Michael R. Hall
Armstrong Atlantic State University

Jennifer Harrison
Kaplan University

Sonia Hazard
Duke University

Alexia Jones Helsley
University of South Carolina–Aiken

Arthur Holst
Widener University

Charles F. Howlett
Molloy College

Jamie L. Huber
Utah State University

Rachel Hynson
University of North Carolina
at Chapel Hill

Katherine Burger Johnson
University Archives and Records Center,
University of Louisville

Wendell G. Johnson
University Libraries, Northern Illinois
University

Sigrid Kelsey
Louisiana State University Libraries

Gary Kerley
North Hall High School
Gainesville, Georgia

Suphan Kirmizialtin
University of Texas at Austin

Jenna L. Kubly
Independent Scholar
St. Paul, Minnesota

Juliana Kuipers
Harvard University Archives

Sarah Hilgendorff List
Independent Scholar

Leonard H. Lubitz
Freelance Writer
Great Neck, New York

Theresa C. Lynch
University of New Hampshire, Manchester

Jodie N. Mader
Thomas More College

Yoshiya Makita
Hitotsubashi University

Ry Marcattilio-McCracken
Oklahoma State University

Ruth E. Martin
Clare College, University of Cambridge

Valerie A. Martinez
University of Texas–Austin

Karen Mason
Charles Evans Inniss Memorial Library
Medgar Evers College, City University
of New York

Jack McCallum
Texas Christian University

Tara M. McCarthy
Central Michigan University

Matthew R. McGrew
University of Southern Mississippi

James McIntyre
Moraine Valley Community College

Emily Meyer
Louisiana State University

Anne M. E. Millar
University of Ottawa

J. Hendry Miller
Florida State University

Jennifer L. Miller
West Virginia University

Alaina M. Morgan
New York University

Cheryl Mullenbach
Iowa Department of Education

Sarah Parry Myers
Texas Tech University

Dana Nichols
Lanier Technical College

Sarah K. Nytroe
Independent Scholar

Patrick J. O'Connor
Independent Scholar

Andrew Orr
Sam Houston State University

Alena Papayanis
Independent Scholar
Toronto, Canada

Edy Parsons
Mount Mary College

Hayden Peake
Independent Scholar

Gwen Perkins
Washington State Historical Society
Tacoma, Washington

Allyson Perry
West Virginia University

Mark Anthony Phelps
University of Arkansas

Allene S. Phy-Olsen
Austin Peay State University

Jeremy L. Piercy
University of North Carolina
at Greensboro

Paul G. Pierpaoli Jr.
Military History, ABC-CLIO, Inc.

Rebecca Jo Plant
University of California, San Diego

Andrew Polk
Florida State University

Estefania Ponti
The Graduate Center, City University
of New York

Tammy Prater
University of Memphis

Rebecca E. Price
University of Texas at Arlington

Laura R. Prieto
Simmons College

Mary Raum
U.S. Naval War College

Stacy W. Reaves
Tulsa Community College Southeast
Campus

Katherine Rohrer
University of Georgia

Jim Ross-Nazzal
Houston Community College

Tanya L. Roth
Mary Institute and St. Louis Country
Day School

Kristen L. Rouse
State University of New York
Jefferson Community College

Margaret Sankey
Minnesota State University–Moorhead

Eva Katharina Sarter
University of Munster

Thomas Saylor
Concordia University—St. Paul

Elizabeth D. Schafer
Independent Scholar

Adriana G. Schroeder
University of Central Oklahoma

Marcus Schulzke
State University
of New York–Albany

Eloise Scroggins
Indiana Historical Society

Debbie Sharnak
University of Wisconsin–Madison

Debra A. Shattuck
University of Iowa

Ashley L. Shimer
West Virginia University

Lisa M. Smith
University of Akron

M. Michaele Smith
College of William and Mary

Betsy Rohaly Smoot
Center for Cryptologic History
National Security Agency

Aeleah Soine
Saint Mary's College of California

Kristen L. Streater
Austin College

Jamie Stoops
University of Arizona

Philippa Strum
Woodrow Wilson International Center
for Scholars
Washington, D.C.

Regina D. Sullivan
Independent Scholar

Lauren K. Thompson
Florida State University

Mike Timonin
Broome Community College

Anthony Todd
University of Chicago

Rebecca Tolley-Stokes
Charles C. Sherrod Library, East
Tennessee State University

Nancy J. Traylor-Heard
Mississippi State University

Bailey L. Trenchard
Kent State University

Spencer C. Tucker
Senior Fellow, Military History
ABC-CLIO, LLC

Antoinette G. van Zelm
Tennessee Civil War National
Heritage Area Center for Historic
Preservation
Middle Tennessee State University

Alison Vick
Virginia Tech

Jay Warner
South Conejos School District RE-10

Aineshia Carline Washington
University of Texas at Arlington

Tim J. Watts
Kansas State University

Tiffany K. Wayne
Independent Scholar

Paula L. Webb
University Library, University of South
Alabama

Kate Wells
Gallucci-Cirio Library, Fitchburg State
University

Victoria Wheeler
Indiana University

Ashanti White
California Institute of Integral Studies

William E. Whyte
Northampton Community College

Natalie Wilson
California State University–San Marcos

Bradford A. Wineman
Marine Corps University, Command
and Staff College

Lia D. Winfield
University of California, Davis

Brett F. Woods
American Military University

Colin Woodward
Sophia Smith Collection, Smith College

Elizabeth Dean Worley
Florida State University

About the Editor

Lisa Tendrich Frank is an independent scholar living in Tallahassee, Florida. She is the author and editor of several books and articles that focus on the history of the United States and the American Civil War. She received her PhD at the University of Florida.